The Concise Code of Jewish Law

Volume Two

הלכות שבת

A Guide to Prayer and Religious Observance

On the Sabbath

Including an Exposition of the

Thirty-nine Principal Melachot

ל"ט מלאכות האסורות בשבת

Other Books by the Author

The Concise Code of Jewish Law, Volume One,
A Guide to Prayer and Religious Observance in the Daily Life of the Jew

A Philosophy of Mizvot: The Religious-Ethical Concepts of Judaism, Their
Roots in Biblical Law and the Oral Tradition

Samuel K. Mirsky Memorial Volume: Studies in Jewish Law, Philosophy,
and Literature (Editor)

ספר הנייר, ספר הלכות של פוסק קדמון מסוף המאה השלש עשרה, חלק ראשון

תורת המצוות באמונת ישראל: ערכי הדת והמוסר במשנתו של בעל ספר החינוך

THE CONCISE CODE
OF JEWISH LAW

COMPILED FROM
KITZUR SHULḤAN ARUCH AND TRADITIONAL SOURCES

A NEW TRANSLATION WITH INTRODUCTION
AND HALACHIC ANNOTATIONS
BASED ON
CONTEMPORARY RESPONSA

by
RABBI GERSION APPEL

VOLUME TWO

הלכות שבת

A GUIDE TO PRAYER AND RELIGIOUS OBSERVANCE
ON THE SABBATH

KTAV PUBLISHING HOUSE, INC./NEW YORK

Library of Congress Cataloging-in-Publication Data
(Revised for volume 2)

The Concise code of Jewish law.
  Bibliography: v. 1, p.
  Includes index.
  Contents: v. 1. A guide to prayer and religious observance in the daily
life of the Jew.—v. 2. A guide to prayer and religious observance on
the Sabbath.
  1. Jewish law. 2. Judaism—Customs and practices.
I. Appel, Gersion. II. Ganzfried, Solomon ben Joseph, 1804-1886.
Kitsur Shulhanarukh. English. 1977.
BM520.9.C66   296.1'8   77-26847
ISBN 0-87068-298-9 (v.1)

Manufactured in the United States of America

In Loving Memory
of Our Grandson
David Judah Kurzman

לזכרן נצח
ולעלוי נשמתו הטהורה
של נכדנו החביב והנעים

דוד יהודה חיים ע"ה
בן משה אהרן ואסתר רחל קורצמאן

נולד ד' כסלו, ונפטר כ"ד אדר, תשמ"ג
ת.נ.צ.ב.ה.

Haskamah of Hagaon Harav Aaron Halevi Soloveichik
Rosh ha-Yeshiva, Yeshivas Brisk and
Yeshivas Rabbeinu Yitzchak Elchanan

Rabbi Gersion Appel, a distinguished Torah scholar, has written a valuable, practical treatise in English on the Kitzur Shulḥan Aruch, dealing with the Sabbath laws.

While I have not been able to thoroughly examine the manuscript in its entirety, I have studied parts of it, and I find it to be an excellent, scholarly work. The author has diligently researched the profound writings of the early and contemporary halachic authorities, and expounded and illumined their teachings with erudition and in a reasoned and insightful manner.

I commend the author for this valuable work, whose publication will be of great benefit, since his halachic annotations provide a reliable guide for the observance and practice of the laws.

To the author, my esteemed friend, I herewith extend my blessings.

Aaron Halevi Soloveichik

For Rabbi Soloveichik's notation בענין מלאכה דאורייתא משום סכנת אבר גרידא see page 489.

הסכמת הגאון הרב אהרן הלוי סולוביציק שליט"א
ראש הישיבה, ישיבת בריסק, וישיבת רבנו יצחק אלחנן

BRISK RABBINICAL COLLEGE 2965 W. Peterson Ave. • Chicago, Ill. 60659 • (312) 275-5166

Rabbi Aaron Soloveichik
President

עיינתי בגליונות של איש האשכולות מופלג בתורה וחכמה, ויראתו קודמת לחכמתו,
ה"ה מוהר"ר גרשון אפעל שליט"א, והוא חבור נאה שמושי באנגלית על קצור שולחן
ערוך הלכות שבת.

ואם כי מסיבות שונות לא עלתה בידי לעיין בו כראוי, אבל גם מהמעט אשר ראיתי
מצאתי בו דברים יקרים, ושהמחבר מעיר ומאיר בבקיאות ובהגיון ובתבונה רבה, ושהוא
טרח ויגע לדלות מים מבארות עמוקים מפוסקים ראשונים ואחרונים.

והריני להחזיק טובותיה למחבר ולאמר לפעלו יישר, כי הדברים ראויין להוציאן
לאור ולזכות את הרבים, משום שהההערות של הרב המחבר ראויין לסמוך עליהן למעשה.

ואני חותם בברכה והוקרה, ידידו המכירו ומוקירו כפי ערכו,

אהרן הלוי סולוביציק

שולי המכתב — הערה בקשר עם מלאכה דאורייתא משום סכנת אבר גרידא — ראה עמ'

.489

מכתב ברכה מאת הגאון הרב דוד ליפשיץ שליט"א
ראש הישיבה, ישיבת רבינו יצחק אלחנן

RABBI DOVID LIFSCHITZ
475 West 186th Street
New York, N. Y. 10033
Tel. 212 – 927-8112

הרב דוד ליפשיץ

[handwritten letter text]

דוד ליפשיץ

בס"ד י"ב אדר שני תשמ"ט,

הנה הובאו לפני גליונות ספר שימושי בשפת המדינה אנגלית, שהנהו מיוסד על הספר "קיצור שלחן ערוך" בהלכות שבת, מאת הרב חריף ובקי מוהר"ר גרשון אפעל שליט"א, וגם טרח ויגע הרבה לאסוף כעמיר גורנה, דיונים ופסקים ממחברים גדולים וגאונים מפורסמים, מהתקופה האחרונה, בהרבה עניני שבת, ובמיוחד בנוגע ההמצאות החדשות בזמננו, והיות שספר "קיצור שלחן ערוך" הנהו מקובל ומפורסם בשער בת-רבים, יהא ספר שימושי זה, לתועלת רבה לצעירי עמנו, ולכל אלה השולטים בשפת המדינה, מכיון שהוא כולל הסברה צחה וקלה וביאורים בהלכות שבת, ומתוך כך יכירו לדעת עניני ודיני שבת כאלה, שלא היו ידועים להם מקודם, ועל ידי העיון והלימוד בזה, יזכו להתחזק בזהירות יתירה בשמירת שבתות קדש, ולכן אמינא לפעלא דא טבא, ויאושר חלקו בזה.

כעתירת הכו"ח לחיזוק שמירת וקדושת השבת,

דוד ליפשיץ

TABLE OF CONTENTS

FROM THE PREFACE TO VOLUME ONE

The essence of Judaism, as taught by our Sages, is *kabbalat malchut shamayim,* acknowledgment of the sovereignty of God, and *kabbalat mitzvot,* acceptance of the commandments ordained by God. Judaism requires a total commitment to Torah as the divine blueprint for a life of holiness in the service of God and of human concern for fellow man, and observance of its laws as defined and explicated by the Halachah.

The continuing discourse and creativity in Halachah, throughout the ages up to our own day, bear witness to the living quality of Torah as *Torat Ḥayyim,* a Torah of life. Addressing itself to every area, personal and social, sacred and worldly, and to every dimension of human experience, its influence is all-pervasive, its authority paramount in Jewish life.

In its root meaning Halachah is the way of the Jew, who stands committed to live his life in accord with Torah law and the Oral Tradition, as expounded by our Sages in the Talmud and by our halachic authorities in the later codes and responsa. While the great code of Jewish law, the *Shulḥan Aruch,* written in the sixteenth century by Rabbi Joseph Karo, has served and continues to be regarded as the major resource for determining the law and for rendering definitive decisions in Halachah, it is the abridged *Kitzur Shulḥan Aruch,* written by Rabbi Shlomo Ganzfried about one hundred years ago, to which the traditional Jew has generally turned for daily guidance in Jewish practice and conduct.

The present work is designed to meet the current need for a concise, contemporary compendium of the traditional laws in the basic areas of Jewish life. The laws are compiled from the *Kitzur Shulḥan Aruch,* and augmented where necessary from the *Shulḥan Aruch* and other traditional codes, such as *Ḥayye Adam, Ḥochmat Adam,* and *Mishnah B'rurah.* The material selected from these primary sources has been translated by the author and arranged in a logical and topical order, following that of the *Kitzur Shulḥan Aruch* as closely as practicable. The basic laws are supplemented by relevant halachic annotations, with particular regard to present-day problems and modern conditions, derived from and based on contemporary responsa by universally recognized halachic authorities. The halachic annotations are meant to be generally informative and are intended essentially as a guide. The reader is advised to consult his Rabbi or appropriate halachic authority for a definitive decision, particularly where the factors in a given case must be examined and evaluated individually.

Volume One endeavors to present the laws, customs, and traditions that pertain to prayer and religious observance in the daily life of the Jew. The Introduction, intended as an overview of the four units which comprise this first volume, provides the reader with halachic and aggadic material bearing upon the subject areas covered. The section on sources and references at the end of the book contains additional halachic notations, as well as divergent opinions, but serves mainly to direct the reader to the sources in the codes and responsa from which the basic laws and the individual rulings are drawn.

This work is, in large measure, the result of a concern and involvement over the years with questions of Halachah and religious practice while serving as Rabbi of several congregations and teaching courses in Jewish law and liturgy at Stern College of Yeshiva University. It is, therefore, for my congregants and my students that it was primarily conceived. The book is presented, however, with a broader objective in mind, namely, to make the knowledge of our laws more widely and more readily accessible, especially for our young people today. It is my hope that it will help to direct them in their daily living in accord with Jewish law, and enable them to identify with the Jewish people and the Jewish faith through the totality of the religious experience as encountered in the world of Halachah.

PREFACE TO VOLUME TWO

The *Kitzur Shulḥan Aruch* remains the definitive work in Jewish Law for ready reference and instruction in day-to-day conduct and religious observance. Hence, it serves as the basic text in this volume, as in the previous volume.

While Volume One is devoted to prayer and religious observance in daily life, Volume Two deals with the laws and customs pertaining to prayer and religious observance on the Sabbath. The *Kitzur Shulḥan Aruch,* however, has only a brief summary of select laws pertaining to some of the *melachot* that are forbidden on the Sabbath. The author explains this by noting that the essential laws are already widely known, and he will therefore write about those that are not well known and that apply to situations which occur with greater frequency. However, this is presently no longer the case. There is often a lack of knowledge and understanding of the Sabbath laws, particularly with regard to the *melachot.* Moreover, with the advances in modern technology and the consequent problems and concerns in Halachah, there is greater necessity for study of the Sabbath laws and for guidance in their practical application.

Volume Two, therefore, includes a separate unit—Part II— devoted to a full discussion of the thirty-nine *melachot* forbidden on the Sabbath. In defining and delineating the laws relating to these principal *melachot,* their derivatives and Rabbinical prohibitions, I follow the classic treatise, *Kalkalat Shabbat,* which is the Introduction of the *Tiferet Yisrael* to the tractate of *Shabbat* in the Talmud. In this unit, as well as in the other parts of this work, I have also drawn extensively upon the traditional codes and primary sources, such as Rambam's *Mishneh Torah,* the *Shulḥan Aruch, Hayye Adam,* and *Mishnah B'rurah.*

The basic text in all of the five units is supplemented by halachic annotations dealing with practical, present-day problems and conditions, derived from and based on contemporary responsa by recognized halachic authorities. The individual rulings and guidelines generally represent a consensus, or the preponderant view, among the authorities consulted. While differing views, where they occur, are usually noted in the annotations or in the references, a detailed discussion and specific attribution of the varying opinions is not always possible within the limitations of a concise work of this nature. For this, and for further exploration of the subject, one should consult the relevant sources provided in the Hebrew references.

I trust the reader will find this work a useful guide to the laws, and the principles involved in determining the laws, that relate to Sabbath observance. As in the first volume, I advise the reader to consult Rabbinic authority where possible in specific cases, particularly in view of the complex nature of the Sabbath laws. Finally, in the tradition of our Sages, I pray that I will not have erred in a matter of Halachah.

I wish to express my thanks to Rabbi Mordechai Willig for reading the final draft of this volume and for his valued comments.

Gersion Appel

Introduction

INTRODUCTION

The Sabbath

The Sabbath is central to Jewish religious thought and practice. As the most vital institution in Judaism, it is at the very heart of Jewish life, determining its religious character and, indeed, its essential nature. As reflected in prayer, in observance, and in its teachings, the Sabbath represents, as well, the fundamental principles of faith, and the eternal ideals of Judaism.[1]

I. The Sabbath—A Memorial of God's Creation of the Universe

The Sabbath is principally a testimony to our belief in God, the Creator and Ruler of the universe.

In the Introduction to the *Guide of the Perplexed,* Maimonides writes, "You should observe that the Almighty, desiring to lead us to perfection and to improve our state of society, has revealed to us laws which are to regulate our actions. These laws, however, presuppose the adoption of intellectual beliefs, the first of which being a conception of the existence of the Creator . . . Therefore, Scripture tells us, 'In the beginning God created the heaven and the earth' (Genesis 1:1)."

The Torah, thus, introduces its exposition of the Divine Laws with Judaism's primary postulate of faith—a belief in the existence of

---

1. See Ramban, *Perush* to Exodus 20:8, ולכן אמרו ז״ל שהששבת שקולה כנגד כל מצות שבתורה, כמו שאמרו בעבודה זרה, מפני שבה נעיד על כל עיקרי האמונה. See also *Ḥayye Adam, Hilchot Shabbat* 1:1; *Mishnah B'rurah, Hakdamah* to *Hilchot Shabbat; Aruch Hashulḥan, Hilchot Shabbat* 242:3.

3

a Divine Being who created the universe. There follows an account of creation, wherein we are informed that the world was brought into existence by God in six primordial days of creation, and that it reached its final stage of completion on the seventh day. The verses of Scripture that depict this climactic stage of creation are a part of the Sabbath eve service (וַיְכֻלּוּ), and form the prelude to the *Kiddush* prayer recited with the advent of the Sabbath.

> And the heaven and the earth were finished, and all the host of them. And on the seventh day God finished His work which He had made; and He rested on the seventh day from all His work which He had made. And God blessed the seventh day and hallowed it, because that in it He rested from all His work which God in creating had made (Genesis 2:1–3).

In the Ten Commandments proclaimed at Mount Sinai, God commands that the Sabbath should be kept as a sacred day, free from all manner of work, to commemorate the Sabbath of Creation.

> Remember the Sabbath day to keep it holy. Six days you shall labor and do all your work. But on the seventh day is a Sabbath unto the Lord your God; you shall not do any manner of work; you, nor your son, nor your daughter, nor your man-servant, nor your maid-servant, nor your cattle, nor your stranger who is within your gates. For in six days the Lord made heaven and earth, the sea and all that is in them, and rested on the seventh day. Wherefore the Lord blessed the Sabbath day and hallowed it (Exodus 20:8–11).

The Sabbath is, thus, in its universal message a memorial of creation, affirming our belief in God, the Creator of the universe.

Maimonides considers this the prime purpose of the Sabbath. "We are told in the Law to exalt this day in order that the principle of the creation of the world in time be established and universally known in the world, when all people keep the Sabbath on the same day . . . We should affirm belief in the creation of the world, which leads to belief in the existence of God" (*Guide of the Perplexed* II, 31).

This purpose is similarly expressed in the *Sefer HaḤinnuch*. "At the root of this *mitzvah* lies the purpose . . . that we should affirm in our hearts our enduring faith in the creation of the world out of non-existence" (Mitzvah 31). The *Ḥinnuch* further notes that this principle "draws with it all the basic tenets of our religion" (Mitzvah 32).

Constructive Work Prohibited

The Divine command, "You shall not do any manner of work" on the Sabbath, as determined in the Halachah, means the prohibition of constructive work done with intention and purpose in mind (מְלֶאכֶת מַחֲשֶׁבֶת אָסְרָה תּוֹרָה). The Sabbath hereby affords a true perspective of the relative position of man in the world. Man was created by God, endowed with reason and a capacity to create by utilizing the resources of nature which God had created. In ceasing all such creative activity on the Sabbath, by refraining from the use of one's skill and intelligence in manipulating and mastering the forces and elements of nature, and by releasing nature from our dominion, we acknowledge that the true Creator and Ruler of the universe is God.[2]

II. The Sabbath—A Sign of God's Choice of Israel as His Covenanted People

Apart from the theological signification of the Sabbath as a memorial of creation, of vital import to all mankind, the Sabbath is of paramount national import to the Jewish People as the sign of God's eternal covenant with Israel, His Chosen People. This is clearly stated in the Torah.

Wherefore the children of Israel shall keep the Sabbath, to observe the Sabbath throughout their generations, for a perpetual covenant. It is a sign between Me and the children of Israel forever (Exodus 31:16, 17).

2. See Rabbi Samson Raphael Hirsch, *The Pentateuch,* trans. by I. Levy, Exodus 20:11; *Horeb* II, 21.

As Rashi notes in a preceding verse (Exodus 31:13), the Sabbath is a sign of God's choice of Israel as His covenanted people, that the nations of the world may know that God consecrated the Jewish People, and bequeathed to them the Sabbath as a holy day of rest, the day on which God rested from His work of creation.

In the Decalogue, as recorded in Deuteronomy, the Sabbath is explicitly associated with the emergence of the Jewish People as a free nation, liberated by God from Egyptian bondage.

> Observe the Sabbath day to keep it holy, as the Lord your God commanded you . . . And you shall remember that you were a slave in the land of Egypt, and the Lord your God brought you out thence by a mighty hand and by an outstretched arm; therefore the Lord your God commanded you to keep the Sabbath day. (Deuteronomy 5:12, 15).

Israel's miraculous deliverance from their enslavement in Egypt, brought about by Divine intervention, made them especially beholden to God for their existence as a free nation, and committed to keep the Sabbath day holy as an everlasting covenant.

Universal in Its Message, Singular in Observance

Thus, while the Sabbath is universal in its message of belief in a Divine Creator, it is singular and particular as regards its observance as a holy day. Its unique laws, both commemorative and prohibitive, are binding only upon Israel.[3]

The Sabbath was given to Israel alone to observe as a sign of God's sanctification of the Jewish People. Commenting on the verse, "For it is a sign between Me and you throughout your generations, that ye may know that I am the Lord who sanctifies you" (Exodus

---

3. See *Aruch Hashulḥan, Hilchot Shabbat* 242:1, see Rabbi S.R. Hirsch, *The Pentateuch,* Exodus 20:8, who cites the *Pesikta,* Chapter 23, אמר ר׳ יודן, זכור נתן לאומות העולם, שמור נתן לישראל.

31:13), the Rabbis say, "For it is a sign between Me and you, and not between Me and the idolatrous nations" (*Mechilta* ad. loc).[4]

This is enunciated in the Sabbath morning *Amidah* prayer (וְשָׁמְרוּ).

> And the children of Israel shall keep the Sabbath, to observe the Sabbath throughout their generations for an everlasting covenant. It is a sign between Me and the children of Israel forever, that in six days the Lord made the heavens and the earth, and on the seventh day He ceased from work and rested. You, Lord our God, have not given the Sabbath to the nations of the world. Nor have You, our King, given it as a heritage to idol worshipers; nor will the uncircumcised abide in its rest. But unto Israel, Your People, have You given it in love, unto the seed of Jacob whom You have chosen.

The dual nature of the Sabbath, as a memorial of creation (זִכָּרוֹן לְמַעֲשֵׂה בְרֵאשִׁית) and as a remembrance of the exodus from Egypt (זֵכֶר לִיצִיאַת מִצְרָיִם) and token of God's choice of Israel, is invoked in the *Kiddush,* the prayer of sanctification, recited in welcoming the Sabbath.

> Blessed are You, Lord our God, King of the universe, Who has sanctified us with His commandments and has taken pleasure in us, and in love and favor has given us His holy Sabbath as an inheritance, a memorial of creation. For it is the first among the days of holy convocation, a remembrance of the exodus from Egypt. For You have chosen us and sanctified us above all nations, and in love and favor have given us Your holy Sabbath as an inheritance. Blessed are You, O Lord, who sanctifies the Sabbath.

III. The Sabbath—A Day of Rest and Holiness

The Sabbath is ordained as a day of rest and holiness (יוֹם מְנוּחָה

---

4. See Rashi, who notes, "It is a great sign between us that I have chosen you, in that I have given you to inherit the day on which I rested as your day of rest." Cf. *Midrash Rabbah,* Genesis 11:9, which states that God paired the Sabbath with Israel, אמר לה הקב״ה [לשבת] כנסת ישראל היא בן זוגך.

וּקְדוּשָׁה). This dimension of *Shabbat* has invested the Sabbath day with an aura of tranquility and a sense of spiritual elevation. This aspect of *Shabbat* is movingly articulated in the Sabbath afternoon *Amidah* prayer (אַתָּה אֶחָד).

> You are One and Your Name is One; and who is like Your people Israel, a nation unique on earth? You have given unto Your people beauty and greatness, a wreath of salvation—a day of rest and holiness. Abraham rejoiced, Isaac was jubilant, Jacob and his sons found rest therein. A rest of love and devotion, a true and trusting rest, a rest of peace and tranquility, serene and secure, a perfect rest with which You are pleased. May Your children recognize and know that their rest comes from You, and by their rest on the Sabbath they hallow Your Name.

A Model for Ideal Living

The Sabbath is a prime factor in molding the character of Jewish family life. After six days of toil and care, the traditional Jewish home, radiant with light and the Sabbath spirit, is transformed on the Sabbath into a haven of contentment and peace.[5] Whether in good times, blessed with material bounty, or in troubled times, amidst poverty and destitution, the family members joyously celebrate the Sabbath, united in a bond of love and trust, their hearts filled with hope and gratitude.

Freed of the bondage of labor and weekday concerns, the Sabbath-observant Jew is contented and at rest. However, Sabbath rest is not meant to be a state of idleness and insensibility. Involving, as it does, both mundane and spiritual pursuits, the Sabbath pulsates

---

5. The Sabbath is traditionally a day of peace, as indeed it is represented by the greeting of *Shabbat Shalom*. The Rabbis exhort one to refrain from discord and contention in the home, especially on the Sabbath. The *Zohar* notes that if one is irascible and given to anger on the Sabbath it is as though he has kindled the fires of Gehinnom. See *Tosafot Ḥayyim* on *Ḥayye Adam, Hilchot Shabbat,* Chapter I, note 12.

with vibrant, lively activity. On the Sabbath one is directed to satisify the material needs of his physical nature by partaking of choice food and drink, and to gratify the innate longings of his spiritual nature by Sabbath prayer and Torah study. In maintaining the physical and spiritual faculties in balance and in harmony, the Sabbath serves as a prototype of the ideal day, the model for ideal living.

Our Sages and religious philosophers believe this to be a guiding principle of the Torah in its counsel as to one's proper conduct in life.[6] This is succinctly stated by Rabbi Yehuda Halevi. "The Divine Law imposes no asceticism. It rather desires that we should keep the balance and grant every spiritual and physical faculty its due . . . Our Law, as a whole, is divided between reverence, love and joy; through each of them you can approach God. Your contrition on a fast day does no more to bring you nearer to God then your joy on the Sabbath and Festivals, if your rejoicing is the outcome of a devout heart . . ."

Expressing a refreshing sentiment, generally associated with the Ḥasidic mode, he remarks further:

"And if your joy leads you to sing and dance, your song and dance become worship and a bond of union between you and the Divine Spirit."

Yehuda Halevi, however, adds a word of caution.

"Our Law, however, did not leave these matters to chance, but they are all prescribed by Tradition" (*Kuzari* II, 50).

Four Elements Comprising the Sabbath

In discussing the Sabbath laws (*Hilchot Shabbat* 30:1), Rambam states that the Sabbath comprises four elements, with distinct duties relating to each. Two are on Scriptural authority, namely, *Zachor* (זָכוֹר), "*Remember* the Sabbath day to keep it holy" (Exodus 20:8), and *Shamor* (שָׁמוֹר), "*Observe* the Sabbath day to keep it holy"

---

6. Rambam advocates a life of moderation, which he considers to be "the way of God," the legacy of Abraham. See *Mishneh Torah, Hilchot De'ot* 1:7.

(Deuteronomy 5:12). Two are on the authority of the Scribes, namely, *Kavod* (כָּבוֹד), *Honor*; and *Oneg* (עוֹנֶג), *Delight*. The latter are mentioned in the Prophets in the verse, "And call the Sabbath a delight, and the holy of the Lord honorable" (Isaiah 58:13).

Remembering the Sabbath

Zachor refers to the positive precepts in remembrance of the Sabbath; to its sanctification over wine with the *Kiddush* prayer in celebration of its coming, and the *Havdalah* blessing marking its departure.

The Sabbath is remembered when identifying the days of the week. Only the seventh day has a name of its own—*Shabbat*—in the Hebrew calendar. All of the other days are reckoned according to the Sabbath, that is, the first day, the second day, etc. יוֹם רִאשׁוֹן בְּשַׁבָּת, יוֹם שֵׁנִי בְּשַׁבָּת וכו'. See *Mechilta*, Exodus 20:8.

Observing the Sabbath

Shamor refers to the negative precepts intended to keep the Sabbath holy by refraining from any desecration through forbidden labors (*melachot*) and prohibited weekday activities.

While some *melachot* may actually entail what is commonly considered work or labor, other activities, such as striking a match or lighting a gas flame, which do not entail any physical exertion, are equally forbidden on the Sabbath. In light of the previously stated purpose of acknowledging the Creator by refraining from constructive, creative acts, the prohibition of such *melachot* is evident. The Halachah, likewise, restricts the movement of people and goods by prohibiting carrying in the public domain on the Sabbath, and by restricting one from going beyond the Sabbath limit, thus preserving the Sabbath as a day of rest and relaxation. By limiting the range of activity on the Sabbath, the prohibitions, moreover, keep it from becoming just another weekday.

These prohibitions and restrictions, however, must be disregarded in a case of emergency, when a human life is in possible danger.[7] In a life-threatening situation the Sabbath laws are suspended. The Halachah demands swift and resolute action. "It is forbidden to hesitate when it is necessary to desecrate the Sabbath for one who is dangerously ill," Maimonides writes, "For it is written, 'Ye shall therefore keep My statutes and Mine ordinances, which if a man do, he shall live by them' (Leviticus 18:5)—and not die by them. From this we learn that the laws of the Torah are not vindictive, but they bring compassion, lovingkindness and peace into the world" (*Mishneh Torah, Hilchot Shabbat* 2:3).

Honoring the Sabbath

Kavod refers to honoring the Sabbath even before the Sabbath, by providing food and drink for oneself and for the needy, cleaning and preparing the house, and bathing and dressing in festive clothing.

The Sabbath is, likewise, honored by lighting Sabbath candles. Maimonides notes[8] that lighting candles is both in honor of the Sabbath and a means of delighting in the Sabbath by bringing light and beauty into the home. Kindling the Sabbath lights is a duty and a privilege especially assigned to the woman of the house.[9] It is customary to light two candles and an additional candle for each child, for the soul is compared to a light.[10] With the lighting of the candles the Sabbath is welcomed. The home becomes a sanctuary, where *shalom bayit,* domestic tranquility and peace, reigns.

---

7. On the verse, "Ye shall keep the Sabbath, for it is holy unto you" (Exodus 31:14), the Rabbis comment, "The Sabbath is given unto you, not you unto the Sabbath; see *Mechilta,* ibid.

8. *Mishneh Torah, Hilchot Shabbat* 2:1, 30:5; cf. *Shabbat* 25b, Rashi and Tosafot ad. loc.

9. The Sabbath candles which the woman lights in the home are considered to be allusive of the *Ner Tamid,* the Eternal Light, kindled by the High Priest in the Sanctuary. See *Perush, Ba'al Haturim,* Exodus 27:20, ואתה תצוה . . . להעלות נר תמיד, תצוה בגימטריא נשים צוה, רמז להדלקת הנר לנשים חובה בשבת . . . נר תמיד בגימטריא בשבת.

10. See Proverbs 20:27; cf. *Shabbat* 32a.

Honor is accorded the Sabbath by joining in Sabbath prayers in the synagogue, and by learning Torah.

The Sabbath prayers are chanted melodiously in accord with the traditional *nusaḥ*. The Rama cites the ruling of the Maharil, who was himself a renowned *ḥazan,* that the traditional melodies should not be changed.[11] These melodies, which go back to antiquity—some believe to the time of the Temple in Jerusalem—have been preserved, and have inspired Jews in prayer through the centuries. In regard to the verse, "Honor the Lord with your substance" (Proverbs 3:9), the Sages comment, "If one has a pleasant voice he should lead the congregation in prayer" (*Midrash Tanḥuma, Parshat Re'eh* 12). The *ḥazan* who employs his musical talent to inspire the worshipers, when leading the congregation in prayer, is deemed praiseworthy. When the *ḥazan* and the worshipers pray reverently, giving sincere expression to the spiritual exultation in their hearts, the *tefillot* are truly *avodat Hashem,* a service of God.[12]

Torah study is an important feature of *Shabbat* in all Jewish communities. According to the Midrash the custom of learning Torah in public was first instituted by Moses. "God said to Moses, 'Gather the people in assemblies so that in generations to come they will assemble every Sabbath in synagogues and in houses of study to learn Torah'" (*Midrash Tanḥuma* cited by *Bet Yosef, Oraḥ Ḥayyim* 290).

Delighting in the Sabbath

Oneg refers to delighting in the Sabbath, according to one's means, by eating three meals (*shalosh seudot*), consisting of tasty food and drinks. Traditionally the meal is accompanied by *zemirot,* Sabbath hymns composed by great religious poets and sung to favorite melodies. Sabbath repose is also a part of the enjoyment of *Shabbat.*

The Sabbath is to be a day of delight. Anything that might disrupt

11. See Rama, *Shulḥan Aruch, Oraḥ Ḥayyim* 281:1, 619:1.
12. See the author's article," The *Sheliaḥ Tzibbur* in Halachah and Jewish Tradition," in *Journal of Jewish Music and Liturgy,* Vol. III, no. 1.

the joyous spirit of the Sabbath is banned. The period of mourning is interrupted on the Sabbath. Public manifestations of grief and fasting are generally forbidden.

The Sabbath is, thus, *ḥemdat yamim,* "the most desirable of days," intended for our benefit, for our spiritual, physical and social well-being. Those who consider it a burden, who see only its restrictions and ignore the joy and spiritual edification of the day, have not truly experienced the beauty of a traditional Sabbath and are ignorant of the true character of *Shabbat.* In this regard the Midrash pointedly notes,

> You may think that I gave you the Sabbath to cause you harm. I gave you the Sabbath only for your good. Sanctify the Sabbath with good food and drink, with clean garments, and delight your soul with pleasure, and I will reward you for it. Whence do we know this? The Prophet says, "And call the Sabbath a delight." What is written afterward? "You shall then delight yourself in the Lord," and I will grant you your heart's desire (*Midrash Rabbah,* Deuteronomy 3:1; cf. Rambam, *Hilchot Shabbat* 30:15).

The laws relating to the above areas of Sabbath observance serve to fashion the ideal Sabbath day, preserving its sanctity and serenity, providing rest and relief from workaday toil and a respite from daily turmoil and travail.

Mindful of the remarkable rejuvenating power of the Sabbath, the Rabbis invoke the imagery of a *neshamah yeteirah* (נְשָׁמָה יְתֵרָה), an additional soul with which the Jew is blessed on the Sabbath.[13]

In the *Zohar,* the classic book of the *Kabbalah,* the Sabbath is said to be "the day from which all of the days of the week draw their blessings." "All blessings from on high and below are dependent on the seventh day" (*Parshat Yitro*).[14] This thought is echoed in the *Lechah*

---

13. *Betzah* 16a, *Ta'anit* 27b. See Rashi ad. loc., who defines *neshamah yeteirah* as the expansiveness and receptivity of the soul for tranquility and joy on the Sabbath.

14. Cf. Ramban, Genesis 2:3. "And God blessed the seventh day" — "The blessing on the Sabbath is the fountain of blessings." See the remarkable statement

Dodi,[15] intoned at the *Kabbalat Shabbat* service. "Come let us go to meet the Sabbath, for it is the wellspring of blessing, ordained from the very beginning; last in creation, first in God's plan."

What is depicted symbolically and poetically in mystical lore is actually to be perceived in the manner in which the Sabbath-observing Jew eagerly awaits the arrival of *Shabbat* and, with its departure, enjoys its lasting beneficial effects, as he greets the new week physically refreshed and spiritually rejuvenated.

IV. The Sabbath—A Portent of a Day That Is All Sabbath

The Sabbath signifies the hallowing of time. "And God blessed the seventh day," the Torah states, "and hallowed it" (Genesis 2:3). The Sabbath is a segment of time, in the eternal flow of time, made holy by God.

On this sacred day, when his spirit is uplifted, the Jew is bidden to rise above the vicissitudes and strivings of his temporal existence, and to view life's trials and yearnings in a timeless, empyrean frame. On the Sabbath the Jew is granted a vision of a brighter, more luminous future, a world of peace and brotherhood, radiant with the glory of God.

According to the Rabbis, this idyllic world envisioned by the Prophets of Israel is intimated in the psalm מִזְמוֹר שִׁיר לְיוֹם הַשַּׁבָּת (Psalm 92) which is recited on welcoming the Sabbath and on the Sabbath day. The psalm begins with praise and thanksgiving to God, the supreme sovereign of the universe.

"A Psalm, a Song for the Sabbath day. It is good to give thanks unto the Lord, and to sing praises to Your Name, O Most High; to

---

of the *'Or Haḥayyim* (Genesis 2:3, Exodus 20:11), based on the *Zohar,* that on every *Shabbat* the divine source of creative power is renewed for the continued existence of the world.

15. *Lechah Dodi* was composed by Rabbi Shlomo Alkabetz Halevi of the Kabbalistic school of Rabbi Yitzḥok Luria in the 16th century. In this beautiful poem the Sabbath is called the bride of the People of Israel.

declare Your lovingkindness in the morning and Your faithfulness in the nights."

After acknowledging the greatness of God's creative works, the psalm proceeds to affirm belief in Divine providence with an expression of trust in God's just rule in the world and the ultimate triumph of the righteous. This is understood to be an allusion to God's providential care of the People of Israel in their perpetual struggle against tyranny and oppression, His faithfulness in protecting Israel in the dark nights of their exile, and the promised dawn of a new day of deliverance and redemption. Psalm 92 is, thus, viewed as a hymn of praise to the Creator, a portrayal of the destiny of the Jewish People, and a prefiguration of the future.[16]

Foretokening the Messianic Era and the World to Come

In his commentary on the first verse, Rashi notes that the psalm speaks of "the World to Come, which is an unending Sabbath." This is clearly enunciated in the Mishnah (*Tamid* 7:4, cf. *Rosh Hashanah* 31a), which states that the psalm was chanted on the Sabbath by the Levites in the Temple.

"On the Sabbath they sang: A Psalm, a Song for the Sabbath Day. A Psalm, a Song for the time that is to come, for the day that shall be all Sabbath and rest in the life everlasting."

In his commentary on the Mishnah, *Tiferet Yisrael* explains that the reason the psalm was sung by the Levites on the Sabbath was because it alludes to a time to come in this world and in the World to Come.

The Sabbath is thus taken to be a foretokening of the ultimate redemption of the Jewish People and the destined day of fulfillment for mankind. Indeed, the coming redemption is associated with observance of the Sabbath. The Talmud quotes Rabbi Shimon ben

---

16. Jewish tradition attributes Psalm 92 to Adam, who composed it amidst the wonders of God's creation. It is said to have been revived by Moses after having been forgotten. See *Midrash Bereshit Rabbah* 22:28; cf. *Bava Batra* 14b, Rashi ad. loc.

Yoḥai as saying, "If Israel were to keep two Sabbaths according to the laws thereof, they would be redeemed immediately" (*Shabbat* 118b).[17]

In a world beset by evil, depravity, and violence, the Sabbath affords us a heartening image of mankind in progress towards the ultimate Sabbath of the Messianic era, when the final redemption of Israel and its spiritual renewal in the Holy Land, as foretold by the Prophets of Israel, will bring about the moral and spiritual regeneration of all mankind.

Thus, the holy Sabbath which stands as a memorial of the Sabbath of Creation is finally a portent of the "Sabbath of history,"[18] the Messianic era, and the day that is all Sabbath[19] in the World to Come.[20]

17. Upon conclusion of the Sabbath, *Eliyahu Hanavi,* the prophet Elijah, is remembered. We pray that in the merit of our having observed the Sabbath he will appear and herald the coming of the Messiah. See *Mishnah B'rurah* 296, note 7. The festive *Melaveh Malkah* meal is referred to as סעודתא דדוד מלכא משיחא, in honor of *Mashiaḥ,* the scion of King David.

18. For the concept of a "Sabbath of history," see *Rome and Jerusalem* (Second Letter) by Moses Hess, the 19th century philosopher of Jewish nationalism. Hess maintains that, while nature attained its Sabbath at the time of creation, history has yet to attain it. The Sabbath of history is the Messianic era envisioned by the Prophets of Israel.

19. Rabbi Yitzḥok Aramah, in his classic work, *'Akedat Yitzḥok (Sha'ar* 55, *Parshat Vayakhel*), states this to be one of the fundamental principles taught by the Sabbath. היום הקדוש הזה רמז גדול, רושם נפלא, אל העולם הנצחי שכלו שבת.

20. The Rabbis state that the *kedushah* of the Sabbath resembles the *kedushah* of the World to Come. See *Mechilta,* Exodus 31:13; cf. *Berachot* 57b. The Sabbath is itself considered a foretaste of the bliss stored up for the righteous in the World to Come. See Ramban, Genesis 2:3. In the Sabbath hymn, *Mah Yedidut,* the poet refers to the Sabbath day of contentment as "a semblance of the World to Come," מעין עולם הבא יום שבת מנוחה. The reference to עולם הבא may be to a celestial world, where the righteous are destined to delight in the splendor of the *Shechinah,* or to the coming Messianic age of harmony and peace in the world. For identification of עולם הבא with Messianic times, see *Ketubot* 111b; *Midrash Rabbah,* Genesis 44:25, Numbers 1:63, and commentaries of *'Etz Yosef* and *Matnat Kehunah.* In the latter instance the *Midrash* cites the prophet Zachariah, who prophesies concerning the Messianic age.

Treasured by Israel Through the Ages

In his work, the *Book of Kuzari,* a classic exposition of Judaism presented in the form of a dialogue between the King of the Khazars and a Jewish sage, Rabbi Yehuda Halevi eloquently depicts the role of the Sabbath in the life of the pious Jew.

> *The Rabbi*: The Sabbath is the choicest day (lit. "the fruit") of the week, because it is appointed to establish the connection with the Divine Spirit (*'Inyan ha-'Eloki*) that he may serve Him, not in sadness but in joy . . . The Sabbath day of rest provides the body and the soul with what it lacked during the six days of toil, refreshing it for the days to come . . .
>
> *Al Khazari*: I have often reflected about you (i.e., the Jewish People), and come to the conclusion that God has secret ways of preserving you, and that He appointed the Sabbath and the Festivals among the most powerful means of sustaining your life and vigor . . . Were it not for these holy days, which you observe so conscientiously because they originate with God . . . you would not enjoy a single day in your lives.[21] By them you spend a sixth part of your life in rest of body and soul. Such is not granted even to kings, for their souls have no respite on their days of rest . . . Whatever you spend on these days is your profit for this life, and also for the next, because it is spent for the sake of God. (*Kuzari* III 5, 10).

The Sabbath has been universally recognized as distinctive of Judaism. Nothing corresponding to it existed in antiquity. No other nation or people in the ancient world is known to have kept the seventh day as a Sabbath day of rest and worship. In fact, those who sought to suppress the Jewish religion placed the Sabbath among the first of the observances to be prohibited, as it was considered to be fundamental to Judaism. Indeed, without the Sabbath, Jewish life would in time atrophy and disappear.

---

21. See *Ketubot* 110b, כל ימי עני רעים, והאיכא שבתות וימים טובים. See *Midrash Rabbah,* Genesis 11:3, אנשי חוץ לארץ בזכות מה [הם חיים] . . . בזכות שהם מכבדים את השבתות וימים טובים. See *Shabbat* 118b, כל המענג את השבת . . . ניצול משעבוד גליות.

Through the ages, the Jewish People have kept the Sabbath, treasuring it as a precious gift from God,[22] complying with its many laws and regulations, even in the face of hardship, often at great sacrifice, in their appreciation of its life-giving sustenance, and in demonstration of their steadfast loyalty to God and their commitment to the Jewish faith.

22. See *Shabbat* 10b, "God said to Moses, I have a precious gift in My treasury whose name is *Shabbat,* and I want to give it to Israel. Go and tell them."

Part I

Welcoming the Sabbath,
Prayers and Reading of the Torah
on the Sabbath

1.   THE HOLINESS OF THE SABBATH

גּוֹדֶל קְדוּשַׁת שַׁבָּת

1.   The holy Sabbath is the great sign and covenant that the Holy
One, blessed be He, has given us so that we may know that in six days
God created heaven and earth and all that is in them, and that He
rested on the seventh day. This belief is the foundation of our faith.
The Rabbis have, therefore, said that the Sabbath is equal to all the
commandments (*Jer. Nedarim* III,14). When one observes the Sabbath properly it is as though he has fulfilled the whole Torah, and
when one desecrates the Sabbath it is as though he has denied the
whole Torah. Thus it is written, "You came down upon Mount Sinai
. . . and gave them right ordinances and laws of truth, good statutes
and commandments; and made known unto them your holy Sabbath" (Nehemiah 9:13,14).[1]

2.   Whoever desecrates the Sabbath publicly is regarded as an

---

1.   Shabbat Is Equal to All the Commandments   The juxtaposition of the
Sabbath to the laws of the Torah given at Mount Sinai is taken by the Rabbis as indicating that observance of the Sabbath is equal to all of the commandments. A similar view is held by the Rabbis regarding the prohibition
of idolatry which is, likewise, taken to be equal to all of the commandments,
as intimated in the verse, "And when ye shall err and not observe all these
commandments which the Lord hath spoken unto Moses" (Numbers
15:22). The error referred to, the Rabbis note, is idolatry, a transgression
that is tantamount to abandoning God and forsaking His commandments.
Desecration of the Sabbath is, therefore, further equated with idolatry, since
both involve a denial of God, the Creator, and His Torah.

21

idolater[2] in every respect.[3] If he touches wine it is forbidden, and the bread he bakes and the food he cooks is like that of an idolater.[4] It is considered a public desecration of the Sabbath if the violation occurs in the presence of ten Jews, or if they know of the violation even if they did not actually witness it.[5]

3.   The prophet, therefore, praises one who observes the Sabbath

---

2.   One Who Desecrates the Sabbath   One who desecrates the Sabbath is considered an idolater with regard to the severe punishment and the restrictions such conduct entails. It does not, however, free him of his religious duties or any obligations which are incumbent upon him as a Jew.

3.   One Raised in a Non-Observant Home   In the opinion of many halachic authorities, only one who habitually and knowingly desecrates the Sabbath and shows no concern for its observance is regarded as an idolater, but not one who is unaware of transgressing and desecrating the Sabbath. Hence, one who grew up in a non-observant home, where he was not taught to keep the Sabbath holy, is not to be regarded as an idolater if he violated the Sabbath laws, since he is regrettably only following in the misguided ways of his parents.

4.   Wine Handled by One Who Violates the Sabbath   Many authorities take a strict view of one who violates the Sabbath, and apply the restrictions herein indicated as regards the wine that he handles, and the bread he bakes, and the food that he cooks. Some, however, are inclined to leniency in these matters, inasmuch as non-observance of the Sabbath presently is not necessarily regarded as a denial of faith. Indeed, many Sabbath violators recite the Sabbath prayers and the *Kiddush,* and observe other fundamentals of Judaism, as circumcision and the laws of marriage and divorce. In view of the general decline in religious observance, they deem it best not to reject these transgressors altogether, lest they become totally alienated from Judaism. For the ruling on counting to the *minyan* one who violates the Sabbath, see Volume One, Part I, Chapter 11, note 3a.

5.   Public Desecration of the Sabbath   This is the law as derived from the Talmud and the Codes. Inasmuch as he is fully aware that his wilful violation of the Sabbath will become known to the public, it is tantamount to a public desecration of the Sabbath.

saying, "Happy is the man who does this, and the son of man who holds fast by it; who keeps the Sabbath from profaning it" (Isaiah 56:2). Whoever observes the Sabbath properly,[6] honoring it and

---

6. Shabbat and the International Date Line God created the earth as a spherical planet in the universe subject to the natural laws of a divinely ordained cosmic order. In rotation on its axis the earth completes a full cycle of 360⁰ in twenty-four hours, thereby effecting a time change of one hour for every 15⁰ of its surface. In more succinct terms the passage of the sun across the meridian at points on the globe separated by 15⁰ of longitude differs by one hour, with the sun thus traversing the entire globe in twenty-four hours.

In order to determine a calendar day it is necessary to designate the following: (1) a focal point on the globe which constitutes the boundary, or date line, where a new calendar day begins; (2) a central, locus point which parallels the date line and determines East and West. The date line thus serves to mark the limits of each calendar day. A new date first begins on the western side of this imaginary boundary, and as the earth rotates on its axis this new date moves westward around the globe spanning it in a period of twenty-four hours. Hence, when traveling westward across the date line, the date changes to one day later, causing the traveler to omit a calendar day. When traveling eastward across the date line, the date changes to one day earlier, causing the traveler to repeat a calendar day.

In an international congress convened in 1884 a system of international time was established in which the world is divided into time zones, each covering 15⁰ of longitude. The meridian passing through the observatory at Greenwich, England was set as the prime meridian, marking 0⁰ of longitude, from which all time is reckoned. For each 15⁰ east of Greenwich the time is advanced one hour, and for each 15⁰ west of Greenwich the time is set back one hour. The meridian 180⁰ from this prime meridian, exactly halfway around the world from Greenwich, was designated as the International Date Line, arbitrarily demarcating each calendar day. The Date Line extends from the North Pole through the Pacific Ocean to the South Pole. It corresponds along most of its length to the 180th meridian of longitude, but deviates eastward through the Bering Strait to avoid dividing Siberia, and then westward to include the Aleutian Islands with Alaska. South of the Equator another deviation allows certain island groups to have the same day as New Zealand.

The Sabbath day, it is evident, does not occur on the same date in differ-

delighting in it according to his ability, is assured by the prophet of his reward in this world, besides the great reward in store for him in the world to come, as it is said, "If you turn away your foot because of the Sabbath from pursuing your business on My holy day; and call the Sabbath a delight, and the holy of God honorable; and shall

_____

ent parts of the world, but varies according to location and time zone. The question of the proper time for the observance of the Sabbath and other holy days, such as Yom Kippur and Pesach, for travelers to distant places on the globe, while of some halachic interest in the past, arose with greater and more dramatic urgency with the arrival in Japan of Torah scholars and religious Jews fleeing the holocaust in Europe, and Jewish soldiers stationed on remote islands in the Pacific Ocean. It has since become a practical question of more widespread interest, in view of the greater accessibility of these distant lands due to modern advances in air and sea travel, and as a result of world wide tourism and international commerce.

Contemporary halachic authorities differ on the principal elements in determining a calendar day, namely, designation of the prime meridian and the corresponding date line. One view, set forth by Rabbi Menachem M. Kasher, advocates acceptance of the International Date Line, adopted by the world community of nations, for determining the Sabbath day in various regions of the world. Rabbi Kasher contends that designation of the date line is not decreed by the Torah, but is the prerogative of Rabbinical authority. Acceptance of the prevailing International Date Line, he believes, will facilitate and assure the observance of the Sabbath by Jews residing in and visiting other regions of the world. Another view, set forth by Rabbi J. M. Tikozinsky, maintains that according to Torah law and Jewish tradition the global center from which time is reckoned is the Holy City of Jerusalem, and consequently the date line is 180° from Jerusalem. A third view, advanced by the *Hazon Ish,* likewise affirms Jerusalem as the focal center. However, in his opinion the calendar day extends 18 hours (270°) west and 6 hours (90°) east, and consequently the date line is to be located in China. In contention, particularly with respect to the latter opinion, is the status of places such as Japan which are farther than 90° from Jerusalem.

While the fundamental issue in the controversy remains unresolved, authorities advise the following procedure for one confronted with the question of observing the Sabbath at the proper time when traveling to distant

honor it, not doing your wonted ways, nor pursuing your business, nor speaking thereof; then shall you delight yourself in God, and I will make you to ride upon the high places of the earth, and I will feed you with the heritage of Jacob, your father; for the mouth of God has spoken it" (Isaiah 58:13,14).

2. PREPARING FOR THE SABBATH

דִּינֵי הֲכָנַת שַׁבָּת

1.   It is written, "Remember the Sabbath day to keep it holy" (Exodus 20:8); which means remember to hallow the Sabbath every day of

---

parts of the world. In general, one must keep the Sabbath, with respect to all the Sabbath laws and restrictions, as well as the Sabbath prayers and observance of *mitzvot,* according to the reckoning of the place of his arrival and as kept by the established Jewish community in the place. Some maintain that in the first week after crossing the date line he should, for the sake of stringency, also keep the Sabbath according to the reckoning of his place of departure. With regard to the latter, he should refrain from doing any *melachah* on this day, irrespective of whether it is a Biblical or a Rabbinical prohibition, but he should consider it a weekday in other respects, and conduct himself accordingly as regards prayer, *tefillin* and other *mitzvot.* One who has crossed the date line while en route on ship at sea should, before reaching his destination, continue counting the calendar days and consider the Sabbath day according to the reckoning of the place of his departure. Some suggest stringency in this case also, and that he should refrain from doing any *melachot* on the Sabbath day according to the alternate reckoning as well.

In view of the complexity of this question and the practical problems involved, it is advisable that one obtain authoritative halachic guidance in each particular instance. In any case, one should not schedule a journey or a flight under circumstances where it will still be *Shabbat* at the time of his arrival at his destination. If in an emergency he must make such a trip, he should conduct himself as one is required to do on *Shabbat.* See Chapter 4 and relevant notes.

the week. Thus, if one should chance upon some food that is a delicacy and not always available, and which will not spoil if kept for a
while, he should buy it in honor of the Sabbath. One should rise early
Friday morning (*erev Shabbat*) in order to procure what is needed for
the Sabbath. He may do so even before reciting the morning prayers,
provided it does not prevent him from joining in the prayer service
with the congregation.[1] It is preferable to buy the provisions on Friday in honor of the Sabbath. However, whatever requires preparation should be bought on Thursday. When buying something for the
Sabbath, he should say לִכְבוֹד שַׁבָּת, "It is in honor of the Sabbath."
One of the ordinances instituted by Ezra is to wash and launder one's
clothes on Thursday, so that they will be ready to wear in honor of
the Sabbath. This should not be left for Friday, as one must then
attend to the immediate needs in preparation for the Sabbath.

2.   It is the duty of all, even one who has many servants, to take part
in some way in preparing for the Sabbath, thereby honoring it in person.[2] This was the custom of the Sages. For example, Rav Ḥisda used
to cut up the vegetables; Rabbah and Rav Yosef would chop wood;
Rav Zeira would kindle the fire; Rav Naḥman would put the house in
order, and bring in the utensils needed for the Sabbath and clear
away those used during the week. Everyone should follow their
example, and not regard it beneath his dignity, for it is to his honor to
honor the Sabbath.

---

1.   Purchasing Sabbath Provisions Before the Morning Prayers   Although
one ought not attend to his personal needs before the morning prayers, he
may purchase provisions, since providing for the Sabbath is considered "in
the interest of heaven." He should, however, recite the *Shema* in the proper
time. In the event that Sabbath provisions will not be available by the time
the congregation concludes the morning service, he should recite the morning prayers privately.

2.   Preparing for the Sabbath   When the days are short, or the hour is late,
it is especially incumbent upon everyone to help prepare for the Sabbath in
order to avoid a violation of the Sabbath.

3. It is a prevailing custom among Jews to bake loaves of bread (*hallot*) in the home in honor of the Sabbath.[3] Those who eat bread baked by a non-Jewish baker on weekdays should be careful to eat Jewish baked bread on the holy Sabbath.[4] And even if one eats bread baked by a Jewish baker on weekdays, he should have bread baked in the home in honor of the Sabbath, so that the woman of the house may perform the *mitzvah* of taking *hallah* from the dough.[5] It is customary to bake three loaves, a large loaf, a medium sized loaf, and a small loaf. The medium sized loaf is for the evening meal, the large one is for the daytime meal to show that the Sabbath day is accorded great honor, and the small loaf is for the third meal (*seudah shelishit*).

4. One should prepare choice meat and fish, tasty food[6] and good

---

3. Hallot Are To Be Baked Erev Shabbat   The Sabbath *hallot* should be baked *erev Shabbat,* that is, on Friday, or on Thursday night if necessary, when the days are short, similar to the show-bread which was prepared *erev Shabbat* and placed on the table in the Temple on the Sabbath.

4. Hallot To Be Baked by a Jew   In honor of the Sabbath one should endeavor to eat *hallot* that were baked by a Jew. However, if need be, he may eat bread baked by a non-Jew, provided it is kosher, and, if necessary, he may make *Kiddush* over it.

5. Mitzvah of Hallah Entrusted to Women   One of the *mitzvot* especially entrusted to the woman, who is mistress of the home, is the *mitzvah* of taking *hallah*. Jewish women have traditionally considered this a great privilege, and are accustomed to bake *hallot* for the Sabbath in order to be able to perform the *mitzvah* of taking *hallah*. For the laws on the separation of the *hallah* portion from the dough in baking bread, see Volume One, Part IV, Chapter 4.

6. Eating Hot Food on the Sabbath   One should endeavor to have hot food to eat on *Shabbat* in honor of the Sabbath and in fulfillment of the *mitzvah* of *Oneg Shabbat*. It is customary among Ashkenazim, in particular, to have *chulent,* a dish consisting usually of meat, beans, barley, and pota-

wine, according to his means. It is desirable to eat fish at every Sabbath meal,[7] but if one finds it harmful or does not care for it, he need not eat it, for the Sabbath is meant to afford us pleasure and not discomfort. The house should be put in order; the beds made, and the table covered with a tablecloth which should remain on the table the entire Sabbath day. Some are accustomed to placing two cloths on the table.[8] The silverware should be polished and the dishes set out in honor of the Sabbath. One should rejoice in the coming of the Sabbath, and consider how assiduously he would go about setting the house in order if he were expecting the arrival of a dear and esteemed guest; how much more so then in honor of the Sabbath Queen. Some

---

toes, that is cooked *erev Shabbat* and kept on the fire overnight to be served hot on *Shabbat*. The Sefardim, likewise, prepare hot food for *Shabbat*. The Rabbis advocated this practice in order to counter the false and misguided views of the Karaite sect and others, who mistook the Biblical admonition, "You shall kindle no fire throughout your habitations upon the Sabbath day" (Exodus 35:3) to mean that one may not leave a fire, which is kindled before the Sabbath, to burn on the Sabbath. This is a denial of the Oral Law (*Torah she b'alpeh*) which teaches that it is permitted. Although it is forbidden to kindle a light or fire, or to cook on the Sabbath, one may, nevertheless, benefit from light and heat, and enjoy a hot meal, if prepared and kept warm in a permissible manner. The Sabbath is to be celebrated as a day of joy, in keeping with the words of the prophet, "And call the Sabbath a delight" (Isaiah 58:13).

7.   Eating Fish at the Sabbath Meals   It is customary to eat fish at the Sabbath meals, especially at the *seudah shelishit*. However, if the price of fish is raised excessively, thereby causing a hardship for the poor, the religious authorities are to instruct the people not to buy any fish until it is offered for sale at a normal price.

8.   Covering the Table With Two Cloths   The table should be covered during all of the Sabbath day. Hence, some are accustomed to placing two cloths, so that when the tablecloth is shaken out, the table will not be left bare.

are accustomed to make a meat pie or stuffed meat for the Sabbath evening meal.[9] One should taste the Sabbath food on *erev Shabbat.*

5.   Even the poorest Jew should endeavor to make the Sabbath a day of delight. He should be frugal during the week so that he will have sufficient funds with which to honor the Sabbath. If one has no money he should borrow in order to provide for the Sabbath. Of such a one our Rabbis, of blessed memory, say, "The Holy One, blessed be He, said unto Israel: My children, borrow on My account and celebrate the holiness of the day, and trust in Me and I will repay" (*Betzah* 15b). All of a man's sustenance for the year is apportioned to him on Rosh Hashanah, except for the expenditures for the Sabbath and for Festivals. If he spends more for these, he is given more. However, if one is in extreme circumstances, he should follow the advice of the Rabbis, of blessed memory, who said, "Treat thy Sabbath like a weekday" (that is, be content with weekday fare) "rather than be dependent on other people" (*Shabbat* 118a). Nevertheless, if possible, he should try to prepare something, however little, such as some small fish or the like, in honor of the Sabbath. If one received some food intended for the Sabbath, he should eat it on the Sabbath and not leave it for a weekday.

6.   One should not do any work on a regular basis on Friday (*erev Shabbat*) from the time of the late afternoon prayer (*Minḥah Ketanah*), that is, from about two and a half hours before nightfall, but if it is work of an incidental nature, it is permitted. When it is required for the Sabbath, one is permitted to work even later. A poor person who wants to earn enough for his Sabbath needs may work all day Friday, just as on the Intermediate Days of a Festival (*Ḥol Hamoed*). Giving a Jew a haircut, even if it is done professionally and

---

9. Eating a Meat Pie   The meat pie (*pashtida*), which consists of meat covered by layers of dough, is in remembrance of the manna which was covered by dew from above and below, and was collected in a double portion for the Sabbath.

for pay, is permissible all day Friday, as it is apparent that it is for the sake of the Sabbath. Shops and businesses should be closed at least one hour before the Sabbath.[10]

7.   During the last quarter of the day on Friday one should refrain from eating a regular meal,[11] even if he usually has one on weekdays. A special meal which one does not usually have on weekdays, even if it is a *seudat mitzvah,* is not permitted all day Friday,[12] even in the morning, provided the *seudah* can be held another day.[13] However, a

---

10.   Closing Shop Early Before Shabbat   Shops and businesses should be closed at a reasonable hour, to allow ample time for people to go home and prepare for the Sabbath, so as to avoid violating the Sabbath. The stipulation of one hour before the Sabbath is, therefore, to be understood to mean one hour before *Kabbalat Shabbat,* which is about an hour and a half before nightfall. The actual closing time would then be at least two and a half hours before nightfall.

11.   Refraining from Eating a Meal Before Shabbat   One should refrain from eating a regular meal *erev Shabbat* after nine hours in the day, which is equivalent to the last quarter of the day. The hours are, in this regard, reckoned according to the length of the day. However, in the winter, when the day is short, it is best not to eat a regular meal even before that time, so as not to spoil one's appetite for the Sabbath meal.

12.   Not Having a Seudah on Friday   One should not have a feast (*seudah*) or a special meal on Friday as he may neglect to prepare properly for the Sabbath as a result of his preoccupation with the feast. Moreover, by having a festive meal on Friday, he detracts from the honor that is to be accorded the Sabbath.

13.   A Wedding or Engagement Seudah on Friday   A *seudah* on the occasion of a wedding may be held *erev Shabbat,* provided the wedding takes place that day, although it is preferable that the feast be postponed until the next day or another day. A feast on the occasion of an engagement is not considered a *seudat mitzvah,* as an engagement is today not similar to a betrothal (*erusin*) which originally had a halachic status in effecting the marriage. Hence, the feast cannot be held *erev Shabbat* even if the engagement

seudat mitzvah that must take place that day, such as on the occasion of a circumcision (*brit milah*) or the redemption of the first born son (*pidyon haben*) and the like, is permitted.[14] Nevertheless, it is proper to make it earlier in the morning and not to prolong the meal, and certainly not to eat to excess, so that the Sabbath meal may be eaten with appetite.

8.   One is required to read each week the portion of the Torah (*parshat hashavua*) that is read in the synagogue. One may begin reading it on Sunday, as that is considered reading the portion together with the congregation, since the congregation already began reading the week's portion at *Minḥah* on the previous Sabbath. However, it is preferable that one read it on Friday afternoon.[15] The procedure to follow is to read the Biblical text twice and the *Targum* once, that is, each section (*parshah*) should be read twice, then its *Targum*,[16] fol-

---

takes place that day. However, it is permitted to serve pastry, sweets, and similar refreshments at the engagement and the writing of the engagement agreement (*tena'im*), as this is not deemed a feast.

14.   A Seudah On Friday for a Brit or Pidyon Haben When Delayed   A *seudah* on the occasion of a *brit* or a *pidyon haben* is held *erev Shabbat,* even if the circumcision or the redemption was delayed and does not take place at its normally appointed time.

15.   Reviewing the Torah Portion by Sabbath Morning   If one has not concluded a review of the weekly Torah portion before the Sabbath, he should endeavor to do so on Sabbath morning before going to the synagogue. Some authorities consider it equally meritorious to start the review at the beginning of the week. Thus, it was the custom of the Gaon of Vilna to read a part of the *Sidrah* and the *Targum* daily after the morning service and to conclude it *erev Shabbat.* One who is pressed for time can fulfill his obligation of reviewing the *Sidrah* by reading with the Reader, and reading the Torah portion a second time, along with the *Targum,* at home.

16.   Procedure for Reviewing the Weekly Torah Portion   The procedure recommended by some authorities, and often followed, is to read each Bib-

lowed by a Biblical verse so as to conclude with a reading from the Torah. It is well not to interrupt one's reading with conversation. It is customary to read the *Haftarah* (the portion from the Prophets) as well.[17] Some are accustomed to recite *Shir Hashirim* (Song of Songs) afterwards. One who has a *Ḥumash* which contains only Scripture without *Targum* should read the text twice, and read the *Targum* when it becomes available. Every devout person should also study Rashi's commentary on the *Sidrah,* and if he is not capable of understanding it, he should read the week's portion of Scripture in translation with commentary in a language that he understands so that he will know the contents of the *Sidrah.*[18]

---

lical verse twice and then the *Targum* of that verse. This would conform to the practice in times past, when the Biblical portion read at the services was translated into Aramaic by the *meturgeman,* one verse at a time. Either procedure is acceptable. Some permit reading the Torah portion, followed by the *Targum,* then the Torah portion again. The Torah reading should be intoned in the traditional chant in accordance with the accents (*ta'amim*) that indicate the cantillation of the verse. It is advisable that the *ta'amim* and cantillation of the Torah and *Haftarah* be learned at an early age. One who is proficient should preferably do the reading from a Torah scroll.

17. Reviewing the Haftarah Assigned for the Sabbath The *Haftarah* to be reviewed is the one assigned to be read on that Sabbath. Thus, on the special Sabbaths, as well as on the Sabbath of *Rosh Ḥodesh,* the Sabbath preceding *Rosh Ḥodesh* and the Sabbath of Ḥanukah, one should read the *Haftarah* designated for that particular Sabbath. The purpose of reviewing the *Haftarah* is so that if one is called to the Torah for *Maftir* he will be able to read it fluently.

18. Reading Targum and Rashi's Commentary The *Targum* is important in that it explains the meaning of the text, while the great value of Rashi's commentary (available in English translation) is that it explains each subject according to the exposition of the Sages in the Midrash and the Talmud. A popular commentary in Yiddish (also available in English translation) is the *Tze'enah Ure'enah,* which includes the commentaries of Rashi and other scholars based on the Midrash, the Talmud and other traditional sources.

9.   One should wash his face and hands with warm water *erev Shabbat*. If possible he should bathe his entire body in warm water, and also immerse himself in a *mikveh*. One should, likewise, wash and cleanse his head, trim his nails, and cut his hair if it is too long.

10.   On *erev Shabbat* one should examine his conduct and repent, and resolve to amend all the wrongs which he committed during the week, for Sabbath eve embodies all the weekdays, just as the eve of *Rosh Hodesh* embodies the whole month.[19]

11.   One should endeavor to have fine clothes as well as a nice *tallit mitzvah*[20] to wear in honor of the Sabbath, for it is written, "And you shall honor it" (Isaiah 58:13), which the Rabbis expound as meaning: "Your garments for the Sabbath should not be the same as those for weekdays" (*Shabbat* 113a).[21] Even while away on a journey among non-Jews, one should wear his Sabbath clothes, because his

---

19.   **Repentance on the Eve of the Sabbath**   *Erev Shabbat* is comparable to the eve of *Rosh Hodesh,* which is like a day of atonement for transgressions one may have committed during the preceding month. It is fitting to turn one's thoughts to repentance *erev Shabbat* in preparation for communion with God on the holy day of *Shabbat.*

20.   **A Tallit in Honor of the Sabbath**   If one has the means, he should endeavor to have a special *tallit* in honor of the Sabbath.

21.   **Wearing Sabbath Clothes**   If possible, one should have a complete change of clothing for *Shabbat*. In any event, one should wear at least one special garment by which to be reminded that it is *Shabbat*. It is not necessary, though commendable, to have special shoes for Sabbath wear. He should, however, polish them for the Sabbath. One who does not put on Sabbath clothes *erev Shabbat* because he is busy and in a hurry, and waits to dress for *Shabbat* on Sabbath morning, is acting improperly and denigrating the sanctity of the Sabbath. One should bathe *erev Shabbat* close to evening and dress immediately in honor of *Shabbat*. The Sabbath clothes should be worn all of *Shabbat* until after *Havdalah.*

special attire on the Sabbath is not in respect for others but in honor of the Sabbath.

12.   Food cooked in a pot placed directly on burning coals* must be removed before the Sabbath. If one forgets, it is forbidden to remove it on the Sabbath, because in picking up the pot he will move the coals surrounding it and cause the fire to flare up. It is permitted to have a non-Jew remove it.

13.   Food that is kept in the oven for the Sabbath day, as is customary, is permitted even if the door of the oven is not sealed with clay. However, it is not permitted to open the door at night, as the food in some of the pots may not be fully cooked and by closing the oven afterwards one will be the cause of its cooking.[22]

14.   The permission to keep food in the oven, even when it is not sealed with clay,[23] applies only to meats, and also to leguminous

---

* While the procedures for storing hot food on the Sabbath outlined here by the *Kitzur Shulḥan Aruch* were intended to serve as a guide, given the cooking facilities available in his time, the underlying halachic principles apply as well today. For a guide to current practice, see the section on Storing Hot Food For Shabbat at the end of this chapter, and Part II, Melachah 11, Baking and Cooking.

22.   Opening and Closing the Oven   On closing the oven door heat is added and the cooking process is accelerated, even if the coals have been removed or covered with ashes. If the coals have not been removed or covered with ashes, it is forbidden for a Jew to open and close the oven door, even if the food was fully cooked before the Sabbath, for at night the coals are in all likelihood still smoldering, and upon opening the door the air entering will cause the coals to flare up, and by closing it he may extinguish the fire.

23.   Keeping a Pot of Food on the Stove   The Sages prohibited placing a pot of food on the stove or in the oven *erev Shabbat* and leaving it to cook on the Sabbath (*shehiyah*) for fear that one may stoke the coals or embers and intensify the fire in order to hasten the cooking process. The prohibition does not apply if one of the following measures is taken to preclude or prevent one from stirring up the fire.

vegetables (such as peas and beans) and dough which have been in the oven for some time before the Sabbath so that they will have been cooked before nightfall to the point where they are edible if need be. But if the legumes and dough are placed in the oven close to nightfall, the oven must be sealed with clay because in all probability the coals have not properly removed or covered with ashes. One must be careful regarding this, for otherwise it is forbidden to partake of the food until such time after the Sabbath as it would ordinarily take to cook it.

15.   An oven that has been sealed with clay should be opened on the Sabbath by a non-Jew. If a non-Jew is not available, it should be opened by a minor. If neither is available, it may be opened by an adult, but he should do it in a manner different from the way it is usually done.

16.   One is not permitted to put a pot of hot coffee in sand *erev Shabbat* in order to keep it warm for the Sabbath, either by burying it completely in the sand or only partially in the sand and covering the rest with pillows and the like.[24] It should rather be done in the follow-

---

(a) If cooking is begun in sufficient time before the Sabbath, so that the food will have been cooked to the point where it is edible, and there will be no further need to stir up the fire for it to be fully cooked. Food is considered edible if it has undergone one-half, or at least one-third of its normal cooking process.

(b) If the coals and embers have been removed or covered with ashes or sand.

(c) If the food is intended for the Sabbath day meal and it is of a kind, such as raw meat, that takes a long time to cook, so that it will not be ready for the Friday evening meal, and provided it is put up to cook just before the Sabbath, so that he will pay no further attention to it, knowing that it will be fully cooked by the next day without intensifying the fire.

(d) If the door of the oven is sealed with clay to serve as a reminder, so as to prevent one from inadvertently stirring up the fire.

24.   Keeping Food Warm Under Covers   The Sages prohibited putting a

ing manner. He should cover only one—half or one—third of the coffee pot with the sand and the rest must remain uncovered. He can then place a board or a vessel over the hole, so that there is a space between it and the coffee pot, and then put a covering of clothing, pillows and the like on top.

17. Shortly before dark one should inquire of his household whether the *hallah* portion had been separated from the dough,[25] and tell them to light the Sabbath candles. He should also caution them to cease whatever work is prohibited on the Sabbath. He should do all of the above in a gentle, pleasant manner.[26]

---

dish or a pot of food under covers on the Sabbath to keep it warm (*hatmanah*). If it is in a substance which generates or adds heat, such as salt or sand, *hatmanah* is forbidden even on *erev Shabbat,* lest one place the pot of food amidst live coals and then stir them up on the Sabbath. However, *hatmanah* applies only where the substance in which the pot is kept is in direct contact with it, and covers it on top and bottom and on all sides. Hence, where the coffee pot is only partially buried in the sand, it is permitted, if covered in the manner indicated. Likewise, for the reason cited, the prohibition of *hatmanah* does not apply to a pot placed in an enclosed oven.

25. Forgetting to Take Ḥallah Before the Sabbath Inquiry about the *hallah* portion is meant to serve as a reminder. In practice, however, if one forgot to separate the *hallah* portion before the Sabbath, it is permitted to eat the bread and then take *hallah* after the Sabbath from what is left over. This procedure may be followed in countries outside the Land of Israel. Hence the reminder is no longer necessary. However, in *Eretz Yisrael* it is not permitted to eat the bread if *hallah* was not taken. For the laws on separating the *hallah* portion, see Volume One, Part IV, Chapter 4.

26. Cultivating a Spirit of Peace and Love in the Home Avoiding contention and quarreling in the family on the eve of the Sabbath is essential to cultivating a spirit of peace and tranquility that should pervade the home (שָׁלוֹם בַּיִת) on *Shabbat*. The man of the house is exhorted to deal kindly with his children and the members of his household, and to show special tenderness and love toward his wife as the Sabbath approaches.

18.   One must examine his clothing *erev Shabbat* before dark to be sure that there is no needle or pin stuck in them, or something in the pockets. This should be done even where there is an *eruv* and it is permissible to carry, because they may contain articles that are *muktzeh* which may not be handled on the Sabbath.

Storing Hot Food For Shabbat

The following is the procedure for leaving food over the fire on a gas or electric stove in order to keep the food hot on the Sabbath. Before the Sabbath:

(a)   The food should be cooked.

(b)   The top burners on the stove that are to be left on should be covered with a *blech,* that is, a metal sheet, such as a tin or aluminum plate.

(c)   The flame should be set at the appropriate level.

(d)   The pot of cooked food should be placed on the *blech* before the commencement of the Sabbath. It may thereafter be moved on the Sabbath to different areas on the *blech* as desired.

All cooked food such as meat, whether as a dry solid or in a broth, and hot liquid, such as soup, may then be kept on the stove to be served hot at the Sabbath meal.

In order to have hot water on *Shabbat* for coffee or tea, and for other purposes, the water should be boiled, and the kettle of boiled water placed on the *blech* before the Sabbath. The kettle may then be kept on the stove overnight and all the Sabbath day, and the water used as needed.

One may also use an electric urn from which water can be drawn on the Sabbath. The electric current should be connected in sufficient time for the water to be boiled before the Sabbath.

The detailed rules on handling and serving hot food and beverages, and the particular laws regarding the use of modern stoves, ovens and electrical appliances on the Sabbath are discussed in Part II, Melachah 11, Baking and Cooking, and Melachah 36, Kindling a Fire, and Electrical Equipment and Appliances.

3. CONTRACTING BEFORE THE SABBATH
FOR WORK BY A NON-JEW

לָתֵת קוֹדֶם שַׁבָּת מְלָאכָה לְאֵינוֹ יְהוּדִי וּלְהַשְׁאִיל וּלְהַשְׂכִּיר לוֹ כֵּלִים

1. A Jew is forbidden to have a non-Jew do work for him on the Sabbath.[1] This prohibition is based on the Biblical verse, "No manner of work shall be done" (Exodus 12:16), which the Sages take to mean even by a non-Jew (*Mechilta,* ibid.).

2. However, if the work is given to the non-Jew before the Sabbath,[2] even though he does it on the Sabbath, it is permitted[3] on the following conditions:

---

1. Prohibition of Work on the Sabbath by a Non-Jew Although a non-Jew is not bound to observe the Sabbath, a Jew may not have him do work on the Sabbath. The Sages instituted this prohibition lest the Sabbath be taken lightly and the Jew will come to profane it himself by work on the Sabbath. The prohibition will also keep the Jew from being preoccupied with activities that would be likely to disturb his Sabbath rest. For additional laws pertaining to work by a non-Jew on the Sabbath see Part V, Chapter 6.

2. Requesting a Non-Jew to Do a Melachah Bain Hashemashot It is permitted to request a non-Jew to do a *melachah* on Sabbath eve during the period of בֵּין הַשְּׁמָשׁוֹת, if it is for a *mitzvah* or if it is urgently needed. Thus, it is permitted to have him put on the lights, or relight the gas if it went out on the stove, and the like. The period of time this is permitted would be up to nightfall, that is, approximately a half hour after sunset.

3. Giving Work to a Non-Jew Before the Sabbath One is not obliged to prevent a non-Jew from working on the Sabbath, if he does the work on his own premises, utilizing his time as he sees fit. Thus, one is permitted to bring garments to the cleaner, or shoes to the shoemaker on Friday, if there is sufficient time before or after the Sabbath to do the work and he does not specify that the non-Jew should do the work on the Sabbath, or that he must have it immediately after the Sabbath, so that he would have to work on the Sabbath.

(a) The work should be taken by the non-Jew and removed from the home of the Jew before the Sabbath. He should not take it on the Sabbath. If the non-Jew does the work in a public place, it should not be commonly known that the work belongs to the Jew.

(b) He should stipulate compensation for the work, so that the non-Jew will then be working for himself in order to receive payment.[4] Therefore, one who employs a non-Jewish servant for a stated period may not allow him to do work on the Sabbath, as the work is solely for the benefit of the Jew. If a Jew gives a letter to a non-Jew to be delivered to a certain place where he is traveling, and he will also be carrying it on the Sabbath, the Jew must pay him, so that he will be doing it for compensation.[5]

(c) The non-Jew should be paid a stipulated amount for the entire job, and not be hired by the day.[6]

(d) It is forbidden to specify, even indirectly, that the work be done on the Sabbath. Nor may one demand that the work be

---

4. Compensation for Work Done   It is permitted to arrange for the work to be done by the non-Jew even if no amount is stipulated, so long as it is agreed that there will be compensation, or it is generally known that there is compensation for such work. Some permit the non-Jew to do the work without compensation if he does it in appreciation, or in anticipation, of a favor. While others dispute this view, it may be followed, especially if the non-Jew takes the initiative in offering his services.

5. Mailing a Letter Erev Shabbat   It is permitted to mail a letter, even registered and express mail, on *erev Shabbat*. It is preferable to refrain from posting mail on *erev Shabbat,* however, if there is a likelihood that some of the postal workers in the local Post Office are Jews. See Part II, Melachah 32, note 23.

6. Contracting for Work by the Week   A non-Jewish worker may also be hired by the week, with the stipulation that he will be paid his wages irrespective of whether or not he works on the Sabbath.

completed by a certain time after the Sabbath, when it is apparent that the non-Jew cannot do so unless he works on the Sabbath,[7] because this would be tantamount to requiring him to work on the Sabbath. Thus, one may not send a letter or a parcel through a non-Jew, specifying a time of delivery that would necessitate his travel on the Sabbath. Similarly one is forbidden to give money to a non-Jew on *erev Shabbat* in order to buy him something which cannot be bought except on the Sabbath. He is, likewise, forbidden to give him anything to sell under such circumstances. However, in these instances, where he does not expressly order him to do it on the Sabbath, it is forbidden only if he gives him the work or the money on *erev Shabbat,* but before then he is permitted to give him work to do or money to purchase an article for him. It is best not to live in a city where the market day is on the Sabbath, as it is bound to lead to transgression. However, if it does not take place in a Jewish neighborhood, one need not be concerned.

(e) The work should not be of such a nature that it is connected with the ground, as in building or farming. It is forbidden to have a non-Jew do work on a building on the Sabbath, even if the Jew agreed to pay him a stipulated amount for the entire work.[8] In case of urgent necessity, one should consult a rabbinic author-

---

7. Leaving a Car for Repair Before the Sabbath It is permitted to leave one's car in a garage for repair at a stipulated price on Friday, provided the operators and workers are non-Jews, and there is time to make the repairs before or after the Sabbath, even if the work is, in fact, done on the Sabbath.

8. Work on a Building by Non-Jews One may not have construction work on a building done by non-Jews on the Sabbath, even under a job contracting agreement, because of the appearance of wrongdoing (*mar'it ha'ayin*), and the *ḥillul Hashem* caused when the public perceives it as a desecration of the Sabbath by a Jew.

ity.[9] It is also forbidden to have a non-Jew quarry stones, or prepare beams for construction, on the Sabbath, if it is known that they belong to a Jew, and the work is done in public. This prohibition applies also to work in the field, such as plowing or reaping, and the like, even if the non-Jew is not a day laborer, but is hired to do the entire work for a stipulated sum. However, if the non-Jew takes a share of the crops as compensation for his work, and it is customary in that locality for the worker in the field to receive a share of the crops, it is permitted.[10] If the field is at a considerable distance and there is no Jew living within two thousand cubits (a *tehum Shabbat*) of the field, it is permitted so long as the non-Jew is paid a stipulated sum for his work, and he is not hired by the day.

3.   If, in violation of the prohibition, the house was built for the Jew by non-Jews who worked on its construction on the Sabbath, it is proper that he act stringently and refrain from dwelling in it. However, there are divergent opinions regarding the law in such a case.[11]

---

9.   Building Homes for Homeless Families   In an extraordinary ruling, the *Hatam Sofer* permitted the building of homes for Jewish families rendered homeless by war, with work done even on the Sabbath by a non-Jewish contractor and non-Jewish workers, in view of the urgent need to provide shelter for the homeless.

10.   Joint Ownership of a Business by a Jew and a Non-Jew   In the case of joint or corporate ownership of a business or a store by a Jew and a non-Jew, competent Rabbinical authority should be consulted for a proper ruling and guidance with regard to conducting the business on the Sabbath.

11.   A House Built by Non-Jews on the Sabbath   Opinions differ in the case where the house was constructed within the city limits on a job contracting arrangement and only the minor prohibition of *mar'it ha'ayin,* the appearance of wrongdoing, is involved. Those who take the lenient view permit

4. One who owns a farm or a mill may rent it to a non-Jew, although he will work there on the Sabbath, but he may not rent a bathhouse to a non-Jew.[12] If the Jew does not own the bathhouse, but is only renting it from a non-Jew, and he wants to sublet it to a non-Jew, he should consult an authority on the matter. Similarly, one who has the rights to collect the taxes levied on an inn, a brick factory, or a glass factory, and the like, should consult an authority as to how he is to conduct himself.

5. One is forbidden, under any circumstances, to allow a non-Jew to do work in his house on the Sabbath.[13] A non-Jewish servant

---

even the Jew who contracted for the work to live in the house. If the house was built by day-workers hired by him, and an actual violation of the law is involved, it is forbidden by law, and not merely improper, for the Jew to dwell there. Other Jews, however, may take up residence after waiting the period of time that it would take to have the work done. Some take a lenient view even in the latter instance, and place the same minimal time restriction as well on the Jew for whom the house was built.

12.   Renting an Establishment to a Non-Jew   It is permitted to rent a farm or a mill to a non-Jew who will be working there on the Sabbath, because it is customary practice, and it is commonly known that he is working for himself. It is not permitted, however, to rent out an establishment such as a bathhouse that is well known as belonging to the Jew, and it is assumed that the non-Jew is only a hired worker. In all these matters, local practice on renting the facilities, and the profit sharing arrangements involved, are taken into account in the final ruling.

13.   A Repairman Working in the House   One may not have an electrician or other repairman do work in his home or apartment on the Sabbath. If a non-Jewish worker or repairman comes on the Sabbath, he must protest and prevent him from doing the work, because it would appear as though he summoned him and directed him to work for him on the Sabbath. In an emergency, as in the case of a breakdown of the furnace in the winter, it is permitted.

should not be allowed to do work in the house on the Sabbath, even if he does the work for himself.[14]

6. If one had a garment made for him by a non-Jewish tailor, who brought it to him on the Sabbath, he is permitted to wear it. But, if it is known that the tailor finished it on the Sabbath, he should not wear it, except in a case of necessity.[15] However, it is forbidden on the Sabbath or on a Festival to take utensils or garments from the house or shop of a craftsman or tailor, even from one who is Jewish. But it is permitted to take it from a non-Jewish storekeeper who did not produce the article. Thus, if he is acquainted with the owner of a shoe store, he may go there on the Sabbath and take a pair of shoes and wear them, provided he does not set the sales price with the owner, and the merchandise was not brought on the Sabbath from outside the Sabbath boundary.[16]

----

14. Work by a Non-Jewish Servant   A non-Jewish servant is not permitted to do work for the Jew that is forbidden him on the Sabbath. Thus, one may not have a servant repair one's clothes in the house. However, according to many authorities, one may allow a non-Jewish servant to do work for himself, such as repairing his own garments in the privacy of his own quarters in the house.

15. Wearing a Garment Completed on the Sabbath   If the non-Jew finished the garment on the Sabbath, one must wait before wearing it until after the conclusion of the Sabbath for the time that it would take to do the work, so that he will not benefit from work done for him by the non-Jew on the Sabbath. However, if he needs the garment for the Sabbath, we follow the lenient view that wherever payment is fixed, the non-Jew is considered to be working on his own behalf, and one is permitted to wear it even on the Sabbath.

16. Taking Merchandise From a Craftsman or a Storekeeper   It is forbidden to take a utensil or a garment from the artisan's premises on the Sabbath because of the appearance of wrongdoing (*mar'it ha'ayin*), as it will be said that he completed the article on the Sabbath at the Jew's bidding. This

7.   It is forbidden to rent out workman's tools, such as a plow and the like, to a non-Jew *erev Shabbat,* even though one is not obligated to have the tools rest on the Sabbath. Since he receives payment for rental of the tools, and he rents them out *erev Shabbat,* it appears as though the non-Jew is acting as his agent and working with the tools at his behest. He may, however, rent them out on Thursday, or before then. He is permitted to lend workman's tools to a non-Jew even *erev Shabbat,* provided he takes them from his house before the Sabbath. Moreover, he may even do so on condition that the non-Jew reciprocate by lending him his tools some other time, and it is not considered as though he were renting them out. In the case of ordinary utensils, which are not workman's tools, it is permitted to rent them out, even *erev Shabbat,* so long as the non-Jew takes them before the Sabbath.

8.   Renting out tools or utensils on the aforestated conditions is permissible only if one is not paid separately for their use on the Sabbath, but payment for the Sabbath is included with the rest of the days, as when they are rented by the month or by the week, and he stipulates payment of a specified amount for the week or the month, or even for every two or three days. One is not permitted to receive separate payment for the Sabbath, even if he rents them out for the year, but he reckons payment for each day separately. Thus, if he rents them out for the year or the month, he may not stipulate payment of a specified amount for each day, even if the non-Jew subsequently pays the full amount at one time. In such a case one may not take the payment due for their use on the Sabbath, even for the rental of ordinary utensils with which no work is done, inasmuch as each day is reckoned separately, and payment for the Sabbath is not

---

would not apply in the case of a storekeeper who is only selling and not producing the articles. Some authorities, however, do not approve the practice of taking merchandise from a storekeeper on the Sabbath, even where no purchase is involved, as it is a weekday activity not in keeping with the spirit of the Sabbath.

included with the rest of the days. The same rule applies in the rental of a room for dwelling.[17] The prohibition of receiving compensation for the Sabbath in the above instances is applicable whether it is from a non-Jew or from a Jew.

4. TRAVEL BY BOAT ON THE SABBATH

דִּין הַמַּפְלִיג בִּסְפִינָה

1.   One may not set out on an ocean voyage in a ship less than three days before the Sabbath, that is, from Wednesday on.[1] But if he is traveling for the sake of a *mitzvah,* he is permitted to embark even on Friday (*erev Shabbat*).[2]

---

17.   Rental of a Car or Hotel Room   Some permit accepting payment on a daily basis for rental of a car or truck, since payment is in compensation for its wear and tear, and especially if it is reckoned by the mile. Similarly, the fee for rental of a hotel room covers the cost of the food served, and includes its use *erev Shabbat* and the use and wear of its bedding and furnishings.

1.   Embarking on an Ocean Voyage Before the Sabbath   One should not embark on a long journey by sea less than three days before the Sabbath, because travel by boat in turbulent waters is likely to cause great discomfort during the first three days of the voyage, thereby preventing one from observing the *mitzvah* of *Oneg Shabbat*. In the view of some authorities, the three restricted days include the Sabbath, beginning with Thursday. Hence, it would. be permissible, according to this view, to set out on a voyage on Wednesday. If it is for a *mitzvah,* the restriction does not apply, in keeping with the principle that one who is engaged in the fulfillment of one *mitzvah* is exempt from another *mitzvah*. Some take a lenient view and consider travel for business or to visit friends, so long as it is not just for pleasure, as being also for the sake of a *mitzvah*.

2.   Travel Erev Shabbat   One who travels on Friday, whatever the mode of transportation, should endeavor to reach home or his destination early in the day, in sufficient time to prepare for the Sabbath. The *Shulḥan Aruch*

2.   One is permitted to set out on a journey by boat on a river even on Friday, and continue his journey on the Sabbath, provided he is not required to do any work on the Sabbath.[3] It is permitted to travel on the vessel even if it is pulled by animals.[4]

3.   When one is permitted to set out on a voyage on Friday, if he goes on board the ship *erev Shabbat* and stays there until nightfall, even if he then returns home and spends the night at home, he is permitted to board the vessel again on the Sabbath, providing it is not

---

states that on *erev Shabbat* one should not travel more than three *parsaot* (a parasang, or Persian mile, is approximately four miles). Inasmuch as travel today is generally not by foot, but by some means of transportation, this limit does not apply. Nonetheless, when contemplating travel on the eve of the Sabbath, one must consider the likelihood of delay en route, which could result in violation of the Sabbath. If, having set out on a permissible journey before the Sabbath, one finds himself in a dangerous situation, where his personal safety is imperiled, necessitating his continuing on the Sabbath, he is permitted to do so.

3.   Travel by Boat on the Sabbath   One is permitted to travel by boat on the Sabbath, provided the boat is operated by non-Jews. He must, however, board the vessel before the Sabbath and establish his Sabbath resting place there, so that it becomes like his home and he has freedom of movement throughout the vessel on the Sabbath (see note 5). If the boat should dock in port on the Sabbath, he may disembark, but he is restricted by all other Sabbath laws. He may not remove his belongings if they are *muktzeh,* or carry them where carrying is not permitted, and he is forbidden to sign documents and perform similar prohibited activities. If one knows, in advance, that the boat is due to dock on the Sabbath, it is advisable that one alter his schedule accordingly, in view of the difficulties he is bound to encounter, or at least arrange to remain on board ship until the conclusion of the Sabbath.

4.   Travel on a Barge Towed by Animals   A barge that is pulled by animals walking alongside on the river bank may be boarded *erev Shabbat* for travel on the Sabbath, since the animals are at a distance from the barge and there is no likelihood of a violation of the Sabbath.

making the journey for Jews only. However, inasmuch as he was at home on the Sabbath, he acquired his Sabbath resting place in his home. Therefore, if the vessel goes beyond the Sabbath limit, that is, farther than 2000 cubits, and it reaches land on the Sabbath, he is confined to within four cubits beyond which he is not permitted to go.[5]

4.   It is permitted to travel by boat on the Sabbath[6] in order to pray

---

5.   Travel on a Boat That Leaves on the Sabbath   One who is to travel on a ship that will set sail on the Sabbath must acquire his Sabbath resting place on board, so that he will have freedom of movement throughout the vessel during the course of the journey. He can do this by boarding ship before the Sabbath and remaining aboard until it sails on the Sabbath. In this case, if it reaches land on the Sabbath, he will be permitted to walk a distance of 2000 cubits in any direction, and if it docks in port, he can walk throughout the city, but as already noted above (note 3) he is bound by all other Sabbath laws.

If one cannot remain on the vessel until it leaves on the Sabbath day, he should board it *erev Shabbat* and stay on board until nightfall. If possible, it is advisable that he also light Sabbath candles, recite the Sabbath prayers and the *Kiddush,* and eat some food while on board. Having thus acquired his Sabbath resting place on the vessel, he may then leave and spend the night at home or in a place of lodging, and return to the ship the next day, on *Shabbat,* before it departs. This latter procedure, however, only permits him to board the vessel again on the Sabbath, but should it reach land or port on the Sabbath, he must remain on board ship until conclusion of the Sabbath. However, he still has freedom of movement throughout the vessel, since he had acquired his Sabbath resting place there. See also Part V, Chapter 11, paragraph 18 and notes.

6.   Travel on the Sabbath by Car, Bus, Train or Airplane   While travel by boat is permitted on the Sabbath under the conditions indicated, it is not permissible by other modes of transportation, such as by car, wagon, bus, train, or airplane, which are subject to various Sabbath restrictions and violations, and disruptive of the spirit of restfulness and holiness of the Sabbath. The prohibition applies even if one purchases a ticket before the Sab-

with a *minyan* or for the sake of another *mitzvah*.[7] Nevertheless, one should board the vessel on Friday while it is still day, and remain there until after nightfall. He may then return home and come back on board the vessel again on the Sabbath. This is permitted if the vessel is making the trip not for Jews only, but for others as well.[8]

5. LIGHTING THE SABBATH CANDLES

דִּין הַדְלָקַת הַנֵּרוֹת

1.   One must cease all work and light the Sabbath candles[1] at least

---

bath. One is not permitted to ride on any of these conveyances, whether public or private, on the Sabbath or on *Yom Tov,* both in the city and outside the city, even if it is operated by non-Jews and most of the riders are non-Jews. Travel on an airplane is not permissible on the Sabbath, whether one boards the airplane on *Shabbat* or *erev Shabbat,* even if he intends upon landing to remain on the airplane or in the airport until after the Sabbath. If one should board an airplane before the Sabbath and it is delayed in flight and lands on the Sabbath, he is subject to the restriction of the Sabbath limit of 2000 cubits as in travel by boat.

7.   Travel to Eretz Yisrael   Travel to settle in *Eretz Yisrael,* and according to some authorities, even if only to visit Israel, is considered a *mitzvah* in this regard. For the very act of walking four cubits in the Holy Land is a *mitzvah,* assuring one of life in the World to Come.

8.   Travel on a Boat With Jewish Passengers   If the vessel follows a regular schedule and it makes the trip regardless of the number of passengers, one is permitted to travel on the Sabbath even if the majority of the passengers are Jews.

1.   The Sabbath Lights   The Sabbath candles are kindled in honor of the Sabbath (לְכָבוֹד שַׁבָּת) and to fulfill the *mitzvah* of delighting in the Sabbath, (עוֹנֶג שַׁבָּת). The Sabbath lights introduce the Sabbath spirit of peace and tranquility into the home, and envelop it with an aura of holiness.

one-half hour before the stars appear in the heavens (צֵאת הַכּוֹכָבִים),[2] signifying night.[3] If, in the synagogue, the congregation recited מִזְמוֹר

---

2. Time of Candle Lighting and Ceasing Work Before Shabbat   The appearance of three stars of medium size betokens the onset of night when all work is definitely forbidden. Work is likewise forbidden during the twilight period (בֵּין הַשְּׁמָשׁוֹת), between sunset and nightfall, when it is doubtful whether it is day or night. The half hour alluded to is presumed to include the twilight period, as well as an additional brief period of time preceding it in compliance with the requirement of extending the Sabbath both at the beginning and at the conclusion of the Sabbath. This reflects one view, that of Rabbeinu Tam, regarding the duration of time within the period designated as *bain hashemashot*. For a discussion of the major opinions on this question, see the following note.

In view of the differing opinions, and the time differentials resulting from variables in locality and time of year, the procedure generally followed is to light the Sabbath candles at least eighteen minutes before sunset, and to cease work with the setting of the sun. Some light the candles twenty to thirty minutes before sunset. In Jerusalem the custom is to light the Sabbath candles even earlier. If the lighting was delayed for some reason, the candles may still be lit until sunset.

If possible, one should refrain from work some time before sunset. The woman who lights the Sabbath candles must cease work immediately upon lighting them, as this signifies her acceptance of the Sabbath, unless she stipulates that she intends to delay her acceptance of the Sabbath, as explained later.

3. Determining בֵּין הַשְּׁמָשׁוֹת and Nightfall   The Talmud in *Pesaḥim* 94a states that the period of time from sunset (שְׁקִיעַת הַחַמָּה) until night (צֵאת הַכּוֹכָבִים) is the equivalent of the time it takes an average person to walk a distance of four *mil*. A *mil* is two thousand cubits, and the time that it represents is variously estimated to be 18, 22 1/2, or 24 minutes, depending on the divergent views as to measurement of the length of the day, whether from sunrise to sunset, or from dawn to night. See Chapter 6, note 1. In *Shabbat* 34b, 35b, it states that the twilight period (בֵּין הַשְּׁמָשׁוֹת) begins with sunset and continues for a time period of three quarters of a *mil* until the appearance of three medium sized stars which signify night. In reconciling these apparently

שִׁיר לְיוֹם הַשַׁבָּת, (Psalms 92), thus ushering in the Sabbath,[4] even if there

---

contradictòry statements in the Talmud, the *Rishonim* present differing views as to what constitutes בֵּין הַשְׁמָשׁוֹת.

According to Rabbeinu Tam there are two sunsets. At first the sun gradually descends below the horizon and disappears from our view within a time span of three and a quarter *mil.* This is called the beginning of the sunset (תְּחִלַת הַשְׁקִיעָה), which is still considered daytime. After this, there occurs the second sunset, which is called the end of the sunset (סוֹף הַשְׁקִיעָה), when all light begins to depart from the sky. This is the period of time mentioned in *Shabbat* 34b as lasting three quarters of a *mil,* which is designated as בֵּין הַשְׁמָשׁוֹת. At its conclusion three medium sized stars appear in the sky, signifying night. This apparently is also the view of the *Shulḥan Aruch.*

However, other authorities, including the Gaon of Vilna (Gra), are of the opinion that בֵּין הַשְׁמָשׁוֹת starts as soon as the sun disappears from view, that is, immediately at the beginning of the sunset, and extends for a time period of three quarters of a *mil,* that is, 13 1/2 minutes, at the end of which time three medium sized stars become visible, when according to Torah law it is considered to be night. The Gaon of Vilna explains that the time period of three quarters of a *mil* mentioned in the Talmud is only for the latitude of Babylonia or *Eretz Yisrael* during the months of *Tishre* and *Nisan,* when the days and nights are of equal length. But for lands that are further to the North the period of בֵּין הַשְׁמָשׁוֹת is of longer duration, and its terminus is determined by the appearance of three medium sized stars.

In practice, the *Mishnah B'rurah* advises that one should give consideration to the more stringent view and cease all work by the time the sun sets and kindle the Sabbath lights even earlier, preferably 20 minutes to a half hour before sunset.

4. Accepting the Holiness of the Sabbath While in the home the woman accepts the holiness of the Sabbath with lighting of the candles, the husband and other members of the household may delay acceptance of the Sabbath and continue activities until sunset. The man accepts the holiness of the Sabbath, customarily in the synagogue, when he recites מִזְמוֹר שִׁיר לְיוֹם הַשַׁבָּת. He is then forbidden to engage in any manner of work, even if it is before sunset and there is still time remaining in the day. Some consider the recitation of לְכָה דוֹדִי, which concludes with בּוֹאִי כַלָה, "Come O Bride," a symbolic welcome to the Sabbath as the bride of the people of Israel, as constituting acceptance of the Sabbath.

are still two hours until nightfall,[5] it is considered Sabbath and the laws forbidding work are binding upon the remaining minority in the community as well.[6] Even a visitor from another city is obliged to observe the Sabbath once the congregation has recited מִזְמוֹר שִׁיר לְיוֹם הַשַּׁבָּת. In a city where there are two or more synagogues, one is not bound by the other.

2.   It is a *mitzvah* to light many candles in the home in honor of the Sabbath. Some are accustomed to light ten, others seven candles. One should light no less than two candles, symbolizing זָכוֹר and שָׁמוֹר, the two words that introduce the Biblical command regarding the Sabbath in the Ten Commandments, as it is written, "Remember (*Zachor*) the Sabbath day to keep it holy" (Exodus 20:8), and "Observe (*Shamor*) the Sabbath day to keep it holy" (Deuteronomy

---

5.   Ushering in the Sabbath Early   If the Sabbath is ushered in earlier than two hours before nightfall, depending upon the length of the day (see Chapter 6, note 1), it is not valid, and one must relight the Sabbath candles and repeat the prayer service. Hence, when some are accustomed to begin the Sabbath early in the summertime, the woman should not light the Sabbath candles at the time that her husband leaves for the synagogue, which could be two or more hours before nightfall. Some authorities advise that she light the candles before the time that he begins the *Maariv* service with בָּרְכוּ. Although the wife is halachically not bound by her husband's early acceptance of the Sabbath, and she can light the candles at the usual time, it is advisable that she lights the candles before he returns from the synagogue.

6.   Congregants in a Synagogue With Early Kabbalat Shabbat Services When a congregation conducts early services for *Kabbalat Shabbat,* as in the summer during daylight savings time, when the days are longer, acceptance of the Sabbath at the early hour is binding upon the worshipers present. However, in view of the fact that people have the option of attending services at other synagogues, and the congregation that schedules the early services does so not for the sake of *mitzvah,* but rather as a temporary convenience, its acceptance of the Sabbath at the early hour is not binding upon those congregants who are not in attendance.

5:12).[7] If necessary, one candle suffices. The candles should be of sufficient size, so that they will burn at least until after the meal. One should endeavor to obtain fine candles that will give a good light. Rav Huna said, "One who regularly lights the Sabbath candles will merit children who are learned in Torah" (*Shabbat* 23b). This is intimated in the verse, "For the commandment (*mitzvah*) is a candle, and Torah is light" (Proverbs 6:23), that is to say, through the *mitzvah* of kindling the Sabbath candles will come the light of Torah (Rashi, *Shabbat* 23b). It is, therefore, proper that when a woman lights the candles she should pray that the Holy One, blessed be He, grant her sons who will be scholars, luminaries of Torah.[8] She should also give some charity before lighting the candles.

3.   The *mitzvah* is best performed by lighting with olive oil. Other oils may be used as well, provided they are readily combustible and do not have a foul odor. The wick should preferably be of cotton, or flax, or such material that will assure a good, steady light. It is customary to use candles made of paraffin. One may also use candles made of tallow.[9]

---

7. Number of Sabbath Candles   Seven candles are taken to correspond to the seven days of the week and the seven lights of the *Menorah* in the Sanctuary, while ten candles would correspond to the Ten Commandments. The prevalent custom is to light two candles and an additional candle for each child in the family. The candles which are kindled in addition to the two that are traditonal in every home need not be on the table where the meal is eaten. When one is away from home one lights the minimum of two candles.

8. Prayer on Lighting Sabbath Candles   An appropriate prayer to be recited on lighting the Sabbath candles is generally included in the prayer books. The *Kitzur Shulḥan Aruch* notes that a woman who has difficulty bearing children, or who is childless, should after lighting the candles recite the *Haftarah* of the first day of Rosh Hashanah (I Samuel 1–2:10), taking care to say it with devotion and attention to its meaning. The *Haftarah* recounts the story of Hannah who was childless, and whose prayers were answered with the birth of a son, the prophet Samuel.

9. Use of Electricity for the Sabbath Lights   In the view of some authori-

4. The following blessing is said upon lighting the Sabbath candles,[10] בָּרוּךְ אַתָּה ה' אֱ־לֹהֵינוּ מֶלֶךְ הָעוֹלָם אֲשֶׁר קִדְּשָׁנוּ בְּמִצְוֹתָיו וְצִוָּנוּ לְהַדְלִיק נֵר שֶׁל שַׁבָּת, "Blessed are You, Lord our God, King of the Universe, Who has sanctified us with His commandments, and commanded us to kindle the Sabbath light."[11]

5. As a rule the blessing for a *mitzvah* is recited before it is performed. However, for the Sabbath candles the blessing is said after lighting them.[12] This is because by lighting the candles the woman

---

ties one may use electricity or gas for the Sabbath lights, to observe the *mitzvah* and say the blessing over them. While others are disinclined to allow the blessing over such lights, the former view can be relied upon in case of necessity, as for a woman confined to the hospital, or an invalid living alone, when use of candles would involve the danger of fire. The lights should, if possible, be specially designated and arranged so that it is evident that they are in honor of the Sabbath. If need be, she can put out the lights in the room and then turn them on, with the thought in mind that it is in observance of the *mitzvah*.

10. A Bride Lighting Sabbath Candles Some have the custom that a bride adds the blessing שֶׁהֶחֱיָנוּ on lighting the Sabbath candles for the first time after the wedding. If a girl has been lighting candles before marriage, as is the custom among the *Ḥasidim* of *Lubavitch,* opinions differ on whether she should say שֶׁהֶחֱיָנוּ on lighting candles for the first time after her marriage.

11. The Blessing Over the Sabbath Candles Some pious women conclude the blessing over the Sabbath candles with לְהַדְלִיק נֵר שֶׁל שַׁבָּת קוֹדֶשׁ "to kindle the light of the holy Sabbath." The basis for this variance in the blessing, which is customary among *Ḥasidim* of *Lubavitch,* is uncertain. It is evidently intended to give fervent expression to the holiness of the Sabbath as it is ushered in with the lighting of the candles. As a rule the pious are accustomed to refer to the Sabbath in this manner, as in the expression לִכְבוֹד שַׁבָּת קוֹדֶשׁ, "It is in honor of the holy Sabbath," when partaking of a special delicacy on the Sabbath.

12. Sefardim Say the Blessing Before Lighting the Candles The *Sefardim* recite the blessing before lighting the Sabbath candles in accord with the general rule that a blessing should be said before performing the *mitzvah*.

signifies her acceptance of the Sabbath, and if she were first to say the blessing, thus in effect initiating the lighting, she would be ushering in the Sabbath and she would no longer be able to light the candles.[13] In order that the blessing should be considered as though it were said beforehand the practice is as follows. The woman lights the candles, spreads her hands before them, and then covers her face so as not to see the candles, and recites the blessing. She then removes her hands and beholds the Sabbath candles. The blessing can then be considered as though it were said before the kindling of the lights. The same procedure is followed when lighting the candles for a Festival, in order not to differentiate. Inasmuch as acceptance of the Sabbath is signified by kindling the candles that are on the table where the Sabbath meal is eaten, one should light these candles last. In case of necessity, as when the woman must go to the *mikveh,* or to a wedding, or she must attend to some other urgent matter, she may light the candles with the reservation in mind, preferably spoken, that she is not accepting the Sabbath with the lighting of the candles. In this case, she can say the blessing and then light the candles,[14] and afterward attend to whatever is necessary until the Sabbath actually begins.

6.   The duty to light Sabbath candles applies to men as well as to

---

13.   A Man Reciting the Blessing   In the case where a man is obliged to light the Sabbath candles, as when he lives alone or the woman of the house is not at home, he too should light them before saying the blessing. Although the man is ordinarily not bound to accept the Sabbath with the lighting of the candles, and he would therefore be permitted to light them after the blessing, he should follow the same procedure as the woman in order not to differentiate.

14.   Reciting the Blessing When Lighting Candles Conditionally   In the view of some authorities, even in a case where the woman does not intend to accept the Sabbath with lighting the candles, she should follow the usual procedure and light the candles before saying the blessing, in order not to differentiate.

women, except that women have the greater obligation because they are at home and attend to household matters.[15] Therefore, if the woman is at home, she takes precedence with respect to this *mitzvah,* and she is accorded the privilege of kindling the Sabbath lights.[16] Nevertheless, the husband should also assist in performing the *mitzvah* by preparing the candles, and by lighting the wicks and snuffing them out, as this will make them easier to kindle. In the case of a woman who has given birth, the husband lights the candles and says the blessing the first Sabbath following childbirth.[17] Thereafter, as well as during the menstrual period, a woman lights the candles and says the blessing herself.

7. It is customary for women to bathe and put on their Sabbath clothes before lighting the candles. They are worthy of praise for honoring the Sabbath in this manner. A woman should also recite the

---

15. Woman's Obligation to Light the Sabbath Candles   Three *mitzvot* are especially incumbent upon women: observing the menstrual laws (*nidah*), taking the *hallah* portion from the dough, and lighting the Sabbath candles. As the mistress of the house, the woman is given the privilege and charged with the responsibility of lighting the Sabbath candles.

16. The Custom for Girls to Light Sabbath Candles   It is customary that a young woman begins lighting the Sabbath candles on the Sabbath following her wedding. A girl who lives at home is not obliged to light Sabbath candles. However, if she wishes, she may light candles without reciting the blessing, but listen to her mother recite the blessing and then say *Amen.* An unmarried woman, as well as a man, who lives independently or away from home, should observe the *mitzvah* and light candles for the Sabbath. Some, such as the *Ḥasidim* of *Lubavitch,* have adopted the custom that girls from three years of age light candles for the Sabbath. This is intended to acquaint them with the *mitzvah* and to inspire them for its observance. Others, however, particularly Sefardim, do not follow this practice.

17. Lighting Candles After Childbirth   In the view of some authorities, the women should light the candles on the first Sabbath following childbirth, if it is possible to provide her with candles and she is able to light them.

Minḥah prayer first, because by lighting the candles she signifies her acceptance of the Sabbath, after which she cannot recite the weekday *Minḥah* prayer. However, if she was delayed and arrived home about half an hour before the Sabbath, so that if she would first wash and dress she might possibly come to desecrate the Sabbath, it is better that she light the candles just as she is, rather than risk desecrating the Sabbath. If the husband sees that she is late in coming, it is the greater *mitzvah* that he light the candles.

8.   If a man lights the candles, and he has some work that he must do afterwards, it is best that he too stipulate that he does not accept the Sabbath with the lighting of the candles. But if he failed to indicate his intention or to have this reservation in mind, he may still do the work, because it is not customary for him to accept the Sabbath with the lighting of the candles.[18]

9.   The candles should be lit in the place where the meal will be eaten, so that it is apparent that they have been kindled in honor of the Sabbath. They should not be lit in one place and then removed to another place,[19] except in times of necessity as when the woman is

---

18.   Activities by Members of the Household After Candle Lighting   Other members of the household are not bound to accept the Sabbath with the lighting of the candles. Thus, if the woman lights many Sabbath candles, the husband may remove some of them and place them elsewhere as needed. He and others in the household may also ride to the synagogue after the kindling of the Sabbath candles, inasmuch as the men accept the Sabbath with *Kabbalat Shabbat* in the prayer service, which is later than candle lighting time. Children who remain at home, however, should accept the Sabbath with lighting of the Sabbath candles.

19.   Where to Light the Sabbath Candles   Since kindling the Sabbath lights constitutes the *mitzvah,* they should be kindled in their proper place where they will be used. The principal Sabbath lights are deemed to be those kindled at the dining table, and the blessing should be recited over them. But if there are several women in the house, they may recite the blessing over the

sick and unable to go to the table. In such a case she may light them while in bed, and the candles can then be set on the table, since the entire house is considered as their proper place. However, women who light the candles in the *Sukkah* and then bring them into the house are acting improperly. If a candle was lit some time before the Sabbath, and it is intended to use it for the Sabbath lights, it should be extinguished and relit for the Sabbath, so that it is apparent that it has been kindled in honor of the Sabbath.

10. There should be lights in all the rooms that are being used, so that the home will be pleasant and tranquil on the Sabbath. Once the blessing is recited by the woman of the house over the Sabbath candles in one room, one need not say the blessing again over candles that are lit in any of the other rooms. If a man is away from home, and he has separate lodging for himself, he must light the Sabbath candles and recite the blessing. If several people are lodged in one place, they should all contribute towards the purchase of candles. One of the group should then light the candles, having in mind to exempt all with his blessing. They, in turn, should also have the intention of observing the *mitzvah* with his blessing. One who is lodged together with his host, who is a Jew, need not light Sabbath candles separately, since his wife lights for him at home. Students who live away from home must light Sabbath candles, and say the blessing, if they are lodged in a separate room. They should contribute towards the purchase of candles, and one should say the blessing and exempt

---

lights in other places as well. Some prefer to light the Sabbath candles in a designated place in the room, and not on the dining table, to indicate that the lights are especially in honor of the Sabbath. It is not permissible, however, to kindle the lights in a room where they will not be used, and then remove them to where they will be used. As a rule, the candles should not be moved from place to place, even if they were kindled where there was a use for them, unless there is a need to do so. If it is necessary to move the candles, it should not be done by the one who kindled them, but by another person who is still permitted to move them.

them all.[20] The candles should burn long enough until they return to their room. But if they have no separate quarters, and they have no wives to light for them, they should contribute towards the purchase of candles by the host, and thereby share with him. One who has his meal with the host is included with his household, and he need not contribute towards the purchase of candles.

11.   If there are several women in the same house, it is still customary that each woman lights her own candles and recites the blessing over them, for the more light the greater the joy. But, if possible, they should light their candles in separate candelabra.

12.   One may not put water into the socket of the candlestick, even when it is still daytime, so that the candle will be extinguished when it burns down to the water level. In case of necessity it is permitted, provided the water is put there when it is still daytime. It is forbidden to place a vessel containing water beneath the candelabra, so that the sparks that fall might be extinguished, even if one would put it there when it is still daytime.[21] However, it is permitted, even after dark, to place a vessel without water under the candles to catch the sparks, since the sparks are not tangible. It is forbidden after dark to place a vessel under the lamp for the oil or tallow to drip into it, because if it drips the vessel is forbidden, and he would be voiding the prospective use of a vessel, which is not permissible. However, it is permitted to

---

20.   Students Lighting Sabbath Candles   Students who are away from home in school, where regulations do not permit lighting Sabbath candles in the dormitory rooms because of the danger of fire, should light the candles in the dining hall. One person may light for all the students, but preferably Sabbath candles should be lit at each table.

21.   Placing Candles Above Water or in Sand   Where there is a danger of fire, it is permitted to place a vessel with water beneath the candles to catch the falling sparks. One is permitted to do so, as well, if a candle is bent over and is likely to fall onto the table. It is permitted to place a candle in sand *erev Shabbat,* although the flame will go out when it reaches the sand.

put it there when it is still daytime. Any of the oil that drips into it is prohibited of use for that Sabbath, and the vessel may not be moved. But if none dripped into it, the vessel may be moved, notwithstanding that it was intended for that purpose.

13.   It is best to place the *ḥallot* on the table before lighting the candles, so that the table becomes a base for both the *ḥallot* and the candles, permitting it to be moved on the Sabbath.[22]

14.   A blind woman should light the Sabbath candles and say the blessing. If she has a husband who can see, he should light the candles and say the blessing. If she lives with others and eats at one table with them, and they have lit the candles and said the blessing, she should light the candles without saying the blessing. If she is the mistress of the home, she should light the Sabbath candles first and say the blessing, and then the others should light the candles and say the blessing.

15.   If a woman once forgets to light the Sabbath candles, she should henceforth light an extra candle, and continue to do so for the rest of her life.[23] If she forgot several times, she should light an additional candle for each time she neglected to light the Sabbath candles. The reason for lighting the extra candle is to remind her to be more careful in the future. Therefore, if her failure to light the Sabbath candles was not due to neglect, but because she was prevented from doing so for some compelling reason, she need not light an additional candle.

---

22.   Forgetting to Put Ḥallot on the Table Before Shabbat   If one forgot to put the ḥallot on the table before sunset and the start of the twilight period (בֵּין הַשְׁמָשׁוֹת), and the table had become a base for the candles which are *muktzeh,* and cannot be moved, it is still permitted to eat at the table as it does not generally involve moving it.

23.   Lighting Candles on Behalf of Someone   If a woman could not light the Sabbath candles, and someone lit candles for her, she need not light an additional candle.

6. PRAYERS ON THE SABBATH AND FESTIVALS

דִּינֵי הַתְּפִלּוֹת בְּשַׁבָּת וּבְיוֹם טוֹב

1. It is customary to recite the *Maariv* prayer on the eve of the Sabbath earlier than on weekdays, provided it is from *Pelag ha-Minḥah* and on.[1] This is proper so as to welcome the Sabbath as early as possible. Even those who customarily recite the *Maariv* prayer on weekdays in its appointed time, that is, with the appearance of the stars, may pray *Maariv* earlier on Sabbath eve.[2] It does not matter that they, at times, recite the *Minḥah* prayer on weekdays in the time that they are now reciting the *Maariv* prayer, since it is a *mitzvah* to add from the weekday to the holy day of the Sabbath.[3]

---

1. Time of Pelag ha-Minḥah *Pelag ha-Minḥah*, literally, half of the short period for *Minḥah*, (see Volume One, page 139) is, according to the *Shulḥan Aruch*, one hour and a quarter before nightfall. In the view of the Gra (Gaon of Vilna) it is one hour and a quarter before sunset. In either case the hours referred to are seasonal, relative to the length of the day, which is divided into twelve parts. According to the *Shulḥan Aruch* the day is reckoned from dawn (עֲלוֹת הַשַּׁחַר) until nightfall (צֵאת הַכּוֹכָבִים), and according to the Gra from sunrise (נֵץ הַחַמָּה) to sunset (שְׁקִיעַת הַחַמָּה). See Chapter 5, note 3 for a discussion of the above views as they relate to determining the twilight period (בֵּין הַשְּׁמָשׁוֹת).

2. Reciting Maariv Early on Sabbath Eve One who recites the *Maariv* prayer early on the eve of the Sabbath should repeat the *Shema* at night. He should also recite the *Minḥah* prayer before *Pelag ha-Minḥah*, so as to avoid the apparent contradiction of reciting the afternoon and evening prayers during the same period of time. In the opinion of some authorities this does not apply when praying with the congregation, or to one who does not ordinarily restrict himself in this regard in his weekday prayers.

3. Reciting Minḥah After Saying שִׁיר מִזְמוֹר If one began the Sabbath prayers early and said מִזְמוֹר שִׁיר לְיוֹם הַשַּׁבָּת and לְכָה דוֹדִי, and then remembered that he had not yet prayed *Minḥah*, he can recite the *Minḥah* prayer so long as he had not responded to בָּרְכוּ, and it is still day. As a rule, one who has not

2.   The blessing הַשְׁכִּיבֵנוּ is not concluded as on weekdays with שׁוֹמֵר עַמּוֹ יִשְׂרָאֵל לָעַד, "Who guards His people Israel forever," inasmuch as this blessing is for the protection of the people of Israel, and the Sabbath is itself guardian of Israel. Instead one should say וּפְרוֹשׂ, and conclude with בָּרוּךְ אַתָּה ה׳ הַפּוֹרֵשׂ סֻכַּת שָׁלוֹם עָלֵינוּ וְעַל כָּל עַמּוֹ יִשְׂרָאֵל וְעַל יְרוּשָׁלָיִם, "Blessed are You O Lord, who spreads the shelter of peace over us and over all His people Israel and over Jerusalem." This is also the conclusion of the blessing on a Festival. If one erred and ended the blessing as on weekdays, then if he became aware of the error right after saying לָעַד, he should immediately say הַפּוֹרֵשׂ סֻכַּת שָׁלוֹם . . . , but if he became aware of the error only after a lapse of time, he need not say it.

3.   In the *Amidah* (in the prayer רְצֵה בִמְנוּחָתֵנוּ) it is customary at the *Maariv* service to say וְיָנוּחוּ בָהּ, at *Shaharit* and *Musaf* וְיָנוּחוּ בוֹ, and at *Minhah* שַׁבְּתוֹת קָדְשֶׁךָ וְיָנוּחוּ בָם.[4]

4.   Following the silent *Amidah* in the Sabbath *Maariv* service the entire congregation recites וַיְכֻלּוּ together. This should be said while standing because it bears witness to God's creation of the world, and witnesses are obliged to give their testimony while standing.[5]

---

yet recited the *Minhah* prayer should not join the congregation in acceptance of the Sabbath by saying בָּרְכוּ for then he cannot pray *Minhah*. He should begin the *Minhah* prayer, even though the congregation is proceeding to accept the sanctity of the Sabbath. If he answered בָּרְכוּ, he must say the *Maariv Amidah* twice, the first for *Shabbat,* and the second to compensate for the missed *Minhah* prayer.

4.   Variations of בָּם, בּוֹ, בָּהּ in the Sabbath Services   The variations of בוֹ, בָהּ, and בָם in the Sabbath services appear in the Ashkenazic *nusah,* although generally preceded by the words שַׁבָּת קָדְשֶׁךָ even in the *Minhah* service. Various reasons have been advanced in explanation of the variations. Some *siddurim* have uniformly שַׁבָּת קָדְשֶׁךָ וְיָנוּחוּ בָהּ, which is taken to be the grammatically correct form, since שַׁבָּת is in the feminine gender.

5.   Saying וַיְכֻלּוּ With the Congregation   The verses of וַיְכֻלּוּ are said three

5. After this the *ḥazan* says בְּרָכָה אַחַת מֵעֵין שֶׁבַע, an abridgement of the
seven benedictions of the *Amidah.* He begins with בָּרוּךְ אַתָּה ה' אֱ-לֹהֵינוּ
אֱ-לֹהֵינוּ וֵא-לֹהֵי אֲבוֹתֵינוּ,⁶ then מָגֵן אָבוֹת, followed by אֱ-לֹהֵי אֲבוֹתֵינוּ רְצֵה
בִמְנוּחָתֵנוּ, and concludes בָּרוּךְ אַתָּה ה' מְקַדֵּשׁ הַשַּׁבָּת. The congregation
should stand and listen attentively to the *ḥazan* as he recites this
blessing.⁷ It is customary for the worshipers to say with him the

---

times: in the *Amidah,* after the *Amidah,* and in the *Kiddush.* One should
endeavor to conclude the silent *Amidah* in time to say וַיְכֻלּוּ aloud with the
congregation. In any event at least two should say it together. When one
prays individually, he may say it, not intending it as testimony, but as if he
would be reading from the Torah. If while reciting the silent *Amidah,* וַיְכֻלּוּ
happens to coincide with the time the congregation is saying it, he should
say it aloud with the congregation, and then repeat it after the *Amidah.*

6. The Ḥazan Bowing for the בְּרָכָה מֵעֵין שֶׁבַע   It is customary for the *ḥazan* to
bow down when saying בָּרוּךְ אַתָּה in the abridged form of the *Amidah* (בְּרָכָה
אַחַת מֵעֵין שֶׁבַע). Although the Halachah stipulates that one should bow down
only in those places ordained by the Sages and that one should not bow
down indiscriminately during prayer, as for example in the prayer נִשְׁמַת,
where the *Shulḥan Aruch* explicitly forbids bowing down when saying לְךָ לְבַדְּךָ
אֲנַחְנוּ מוֹדִים, one should not object to the practice. To the contrary, it is a
time-honored custom similar to bowing down when saying בָּרְכוּ. The custom
evidently stems from the notion that the בְּרָכָה מֵעֵין שֶׁבַע is in effect the *ḥazan*'s
repetition of the *Amidah.*

7. Use of a Tuning Fork by the Ḥazan   *Ḥazanim* who are musically trained
customarily use a tuning fork to ascertain the correct pitch for their musical
renditions. The permissibility of its use on the Sabbath has been questioned,
in view of the prohibition of producing a sound with a musical instrument,
lest one come to prepare a musical instrument for this purpose, which would
be a transgression of forming a utensil (תִּקּוּן מָנָא), a subsidiary of the *melachah* of מַכֶּה בְּפַטִּישׁ. The *Mishnah B'rurah* prohibits its use on these grounds.
However, other authorities endeavor to find some permissible grounds for
this widespread practice. The *Aruch Hashulḥan* condones it, reasoning that
since the sound is momentary and is heard only by the *ḥazan* it may not
come under the Rabbinical prohibition of instrumental music. In a paren-
thetical comment, he also finds no prohibition in the *ḥazan*'s use of musical

verses from מָגֵן אָבוֹת until זֵכֶר לְמַעֲשֵׂה בְרֵאשִׁית.[8] One who prays alone may also say זֵכֶר לְמַעֲשֵׂה בְרֵאשִׁית until מָגֵן אָבוֹת, but no further.

6. This benediction is recited every Sabbath throughout the whole year, even if it falls on a Festival or after the close of a Festival. However, it is omitted on the Sabbath which occurs on the first day of Passover.[9]

7. The benediction is recited only at services where the *minyan* assembles regularly for worship, but where they assemble only on

———————

notations at the *amud*. Others point to the lenient view cited by the Rama that we are not ordinarily capable of making musical instruments nowadays, and therefore there is no reason to fear that one may improvise and prepare a musical instrument in full public view of the entire congregation. Besides, the *ḥazan* is engaged in performing a *mitzvah* and his main concern is to lead the prayers, to which use of the tuning fork is incidental. It may, furthermore, be suggested that the decree of שֶׁמָּא יְתַקֵּן, which is the basis of the prohibition, would not apply to a tuning fork which is not really a musical instrument. It is simply an implement, consisting of a metal rod in the shape of a U, with a stem at the end, which when struck and vibrated emits a fixed tone, and it is, moreover, not readily subject to being fashioned or repaired by the person using it. It would seem that use of a pitch pipe, however, would not come under the above lenient ruling. See also Part II, Melachah 38, note 17.

8. **Reciting מָגֵן אָבוֹת Aloud**   The procedure generally followed in synagogues is that the congregation recites מָגֵן אָבוֹת together. After the congregation has concluded, the *ḥazan* must say it aloud, as it is an integral part of the בְּרָכָה אַחַת מֵעֵין שֶׁבַע which he is required to recite.

9. **Omitting the בְּרָכָה מֵעֵין שֶׁבַע on Passover Night**   The בְּרָכָה אַחַת מֵעֵין שֶׁבַע recited by the *ḥazan* after the *Amidah* was originally instituted by the Sages as a protective measure, when synagogues were located in the field outside the city, in order to allow all of the worshipers, especially latecomers, to conclude their prayers and return home together. It is not said on Passover because it is לֵיל שִׁמּוּרִים, the night when Israel is accorded special divine protection. However, וַיְכֻלּוּ is recited aloud.

occasion, as in the home of a bridegroom or of a mourner, it is not said. However, if they assemble for worship at an appointed place for several weeks, it should be recited.[10]

8.   It is customary that the *ḥazan* recite the *Kiddush* in the synagogue at evening services on Sabbaths and on Festivals, except for the first two nights of Passover.[11] Inasmuch as he is not exempt thereby from saying *Kiddush* at home, and since he may not partake of any food or drink before *Kiddush,* therefore in order that his blessing not be in vain, some of the wine should be given to a child who has reached the age of training in the observance of *mitzvot*. The child should hear the blessing, and being thereby exempt from saying it himself should then drink the wine, and thus the blessing will not have been said in vain. If there is no child in the synagogue, then the one who recites the *Kiddush,* or someone else, should have in mind to fulfill his obligation by the *Kiddush* that is being said and drink an amount equal to a *reviit,* so that he will be able to say the concluding blessing. Notwithstanding, he recites the *Kiddush* again at home for his wife

---

10.   Reciting the בְּרָכָה מֵעֵין שֶׁבַע at a Regular Service   Where a *minyan* of worshipers assembles for regular services at an appointed place with a *Sefer Torah,* if only for several days, it is considered an established place of worship in this regard and the בְּרָכָה מֵעֵין שֶׁבַע is said.

11.   Reciting Kiddush in the Synagogue   *Kiddush* is not recited in the synagogue on the first two nights of Passover, because everyone has wine for *Kiddush* at the *Seder.* Reciting *Kiddush* in the synagogue at the Sabbath evening service is a custom of long standing, originally instituted for guests and wayfarers who were served meals following the services. The custom is generally maintained in synagogues as a public sanctification of the Sabbath, serving to enhance the spirit of *Shabbat.* It is also intended for those who may not make *Kiddush* at home. *Kiddush* is not recited in synagogues in *Eretz Yisrael.* In synagogues in the Diaspora, where the custom prevails, it should not be abolished.

and family.[12] While *Kiddush* may only be recited where the meal takes place, he nevertheless fulfills his obligation with the *Kiddush* in the synagogue, for in a case of necessity, we rely upon those authorities who maintain that it suffices if he drinks a *reviit* wine from the *Kiddush* cup. Hence it is best that he drink a *reviit* in addition to the first mouthful of wine; the first mouthful for the *Kiddush* and the *reviit* in place of the meal.

9.   It is customary to recite בַּמֶּה מַדְלִיקִין (*Mishnah, Shabbat,* Chapter 2). However, this chapter is not said when a Festival occurs on the Sabbath or on the eve of the Sabbath, or on the Sabbath of *Ḥol Hamoed.*[13]

10.   It is customary on Sabbath morning[14] not to arise to go to the

---

12.   Reciting Kiddush for Those Unable to Say It Themselves   One may recite *Kiddush* for others who are unable to make *Kiddush* themselves, or for young children in order to train them in performing *mitzvot,* even if they are not of one's household and one does not eat the meal with them. See also Chapter 7, note 11.

13.   Reciting בַּמֶּה מַדְלִיקִין   While some are of the opinion that בַּמֶּה מַדְלִיקִין should be said after *Kiddush,* the prevailing practice is to say it before *Kiddush.* In many congregations it is said after *Kabbalat Shabbat,* before *Maariv.* Some congregations recite instead כְּגַוְנָא and רָזָא דְשַׁבָּת, passages taken from the *Zohar* (*Parshat Terumah*), after מִזְמוֹר שִׁיר לְיוֹם הַשַּׁבָּת, before בָּרְכוּ. It is also customary not to say בַּמֶּה מַדְלִיקִין when Yom Kippur occurs on the Sabbath. In Sefardic congregations it is likewise not said on the Sabbath of Ḥanukah.

14.   Tefillin Not Worn on Shabbat   *Tefillin* are not worn on *Shabbat* or *Yom Tov* because the *tefillin* are called "a sign" (Exodus 13:9) and it is not proper to have this additional sign, when the Sabbath and Festivals are themselves covenantal signs between God and Israel (Exodus 31:17).

synagogue for prayer[15] as early as one does on weekdays,[16] since sleep is one of the comforts enjoyed on the Sabbath, which is intended to be a day of delight. However, one should take care not to delay reciting the *Shema* and the *Amidah*[17] past their prescribed times.

---

15. Wearing a Tallit During Prayer Sabbath Morning   Before beginning prayer the worshiper puts on a *tallit,* preferably a special *tallit* in honor of the Sabbath. This he does while standing, wrapping it about the head. Taking hold of the right side of the *tallit,* he throws it over his left shoulder, and after saying the blessing he lowers it over his body. It is best to wear the *tallit* over one's head during prayer, as this tends to bring one to a feeling of humility and reverence. Those who wear the *tallit* wrapped around the neck like a shawl are not observing the *mitzvah* properly. It is common practice not to wear a *tallit* for prayer until one is married. The *ḥatan* customarily begins wearing a *tallit,* usually a gift from his bride, on the Sabbath before the wedding, when he is called to the Torah. However, as this often results in not observing the *mitzvah* for years, and in some cases not observing it at all, some authorities deem it advisable that young men of *Bar Mitzvah* age should wear a *tallit* for prayer.

16. Time of Prayer on Sabbath Morning   The custom to begin the Sabbath morning service later is inferred from the Biblical verses concerning the daily sacrifices. On weekdays the Torah states that they were to be offered "in the morning" (Numbers 28:4), while on the Sabbath it says "on the Sabbath day" (Ibid. 28:9), which implies a later hour for the Sabbath morning sacrifice. Hence, a later hour is indicated for the Sabbath morning prayers as well, since the prayers were instituted to correspond to the sacrificial offerings brought in the Temple. Some are accustomed, however, to begin the morning prayers early, even on the Sabbath, in order to recite the *Shema* at sunrise as did the pious men of old.

17. Listening to the Repetition of the Amidah   One should remain standing after the *Amidah* while the *ḥazan* repeats the first three benedictions, and concludes with הָאֵ־ל הַקָּדוֹשׁ. He may then be seated, provided he is not within four cubits of the *ḥazan*. He should rise again at מוֹדִים, bow and remain standing until he concludes מוֹדִים דְּרַבָּנָן. It is commendable to stand during the repetition of the entire *Amidah*. In any event, one must listen attentively

11.   The time for reciting the *Musaf* prayer[18] is immediately after *Shaharit*.[19] One must not delay it[20] past seven seasonal hours in the day (approximately one o'clock).[21] If he recites it after seven hours he is considered to have transgressed, but he nevertheless fulfills his obligation, inasmuch as the time for its recitation is all day.

12.   If one delayed reciting *Musaf* until past six and a half hours in

---

to the *hazan*'s repetition of the *Amidah,* and not even converse in Torah learning, or engage in the study of Torah.

18.   One Who Arrives for Prayer Before Musaf   One who comes to the synagogue late, and arrives when the congregation is about to start the *Musaf* service, should forego joining the congregation in prayer and proceed to say his prayers in their proper order, first *Shaharit* and then *Musaf.*

19.   Prescribed Order of the Sabbath Morning Service   The prescribed order for the Sabbath morning service is reciting the *Shaharit* prayer, reading of the Torah portion, followed by the *Musaf* prayer. This order should, as a rule, not be changed. However, when it is deemed necessary in an exceptional circumstance, it is permitted to have the *Musaf* prayer precede the Torah reading.

20.   Delivering the Sermon Before Musaf   The practice in many synagogues of delivering the sermon at the Sabbath morning service before *Musaf* has support in Jewish tradition, and it is not considered an interruption in the service. However, the Rabbi is well advised to keep the sermon to a moderate length, so that it does not result in undue delay of the *Musaf* prayer and a protracted service (see the following note).

21.   Concluding the Prayer Service Early   The prayers should be concluded early on the Sabbath, in ample time for the congregation to leave the synagogue by noon, especially in the winter when the days are short, so that people may go home and enjoy the rest of the Sabbath day in fulfillment of the *mitzvah* of *Oneg Shabbat*. The *hazan* is, therefore, advised not to prolong the prayers unduly with musical renditions. The service should not be extended beyond the sixth hour, that is past noon, on *Shabbat* and particularly on *Yom Tov,* with the exception of Rosh Hashanah.

the day (approximately twelve-thirty o'clock), and he is then obliged
to pray both *Minḥah* and *Musaf,* he should first recite *Minḥah* and
then *Musaf,*[22] because *Minḥah* is recited daily, and the rule is that
what occurs regularly takes precedence over that which is occasional.
This procedure, however, is to be followed only by one who is praying privately, but not by the congregation.

13.   In the *Kedushah* of *Musaf,* when reciting שְׁמַע יִשְׂרָאֵל ה׳ אֱ־לֹהֵינוּ ה׳
אֶחָד, the congregation errs if it immediately repeats the word אֶחָד
before הוּא אֱ־לֹהֵינוּ, because it is forbidden to say the word אֶחָד here
twice in succession.[23] One should just say ה׳ אֶחָד, הוּא אֱ־לֹהֵינוּ. However,
the *ḥazan* can begin the response by repeating the word אֶחָד, since he
has paused while waiting for the congregation to respond.[24]

---

22.   Reciting Musaf and Minḥah   The procedure of reciting *Minḥah* before
Musaf, according to some authorities, applies when it is already time for
Minḥah Ketanah (the short period for *Minḥah,* i.e. at nine and a half hours
of the day and thereafter). In the event that there is not enough time to say
both, one should recite the *Musaf* prayer, inasmuch as the *Minḥah* prayer if
omitted can be made up at the *Maariv* service, while *Musaf* if omitted cannot be made up once the appropriate time has passed. See Volume One, Part
I, Chapter 39.

23.   Repeating the Word אֶחָד in the Kedushah   A repetition of the word אֶחָד
in this context would appear to be an acknowledgment of two divine
powers, hence it is forbidden. The *ḥazan* may repeat it, after pausing for the
congregation's response, as it is then not in succession.

24.   Repetition of Words by the Ḥazan   The practice of some *ḥazanim* to
repeat words in the prayer for emphasis, or in order to achieve a desired
musical effect, is inappropriate because it alters the traditional form of the
tefillot as instituted by the Sages. It is not considered an interruption,
however, and it does not invalidate the prayer, provided it does not distort
its meaning. However, the *ḥazan* should not repeat words in the *Amidah,*
in the benedictions related to the *Shema, Hallel,* or in Biblical verses. The *Piyutim* and other prayers which do not constitute the body of the prayers afford
greater latitude in this regard. In general, however, the *ḥazan* should be

14.   At the *Minḥah* service, before the reading of the Torah, one recites the verse, וַאֲנִי תְפִלָּתִי, "But as for me, I offer my prayer unto You, O Lord, in an acceptable time. O God, in the abundance of Your mercy answer me with the truth of your salvation" (Psalms 69:14). This practice is based on a *Midrash* on the preceding verse, "They that sit in the gate talk of me; and of me are the songs of the drunkards" (Psalms 69:13). Our Rabbis, of blessed memory, comment as follows: "David addressed the Holy One, blessed be He, saying, Master of the world. Our nation is not like the other nations. They drink and become wantonly drunk. But we are not so. Although we drank, I offer my prayer unto you, O Lord" (*Midrash* cited in *Tur, Oraḥ Ḥayyim,* Chapter 292). This verse is therefore said before reading the Torah to give thanks to our Creator who did not let our portion be like theirs, for even the worthless among us come to hear the Torah read. It is therefore not said on a Festival which falls on a weekday, when the Torah is not read. However, it is said on the Sabbath even where there is no *Sefer Torah* from which to read. In this case it is said before the half-*Kaddish* is recited, so as not to interrupt between *Kaddish* and *Shemoneh Esreh.*

15.   After the repetition of the *Shemoneh Esreh* by the *ḥazan* it is customary to recite the three verses of צִדְקָתְךָ צֶדֶק, "Your righteousness is an everlasting righteousness . . ."[25] This is a form of צִדּוּק הַדִּין (the prayer recited by mourners at the interment of the dead, in justification of the divine decree) for Joseph, Moses and David, the righteous three who died on the Sabbath at this hour. However, צִדְקָתְךָ צֶדֶק is not

---

faithful to the traditional form of the prayers, enunciating the words clearly and accenting them properly. For laws relating to the *ḥazan* and his conduct of the services, see Volume One, Part I, Chapter 12.

25.   Reciting the Verses of צִדְקָתְךָ   In the Sefardic *nusaḥ* the three verses of צִדְקָתְךָ are recited in the order in which they appear in the Psalms (36:7, 71:19, 119:142). However, in the Ashkenazic *nusaḥ* they are recited in reverse order. One reason given is so that the Divine Name would then immediately precede the *Kaddish.*

said when, if it were a weekday, *Taḥanun* (תַּחֲנוּן) would not be said.[26] When praying with a *minyan* in the house of a mourner it should be said, for its omission would indicate a public display of mourning, and mourning is not observed publicly on the Sabbath.

16.   If one erred on a Sabbath or on a Festival and began to say the intermediate benedictions of the weekday *Shemoneh Esreh,* and he became aware of the error in the middle of the benediction, he should conclude it and then say the intermediate benediction of the Sabbath or of the Festival. The reason for this is that in fact the intermediate weekday benedictions should have been instituted for Sabbaths and Festivals as well, and mention made of the holiness of the day in the benediction of רְצֵה, as on *Rosh Ḥodesh* and *Ḥol Hamoed,* but in honor of the Sabbath and the Festival, so as not to burden the people, the Sages reduced the number and instituted one intermediate benediction on the holiness of the day. Hence, one who began a weekday benediction should complete it, since, in fact, it would have been proper to say it.

17.   Even if he only said the first word of the weekday benediction, and immediately became aware of the error, he must conclude the entire benediction. An exception to this is the benediction of אַתָּה חוֹנֵן, since the intermediate Sabbath benedictions in the *Amidah* for *Maariv* and *Minḥah* also begin with the word אַתָּה, namely אַתָּה קִדַּשְׁתָּ and אַתָּה אֶחָד. Hence, in these instances, if he forgot it was *Shabbat* and said the word אַתָּה with the intention of saying אַתָּה חוֹנֵן and he immediately remembered that it was *Shabbat,* he need not conclude the weekday benediction of אַתָּה חוֹנֵן but he should continue with the benediction for the Sabbath. But if this should occur in the *Amidah* of *Shaḥarit,* and he erred in thinking that it was a weekday, he must

---

26. When צִדְקָתְךָ Is Not Said   The verses of צִדְקָתְךָ are not recited if *Shabbat* falls on *Rosh Ḥodesh* or on the day before *Rosh Ḥodesh,* on a Festival or on the day following a Festival, on *Ḥol Hamoed,* or on Ḥanukah, since *Taḥanun* would not be said then if it were a weekday.

conclude the benediction of אַתָּה חוֹנֵן. However, if he was aware that it was *Shabbat* and that he should say יִשְׂמַח מֹשֶׁה, but by force of habit he erred and said the word אַתָּה, he need not conclude the benediction of אַתָּה חוֹנֵן, but he should say יִשְׂמַח מֹשֶׁה. Since he is aware that it is *Shabbat,* and there are other prayers in the Sabbath *Amidah* that begin with אַתָּה, and that is the only word he said, it is as though he were mistaking one Sabbath prayer for another.

18. If he did not become aware of his error until the concluding benedictions, that is from רְצֵה and further, he must stop at the place that he reminds himself and say the benediction for the Sabbath or the Festival and the concluding benedictions in the proper order. But if he did not become aware of the error until he began saying יִהְיוּ לְרָצוֹן he must repeat the *Amidah* from the beginning.[27]

19. If by error one began to say a weekday benediction in the *Amidah* of *Musaf,* he must stop wherever he reminds himself and say the intermediate benediction of *Musaf,* because there was never any consideration of including the intermediate weekday benedictions in the *Musaf* service.

20. It is considered a bad sign for one to be so unmindful of the Sabbath as to err in his prayers and begin to say the weekday benedictions. If this occurs he should examine his conduct during the coming week and repent.

21. If one erred in the intermediate benedictions of the Sabbath *Amidah,* substituting one for another, and he became aware of the error before saying the Divine Name at the conclusion of the benediction, he must go back and recite the benediction designated for that

---

27. **Repeating the Amidah in case of Error** According to some authorities one must repeat the *Amidah* from the beginning, if he failed to say the benediction for the Sabbath or the Festival, only if he has concluded the verse of יִהְיוּ לְרָצוֹן, or in the view of *Ḥayye Adam* if he actually stepped backward, thus signifying completion of the *Amidah.* Otherwise, he need return only to the place in his prayers where he erred.

prayer service. However if he became aware of the error after he had pronounced the Divine Name, he should conclude the benediction and say מְקַדֵּשׁ הַשַּׁבָּת. He will thereby have fulfilled his obligation, inasmuch as the essential part of the intermediate benediction is the prayer רְצֵה נָא בִמְנוּחָתֵנוּ, which is uniform in all the prayer services on the Sabbath.

22.   The aforesaid is applicable only for the *Maariv, Shaharit* and *Minhah* services. However, if he substituted another prayer in the *Musaf* service, he has not fulfilled his obligation, because he will not have made mention of קָרְבַּן מוּסָף, the additional Sabbath offering referred to in the designated prayer. Likewise, if he substituted the *Musaf* prayer for the one designated for *Maariv, Shaharit* or *Minhah*, he has not fulfilled his obligation inasmuch as in mentioning the קָרְבַּן מוּסָף, he is stating a falsehood.

23.   If one erred in the Festival prayer, and instead of concluding the benediction with מְקַדֵּשׁ יִשְׂרָאֵל וְהַזְּמַנִּים, "Who hallows Israel and the Festivals," he concluded with מְקַדֵּשׁ הַשַּׁבָּת, "Who hallows the Sabbath," then if he immediately corrected himself and said מְקַדֵּשׁ יִשְׂרָאֵל וְהַזְּמַנִּים, he has fulfilled his obligation.[28] If not, he must repeat the benediction, beginning with אַתָּה בְחַרְתָּנוּ.

7. KIDDUSH AND THE SABBATH MEALS
דִּינֵי הַקִּידוּשׁ וְהַסְעוּדוֹת בַּלַּיְלָה וּבַיּוֹם

1.   It is a positive commandment in the Torah to sanctify the Sabbath in words, as it is written, "Remember the Sabbath day to keep it

---

28.   Failing to Say מְקַדֵּשׁ יִשְׂרָאֵל וְהַזְּמַנִּים **on a Festival**   The error can be rectified by immediately saying מְקַדֵּשׁ יִשְׂרָאֵל וְהַזְּמַנִּים, provided one has not yet begun the following benediction of רְצֵה. If a Festival occurs on the Sabbath and one concludes either with מְקַדֵּשׁ הַשַּׁבָּת or מְקַדֵּשׁ יִשְׂרָאֵל וְהַזְּמַנִּים, he has fulfilled his obligation according to some authorities, provided he made mention of both the Sabbath and the Festival in the course of the benediction.

holy" (Exodus 20:8); that is to say, remember the Sabbath by sancti-
fying it.[1] One must, therefore, remember the Sabbath when it arrives
by reciting *Kiddush*,[2] and when it departs by reciting *Havdalah*. The
Sages have instituted that both *Kiddush* and *Havdalah* be said over a
cup of wine.

2.   It is permitted to recite the *Kiddush*[3] and to eat the Sabbath meal[4]

---

1. Welcoming the Sabbath in the Home Following the services in the
synagogue, one should proceed to go home without delay in order to make
Kiddush and join his family in welcoming the Sabbath. Upon arriving, one
extends greetings, such as *Gut Shabbbos* or *Shabbat Shalom*. He then says
שָׁלוֹם עֲלֵיכֶם in welcome to the angels who are said to accompany one on the
eve of the Sabbath from the synagogue to his home, and אֵשֶׁת חַיִל (Proverbs
31:10–31) in honor of his wife who has prepared the home for *Shabbat*.
Before *Kiddush*, it is customary for the parents to bless the children. One
places his hands on the child's head and bestows the traditional blessing. To
a son one says יְשִׂימְךָ אֱ-לֹהִים כְּאֶפְרַיִם וְכִמְנַשֶּׁה, "God make you as Ephraim and
Menasheh." (Genesis 48:20); to a daughter one says, יְשִׂימֵךְ אֱ-לֹהִים כְּשָׂרָה, רִבְקָה,
רָחֵל וְלֵאָה "God make you as Sarah, Rebecca, Rachel and Leah." One then
continues with the benediction, יְבָרֶכְךָ ה' וְיִשְׁמְרֶךָ, יָאֵר ה' פָּנָיו אֵלֶיךָ וִיחֻנֶּךָּ, יִשָּׂא ה' פָּנָיו
אֵלֶיךָ וְיָשֵׂם לְךָ שָׁלוֹם. "God bless you and keep you; God make His face to shine
upon you and be gracious unto you; God turn His face unto you and give
you peace" (Numbers 6:24–26). One may add any other blessing that he
deems appropriate to bestow upon the child.

2. Neglecting to Say Kiddush Friday Night If one failed to recite the *Kiddush* on Friday night he may make it up throughout the following day. He
then recites all of the *Kiddush*, except for וַיְכֻלּוּ as it refers to the completion of
God's work of creation which occurred on Friday night.

3. Reciting Kiddush Early for Others As a rule, one should not recite the
Kiddush on behalf of others who start the Sabbath early, if he himself does
not accept the Sabbath at the time. In case of emergency, when one must
recite *Kiddush* for patients in a hospital or in an institution, he may do so,
having in mind not to accept the Sabbath, and then drive home for *Shabbat*.

4. Eating the Sabbath Eve Meal Early While one may pray, recite the

even though it is not yet night. However, those who are accustomed on weekdays to pray *Maariv* at the proper time, but pray earlier on Sabbath eve, are forbidden to eat if it is within a half hour before nightfall. They must wait until it is night so that they may read the three sections of the *Shema* again, and then they can recite the *Kiddush*.

3.   It is not permitted to partake of anything, even water, before *Kiddush*.[5]

4.   One should, if possible, recite the *Kiddush* over old wine of good quality, preferably over wine that is red.[6] Where kosher grape wine is not available, *Kiddush* may be said over raisin wine.[7] If one has no

---

Kiddush and eat the Sabbath evening meal earlier, he should if possible extend the meal and eat a *kezayit* at night, so as to fulfill the requirement of eating three *seudot* on the very day of the Sabbath.

5.   Eating and Drinking Prohibited Before Kiddush   The Rabbis prohibited partaking of food or drink before *Kiddush,* inasmuch as one is obligated to make *Kiddush* with the arrival of the Sabbath. Hence the prohibition is from sunset, or before sunset from the time that one has ushered in the Sabbath with the lighting of the Sabbath candles or the evening prayer. This does not apply to young children, who may eat and drink prior to *Kiddush* on Sabbath eve as well as Sabbath morning, as it is forbidden to make them suffer from hunger or thirst.

6.   Adding Some Water to the Wine for Kiddush   Some are accustomed to add a little water to the wine for *Kiddush*. Inasmuch as wine is deemed to have brought lament to the world, mixing it with some water is taken to signify a desire to turn it to blessing instead.

7.   Raisin Wine and Grape Juice for Kiddush   Raisin wine is properly prepared by crushing the raisins and soaking them in water for three days, allowing them to ferment. The raisins should be in a ratio of more than one to six in proportion to the water, so that it will have the taste of wine. See Volume One, Part II, chapter 13, paragraph 6. One may use grape juice for *Kiddush,* if wine is not available or harmful.

wine, he should say *Kiddush* over bread (the *ḥallot*),[8] but not over any other beverage. In reciting the *Kiddush,* one should stand while saying וַיְכֻלוּ, looking all the while at the Sabbath candles. Afterward he should sit down and look at the cup of wine while saying the blessings אֲשֶׁר קִדְּשָׁנוּ בְּמִצְוֹתָיו and בּוֹרֵא פְּרִי הַגָּפֶן.[9]

5.   *Kiddush* is also obligatory upon women.[10] They should, there-

---

8.   Saying Kiddush Over the Ḥallot   When saying *Kiddush* over the *ḥallot,* one places his hands upon the cloth covering the two loaves and says the verses of וַיְכֻלוּ. He then lifts the cover and places his hands over the *ḥallot* and says the blessing הַמּוֹצִיא, raising both loaves when mentioning the Divine Name. Upon completing the blessing he replaces the cover and again places his hands upon the cloth covering the *ḥallot* until the *Kiddush* is concluded. *Kiddush* may be recited over bread only Friday evening. When necessary, it may be said over one loaf, and even over a piece of bread the size of a *kezayit.*

9.   Procedure for Reciting Kiddush   It is customary to begin the *Kiddush* with יוֹם הַשִּׁשִּׁי, וַיְכֻלוּ הַשָּׁמַיִם, (Genesis 1:31, 2:1), so that the first letters spell out the Divine Name. It is advisable to pause between יוֹם הַשִּׁשִּׁי and וַיְכֻלוּ to indicate that it is not one continuous verse. Some say the preceding words וַיְהִי עֶרֶב וַיְהִי בֹקֶר silently before saying יוֹם הַשִּׁשִּׁי aloud. One stands while saying וַיְכֻלוּ because it bears witness to God's creation of heaven and earth, and testimony has to be given while standing. The reason for sitting down for the rest of the *Kiddush* is because it has to be said at the meal, which is normally eaten while seated. Customs vary in the manner in which *Kiddush* is recited. Some, particularly those who follow the Sefardic custom, stand as they recite the entire *Kiddush.* Those who follow the view of the Rama sit while saying the *Kiddush,* but first stand for a moment as the Divine Name is alluded to at the outset. The family and others who are present should stand nearby, and sit together as a group, not dispersed or walking about, and listen attentively so as to fulfill their obligation by the *Kiddush* being recited for them.

10.   A Woman's Obligation for Kiddush   *Kiddush* is a Biblical command which women, just as men, are obligated to keep, even though it is a positive commandment that is performed at a fixed time, which women are ordinari-

fore, listen attentively while it is being said[11] and respond אָמֵן, but not בָּרוּךְ הוּא וּבָרוּךְ שְׁמוֹ.[12] A boy who has not yet become *Bar Mitzvah* cannot exempt a woman by reciting *Kiddush* for her. In such a case she must recite the *Kiddush* herself. If she does not know how to say it, she should repeat after him word for word. Even when she hears the

---

ly not required to observe. The reason for this is that the two commandments of *Shabbat,* namely *Zachor* (זָכוֹר), "Remember the Sabbath day to sanctify it" (Exodus 20:8) which refers to the positive commandment of making *Kiddush,* and *Shamor* (שָׁמוֹר), "Keep the Sabbath day to sanctify it" (Deuteronomy 5:12), which refers to refraining from doing work, are equated to each other. Since women are obligated in the commandment of *Shamor,* that is the prohibition against work on the Sabbath, for they are bound by all prohibitive commandments regardless of any time factor, they are also obligated in the commandment of *Zachor,* that is the positive commandment of *Kiddush* on *Shabbat.* Therefore, since women and men have the same Torah obligation with regard to the *mitzvah* of *Kiddush* on *Shabbat,* a woman can recite the *Kiddush* on behalf of others, including men. However, for the sake of propriety, she should say it only for the members of her family when her husband is unable to do so, or when circumstances require it.

11.   Reciting Kiddush on Behalf of Others   One who recites the *Kiddush* for others must have in mind to include them in the *mitzvah,* and they in turn must have in mind to fulfill their obligation by listening to the *Kiddush* being recited. This applies in all instances when one performs a *mitzvah* on behalf of others. One may recite *Kiddush* for others, even if he does not eat the meal with them. Likewise, one who has already said *Kiddush* for himself may say it again for others. One may recite *Kiddush* when necessary, such as for patients in a hospital or nursing home, even if they already ate their meal.

12.   Responding to a Blessing Said on One's Behalf   When one hears a blessing which is said on his behalf in fulfillment of his own obligation he does not respond בָּרוּךְ הוּא וּבָרוּךְ שְׁמוֹ at the mention of the Divine Name, as this would be an interruption in the blessing. He must listen attentively to the entire blessing, and then say אָמֵן which is an acknowledgment on his part of the blessing recited. See Volume One, Part I, Chapter 15.

Kiddush recited by her husband or by another man, it is best that she say it with him word for word.[13]

6.   One should not recite *Kiddush* over wine that has turned sour, or if it has a bad odor. In this regard we are guided by the admonition of the prophet, "Present it now to your governor, will he be pleased with you?" (Malachi 1:8). Moldy wine should be strained. If it is not possible to strain it, one may still say *Kiddush* over it. But if it is covered by a white film, *Kiddush* should not be said over it, because it has presumably become stale. One may say *Kiddush* over boiled wine[14] or wine that contains honey. However, some are of the opinion that such wine should not be used for *Kiddush,* since similar wine was not fit for the altar in the Temple. If possible, therefore, one should try to obtain other wine for *Kiddush.*

7.   The cup used for *Kiddush* must be whole, that is without defect, and it should be clean. All of the rules that pertain to the cup used for Grace after meals apply also to the cup used for *Kiddush* at night and in the daytime.[15] They apply, as well, to the cup used for *Havdalah.*

---

13. Reciting Kiddush in Unison   When several families partake of their meal at the same table it is best that the *Kiddush* be recited in turn, one at a time, lest the words be drowned out in the babble of voices. Those accustomed to recite the *Kiddush* together, should say it in unison, so that it may be heard distinctly by all. In the latter case, one should not respond אָמֵן for the other's blessing, as this would be an interruption between saying the blessing and drinking the wine.

14. Kiddush Over Pasteurized Wine   Wine that was pasteurized retains its taste and aroma, and may be used for *Kiddush* on the Sabbath and *Yom Tov.*

15. The Kiddush Cup   One should recite *Kiddush* over a full cup of wine. The cup should be of a size to contain at least a quantity of wine equal to a *reviit* (approximately 3–5 ounces). It should be taken with both hands and held in the right hand. One who is left-handed may hold it in his left hand. The cup should be raised over the table more than a handbreadth so that all may see it. A paper cup, usually discarded after use, should not be used for

8. The *ḥallot* should be covered while *Kiddush* is recited. Even when *Kiddush* is said over the *ḥallot* they should be covered, in remembrance of the manna which was covered above and beneath with dew.

9. The one who said *Kiddush* should drink at least a mouthful of wine from the cup without interruption. It is a *mitzvah* that all present should likewise sip some of the wine over which the blessing was recited.[16] One who does not drink wine by reason of abstinence or because it is harmful to him, and the like, should not recite *Kiddush* over wine, relying on others present to drink it.[17]

10. Since the wine over which *Kiddush* is recited is essential for the meal, it does not require that a concluding blessing be said after drinking it, inasmuch as it is exempted by Grace said after the meal. However, since some authorities are of the opinion that it is not exempted, if possible one should say a blessing over a cup of wine after Grace, and after drinking a *reviit* say the concluding blessing

---

Kiddush and *Havdalah* unless no other cup is available. Some permit the use of paper or plastic cups that are well constructed and more durable. See Volume One, Part II, Chapter 7, note 3.

16. Drinking the Kiddush Wine   The amount of wine one must drink after saying the *Kiddush* is מְלֹא לוּגְמָיו, that is, a quantity filling one's cheek. While it is preferable that all present partake of some of the wine, they should not drink from the *Kiddush* cup from which he drank, as it is unsanitary and a possible danger to health. Moreover, some consider the wine impaired (פָּגוּם) once he drank from it. Therefore, after reciting the *Kiddush,* and before drinking the wine, one should pour some of it into separate cups for those present at the table. They may then drink the wine without saying the blessing בּוֹרֵא פְּרִי הַגָּפֶן. Many, however, prefer to say the blessing themselves.

17. Kiddush by One Who Does Not Drink Wine   According to the *Magen Avraham* one who does not drink wine should say *Kiddush* over the *ḥallot* and the others present should make *Kiddush* for themselves over wine. Some authorities, however, are of the opinion that he may recite the *Kiddush* over the wine, relying on the others present to drink it.

with the intention of also exempting the wine that he drank for *Kiddush.*

11.   One need not say any blessing over wine that he drinks during the meal, as it was exempted by the blessing בּוֹרֵא פְּרִי הַגָּפֶן in the *Kiddush.*[18]

12.   If one said *Kiddush* over the cup, thinking it contained wine and then he discovered that it contains water or some other beverage, he must repeat the *Kiddush* over wine. However, if there was wine on the table which he intended to drink during the meal, he need not repeat the *Kiddush,* as it is considered as though he had said *Kiddush* over wine. If there was no wine on the table, but there was some in the house and he intended to drink wine during the meal, he need not repeat the blessing, בּוֹרֵא פְּרִי הַגָּפֶן, but only the blessing אֲשֶׁר קִדְּשָׁנוּ. If the cup contained a beverage such as beer or mead, where these are the native drinks, he need not in any event repeat the *Kiddush,* but he should say the blessing שֶׁהַכֹּל and drink it. Where it is the custom to say *Kiddush* after washing the hands and before breaking bread,[19] he

---

18.   A Blessing Over Wine During the Meal   The *Mishnah B'rurah* maintains that one who is not accustomed to drinking wine in the course of the meal must say a blessing over the wine, unless he had it in mind when he made *Kiddush* and said the blessing that he would also drink wine during the meal.

19.   When to Recite the Kiddush Before the Meal   The practice generally followed is to recite the *Kiddush* and then wash for the meal, so as not to have an interruption between washing the hands and saying the blessing הַמּוֹצִיא. Some, however, do not consider the *Kiddush* an interruption, since it is a requirement of the Sabbath meal. Hence, for the sake of uniformity, whether one makes *Kiddush* over wine or over bread, they deem it preferable to wash the hands first and then recite the *Kiddush,* and after drinking the wine say the blessing הַמּוֹצִיא over the *ḥallot.* The prevalent practice, as noted above, is to make *Kiddush* first, before washing for the meal, but the other members of the family who do not make *Kiddush* themselves may wash their hands before *Kiddush.*

likewise need not repeat the *Kiddush,* but he should say the blessing הַמּוֹצִיא, and it is considered as though he said *Kiddush* over bread.

13.   *Kiddush* is recited over a cup of wine also at the Sabbath day meal. In this instance it is simply the blessing בּוֹרֵא פְּרִי הַגָּפֶן.[20] This *Kiddush* is equally obligatory upon women. Before reciting the *Kiddush* it is forbidden to partake of anything, even water.[21] It is best to recite this *Kiddush* too over wine. However, if one prefers to say it over whiskey,[22] he fulfills his obligation. However, he should see to it that

---

20.   Kiddush on Sabbath Day   *Kiddush* at the Sabbath day meal is euphemistically called *Kiddusha Rabba,* the Great *Kiddush,* as it is not obligatory by Torah law, but was instituted by the Rabbis in honor of the Sabbath. It is customary to begin by first reciting the verses וְשָׁמְרוּ בְנֵי יִשְׂרָאֵל (Exodus 31:16,17) and זָכוֹר אֶת יוֹם הַשַּׁבָּת (Exodus 20:8–11) until וַיְקַדְּשֵׁהוּ, preceding the blessing בּוֹרֵא פְּרִי הַגָּפֶן. One should not just begin with עַל כֵּן בֵּרַךְ, as this is not a complete verse. Some begin with אִם תָּשִׁיב מִשַּׁבָּת רַגְלֶךָ (Isaiah 58;13,14).

21.   Eating and Drinking Before Kiddush on Shabbat Morning   The prohibition not to partake of anything, even water, applies when it is already incumbent on one to make *Kiddush,* namely after the *Shaharit* prayers. In any case, water, tea, or coffee may be drunk before the morning prayers. If, for health reasons, one must eat in the morning before *Shaharit,* he should first make *Kiddush* if he intends to eat bread or pastry at his meal. A woman may eat on Sabbath morning, even if she has not heard *Kiddush* recited. However, once the morning service is concluded she must wait until *Kiddush* has been said. For the rules pertaining to eating and drinking in the morning before prayers, see Volume One, Part I, Chapter 5, paragraph 2.

22.   Sabbath Day Kiddush Over Whiskey or a Beverage   If no wine is available for the Sabbath day *Kiddush,* one should say it over whiskey or some other beverage, but not over bread. In the view of some authorities one who says the *Kiddush* over whiskey is not required to use a cup that holds a *reviit,* and he need drink only the customary amount of whiskey that one usually drinks.

the cup for the *Kiddush* holds a *reviit,* and that he drinks a mouthful without interruption.[23]

14.   Both on Friday evening and on Sabbath day *Kiddush* should be recited where the meal is eaten, as it is said, "And you shall call the Sabbath a delight" (Isaiah 58:13), which our Rabbis of blessed memory have expounded to mean: Where you proclaim the Sabbath (i.e. with *Kiddush*) there shall you have delight (i.e. the meal). Therefore, if one says *Kiddush* in one house and eats in another, even if he had that in mind when he said *Kiddush,* he has not fulfilled his obligation. One must also begin eating immediately after saying *Kiddush,*[24] and if he does not do so he has not fulfilled his obligation of making *Kiddush.* On the Sabbath day if one does not care to eat a full meal right after *Kiddush,* he may recite *Kiddush,* and eat some pastry and drink a *reviit* wine,[25] in order to say the blessing עַל הַמִּחְיָה and עַל פְּרִי הַגָּפֶן. This he can do even before *Musaf* if he feels weak. A *Mohel* who

---

23. Blessing Over a Beverage After Kiddush   If one wishes to drink a beverage such as whiskey or coffee after *Kiddush,* it is suggested that he say the blessing *Shehakol* over some confection first, which would suffice for the beverage as well. Some authorities, however, maintain that one who recites *Kiddush,* or listens to it with the intention of fulfilling his obligation, need not recite an additional blessing over another beverage provided he drank some of the wine, as the blessing over the wine exempts him from the additional blessing.

24. Delaying the Meal After Kiddush   Some are of the opinion that one may delay the meal for a brief period of time, even for an hour after *Kiddush,* especially on Sabbath day when the obligation to make *Kiddush* is Rabbinical.

25. Kiddush Where the Meal Is Held   *Kiddush* is considered as having been made where the meal is held (קִידּוּשׁ בְּמָקוֹם סְעוּדָה) even if one eats a small amount of food (at least a *kezayit*), such as a piece of cake made of one of the five species of grain, or drinks a cup of wine of a sufficient quantity (i.e. a *reviit*), to require a blessing afterward.

must say the blessing over a cup of wine at the circumcision but has not yet made *Kiddush,* should drink a mouthful from the cup, and an additional *reviit* wine.

15.   It is permitted to refresh oneself with some food after the *Sha-ḥarit* service, before *Musaf.* One may eat a piece of bread, no larger than the size of an egg, but as much fruit as he desires.[26] However, he must first say *Kiddush* and either drink a mouthful and an additional *reviit* wine (the latter being considered in place of the meal), or drink a *reviit* wine and eat a *kezayit* of some food made of one of the five species of grain.

16.   Every Jew, both man and woman, is duty bound to eat three meals on the Sabbath,[27] one in the evening and two during the day.[28] At each of the meals one must eat bread, and since he washes his hands and says the blessing עַל נְטִילַת יָדָיִם,[29] he should eat a piece of

---

26.   Refreshments Before Musaf   One who made *Kiddush* before *Musaf* may eat some meat, fish and cheese, which like fruit are considered to be refreshments and not a complete meal. He may also eat some pastry in an amount less than would be sufficient for a meal (see Volume One, Part II, Chapter 10, paragraph 3). If one feels weak he may eat pastry, and even bread, more than the size of an egg until he feels refreshed.

27.   Three Meals On Shabbat   The obligation to eat three meals on the Sabbath is derived from the Biblical account of the portion of manna reserved for the Sabbath. The Rabbis note the threefold expression "today" (הַיּוֹם) in the verse, "And Moses said: 'Eat that today, for today is a Sabbath unto the Lord; today you shall not find it in the field'" (Exodus 16:25), which they take to allude to the three Sabbath meals.

28.   One Who Omitted the Evening Meal   One who failed to eat the Friday night meal should eat the three meals on the Sabbath day. If he also did not make *Kiddush* at night, he must recite the nighttime *Kiddush* in the morning, except for וַיְכֻלּוּ (see note 2).

29.   Washing For the Meal and Breaking Bread   After washing and before reciting the blessing עַל נְטִילַת יָדָיִם it is customary to raise one's hands and say,

bread the size of an egg. One should not eat to excess at the morning meal so that he will be able to observe the *mitzvah* of *shalosh seudot,* and eat all three of the Sabbath meals.[30] One should endeavor to eat bread at the *seudah shelishit,* but if he cannot eat any bread he should at least eat some pastry or another food that is made from one of the five species of grain and over which the blessing בּוֹרֵא מִינֵי מְזוֹנוֹת is said, as this too is considered a meal. If he cannot eat this, let him eat some food that is usually eaten with bread, such as meat or fish and the like. And if this is also not possible, then he should at least eat some cooked fruit.[31] The time for eating the *seudah shelishit* is from the time of *Minḥah gedolah* (the greater period for *Minḥah*), that is, at six and a half hours of the day.[32]

שְׂאוּ יְדֵכֶם קֹדֶשׁ וּבָרְכוּ אֶת ה'. וָאֶשָּׂא כַפַּי אֶל מִצְוֹתֶיךָ אֲשֶׁר אָהַבְתִּי וְאָשִׂיחָה בְחֻקֶּיךָ. "Lift up your hands to the sanctuary, and bless the Lord (Psalms 134:2). "I will lift up my hands unto thy commandments which I have loved, and I will meditate in thy statutes" (Psalms 119:48). The one who will break bread and say the blessing over the *ḥallot* should wait until all present have washed their hands and are seated at the table, so that he may include them all in the *mitzvah* of *leḥem mishneh.* For the procedure in washing the hands and other laws pertaining to the blessings and proprieties during the meal, see Volume One, Part II, Chapters 2–5.

30.   Saying רְצֵה in Birkat Hamazon   In the Grace recited after the meal (*Birkat Hamazon*) the prayer רְצֵה is included in the benediction בּוֹנֵה יְרוּשָׁלַיִם. If one failed to say רְצֵה, he must repeat the Grace from the beginning if this occurs at the first two Sabbath meals, but not at the third meal, when eating bread is not obligatory. For the procedure to follow if one failed to say רְצֵה, and other rules pertaining to Grace after the meal, see Volume One, Part II, Chapters 6,7.

31.   Eating a Third Meal on Shabbat   One may eat uncooked fruit for the *seudah shelishit* if he prefers it. Indeed, if he is unable to eat anything he is not obligated to eat at all, as the meal is intended for his pleasure and not to cause him discomfort.

32.   Time for Seudah Shelishit   It is customary to eat *seudah shelishit* after

17. One is obliged to break bread at every Sabbath meal over two whole loaves[33] (*ḥallot*), known as *leḥem mishneh*.[34] It is customary before saying the blessing to make a slight incision with the knife, marking the place where he intends to cut the *ḥallah*. The *ḥallot* should be placed in such a way that the one he intends to cut is at hand before him. He should hold both *ḥallot* in his hands while saying the blessing הַמּוֹצִיא, and then cut one of them.[35] Even if one eats

---

the *Minḥah* service, but if need be one may eat it before *Minḥah*. If one should begin the *seudah shelishit* before noon, he will still have fulfilled his obligation if the meal extends after the time of *Minḥah gedolah,* that is a half hour after noon.

33. Using Matzot for Leḥem Mishneh One can use *matzot* for *leḥem mishneh*. Even though they are generally baked in the form of sheets of dough and separated into individual *matzot* upon removal from the oven, they are nevertheless considered whole and may be used for *leḥem mishneh* on the Sabbath and on *Yom Tov*.

34. Women Required to Have Leḥem Mishneh The two *ḥallot* (*leḥem mishneh*) are in remembrance of the double portion of manna that the people of Israel gathered on Friday (Exodus 16:22), which sufficed them for food for the Sabbath as well. The requirement of *leḥem mishneh* applies also to women, since they too experienced the miracle of the manna from heaven which nourished the Israelites in the wilderness for forty years. The woman fulfills her obligation by listening to the blessing over the *ḥallot* made on her behalf and the others at the table (see also note 29).

35. Making an Incision and Cutting the Ḥallah The reason for making an incision in the *ḥallah* before saying the blessing is in order to avoid delay afterward while determining the number of portions to cut. On a weekday the incision is made all around the bread on the top and the bottom. On the Sabbath this cannot be done because the loaves have to be whole while the blessing is recited. Hence, the incision is only slight, just enough to mark the place where he intends to cut. At the Friday evening meal one cuts the lower loaf, and at the Sabbath day meal the upper loaf (see Chapter 2, paragraph 3).

many meals he should have two whole loaves at each of them.[36] If, after *Kiddush* in the morning, he eats some pastry before the meal, he should also take two whole pieces of cake.

18.   If only one of those present at the table has *lehem mishneh* before him, he should break bread on behalf of all. He may also say the blessing הַמּוֹצִיא on their behalf. Before saying the blessing he should request their permission and say בִּרְשׁוּת מוֹרַי וְרַבּוֹתַי. After eating some of the bread over which he said the blessing, he should give each one a piece, which they should then eat.

19.   If one failed to read the weekly portion of the Torah on the eve of the Sabbath, he should read it Sabbath morning before the meal.[37] If he did not read it then, he should do so at least before *Minhah,* and if need be before Tuesday evening.

20.   It is forbidden to fast on the Sabbath, even for a short time, if it is for the expres purpose of fasting. And in any case, it is forbidden to fast until midday,[38] even if it is not for the express purpose of fasting.

---

36.   Using a Frozen Hallah for Lehem Mishneh   One may use a *hallah* from the freezer for *lehem mishneh,* even if it is still frozen and inedible. It is considered bread because in time it will be edible when it is unfrozen.

37.   Reviewing the Torah Portion Before the Meal   One who did not complete a review of the weekly portion of the Torah should not delay the meal on that account past noontime, nor need he delay the meal if he has guests for the Sabbath who will be inconvenienced by the delay. For the requirement to review the weekly portion of the Torah, see Chapter 2, paragraph 8.

38.   Delaying the Meal For Prayer and Torah Study   Since the Sabbath meal should be eaten by noon, it is improper to prolong the services so that the worshipers cannot leave the synagogue in time, especially in the winter when the days are short. Services should not be unduly prolonged, particularly on the Festivals, except for Rosh Hashanah. Some authorities, however, take a lenient view, and permit delaying the Sabbath meal for prayer and Torah study, or if one finds it more convenient to have his meal at a later hour.

21. It is forbidden to grieve on the Sabbath,[39] but one should pray for mercy from God, the Merciful One.[40]

22. One should partake generously of fruits and delicacies, and enjoy pleasant aromas, in order to complete the total of one hundred blessings for the day.[41] It is a *mitzvah* to delight in things that give one pleasure, as it is written, "And you shall call the Sabbath a delight" (Isaiah 58:13).[42]

23. After the Sabbath day meal, one who is accustomed to take a nap should do so, as sleep is deemed to be one of the delights of the

---

39. Visiting a Mourner on Shabbat It is permitted to visit a mourner to console him on the Sabbath. However, it is not proper to delay the visit all week for one's own convenience, and to leave it for the Sabbath.

40. Visiting the Sick and Offering a Prayer for Recovery It is permitted to visit the sick on the Sabbath. It is likewise permitted to offer a prayer for one who is ill. However, the prayer should include the statement, שַׁבָּת הִיא מִלִּזְעוֹק וּרְפוּאָה קְרוֹבָה לָבוֹא, "It is the Sabbath, when one must not cry out, and healing will soon come."

41. Reciting One Hundred Blessings During the Day One normally recites one hundred blessings during the course of the day. However, since the *Amidah* on the Sabbath consists of seven benedictions, rather than nineteen as on weekdays, one should endeavor to compensate for them in order to complete the total of one hundred blessings for the day.

42. Making the Sabbath a Delight In addition to the regular meals on the Sabbath, consisting of fish, meat and tasty foods, one should partake of other delicacies and drinks according to one's means. It is also customary to adorn the house with flowers. It is traditional to sing *Zemirot*, lyrical poems depicting the beauty of *Shabbat* and God's abiding love for the Jewish People. Sung to a variety of melodies the *Zemirot* serve to enhance the Sabbath spirit, and to create a warm, pleasurable feeling of fellowship around the Sabbath table. The Sabbath meal is also a time for sharing Torah thoughts and for family communion, Thus, the Sabbath is a day of delight, affording those who observe it a uniquely joyous spiritual experience.

Sabbath. But he should not say, "I will sleep because I must work or go on a journey at night."

24.   Afterward one should set aside a time for Torah study. In the section of the Bible relating to the Sabbath, it is written, "And Moses assembled all the congregation of the children of Israel" (Exodus 35:1). Our Rabbis, of blessed memory, expound upon this as follows: "Why does it say here 'And Moses assembled,' and not elsewhere in the Torah? The Holy One, blessed be He, said to Moses: 'Go down and make assemblies for Me on the Sabbath, so that the generations who will come after you will learn to convoke assemblies every Sabbath for the study of Torah.'"[43] The Rabbis have further said, "The Sabbaths and Festivals were given to Israel in order to enable them to engage in the study of Torah. For many people are occupied with their work all week and cannot set aside time regularly for Torah study. But on a Sabbath and a Festival, when they are free from work, they can devote themselves properly to the study of Torah." Therefore, all those who are occupied with their work or business and cannot study Torah all week, are all the more obliged to devote themselves to Torah study on the holy Sabbath, each one according to his capacity and ability.

---

43.   Torah Study on the Sabbath   Torah study should include study of the laws, especially the Sabbath laws, reading of the Prophets and *Aggadic* passages, so that people will learn the laws, and be inspired by the divine teachings, and be instilled with reverence for God. Hence, it is customary in all Jewish communities to gather for Torah study, and to assemble in the synagogue for public lectures on the Sabbath.

8. READING THE TORAH ON THE SABBATH AND FESTIVALS

הִלְכוֹת קְרִיאַת סֵפֶר תּוֹרָה בְּשַׁבָּת וְיוֹם טוֹב וְחִיוּבָם

1. On Sabbath morning, after the *Shaharit* service, the *Sefer Torah** is taken from the Holy Ark[1] and the Torah portion of the week is read. Seven worshipers are called for the reading,[2] but if need be more may be called.[3] A *Kohen* is called up first, then a *Levi,* and fol-

---

*For the detailed laws regarding the *Sefer Torah,* those called to the Torah, and rules for reading the Torah, see Volume One, Part I, Chapters 26–28.

1. Carrying the Sefer Torah to the Bimah When the *Sefer Torah* is taken from the Ark and carried to the *bimah* the congregation should stand. It is customary to kiss the Torah and to accompany it to the *bimah.* It is not proper or an honor to the Torah, however, for the one who is carrying it to turn off to the sides, or to hold the Torah out to the worshipers so that it may be kissed.

2. Calling to the Torah One Who Does Not Observe the Sabbath As a rule, a worshiper is not to be denied the privilege of an *aliyah,* that is, being called to the Torah, provided he has not married out of the faith or forsaken the faith. While it is fitting that the honor be accorded to those who keep the laws of the Torah, nonetheless, one who does not observe the Sabbath is not, in our time, considered an apostate. The decision to give him an *aliyah* or not should be made by Rabbinical authority, depending on the circumstances, as on the occasion of a *Yahrzeit,* with due consideration to the effect it will have on the individual in encouraging him to observe the Law, and upon the community in preserving and strengthening Torah life. In any case, he should preferably not be called up as one of the requisite seven, but among the additional number called to the Torah. See Volume One, Part I, Chapter 27, note 20.

3. Calling to the Torah More Than the Required Number It is not proper to have more *aliyot* than the requisite number, thereby prolonging the service and inconveniencing the congregation, unless the occasion warrants it,

lowing him an Israelite. If there is no *Levi* present the same *Kohen* is called again instead, and they say בִּמְקוֹם לֵוִי. If there is no *Kohen* present, a *Levi* or an Israelite is called up instead, and they say אִם אֵין יִשְׂרָאֵל בִּמְקוֹם כֹּהֵן or כַּאן כֹּהֵן, לֵוִי בִּמְקוֹם כֹּהֵן. If a *Levi* or an Israelite was called up in place of a *Kohen*, then a *Levi* is not called up next after him.

2.   It is customary not to call a *Kohen* or a *Levi* after their turn among the required number to be called. However, if more than seven are called, it is permitted to call a *Kohen* or a *Levi* last, as *aharon* (אַחֲרוֹן), since the requisite number has already been called. A *Kohen* or a *Levi* may also be called for *Maftir* (מַפְטִיר). Indeed, one *Kohen* may be called for *aharon* and another for *Maftir,* since recitation of the *Kaddish* separates the two. On *Simhat Torah,* when the reading is done from three scrolls of the Torah, one *Kohen* may be called up as *Hatan Torah* for the reading of the last verses of the Torah, a second as *Hatan Bereshit* for the opening verses, and a third for the *Maftir,* since the reading for each is from a separate scroll. However, if *Rosh Hodesh Tevet* occurs on the Sabbath, even though the reading is from three scrolls, and eight are being called up for the reading from the first scroll, a *Kohen* may not be called as the eighth one, because the reading is not concluded in the first but rather in the second scroll where the portion for *Rosh Hodesh* is read and to which the *Kohen* can be called. The latter rule applies as well to *Shabbat Shekalim* and *Parshat Hahodesh* when they occur on *Rosh Hodesh.*

3.   If a *Kohen* or a *Levi* is mistakenly called up out of turn, someone else should go up to the Torah in his place, and he should wait at the reading desk and go up for *Maftir,* or for *aharon* after the requisite number has been called.[4]

---

as for a wedding, or a *Brit Milah,* and the like. However, this rule may be further relaxed, if need be, to avoid dissension.

4.   A Kohen or Levi Called to the Torah Out of Turn   If a *Kohen* or a *Levi* is

4. On a Sabbath when two *sidrot* are read, they are combined in the Torah portion read for *revii,* that is for the fourth person called up to the Torah.

5. There should be no interruption in the reading of the curses in the sections of *Parshat Beḥukotai* (Leviticus 26:14–43) and *Parshat Ki tavo* (Deuteronomy 28:15–68), known as the *Tochaḥah* (תּוֹכָחָה) or Admonition. The reading should begin with the preceding verse. However, so as not to start where there are less than three verses left to the section, one should begin the reading with the preceding three verses. At the end one should likewise read an additional verse, but he must take care not to conclude the reading where there are less than three verses left to the following section. In *Parshat Ki tisa* the entire section (Exodus 31:18–33:11) dealing with the golden calf until the concluding verse, "But his minister Joshua, the son of Nun, a young man, departed not out of the Tent" (Ibid. 33:11), should be read for the *Levi,* because the Levites did not participate in the mak-ing of the golden calf. It is customary to read in a low voice the verses beginning with וַיִּתֵּן אֶל מֹשֶׁה כְּכַלֹּתוֹ (Ibid. 31:18), and then to raise his voice for the verses beginning with וַיְחַל מֹשֶׁה (Ibid. 32:11–14). He lowers his voice again with וַיִּפֶן וַיֵּרֶד מֹשֶׁה until וּמֹשֶׁה יִקַּח אֶת הָאֹהֶל (Ibid. 32:15–33:6); after which he resumes reading aloud to the end of the portion. The curses in *Parshat Beḥukotai* and in *Parshat Ki tavo* should similarly be read in a low voice. In *Parshat Beḥukotai* the verse וְזָכַרְתִּי אֶת בְּרִיתִי יַעֲקוֹב. "Then will I remember My covenant with Jacob . . ." (Leviticus 26:42) should be read in a loud voice and the next verse וְהָאָרֶץ תֵּעָזֵב. "For the land shall be forsaken . . ." in a low voice. He then raises his voice again at the following verse, beginning with וְאַף גַּם זֹאת until the end of the portion. In *Parshat Ki tavo* he should raise his voice, beginning with the words לְיִרְאָה אֶת הַשֵּׁם הַנִּכְבָּד (Deuteronomy 28:58) to the end of the verse, and then continue in a

---

mistakenly called up for an *aliyah* out of turn, and it is not possible to give him *aharon* or *Maftir* instead, he should say the blessing for the Torah read-ing to which he was called.

low voice until the words וְאֵין קֹנֶה (Ibid. 28:68). In *Parshat Beha'alot-cha* it is likewise customary to read in a low voice the verses from וַיְהִי הָעָם כְּמִתְאֹנְנִים until וְהָמָן כִּזְרַע גַּד (Numbers 11:1–7), which deal with the rebelliousness of the people. The portions that are read in a low voice must nonetheless be read loud enough for the worshipers in the congregation to hear since they would otherwise not fulfill their obligation of reading the Torah. There should be no interruption in the reading of the forty-two stages of the journey of the Israelites, recounted in *Parshat 'Eleh Mas'ei* (Numbers 33:5–49), as it is symbolic of the Divine Name comprised of forty-two letters.[5]

6. During the intervals between *aliyot* the Torah scroll should be rolled up, but it need not be covered. However, before *Maftir,* when *Kaddish* is recited and there is a longer interval between the readings, the scroll should also be covered with its mantle. The scroll should likewise be covered whenever there is a longer interval, as when a benediction is chanted for a bridegroom, or when the blessing מִי שֶׁבֵּרַךְ is recited.[6]

7. If by error the reading of the entire *sidrah* on the Sabbath was concluded with the sixth person called, the *Kaddish* should not be

---

5. The Divine Names The Name that is associated exclusively with God, denoting His essence and existence as the Divine Being, consists of four letters (the Tetragrammaton). It is the ineffable Name of God referred to in the Mishnah and Talmud as the *Shem hameforash,* the proper or expressed Name. The Sages cite other names of God consisting of twelve letters and of forty-two letters. It is believed that these Names signified certain profound theosophical ideas.

6. Reciting a מִי שֶׁבֵּרַךְ It is customary to recite a blessing (מִי שֶׁבֵּרַךְ) on behalf of the person called to the Torah after the reading, as well as special blessings on the occasion of the birth of a child, and for a sick person. Although it is permitted to recite a מִי שֶׁבֵּרַךְ for a sick person while he is present, it is best under the circumstances not to use the one usually recited for the sick, but rather the regular מִי שֶׁבֵּרַךְ which also petitions God for protection and deliverance from "distress and illness."

recited then, but the *Maftir* should be called up immediately to complete the required seven that must be called for the Torah reading.[7] After he concludes the *Haftarah* and the blessings, the *Kaddish* is recited. Similarly on a Festival, if by error the prescribed portion is completed with the fourth person called, the *Kaddish* is not recited then, but the *Maftir* should be called immediately for the reading from the second scroll, and after he concludes the *Haftarah* and the blessings the *Kaddish* is recited.

8. When three Torah scrolls are required for the readings and there are only two available, the second scroll should not be rolled to the portion that would ordinarily be read in the third scroll, but the first scroll should be taken for the reading of that portion.

9. The *Sefer Torah* must be in perfect condition, free of disqualifying defects. If a serious defect involving a change in the form of a letter or a word is found in the scroll it is not permitted to read from it, and another *Sefer Torah* must be taken out of the Ark for the reading.* If the defect is found in the reading of the *Maftir,* and it is a special *Maftir* that it is obligatory to read on that day, as on a Festival, or on *Shabbat Rosh Ḥodesh,* or *Shabbat Parshat Shekalim,* and the like, when an additional *Sefer Torah* is taken out for the *Maftir,* then the rules and procedure to be followed are the same as apply to any of the other sections of the Torah that are read. However, if it is

---

*For the rules regarding a defective scroll and the procedure to be followed when the defective scroll must be returned and another *Sefer Torah* taken out of the Ark, see Volume One, Part I, Chapter 29.

7. Torah Reading Mistakenly Concluded With the Sixth Person   The *Maftir* is called as the seventh person only where by error the reading has been completed and *Kaddish* already recited. But if they become aware of the error before *Kaddish* has been said, then a seventh person is called up and the section that was read previously for the sixth person is repeated, thus again concluding the reading with him. Following this, *Kaddish* is recited, and the *Maftir* is called for the reading of several verses as usual.

an ordinary Sabbath when the reading for the *Maftir* is but a repetition of what was read for the seventh person called, then another *Sefer Torah* should not be taken out. For the reason a portion of the Torah is read for the *Maftir* is out of respect for the Torah, so that it may not appear as though the honor accorded the Torah and the honor accorded the Prophets are equal, since the readings from both the Torah and the Prophets are preceded and followed by their respective blessings. Therefore, it was instituted that for the *Maftir* there should first be a reading from the Torah in order to show that the essential reading is from the Torah. Accordingly, when a defect is found in the reading for the *Maftir* on an ordinary Sabbath, and as indicated another *Sefer Torah* is not taken out, the reading is completed in the same scroll, but the concluding blessing is not said. The *Haftarah* is then read with its blessings. If the defect is discovered before he said the blessing prior to the reading, another scroll should be taken out.[8] If there is no other scroll available, then the one who was called up last should read the *Haftarah* with its blessings, and if the *Kaddish* was not yet recited, it should be said after their conclusion.

10.   If a defect is discovered that is not considered to be serious but involves only an error in the transcription of a word, such as the omission or addition of the letter *vav* or *yud* (that is not part of the root), and neither the pronunciation or the meaning is changed, another scroll is not taken out. However, if such an error is dis-

---

8. A Defect Found After Concluding the Torah Reading   In the view of some authorities, if the defect is discovered after the Torah reading has been concluded, but before *Kaddish* was recited, another scroll is not taken out for *Maftir,* but the one who received the last *aliyah* proceeds to read the *Haftarah* with its blessings, following which the *Kaddish* is recited. If the defect is discovered only after *Kaddish* has been said, three verses of the Torah are read for the *Maftir* from the same scroll, without the blessings before and after the reading, followed by the *Haftarah* and its blessings. In the latter instance, the *Kaddish* is not said again afterward.

covered on the Sabbath, although another scroll is not taken out, nonetheless no more than seven should be called for the reading in that scroll. The seventh person called should read the *Haftarah* as well, with its blessings, after which *Kaddish* is recited. This procedure is followed on an ordinary Sabbath. But if it is obligatory to read a special *Maftir* for that day, as on *Shabbat Rosh Ḥodesh* or *Shabbat Parshat Shekalim,* another person must be called for *Maftir.* The defective scroll, however, should not be used later at the *Minḥah* service.

11.   On a day when two scrolls of the Torah are taken out and the first is found to be defective, and there is a third scroll in the Ark, the second scroll may not be used for the reading in place of the first, and the portion of the second scroll read from the third scroll. In such a case the third scroll should be taken from the Ark for the reading of the first portion, replacing the defective scroll, and the second portion read from the second scroll, because each reading must be in the scroll that was originally designated for it. This rule applies as well on a day when three scrolls are taken out for the prescribed readings. Likewise, if the scrolls were interchanged, and the second scroll was taken by error in place of the first, it must be rolled up and the other scroll must be used for the first reading, so that the readings will be in the scrolls intended for each.

12.   The following is the order of precedence in *aliyot* for those who are obliged to be called to the Torah: (1) A bridegroom on the day of his wedding. A bridegroom on the Sabbath before his wedding, if he had never been married, when special blessings are chanted in honor of the occasion,[9] and (2) a boy who has become *Bar Mitzvah*[10] during

---

9.   Precedence to a Bridegroom for an Aliyah   The degree of precedence given to a bridegroom on the Sabbath before his wedding applies even when the wedding will not take place in the coming week, but only later because he must travel a great distance to the wedding, or for some other pressing reason.

10.   A Bar Mitzvah Leading the Prayers and Reading the Torah in a Different

that week, are equal in their right to be called. (3) A *sandak,* who holds the baby during the circumcision, on the day of the circumcision. (4) A *sandak,*[11] who carries the baby to the synagogue to be circumcised, on the day of the circumcision. (5) The husband of a woman who has given birth to a daughter, when his wife comes to the synagogue. (6) The husband of a woman who has given birth to a son, when his wife comes to the synagogue. But if she does not come to the synagogue her husband is not obliged to be called to the Torah, unless it is forty-one days on the birth of a son, or eighty-one days on the birth of a daughter, as it was at these times that an offering was brought in the Temple. (7) A bridegroom on the Sabbath after the wedding, when the wedding took place on Wednesday or thereafter and it is the first marriage for either the bridegroom or the bride. (8) One who has *Yahrzeit* on that day. (9) The father on the day of his son's circumcision. (10) One who will have *Yahrzeit* during the week following the Sabbath. (11) The *mohel* (one performing the circumcision) on the day of the circumcision. (12) The *sandak,* then the father, then the *mohel,* on the Sabbath before the circumcision.

If two people have equal claims to be called, the decision rests with the *Gabai,* or they decide by lots. One who is not a resident does

---

Pronunciation   A *Bar Mitzvah* who has been taught the Sefardic pronunciation may lead the prayer service and read the Torah and *Haftarah* in an Ashkenazic congregation, inasmuch as people are by now familiar with the Sefardic pronunciation as well. As a rule, however, a congregation should not change its tradition. If the *Bar Mitzvah* reads the entire Torah portion, and not just the *Maftir,* Rabbi M. Feinstein ל״ז advises that the Torah portion be read in the Ashkenazic pronunciation, in keeping with the established custom of the congregation, at a *minyan* assembled elsewhere in the synagogue.

11.   Aliyot for the Sandak and Mohel   Some include the *sandak* and *mohel* among those obliged to be called to the Torah. In other congregations, however, it is not customary to give them preference for an *aliyah,* but they are accorded the honor of *Hagbah* and *Gelilah,* raising and rolling up the scroll after the reading of the Torah is concluded.

not take precedence over a resident who is obliged to be called to the Torah. It is customary to call one who is embarking on a journey after the Sabbath, or who has returned from a journey. It is also customary to honor a worthy visitor by calling him to the Torah.[12] However, none of these takes precedence over one who is obliged to be called to the Torah.[13]

13.　One who is called to the Torah[14] should wrap himself in a *tallit,* proceed to the reading desk and take his place to the right of the Reader. When the Torah Scroll is opened, he should look for the place where the reading is to begin, and after reciting the blessing,[15],

---

12.　One Who Is Accorded an Honor at the Torah　The sixth *aliyah* (ששי) is deemed to be the most prominent, and is usually reserved for a person of distinction. However, one who is called to the Torah should not refuse any *aliyah* or decline any honor accorded him, but he should accept it with grace and humility.

13.　An Aliyah to One Recovering From Illness　One who has occasion to recite the blessing of *Hagomel* (see Volume One, Part II, Chapter 21), as on recovering from a serious illness and the like, should be given preference for an *aliyah,* but he does not take precedence over any of those who are obliged to be called to the Torah. Although the blessing *Hagomel* is customarily recited at the reading of the Torah, it can be recited as well at any time in the presence of a *minyan.*

14.　Calling to the Torah by Name　One who is called up to the reading of the Torah should be called by name, that is, by calling out his Hebrew name and that of his father. This is a hallowed tradition, of great importance in the retention of Jewish names and in the preservation of Jewish identity which should not be abandoned. One who was adopted and raised by foster parents may be called to the Torah as the son of his adoptive father, if he prefers using the latter's name for that of his father.

15.　Reciting the Torah Blessings　Some are accustomed to roll up the

he should read along silently with the Reader. After the portion has been read,[16] he recites the blessing and waits for the next reading. When the person called after him has said the final blessing, he departs.

14.   A boy who is not yet *Bar Mitzvah* should not be called to the Torah, nor should he act as a Reader of the Torah.[17]

---

scroll before reciting the first blessing. The *Mishnah B'rurah* is of the opinion that the scroll may remain open, so that the Torah reading will proceed without delay. One may follow either custom. After the reading, the scroll should be rolled up and the concluding blessing recited. The one who is called to the Torah for an *aliyah* should say the blessings aloud so as to be heard by the congregation, thus providing an opportunity for the worshipers to respond to the blessings.

16.   An Error in the Torah Reading   The Reader should prepare in advance for reading the Torah portion and read it carefully for the congregation without any mistakes. If the Reader is required to correct an error in the reading, and he had already read part of the verse which contained the Divine Name, he should conclude the verse and then repeat it from the beginning. However, if the rest of the verse also contains the Divine Name, he should leave the latter part of the verse unread, and begin again immediately from the beginning of the verse.

17.   An Aliyah and Torah Reading by a Minor   A boy who is not yet *Bar Mitzvah*, but has reached the age of religious training and knows to whom the blessings are directed, may be called to the Torah for *Maftir*, provided he can pronounce the words and intone them correctly (see Chapter 9, paragraph 9). However, one who is not yet *Bar Mitzvah* may not act as Reader of the Torah portions for others to fulfill their obligation. Some permit it in an emergency, when there is no one else available to read from the Torah scroll, so that the reading of the Torah will not be entirely omitted.

15. All of the congregation[18] must listen attentively[19] while the Torah portion is read.[20] It is forbidden to converse during the reading, even on subjects relating to Torah, nor may one leave the synagogue at this time. In the intervals between the readings, when the scroll is rolled up, one may leave if it is urgent.

16. In a place where there is no *Sefer Torah*,[21] one of the congrega-

---

18. Standing During the Torah Reading The *Shulḥan Aruch* writes that the worshipers need not stand while the Torah is being read. Following this ruling of the *Meḥaber,* the Sefardim do not stand. The Rama, however, states that those who are more stringent stand during the Torah reading. While the prevailing view among the authorities is that one is not duty-bound to stand, some deem it proper to do so, with the thought in mind that when one hears Torah read it is as though he were receiving it from Sinai, and the people of Israel stood at the foot of the mountain when the Torah was revealed to them at Sinai. One who finds it difficult to stand, should rather sit so that he may concentrate on the reading. In any case, one should stand while the one called to the Torah says בָּרְכוּ and the congregation responds בָּרוּךְ ה' הַמְבֹרָךְ. One need not stand during the intervals between the *aliyot.*

19. Correcting the Reader If the Reader misreads a word in the Torah he should be corrected, and he must repeat it correctly. However, if the error is in the intonation, or it is in the punctuation, and the mispronunciation does not change the meaning, he need not repeat the word. Hence, if he reads אַת instead of אֶת, or vice versa, he should not be corrected.

20. Use of a Microphone or Loudspeaker for the Torah Reading Apart from the prohibitions involved in their use on *Shabbat* and *Yom Tov,* one's obligation for the reading of the Torah, according to many authorities, is not fulfilled when it is heard through a microphone and other electrical or electronic devices and instruments such as a loudspeaker and telephone, or from a radio, television or tape recorder. In the operation of these instruments the sound of the voice is converted into electrical impulses, and one does not hear the natural voice. For a discussion of their prohibited use on the Sabbath, see Part II, Melachah 36, Electrical Equipment and Appliances.

21. Failure to Read the Torah on Sabbath Morning In the event that the

tion should read the Torah portion aloud from a printed *Ḥumash*,[22] while the rest of the worshipers listen.

9. READING THE MAFTIR AND HAFTARAH

דִּינֵי מַפְטִיר

1. After the reading of the Torah, and before one is called up for *Maftir*, the half-*Kaddish* is recited.[1] While the *Kaddish* is being recited the scroll from which the Torah portion has just been read should be on the table, as well as the second scroll if the *Maftir* portion is to be read from it. When the readings are from three scrolls it is not necessary to place the first scroll on the table.

2. The one called for *Maftir* should not begin saying the blessings for the *Haftarah* until the scroll has been bound up and wrapped in its mantle.

-----

congregation failed to read the Torah portion at the Sabbath morning service, it should be read on the following Sabbath, together with the designated portion for that Sabbath. It may not be read, however, on Monday and Thursday mornings, as it would inconvenience worshipers who must go to work. In the view of some authorities the Torah and *Haftarah* portions should be read, and the blessings recited, that very Sabbath afternoon before *Minḥah*, followed by the regular *Minḥah* service. If special circumstances warrant it, as in the case of hospital patients who cannot assemble for services on Sabbath morning, the latter arrangement can be followed.

22. Reading the Torah Portion From a Ḥumash When a *Sefer Torah* is not available and the Torah portion is read from a *Ḥumash*, the blessings over the Torah are not recited. If there is a *Sefer Torah* available, but no one present is proficient in reading from it, one may read from the *Sefer Torah* with the help of another person who reads from a *Ḥumash*.

1. Kaddish After the Torah Reading As a rule, whenever the Torah is read a half-*Kaddish* is said afterward, except at the *Minḥah* service on the Sabbath, and at the *Minḥah* service on a Fast Day, when the *Kaddish* said before the *Amidah* is meant for the Torah reading as well.

3. The blessing said before the *Haftarah* does not end with הַנֶּאֱמָרִים בֶּאֱמֶת. Hence, one does not respond with *Amen* until after וָצֶדֶק, which concludes the blessing. This also applies to the first of the blessings said after reading the *Haftarah*. One does not respond with *Amen* after אֱמֶת וָצֶדֶק, as the blessing does not end there, but continues with נֶאֱמָן אַתָּה. Since some mistakenly respond with *Amen* in these places, it is advisable that the one reciting the blessings should not pause there, so as to indicate that the blessing is not yet concluded.

4. It is not permitted to converse while the *Haftarah* is being read.

5. The *Haftarah*[2] should be read aloud only by the one who is called up to *Maftir*;[3] the worshipers are to read it along with him quietly.[4] In some congregations the worshipers read the *Haftarah* aloud. This custom is due to ignorance and should be abolished.[5] There are also some worshipers who are slow in reading the *Haftarah,* and they con-

---

2. Haftarah Readings Designated for Sefardim References in the *Humashim* to *Haftarah* readings according to the custom of the Sefardim do not apply to those who are not Sefardim, but have only adopted the Sefardic *nusah* in prayer as established by the Ari. With respect to the *Haftarah* to be read in conjunction with the Torah reading they should follow the Ashkenazic custom.

3. Calling to Maftir One Who Only Says the Blessings In order to avoid embarrassment and controversy it is permissible to call to *Maftir* one who will only say the blessings, and the Reader will recite the *Haftarah.*

4. Reading the Haftarah From a Scroll The practice in most synagogues, where the worshipers read along silently, is that the *Maftir* reads the *Haftarah* from a *Humash* or from a book containing the individual *Haftarah* readings. In some synagogues, however, it is the custom to read the *Haftarah* from a scroll of the Prophets. In the latter case, the *Maftir* alone should read the *Haftarah,* while the congregation listens.

5. Worshipers Reading the Haftarah Aloud Some authorities are of the opinion that the custom followed in some synagogues where the worshipers join the *Maftir* in reading the *Haftarah* aloud serves to keep those who are

tinue reading it after the *Maftir* has already concluded and has begun to say the blessings. They are acting improperly, because if they continue reading it aloud, they do not hear the blessings and in all likelihood prevent their neighbors from hearing them as well. And even if they lower their voices, they still do not hear the blessings themselves. Therefore, it is best that when the *Maftir* has finished reading the *Haftarah* and begins the blessings one should remain silent until the blessings are concluded, and afterwards he may finish reading the *Haftarah* himself. The *Maftir* should also take care not to begin saying the blessings until the voices of the congregants have entirely subsided.

6.   On a Sabbath when two *sidrot* are read jointly, the *Haftarah* of the second *sidrah* is read, except when the *sidrot Aharei* and *Kedoshim* are joined in which case the *Haftarah* read is הֲלוֹא כִבְנֵי כֻשִׁיִּים (Amos 9:7–15). In some *Humashim* it is erroneously noted that the *Haftarah* of *Parshat Vayishlah* is וַיִּבְרַח יַעֲקֹב (Hosea 12:13–14:10). This *Haftarah,* however, is read in conjunction with *Parshat Vayetze* while the *Haftarah* of *Vayishlah* is חֲזוֹן עוֹבַדְיָה (Book of Obadiah).

7.   On *Rosh Hodesh* which occurs on the Sabbath the *Haftarah* reading is הַשָּׁמַיִם כִּסְאִי (Isaiah 66:1–24). If instead one read the *Haftarah* selection for the *Sidrah* of that week, and he becomes aware of the error before reciting the concluding blessings, he should also read הַשָּׁמַיִם כִּסְאִי and then say the blessings. But if he becomes aware of the error after saying the blessings, he should read הַשָּׁמַיִם כִּסְאִי without repeating the blessings. When *Rosh Hodesh* occurs on Sunday, the *Haftarah* מָחָר חֹדֶשׁ (I Samuel 20:18–42) is read. If he erred, he should follow the above procedure as on *Shabbat Rosh Hodesh*. When *Rosh Hodesh* occurs on *Shabbat* and on Sunday the *Haftarah* הַשָּׁמַיִם כִּסְאִי is read.

8.   On *Shabbat Hol Hamoed Pesach* (the Sabbath of the Interme-

---

unable to read the *Haftarah* with its traditional intonation and melody from embarrassment, and need not be abolished.

diate days of Passover) no mention of Passover is made, neither in the middle nor at the end of the concluding blessings of the *Haftarah,* and the blessing concludes only with מְקַדֵּשׁ הַשַּׁבָּת. However, on *Shabbat Ḥol Hamoed Sukkot* (the Sabbath of the Intermediate days of Sukkot), when complete *Hallel* is recited, and the sacrificial offerings differ each day, mention is made of the Festival, and the blessing concludes מְקַדֵּשׁ הַשַּׁבָּת וְיִשְׂרָאֵל וְהַזְּמַנִּים as when the first days of Sukkot occur on the Sabbath.

9.   A minor who has reached the age of training in *mitzvot,* who knows to whom the blessings are addressed, and who can pronounce the words distinctly, may be called to *Maftir* on the Sabbath and on a Festival, except on the Sabbath of *Parshat Zachor* and *Parshat Parah,*[6] and on *Shabbat Shuvah.* It is also customary not to call a minor to *Maftir* on the seventh day of Passover, when the *Haftarah* reading is the *Shirah,* the Song of David (II Samuel 22:1–51, and on the first day of Shavuot, when the *Haftarah* reading is the *Merkavah,* the chariot of Ezekiel (Ezekiel 1:1–28, 3:12). On these occasions it is customary to call an adult, who is also a learned man. It is, likewise, customary to call the Rabbi to *Maftir* on *Shabbat Ḥazon,* when the *Haftarah* reading is חֲזוֹן יְשַׁעְיָהוּ (Isaiah 1:1–27), the Vision of Isaiah.

10.   The *Haftarah* was instituted to be read with its blessings only after the Torah has been read with its blessings for the required number of people that are to be called.[7] But, if on an ordinary Sabbath the

---

6.   Calling a Minor to Maftir on the Four Special Sabbaths   Some authorities are of the opinion that a minor may be called only when the Torah portion that is read for the *Maftir* is a repetition of what was read for the previous *aliyah.* According to this view a minor should not be called up to *Maftir* on any of the four Sabbaths (*Arba Parshiot*) when a special section of the Torah designated for that Sabbath is read for the *Maftir.* This would mean that, in addition to *Parshat Zachor* and *Parshat Parah,* a minor is also not to be called to *Maftir* on the Sabbath of *Parshat Shekalim* and *Parshat Haḥodesh.*

7.   Haftarah Reading on the Occasion of Two Bar Mitzvahs   In the event

Torah scroll is found to be defective, even in the reading for the seventh *aliyah,* and there is no other *Sefer Torah* available, and he therefore has not said the concluding blessing over the Torah, the blessings for the *Haftarah* are not said.[8] Neither are the blessings for the *Haftarah* said on a Sabbath when it is obligatory to read a special portion for the *Maftir* on that day, even if the defect is found to be in the portion read for the *Maftir.* In these instances the *Haftarah* is read, but without the blessings. However, if on an ordinary Sabbath the defect is found after seven people have been called and they said the blessings over the Torah, whether the defect was found in the reading for the additional people called up, or in the reading for the *Maftir,* the *Haftarah* should be read with its blessings.

––––––––––

there are two boys in the synagogue who are celebrating their *Bar Mitzvah* on the Sabbath, it is not permitted to have them read the *Maftir* and *Haftarah* twice, that is, to call the first *Bar Mitzvah* to read the *Maftir* and the *Haftarah* and to recite the blessings, and then to call the second *Bar Mitzvah* to repeat the readings and the blessings. In such a case they should be advised to schedule the *Bar Mitzvah* celebrations on different Sabbaths. If scheduled on the same Sabbath, they should divide the honors, one to be called for *Maftir* and the second for another *aliyah,* or the congregation can form separate groups and the Torah and *Haftarah* read in two places. If this arrangement is not acceptable, and it is necessary to avoid discord and re-criminations, some authorities permit individual consecutive readings for each *Bar Mitzvah,* provided a *minyan* of worshipers resolve not to fulfill their obligation with the first reading. They should leave the synagogue and return for the readings by the second *Bar Mitzvah.* The Torah scroll should not be raised and rolled up, but only covered, in the interval between the readings. On the observance of *Bar Mitzvah* and *Bat Mitzvah,* see Volume One, Part II, Chapter 21, paragraph 8, and notes.

8. Haftarah Blessings After Torah Reading From a Defective Scroll   In the view of some authorities, where the scroll is found to be defective and no other scroll is available, the concluding blessing over the Torah is said, and hence the *Haftarah* is read with its blessings as well. See Chapter 8, paragraph 9, and notes.

* The *Kitzur Shulḥan Aruch* does not include a comprehensive discussion of the principal *melachot* and their subsidiaries, except for a brief summary of select laws which constitutes Part III of this volume.

Part II, which follows here, is intended as a supplementary exposition of the thirty-nine classes of labor and related activities forbidden on the Sabbath.

Part II

Principal Classes of Labor (Melachot)
Forbidden on the Sabbath
ל״ט מְלָאכוֹת הָאֲסוּרוֹת בְּשַׁבָּת

INTRODUCTION

THE NATURE OF MELACHAH

Determining the Nature of Melachah

We are commanded by God not to work on the Sabbath, as it is written, "Six days you shall labor and do all your work. But the seventh day is a Sabbath unto the Lord your God; in it you shall not do any manner of work" (Exodus 20:9,10; Deuteronomy 5:12,13). The Torah does not explicitly define the term *melachah* (מְלָאכָה)[1] which it uses here in forbidding "work" on the Sabbath. We are, however, informed by the Halachah as to what is encompassed by this prohibition. Physical exertion and toil are not the deciding factors in establishing whether an activity is a *melachah* which the Torah forbids on the Sabbath. The Sages have determined that the various activities that were necessary for the *Mishkan,* the Tabernacle that the People of Israel erected in the wilderness, are the main classes of labor forbidden on the Sabbath. They note the juxtaposition of the commands regarding observance of the Sabbath and the building of the *Mishkan,* where the Torah also uses the term *melachah* to describe

---

1. Melachot Mentioned in the Torah Several *melachot* are specifically mentioned in the Torah as forbidden on the Sabbath: Plowing and Reaping, "In plowing time and in harvest you shall rest" (Exodus 34:21); Kindling a Fire, "Ye shall kindle no fire throughout your habitations upon the Sabbath day" (Exodus 35:3); Carrying from one domain to another, "Let no man go out of his place on the seventh day" (Exodus 16:29). The latter statement is understood as forbidding the people from going out with vessels on the Sabbath to gather the manna.

the work in connection with construction of the Tabernacle which was forbidden and discontinued on the Sabbath.[2] (See *Shabbat* 49b, 73b; Exodus 35:2, Rashi and *Mechilta,* ibid.; Exodus 31:13, Rashi, ibid).

The Principal Classes of Melachah

The Mishnah (*Shabbat* VII, 2) enumerates thirty-nine principal classes of labor (ל"ט מְלָאכוֹת) that are forbidden on the Sabbath. They are the following:

(1) Sowing (הַזּוֹרֵעַ),[3] (2) Plowing (הַחוֹרֵשׁ), (3) Reaping (הַקּוֹצֵר), (4)Binding Sheaves (הַמְעַמֵּר), (5) Threshing (הַדָּשׁ), (6) Winnowing (הַזּוֹרֶה), (7) Selecting (הַבּוֹרֵר), (8) Grinding (הַטּוֹחֵן), (9) Sifting (הַמְרַקֵּד), (10) Kneading (הַלָּשׁ), (11) Baking (הָאוֹפֶה),[4] (12) Shearing Wool (הַגּוֹזֵז אֶת הַצֶּמֶר), (13) Cleaning (הַמְלַבֵּן), (14) Combing (הַמְנַפֵּץ), (15) Dyeing

---

2. Melachot Associated With the Tabernacle The main classes of labor on the Sabbath are activities that the Sages have determined were involved in constructing the Tabernacle, which were forbidden even for such a holy purpose as building a Sanctuary to God. Some authorities include, as well, the activities that were involved in preparation of the offerings in the dedication of the Tabernacle. According to this view the first eleven *melachot,* from Plowing to Baking, involved production of the loaves of bread for the sacrificial offerings.

3. Sowing and Plowing as Listed in the Mishnah The Mishnah lists Sowing first, and then Plowing, in the order of the thirty-nine *Avot Mela chot.* Some of the Codes follow the same order. Other Codes, however, such as the *Mishneh Torah, Semag,* and *Ḥayye Adam,* list Plowing first, in accord with the usual practice in tilling the soil. The Talmud explains the reverse order of the Mishnah by stating that it refers to the Land of Israel, where the soil is hard and requires additional plowing after the seed is sown and planted in the ground. The intent of the Mishnah is to let us know that the second plowing is also considered a prohibited *melachah* on the Sabbath.

4. Baking and Cooking The Mishnah lists Baking among the principal labors, rather than Cooking, although it was the boiling of ingredients for dyes that was involved in preparing the hangings and curtains for the Taber-

(הַצּוֹבֵעַ), (16) Spinning (הַטּוֹוֶה), (17) Stretching the Threads (הַמֵּיסֵךְ), (18) Making Loops (הָעוֹשֶׂה שְׁתֵּי בָתֵּי נִירִין), (19) Weaving Threads (הָאוֹרֵג שְׁנֵי חוּטִין), (20) Separating the Threads (הַפּוֹצֵעַ שְׁנֵי חוּטִין), (21) Tying a Knot (הַקּוֹשֵׁר), (22) Untying a Knot (הַמַּתִּיר), (23) Sewing (הַתּוֹפֵר שְׁתֵּי תְפִירוֹת), (24)Tearing (הַקּוֹרֵעַ עַל מְנָת לִתְפּוֹר), (25) Trapping (הַצָּד צְבִי), (26) Slaughtering (הַשּׁוֹחֵט), (27) Skinning (הַמַּפְשִׁיט), (28) Salting (הַמּוֹלֵחַ),[5] (29) Tanning (הַמְעַבֵּד אֶת עוֹרוֹ), (30) Scraping (הַמְמַחֵק), (31) Cutting (הַמְחַתֵּךְ), (32) Writing (הַכּוֹתֵב שְׁתֵּי אוֹתִיּוֹת), (33) Erasing (הַמּוֹחֵק עַל מְנָת לִכְתּוֹב שְׁתֵּי אוֹתִיּוֹת), (34) Building (הַבּוֹנֶה), (35) Breaking Down (הַסּוֹתֵר), (36) Extinguishing a Fire (הַמְכַבֶּה), (37) Kindling a Fire (הַמַּבְעִיר), (38) Striking the Final Hammer Blow (הַמַּכֶּה בַּפַּטִּישׁ), (39) Carrying (הַמּוֹצִיא מֵרְשׁוּת לִרְשׁוּת).

Avot Melachot

The thirty-nine classes of labor listed above are referred to in the Mishnah as *Avot Melachot* (אֲבוֹת מְלָאכוֹת), that is, principal or primary categories of labor. However, *Avot Melachot* are not limited to the specified activities involved with the Tabernacle. Any activity may be considered an *Av Melachah* if it is similar to one of the principal categories of *melachah* (1) by reason of the purpose or objective, as well as the nature of the activity, or (2) by virtue of a common purpose or objective alone, even where the activity itself is not the same.

An example of the first (1) is the act of embedding a branch of a tree in the ground so that it will take root and grow into a separate

---

nacle. The Talmud explains that the Mishnah follows the order of making bread and enumerates the various activities associated with it. Baking and Cooking are in fact considered as of the same category of *melachah*.

5. The Substitution of Marking for Salting The listing of the *melachot* in the Codes differs from that of the Mishnah in this instance to accord with the ruling in the Talmud (*Shabbat* 75b) that Marking (הַמְשַׂרְטֵט) is to be substituted for Salting. This is because salting is held to be part of the tanning process, while marking is a necessary operation preparatory to cutting or writing.

tree. This activity is similar to the principal category of sowing or planting in the nature as well as in the objective of the act, since in both instances it entails putting something in the ground for the purpose of growth. An example of the second (2) would be pruning the branches of a tree. While the act of cutting the branches is not similar to the principal category of the *melachah*, namely Sowing or Planting, it nevertheless shares with it the common purpose of growth, in that pruning the branches of the tree will facilitate and enhance its growth.

Toladot

Each of the principal categories of labor subsumes other derivative or subsidiary acts of labor which are known as *Toladot* (תּוֹלָדוֹת). As to determining whether an act is an *Av Melachah* or a *Toladah*, the following rules apply.

1. If the act is similar to a principal category of *melachah* by virtue of a common purpose or objective, it is considered an *Av Melachah* when it is directly carried out on the object for which it seeks to achieve the purpose intended, but not where it directly involves another object. Thus, watering a plant or a tree, although it shares with the principal category the common purpose of growth, is not considered an *Av Melachah*, because the act directly involves the water and not the plant or the tree. Watering is, consequently, subsidiary to, or a derivative of the *melachah*, and is therefore a *Toladah*. Another illustration of this distinction would be removing a mound of earth, thereby leveling the ground. Since it serves the same objective of preparing the soil for seeding or planting as the principal category of plowing, and the act is carried out on the ground itself, it is considered an *Av Melachah*. However, removing weeds from the ground, where the act does not directly involve the ground, is a *Toladah*, even though it has the same objective of preparing or improving the soil as does the principal category.

2. If the act is similar to a principal category of *melachah* only in the nature of the act, but it does not share a common purpose, it is considered to be a *Toladah*. Thus, filing metal, which is similar to

grinding corn or other grain in the nature of the act, but not in its purpose, which in the case of corn or grain is for food, is therefore considered to be only a *Toladah* of the *Av Melachah* of Grinding. Similarly, mixing earth with water and kneading it is a *Toladah* of the *Av Melachah* of Kneading, and cheese-making is a *Toladah* of Building, since each resembles the *Av Melachah* only in the act, but not in its purpose.

Apart from certain halachic considerations, the *Toladot* are for all practical purposes equal to *Avot Melachot* in that they are also considered to be Biblically prohibited.[6] Thus, the performance of a forbidden act which is considered to be a *Toladah* constitutes a violation of Torah law.

The Juridical Status of Melachot

The juridical status of *melachot* on the Sabbath is characterized by the following terms. The term חַיָּיב, liable or culpable, and hence punishable, is used to indicate an act that is Biblically forbidden, and subject to the penalties which such a violation incurs. The term פָּטוּר, exempt, is used to indicate an act that is not Biblically forbidden, but is nevertheless Rabbinically forbidden (פָּטוּר אֲבָל אָסוּר), and subject to a penalty incurred for the violation of a Rabbinical prohibition. The term מוּתָּר, permissible, is used to indicate an act that is not subject to any Biblical or Rabbinical prohibitions and may be performed on the Sabbath.

Applicable to all Sabbath prohibitions, whether Biblical or Rabbinical, is the overriding rule (*Shabbat* 132a; Yoma 85b; Rambam, *Mishneh Torah, Hilchot Shabbat* 2:1) that the saving of life supersedes

---

6. Transgression of a Melachah   An intentional transgression of a Biblical prohibition involving an *Av Melachah* or a *Toladah* is considered a desecration of the Sabbath subject to severe punishment (see Exodus 31:14, *Mechilta,* and Rashi, ad loc.) An unintentional transgression, which in the time of the Temple required a sin-offering, is today subject to atonement by means of fasting and charity.

the Sabbath (פְּקוּחַ נֶפֶשׁ דוֹחֶה אֶת הַשַּׁבָּת). Hence, whatever their designation, whether *Avot Melachot* or *Toladot,* activities that are otherwise forbidden are permissible when there is a possible danger to human life.

Halachic Conditions Determining a Melachah

A guiding principle underlying the Sabbath laws enunciated in the Talmud is that מְלֶאכֶת מַחֲשֶׁבֶת אָסְרָה תּוֹרָה, "the Torah prohibits work of craftsmanship," in which manner the work of the Sanctuary is characterized in the Bible (Exodus 35:33).[7] The Sages understood this to mean that the *melachah* that is forbidden on the Sabbath must be constructive, done with intention and purpose.

In keeping with the above principle, the Halachah sets forth certain conditions which determine whether a *melachah* is to be considered in violation of a Biblical prohibition, thereby rendering one liable to a penalty for its transgression.

(a) A *melachah* must be done intentionally with the result due to direct action (עֲשִׂיָּיה הוּא דְאָסוּר). An indirect action (גְּרָמָא) does not come under the Biblical prohibition.[8]

---

7.   The Principle of מְלֶאכֶת מַחֲשֶׁבֶת   The principle of מְלֶאכֶת מַחֲשֶׁבֶת, namely that the Torah forbids work of craftsmanship, is intimated by the congruity of the terms and the confluence of the passages in the Bible dealing with the building of the Tabernacle and the laws of the Sabbath. In his work on the *Mishkan* Bezalel, the chief architect, is commissioned to work as a craftsman in all manner of skillful workmanship. This is followed by the laws concerning the Sabbath (see Exodus 31:4,5,12–17; 35:33).

8.   A Melachah Done Indirectly   The prohibition of *melachah* as given in the Torah, "You shall not do any manner of work" (Exodus 20:10), is taken by the Sages to mean that direct action (עֲשִׂיָּיה) is forbidden, but indirect action (גְּרָמָא) is not forbidden. However, while גְּרָמָא is not Biblically forbidden, it is nevertheless Rabbinically prohibited. In certain instances, as in cases involving substantial financial loss (פְּסֵידָא), a *melachah* may be permitted when it is done indirectly (גְּרָמָא). Thus, one may make a water barrier

(b) One must do the whole of the *melachah* by himself (שֶׁיַעֲשֶׂה כָּל הַמְּלָאכָה) for him to be liable, unless it is a *melachah* that he cannot do alone. In such a case, if two people do it together they are both liable.[9]

(c) One must do the *melachah* because it is required on its own account (מְלָאכָה הַצְּרִיכָה לְגוּפָה), and not for some other purpose.[10]

---

to intercept and indirectly extinguish a fire when there is a financial loss involved. Of course, where there is a possible danger to life one should take direct and prompt action to extinguish the fire.

9. Doing the Whole Melachah   The condition that one must do the whole of the *melachah* himself to be liable is derived from the Biblical admonition, "And if any one sin . . . in doing any of the things which the Lord has commanded not to be done and be guilty" (Leviticus 4:27). The Sages expound the verse as follows: "Only he who performs the whole of it, but not he who performs a portion thereof. If a single person performs it, he is liable; if two perform it, they are exempt" (*Shabbat* 3a). Hence, if two people take hold of a pen and write with it on the Sabbath, they are exempt. However, if one person cannot do the *melachah* alone, and two do it together, they are both liable. Thus, if two people should move an object that is too heavy for one to move alone from one domain to another on the Sabbath, they are both liable. If one is able to move it alone, and the other is not, the one who can move it is liable, while the other is exempt. In the above, as in other similar instances, the exemption is only with regard to culpability for the Biblical violation. The *melachah* is, nonetheless, Rabbinically prohibited.

10. A Melachah Not Required on Its Own Account   An example of a *melachah* which is not required on its own account (מְלָאכָה שֶׁאֵינָה צְרִיכָה לְגוּפָה) is if one digs a hole on the Sabbath, and he needs only the earth, but not the hole itself. Another example would be if one extinguishes a lamp, not because he wants the light extinguished, but because he wants to spare the oil or the wick. Whether one is liable for such an act is the subject of debate in the Talmud. The *Rishonim* differ in the matter as well. Rambam rules that one is culpable for a *melachah* which is not required on its own account. The *Shulhan Aruch* and most authorities maintain that a *melachah* which is not done for its own sake is not forbidden by Torah law, but the act is nevertheless Rabbinically prohibited, especially in the case of extinguishing a fire, where the prohibition is more severe than other Rabbinic prohibitions.

(d) One must do the *melachah* in the manner that it is customarily done, without any change (כְּדַרְכָּהּ בְּלִי שִׁינוּי). But, if he did not do it in the usual way, it is as though it was done כִּלְאַחַר יַד, literally, with the back of the hand, and he is not liable.[11]

(e) One must intend doing the *melachah* (מְתְכַּוֵּין), that is, his intention must be to do the prohibited act in the manner that it is prohibited, involving the same object, and in the intended order. But, if he intended to do a permitted act and instead he did a forbidden act he is not liable. However, it is only when it is possible to do the act intended without violating a prohibition, that one is exempt.[12] But, if it is not possible to do the permitted act without doing a forbidden act, even though he does not intend the forbidden act, he is liable. This is because, in the latter instance, the forbidden act is inevitable (פְּסִיק רֵישָׁא).[13]

---

11. A Melachah Done in an Unusual Way   While one is not liable for a *melachah* when it is done in an unusual manner (עַל יְדֵי שִׁינוּי), it is nevertheless Rabbinically prohibited. Thus, one is not liable if he pulls his nails off by hand or by biting them off, since the Biblical prohibition applies when the nails are removed in the usual way, that is with a scissors or some other cutting implement. It is nevertheless Rabbinically forbidden even when it is not done in the usual way. Similarly, one who is right-handed is Rabbinically forbidden to write with his left hand, although he would not be culpable, since it is not his usual way of writing.

12. An Act Where a Transgression Is Not Intended   One is not liable for an act that results in a transgression which is neither intended nor inevitable. In such a case one is permitted to do the act at the outset. Thus, one is permitted to pull a chair or a table along the ground, as long as he does not intend making a groove in the earth, since it is possible to do so without making a groove. Similarly, one may walk on grass, as long as he does not intend tearing the grass, because it is possible to walk on grass without tearing or uprooting it.

13. An Act Where a Transgression Is Inevitable   The expression פְּסִיק רֵישָׁא וְלֹא יָמוּת, "Cut off his head, but let him not die!," is employed in the Talmud (*Shabbat* 75a) to indicate a situation where an act must inevitably result in a violation of the Sabbath. If the result is one that he desires and he is satis-

(f) One must do a *melachah* that is constructive (מְתַקֵּן). If it is merely destructive (מְקַלְקֵל) he is not liable. However, if he has a useful or constructive purpose in mind, for example if he destroys in order to build, he is liable.[14]

(g) One must do a *melachah* which endures (מִתְקַיֵּים). If it is not of an enduring nature he is not liable.[15] This applies only to certain *melachot,* such as Writing, Dyeing, and Building, but not to such *melachot* as Plowing and Sowing.

---

fied with it (פְּסִיק רֵישָׁא דְנִיחָא לֵיהּ), he is liable. Thus, one who pours water on grass or on a plant, even when he does not do so in order to promote its growth, but he is nonetheless satisfied by the prospect of its growth, is liable because it is as though he intended the forbidden act from the start. However, if he is not desirous of the result (פְּסִיק רֵישָׁא דְלָא נִיחָא לֵיהּ), or he is indifferent to it (פְּסִיק רֵישָׁא דְלָא אִיכְפַּת לֵיהּ), he is not liable. In the latter case, some take it to be permissible, but most authorities believe it to be Rabbinically forbidden.

14. Destructive and Constructive Acts Since the *melachot* in the Tabernacle were all of a constructive nature, a destructive act does not conform to the concept of *melachah,* and therefore does not incur a penalty. Hence, if one should tear or burn clothing, or deliberately break an object, he is not liable. However, if he has a constructive objective in mind he is liable. Examples of the latter would be tearing a garment in order to sew it properly, erasing in order to write in the place of the erasure, demolishing a building in order to build another one on its site. It should be noted, however, that even acts that are wholly destructive, for which one is not liable, are nevertheless Rabbinically prohibited.

15. Melachot That Are Not Durable While one is not liable for a *melachah* if the end result is not enduring, the act may still be Rabbinically forbidden (פָּטוּר אֲבָל אָסוּר). An example would be coloring an article with a dye which will not last, or writing with material or on a surface where the writing will not endure. In certain instances, however, the act may be permissible. Thus, tying or untying a durable knot, such as a double knot, is forbidden on the Sabbath. It is permitted, however, to tie or untie a bow which is not a durable knot. As to the length of time required for an act to be considered of an enduring nature, it should last at least through the Sabbath, although some require that it endure for a longer period of time.

A *melachah* that does not meet the above conditions, while it does not incur liability as a transgression of a Biblical prohibition, is nonetheless Rabbinically prohibited (פָּטוּר אֲבָל אָסוּר), and may therefore not be done on the Sabbath.

Prohibition of Benefits From a Melachah

One may not benefit from work that is done by a Jew in violation of the Sabbath. The prohibition of benefits resulting from doing a *melachah* is a penalty which the law imposes even when the transgression is unintentional, lest one comes to do the *melachah* willfully. The prohibition applies to the transgressor, and may affect others as well, in accordance with the following rules.

If one willfully transgresses (מֵזִיד), and he does a *melachah* which is Biblically prohibited (מְלָאכָה הָאֲסוּרָה מִדְּאוֹרַיְיתָא), for example, if he cooks on the Sabbath, it is forever forbidden to him. To others it is forbidden on that Sabbath,[16] but it is permitted immediately upon conclusion of the Sabbath.[17] But if he did the *melachah* unwittingly (שׁוֹגֵג), either because he forgot that it was *Shabbat*, or he thought that it was permissible, it is forbidden to everyone on that Sabbath day, but immediately after *Shabbat* it is permitted to all, even to him. If

---

16. Drinking Coffee or Tea in a Non-Observant Home One who is visiting on *Shabbat* in a Jewish home where the people are not observant of the Sabbath should not partake of any food or drink, such as coffee or tea, even when there is no question whether it is *kosher,* if he thinks that it may have been cooked on the Sabbath.

17. Benefit From a Melachah by a Non-Jew In the case of a *melachah* that was done by a non-Jew for a Jew one must wait after *Shabbat* until such time as would be required to have the work done (בִּכְדֵי שֶׁיַּעֲשֶׂה) before benefitting from it. This is because the prohibition against instructing a non-Jew to do work on the Sabbath is regarded lightly, and if one were allowed to benefit from the work as soon as the Sabbath is over one would instruct a non-Jew to do work for him on other occasions. This precaution is not deemed necessary in the case of a *melachah* done by a Jew.

one willfully transgresses (מֵזִיד) and he does a *melachah* that is Rabbinically prohibited (מְלָאכָה הָאֲסוּרָה מִדְּרַבָּנָן), it is forbidden to everyone on that Sabbath day, but immediately after *Shabbat* it is permitted to all, even to him. But if he did the *melachah* unwittingly (שׁוֹגֵג), it is permitted to all, even to him, on that Sabbath day.

Rabbinical Enactments

In keeping with their historic role as guardians of the Torah, its laws and institutions, the Sages have adopted safeguards, and enacted laws and prohibitions designed to preserve the sanctity of the Sabbath and its unique character as a holy day of rest. These prohibitions with respect to the Sabbath carry Biblical sanction, and are regarded as being more severe than other Rabbinical prohibitions.[18] In accord with the Biblical exhortation (Exodus 23:12) to "rest" on the Sabbath (וּבַיּוֹם הַשְּׁבִיעִי תִּשְׁבּוֹת) such prohibitions are known by the term *shevut* (שְׁבוּת).

Accordingly, in their endeavor to prevent any possible desecration of the Sabbath, in the unwitting transgression of a *melachah,* the Sages prohibited certain activities,[19] although the activity of itself does not constitute a *melachah,* for the following reasons (Rambam, *Hilchot Shabbat* 21:1):

1. The activity resembles a *melachah,* and if permitted one might mistakenly come to do the actual *melachah.*

Thus, pressing olives or grapes is a *melachah* (Pressing is a *Toladah* of דִּישָׁה, Threshing) which the Torah forbids, since olives and

---

18. Rabbinical Authority Presently Limited   The Rabbis are presently not empowered to enact similar decrees of their own accord. Such authority could no longer be exercised after the close of the Talmud and the age of the Gaonim.

19. Transgression of a Rabbinical Prohibition   An intentional violation of the Sabbath involving a Rabbinical prohibition is likewise subject to punishment as authorized by the Rabbis. If one transgresses unintentionally, he should make amends by fasting and giving charity to the poor.

grapes are used principally for the oil and wine which is extracted when these fruits are pressed and processed. However, squeezing mulberries, pomegranates and similar fruits for their juice is not a *melachah,* since these fruits are generally intended to be eaten as food, but it nevertheless is Rabbinically forbidden (Rambam, ibid. 21:12).

2. The activity normally involves, or may lead to doing a *melachah.*

Thus, one is Rabbinically forbidden to transact business such as buying and selling on the Sabbath, as it may lead to transgressing the *melachah* of Writing. It is likewise Rabbinically forbidden to make a loan, or to conduct judicial proceedings on the Sabbath, as these activities customarily involve writing (Rambam, *Hilchot Shabbat* 23:12,14).

3. The Sages have, futhermore, prohibited certain additional activities in keeping with the Prophet's directive, "If you turn away your foot because of the Sabbath, from pursuing your business on My holy day . . . and shall honor it, not doing your wonted ways, nor pursuing your business, nor speaking thereof" (Isaiah 58:13). The Sages take this to mean that on the Sabbath one should refrain from weekday activities and concerns (עוּבְדִין דְחוֹל).

Thus, one may not speak of business matters, or handle objects that are not for Sabbath use, or engage in excessively strenuous activity, or engage in activities that are of a distinctly weekday nature. The purpose of these Rabbinic enactments is to keep the Sabbath from becoming an ordinary weekday, with people occupying themselves with their usual weekday pursuits (Rambam, *Hilchot Shabbat* 24:1,12,13).

The Principle of Shevut De-Shevut

The concurrence of two independent Rabbinical prohibitions is termed a *shevut de-shevut* (שְׁבוּת דְּשְׁבוּת), which renders the act permissible in certain circumstances.

Thus, a Jew may instruct a non-Jew to do something on the Sabbath, such as an activity that is not a transgression of a *melachah,* but is forbidden to be done on the Sabbath on account of a Rabbinical prohibition, provided it is urgently necessary to have it done for a person who is slightly ill, or it is essential that it be done, for example, to save one from a considerable loss, or for a *mitzvah,* because it is a *shevut de-shevut,* that is, an act involving two separate Rabbinical prohibitions (*Shulḥan Aruch, Oraḥ Ḥayyim, Hilchot Shabbat,* 307:5; 331:6). Since the prohibition involved is Rabbinical in nature, and the prohibition to instruct a non-Jew to do anything a Jew is forbidden to do on the Sabbath is likewise Rabbinical, it is not prohibited by the Sages in such a circumstance.

The principle of *shevut de-shevut* as a mitigating factor applies to a Jew as well, allowing for leniency in such emergency situations, when there is a combination of two prohibitions that are Rabbinical in nature.

Performing an Act in a Different Manner

As already indicated, performing a *melachah* in a backhanded manner (כְּלְאַחַר יָד), or in an unusual way (עַל יְדֵי שִׁינוּי) renders the act a *shevut,* and the one performing the *melachah* is not culpable, but the act is Rabbinically prohibited.

When applied to Rabbinical prohibitions שִׁינוּי and כְּלְאַחַר יָד are further mitigating factors. Thus, preparing a soft, thin mixture on the Sabbath, which does not violate the Torah prohibition of Kneading but is Rabbinically prohibited, requires that the mixing be done in an altered manner (עַל יְדֵי שִׁינוּי). Mashing fruits and vegetables in a manner different from the usual, for example, with the handle of a knife or spoon, is likewise permissible on the Sabbath.

The rationale for שִׁינוּי as a mitigating factor is that, when one does something in a manner different from the way he would do it on weekdays, we need not fear that he will come to do the *melachah* which is forbidden by Torah law.

The principle of שִׁינוּי and כְּלְאַחַר יָד applies in the case of Rabbinical prohibitions relating to the transgression of a *melachah* (אִיסוּרֵי מְלָאכָה

דְּרַבָּנָן), but not to certain decrees enacted by the Sages (גְזֵרוֹת) prohibiting individual activities on the Sabbath as a preventive measure to safeguard observance of *Shabbat*.

The Prohibition of Mar'it Ha'ayin

The Rabbinical prohibition of *mar'it ha'ayin* (מַרְאִית הָעַיִן), that is, prohibition of an act because of the appearance of wrongdoing, which applies generally, imposes restrictions on the Sabbath as well. An apparent reason for this restriction, aside from one's obligation to present an appearance of upright conduct and to avoid a *ḥillul Hashem,* profaning the Name of God, in compliance with the Torah's admonition, "Ye shall be clean before the Lord and before Israel" (Numbers 32:22), is that one's action could be misconstrued and might lead others to actually violate a *melachah.* Thus, if one's garments become soaked in water, he may not spread them out to dry, lest people suspect him of having laundered them on the Sabbath. *Mar'it ha'ayin,* although a Rabbinical prohibition, applies with regard to both Biblical and Rabbinical prohibitions. However, while in the case of a Biblical prohibition an act that has the appearance of wrongdoing and is subject to *mar'it ha'ayin* is forbidden even in private, in the case of a Rabbinical prohibition it is only forbidden in public.[20]

---

20. Acts Prohibited Because of Mar'it Ha'ayin   The Sages did not, as a rule, differentiate and make exceptions in their enactments with regard to Biblical prohibitions. Hence, in such a case an act that is subject to *mar'it ha'ayin* is forbidden even in private. In the case of a Rabbinical prohibition they were stringent in prohibiting the act in public, but not in private. The restriction in private (בְּחַדְרֵי חֲדָרִים), even in one's innermost chamber, applies to acts that are customarily performed in public, but not to acts that are normally performed in private. It should be noted, as well, that the restriction of *mar'it ha'ayin* is not applied indiscriminately. Thus, one is not forbidden to perform an act that is manifestly permissible merely because some people might mistakenly believe it to be prohibited.

Exposition of the Melachot*

In setting forth and expounding the ל״ט מְלָאכוֹת we shall endeavor (1) to define the objective of each of the *melachot,* that is, the end toward which the act is directed, (2) to determine the forbidden primary activities of the *Av Melachah,* the subsidiary activities prohibited as *Toladot,* and the Rabbinical prohibitions relating to the *melachah,* (3) to indicate practical applications of the Halachah that pertain to the *melachah.*

The synoptic exposition of the *melachot* is based primarily on the following authoritative works: *Tiferet Yisrael*'s Introduction to the tractate *Shabbat,* entitled כַּלְכָּלַת שַׁבָּת; *Hayye Adam,* הִלְכוֹת שַׁבָּת; Rambam, *Mishneh Torah,* הִלְכוֹת שַׁבָּת; *Shulhan Aruch,* הִלְכוֹת שַׁבָּת, with commentaries, particularly *Magen Avraham* and *Mishnah B'rurah,* as well as other Codes, and Responsa literature by past and contemporary authorities.

---

* The thirty-nine *melachot* which follow are given according to the order in the Mishnah, *Shabbat* VII, 2, except in several instances. The *melachah* of Plowing is listed first in accord with the usual practice in tilling the soil, and as it appears in some Codes (*Mishneh Torah, Semag, Hayye Adam*). The *melachah* of Sifting is placed before Grinding, although the order is reversed in the Mishnah, because of its similarity to the preceding *melachot* of Winnowing and Selecting. The *melachah* of Marking is substituted for Salting in accord with the ruling in the Talmud and the listing in the Codes. The *melachah* of Kindling is placed before Extinguishing, in a more practical sequence as listed in the *Mishneh Torah,* although the order is reversed in the Mishnah in this case as well.

1. PLOWING

חֲרִישָׁה

1.   The objective of this *Av Melachah* is to prepare the soil for seed-ing or planting. Plowing is forbidden in any degree and in any form, whether with a plow or another implement, or by hand.

The *melachah* comprises such forbidden primary activities in the field as plowing, digging,[1] making a furrow,[2] leveling a small mound of earth, and filling up a hole or hollow in ground that is suitable for sowing.

2.   The *melachah* includes forbidden subsidiary activities (*Toladot*) which do not involve working directly with the soil, but are equally designed to prepare and improve the soil, as for example, fertilizing in order to prepare the soil for planting, removing weeds from around the roots of trees, removing stones from the ground, and breaking up clods of earth.

---

1.   **Wheeling a Carriage on a Dirt Road**   One is permitted to wheel a baby carriage, or a wheel chair for an invalid, on an unpaved street or on a dirt road where there is an *eruv,* since one does not intend making a track or leveling the ground. Moreover, the wheels only cause a depression in the ground, while the prohibition entails digging out the earth and causing a furrow or groove in the ground. One is, likewise, permitted to walk on sand or dirt with shoes that leave the impress of markings or designs that are on the heels.

2.   **Pulling a Chair or Table on the Ground**   It is permitted to pull a chair, a bench, or a table along the ground, provided one does not intend making a groove in the ground. However, if the object is very heavy and bulky, and it is inevitable that it will make a groove, it is not permitted.

3. An activity such as sweeping an earthen floor[3] is Rabbinically prohibited[4] because it may involve leveling holes in the ground.[5]

2. SOWING

זְרִיעָה

1. The objective of this *Av Melachah* is to promote and facilitate the

---

3. Sweeping Unpaved Ground Loosening the earth and leveling the ground in the field is prohibited under the *melachah* of Plowing, since it renders the ground suitable for planting. If one does it in the house, it involves the prohibition of Building. (See Melachah 34, paragraph 10.) Sweeping unpaved ground or an unpaved floor is deemed to be Rabbinically forbidden because it is bound to result in displacing earth and leveling the ground or making grooves and holes in the ground. Even when one does not intend to do so, it is still forbidden inasmuch as it is inevitable (פְּסִיק רֵישָׁא), or because while preoccupied with sweeping he may forget and intentionally level the ground.

4. Sweeping and Cleaning a Floor It is permitted to sweep a floor, where the surface is paved or covered with a flooring such as wood or linoleum, with a soft broom or a dust mop, but not with a hard broom made of bristles that are likely to break. One may not clean the carpet with a carpet sweeper, even if it is operated manually and not electrically. It is not permitted to wash or mop the floor, but one may sprinkle water on the ground or on the floor in the house in order to keep the dust from rising. It is not permitted to wax or polish the floor.

5. Ball Playing One is not permitted to play soccer, golf, or football on earth or grass lest he come to level the ground. Some permit ball playing by children, except for the kind of games mentioned above, where there is an *eruv,* or in a private area where there is no likelihood that the ball will fall out of bounds. Table tennis is likewise permitted. Older children should refrain even from these games, and should engage in learning Torah and in activities more in keeping with the spirit of *Shabbat.*

growth of plants[1] for whatever purpose. Sowing is forbidden in any amount and in any form, whether with an implement, a machine, or by hand.

The *melachah* comprises such forbidden primary activities as sowing seed in soil (זוֹרֵעַ), planting a tree (נוֹטֵעַ), bending a vine or twig under ground to produce an independent plant (מַבְרִיךְ), grafting (מַרְכִּיב), and pruning the branches of a tree (זוֹמֵר).

2. The *melachah* includes forbidden subsidiary activities (*Toladot*) which have the same purpose, although the nature of the *melachah* is different, as for example, weeding out harmful plants, watering[2] plants,[3] flowers,[4] or trees, soaking seeds such as wheat and barley in

---

1. Growing Plants in a Flower Pot It is forbidden to sow seed or to plant for growth, whether in the ground or in a flower pot that contains soil. The prohibition applies to a flower pot made of clay, wood, or other material, irrespective of whether it has an opening on the bottom and rests on the ground, or it has no opening. A large flower pot that is fixed and immovable is in any case considered like planting in actual earth. Since the object of the *melachah* is to promote growth, it is also forbidden to remove a flower pot from a table or some other surface and place it on the bare ground if the pot has an opening on the bottom, as contact with the ground will facilitate its growth. It is, likewise, forbidden to remove it from the ground and stand it on planks or stakes, as this would be in violation of the *melachah* of Reaping (קוֹצֵר). In practice it is Rabbinically forbidden to merely lift a perforated flower pot from the ground and suspend it in the air. It is also forbidden to place even a non-perforated flower pot on the ground or remove it from the ground. Indeed a flower pot is considered *muktzeh* and may not be moved altogether.

2. Watering the Lawn by Means of a Time Clock One should not water the lawn on the Sabbath, even by means of a time clock that is set before *Shabbat* to turn the water on and off at designated times.

3. Watering Plants in a Flower Pot It is forbidden to water flowers or plants, whether they are growing in the ground or in a flower pot. In the latter case, it is forbidden even if the pot has no opening on the bottom and is not set on the ground.

water thereby causing them to sprout and grow,[5] coating a tree with a substance to protect it from insects or from injury and decay, and smoking out insects, or otherwise removing them from a bush or a tree.

3.   It is not permitted to throw seeds on ground that is wet or damp from the rain, as they may sprout or take root in the soil. One may not wash his hands on the grass, even if he does not intend to water it.[6]

3. REAPING

קְצִירָה

1.   The objective of this *Av Melachah* is to sever a plant from its place of growth.

---

4.   Placing Cut Branches and Flowers in Water   Cut branches and flowers should not be put into a vase with water on the Sabbath. It is not permitted to add water or to change the water on *Shabbat*. It is permissible, however, to move a vase containing flowers on the Sabbath.

5.   Washing and Soaking Vegetables and Dried Fruits   It is permitted to wash cut vegetables to keep them from withering so that they may be eaten on the Sabbath. Grain may be soaked in water to soften it for feeding one's cattle and animals, since he does not intend to have it sprout, but only to soak for a short time and then to be used as fodder. Seed may be spread as feed for one's chickens and fowl in small quantities, so that they will be consumed in a day or two and will not remain on the ground longer in the event that it should rain. It is likewise permitted to soak raisins and dried fruits to be eaten on the Sabbath, but not in order to make preserves.

6.   Eating and Drinking in the Garden   It is best not to eat and drink in the garden on the Sabbath if water and beverages are served, as it is difficult to avoid spilling some of it on the grass. Some authorities take a lenient view with regard to serving wine and similar drinks, which if spilled onto the grass would tend to inhibit rather than to promote its growth. An additional concern should be the permissibility of carrying from the house into the garden and in the garden itself.

The *melachah* comprises such forbidden primary activities as cutting the grain crop and produce in the field, and cutting grapes from the vine, or dates, figs and other fruit from the tree, when these acts are done with a cutting implement or a machine.

2. The *melachah* includes forbidden subsidiary activities (*Toladot*) which involve detaching something from where it grows, when it is done by hand (תּוֹלֵשׁ)[1], as for example, plucking plants, flowers,[2] berries and fruits that grow on trees, on bushes and in the soil,[3] or shaking a bush or a tree and knocking off its fruit. One is also liable if he detaches mushrooms, moss and other fungi from wherever they are growing, or plants that are growing in a perforated flower pot set directly on the ground or over it with no obstruction beneath it, or if he removes the perforated flower pot with the plant from the ground and places it on another surface.

----

1. Reaping and Plucking Plucking (תּוֹלֵשׁ) when it is done by hand is a derivative of the primary *melachah* of Reaping (קוֹצֵר) which is done with an implement.

2. Smelling Fragrant Fruit and Flowers One is forbidden to smell any edible fruit, such as an *etrog* or an apple, while it is still attached to the tree or to the ground, lest he pluck it in order to eat it. One is permitted to smell a flower or an aromatic plant that is not edible, for we need not fear that he will pluck it, since one can enjoy its fragrance without plucking it. However, while the authorities permit it, prevailing custom takes a stricter view, lest one forgets himself and plucks it. The restriction does not apply to cut flowers in a vase which may be handled and their fragrance savored. See also Part V, Chapter 3, note 17.

3. Putting Cattle Out to Graze It is permitted to put one's cattle out to graze and feed on the grass and herbage in the field. This is in compliance with the Biblical command, "That your ox ... may have rest" (Exodus 23:12). The Rabbis take this to mean, "Let it have satisfication by allowing it to pull up and eat grass from the ground as it pleases," for otherwise the cattle would be in pain and would have no rest.

3. The Rabbis prohibited certain activities which may lead to a violation of the *melachah*,[4] such as eating fruit that fell from a tree, or vegetables that were detached from the ground on the Sabbath.[5] One is not permitted to remove a honeycomb or honey from a beehive, or climb a tree,[6] or make use of a tree by placing an object on it or removing the object from it. One is likewise forbidden to ride an animal on the Sabbath, lest he cut or break off a branch to use it as a whip to direct the animal.[7] It is not permitted to detach a plant that is growing in a non-perforated flower pot, or to lift the pot from the ground onto posts or onto the table or some other surface.

---

4. Walking on the Grass   One may sit or walk on the grass, whether it is dry or moist, even if the grass is tall, and irrespective of whether he has shoes on or is walking barefoot, since he does not intend to tear the grass.

5. Fruit Fallen From the Tree   Fruit that may have fallen from the tree, or vegetables that may have dropped to the ground on the Sabbath may not be eaten until the conclusion of *Shabbat*. They may not be handled, as well, because they are *muktzeh*. Fruit that fell before the Sabbath may not be gathered on the Sabbath, but may be picked up and eaten one at a time.

6. Climbing and Leaning on a Tree   One is not permitted to climb a tree for fear that he will come to pluck its fruit or tear off its leaves. The prohibition applies even to a tree that is barren of fruit or leaves, so as not to make any exceptions. It is likewise not permitted to lean against a tree, or even to touch it if it will move with his touch. If the tree is sturdy and immovable, he may lean against it if he does not support his full weight on it. One may lean or sit on a tree stump, irrespective of its height.

7. Riding an Animal or in a Wagon Drawn by an Animal   One is forbidden to ride an animal even when there is no likelihood that he will break off a branch to use as a whip. One is likewise forbidden to make use of an animal by sitting or leaning on it while it is standing still, or by placing an article on it, unless it is for its own benefit, such as a blanket to keep it warm. This applies to all animals regardless of their size. It is also forbidden to sit in a wagon drawn by an animal, even when it is led or driven by a non-Jew. Apart from the fear of violating the Sabbath by tearing off a branch in order to prod and lead the animal, one is also duty-bound to allow the animal its due rest on the Sabbath.

4. BINDING SHEAVES

עִימוּר

1.　The objective of this *Av Melachah* is to gather products that grow in the soil (גִידוּלֵי קַרְקַע), after they have been detached from the ground (תְּלוּשִׁין), in the place where they were grown (בִּמְקוֹם גִידוּלָן), and binding or heaping them up, as is customarily done with sheaves of grain.

The *melachah* comprises such forbidden primary activities as gathering corn, fruit, vegetables, flowers, wood, and other products that grow in the soil, and piling them up in a heap for storage or for sale.[1] It is forbidden to gather these products in the field or in the garden in a quantity or in amounts in which they are minimally collected, such as two plants or two flowers, even if they were cut and detached before the Sabbath.[2]

2.　The *melachah* includes forbidden subsidiary activities (*Toladot*) of a similar nature, such as collecting and pressing figs into a round cake, or pressing other fruits into one mass, or piercing figs and inserting a cord through them and tying them together. This is forbidden even when done in a place other than where the fruit was grown, as it is normal to process the product in this manner in a building as well as in the field or orchard.

3.　It is Rabbinically forbidden to gather products such as salt and other minerals from where they are mined, even though they are not

---

1.　Gathering Natural Products　The *melachah* involves only raw products in their natural state. It does not apply to grain or fruit that has been ground, cooked or baked. It also applies only to gathering natural products in their place of growth, but not in the house or in the courtyard.

2.　Making a Bouquet of Flowers　Making a bouquet of flowers is a violation of the *melachah* if it is done in the place where the flowers were grown. One may not, however, arrange flowers into a bouquet on the Sabbath elsewhere as well.

products that grow in the soil. Some authorities, however, are of the opinion that this would be in actual violation of the *melachah,* as they maintain that the *melachah* applies even to products that are not grown in the soil. It is not permitted to gather fruit that is strewn about over a considerable area in the courtyard, and to heap them in a pile or put them into a basket, as this is considered a weekday activity (עוּבְדָא דְחוֹל). However, one may collect them individually and eat them. It is permissible to gather fruit, and to collect other articles such as household utensils, that are scattered about the house.

5. THRESHING

דִּישָׁה

1. The objective of this *Av Melachah* is to separate a natural product which grows in the soil (גִּידוּל קַרְקַע) from its husk or outer covering, or its constituent part, to which it is by nature attached.

The *melachah* comprises such forbidden primary activities as threshing grain to separate the seed, which is considered edible or desirable matter (אוֹכֶל), from the chaff, which is considered inedible or undesirable matter (פְּסוֹלֶת). Beating flax or cotton are forbidden activities of this nature. One is liable for violation of the prohibition as an *Av Melachah* when done with an implement or by machine.

2. When the edible or desirable matter is separated from the inedible or undesirable matter by hand it is considered a *Toladah* (מְפָרֵק).[1] The *melachah* includes such forbidden subsidiary activities (*Toladot*) as stripping the husks from ears of corn, and removing peas

---

1. **Removing Honey From a Honeycomb** Removing a honeycomb or honey from a beehive is prohibited because it resembles plucking (תּוֹלֵשׁ) a derivative of the *melachah* of קְצִירָה. Removing honey from the wax, or crushing a honeycomb to extract the honey is forbidden as a *Toladah* (מְפָרֵק) of the *melachah* of דִּישָׁה. Honey that flows out of a honeycomb of its own accord on the Sabbath may not be eaten until after the Sabbath.

or beans from dry, inedible pods. If the pods are fresh and edible it is permitted to remove them in small quantities for immediate consumption, since the prohibition does not apply to extracting a product that is edible from something that is also edible (מְפָרֵק אוֹכֶל מֵאוֹכֶל). Cracking and removing the hard shell from nuts such as almonds, walnuts and hazelnuts even with a nutcracker or some other instrument is permissible. It is likewise permitted to extract the marrow from bones. Fruits and vegetables, such as oranges, bananas, onions, garlic, and carrots, whose rind or outer covering is not normally eaten, may be peeled even with a knife for immediate consumption. Removal of the undesirable matter is in this case permitted as it is the normal way of eating this kind of food (דֶּרֶךְ אֲכִילָה).

3.   The *melachah* also includes squeezing (סְחִיטָה) olives to extract oil and grapes for wine. This is forbidden because of the prohibition of separating (מְפָרֵק) which is a *Toladah* of דִּישָׁה. As a precautionary measure the Sages have additionally prohibited squeezing out such fruits as mulberries and pomegranates, which are generally intended to be eaten but are also squeezed for their juice. This Rabbinical prohibition would therefore apply as well to similar fruits such as oranges, lemons, apples, tomatoes, grapefruits, and the like which are commonly squeezed out in order to drink the juice. Where the prohibition applies, it is forbidden irrespective of whether the fruit is squeezed with an instrument or by hand. It is not permitted to squeeze the juice into another liquid, as for example squeezing the juice out of a lemon into a cup of tea,[2] but one may squeeze the juice onto solid food, such as fish or a salad, because when liquid is added to food to improve it or to enhance its taste it is regarded as food (מַשְׁקֶה הַבָּא לָאוֹכֶל כְּאוֹכֶל דָּמֵי). It is permitted to squeeze the juice out of fruits and vegetables other than olives and grapes if one intends to

---

2.   Putting Lemon into Tea   While some permit squeezing the lemon onto sugar and putting it into the tea, it is best to prepare the lemon juice before the Sabbath, or to put a slice of lemon into the tea without squeezing it. See Part III, note 15.

remove the juice in order to enhance the taste of the fruit or vegetable,[3] even if the juice is squeezed into a container so that it does not go to waste. It is permitted to suck the juice out of fruits, vegetables and other kinds of food, as for example soup and gravy from meat, or wine that was soaked up in bread. Fruits and vegetables whose juice is not normally extracted for drinking do not come under the prohibition altogether and may be squeezed out, unless there is prevailing local custom prohibiting it.

4.   Milking an animal is forbidden as a *Toladah* (מְפָרֵק) of the *melachah* of דִּישָׁה, and one is in violation of the *melachah* if he expresses the milk into an empty vessel. Milking into a vessel containing food is Rabbinically prohibited. It is permitted to request a non-Jew to milk an animal on the Sabbath.[4] A woman may not express milk from her breast into a vessel on the Sabbath.[5] It is, of course, permissible to breast feed and nurse an infant on the Sabbath.

---

3.   Removing Excess Water or Oil From Food   It is permitted to squeeze vegetables, meat and other foods to remove the water soaked up in cooking. Food that was fried in fat or oil may be squeezed to extract the excess fat or oil in order to make it more palatable.

4.   Milking on the Sabbath   Although telling a non-Jew to do a *melachah* on the Sabbath is ordinarily Rabbinically forbidden, it is permitted under the circumstances in order to relieve the animal from suffering (צַעַר בַּעֲלֵי חַיִּים). It is advisable that he milk into a vessel containing food. The milk, however, may not be used or handled until after the Sabbath. If a non-Jew is not available, the Jew may do the milking himself for the above-stated reason. In such a case he can milk to waste by letting the milk flow onto the ground, or by milking into a dirty pail or into a solution which will spoil the milk. The milk may not be used but must be discarded. Milking may also be done by means of a milking machine that operates automatically and is activated by a time clock which turns the machine on and off at pre-set times. The machine should be attached to the animal while it is not in operation. In this case the milk is permitted after the Sabbath.

5.   Expressing Milk From the Breast   A woman may express milk from her breast into a vessel on the Sabbath if the baby must be fed only the mother's milk and cannot or will not nurse at the mother's breast. If the baby is in the

5.   It is forbidden to wring out a cloth which has absorbed wine or some other liquid.[6] It is not permitted to crush[7] snow[8] or ice in order to make use of the water thus extracted. However, it is permitted to put pieces[9] or cubes of ice[10] into water or in a beverage to cool it.[11]

---

hospital and must have mother's milk fresh daily, she is likewise permitted to express the milk into a vessel. A woman who is nursing may express some milk into the baby's mouth while breast feeding in order to induce the baby to begin nursing. If the woman is in pain because of excess milk in her breasts, she may express some of the milk manually or if necessary with a hand pump, and let it flow out on the ground, into the sink, or into a disposable diaper where it will go to waste. Some suggest expressing the milk directly from the breast into a vessel containing a solution of soap and water. If the woman is in the hospital and the only means of expressing the milk is with an electrically operated pump, she should have it done by the non-Jewish nurse. See Part V, Chapter 9, note 10.

6.   Squeezing Out a Wet Cloth   The prohibition of סְחִיטָה is a *Toladah* of דִּישָׁה when it is done for the sake of the liquid. Wringing water from a wet cloth or garment is a violation of the *melachah* of לִיבּוּן, since the intention is to clean the cloth or garment by removing the water it soaked up.

7.   Making Snowballs or a Snowman   Although snow that falls on the Sabbath is not *muktzeh,* it is nevertheless not permitted to make snowballs or a snowman, as this involves squeezing and crushing the snow. Children who are of age, and even those over nine years old, should not be allowed to make and throw snowballs on the Sabbath. Even younger children should not be permitted to make a snowman on the Sabbath.

8.   Washing One's Hands in Snow   One should not wash or clean his hands by rubbing them with snow. If one must wash his hands in water containing snow or ice he should take care not to squeeze and crush the snow or ice between his hands.

9.   Melting Sugar or Butter   It is permitted to put a lump of sugar into a liquid or to pour hot water over it to dissolve it. It is likewise permitted to put a pat of butter on hot food so that it will melt over it.

10.   Making Ice Cubes and Removing Them From the Tray   One may remove ice cubes from the ice tray taken from the freezer by breaking them

But it is not permitted to put ice into an empty vessel in order to drink the water when the ice melts. It is permitted to walk on snow, even though it will be crushed and will melt underfoot.

6. WINNOWING

זְרִיָּה

1.   The objective of this *Av Melachah* is to separate the grain from the chaff which remain mixed together after the threshing.

The forbidden primary activity of this *melachah* involves propelling the mixture of grain and chaff into a current of air by means of a winnowing fork, a shovel, or some other implement or machine used for winnowing, and thereby removing the chaff by scattering it to the wind.

2.   The *melachot* of Winnowing (זְרִיָּה), Selecting (בְּרֵירָה), and Sifting (הַרְקָדָה) are similar, in that they comprise activities intended to separate what is fit for food (אוֹכֶל) from its undesirable elements (פְּסוֹלֶת). They are, however, counted as individual *melachot*[1] because they were separate *melachot* performed for the Tabernacle.

---

out of the tray, or by pouring water on the cubes in the tray. One should refrain from making ice cubes on the Sabbath since opinions differ as to its permissibility. In case of necessity, however, as when needed in hot weather, or to reduce swelling or to lower temperature and the like, it is permissible to fill an ice tray with water and put it in the freezer on the Sabbath to make the ice cubes. See Melachah 38, note 22; Part V, Chapter 3, note 9.

11.   Cooling Beverages and Bottles With Ice   It is permitted to break off pieces of ice to put into a beverage, even though some water will flow. Ice may be placed on fruit and around bottles containing drinks to cool them. Ice may be placed in the sink and allowed to melt. See Melachah 38, note 20.

1.   Winnowing, Selecting, Sifting   While winnowing, selecting and sifting are similar in purpose, in that their common object is to separate fit food or desirable matter (אוֹכֶל) from unfit food or undesirable matter (פְּסוֹלֶת), they

3. The *melachah* includes as forbidden subsidiary activities (*Tolados*) taking a mixture of grain and chaff in hand and throwing it into the wind, thereby removing the chaff from the grain, or blowing the chaff away by mouth.

4. One is Rabbinically forbidden to remove the chaff from ears of grain, which were crushed before the Sabbath, by rubbing the ears with both hands. One is also forbidden to sift the grain by transferring it from one hand to another.

7. SELECTING

בְּרֵירָה

1. The objective of this *Av Melachah* is to separate what is fit or desirable (אוֹכֶל) from what is unfit or undesirable (פְּסוֹלֶת).

The following methods of selection render one liable for violation of the *melachah*.[1]

---

are actually separate *melachot* involving distinctly different activities. Winnowing (זְרִיָה) involves removing the chaff from the grain by means of the wind. Selecting (בְּרֵירָה) involves removing the remaining undesirable elements such as earth and stones by hand. Sifting (הַרְקָדָה) involves separating the fine bran flour from the coarse bran flour by means of a sieve.

1. Selecting Food and Articles for Use on the Sabbath The *melachah* of Selecting generally applies when it is done in a way that one usually selects or sorts out things on weekdays. It does not apply to choosing or selecting food and articles in the course of their normal use, if one meets the following conditions:

(1) One selects the food or the desired article from what is not desired.

(2) The selection is not done by means of an instrument or a utensil such as a sieve specially designed for that purpose.

(3) The food that is selected is intended for immediate consumption, that is for the meal at hand, and the article selected is intended for immediate use, and not for use at some time in the future.

(1) Selecting and separating[2] undesirable matter[3] from food[4] (פְּסוֹלֶת מִתּוֹךְ אוֹכֶל),[5] whether it is done with a utensil or by hand, and even for immediate consumption.

In view of the complex nature of the rules pertaining to this *melachah*, and in order to assure the restfulness of the Sabbath, it is advisable that such activities and preparations of this kind be done before the Sabbath.

2.   Removing Shells, Skins, Peels, and Casings From Food   It is permissible to remove inedible shells, peels and skins prior to the meal. Thus, for example, one may remove the shells from eggs and nuts, the peel of onions, potatoes, melons and bananas, and the casings from sausages and *kishke,* as this is the manner in which they are eaten. This may be done by hand or with a knife and similar utensils which are not instruments made specifically for that purpose. However, one may use a nutcracker, and even a hammer if necessary to crack nuts. One may remove a bakery label from a *ḥallah,* taking care not to tear the print on the label. One may remove the edible skin from chicken and fish, even for a later meal, as it is considered to be a part of the food itself. One may remove the paper or foil that is stuck to food.

3.   Removing Bones From Fish and Meat   The preferred method of removing chicken or meat bones and fishbones is to remove them from one's mouth after chewing off the meat or fish. If this is not practicable, one may remove the meat or fish from the bone while eating, and chewing and sucking the bones as well. Some permit removing the bones, especially small fish bones in the normal manner while eating, preferably along with some of the meat or fish on the bones. The custom of eating *gefilte* fish on *Shabbat,* the fish having already been deboned and prepared before the Sabbath, reflects the care with which Jewish families have sought to comply with the Sabbath laws in this instance.

4.   Removing Seeds From Melons and Other Fruits   When eating a watermelon or a grapefruit which contains seeds throughout the fruit, one should shake the loose seeds off and then he may remove the seeds that remain during the meal, as this is the normal way of eating it. Some, however, advise taking a piece of the melon into one's mouth and then removing the seeds. In the case of a melon which contains seeds in the center of the fruit, such as a cantaloupe or a honeydew, the seeds may be removed prior to the meal. Fruits such as dates, plums, peaches and apricots which

(2) Selecting and separating food[6] from undesirable matter (אוֹכֶל מִתּוֹךְ פְּסוֹלֶת) with an instrument or a utensil used specifically for that purpose, even for immediate consumption.

Hence, the selection and separation of food[7] from undesirable matter (אוֹכֶל מִתּוֹךְ פְּסוֹלֶת) is permissible only when in compliance with the following conditions: (a) the food (אוֹכֶל) is of greater quantity than the undesirable matter (פְּסוֹלֶת); (b) the food is separated from the undesirable matter, and not the reverse; (c) the separation is done by hand;[8] (d) it is for immediate consumption.[9]

---

contain a single pit may be opened and the pit discarded while eating or removed prior to the meal, as this is the way these fruits are normally eaten. Grapes and similar fruits which contain several pits should be taken in the mouth and the pits discarded while eating, as this is the usual manner of eating such fruit.

5. Removing an Insect and Undesirable Matter From Food or Drink If an insect or some other undesirable matter fell into one's food or drink he may remove it with his hands or with a spoon. However, he should take out some of the food or drink along with it. Some permit removing it only by pouring off some of the food or drink. One should remove an insect from a lettuce leaf together with part of the leaf.

6. Selecting Food to Be Served at a Meal One is permitted to select the food for the meal at hand for himself and for others who will partake of it. This includes all the food that one intends to serve, regardless of the duration of the meal, even if it extends for several hours. It does not matter if some of the food remains after the meal. However, he may not deliberately select more than needed with this in mind.

7. Preparation of Food for Animals Preparation of food, including selecting the food and cutting it up into edible pieces may be done not only for humans but also to feed one's fowl and cattle, and other animals.

8. Use of an Ordinary Utensil Use of an ordinary utensil such as a knife, spoon or fork is the same as the hand. If the selection can just as well be accomplished by hand and one uses a knife, spoon or fork so as not to soil his hands, or to grasp more easily, the utensil is like his hand and he may use it to remove food for immediate consumption.

(3) Selecting and separating one food from another, if they are of different kinds, such as two or more kinds of fish cooked together.[10] In such a case the ones he wishes to eat immediately are considered as the food (אוֹכֶל) and the others as undesirable (פְּסוֹלֶת). Hence, if he selects the ones he wishes to eat immediately, the law of אוֹכֶל מִתּוֹךְ פְּסוֹלֶת applies as in (2) above, and if he selects the others, the law of פְּסוֹלֶת מִתּוֹךְ אוֹכֶל applies as in (1) above.

The prohibition of selecting and separating one food from another applies when the different kinds are mixed together, but not when they are distinctly separate and readily distinguishable.[11] It also does not apply when there are so few as not to constitute a mixture.

One is permitted to select and separate the larger pieces of food from the smaller pieces, and vice versa, whether they are of the same kind or of two different kinds provided he selects in the latter instance from both kinds.

Removal of the inedible parts of a food from that which is edible

---

9. Selecting for Immediate Consumption Selecting is generally done in order to store the food for later use. When one intends to eat it immediately, the usual procedure is to select the portion of food that he desires to eat. Selecting the food to be eaten is then part of the normal process of eating (דֶּרֶךְ אֲכִילָה), hence it is permissible. The selection must be done prior to the meal, or within the time it normally takes to prepare the forthcoming meal, depending on the number of people and the courses to be served.

10. Selecting From Food Prepared Differently The prohibition of selecting applies as well to food of the same kind if prepared in a different manner; for example, fish cooked plain and stuffed (*gefilte* fish), meat or chicken cooked and roasted, white and black bread, food that is fresh and of good quality and food that is spoiled or burnt. In the above instances one should select those he intends to eat immediately.

11. Selecting From a Platter of Different Foods If there are different kinds of food on a platter, one is permitted to remove the pieces on top in order to reach the ones on the bottom that he wishes to eat.

is permissible, as this is not considered selection but the normal way of preparing food before it is eaten.[12]

(4) The *melachah* of Selecting and the laws pertaining to it apply also to non-edible items, such as utensils,[13] garments,[14] and the like.[15] In such cases the articles that he does not wish to use are regarded as undesirable matter (פְּסוֹלֶת).

2. The *melachah* includes such forbidden subsidiary activities (*Toladot*) as filtering or straining liquids[16] through a filter or strainer[17]

---

12.   Removal of Inedible Parts of Food   It is permitted to remove the outer leaves from a head of lettuce and similar leafy vegetables when the leaves are wormy, moldy, rotted or soiled. In this case it is considered as though one were removing the outer peeling in order to eat the edible part. It is, likewise, permissible to cut away the stem and rotted part of fruit, the burnt part of bread, the fatty part of meat, and the like.

13.   Selecting Dishes and Silverware for the Meal   It is permitted to select the utensils, such as dishes, pots, silverware and the like, that one intends to use for the forthcoming meal. After washing and drying, the utensil may be put in its allotted place.

14.   Selecting Clothes to Wear   In dressing on the Sabbath one should select the clothes that he intends to wear presently. In making the selection one is permitted to choose from a pile of clothes or articles of clothing in a drawer or among garments hanging in the closet, even if it is necessary to remove the clothing or the garments that he does not intend to wear in order to reach the ones that he wants to wear. However, one may not sort clothing or select garments for storage.

15.   Selecting Books to Read   One may select *sefarim* or books that he wishes to read. If he intends to read one later, but finds it convenient to remove it from the bookcase before then, he should peruse it briefly before setting it down. One may not sort books in order to stock them on the shelf or in the bookcase.

16.   Pouring Coffee, Tea and Other Drinks   Care should be taken in pouring coffee and tea so that the coffee grounds and tea leaves remain at the bottom. One should not drain out the residual drops, as this would involve their separation from sediment, and would be prohibited unless the coffee or

used principally for that purpose, churning milk or cream to make butter, and causing milk to curd, whereby the curd is separated from the whey in the process of making cheese.

3.   Rabbinical prohibitions include removing the cream from milk[18] unless it is for immediate consumption, putting food into water to remove impurities,[19] and peeling fruits and vegetables to be eaten later in the day.[20].

---

tea is for drinking immediately. The same procedure should be followed in pouring other drinks, such as wine, that contain sediments.

17.   Pouring From a Coffee or Tea Pot Through a Strainer   One is permitted to pour coffee and tea or tea essence from a coffee pot or a tea kettle that has a strainer in its spout to keep the tea leaves and the coffee grounds from falling into the cup, as he is only pouring out the liquid and not straining it. He may pour as long as the liquid flows freely. But he should not empty out the last drops that remain with the sediment.

18.   Skimming Cream and Fat   When skimming the cream from milk the following procedure is permissible. One should either leave some cream in the milk or take some milk with the cream. Likewise, in skimming the fat from soup, one should remove some soup as well.

19.   Washing Fruits and Vegetables   It is not permitted to soak potatoes and other such vegetables in water to remove the dust and earth from them. Fruits and vegetables may be washed for sanitary reasons. It is accepted practice to wash such fruits as apples, pears, peaches and grapes before eating. Some authorities draw a distinction, even with regard to vegetables, between soaking them in a vessel, and washing them with water which they permit.

20.   Peeling Fruits and Vegetables   The peel, skin or shell of fruits and vegetables may be removed prior to the meal. The prohibition of peeling for later consumption applies to fruit such as oranges and bananas, to nuts, and to vegetables such as garlic and onions, whose peel, or skin or shell is not eaten. Some maintain that it applies as well even to fruit such as apples, whose peel is edible. Other authorities, however, permit peeling apples, pears, peaches and similar fruit, whose peel is eaten by most people, even when one intends eating the fruit later on during the Sabbath.

8. SIFTING

הַרְקָדָה

1.   The objective of this *Av Melachah* is to sift flour by passing it through a sieve, and separating and removing its impurities and other worthless matter.

The *melachah* includes sifting ordinary flour from bran flour, and sifting oats in a sieve to remove the chaff and to cleanse it of undesirable matter.

2.   Forbidden subsidiary activities (*Toladot*) include sifting fine flour from ordinary flour, and placing wine lees into a strainer[1] in order to filter[2] the wine.[3]

---

1.   Use of a Water Faucet With a Strainer   Water that is fit for most people to drink may be filtered to strain out some sediment that it may contain. Hence, it is permissible to use a water faucet equipped with a strainer designed to keep out sediment and impurities when the water is drawn from the faucet.

2.   Drinking Through a Filter   The prohibitions of Selecting (בְּרִירָה) and filtering or Sifting (הַרְקָדָה) apply only in the preparation of the drink or food beforehand, but not if one filters the liquid as he is drinking it.

3.   Straining and Filtering Beverages and Fruit Juices   Turbid liquids, such as wine roiled with sediment and impurities, which are not fit to drink at all, or which one is particular not to drink unfiltered, may not be filtered, neither with a cloth nor a strainer or filter. Where the beverage is drinkable (or the food is edible) for most people with the impurity present, and he is not particular about it as well, filtering (or sifting) is permissible. Thus it is permitted to filter wine that has some sediment or mold in it, and water that contains some sediment, since it is fit to drink for most people without being filtered. Some permit straining fruit juice, such as orange juice in order to filter out small particles of the orange, especially for infants to prevent the particles from clogging the nipple in the baby bottle, since most people are able to drink it without straining.

3.   The Rabbis prohibited sifting food from food [4] where there is no undesirable matter, as when ground *matzah* meal is sifted in order to separate the fine particles from clods that are lumped together.[5]

9. GRINDING

טְחִינָה

1.   The objective of this *Av Melachah* is to grind a substance into small, fine particles by means of a utensil or instrument used for the purpose, such as a hand mill, a mortar, a grater, a blender, and the like.

The *melachah* comprises such forbidden primary activities as milling grain to produce flour, grinding coffee in a mill, and pounding or crushing spices,[1] drugs, or other substances in a mortar.

---

4.   Use of a Perforated Utensil to Strain Food   A colander, a straining spoon or ladle, or a similar utensil that is perforated and used for draining food is considered like a strainer. It may be used only to strain foods and liquids that are of one kind. Hence, one may use a salad spoon to serve coleslaw, since he desires the liquid dressing as well. While some take a stringent view, other authorities permit straining the liquid from vegetables as well.

5.   Pouring Food Waste Down a Sink Drain   It is permitted to pour food and liquid waste down a sink drain that is fitted with a receptacle and a perforated cover to strain out the thick pieces of refuse and prevent the pipe from becoming blocked. The waste matter that has accumulated in the receptacle may be emptied into the garbage can. Since one does not intend to separate the food in order to retain it, but rather to discard all of it as waste, there is no prohibition of straining or selecting involved.

1.   Crushing Spices   It is permissible to crush pepper, garlic, salt and other spices, as needed for the Sabbath meal. However, it is not permitted to do it in the usual manner in a utensil designed for the purpose. It should be done in some other way, such as placing the spices in a plate or on the table, and crushing them with a knife, rather than in a mill or with mortar and pestle.

2. The *melachah* includes other forbidden subsidiary activities (*Toladot*), such as cutting up[2] radishes, onions and other vegetables[3] into fine pieces for later use, filing metal for use of the metal chips, sawing wood for use of the sawdust, chopping wood into small pieces for firewood and crushing a clod of earth for some use of the earth.

3. It is Rabbinically prohibited to grate *matzah* or cheese on a grater, as this is a weekday activity. It is permitted, however, to crumble bread by hand, as the prohibition of grinding does not apply to something that was already ground (אֵין טוֹחֵן אַחַר טוֹחֵן).[4] One may also

---

2. Cutting Up Fruits and Vegetables The *melachah* is not relevant unless one cuts the food into small pieces with the intention of setting it aside for later, but not if he intends to eat it immediately. Hence, one is permitted to cut up fruits and vegetables into small pieces to be eaten immediately. He may do it for himself, his family and guests, and to feed his animals. Some recommend stringency and advise cutting them into somewhat larger pieces, but nevertheless also advise a tolerant view of those who are more lenient and cut up vegetables such as onions and radishes into small pieces. In any event, this should be done only before the forthcoming meal. One should not cut up the vegetables with a utensil used principally for that purpose, but rather with a knife. Some permit use of a chopping knife as well.

3. Mashing Fruit and Vegetables Some permit squashing and mashing fruits and cooked vegetables to be eaten immediately, if done in a manner different from the usual. Thus one may squash a banana with a spoon for a young child. Cooked vegetables, such as cooked potatoes, may not be mashed with a strainer or a potato masher, but only with a spoon or fork, and the like. Some only permit one to complete mashing cooked potatoes if they were partly crushed before or during cooking.

4. Crumbling Bread The prohibition of grinding does not apply to bread, which already underwent a process of grinding when the grain was ground into flour. Hence, it is permitted to crumble bread, even to feed it later to one's chickens. One may likewise crumble other bakery products, such as *matzah,* to be eaten later. However, one should not use a grater or grinder, or a similar utensil for grinding, as it would be a weekday activity.

cut thin slices of cheese or meat with a knife.[5] It is not permitted to rub off dried mud from one's clothing, or to scrape it off with one's fingernail, as it is similar to grinding.[6] One is not permitted medication for the relief of a slight ailment, because of the prohibition of compounding medicines on the Sabbath.[7] One may not feed one's animals on the Sabbath in the same manner that he feeds them on a weekday, lest he crush legumes in order to feed them.[8] Therefore one

---

5. Cutting Up Meat, Fish, Eggs and Cheese   Food which is not grown in the earth and is generally edible without being ground, such as cooked and roasted meat, fish, eggs, and cheese, may be ground or cut up into small pieces, even for later use, provided it is not done with an instrument used for the purpose, such as a grater or a grinder. One may use a knife, and even a manually operated slicer for meat, cheese and eggs. Boiled eggs, cooked meat and fish may be mashed with a fork.

6. Removing a Mud Stain From Clothing   If there is only a mud stain, but no actual mud on the garment for any particles to fall off when scraped, so that it does not resemble the *melachah* of Grinding, some permit scraping the garment to remove the stain. Other authorities, however, indicate that while grinding is not involved, it may involve the *melachah* of Cleaning (לִיבּוּן).

7. Use of Medicines and Medical Treatment   The use of medicines in the treatment of a minor ailment is not permitted one who is in general good health, and is only mildly indisposed or experiences slight pain. The prohibition does not apply to one who is ill. Treatments which do not involve the use of drugs or medicines do not come under the restriction, provided they are not otherwise prohibited on the Sabbath. For a detailed discussion of the laws pertaining to the use of medicines and medical treatment on the Sabbath, see Part V, Chapters 7,8.

8. Cutting Up Vegetables and Meat for One's Animals   One is obligated to provide food for his animals. It is therefore permissible to make the food edible on the Sabbath, if it is otherwise inedible, in order to prevent the animal from suffering. However, if the food is already edible and fit to be eaten, one may not exert himself on the Sabbath to make it more appropriate and suitable, even for immediate consumption. Hence, one is permit-

may not stuff or force feed one's cattle, animals, or fowl on the Sabbath.[9]

10. KNEADING

לִישָׁה

1. The objective of this *Av Melachah* is to combine separate particles of a substance by means of a liquid to form a mass wherein the particules fuse into one mixture.[1]

Combining flour with water, or some other liquid such as honey or fat, to form a dough-like mixture constitutes a primary activity of the *melachah* of Kneading.

The prohibition applies even if the kneading is done immediately prior to the meal at which the food that is being prepared is to be eaten.

---

ted to cut up vegetables or meat in order to render them edible as feed for his fowl, his dogs and his animals for immediate consumption. However, if the vegetables and the meat are edible in their present state, one may not exert himself to cut them up, even for immediate consumption, because it resembles grinding.

9. Feeding One's Animals   One may feed one's animals, cattle and fowl on the Sabbath, as it is his obligation to see to it that they do not suffer from hunger. While force feeding is prohibited, it is permitted to put food into their mouths. In the case of geese who are accustomed to being force fed, and they cannot eat in any other way, it is permissible to instruct a non-Jew to stuff them. If a non-Jew is not available, the Jew is permitted to stuff them so that they should not suffer. For a full discussion of the laws pertaining to the care and feeding of animals on the Sabbath, see Part V, Chapter 2, especially paragraphs 8, 10–16 and notes.

1. Preparing a Vegetable or Fruit Salad   One may prepare a vegetable salad on the Sabbath, and pour oil, vinegar, or mayonnaise on the vegetables, and add salt and seasoning as usual. One may, similarly, make a fruit

2.   The *melachah* includes as forbidden subsidiary activities (*Tola-dot*) mixing earth,[2] or clay,[3] plastic, and the like with water.[4]

3.   The *melachah* of Kneading applies only when it results in a thick mass, such as bread dough or cake dough. Kneading that results in a soft, thin mixture, which can be poured but is still not a liquid, does not violate the Biblical prohibition but is nevertheless Rabbinically prohibited.

It is consequently permissible to prepare a soft, thin mixture on the Sabbath if it is done in a manner different from the usual (עַל יְדֵי שִׁינוּי), (a) by reversing the order in which the ingredients are mixed, and (b) by mixing the ingredients in a different way.

Thus, in mixing a relish, such as mustard or horseradish with

---

salad with condiments added. In the above instances the ingredients do not fuse into one mixture, and it does not involve the *melachah* of Kneading.

2.   Substances Not Subject to Kneading   Opinions differ as to whether the *melachah* applies to substances, such as ash and coarse sand, which cannot be kneaded into a dough-like mixture. Some maintain that in such cases the *melachah* does not apply, and it is only Rabbinically prohibited. Many *Rishonim,* however, are of the opinion that the *melachah* applies and the addition of water to the substance is a transgression of the *melachah.*

3.   Children Playing With Sand and Clay   Children are permitted to play in a sandbox with sand that has been prepared for this purpose before the Sabbath, provided it is dry, loose sand so that it will collapse and refill the hole when the sand is removed. It is not permitted to mix the sand with water or to pour water over it. Children should not play with clay, plastic, wax and similar substances that can be molded.

4.   Use of Adhesive Powder and Paste for Dentures   One may use a denture adhesive paste. Some authorities also permit the use of adhesive powder on dentures which, when it dissolves in the mouth, forms a thin paste, allowing the false teeth to adhere to the gums. Others, however, do not permit the use of adhesive powder, as it involves kneading.

vinegar, and the like, to be used as a condiment,[5] one should make a thin mixture by pouring a sufficient amount of the liquid at the outset. He should prepare the mixture in a manner different from the usual way by reversing the order, that is, by pouring the liquid first. He should then mix the ingredients in a different manner, that is, with the handle of the spoon, or by shaking the vessel, by stirring with an altered motion, and the like. It is, likewise, permitted to mix *matzah* meal with wine or honey, or some other liquid by doing it in a different way than the usual. When Pesach occurs on the Sabbath and one forgot to prepare the *haroset* before *Shabbat,* he should also do it in a manner different from the usual, by pouring the wine first and then adding the apples, nuts, and other ingredients.

4.   If, due to the amount of liquid in the mixture, it results in a thick, turbid liquid it is permissible to prepare the mixture, even if it is not done in a manner different from the usual. Where the mixture involves dissolving a soluble powder which yields a liquid solution, the prohibition does not apply.[6]

5.   Instant, pre-cooked and ready-to-eat, solid foods, such as rice pudding and mashed potatoes, which are made by mixing the powder

---

5.   Preparing a Salad of Fish, Eggs, Chopped Liver   One may prepare a salad of fish, such as tuna or herring, eggs, and chopped liver, with onions or other vegetables, and add oil, mayonnaise or fat, provided it is prepared immediately before the meal. The tuna and eggs should be mashed with a fork, and the vegetables cut into somewhat larger pieces. Some permit cutting the vegetables into smaller pieces immediately before the meal. See Melachah 9, note 2.

6.   Dissolving Soluble Powders and Other Substances   One may dissolve soluble powders in water, sugar in tea or coffee, instant coffee or tea in water, milk powder in water, cocoa in water or milk, beverage mixes in water, and the like. Some require a variation in the way of preparing the mixture in liquid mixtures made with cocoa and milk powder and the like, where some of the substance forms into lumps as it settles at the bottom.

with water, or some other liquid may not be prepared on the Sabbath.[7]

11. BAKING AND COOKING

אֲפִיָּה וּבִישׁוּל

1.   The objective of this *Av Melachah* is to change the material state of a substance by means of heat in order to make it edible or fit for some use. This may be effected directly through fire, or through heat derived from fire[1] and other sources[2] such as gas or electricity.

---

7.   Preparing Cereal and Pudding for a Baby   One may prepare baby cereal, which requires that the cereal be mixed with water or milk, but it should be done by reversing the usual order, and mixing moderately in an altered manner. A sufficient amount of the liquid should be poured at the outset to make a thin mixture. Rabbi Moshe Feinstein ז"ל permits making pudding if it is needed for a baby. It may be prepared from instant pudding powder in a thin mixture by employing a variation from the usual method of preparation, as indicated. It is permitted to beat an egg to put it into a cereal or porridge for an infant, or into a cup of coffee. See Melachah 11, paragraph 3.

1.   Cooking With Steam Heat   Cooking food by means of steam heat is a violation of the prohibition of cooking on the Sabbath, although a steam heating system involves fewer problems of a halachic nature with regard to leaving and replacing food to be heated on *Shabbat*. Its use on the Sabbath, generally in institutions and larger establishments, is preferable to other modern heating devices, provided the requisite halachic regulations are complied with in consultation with Rabbinical authority.

2.   Cooking in a Microwave Oven   Heating in a microwave oven is effected by electromagnetic waves which penetrate and heat the food without heating up the surrounding area, thereby greatly reducing cooking time as compared with the time required by a conventional oven. The heat generated in a microwave oven has the same status as heat generated by fire with regard to the prohibition of cooking on the Sabbath.

The *melachah* includes baking, cooking,[3] boiling, frying or roasting, and comprises such forbidden primary activities as baking bread; cooking food; heating water[4] or other liquids,[5] boiling ingredients

---

3. Stages of Cooking and Baking A liquid, or food containing a liquid, is considered to be cooking when it is heated to the degree of *yad soledet bo* (literally, when "the hand recoils from it"), the minimum temperature of which is taken to be between 110⁰ and 120⁰ Fahrenheit. Some estimate it at 113⁰F (45⁰C). The degree of heat of *yad soledet bo* can be assumed when it is too hot to touch, or it is so hot that one would refrain from eating or drinking it. Dry, solid food is considered cooked when cooked כְּמַאֲכַל בֶּן דְּרוֹסָאִי (literally, "the food of Ben Derusai," a notorious robber, who ate food when only partially cooked). Some estimate it to be one third cooked, others one half cooked, with the time varying according to how long it takes to cook the particular food to completion. Bread is considered baked when it has formed a crust on the bottom and top of the bread. One is liable for transgressing the Biblical prohibition of the *melachah* when cooking and baking to these stages.

4. Drawing Hot Water From the Faucet Hot water systems generally operate on the principle that water stored in a boiler is heated by gas, oil or electricity to a given temperature as the heating unit is activated by means of a thermostat. When the hot water is drawn from the boiler, it is automatically replaced by an inflow of cold water, which is then heated by the hot water in the boiler, or by the heating element. In drawing hot water from the faucet one is thereby causing the cold water to enter the boiler and to be heated.

Some authorities permit the use of hot water from the faucet, especially in case of necessity, if one of the following steps is taken before the Sabbath.

(1) The water valve is shut off so that no cold water flows into the boiler. One should take care that the procedure is safe and will not damage the boiler.

(2) The thermostat is adjusted so that the water temperature is always below the degree of *yad soledet bo*.

(3) The heating apparatus is turned off several hours before the Sabbath, allowing the water in the boiler to cool sufficiently so that the cold water flowing into the boiler will not be heated to the degree of *yad soledet bo*.

(4) The hot water faucet is opened before the Sabbath and the hot water is left running on the Sabbath. The flow of hot water may not be increased, nor should one draw hot water from another faucet. If cold water is drawn

used to make dyes; adding spices or other ingredients that cook readily in a boiling pot; and pouring hot water onto a solid, such as a piece of meat, causing the surface to be cooked.

2.   The *melachah* includes such forbidden subsidiary activities (*Toladot*) as stirring food that is not fully cooked in a boiling pot on the fire to hasten the cooking; melting or heating metal until it glows in order to soften it; heating and melting wax, butter, animal fat, pitch, or any other substance that is naturally congealed; baking a clay vessel in a furnace; drying damp wood in a hot oven; and hardening a naturally soft substance, or softening a naturally hard substance by means of fire.

3.   In order to prevent one from transgressing the *melachah* of Cooking the Rabbis extended the prohibition to include leaving food over the fire on *Shabbat* (*shehiyah*), returning a pot of cooked food to the stove over the fire (*ḥazarah*), and retaining the heat of food by covering it (*hatmanah*). These are Rabbinically prohibited unless certain conditions are complied with (see paragraphs 12–15).

In addition, the Rabbis also prohibited, as a further precaution, what appears as cooking (נִרְאָה כִּמְבַשֵׁל).[6] Thus, while solid food that is

---

from a faucet that connects to the same outlet as the hot water, it should be turned on in a way that the cold water will flow at once in such a quantity that the mixture will not be of the degree of *yad soledet bo*.

5.   Opening and Closing a Radiator   It is not permitted to open the valve of a radiator on the Sabbath to allow the steam from the furnace to come up, because it will heat the water or residual moisture in the radiator. Some permit closing the radiator valve, but others forbid it. In case of hardship, as when there is a sudden, severe cold spell, and there are young children or old and sick people in the house, and a non-Jew is not available, one may open and close the radiator valve, but he should do it in an indirect, irregular manner (כִּלְאַחַר יַד).

6.   Activities That Appear as Cooking   In the opinion of Rambam and the *Shulḥan Aruch,* pickling preserves resembles cooking and is therefore Rabbinically prohibited. Hence, it is not permissible to salt a large quantity of radishes, cucumbers, or other vegetables that are salted and pickled. It is

fully cooked is not subject to cooking again, and therefore would not involve a transgression of the Torah prohibition, it is nevertheless Rabbinically prohibited to place the food in a heated oven because of the appearance of cooking (see paragraph 14).

Since the *melachah* fobids cooking by means of heat derived from fire and from a fire-heated object, the Rabbis also prohibited cooking by means of an object that was heated by the sun. It is therefore not permitted to roast or cook an egg on a pan, on a cloth, in sand, earth, or water that was heated by the sun. However, it is permitted to cook by the heat of the sun itself.[7] Hence, one may place an egg or water in the sun[8] in order to warm it. It is not permitted to cook in natural hot spring water, such as the hot springs of Tiberias.

It is not permitted to wash one's entire body or the greater part of

---

also not permitted to beat several eggs in a bowl because it appears as though one is preparing them for cooking. However, one may mix a raw egg with some water and put it into a cup of coffee instead of milk, provided the water and coffee are not so intensely hot as to cook the egg.

7. Cooking With Heat From the Sun   The decree enacted by the Sages that prohibits cooking with a sun-heated object was intended to prevent one from cooking with objects heated by fire, since it might mistakenly be assumed that the object was heated by fire and not by the sun. The Sages did not prohibit cooking by the heat of the sun itself, because it is not customary to cook in this fashion and people will not confuse the sun with fire. Some authorities, however, question the permissibility of cooking by the heat of the sun, in view of the fact that solar energy is being utilized increasingly and is becoming a customary way of heating.

8. A Water Heater Operated by Solar Energy   It is advisable to refrain from using hot water from a heater operated by solar energy, when it is automatically replaced by a flow of cold water, which in turn will be heated by the hot water remaining in the tank. It is permissible if the flow of cold water is shut off. The hot water from a solar heater is to be considered as coming from a *keli rishon* (see paragraph 4), with its attendant restrictions, but it should, nevertheless, not be poured into a *keli rishon,* since it was not heated by fire in the usual way.

the body with hot water, even if the water was heated before the Sabbath, lest he come to heat it on the Sabbath. It is forbidden even if one does not wash his body all at once, but only a part of the body at a time.[9]

4.   A vessel which is on the fire is called *keli rishon* (כְּלִי רִאשׁוֹן), the "first vessel." The vessel is considered a *keli rishon* and capable of cooking, even after it is removed from the fire, as long as it retains sufficient heat to be *yad soledet bo* (יָד סוֹלֶדֶת בּוֹ), that is, the heat of the vessel would cause the hand to recoil from it. It is, therefore, forbidden to put anything that is subject to cooking into a *keli rishon*.[10] It is

---

9.   Washing, Showering, and Bathing   One may not wash his entire body or the greater part of his body with hot water, irrespective of whether he bathes, showers or washes a part of his body at a time. The degree of heat in this instance is not *yad soledet bo,* as people do not wash themselves with scalding water, but what is generally considered to be hot water. One may wash his hands, face, or other individual parts of the body, even with hot water if it was heated in a permissible manner or before the Sabbath. In washing one's head or beard care should be taken not to squeeze the water out of his hair. While it is not prohibited, one should refrain from showering or bathing in cold or lukewarm water as well, unless he experiences great discomfort, as on a very hot day. In view of certain complications and prohibitions involved, the prevailing custom is not to bathe in a pool, or in a body of water such as a lake, a river, or in the ocean. Swimming, whether in a pool or in a body of water, is not permitted. However, a woman may immerse herself in a *mikveh* at the prescribed time following her menstrual period. A man who wishes to cleanse himself after a nocturnal, seminal emission, and according to some authorities for purposes of additional sanctification, may likewise immerse himself in a *mikveh* on a Sabbath morning. The water in the *mikveh* should be lukewarm, and one should be careful to avoid squeezing water out of one's hair. When bathing or showering is permissible, as in the instances cited above, it is advisable to wear a nylon or rubber shower cap. See Part V, Chapter 1.

10.   Putting Salt and Sugar into a Pot on the Fire   Salt and sugar, although already boiled in the refining process, should not be put into a pot of soup or broth that is on the fire, or even when the pot is removed from the fire, if it is

also forbidden to pour from a *keli rishon*[11] onto something[12] that is subject to cooking,[13] because pouring from a *keli rishon* (עִירוּי מִכְּלִי רִאשׁוֹן)[14] has the effect of cooking[15] its surface or outer layer (מְבַשֵּׁל כְּדֵי קְלִיפָּה).

---

yad soledet bo. The soup or broth should first be poured into a *keli sheini* (see paragraph 5) and the salt and sugar then added. If one should put the salt and sugar into a pot that is on the fire the food may still be eaten.

11. Warming a Baby Bottle in Hot Water One may pour hot water, even from a *keli rishon,* onto a baby bottle containing milk, or on a container of soup or baby food, in order to warm it. However, one may not warm a baby bottle or some other container by placing it in hot water in a *keli rishon* if the contents will be heated to the degree of *yad soledet bo.* One may warm it by placing it in a *keli sheini* containing hot water, even if it is *yad soledet bo.*

12. Pouring Hot Soup onto Bread Hot soup should not be poured directly from the pot in which it was cooked onto pieces of bread or *matzah.* The soup should first be poured into the plate, and after it has cooled somewhat the bread or *matzah* may be added. One can also remove the soup from the pot with a spoon or ladle, and add the bread or *matzah* immediately, since the plate will have the ruling of a *keli shlishi* (see paragraph 6).

13. Pouring Hot Water onto Instant Coffee and Tea One should not pour boiling hot water from a *keli rishon* onto instant coffee or instant tea, although they have been pre-cooked and dried in the process of production. They should be added after the water is first poured into a cup. Some advise the use of a *keli shlishi* (see paragraph 6), that is, pouring the hot water from the kettle into a second vessel and then into a third vessel. The above ruling applies as well to other similar products, such as milk powder, soup powder, and instant cocoa.

14. Preparing Tea for the Sabbath In preparing tea on the Sabbath it is not permitted to pour hot water from the kettle that was on the fire onto tea leaves, or to place a tea bag into hot water either in a *keli rishon* or in a *keli sheini* (see paragraph 5). The proper method is to cook the tea leaves or pour hot water over them before the Sabbath. On the Sabbath the liquid tea

5.   A vessel that is not on the fire into which food or liquid is transferred from a "first vessel" in which it was cooked, is called *keli sheini*
(כְּלִי שֵׁנִי), the "second vessel." While a *keli sheini* is generally not capable of cooking, even when it retains sufficient heat to be *yad soledet
bo,* there are some foods that will cook in it. As we are not certain
which foods are of this nature, one should not put any food which is
not cooked into a *keli sheini* when it is sufficiently hot to be *yad
soledet bo.*[16] While it is generally assumed that pouring from a *keli
sheini* does not effect cooking and is therefore permissible, it is
advisable to follow the stricter view and to refrain from pouring from
a *keli sheini* that is still sufficiently hot to be *yad soledet bo* onto

---

essence may be put into hot water that was poured from the kettle into a *keli
sheini* (or a *keli shlishi* as previously noted). If the tea essence is kept warm
on the *blech* (see paragraph 12) one may put it into a cup and pour hot water
on it from the kettle. If one did not prepare tea essence before the Sabbath
some permit doing it on the Sabbath by putting a tea bag into cold or lukewarm water.

15.   Washing Dishes With Hot Water   When washing soiled and greasy
dishes for further use on the Sabbath one should not pour hot water from a
keli rishon directly over the dishes. One should first pour the hot water into
another vessel and then put the dishes into it. Hot water from a boiler drawn
from the faucet, and from a heater or urn is considered as from a *keli rishon,*
if it is of the degree of *yad soledet bo.* See also Melachah 13, note 1.

16.   Putting Food or Liquid into a Keli Sheini   One should not put a slice of
lemon into a hot cup of water or tea which is a *keli sheini* that is *yad soledet
bo.* But one may put into a *keli sheini* boiled or pasteurized milk, tea essence
that was boiled before the Sabbath, processed lemon juice and soup essence
which were cooked when produced, and other products that were similarly
pre-boiled or pre-cooked in the process of production, such as salt, sugar,
saccharin, soup powder, soup cubes, milk powder, instant powdered cocoa,
instant coffee, and instant tea. One should not pour from a *keli rishon* into a
keli sheini containing the above substances. See note 13 on the preferred use
of a *keli shlishi* for instant coffee or tea.

uncooked food such as a raw egg[17] which is more readily subject to cooking.[18]

6.   A vessel that is not on the fire into which food or liquid is transferred from a "second vessel" is called *keli shlishi* (כְּלִי שְׁלִישִׁי), the "third vessel." While the prohibition of cooking is generally considered as not applying to a *keli shlishi,* some do not differentiate between a *keli sheini* and a *keli shlishi,* and advise not to put uncooked food that is easily cooked even into a *keli shlishi,* when it is sufficiently hot to be *yad soledet bo.*[19]

7.   Any solid food that is hot to the degree of *yad soledet bo* is capable of cooking irrespective of the vessel from which it was transferred, because it stores the heat and the walls of the vessel that it is in, even a

---

17.   Adding Eggs to a Hot Plate of Borscht   It is permitted to add eggs to borscht in a *keli sheini* provided the eggs were beaten before the Sabbath. However, if the borscht is very sour it is advisable not to do it, as the eggs may be cooked even in a *keli sheini.* One should not pour hot water on an egg yolk, even from a *keli sheini,* as eggs are subject to cooking with moderate heat.

18.   Rinsing Herring to Remove the Salt   Some salty food is not edible unless it is first rinsed in hot water. Consequently, rinsing is the final stage in its preparation and is forbidden because it is considered as cooking, since it makes the food fit for eating. Herring, however, although it is salty, is nevertheless edible when rinsed in cold water, or even if it is not rinsed at all. Hence it would be permitted to rinse the herring with hot water poured from a *keli sheini.* However, it is advisable to be more stringent and rinse it with cold water.

19.   Status of a Keli Shlishi   Opinions differ regarding the status of a *keli shlishi.* Many authorities do not differentiate between a *keli sheini* and a *keli shlishi,* maintaining that the only valid considerations are whether the vessel is *yad soledet bo,* and the nature of the food and how readily it is cooked. However, some authorities, such as Rabbi Moshe Feinstein, are of the opinion that cooking does not take place in a *keli shlishi.* Where additional factors can be taken into account one may follow the lenient view.

keli shlishi, do not cool it. It is, therefore, forbidden to put seasoning onto meat, or to put a piece of meat into cold soup, if the meat is hot to the degree of *yad soledet bo.*[20]

8.   A dish of food containing soup that was cooked before the Sabbath is subject to cooking again once it has cooled off, because a liquid is subject to repeated cooking (יֵשׁ בִּישׁוּל אַחַר בִּישׁוּל בְּדָבָר לַח).[21] Solid, dry food that was fully cooked before the Sabbath is not subject to cooking again (אֵין בִּישׁוּל אַחַר בִּישׁוּל בְּדָבָר יָבֵשׁ), even if it has cooled off. Hence, it is permitted to soak it in a *keli rishon,* provided it is not on the fire. Solid, dry food that was not cooked before the Sabbath may not be soaked, even in a *keli sheini,* because it appears as though it is being cooked. But it is permitted to pour onto it from a *keli sheini.*

9.   If the food in a *keli rishon* is not fully cooked, one is not permitted to stir it or remove some of the food with a spoon or ladle, or to put a lid or a cover on the vessel, whether it is on or off the fire, so

---

20.   Putting Gravy, Butter, Salt and Ketchup on Hot Food   It is not permitted to pour cold soup or gravy onto a hot piece of meat, nor may one put butter on hot potatoes. It is permitted, however, to put salt and ketchup which are pre-cooked in the process of production onto hot meat when it is on the plate, that is, in a *keli sheini.*

21.   Reheating Fluids and Food Containing Liquid   The prohibition of repeated cooking applies to fluids such as water, wine, oil, fat, fruit juices, and the like. It applies as well to cooked food, such as meat in soup or in a broth. It is forbidden to heat them again to the degree of *yad soledet bo* once they have cooled off completely. Hence, it is not permitted to pour cold food or fluid into a *keli rishon,* whether it is on or off the fire, nor may one pour onto it from a *keli rishon.* If it was previously fully cooked, and it has not cooled off completely, but it is warm enough to be edible, it may be reheated by placing it some distance from the fire, or on top of a vessel that is on the *blech* over the fire, or on the radiator, or on a hot plate used to keep food warm. It may also be heated by pouring on it from a *keli rishon,* or putting it in a *keli rishon* which is not on the fire.

long as it is *yad soledet bo,* because he would be causing it to cook. If it is fully cooked one is permitted to stir or remove some of the food and to cover the vessel, provided it is not on the fire.[22] It is permitted in any case to uncover the vessel, even when it is on the fire and the food is not fully cooked.

10.   Just as solid food that is fully cooked is not subject to cooking again (אֵין בִּישׁוּל אַחַר בִּישׁוּל),[23] so it is also not subject to roasting if it was already roasted (אֵין צָלִי אַחַר צָלִי), and not to baking if it was already baked (אֵין אֲפִיָה אַחַר אֲפִיָה). However, according to some authorities whatever is roasted or baked is subject to cooking (יֵשׁ בִּישׁוּל אַחַר צָלִי וּבִישׁוּל אַחַר אֲפִיָה), and whatever is cooked is subject to roasting or baking (יֵשׁ צָלִי אַחַר בִּישׁוּל וְאֲפִיָה אַחַר בִּישׁוּל). Therefore, one should not put cooked meat without soup near the fire where it can be heated to the degree of *yad soledet bo,* as it would then be roasted. Likewise, one should not put roasted meat, bread crumbs or *matzah*

---

22.   Stirring and Removing Food From a Pot on the Fire   Some maintain that it is a transgression of the *melachah* if one stirs the contents of a pot that is standing on the fire, even if the food is fully cooked. One should, therefore, refrain from stirring a pot of food that is on the fire or on a *blech* directly over the fire. It is, likewise, Rabbinically prohibited to stir food that is not fully cooked in a pot that is sufficiently hot to be *yad soledet bo,* even after it has been removed from the fire. Opinions also differ as to the permissibility of removing some of the food with a spoon, or some other implement, from a pot on the fire, even when the food is fully cooked. It is advisable to follow the stricter view and to refrain from removing food, regardless of the extent to which it was cooked, from a pot that is on the fire or on the *blech* directly over the fire. One should first remove the pot from the fire before taking out any of the food.

23.   Putting Fried or Cooked Noodles into Hot Soup   Food that is fried in oil is considered as cooked and not subject to cooking again. Baked products that were cooked are, likewise, not subject to being cooked again. It is, therefore, permitted to put noodles that were fried in oil or cooked into a pot of hot soup after it was removed from the fire, or to pour the hot soup from the pot onto the noodles.

into hot soup or gravy that is in a *keli rishon* where it would be cooked, or even into a *keli sheini,* as some foods cook in a *keli sheini* as well.[24]

11.   Raw fruit, cold food, or liquid that is subject to cooking again may not be placed near the fire, or on the stove[25] after it was lit, even before it has heated up, when if left there for a long time it would be heated to the degree of *yad soledet bo,* lest one forgets and lets it stand there until it reaches that degree of heat and begins to cook. It is permitted, however, to put it at a distance from the fire or on the stove in a place where even if left there for a long time it would not be heated to the degree of *yad soledet bo.*[26] It is, likewise, permitted to put a pot

---

24.   Using a Spoon or Ladle to Remove Soup From a Pot   If a spoon or ladle is used to remove the hot soup from the pot in which it was cooked into a bowl or plate, the bowl or plate may be considered a *keli shlishi,* provided the ladle was not left in the pot for any length of time. It would then be permitted to put the bread or *matzah* into the soup.

25.   Heating Food by Means of a Timer   It is not permitted to cook food that was not cooked or only partially cooked by putting it on an electric stove which is ignited on the Sabbath by means of a time clock set before the Sabbath. It is forbidden to cook the food in this manner, irrespective of whether it is placed on the stove on the Sabbath or before the Sabbath, and even before the fire is kindled. Opinions differ on whether it is permitted to heat food that was already cooked by setting the timer before the Sabbath to light the stove on the Sabbath. Some authorities forbid it. Others permit it, especially if necessary for a sick person, if the food is placed on the *blech* before the Sabbath. If it is feared that the food will spoil if left there overnight, one may have a non-Jew place it on the stove on the Sabbath before the fire is kindled. In this case the pot of food should preferably be placed on top of another vessel, and precautions taken to prevent one from inadvertently adjusting the timer or the control knobs on the stove. See also note 47.

26.   Warming Cold Food to Make It Edible   A piece of cooked meat, chicken, or *kugel* that was kept in the refrigerator and completely cooled may be reheated by putting it into hot gravy or soup in a *keli rishon* that is not on the fire, or by placing it some distance from the fire, or on top of a

of cooked food[27] that has not cooled off completely or solid, dry food that is not subject to cooking again,[28] on top of a vessel which is on the fire, inasmuch as the latter vessel separates it from the fire (הֶפְסֵק קְדֵירָה). Similarly, if the food that is already cooked is beginning to burn, and he wishes to prevent it from burning, he may put an empty used vessel on the fire and place the pot of food on top of it.

12.   A vessel containing food, even if not subject to cooking again, may not be kept on the stove[29] from before the Sabbath, or replaced on the Sabbath, unless the fire is covered with some material, such as a metal sheet (a *blech*)[30] and the like, as a reminder to prevent one

---

vessel that is on the *blech* over the fire, or on a radiator, or on a non-adjustable hot plate made to keep food moderately warm. In the view of some authorities the above procedures are permissible only if it will not be heated to the degree of *yad soledet bo*. Other authorities do not set this restriction.

27.   Warming Cooked Food on Top of Another Vessel   A pot of soup that was fully cooked and is still warm, or a piece of cold meat that was fully cooked may be heated up again by placing it on top of a vessel of food or liquid, such as a pot of *chulent,* or a water kettle, that is on the fire, even if the soup or meat is heated to a high temperature. Care should be taken that the meat is not placed where it will roast.

28.   Warming a Kugel or Meat Pie   It is permitted to heat a *kugel* or a meat pie, as the small amount of fat that dissolves will remain within the pie or the *kugel*. It is, likewise, permitted to heat a piece of fatty meat, since the amount of fat that melts and flows off is negligible.

29.   Status of Gas Ranges and Electric Stoves   Present day gas ranges and electric stoves and ovens are deemed to be similar to the *kirah* (כִּירָה) type of stove referred to in the Talmud, whose heat was less intense and to which the least stringent restrictions applied. These cooking appliances must also be covered with some suitable material, such as a *blech*. See the following note.

30.   Covering the Stove With a Blech   An electric stove must likewise be covered with a *blech* even if, unlike a gas range, the fire and the electric elements are not visible. An electric hotplate which maintains a set temperature

from stirring the fire, or adjusting the flame, (lit. "lest he rake the coals," שֶׁמָּא יְחַתֶּה בַּגֶּחָלִים). A vessel containing cooked food, and a kettle of boiled water may be moved to and from areas on the *blech* where the heat is at the degree of *yad soledet bo,* and according to some authorities, to and from any warm part of the *blech* to any other part of the *blech,* provided the food and the liquid have not cooled off completely.[31] One may place cold foods or liquids to warm on a part of the *blech* where they cannot heat up to the degree of *yad soledet bo,* even if left there all day.[32]

---

that cannot be adjusted, and is designed to keep food hot but not to cook it, in the opinion of many authorities does not require a *blech.* The covering placed on the stove should be of a material not used to cook on during the week. If need be, a sheet of aluminum foil will suffice. Since the fire on a gas range or an electric stove can be raised or lowered, it is best that the control knobs be removed, covered, or taped as a reminder not to adjust it. If one finds it difficult to cover the knobs it is sufficient if the stove is covered. A pot of food and a kettle of water may then be kept hot on the stove on the Sabbath. If one forgot to put a *blech* on the stove before the Sabbath, it is permissible to do so on the Sabbath, provided the fire will not heat the metal covering to a glow, and he is careful not to extinguish the flame while covering it. In any event, the food may be eaten on *Shabbat* if it was fully cooked before the Sabbath, even if the stove was left uncovered.

31. Moving a Pot on the Blech and From Stove to Stove One may move a pot of food on the *blech* from a smaller flame to a larger flame, provided the food is fully cooked. It is permitted to move a pot of cooked food from a part of the *blech* where it is not over the fire to a place over the fire, if the food is still warm. It is, likewise, permitted to remove the pot of cooked, hot food from one stove to another, as well as from a gas stove to an electric stove, and vice versa, provided the stoves are covered.

32. Melting Congealed Fat and Ice Near the Fire A vessel containing broth that has congealed or liquid that has frozen may be placed at a distance from the fire in order to melt the fat or the ice if it is needed for the Sabbath, provided it is put where it will not heat up to the point of *yad soledet bo.*

13.   In preparation for the Sabbath meals all food must be cooked
and water boiled before *Shabbat*. Food cooked[33] and water boiled
before the Sabbath may be left on a stove (שְׁהִיָּיה) that is covered with
a metal sheet (a *blech*) and the like, with the heat set to keep the food
hot[34] on the Sabbath. The food may then be eaten[35] and the water
used for drinking and other purposes on the Sabbath.[36] One may

---

33.   Food Must Be Cooked Before the Sabbath Until It Is Edible   Food that
is left on the stove to continue cooking on the Sabbath should be fully
cooked before the Sabbath, or cooked until it is considered edible, that is,
one half cooked, and in case of emergency, at least one third cooked.

34.   Eating Hot Food on Shabbat   It is a *mitzvah* to eat hot food on *Shabbat*. One who prepares good food, and preserves its heat in a permissible
manner, honors the Sabbath and makes the Sabbath a day of delight. While
the Sages permit the use of fire kindled before the Sabbath, some sects who
denied the validity of the Oral Law forbade it. One who endeavors to have
hot food on the Sabbath affirms his faith in the authority of the Sages and
will merit the End of Days. See Part I, Chapter 2, note 6.

35.   Serving Hot Chulent on the Sabbath   It is customary to keep a pot of
chulent that was cooked before the Sabbath on the stove or in the oven in
order to have a hot dish to serve on the Sabbath. If the *chulent* is drying up,
it is permitted to add hot water to it from a kettle on the *blech*. This should
be done by lifting the pot of *chulent* from the *blech,* or moving it to another
part of the *blech* not directly over the fire, and then adding the water. The
pot may then be returned to its former place on the *blech*. It is advisable to
use the same procedure when removing some of the *chulent* from the pot.
One should not stir the pot while it is over the fire, even if the *chulent* is fully
cooked.

36.   Use of an Electric Hot Water Urn   It is permitted to use an electric urn
for hot water that is kept at an even temperature on the Sabbath. It should
be connected to the electric current in ample time for the water to boil
before the Sabbath. It is not permitted to have water flowing into the urn, or
to add water to the urn on the Sabbath, even hot water from a kettle on the
blech. The water should be drawn from the tap, which should not be at the
very bottom of the urn lest one might add water to keep the heating element
from burning out.

transfer the cooked food and the boiled water from one vessel to another if necessary, provided both vessels are on the *blech* and the contents of both are still warm. If the food in one vessel is becoming dried up one may pour hot water into it from another vessel on the *blech*. It is preferable that the above be done by first lifting the vessel to which the food or water is being transferred off the *blech,* or moving it to another part of the *blech* not directly over the fire.[37]

14. A vessel containing food that one placed on the stove before the Sabbath, and was removed on the Sabbath, may not be returned onto the stove (חֲזָרָה), because it appears as though he is cooking on the Sabbath, or according to some authorities, because he may stir the fire to reheat it.[38] However, one may return the vessel onto the stove if the following conditions are met:[39] (1) the food is fully cooked;

---

37. Pouring Hot Water to Keep Food From Drying Up   Opinions differ on pouring hot water from a kettle standing on the *blech* onto food that is becoming dried up to keep it from burning. Ashkenazic authorities, such as Rabbi Moshe Feinstein ז"ל, permit it after the pot of food has been moved to another part of the *blech* not directly over the fire. Sefardic authorities forbid it while the food is in a *keli rishon,* but permit it in a *keli sheini.*

38. Prohibition of Returning Food to the Stove   The reasons alternatively advanced for the Rabbinical prohibition of replacing cooked food over the fire (חֲזָרָה) on the Sabbath are: (1) to prevent the likelihood of stoking the fire (שֶׁמָּא יְחַתֶּה), (2) returning the food over the fire has the appearance of cooking (נִרְאֶה כִּמְבַשֵּׁל). The implications of these alternative reasons in application to modern heating appliances are significant. While the likelihood of stoking may not be applicable under conditions that would preclude that possibility, the prohibition on the ground that it appears as cooking would in certain cases apply.

39. Returning Food to the Blech   The restrictions on returning a pot of food to the stove apply only if it is placed on a part of the *blech* where it will be heated to the degree of *yad soledet bo.* However, if it will not attain that degree of heat it is permitted to return food, both solid and liquid, even if it has cooled off, without regard to the prescribed conditions, because it is incapable of cooking and it does not appear as though one were cooking on the Sabbath.

(2) the food has not cooled off completely, but is still warm; (3) the stove is covered with a *blech*; (4) when the vessel was removed from the stove one intended to return it; (5) the vessel continues to be held in the hand, even if placed on the table but not set down on the ground.[40]

One should not put or return a vessel containing food into a heated oven on the Sabbath, even under the above conditions.[41]

15. It is permissible before the Sabbath to cover and envelop a vessel containing food (הַטְמָנָה) with a substance or material that will retain the heat (מַעֲמִיד הֶבֶל) on the Sabbath. It is not permissible to

---

40. Replacing a Pot of Food on the Stove   In case of need one may return a vessel onto the stove if, in addition to the first three conditions, either of the last two conditions are complied with. In case of extreme need, where one would be left without warm food on *Shabbat,* the vessel may be returned to the stove even if he did not have in mind to return it, and he set it down on the table or on another surface. The restriction is eased in this case if the remaining three conditions are complied with.

41. Use of an Oven Regulated by a Thermostat   A gas or electric oven that is regulated by a thermostat may not be used on the Sabbath, because on opening the door one is likely to ignite the flame or turn on the electricity. One is, therefore, not permitted to open the oven door to remove any food unless the fire is on, or the thermostat is set so that it is certain the fire will not go on as the door is opened. Opinions differ on returning food into the oven if it is not regulated by a thermostat, or even if it is thermostatically controlled and it is set so that the fire will not go on when the door is opened. According to some authorities it is similar to returning the food onto the stove and is permissible under the same conditions. Others, however, do not permit it, because the heat inside an oven is more intense and it appears as though he is cooking on the Sabbath. The restrictions regarding returning food, whether on the stove or into the oven, apply only if the food could be heated to the degree of *yad soledet bo,* but not if it cannot reach that degree of heat. Hence, it is permissible to remove food from the oven, and to return the food to the oven, when the fire is completely off and only the pilot burner is on, so that the food would surely not be heated to the degree of *yad soledet bo.* See also Melachah 36, note 7.

cover and envelop the vessel with a substance or material that will generate or add heat (מוֹסִיף הֶבֶל) to the food.[42] It is forbidden on the Sabbath to cover and envelop a vessel containing food, whether or not it is fully cooked, even with material that only retains the heat of the food.[43] The Sages prohibited *hatmanah* lest one forgets and places the pot in ashes containing coals and then stirs the fire in order to reheat the food if he should find that it has cooled in the interim. The prohibition applies only when the food remains in the vessel in which it was cooked (*keli rishon*), and not if it is transferred to another vessel,[44] even if the food is still *yad soledet bo,* and even if it is returned to the original vessel. If the food has cooled below *yad soledet bo,* even if it remains in the vessel in which it was originally cooked, *hatmanah* is

---

42. Keeping a Pot of Food in the Oven   Placing a pot of fully cooked food, such as *chulent,* in the oven before the Sabbath to keep it hot for serving on the Sabbath is not considered *hatmanah* because the pot is not enveloped with material, and it is therefore permissible. If the oven is so constructed that the pot fits into it snugly and is completely enclosed, it is considered *hatmanah* and it is not permissible.

43. Covering a Pot With a Lid or Aluminum Foil   Putting a lid on a pot containing fully cooked food is permissible on the Sabbath, even if it helps to preserve the heat, as this is normal procedure and is not considered *hatmanah.* Covering a pot with some other article or material, such as aluminum foil, is likewise not considered *hatmanah* and is permissible, provided one's intention is to protect its contents. If the pot was already covered before the Sabbath in a permissible manner with material that retains heat, one may add to or replace the covering on the Sabbath with similar material in order to preserve the heat.

44. Filling a Thermos or Hot Water Bottle   It is permitted to pour liquid from a *keli rishon,* such as hot soup from a pot on the stove, or hot water from the kettle on the stove, into a thermos on the Sabbath. Although it is intended to retain heat, it is not prohibited because the thermos is considered a *keli sheini* and it is, moreover, not the manner of making *hatmanah.* It is likewise permitted to fill a hot water bottle on the Sabbath. The thermos and the hot water bottle should be dry before being filled.

permitted in case of need. It is permitted on the Sabbath to cover and envelop cold food or liquid with material that retains heat, but does not add heat, in order to remove the chill or to keep it from cooling further.

16.   If one cooked food on the Sabbath in deliberate transgression (מֵזִיד) of the Sabbath, the food is forbidden to him and his family forever,[45] but it is permitted to others at the close of the Sabbath.[46] The vessel in which he cooked the food may also not be used by him for cooking until it is *kashered*. If one cooked food on the Sabbath unintentionally or in ignorance of the fact that it is a transgression (שׁוֹגֵג), it is forbidden on the Sabbath but permitted to all at the close of the Sabbath. In the latter instance it may be eaten on the Sabbath as well in case of need.

17.   One is forbidden to tell a non-Jew to cook or bake for him on the Sabbath. Food cooked and bread baked by a non-Jew for a Jew on the Sabbath may not be eaten until such time has elapsed after the Sabbath as it would take to cook the food and bake the bread. Where a non-Jew has been instructed to heat the house, it is permitted to

------

45. Food Cooked and Bread Baked by a Jew on the Sabbath If one instructs a non-observant Jew to cook or bake for him on the Sabbath the food is forever forbidden. Food cooked and bread baked on the Sabbath by Jews in a restaurant, hotel or bakery for a Jewish clientele is likewise forever forbidden. When purchasing bread and other baked products one should not only ascertain that it was not baked on the Sabbath, but also that the dough was not kneaded on the Sabbath.

46. Food Cooked for One Critically Ill If, in an emergency, one must cook on the Sabbath for a dangerously ill person, the food is permitted only to him, or to one who is in the same critical condition. It is not permitted to others until the close of the Sabbath. The vessel in which the food was cooked is permitted to be used afterwards. See Part V, Chapter 8, paragraph 8,9 and notes, for the laws pertaining to providing food for one who is critically ill.

have him put the cold pots of cooked food and liquids on the oven before lighting the fire in order to reheat them for the Sabbath meal.[47].

12. SHEARING

גְּזִיזָה

1. The objective of this *Av Melachah* is to sever from its natural source the outer covering of wool or hair of an animal.

The *melachah* comprises such forbidden primary activities as shearing wool or hair from a domestic or non-domestic animal or fowl, irrespective of whether it is alive or dead, and even from its detached skin or hide.

2. The *melachah* includes such forbidden subsidiary activities (*Toladot*) as plucking feathers[1] from a bird or fowl, pulling off or cutting

---

47. Having a Non-Jew Put Cooked Food on a Stove to Be Heated It is not permitted to instruct a non-Jew to do anything on the Sabbath that a Jew is forbidden to do, even if it is only a Rabbinical prohibition. Hence, one may not request a non-Jew to put a pot of cooked food, that has cooled completely, on a heated stove which is used exclusively for cooking, where the food will be heated to the degree of *yad soledet bo*. Some permit having the non-Jew put it on the stove to be heated before it is lit, in case of need, and on an electric stove while it is not in operation but will begin to operate when the current is connected by means of a time switch. He may set the food to be warmed on the *blech* over the stove or on a hot plate, even when already in operation, in a way that it will not reach the degree of *yad soledet bo*. See also note 25.

1. Removing Feathers From a Cooked Chicken Some authorities caution against removing the small feathers that remain on the skin of the chicken after it has been cooked. Others, however, maintain that the prohibition does not apply after it is cooked, especially since the feathers are loose and practically detached.

off one's nails or hair, or another person's nails or hair with an implement.[2]

3. Rabbinical prohibitions include pulling off nails,[3] or pulling out hair by hand, and removal of a wart by hand or with an implement. It is not permitted to pull off a scab or a cuticle. It is not permitted to comb the hair[4] or to brush[5] it with a hard brush, as one is likely to tear out some hair.

13. CLEANING

לִיבּוּן

1. The objective of this *Av Melachah* is to remove stains, dirt or coloring from wool, linen and other fabrics.

The *melachah* comprises such forbidden primary activities as bleaching a cloth or a fabric, or cleaning it by rubbing the fabric on a washboard.

---

2. Removal of Hair From the Face, Head or Body   Removal of hair from the face, the head, or the body, whether by scissors, razor, shaver, and depilatory paste or ointment is in violation of the *melachah* and is forbidden on the Sabbath. In the case of a razor there is the additional prohibition of its use to shave a man's beard and the hair of his temples (see Volume One, Part IV, Chapter 2).

3. Removing a Hangnail That Is Painful   A hangnail that is mostly detached, and is causing pain, or is likely to cause pain, may be removed by hand or with the teeth, but not with an implement.

4. Combing or Brushing a Wig   One should refrain from combing out a wig on the Sabbath, as it is likely to tear out some hair. However, one may use a soft-haired brush to smooth the hair.

5. Brushing the Hair   It is permitted to part the hair by hand, and to brush the hair lightly with a soft brush that is not likely to tear out any of the hair, preferably one that is kept expressly for use on the Sabbath.

2. The *melachah* includes such forbidden subsidiary activities (*Toladot*) as laundering a garment by soaking it in water, or by pouring water or some other cleaning agent over it, and wringing or pressing water out of a cloth or a garment (סְחִיטָה).[1]

3. Rabbinical prohibitions include mopping up water[2] with a cloth,[3] or wiping up water with a sponge,[4] lest one will wring out the

---

1. Washing and Drying Dishes With a Cloth In washing dishes and utensils one should not use a cloth that will absorb the water, because it will lead to pressing out the water in violation of the prohibition of *seḥitah*. One may use a dish scrubber made of plastic or other non-absorbent material. In drying the dishes and utensils, a cloth designated for that purpose should be used, so that one will not be concerned with its condition and will not squeeze the water out of it. For further discussion of the rules pertaining to washing dishes and utensils on the Sabbath, see Melachah 11, note 15 and Part III, paragraph 26 and notes.

2. Use of a Paper Towel It is permitted to dry one's hands and to soak up water, or other liquid that has spilled, with a paper towel or a paper napkin, as it is afterward discarded.

3. Wiping a Table and Tablecloth Clean One should use a dry, not a wet cloth to wipe a table clean. If liquid spilled on a tablecloth made of cloth or a synthetic material which is absorbent, one may remove the liquid with a spoon or knife, but without pressing down and squeezing it. Liquid that spilled onto the table or tablecloth may be mopped up with a paper towel, or with a cloth or rag one does not mind being wet, but one should not wring it out. If liquid spilled onto a plastic tablecloth one may clean it with a rag or non-absorbent cloth or scourer. If it is soiled one may pour water on it and clean it with a paper towel or a paper napkin, taking care not to wring it out.

4. Washing a Baby Bottle With a Brush It is permitted to wash the inside of a baby bottle with a brush made of synthetic bristles, inasmuch as they do not absorb the water, and hence the prohibition of *seḥitah* does not apply.

water;[5] handling wet[6] washed clothing;[7] hanging washed clothing out to dry; rubbing clothes after laundering to make them shine; wring-

---

5.   Drying Oneself With a Towel   It is permitted to dry one's whole body with a towel. When drying one's hands, some are careful to let the excess water drip off before drying them. See Part III, paragraph 32 and notes.

6.   Handling a Wet Baby Diaper   It is permitted to place a cloth or a diaper under an infant while bathing him, since one is not particular about pressing the water out if it gets wet. It is permitted to hang up a baby diaper to dry, if it is needed to be used again that day, as it is evident that a wet or soiled diaper is dried in this way. But it should not be placed on or near a heater where it will be heated to the degree of *yad soledet bo*. One may store soiled diapers and clothing in the washing machine in order to keep the house free of a foul odor, provided there is no water in the machine.

7.   Wearing Wet Clothes and Drying Them Out   If one's clothes were soaked in the rain he may continue to wear them, but he may not dry them near a heater or near the oven where they will be heated to the degree of *yad soledet bo*. After removing them he should not spread them out to dry, as it would appear that he had them laundered on the Sabbath. He may, however, hang them in their usual place.

8.   Drying One's Hair   While it is not permitted to squeeze the water out of one's hair, it is permitted to dry the hair with a towel, and even to rub it to relieve any discomfort.

9.   Brushing and Removing Dirt From Clothing   One may not use a brush to remove dirt from clothing. If one is not particular about its cleanliness, he may clean it off with his hand or with a dry cloth, or by shaking it lightly. However, a dark, new suit or garment about which one is particular may not be cleaned in this manner. Dust and surface dirt may be brushed off with one's hands or with a dry cloth. Some permit use of a clothes brush with soft bristles.

ing water out of one's hair;[8] and brushing dust or dirt from a suit,[9] or garment,[10] or one's shoes.[11]

14. COMBING RAW MATERIALS

נִיפּוּץ

1.   The objective of this *Av Melachah* is to prepare the raw material by combing, hackling and separating it into strands or fibers to be used for spinning, twining and weaving.

The *melachah* comprises such forbidden primary activities as carding or combing out raw wool and flax to make the fibers and felts.

2.   The *melachah* includes such forbidden subsidiary activities (*Toladot*) as hammering out or pounding dried sinews until they form strands fit for spinning, and combing out various fibers until they become threadlike and fit for weaving and braiding into rope.

3.   Rabbinical prohibitions include winding thread and yarn onto a cylinder or spindle, and unwinding a ball or coil of wool or other threads.

---

10.   Cleaning a Carpet   It is not permitted to use a carpet sweeper to clean the carpet or rug on the Sabbath, even if it is operated manually and not by electricity. It is permitted, however, to use a broom with soft bristles to remove the dirt and refuse.

11.   Cleaning Shoes of Dirt and Mud   Shoes made of leather or a similar non-absorbent material may be cleaned of dirt by pouring water over them. Mud that is still wet may be removed by scraping lightly with a scraper or some other article that may be handled on the Sabbath, but not with a knife. Dry mud may not be scraped off, but may be washed off with water. Suede and cloth shoes are governed by the laws that apply to cleaning clothes.

15. DYEING

צְבִיעָה

1. The objective of this *Av Melachah* is to change the color of an object or substance.

The *melachah* comprises such forbidden primary activities as dyeing wool or linen and other fabrics; dyeing a garment; painting a utensil or a wall. If one applies a coat of whitewash or plaster to a wall he transgresses both the *melachot* of Dyeing and of Building, since he is also adding to the wall surface. One is culpable for a violation of the *melachah* if he uses a dye or paint that is durable.[1]

2. The *melachah* includes such forbidden subsidiary activities (*Toladot*) as mixing or blending colors;[2] mixing chemical solutions that effect a change in color; making color reaction tests for medical diagnosis; dissolving coloring matter in water.[3] The prohibition

---

1. Applying a Color That Is Not Durable   While one is not culpable when applying a color that is not durable it is still Rabbinically prohibited. Thus, one may not rub colored chalk onto a surface, even though he only applies it temporarily and the color will not last.

2. Wearing Photochromatic Eyeglasses   Eyeglasses that are fitted with photochromatic lenses that darken and change color in sunlight may be worn on the Sabbath inasmuch as the color modification takes place in the lenses which have been sensitized to react when exposed to light. The person wearing the eyeglasses is not involved in any actual coloring of the lenses. Unlike sunglasses which one is likely to remove in the shade, these photochromatic eyeglasses resume their original achromatic state in ordinary light and, therefore, may be worn in the street, even where there is no *eruv*.

3. Flushing a Toilet Containing a Cleansing Agent   It is permitted to flush a toilet where the tank contains a bowl cleaner and deodorizer that colors the water which flows into the toilet bowl, cleaning and disinfecting it and producing a pleasant odor. However, unless it is needed to dispel a malodor in the room, it is advisable to be stringent, and refrain from keeping it in the tank on the Sabbath.

against dyeing does not apply to coloring food if it is required for immediate consumption.

3. Rabbinical prohibitions include adding coloring matter to food to improve its appearance for ornamental purposes or, as is the practice of merchants, so that the food will retain its color and fresh appearance for a longer time in order to facilitate its sale;[4] applying a coloring to the face, around the eyes or on other parts of the body.[5] One should if possible refrain from wiping his hands or lips with a cloth, when they are stained from eating or handling certain fruits, such as cherries and blackberries.[6] One should, likewise, refrain if possible from applying a cloth to the nose or to a wound that is bleeding.[7]

---

4. Coloring Food and Beverages It is permitted to put coloring into food or into a beverage that is being prepared for the meal on the Sabbath, so long as it is not intended merely to add color, but rather to improve its flavor. Hence one may add instant tea or coffee to water, mix raspberry juice with water, put paprika into soup, and pour red wine into white wine, and the like. It is not permitted to add coloring to cakes and other food products for ornamental and commercial purposes.

5. Use of Cosmetics A woman may not color her face, paint her eyebrows or eyelids, dye her hair, or color her fingernails on the Sabbath. It is forbidden to apply nail polish, irrespective of whether it is colored or colorless. A woman may apply make-up powder to her face, as it does not adhere to the skin, provided it is not oil based or mixed with cream or ointment. As a practical measure, women are well advised to apply cosmetics before the Sabbath which last over the Sabbath.

6. Wiping One's Stained Hands and Lips With a Napkin As it is common practice to cleanse one's hands and lips while eating, one may be lenient in wiping his stained hands on a cloth napkin if it is unavoidable. It is advisable to wash one's hands first, or to use paper napkins which are discarded after the meal.

7. Covering a Bleeding Wound In the case of superficial bleeding, if possible one should first wash the blood off with water and then apply a cloth. If

16. SPINNING

טְוִיָּה

1.   The objective of this *Av Melachah* is to draw out and twist fiber into yarn or thread, rendering it fit for weaving, sewing and the like.

The *melachah* comprises such forbidden primary activities as producing yarn and thread from wool, flax, cotton, silk, hair, sinews, and other raw materials, irrespective of whether it is spun by hand[1] or with a device such as a spinning wheel.

2.   The *melachah* includes such forbidden subsidiary activities (*Toladot*) as manufacturing plush and felt; twining threads; and twisting or braiding strands together to form a cord or rope.

3.   Rabbinical prohibitions include retwining a thread or strand that has unraveled.

17. STRETCHING THE THREADS

הַנָּסָכַת הַמַּסֶּכֶת

1.   The objective of this *Av Melachah* is to stretch out the threads of the loom, extending them from the top to the bottom and thus forming the warp of the loom.

---

the bleeding is severe the cloth should be directly applied to cover the wound and to stem the flow of blood. A gauze bandage and absorbent cotton intended for this purpose and discarded may be used in any case.

1.   Spinning Wool Directly on the Animal   If one spins wool when it is still attached to a living animal he is not culpable, as it is not normal to do the *melachah* of Spinning in this way. According to the Talmud (*Shabbat* 74b, 99a) such spinning, which required superior skill, was performed by the "wise-hearted" women who spun the goats' hair by hand in this manner for the curtains in the Tabernacle (Exodus 35:25, 26).

2. The *melachah* includes such forbidden subsidiary activities (*Toladot*) as beating the threads so as to straighten and position them in the loom.

3. Stretching out yarn or threads of wool, silk and the like on a frame for knitting is likewise considered a transgression of this *melachah*.

18. MAKING MESHES

עֲשִׂיַּת הַנִּירִין

1. The objective of this *Av Melachah* is to insert and arrange the threads of the warp in the upper and lower sections of the loom in such a manner that when one is raised the other is lowered, thereby enabling the cross-rods of the shuttle to intersect and the threads of the woof to interlace with the threads of the warp.

2. The *melachah* includes such forbidden subsidiary activities (*Toladot*) as meshing material in making a sieve, a sifter, a basket or a net, and interweaving ropes or other material to make a bed. One who forms two meshes in construction of the above, or of anything that is made in this way, transgresses this *melachah*.

3. Prohibited activities include intertwining flowers to form a wreath or a garland of flowers and meshing wires to make a wire netting.

19. WEAVING

אֲרִיגָה

1. The objective of this *Av Melachah* is to form a cloth by interlacing the threads of the warp and the woof in the loom.
   The *melachah* comprises such forbidden primary activities as weaving, knitting, and embroidering.

2.   The *melachah* includes such forbidden subsidiary activities (*Toladot*) as smoothing and disentangling threads in order to even the woof, plaiting threads, braiding strands of detached hair, and interweaving slats of wood or other materials, as in the construction of a fence, a window shutter, or a cane chair.

3.   Rabbinical prohibitions include braiding the hair of a wig.[1]

20. SEPARATING THE THREADS

בְּצִיעָה

The objective of this *Av Melachah* is to separate woven material into its component threads for some constructive purpose.

The *melachah* comprises such forbidden primary activities as separating the threads of the warp from those of the woof, or vice versa, for the purpose of repairing the weave; detaching the threads in order to remove the woven fabric from the web of the loom; and separating threads in order to interweave a torn thread.

2.   The *melachah* includes such forbidden subsidiary activities (*Toladot*) as unraveling the threads of a woven or knitted garment, or removing threads from a sewn or stitched garment for the purpose of repairing or improving it.

3.   Rabbinical prohibitions include separating tangled threads and

---

1.   Braiding Hair   The *melachah* of Weaving applies in the case of braiding hair when it is detached. Braiding a wig, however, as the *Mishnah B'rurah* explains, is only Rabbinically prohibited, since the braids are not permanent and will eventually be undone. Indeed, where the admonition is likely to go unheeded, it is advisable not to remonstrate against the practice. Braiding hair that is attached to the head is Rabbinically forbidden, not under the *melachah* of Weaving, but rather under the *melachah* of Building. See Melachah 34, paragraph 11 and notes.

tearing off a piece from a layer of cotton.[1] Removing the basting threads from a sewn garment violates this *melachah* and is also prohibited because it is the finishing touch to the garment.

21. TYING A KNOT

קְשִׁירָה

1. The objective of this *Av Melachah* is to join ropes, cords, threads, and the like by tying a lasting knot.[1]

The *melachah* comprises such forbidden primary activities as

---

1. Use of Absorbent Cotton One who may need to use absorbent cotton to bandage or swab a wound, or to clean a baby on the Sabbath is advised to prepare a supply of individual cotton balls before the Sabbath.

1. Tying a Knot on the Sabbath The prohibited *melachah* entails tying a permanent knot (קֶשֶׁר שֶׁל קַיְּמָא). According to Rif, Rambam and the *Shulḥan Aruch* one has transgressed the *melachah* and is culpable if he tied a knot that is generally left tied, without setting a time when one intends to undo the knot, and it is the kind of knot that is made by a craftsman, such as a sailor, a stevedore, or a shoemaker. If it is a knot that is meant to remain tied, but it is not one that a craftsman would make, or vice versa, he is not culpable, but it is nevertheless Rabbinically prohibited. If it is neither, it is permissible. In the view of Rashi, Rosh, and other authorities the nature of the knot, that is, whether it is that of a craftsman or not, is of no consequence. If it is meant to be a permanent knot, namely, that it is usually left to remain tied, he is culpable. If it is a knot that is usually left tied for only a limited period of time, he is not culpable, but it is nevertheless Rabbinically prohibited. If it is one that is customarily untied on the same day, it is according to these authorities permissible to tie such a knot on the Sabbath.

In practice one is permitted to make a knot so long as it is not firmly tied, if it is one that is usually, and in that particular instance actually intended to be untied within a period of twenty-four hours. Thus, a woman may tie her head scarf with a loose double knot if she is in the habit of untying it when she takes it off. Where there is an urgent need and there is no

tying a craftsman's knot; tying a tightly-drawn double knot; tying a single knot at the end or in the middle of a string or thread; tying two adjacent cords with a single knot; and tying other knots that are meant to remain permanently tied.

2.   The *melachah* includes such forbidden subsidiary activities (*Toladot*) as twining strands of rope so that they remain joined and cannot be parted without untwining them.

3.   Rabbinical prohibitions include making a knot that one intends to untie, but which one sometimes reconsiders and decides to leave permanently tied. It is permissible, however, to tie a bow, that is a knot formed by doubling a lace or a string into two or more loops,[2] as it is meant to be untied on the same day,[3] and it is easily untied.

22. UNTYING A KNOT

הַתָּרָה

1.   The objective of this *Av Melachah* is to separate ropes, cords, threads and the like that have been tied together with a lasting knot.

---

other way but to tie a knot, or it is necessary to prevent or to alleviate pain or discomfort, or in the performance of a *mitzvah,* it is permissible to tie a knot that is to be untied within seven days.

2.   Tying and Untying Shoelaces   It is permitted to tie and untie one's shoelaces on the Sabbath, since they are customarily untied when the shoes are removed the same day, and they are moreover tied in a bow over a single tie which is not considered a permanent knot. If the shoelace is knotted and one is unable to untie it, he may tear or sever it in order to remove the shoe. It is permitted to reinsert a shoelace that has slipped out of the eyelet of one's shoe, if it can be done without undue difficulty.

3.   Tying a Necktie   One is permitted to tie a necktie, if he regularly unties it when he removes it.

2. The forbidden primary activities (*Avot Melachot*) and subsidiary activities (*Toladot*) that this *melachah* comprises correspond to the previous *melachah*. For whatever knot one is culpable for tying, one is culpable for untying, and vice versa. Whatever knot one is permitted to tie, one is likewise permitted to untie.[1]

3. It is permitted to untie the string or cord that is bound around food or containers of food, beverages, medicine and the like, if the food or contents are required for use on the Sabbath.[2]

23. SEWING

תְּפִירָה

1. The objective of this *Av Melachah* is to join two pieces of cloth or other materials by sewing them together with thread, and the like, in a lasting manner.

The *melachah* comprises such forbidden primary activities as sewing two stitches and knotting each end of the thread, or knotting both ends of the thread together; sewing three or more stitches, even without knotting the threads, so that the stitches will not come apart.

2. The *melachah* includes such forbidden subsidiary activities (*Tola-*

---

1. Untying a Tie on a Garment It is permitted to tie and untie a dress or a nightgown with a bow neckline, or pajamas with a tie at the waist, which are customarily tied in a bow and intended to be untied the same day. If the cord should become knotted and it is not possible to untie it, one is permitted to cut or tear it in private.

2. Untying a Container of Food It is permitted to untie a string used to tie fruit, such as figs and clusters of grapes, or food, such as stuffed fowl or roast meat. If it is not possible to untie or remove the string or cord from the fruit or food, or from a container of food, and the like, one may tear or sever it, even with a knife, provided it is not done in a way intended to preserve the string or cord for further use.

dot) as pulling the thread of a seam[1] so as to draw the cloth or other materials together[2] and to hold them fast; joining sheets of paper,[3] strips of leather, or other materials with an adhesive substance,[4] or by some other means,[5] in a lasting manner.[6]

3. Rabbinical prohibitions include filling a pillow or a quilt with down or feathers, or similar material, lest it lead to sewing them. However, it is permitted to reinsert the down or the feathers that have fallen out.

---

1. Tightening the Thread of a Seam or a Loose Button   It is not permitted to pull the thread of a seam in order to tighten it, or of a loose button in order to secure it, even without making a knot to hold it fast.

2. Tightening a Band on a Garment   One may draw a band or a cord through the eyelets of a garment, as for example to tie up the opening of a dress or an undergarment, provided it is customary to draw it when putting on the garment and to loosen it when taking off the garment.

3. Stapling Papers and Other Materials   It is not permitted to join sheets of paper or other materials by stapling them together.

4. Use of Disposable Diapers   Disposable diapers that are made to be secured with adhesive tape may be used on the Sabbath. The tape may be fastened so that the diaper will hold after it is placed on the infant, and it may later be unfastened and torn off if need be. The protective covering on the tape should be removed before the Sabbath.

5. Fastening a Garment or a Diaper With a Pin   One may use a straight pin, as well as a safety pin, to fasten a garment or a baby diaper, whether made of cloth or of paper, since the pin is only used to fasten it temporarily.

6. Opening and Closing a Zipper   One may open and close a zipper on a garment, even if the zipper can be completely disconnected and reconnected as in a detachable raincoat lining.

24. TEARING

קְרִיעָה

1. The objective of this *Av Melachah* is to tear apart or separate materials that have been sewn or joined together in a lasting manner for the purpose of resewing or rejoining them.

The *melachah* comprises such forbidden primary activities as undoing the stitches in a garment, and tearing apart cloth or other material in order to resew it.[1]

2. The *melachah* includes such forbidden subsidiary activities (*Toladot*) as separating paper, cloth, leather, wood and other materials that have been joined together with an adhesive substance or by some other means in a lasting manner.[2]

3. Rabbinical prohibitions include tearing,[3] even when it is not in

---

1. Tearing a Cloth or Garment While Using It One need not avoid ordinary use or handling of a garment on the Sabbath for fear that it may be torn. Thus, one may wear a new garment even if it should prove to be too tight and tears. One may remove thorns that became entangled in a garment even if it should tear. However, one should do so in private and with care to avoid tearing if possible. One may crack nuts wrapped in a cloth even if it should tear. In the above instances it is permitted because one does not intend to tear the cloth or garment.

2. Removing Staples From a Bag or Envelope While it is not permissible to staple sheets of paper together or to staple an envelope to close it, it is permitted to remove the staples from an envelope or folder, and from a paper or plastic bag.

3. Tearing Bathroom Tissues It is not permitted to tear paper off a roll, irrespective of whether the paper is perforated or not. Thus, one may not tear off absorbent paper towels or toilet paper from a roll, or facial tissues that are attached. One should, therefore, prepare a supply of bathroom tissues before the Sabbath. Some permit tearing toilet paper, if necessary, even from a perforated roll.

order to resew or repair the material.[4] It is likewise not permitted to tear one's garment in order to vent one's anger, or to relieve one's grief.

4.   It is permissible to break open a sealed vessel or container of food, or to tear the cord binding it, if its contents are needed for the Sabbath.[5] It is permitted to separate pages of a book that were inadvertently stuck together by paste or wax.[6]

------

4.   Opening a Sealed Envelope   It is not permitted to tear open a sealed envelope on the Sabbath. If it is urgent one may request a non-Jew to open the envelope. He should do so indirectly, if possible, by informing him that he cannot read the letter as it is sealed in the envelope.

5.   Opening a Sealed Container   One is permitted to break open a sealed container of food, beverages, medicine, and the like, whose contents are needed for immediate consumption or use on the Sabbath. One may likewise tear the wrapping or cut the cord binding or break the seal on a container, provided he avoids tearing any lettering or pictures. Since the container was not meant to be permanently sealed, and he does not intend to reuse it after its contents are removed, breaking or tearing the container is not a constructive act. However, it is not permitted to make an opening of a particular shape in the container in order to render it reusable as a utensil after its contents are removed. Some advise that milk and juice containers that form a spout upon opening should preferably be opened by cutting off from the top of the container or by making a hole in its side. Opinions differ on the permissibility of opening a bottle of wine or some other beverage by twisting the cap so that the bottom ring breaks off, leaving the upper part of the cap to form a reusable cover for the bottle. While some authorities forbid it, others permit it, inasmuch as the cap served as a cover before the bottom ring was separated from it and only continues to serve as such afterward. In view of the varied nature of sealed containers and the complexities in determining the permissibility of opening them on the Sabbath, one should endeavor to open the cans, cartons, bottles and other containers before the Sabbath. See Part III, note 64.

6.   Separating Pages of a Book   While it is permitted to separate pages of a book that were inadvertently glued together, one may not do so if they are

25. TRAPPING

צֵידָה

1. The objective of this *Av Melachah* is to restrict, by trapping, snaring and capturing, the freedom of movement of a living creature, of the kind that is ordinarily trapped or hunted, for the purpose of bringing it under human control.

The *melachah* comprises such forbidden primary activities as trapping animals,[1] birds or fish, whether by hand, with a snare, a trap or net,[2] or by entrapping them and confining them in an enclosed area where one will not have to catch them again. Thus, one would be in violation of the *melachah* if he pursued an animal and drove it into the house or into the yard and shut it in, or if he caused a bird to fly into the aviary and shut it in, or if he drew fish from the sea into a tank of water.[3] He is likewise liable if the animal should enter the

---

stuck together on the words and in separating the pages the words will be torn. It is forbidden to cut or tear apart the uncut pages of a book on the Sabbath.

1. Freeing a Trapped Animal One is permitted to free an animal from a trap on the Sabbath, but he should if possible avoid handling the animal as it is considered to be *muktzeh.*

2. Setting a Trap Before the Sabbath It is permissible to set a trap or spread out a net before the Sabbath to trap wild animals, birds, or fish, even if they will be caught on the Sabbath. It is not permitted to do so on the Sabbath.

3. Catching Fish on the Sabbath Fish are classed as creatures that it is customary to trap. If one catches a fish and removes it from the water, he is in violation of this *melachah,* even if he immediately puts it into a tank or bowl of water. If he takes it out of water until it dies, or for such time that it cannot be revived, he is also liable for taking a life (*netilat neshamah*), even if he returns it into the water while it is still alive. If one draws the fish into a

house or yard of its own accord and he shut it in. Similarly, if a small bird such as a sparrow should enter a box or cage and he shut it in, or a large bird entered the house and he shut it in, he is liable. However, if a small bird should enter or be made to fly into the house, and he shut it in, he is not liable, inasmuch as it still has to be caught. It is, nevertheless, Rabbinically forbidden to do so.

In the case of animals and birds that are domesticated it is permitted to shut them in, so long as it is not necessary to snare and catch them. However, if they are not yet domesticated, or if they rebelled and fled and fail to return at night, it is forbidden to capture them or to shut them in, as it would be a violation of the *melachah*.[4]

2.   The *melachah* includes such forbidden subsidiary activities (*Toladot*) as setting a dog after a wild animal[5] such as a fox or a rabbit, or sending out a predatory bird such as a hawk to hunt other birds. In these instances he is culpable if he actively participates in the hunt, as for example by frightening the animal and blocking its path until it is overtaken. If one takes no active part, but only sends the dog or the hawk after its prey, the trapping is Rabbinically forbidden.

---

tank of water or some other receptacle where it can readily be retrieved, he is culpable. If he draws the fish into a pool of water where it can elude him and must be caught again, he is not culpable. One may not instruct a non-Jew to catch fish for him on the Sabbath. If a non-Jew caught fish on the Sabbath, they are even forbidden to be handled by a Jew on the Sabbath, but are permissible after the Sabbath.

4.   Retrieving a Domesticated Animal   If one's domesticated animal or fowl has wandered away from the house and he fears that it will be lost or stolen, he may drive it into the yard or house or request a non-Jew to capture it.

5.   Hunting With Dogs for Sport   One is not permitted to hunt with dogs for sport even on weekdays. One who engages in such an abhorrent pastime is held in contempt and is deemed as participating in a "gathering of the scornful" (Psalms 1:1).

3.   Rabbinical prohibitions include setting a trap for mice;[6] catching flies or other creatures of the kind that are not customarily trapped for food or for other use; catching fish with a fish hook or in a net without taking the fish out of the water.

4.   One is permitted to snare and trap a dangerous animal or a venomous reptile or insect whose bite is deadly, even if it is not pursuing or threatening him.[7] One is also permitted to snare and trap any animal or reptile that can cause injury if it is pursuing or threatening him.[8]

---

6. Setting a Trap for Mice   One may not set a trap on the Sabbath to catch mice or other creatures and insects. It is, however, permitted to do so before the Sabbath. If one should find a dead mouse on the Sabbath he may remove it, even though it is *muktzeh*, because it is permitted to remove anything that is repulsive.

7. Trapping and Killing a Dangerous Animal or Reptile   One may trap and kill a dangerous animal or reptile, such as a mad dog or a venomous snake, even when it is in flight. Other creatures that are not deadly, but are by nature harmful and can cause serious injury may be trapped and killed when they are pursuing or threatening one. See Melachah 26, paragraph 4.

8. Trapping and Killing Insects   If an insect whose bite or sting is not deadly, but can cause severe pain or injury, is not pursuing him at the moment, but he fears that it may do so, one is permitted to trap it by covering it with a vessel or otherwise restraining it, but he may not kill it. If it pursues him and he cannot trap it, he may kill it. One may kill a wasp or a bee that is near an infant or someone who is allergic to its venom, as its sting can be dangerous. One may also kill insects of the kind that are known to spread dangerous disease. Insects, such as mosquitoes and fleas, whose bite or sting causes only minor pain or discomfort can only be chased away, but may not be killed. If it is biting or stinging him, or it is on his body or on his clothes, and he cannot chase it away, he may catch it and remove it, but he may not kill it. On the use of an insect repellent see Melachah 26, note 4. See also Part III, paragraph 52, 53.

26. SLAUGHTERING

שְׁחִיטָה

1.   The objective of this *Av Melachah* is to terminate the life of a living being.

The *melachah* comprises such forbidden primary activities as killing animals, cattle, fowl, fish and insects by slaughtering, stabbing, striking, and similar means. The prohibition applies to any living creature irrespective of its size. One who kills a spider, a worm, a flea or a fly is as culpable as though he had killed an animal of greater size.

2.   The *melachah* includes such forbidden subsidiary activities (*Toladot*) as taking a fish out of the water or pouring out the water, thereby causing the fish to die, and drawing blood from a living being for a constructive purpose.

3.   Forbidden activities include inflicting a wound that causes bleeding;[1] sucking blood from a wound; pressing a wound and drawing out blood; extracting a tooth[2] and drawing blood; bleeding by the use of leeches; drawing blood to the surface of the body by means of cupping. Drawing blood is permissible in a case of emergency for one who is critically ill.[3]

---

1.   Removing a Splinter   It is permitted to remove a splinter on the Sabbath even with a needle, but one should take care not to cause unnecessary bleeding.

2.   Extracting a Tooth   It is forbidden to extract a tooth on the Sabbath. However, if the pain is severe one may treat it medicinally, and if necessary he may have it extracted by a non-Jewish dentist. For the law in case of emergency, see Part V, Chapter 8, paragraph 4 and note 17.

3.   Drawing Blood for One Who Is Critically Ill   Drawing blood as a therapeutic measure, or taking a sample of blood for testing and diagnosis is permissible when it is necessary for one who is critically ill. It is, likewise,

4.   It is permitted to kill a dangerous animal, such as a mad dog or a poisonous snake whose bite is deadly, even if it is not pursuing one. In the case of other destructive creatures, such as snakes that can cause injury but are not a threat to life, it is permitted to kill them only if they are pursuing him. It is nevertheless permitted to trample them while walking, even with intent, provided he does not appear to be doing so intentionally. It is forbidden, however, to kill ants, insects,[4] or creeping creatures, that are not harmful,[5] whether by trampling them intentionally while walking,[6] or by other means.

27. SKINNING

הַפְשָׁטָה

1.   The objective of this *Av Melachah* is to separate the skin from the flesh of a dead animal.

---

permitted to donate blood and to draw blood for a transfusion when it is needed for one who is critically ill.

4.   Spraying an Insect Repellent   One may not trap or kill ants, worms, flies, and other such insects which do not bite or sting. One may not spread poison in order to kill them, but he may pour some other substance in their path that will keep them away. One may spray a room with an insect repellent in order to drive flies and other insects away from an infant or an invalid, but he may not direct the spray on the insects so that it will kill them. He should leave a door or window open to allow the insects to disperse. See also Melachah 25, note 8.

5.   Spreading Poison for Rodents   One may not spread poison on the Sabbath to kill mice and other creatures or insects. It is, however, permitted to do so before the Sabbath.

6.   Stepping on Ants and Other Insects   One should avoid deliberately stepping in a place where there are many insects, such as ants and the like, inasmuch as he will surely crush and kill them, even though he does not intend to kill them.

The *melachah* comprises such forbidden primary activity as stripping the skin off of animals, fowl, and fish.

2.   The *melachah* includes such forbidden subsidiary activities (*Toladot*) as splitting the hide of an animal, and separating the inferior part that lies opposite the flesh from the part opposite the hair that is of superior quality for the manufacture of parchment.[1]

28. TANNING

עִבּוּד הָעוֹר

1.   The objective of this *Av Melachah* is to process the hide and prepare it for a useful purpose.

The *melachah* comprises such forbidden primary activities as salting the hide; treating it with lime or a substance of plant origin, such as tannin-rich bark; or treating it with a chemical agent of similar effect in order to convert the hide into leather.

2.   The *melachah* includes such forbidden subsidiary activities (*Toladot*) as hardening leather by treading on it, softening leather by oiling it or bending it by hand; and smoothening leather by pulling it or stretching it on a frame.

3.   Rabbinical prohibitions include oiling or polishing shoes; salting and pickling in order to preserve meat, fish, radishes, cucumbers,

---

1.   Manufacture of Parchment   The manufacture of parchment involves stripping off the hide, removing the hair, and treating the hide and the skins in a prescribed process. Parchment made of the whole hide leather (גְּוִיל) is suitable for writing a *Sefer Torah*. Parchment is also produced by splitting the hide through its thickness into two parts, thus forming two skins. Parchment made from the thick, inner skin next to the flesh (דּוּכְסוּסְטוֹס) is suitable for writing a *mezuzah*. Parchment made from the thin, outer skin next to the hair (קְלָף) is of superior quality and suitable for writing *tefillin*.

onions and the like.[1] It is likewise forbidden to salt meat or to soak meat in water[2] in order to *kosher* it for cooking.

29. MARKING

שְׂרְטוּט

1.   The objective of this *Av Melachah* is to mark a line on a surface in preparation for cutting[1] or for writing.

The *melachah* comprises such forbidden primary activities as tracing a line on leather in order to cut it to measure, and tracing lines on parchment in order to write on it. The prohibition applies to tracing

---

1.   Salting Food for the Sabbath Meal   It is permitted to salt cooked meat, eggs, vegetables, and other foods that one intends to eat at the meal on the Sabbath. See Part III, paragraph 22.

2.   Soaking Meat Before Three Days Have Elapsed   Meat kept for three full days (seventy-two hours) without being soaked or washed cannot be made *kosher* for cooking purposes by soaking and salting it, because the blood will not come out by merely salting. The meat may not be cooked, but must be broiled. If the third day falls on the Sabbath it is not permitted to soak the meat, because soaking softens it and prepares it for salting. However, in a case involving a loss, it is permissible to have the meat soaked on the Sabbath by a non-Jew, and when this is not possible it may be done by a Jew, preferably indirectly by pouring the water over one's hands and onto the meat.

1.   Marking Food Before Cutting   The prohibition of marking does not apply to food preparatory to cutting and eating it. It is therefore permissible to mark lines with a knife on bread or on cake in order to cut it into slices, or to cut lines around an orange in order to peel it. Indeed, it is customary on the Sabbath to mark the *ḥallah* with the knife before reciting the blessing.

and scoring lines with ink, a dye, an instrument, or with anything[2] that will make a lasting mark.[3]

2.   The *melachah* includes such forbidden subsidiary activities (*Toladot*) as marking out a line on wood or tracing a line on stone in preparation for cutting, as is customarily done by woodcutters and stonecutters.

30. SCRAPING AND SMOOTHENING

מְחִיקַת הָעוֹר

1.   The objective of this *Av Melachah* is to remove coarse matter from the hide, and smooth its surface for further use.

The *melachah* comprises such forbidden primary activities as removing hair or wool from the hide of a dead animal by plucking or scraping with a sharp instrument in order to smoothen it.

2.   The *melachah* includes such forbidden subsidiary activities (*Toladot*) as plucking feathers from the wing of a chicken; scouring a utensil[1] with powder or an abrasive material or substance in order to

---

2.   Marking a Book or Paper With One's Fingernail   While some permit it, one should nevertheless refrain from making a mark in a book or on a sheet of paper with his fingernail, even though it does not leave a lasting impression. Tracing the form of a letter with one's fingernail is definitely not permitted. It is likewise not permitted to trace a line on paper, or on wood with an implement that will make a deep impression.

3.   Ice Skating on Shabbat   One should not skate on ice on *Shabbat* because the runners on the skates will leave a mark, even if it is not a lasting impression, apart from other prohibitions that are likely to be encountered while engaging in the sport.

1.   Washing Dishes With Liquid Soap   Dishes and utensils may be washed with liquid soap and dish washing substances that are not abrasive. On washing and drying dishes, see Melachah 11, note 15; Melachah 13, note 1; and Part III, paragraph 26 and notes.

polish and smoothen it; sharpening a knife on a grindstone; smearing (מְמָרֵחַ) wax, pitch, grease, salves,[2] creams,[3] ointments[4] and the like[5] on material or some other surface;[6] and polishing shoes with shoe polish.[7]

---

2. Applying a Salve and Bandaging a Wound   One is permitted to apply an antiseptic in liquid form or an antibacterial liquid directly to a wound on the Sabbath. It is permitted to apply a medicated bandage or dressing that was prepared before the Sabbath to a sore or a wound in order to protect it from irritation or infection. If a prepared bandage is not available, one may apply a salve, Vaseline, or ointment by squeezing it from the tube onto the wound or on the bandage, or by taking it from the jar or container with a stick and placing it on the bandage, or on the wound and covering it with a bandage, without smearing or rubbing it on. It is permitted to apply Vaseline to an infant in a similar manner to relieve a diaper rash or to prevent it. See Part V, paragraph 9 on bandaging a wound and applying medication on the Sabbath.

3. Use of Hair Cream, Oils, and Lotions   One may not apply hair cream or a pomade on the hair or scalp on the Sabbath. One may apply a small amount of hair oil or brilliantine to impart a sheen to the hair. It is permissible to apply a liquid lotion or oil to one's chapped hands or lips.

4. Use of Deodorants and Perfumes   One may apply or spray a perfume on one's body, but not onto clothing. One may use a roll-on underarm deodorant, and a deodorant spray on one's body, but not a deodorant stick. According to some authorities the deodorant should be unscented, so as not to perfume the hair. Some permit spraying a non-stiffening perfume on natural hair. However, it may not be sprayed on a wig. One may spray a deodorizer to freshen the air in a room.

5. Washing With Soap   One may not wash with a bar of soap on the Sabbath. However, the use of liquid soap is permitted.

6. Brushing One's Teeth   While some authorities take a lenient view, it is customary practice not to brush one's teeth with toothpaste on the Sabbath, and even without toothpaste, especially when it may cause bleeding of the gums. However one may rinse one's mouth with a mouthwash.

7. Polishing and Cleaning Shoes   It is not permitted to polish or shine

3.   Sealing a hole with wax, tar, and the like,[8] is Rabbinically forbidden, lest one transgress the *melachah* by smearing it on.

4.   The prohibition does not apply to food which is edible without being smeared or smoothened. It is therefore permissible to smoothen a dish of cereal, and to spread butter, margarine, cheese, jam, and the like, on bread.

31. CUTTING

חִיתּוּךְ הָעוֹר

1.   The objective of this *Av Melachah* is to cut off a portion of the hide to measure.

The *melachah* comprises such forbidden primary activities as cutting or tearing hides, leather, parchment or paper[1] to a particular size or shape, when it is cut or severed as it is usually done by hand or with an implement.

---

shoes on the Sabbath, but one may remove dust by hand or with a cloth, without shining. It is also permitted to remove dirt or mud that is still moist by rubbing the shoes lightly on a piece of wood, a doormat, and the like. Dry mud may not be removed by hand or with an instrument. One may pour water on one's leather shoes to remove even dry mud or dirt. One is not permitted to have a non-Jew polish his shoes on the Sabbath. If the non-Jew polished them, they may not be used until after *Shabbat*.

8.   Molding Clay   It is forbidden to mold or shape clay, wax, plastic, and the like, on the Sabbath. Children should be advised to refrain from shaping models out of such substances on the Sabbath.

1.   Tearing Paper Towels, Toilet Paper, and Tissues   It is not permitted to tear paper towels or toilet paper off a roll on the Sabbath, whether one tears along the perforation or not. In case of necessity one may tear the toilet paper, but he should do so in an indirect manner and not along the perforation. Tissues that are not completely separated and are still attached may not be torn apart. It is permitted to use tissues and paper towels on the Sabbath even if they are likely to tear.

2.　The *melachah* includes such forbidden subsidiary activities (*Toladot*) as trimming feathers for use in pillows and bedding; shaping a quill; sharpening a pencil; and cutting and shaping a piece of wood for some useful purpose. The prohibition applies as well to cutting, tearing or breaking metal, plastic, cloth and other materials to a desired shape or pattern.

3.　The prohibition does not apply to cutting up food that is edible and is being prepared for consumption.[2]

4.　Cutting materials wastefully, or without regard to size, but only playfully or for no purpose is not a transgression of the *melachah* but is nevertheless Rabbinically prohibited.

32. WRITING

כְּתִיבָה

1.　The objective of this *Av Melachah* is to write with a durable substance on durable material so that the writing will last.[1]

　　The *melachah* comprises such forbidden primary activities as

---

2. Cutting Up Food　It is permitted to cut food into portions to serve at a meal. However, one should not use a specially designed implement to cut food, such as fruits and vegetables, into particular shapes and designs.

1. Writing That Endures　One is in violation of the Biblical prohibition against writing, as in the case of all *melachot* on the Sabbath, only if it endures. The Mishnah states, "This is the general principle, whoever does work on the Sabbath, and his work endures is culpable" (*Shabbat* XII,1). Authorities differ as to the intent of the stated principle of the Mishnah. Rambam maintains that one is culpable if it lasts for the Sabbath day. However, authorities such as Rashi, Ran, and others understand the Mishnah to mean that the Biblical prohibition applies only if the work is of an enduring nature and is complete in itself, and it is not necessary to add to it.

writing[2] letters or numbers, in any script[3] and in any language, with pen, pencil, crayon or some other durable substance,[4] on any durable material such as paper, parchment, wood, cloth, clay, metal and the like.

2. The *melachah* includes such forbidden subsidiary activities (*Toladot*) as making marks or signs; tracing lines, designs or figures; reproducing[5] graphic material by means of printing,[6] typewriting and the like.[7] Making impressions[8] on wax[9] or other materials;[10] tearing

---

2. Writing in an Unusual Manner While the Biblical prohibition applies only if one writes in a normal fashion, it is Rabbinically forbidden to write on the Sabbath with the back of the hand, with one's foot or mouth, or in some other unusual manner. If a right-handed person writes with his left hand, and a left-handed person writes with his right hand, he is not culpable, but it is Rabbinically forbidden. If one is ambidextrous he is culpable if he writes with either hand.

3. Writing in Shorthand One is not permitted to write on the Sabbath using any script. Hence stenographic writing or shorthand, where characters or symbols are substituted for letters is a transgression of the *melachah.*

4. Writing With Chalk Writing with chalk on a blackboard on the Sabbath is a transgression of the *melachah,* since the writing will remain for a considerable time until it is erased.

5. Taking a Photograph It is not permitted to take a photograph with a camera, to develop the film, or to make prints from the film on the Sabbath. One may not have a non-Jew take his photograph unless it is an emergency and cannot be delayed until after the Sabbath.

6. Use of a Rubber Stamp It is not permitted to make an impression with a rubber stamp, or to arrange the letters in the rubber stamp on the Sabbath.

7. Xeroxing and Photocopying Xeroxing or making a photocopy of written material is a transgression of the *melachah* of Writing and is forbidden on the Sabbath.

8. Having Fingerprints Taken It is not permitted to have one's finger-

paper, leather, or other materials to form letters is likewise in violation of this *melachah.*

3. Rabbinical prohibitions include[11] writing and drawing with a substance or on materials that will not last.[12] It is therefore not permitted to write letters or draw designs on a misty or frosty window-pane, in sand, or on a dusty surface. However, one is permitted to make the shape of letters with one's finger in the air or on the table, since there is no visible impression.[13] It is not permitted to attach

---

prints taken on the Sabbath. If he cannot avoid it, one may have it done with a non-Jew pressing down on his finger.

9. Recording on a Phonograph or on Tape It is forbidden to make a recording on a phonograph disc or on magnetic tape on the Sabbath, for apart from other prohibitions, such as the use of electricity, it is also according to some authorities a violation of the *melachah* of Writing.

10. Writing on an Erasable Writing Pad It is not permitted to make impressions of letters or designs on a pad from which they can be erased by separating the upper sheet from the bottom part of the pad.

11. Instructing a Non-Jew to Write a Letter One is not permitted to instruct a non-Jew to write a letter or to send a telegram for him unless it is urgently necessary to do so, as for a sick person, or to perform a *mitzvah,* or if a great loss is involved.

12. Making Letters or Designs on a Cake or in Fruit It is not permitted to decorate a cake with icing in the form of letters or designs. It is permissible to squeeze icing or whipped cream onto a cake, so long as one does not form letters or special shapes or designs. One may use a scoop to dish out ice cream and the like. It is forbidden to cut letters or designs into the peel of an orange or other fruit.

13. Use of a Combination Lock One is permitted to use a combination lock on the Sabbath, which is operated by combining a series of numbers or letters, whereby the correct combination opens the lock.

letters¹⁴ or numbers made of silver and the like to material, as for example on a curtain or on clothing.¹⁵

4.   The Sages prohibited the transaction of business¹⁶ on the Sabbath, as it usually involves writing and it might lead to a violation of the *melachah.* The prohibition of doing business on *Shabbat* is, moreover, alluded to in the Prophets (Isaiah 58:13,14): "If you turn away your foot because of the Sabbath, from pursuing your business on My holy day; and call the Sabbath a delight, and the holy of the Lord honorable; and shall honor it, not doing your wonted ways, nor pursuing your business, nor speaking thereof. Then shall you delight yourself in the Lord, and I will make you to ride upon the high places of the earth, and I will feed you with the heritage of Jacob your father; for the mouth of the Lord has spoken it." The Rabbis understood this to mean that one may not attend to one's business affairs, or even speak of them on the Sabbath (*Shabbat* 113a, b). Inasmuch as there are scriptural allusions to the prohibition of transacting business on the Sabbath, as in the above verses in Isaiah, and in Nehemiah where it is declared to be "a desecration of the Sabbath"

---

14.   Combining Letters and Parts of a Puzzle   Children are permitted to play games where letters are combined to form a word, or to put together parts of a jig-saw puzzle to form a complete picture, provided the word or the picture is not set tightly in a frame or tightly interlocked. Young children need not, in any case, be forbidden to play such games. In a game where letters or designs are imprinted on squares that are set in a frame, it is permissible to move and rearrange the squares.

15.   Arranging Page Numbers During the Sabbath Services   It is permitted to arrange and rearrange page numbers on cloth or cardboard during services in the synagogue on *Shabbat* and *Yom Tov* to keep the congregation informed of the prayers in the *Siddur* or *Maḥzor,* provided they are not firmly fastened in place.

16.   Conducting Business on the Sabbath   In addition to the prohibition of writing there are other *melachot,* such as cutting to measure (חִיתּוּךְ) and the like, which are liable to be transgressed in the course of buying and selling and conducting business on the Sabbath.

(Nehemiah 10:32, 13:17), it is considered a "traditional law" (*divrei kabbalah*), which is as authoritative as Biblical law. Its transgression is, therefore, more severe than in the case of other Rabbinical prohibitions.[17]

5. Hence, it is forbidden on the Sabbath to buy[18] or sell, to hire[19] or rent, to borrow[20] or lend, whether by verbal agreement or by handing

---

17. Transacting Business Desecrates the Sabbath In discussing the halachic nature of the prohibition of transacting business on the Sabbath, *Ḥatam Sofer* notes that it is a transgression of a Rabbinical decree only if it is of an infrequent or occasional nature. But if one is regularly involved in conducting business on the Sabbath in his store or shop, or in shopping and the like, he desecrates the Sabbath and is in violation of a Biblical command, even if it does not involve an actual transgression of a *melachah*. The Torah ordained the Sabbath as a day of solemn rest, free of occupational and week-day activities that are not in accord with the spirit and observance of *Shabbat* as a holy day of rest.

18. Buying Property From a Non-Jew in Eretz Yisrael A Jew is permitted to buy property from a non-Jew in *Eretz Yisrael,* and have the non-Jew sign and register the deed of sale on the Sabbath. The Sages permitted this to be done for the sake of Jewish settlement of *Eretz Yisrael.*

19. Compensation for Services Rendered on Shabbat One who is hired to perform duties on the Sabbath, which in themselves are permissible, should not receive wages specifically for services rendered on *Shabbat,* but should be compensated by the week, the month, or the year. If it is for the performance of a *mitzvah,* as in the case of a doctor or a nurse, or a *ḥazan* for conducting the services, or a Reader for reading the Torah, it is permissible to compensate them for services rendered on *Shabbat.* However, it is best, even in the latter instances, to have the salary or compensation cover some duties performed during the week as well. The time and effort spent in preparation before *Shabbat* may be taken into consideration in this regard.

20. Borrowing on the Sabbath Borrowing and lending, where the loan passes into the possession of the borrower and is repayable after a considerable time, is not permitted on the Sabbath, for fear that the lender may write down the details of the loan. It is permitted, however, to borrow something

over the article in token of the transaction. It is, likewise, not permitted to weigh and measure, whether with a scale, a measuring utensil, or by hand. One may not repay a loan[21] on the Sabbath, or engage in other activities[22] that usually involve writing.[23]

6. In case of necessity, as when one needs food on the Sabbath, he may obtain it from the storekeeper, but without reckoning his account. One should, likewise, avoid mention of price, and the use of terms relating to buying and selling in requesting the article.

7. One may not give a gift on the Sabbath, as it resembles buying and selling, since the article leaves the possession of the donor and comes into possession of the recipient.[24] However, it is permitted if it

---

that one wishes to use and will itself be returned. When borrowing one should not say "lend me" (הַלְוִינִי), which implies that he wishes to keep the article for a lengthy period, and there is reason to fear that in this instance, as well, the lender may note it down in order to remember it. He should rather say "give me" (הַשְׁאִלֵינִי).

21. Repayment of a Loan If one obligates himself to repay a loan on a specified date which occurs on the Sabbath, he may do so by means of a pledge, or he may have a non-Jew repay it for him. If a non-Jew comes to repay a debt on the Sabbath, one may allow him to leave the money and to redeem his pledge or to exchange it, but he should not handle the money or make a reckoning of the loan. It is best that he not handle the pledge as well.

22. Having a Passport Validated Where it is urgently necessary, one may have his passport validated or stamped by a non-Jew on the Sabbath.

23. Mailing a Letter on Friday Opinions differ on the question of mailing a letter or a package on Friday. While authorities generally do not deem it to be prohibited, it is advisable not to post mail *erev Shabbat* in a district where there are Jewish employees in the Post Office who may handle the mail on the Sabbath. Where it is not probable that there are Jewish employees one need not avoid posting mail *erev Shabbat*.

24. Giving a Gift to a Bar Mitzvah Gifts on the occasion of a *Bar* or *Bat Mitzvah* should be given before or after *Shabbat*. Likewise, when the reci-

is needed for the Sabbath or if it is for the sake of a *mitzvah*. It is not permitted to cast lots on the Sabbath, as it may lead to writing.

8.   Judicial proceedings, both civil and criminal, marriage,[25] divorce, and *ḥalitzah* are forbidden on the Sabbath, as they are customarily accompanied by writing. It is also forbidden to confirm an agreement by handing over an object from one to the other of the contracting parties, because it is like a business transaction, except in the case of a dangerously ill person who has made a verbal declaration of his will. In such a case it is permitted in order to put his mind at rest. One is not permitted to perform the *mitzvah* of redeeming his son on the Sabbath, even with an article worth five *shekalim*, as it is similar to a business transaction.

9.   It is not permitted to gamble or to play games for profit, as it is like transacting business. One should likewise refrain from playing games that usually involve writing.[26]

---

pient is presented with a gift from the congregation, such as a *Siddur* or *Ḥumash*, as is customary in many synagogues, it should be given to him with the understanding that he only acquires it after *Shabbat*. Apart from the question of taking possession of the article on *Shabbat*, there is also the possibility of transgressing the prohibition of carrying on *Shabbat* where there is no *eruv*. Care should, therefore, be taken that the gift is not taken out of the synagogue until after *Shabbat*.

25.   A Wedding Delayed Until Shabbat   In an emergency, as when a wedding that was to take place on Friday is delayed until after nightfall, the marriage may be performed on *Shabbat* in order to avoid embarrassment to the bride and groom, and the considerable monetary loss that is likely to be incurred. The decision to have the wedding take place on the Sabbath, which is subject to certain conditions, should be made by Rabbinical authority. It is advisable that weddings should not be scheduled for Fridays, especially late in the day close to *Shabbat*.

26.   Games That Involve Score Keeping and Word and Picture Building   Games in which points are recorded and score is kept should not be played on the Sabbath, since such games usually involve writing. Games such as chess, checkers, and dominoes are permissible. A game, such as scrabble,

10. One may not read or examine commercial documents, such as bills of sale, invoices, promissory notes, contracts, business correspondence, and the like. One may not attend to or discuss his business affairs.[27] One should likewise refrain, as far as possible, from thinking of business matters on the Sabbath.

33. ERASING

מְחִיקָה

1. The objective of this *Av Melachah* is to erase writing of a durable nature in order to prepare the surface for new writing.

The *melachah* comprises such forbidden primary activities as erasing or obliterating writing that is durable by rubbing, smearing, blotting and scraping, whether by hand, by use of an eraser or an instrument, or by means of a chemical.

2. The *melachah* includes such forbidden subsidiary activities (*Toladot*) as erasing or obliterating markings, signs, designs, figures and the like.

3. The Rabbinical prohibition includes any erasures, even if not for the purpose of preparing space for new writing. It is, likewise, not

---

where the letters are put together loosely is permissible, but not if the letters are wedged tightly in a frame. Assembling a jig-saw puzzle is likewise prohibited. It is best to refrain from playing games such as Monopoly that use play money. Young children may play with puzzles and play paper money. Adults, and children who have reached the age of religious training, however, should not occupy their time with such games, but should devote themselves to learning Torah and to enjoyment more in keeping with the spirit of the holy Sabbath.

27. Attending to Communal and Charitable Affairs While it is not permitted to calculate or discuss business accounts on the Sabbath, one may do so in connection with a *mitzvah,* such as contributions to charity, attending to communal needs, donations to the synagogue and philanthropic and educational institutions, and purchasing *aliyot,* and other *mitzvot.*

permitted to remove letters or numbers that have been attached to some material, such as to clothing or to a curtain.[1]

4.   It is not permitted to tear or cut through writing in order to open a sealed letter or envelope, a sealed food wrapper, or a sealed wine or whiskey bottle. It is permissible to open and close a book that has letters or words stamped on the edges of the pages along its side.[2]

5.   A cake that is decorated with coloring in the form of letters or designs should not be cut in a way that the lettering and designs are spoiled when the cake is cut.[3] If the lettering and designs are made of the same ingredients, or of sugar, honey, jelly, chocolate, and similar food stuffs of a non-durable nature one may cut the cake without regard for the letters or designs. If it is in the course of eating the cake, one may break the letters or designs regardless of the nature of the ingredients.[4]

---

1.   Opening a Parochet With Lettering on It   The *parochet* covering the holy Ark generally consists of one piece of cloth. If it is made of two sections, care should be taken to construct it so that any words inscribed on the *parochet* are not parted as it is opened. However, if it was so constructed that a word is divided as the *parochet* is opened, it is still permitted to open and close the *parochet* on the Sabbath since this has no effect on the lettering itself. However, it is best to part the curtains somewhat before the Sabbath.

2.   Opening a Book With Lettering on the Edges   Most authorities do not consider opening a book with lettering on the edge of the pages to be subject to the prohibition of writing or erasing, as it is made to be opened and closed and the letters remain intact. It is advisable, however, to take account of the stricter view and to refrain from stamping books in this manner. One should preferably use another copy of the book if available.

3.   Removing a Slice of a Cut Cake   If the cake was cut before the Sabbath it is permitted to remove a portion in any case, even if the letters or designs are broken up in the process.

4.   Cookies Shaped or Impressed With Letters or Designs   It is permitted while eating to cut or break cakes or cookies that are baked in the shape of letters or designs, as well as cookies, crackers, biscuits, and chocolates that have a name or a trademark impressed on them. See Part III, paragraph 63 and notes.

34. BUILDING

בְּנִיָּיה

1.   The objective of this *Av Melachah* is to construct, erect, add to, or assemble a structure.

The *melachah* comprises such forbidden primary activities as (a) building a permanent structure on the ground, constructed of wood, stone, brick, mortar, or other building materials; (b) preparing or improving the ground, or whatever is attached to the ground, by digging or filling a hole, or leveling the ground and the like for the purpose of building or for habitation; (c) repairing, improving or adding to a structure, including hanging a door on its hinges, resetting a window, making a hole in the wall, opening a hole in the floor, or knocking a nail into the wall.

2.   The *melachah* includes such forbidden subsidiary activities (*Toladot*) as erecting a permanent tent, even if not attached to the ground; joining two boards or pieces of wood together, whether with a nail or glue, or by interlocking them in such a manner that they remain joined;[1] setting type in a printing press; making a vessel from earth, clay, glass or other materials; and assembling parts of a vessel or an implement,[2] as for example inserting the handle into an axe or a hammer. The *melachah* also includes activities of this nature involving

---

1.   Playing With Building Blocks   A child may play on the Sabbath with building blocks and similar toys where the pieces are placed on top or alongside each other, or loosely interconnected, but are not screwed or tightly joined together. It is permissible for an adult to help and instruct the child as well.

2.   Adjusting Binoculars   One is permitted to use binoculars or some other optical instrument, such as a telescope, on the Sabbath. It is permissible to adjust the instrument in order to focus it, as this is its normal use and does not involve assembling or disassembling any of its parts.

food stuff, as in making cheese, or pressing fruits such as figs or dates into a particular shape or mold.[3]

3.   As previously stated, it is forbidden to build a permanent structure, and to enlarge it or add to it in any manner. This includes plastering or cementing a wall, driving a plank into the wall or into the floor, inserting a peg and driving a nail into a wall, hanging a door on its hinges and setting a window in its frame. If the door or window is made to be opened and closed regularly in this fashion it is permissible. Thus, a window set on the roof as a skylight, or a door covering the entrance to the cellar, may be removed and set in place again. It is, likewise, permitted to lock a door or a window with a bolt or a latch. However, it is forbidden to close an opening in a wall or in a window with anything that is to be left there permanently. It is permitted to close the opening with something that will only be kept there temporarily.

4.   Erecting a permanent tent, even if it is not attached to the ground, is in violation of the *melachah* of Building, provided (1) the tent is set up for an extended period of time, that is for at least eight or nine days; (2) it consists of at least three partitions with a covering over them; and (3) it measures at least one handbreadth (*tefah*) by one handbreadth to the height of a handbreadth at the top or within three handbreadths from the top.

5.   Rabbinical prohibitions include building a temporary[4] struc-

---

3.   Cutting Food into Decorative Shapes   One should not mold food into a particular form, or use an instrument designed to cut fruit such as melons into particular shapes for decorative purposes.

4.   Opening and Closing Folding Chairs, Tables and Beds   It is permitted to open and close a folding chair and a folding table on the Sabbath, as they are constructed to be used in this manner. One may extend the length of a table by lifting or adding a leaf. It is permitted to open and close a folding cot or a bed, such as a hi-riser or a convertible couch. See Part III, note 95.

ture;[5] erecting a tent that is temporary; digging or filling a hole in the ground without any intention to build, and certain activities that might lead to digging a hole or leveling the ground, such as dragging heavy furniture on the ground.

6.   It is not permitted to spread a cloth or other covering over partitions, even if there are less than three partitions, if it is for the purpose of shade or protection.[6] However, it is permissible if the cover was already partly extended before the Sabbath at least over an area of one handbreadth by one handbreadth or there are less than three handbreadths between the rings or loops upon which the cover is hung, as this is considered adding to a temporary tent which is permissible. If there are three or more partitions that extend to the ground it is not permitted to spread a covering over them, even if it is not for shade or protection, unless the covering was designated for the purpose before the Sabbath, or it is not intended as a covering. If there are not three partitions, and the covering is not for shade or protection or for some other use beneath it, it is permissible. Hence, it is permitted to place a board on table legs, as there are no partitions, nor is it intended to make a tent but only to use the board as a table. If the temporary structure does not in any way serve as a tent it is likewise permissible. One may not open an umbrella or a parasol, as it forms a tent and is intended for shade or protection from the rain.[7]

---

5.   Opening and Closing a Playpen or a Crib   It is permitted to open and close a collapsible playpen or crib. One may slide the latch and lock it in place, and lower or raise the mattress. However, it is not permitted to loosen or tighten any screws.

6.   Extending the Hood on a Baby Carriage   It is permitted to open and extend the hood on a baby carriage, provided it was attached to the carriage before the Sabbath. Some require opening the hood a handbreadth before the Sabbath and then extending it fully on the Sabbath. One may, likewise, spread a net over the carriage. See Part III, note 90.

7.   Opening and Carrying an Umbrella   One may not open or close an

7. Setting up a partition without a covering over it is permissible if it is intended for privacy or for beauty, such as hanging tapestry on the wall, in the home, or in a *sukkah,* or a curtain on the window or in a doorway, provided it does not require much effort or special skill. However, it is forbidden to set up such a partition if it is for the purpose of rendering something permissible, which for the lack of a partition would be prohibited or invalid. Thus, it is not permitted to put up a partition in order to create a private area so as to permit carrying on the Sabbath, or to put up a partition to serve as a necessary third wall for a *sukkah.* However, if the partition was already opened and extended up to a handbreadth (*tefaḥ*) before the Sabbath, one may open it fully on *Shabbat,* even if it is in order to render something permissible. Hence it is permitted to open out a folding screen or a folding door if it was already opened a handbreadth before the Sabbath.

8. A partition that is not fastened at the bottom and will therefore blow and flap in the wind is not considered a partition at all and may be put up on the Sabbath for any purpose.

9. It is forbidden to make a hole in a wall, or in anything that is attached to the ground. It is forbidden, as already noted, to dig a hole in the earth or to level the ground.[8] It is likewise not permitted to spread sand in the yard or on an unpaved floor in the house. If the

---

umbrella on the Sabbath. Nor should one carry an umbrella that was opened by a non-Jew or opened before the Sabbath, even where there is an *eruv.* See Part III, paragraph 82.

8. Playing Ball on Unpaved Ground   One may not play with a ball on ground that is not paved or surfaced. Playing ball on a table, a court or other area that is paved or surfaced is permitted, provided it is indoors, or where one may carry, and the ball is not likely to fall out of bounds. Children need not be prevented from playing ball games, even on unpaved ground. However, older children and adults are advised to refrain from playing ball on the Sabbath, and to devote their time to learning and to activities more in keeping with the holiness of the day.

sand was set aside before the Sabbath and kept in a designated place it is permitted to use it to spread over a paved floor or to cover excrement, provided the sand is not moist so that when one removes some of it one will not leave a hole in the sand pile.

10.   It is not permitted to sweep an unpaved floor as it may lead to leveling the holes or depressions in the earth. It is permitted to sprinkle water even over an unpaved, earthen floor in order to keep the dust from rising. One is permitted to pull a chair, a bench, or some other object over the ground, since he does not intend to make holes and tracks in the earth, provided the object is not so large or heavy as to inevitably leave holes or tracks in the earth. It is not permitted to pull up an object that is embedded in the ground, lest he come to level the hole in the earth. If one stored radishes in the field and some of the leaves are uncovered, he may grasp the leaves and pull them up, because he will not come to level the earth in the field.

11.   It is not permitted to set [9] one's hair[10] in braids or to undo one's braids on the Sabbath, as the interweaving of the strands of hair resembles building (בְּנִיָּיה), and undoing the braid resembles its demolition (סְתִּירָה).[11]

---

9. Setting the Hair   A woman may not set her hair in curlers on the Sabbath. However, she may gather the hair and arrange it by hand. She may also use a hairband, ribbon, hairpins, clips, or decorative combs to keep the hair in place, and she is permitted to wear them in the street, even where there is no *eruv*.

10. Use of a Hairspray   One may not use a hairspray, thickener, or lotion to stiffen and set the hair in place on the Sabbath. Some permit use of a hairspray to impart a sheen to the hair.

11. Braiding the Hair   Braiding the hair was forbidden as a Rabbinical ordinance. Some authorities, however, counsel against protesting the practice, inasmuch as women are greatly concerned with the appearance of their hair and may not heed the admonition. See Part III, paragraph 31 and notes.

35. DEMOLISHING

סְתִירָה

1. The objective of this *Av Melachah* is to demolish or break down any permanent structure, whether made of wood, stone, brick, mortar, or other materials, for a constructive purpose.

Forbidden primary activities involve the undoing of any of the operations that are indicated in the previous *melachah* of Building.

2. The *melachah* includes such forbidden subsidiary activities (*Toladot*) as dismantling a permanently erected tent; detaching and removing a plank from the wall or from the floor; separating boards or pieces of wood that were fastened together.

3. Whatever activity is considered a Biblical or a Rabbinical transgression of the *melachah* of Building similarly constitutes a Biblical or a Rabbinical transgression of the *melachah* of Demolishing when it involves the demolition of something that was constructed,[1] or undoing any of the operations that comprise the *melachah* of Building.

4. Rabbinical prohibitions include dismantling a temporary tent[2] and closing a folding partition which may not be erected or set up on the Sabbath. It is permissible to remove and replace the covers or side

---

1. **Opening a Locked Door**   If the key to the door of the house is lost one is not permitted to remove the door hinges or to break the lock. He may, however, open the lock with a knife or a pin. If a young child is locked in, it is permitted to remove the door or to break the door open, if need be, in order to free him. One may not delay and and seek to distract him until the key is found, as the child may be endangered by the severe fright.

2. **Opening and Closing the Roof or Covering Over a Sukkah**   When a *sukkah* is made with a roof that is attached and opens and closes on hinges, it is permitted to open and close the roof on *Shabbat* and on *Yom Tov*. It is also permitted to cover the *sukkah* with a plastic covering in order to protect it from the rain, and to uncover it on *Shabbat* and *Yom Tov*, taking care not to move the *schach* which is *muktzeh*.

panels of boxes and vessels if they are so constructed that they are normally opened and closed in this manner.

5.   It is not permitted to break open a vessel, or to take it apart, or to make a hole in it .[3] If it is necessary in order to have food on the Sabbath, or wine for *Kiddush,* it is permitted to break open a container or to open a carton, provided one does not thereby construct or form a vessel.[4]

36. KINDLING A FIRE

הַבְּעָרָה

1.   The objective of this *Av Melachah* is to kindle a fire that produces, prolongs or increases heat or light for the purpose of igniting, heating, lighting, cooking, baking, operating an engine or a motor, and the like.

The *melachah* comprises such forbidden primary activities as kindling a fire[1] by striking a match, or by lighting one fire from another, as well as increasing or prolonging a fire by raking the coals,

---

3.   Removing the Cork From a Bottle   It is permissible to remove the cork from a wine bottle with a cork screw, if necessary, even though it will make a hole in the cork.

4.   Opening Containers of Food   Cartons and containers of food should be opened before the Sabbath. For a discussion of the laws pertaining to opening them on the Sabbath when it becomes necessary to do so, see Melachah 24, note 5, and Part III, paragraph 51 and notes.

1.   Kindling a Fire With a Magnifying Glass   Igniting a fire by using a magnifying glass to concentrate the rays of the sun on combustible material is forbidden on the Sabbath.

and igniting a fire or producing heat or light[2] with a chemical substance.

2.   The *melachah* includes such forbidden subsidiary activities (*Toladot*) as adding oil to a lamp to keep the light burning; tilting or adjusting the lamp to facilitate the flow of oil to the flame; adding gasoline, wood, coal or other fuel to a tank or furnace to prolong the fire; heating metal to a glow.

3.   Rabbinical prohibitions include reading alone or examining an article closely by lamplight, lest one tilt the lamp for the oil to flow more freely in order to increase the light;[3] moving a lighted candle or lamp.

4.   Among the activities prohibited[4] under this *melachah* are smoking a cigarette, cigar or pipe; turning on or regulating the flame of a gas burner; starting the furnace;[5] opening a coal furnace, or a ther-

---

2.   Handling Synthetic Fabrics That Emit Sparks   Clothing made of synthetic fabrics that create static electricity and emit sparks when handled may be worn on the Sabbath.

3.   Reading by Electric Light   It is permissible to read by electric light, and perform other activities that require close concentration. The restriction does not apply to electric lights, even if the intensity of light in the bulb can be increased. The restriction also does not apply to gas light, or to lamps and candles which give off a good, steady light.

4.   Dropping Garbage into the Incinerator   In an apartment house, where the garbage is incinerated daily, it is not permitted on the Sabbath to drop garbage into the chute that leads to the cellar, where it is collected and burned in an incinerator on the Sabbath.

5.   Having a Non-Jew Light the Furnace   It is permissible to have a non-Jew light the fire in the furnace on the Sabbath in order to heat the house in cold weather, because everyone is susceptible to sickness in the cold. While it is permitted to explicitly request him to light the furnace on the Sabbath, it is best to arrange for it in advance, preferably on a contractual basis for the winter season.

mostatically controlled[6] gas oven,[7] and thereby igniting or intensifying the fire.[8]

5.   The use of electricity on the Sabbath is considered to be a violation of the *melachah* of Kindling a Fire (הַבְעָרָה).[9] Hence, activities involving the use of electricity, such as turning on an electric light and

---

6.   Activating the Thermostat That Controls Operation of the Furnace   In a heating system where a thermostat automatically controls the operation of the furnace, one may not raise the temperature setting on the Sabbath when the furnace is not in operation, as it is bound to start the fire in the furnace. One should refrain from raising the temperature setting even when the furnace is in full operation. However, one may open a door or a window in the room where the thermostat is located, even though it will lower the temperature in the room and activate the thermostat, thereby causing the furnace to operate and the heat to come up in the house.

7.   Use of an Oven With Thermostat Control   Many authorities prohibit keeping food warm on the Sabbath in a thermostatically-controlled gas or electric oven, because on opening the door of the oven to remove the food, thereby lowering the temperature, one may cause the thermostat to ignite the flame, or to intensify and prolong the fire if it is burning. Some, however, permit removing the food if necessary when the fire is off. See also Melachah 11, note 41.

8.   Opening a Door Near a Fireplace   One may not open a door or window directly opposite and near a fireplace if the wind will fan the fire causing it to burn more intensely. If there is no wind it is allowed, provided he does not cause a draft. Closing the door or window is allowed, even if it will restrict the supply of air in the room, causing the fire eventually to go out.

9.   Halachic Basis for the Prohibited Use of Electricity   The halachic status of electricity relative to its prohibited use on the Sabbath is problematic. The precise nature of the prohibition, and whether the proscription is Biblical or Rabbinical, is uncertain and the subject of controversy among halachic authorities. In the view of many authorities the use of electricity comes under the *melachah* of הַבְעָרָה, as it is presumed to involve kindling a fire and generating a spark when the electrical circuit is made. It is also classified by some authorities under the *melachah* of Cooking (בִּישׁוּל) on the

operating electrical equipment and appliances, are forbidden on the Sabbath. Although one is forbidden to switch the electric lights and appliances on during *Shabbat,* it is permitted to have lights burning on the Sabbath that were turned on *erev Shabbat* or automatically switched on during *Shabbat,* and to have certain appliances in operation on *Shabbat* that were switched on or set for operation *erev Shabbat.*[10]

---

presumption that the electrical current causes the wires to be heated. A novel view has been advanced by the *Ḥazon Ish* that making the electrical contact and completing the circuit, or breaking the contact and the electrical circuit are activities of the nature of Building (בְּנִיָּיה) and Demolishing (סְתִירָה). Some authorities ascribe it as well to the prohibition of forming or repairing a utensil (תִּקּוּן מָנָא), and of creating (מוֹלִיד), insofar as it entails the completion of an electrical circuit. While opinions thus vary as to the halachic basis of the prohibition, there is general agreement that it is forbidden on the Sabbath to switch the electric lights on and off, and to operate electrical appliances and equipment. For analysis of the technical and halachic principles involved in the analogies that are drawn, see the sources and references cited.

10. Operating Electrical Appliances by Means of a Time Clock The use of a timing device known as a time clock or time switch connected to an electrical circuit, that is set before the Sabbath to operate electrical equipment and appliances on the Sabbath is the subject of a difference of views among halachic authorities. Rabbi Moshe Feinstein permits use of the device when it is set before the Sabbath to put on the electric lights and to turn them off, but does not permit its general use for appliances. The prevailing view among authorities, however, permits use of the device, when set before the Sabbath, to turn the current on and off on the Sabbath on certain, select appliances as well. Opinions differ also as to the permissibility of adjusting the device on the Sabbath either to advance or delay the operation. While some authorities consider it a violation of a Biblical prohibition if the electrical current is on, and a Rabbinical prohibition if the current is off, others take a lenient view and permit adjusting the device on the Sabbath so that it will turn the current on or off at a later time, but not at an earlier time. See the following section, *Electrical Equipment and Appliances,* for particulars on use of the timing device with electric lights (#1), air conditioner (#4), radio and TV (#5), tape recorder (#10), dishwasher (#17), and an electric stove (see Melachah 11, note 25).

ELECTRICAL EQUIPMENT AND APPLIANCES

The following are additional notations on operating electrical equipment and appliances on the Sabbath. In view of technological advances in this field, one is advised to obtain technical and halachic guidance.

1. Turning Lights On and Off

Lighting an electric light involves the flow of an electric current through the wire or filament in the electric bulb, thereby heating it to incandescence and causing it to give off light. Lighting a fluorescent lamp entails the conduction of electricity through mercury vapor resulting in the emission of visible light. Turning on electric lights thus involves prohibited activities in the completion of an electric current and in the production of heat and light. It is permissible, however, to turn lights on and off at designated times on the Sabbath by means of a time clock set before the Sabbath. One should not reset the time on the clock on *Shabbat,* neither to advance or delay the operation.

2. Opening an Electric Refrigerator and Freezer

A standard electric refrigerator and freezer that is thermostatically-controlled operates automatically to cool the air when the temperature in the unit reaches a preset degree. By opening the door of the refrigerator, and allowing warm air to enter, the thermostat is activated, causing the compressor and the cooling mechanism to operate.

While some authorities permit opening the refrigerator and the freezer on the Sabbath to remove food or to put it in at all times, others require that it be opened only when it is in operation. However, one may not raise or lower the temperature setting at any time, whether it is in operation or not. Some recommend opening the door of the refrigerator in an indirect manner (כְּלְאַחַר יָד) when it is not in operation. Those who wish to comply with a more restrictive view are advised to install a timing device that will turn the motor off at designated times, allowing the unit to be opened at such times. In view of the new models of refrigerators and freezers that appear on the market periodically, one should ascertain the nature of the operation of a particular model in order to take the proper measures to remove any restrictions.

In any case, the light bulb that lights up when the door is opened and goes out when the door is closed should be removed or the switch taped before the Sabbath. If one failed to deactivate the light, he should have a non-Jew open the refrigerator to remove the food. In case of emergency, and a non-Jew is not available, one may unplug the cord of the refrigerator when it is not in operation. This should be done in an indirect manner, as with one's foot and the like.

3. Adjusting an Electric Fan

One is not permitted to adjust the speed on an electric fan on the Sabbath. However, one may move it and turn it to direct the flow of air in a desired direction.

4. Regulating Operation of an Air Conditioner

One is not permitted to adjust the controls of an air conditioner on the Sabbath in order to raise or lower the temperature. However one may open the door or window, although it will result in altering the temperature in the room. It is permitted to adjust the grille or the partitions while the air conditioner is in operation, so as to direct the flow of air. Many authorities permit use of a timer set before the Sabbath to turn on the air conditioner on the Sabbath. On a hot day it is permissible to request a non-Jew to turn on the air conditioner to obtain relief from the heat, even as it is permitted to have a non-Jew make the furnace to obtain relief from the cold. It is likewise permitted to have the non-Jew turn off the air conditioner if the weather should turn cold.

5. Listening to the Radio or Stereo and Viewing Television

One is not permitted to listen to the radio or to watch television on the Sabbath, even when it is turned on by means of a timing device that is set before the Sabbath, or it is turned on before the Sabbath. The prohibition applies to a transistor or battery operated radio, as well as one that is operated electrically. It is likewise prohibited to listen to music on a stereo or on a similar musical apparatus. Apart from the likelihood of turning the dials to adjust the volume or the picture, or to change stations, and even if one should take measures to prevent turning the dials, it is disruptive of the spirit of *Shabbat* and not in keeping with the holiness of the Sabbath day. In case of emergency, when it is essential to be informed of weather conditions and the like, one may set the radio before the Sabbath to go on at a designated time and listen discreetly, taking precautions to prevent turning the knobs.

6. Monitoring the Doorway With a TV

A television that monitors the area surrounding the doorway may be kept going on the Sabbath, if it is deemed necessary to screen those who come to the door, in order to protect one's home and family.

7. Using the Telephone

One is not permitted to use a telephone on the Sabbath, for on lifting the receiver one effects the completion of an electrical circuit, and by talking into the phone the sound of one's voice is converted into electrical impulses for transmission over the telephone wires. On replacing the receiver one breaks the circuit. In an emergency, as in the case of one who is critically ill, it is permissible to make a telephone call. Thus, one may phone for an ambulance, to summon a car for a woman in labor, for police in case of a break-in by a robber, for firemen in case of a fire and a possible danger to life, however remote. If possible, one should lift the receiver and replace it in a manner different from the usual.

8. Use of a Telephone Answering Machine

One may use a telephone answering machine that is programmed before the Sabbath to answer a call and to convey a message to the effect that one cannot answer the phone, or that the office or business is closed and will be open at a certain time, and requesting the caller to leave a message. It is best not to ask the caller to place an order on the phone unless one is concerned that he will suffer a considerable loss of business. It is permissible to use an answering service operated by non-Jews to convey a similar message as on an answering machine.

9. Use of a Microphone and Loudspeaker

One is not permitted to use a microphone or loudspeaker on the Sabbath, irrespective of whether it is operated by electrical current or by means of a transistor. It is not permissible even if the apparatus was turned on before the Sabbath or by a non-Jew on the Sabbath.

10. Operating a Tape or Video Recorder or a Phonograph

Operating a tape or video recorder involves the conversion of sounds or pictures into electric waves, which are recorded on magnetic tape, and the reconversion of the electric signals into sounds or pictures when the tape is played back. It is therefore forbidden to record or to operate a tape or video recorder on the Sabbath, even if it was turned on before the Sabbath, or set for operation by means of a timing device. It is likewise forbidden to operate a phonograph on the Sabbath.

11. Ringing an Electric Doorbell

It is not permitted to ring an electric doorbell on the Sabbath because on pressing the button one completes an electrical circuit that operates the bell. If one is in danger of being locked out at night, or in a similar emergency, some permit ringing the doorbell in order to enter the house or to summon help. In such a case he should do it in a manner different from the usual, such as with his elbow, his foot, his left hand, and the like. For the ruling regarding a doorbell that operates mechanically, see Melachah 38, note 19.

12.   Opening a Door That Operates Automatically

One may not enter or exit a doorway, if in opening the door he causes a light to go on, or if in stepping on or across the threshold he activates a photo-electric or an electromagnetic mechanism, causing the door to open automatically. In case of doubt, whether or not the door opens automatically, one is permitted to enter.

13.   Installing a Burglar Alarm System

There are various types of alarm systems designed to protect the home from intruders. They are mainly operated by an electrical circuit which sounds a bell or a siren when a door or window is forced open. In installing a burglar alarm system one must take into consideration the halachic problem of closing and breaking the electrical circuit on entering and leaving the premises. Several systems have been proposed, though not all of them are universally accepted or fully operable, as solutions to the halachic problem, including the open circuit system, a system utilizing a bypass switch, and the use of a time clock. It is advisable that one obtain technical and halachic guidance regarding the security system to be installed.

14.   Riding in an Elevator

One is forbidden to use an elevator on the Sabbath when it entails activating an electrical current by pressing a button to summon the elevator and to open the doors, or to operate the elevator.

Halachic literature reflects differing opinions on the question of riding in an elevator that operates automatically, either continually or at designated intervals, and the doors open and close automatically. Automatic elevators, such as the standard traction elevator or the hydraulic elevator, may pose halachic problems by virtue of the technical nature of their operation, including speed of descent, switching signal lights, and braking, which are affected by the presence or absence of passengers. According to some authorities one is permitted to ride in an automatic elevator, taking care not to touch the doors with his hands or any part of the body when they are closing, lest he cause the doors to open. Others permit riding in an automatically operated elevator only in case of extreme need, as when one is ill or elderly, or to enable one to pray with a *minyan*.

One may not ride in an elevator that is operated by a Jew. If it is operated by a non-Jew, some permit one to ride in the elevator, provided he enters and leaves along with other non-Jews, and does not request that it stop on his floor. Others do not permit it, except in case of illness or in an emergency. One accompanying a critically ill person may ride the elevator with him.

In general, it is recommended that when one must use the elevator, he should do so, if possible, only for ascent, and use the stairs for descending.

15.   Riding on an Escalator

An escalator that is set in motion when one approaches it, or when one steps on it, may not be used on the Sabbath. However, if it operates automatically, either continually or at designated times, it is permitted to ride the escalator up or down.

16.   Use of an Intercom or an Apnea Monitor

An intercom, consisting of a two-way communication system with a microphone and loudspeaker at each station, may not be used on the Sabbath. Thus, one may not use an intercom in one's apartment to communicate with someone seeking entrance to the apartment house. Nor is it permissible under normal circumstances to use an intercom to monitor children in another part of the house. This restriction, however, does not apply in a dangerous situation, or in the case of a child with a critical condition, such as one prone to apnea, a serious respiratory condition that requires the use of an apnea monitor to monitor the child when asleep. In such a case it is permitted and one should consult halachic authority for guidance.

17.   Use of a Dishwasher

One is not permitted to use a dishwasher to wash the dishes on the
Sabbath, even if it is set for operation on a timer before the Sabbath.
However, one may stack the soiled dishes in the machine on the Sabbath without sorting them. It is likewise permissible to remove dishes
from the dishwasher. One should ascertain the nature of the operation of the newer models, however, to determine if it is permissible to
open it on the Sabbath. See Part V, Chapter 5, note 8.

18.   Use of a Heating Pad

One may use an electric heating pad on the Sabbath if it is turned on
before the Sabbath. The temperature controls and the outlet should
be taped to prevent one from inadvertently resetting the temperature
or turning it off. It is permissible to have a non-Jew turn it on and
regulate the temperature on the Sabbath.

19.   Use of an Electric Blanket

One is permitted to use an electric blanket on the Sabbath, provided
it is plugged into the electrical currrent and turned on before the Sabbath. The temperature controls and the outlet should be covered or
taped to prevent one from inadvertently adjusting the heat or turning
it off. The above deals only with the halachic considerations in the
matter. It does not address the safety factors that should be considered in the use of an electric blanket generally, and in particular
under such circumstances.

20.   Using Electronic and Battery-Operated Devices

A device or an instrument that utilizes a transistor to control the flow
of electricity in its operation, as in computers and other electronic
devices and equipment, may not be used on the Sabbath. An
appliance, such as a flashlight or a portable radio, that operates on
electric current produced by batteries, is likewise forbidden on the

Sabbath. In the case of toys that operate with batteries, the batteries should be removed before the Sabbath.

21. Doors Equipped With Electronic Locks

Various types of electronic locks are being installed in hotels and institutions as a substitute for ordinary locks in order to prevent theft. The plastic coated card that serves as a key is outfitted with a magnetic tape. The magnetic code on the key aligns the tumblers within the lock body to free the bolt and open the door. Each room is given a number combination and the numerical code is changed when the hotel room is vacated or the card is lost or stolen. It is not permitted on the Sabbath to insert the card into the electro-magnetic lock to open the door, in view of the halachic problems and prohibitions currently involved in activating electrical sensors and the switching on of lights in the mechanism. When encountering such an unavoidable situation, one should arrange before the Sabbath for a non-Jewish attendant to open the door.

22. Wearing a Digital or Battery-Powered Watch

It is permissible to wear a watch that is powered by a battery, where it is permitted to carry on the Sabbath, but one may not insert the battery to make it work. A digital watch that lights up the time by pressing a button may be worn, according to some authorities, if the time is visible without the light, and the button is taped as a precaution against pressing it on the Sabbath.

23. Wearing a Hearing Aid

One who is hard of hearing may wear a hearing aid on the Sabbath. If it is battery operated it should be turned on before the Sabbath. It is permissible to adjust the volume, if necessary, but not to turn it on or off, or to replace the battery. Precautions should be taken to prevent turning it off inadvertently. A hearing aid that operates automatically without batteries for an extended period of time is preferable. Technical and halachic guidance is advised as regards the operation of modern hearing aid devices that are being produced. If the hearing aid is attached to one's eyeglasses or worn in the ear, it may be worn outdoors. Some also permit wearing one that is attached to one's clothing. See Part IV, Chapter 4, note 18.

37. EXTINGUISHING A FIRE

כִּיבּוּי

1.   The objective of this *Av Melachah* is to extinguish a fire, or to decrease it, or to slow its progress for some productive purpose.

The *melachah* comprises such forbidden primary activities as blowing out a flame, raking the coals to put out a fire, extinguishing a fire with one's hands, stamping on it, pouring water over it, covering it with sand or earth, spraying it with chemicals, and the like. The *melachah* of Extinguishing a Fire is applicable to any of the processes described in the previous *melachah* of Kindling a Fire.

2.   The *melachah* includes such forbidden subsidiary activities (*Toladot*) as removing oil from a burning lamp, tilting or adjusting it so as to impede the flow of oil to the flame, removing some fuel from a tank or other container that is supplying the fuel to feed the fire.

3.   It is not permitted to extinguish a fire[1] for any reason, even if it is not for some productive purpose. Among the prohibited activities are

---

1.   Opening a Door or Window Opposite a Burning Candle   One should not open a door or a window directly opposite a burning candle lest it be extinguished by the wind blowing in from the outside. In case of necessity one may open the door or window gradually so as not to cause a sudden draft that might extinguish the flame. The Sabbath candles should therefore be placed where they will be protected from a draft or the wind blowing in from the outside.

turning off or lowering the flame of a gas[2] or electric burner, extinguishing a fire by closing off its supply of air, shutting off a motor, turning off an electric light[3] or a battery powered flashlight, disconnecting[4] or turning off[5] any electrical equipment or appliance.[6]

2. Turning Off the Gas if the Flame Goes Out on the Stove If the gas flame on the stove is accidentally extinguished on the Sabbath it is permitted to turn off the gas, as the continued flow of gas constitutes a danger. If possible it should be done in a manner different from the usual.

3. Extinguishing a Light for a Dangerously Ill Person In the case of a dangerously ill person it is permissible to put out a light if it keeps him from falling asleep or causes him discomfort. One should first try to shade the light or move the sick person to another room, provided moving him will not aggravate his condition. If need be, one should remove the lighted candle or lamp, rather than extinguish it. If a non-Jew is readily available, he should be requested to remove or extinguish the light. The lenient ruling above in the case of a dangerously ill person applies as well to kindling a light on his behalf if it should be necessary to do so.

4. Turning a Switch Off When the Current Is Disconnected One should not remove a plug from an electric socket or turn an electric switch off on the Sabbath, even when the electric current is disconnected, as the plug and switch are *muktzeh*. Some permit removal of the plug and turning the switch off when the current is disconnected, if necessary, to prevent it from coming on again, by doing so in some manner different from the usual, such as with the elbow or with one's foot.

5. Turning the Switch Off and On During a Power Failure In the event that the electricity is cut off as a result of a general power failure it is permitted, in the opinion of some authorities, to turn the switch off to keep the lights and electrical appliances from going on when the current returns. If possible this should be done in a manner different from the usual. In a case of extreme necessity some permit turning the switch on so that the lights and electrical equipment will go on again when the current is reconnected.

6. Disconnecting an Electric Current When an electric current is disconnected, and an electric light or electrical equipment is turned off, it is a transgression of the *melachah* of Extinguishing (כִּיבּוּי). As with regard to the use of

4.   The prohibition against extinguishing a fire does not apply where there is possible danger to human life. In such a case, when a fire breaks out and there is cause to fear that it may spread, it should be promptly extinguished.[7] One may not directly extinguish a fire only to save material possessions.[8] But one may take indirect measures to keep it from spreading and to cause it to be extinguished, such as pouring water in its path, and the like. Likewise, if a burning candle should fall onto the table[9] one may shake it off the table, even if it is thereby extinguished.

---

electricity and electrical equipment and appliances, while opinions differ as to the basis of the prohibition and whether it is Biblical or Rabbinical (See Melachah 36, note 9), there is general agreement that it is forbidden on the Sabbath.

7.   Putting Out a Fire in a House or Apartment   If a fire breaks out in an apartment or in a house on the Sabbath, whether it is in one's own house or apartment or in that of a neighbor, one is duty bound to extinguish it, inasmuch as under present-day conditions it constitutes a possible danger to life. It is permitted to sound the alarm and to use the telephone to summon the fire department. If it is certain that there is no possible danger, one can resort to other measures to contain the fire and keep it from spreading, by hosing down the area around it, or by covering it without actually extinguishing it.

8.   Saving Money and Other Valuables From Loss   It is permitted to handle money and other valuables on the Sabbath, even if they are *muktzeh,* in order to save them from loss by fire, flood, or robbery. For further discussion of the rules with regard to saving valuables in case of a fire, see Part IV, Chapter 5.

9.   Placing a Vessel Under a Burning Candle   It is permitted to place a vessel under a candle or a lamp in order to catch the falling sparks, but one may not fill it with water even before the Sabbath. If there is a danger of fire, should the sparks or the burning candle fall onto the table, one may have a vessel placed under it, with water if necessary.

38. STRIKING THE FINAL HAMMER BLOW

מַכֶּה בַּפַּטִּישׁ

1.   The objective of this *Av Melachah* is to put the finishing touch in the manufacture of an article, to "strike the final hammer blow," as it were, in any type of construction.

The *melachah* comprises forbidden acts, however slight, that signify the final stage in completion of the work, such as the craftsman's final blow with the mallet to level out any unevenness in a vessel he has made and the bricklayer's final tap with the trowel on a brick to set it in the foundation and to align it with the row of bricks he has laid.

2.   The *melachah* includes such forbidden subsidiary activities (*Toladot*) as blowing glass to shape it;[1] inscribing a figure on a vessel; putting a glossy finish on an article; boring a hole that can serve as an opening for putting in and taking out in a vessel or in a building; chiseling a stone to make it smooth; opening a buttonhole or neck-opening in a garment when the hole and the opening had been sewn together;[2] removing the knotted ends of wool or the protruding

---

1.   **Blowing Up Rubber and Plastic Articles**   Articles made of rubber or plastic, such as a cushion, a pillow, a ball, and balloons of all shapes with pictures and designs may be blown up with air on the Sabbath. One may use a stopper or a rubber band to plug the opening, but one may not tie the balloon or the article itself, nor may he tie it with a string.

2.   **Separating Clothing Tied or Sewn Together**   Articles of new clothing, such as a pair of socks or gloves, that come sewn or tied together should be taken apart before the Sabbath. If one failed to do so, he may not untie the knot on the Sabbath. Some permit severing the connecting thread, since the articles were intended to remain tied only for a period of time and not permanently.

threads from a woven garment, and the stitching or basting thread from a sewn garment.[3]

3.   Forming or improving a utensil (תִּיקוּן מָנָא) is, likewise, a derivative (*Toladah*) of the *melachah*. Hence, the repair[4] of any instrument, equipment[5] or appliance is forbidden.

Prohibited activities include also sharpening a knife, straightening a crooked pin;[6] inserting shoelaces into new shoes,[7] or laces into a new garment.[8]

---

3.   Removing Pins From a New Shirt   It is permissible to remove the pins with which a new shirt is secured during packing to keep it from being creased.

4.   Winding Up a Mechanical Toy   It is not permitted to wind up a mechanical toy on the Sabbath. However, one need not prevent children from playing with such toys as racing cars or robots that have to be wound up, provided they do not produce sparks or a distinctive sound.

5.   Use of a Plunger to Unclog a Sink or Toilet   One may clear a temporarily clogged sink or toilet with a plunger or a snake, if it is urgently necessary to do so. One may cover the drain in the sink with a perforated cover, or plug it with a stopper.

6.   Repairing Eyeglasses   One may not repair eyeglasses by straightening a bent frame, or replacing the lens that fell out of the frame.

7.   Inserting Laces into Shoes   Shoes today are so constructed that the laces no longer serve to bind the shoe together, as in the past, hence the insertion of laces does not constitute a transgression of the *melachah*. The only consideration is whether inserting the laces involves undue effort. Therefore, if the shoelaces have metal or plastic tips, or the eyelets are large enough, or they are reinforced with metal or plastic, thereby facilitating the insertion of laces, it is permitted to insert the shoelaces, irrespective of whether the shoes or the laces are old or new.

8.   Inserting a Belt into a Garment   It is permitted to insert a belt into a new pair of trousers or into a new dress, since it is not left there but is regularly removed.

4. Rabbinical prohibitions include immersing a vessel in a *mikveh* for ritual purification, since that would render it finally fit for use;[9] separating the *hallah* portion from dough, as that would make it finally fit to be eaten;[10] winding[11] a watch[12] or a clock.[13]

---

9. Immersing a Vessel in a Mikveh If necessary, one can immerse the vessel on the Sabbath by dipping the vessel and drawing water with it. In such a case the blessing should not be recited. If lack of the utensil will deprive him of a meal on the Sabbath, one may immerse it in a *mikveh* in the usual way. For the laws pertaining to the ritual immersion of utensils, see Volume One, Part III, Chapter 11.

10. Separating the Hallah Portion If one forgot to separate the *hallah* portion before the Sabbath he may still eat the bread on *Shabbat*, but he should leave a piece of it uneaten and set it aside. After *Shabbat* he must take *hallah* from the portion that was set aside. This procedure may be followed outside the Land of Israel, but not in Eretz Yisrael. For the laws regarding separation of the *hallah* portion, see Volume One, Part IV, Chapter 4.

11. Winding a Watch Opinions differ on the question of winding a watch or a clock on the Sabbath. Some consider winding it when it has stopped as coming under the prohibition of repairing an instrument (תִּיקוּן מָנָא). Others, however, contend that this is the way it is designed to operate and they do not consider it a violation of the *melachah*. While most authorities permit winding a watch or a clock while it is still going and setting the hands to the correct time, it is common practice to refrain from doing so unless it is needed to determine the time for some urgent matter, as for the sake of a sick person to enable him to take his medicine at specified times, or for the performance of *mitzvot*, such as prayer and Torah study. See Part III, paragraph 86 and notes.

12. Wearing a Self-Winding Watch A wristwatch that winds itself automatically with the movement of the wrist may be worn on the Sabbath as long as it is working. On wearing a wristwatch in the street where there is no *eruv*, see Part IV, Chapter 4, paragraph 2 and notes.

13. Setting an Alarm Clock to Ring on Shabbat An alarm clock that operates mechanically may be set *erev Shabbat* to ring on the Sabbath. When the alarm rings one may shut it off. It is also permitted to shut off the

5. The Rabbis have also prohibited certain activities because they might lead one to make or repair an instrument to be used for that activity.[14] Thus it is not permitted to swim in a body of water, such as the ocean, a river or a lake, lest one fashion a tube or a raft to keep afloat.[15] Sailing and rowing in a boat and riding a bicycle[16] are similarly prohibited. It is not permitted to play a musical instrument lest

----

alarm on Friday evening to keep it from ringing, and then to release the alarm so that it will ring at the appointed time on Sabbath morning, if it is necessary for the sake of a *mitzvah* and the like. One may not shut off the alarm on an electric alarm clock, as it involves breaking an electrical circuit.

14. Clapping One's Hands and Dancing Pursuant to this decree the Rabbis prohibited clapping one's hands and dancing on the Sabbath, lest one come to prepare a musical instrument. Rabbi Yosef Karo records this prohibition in the *Shulḥan Aruch*. The Rama, however, advises against protesting the practice, stating that it is preferable that people transgress in ignorance (בְּשׁוֹגֵג), since they will not heed any admonition in this regard. He also cites the view of some authorities that it is permitted nowadays, because we are not ordinarily capable of making musical instruments, and it would be rare for one to do so. Ashkenazim follow the lenient view of Rama and permit clapping and dancing, provided it is done in honor of the Torah, or for the sake of a *mitzvah,* as on Simḥat Torah and in honor and rejoicing for a bride and groom, or to soothe an infant and keep it from crying. Sefardim adhere to the stricter view of the *Shulḥan Aruch*.

15. Swimming on the Sabbath While swimming is prohibited, it is also customary not to bathe even without swimming in a natural body of water, or in a pool, as it is likely to lead to the transgression of Sabbath laws. Immersion in a *mikveh* when necessary, however, is permissible. For the laws of bathing on the Sabbath, see Part V, Chapter 1.

16. Riding a Bicycle One is not permitted to ride a bicycle on the Sabbath lest he come to repair it. However, a child may be allowed to ride a tricycle or a bicycle with training wheels, and the like, when it is evident that it is designed for use by children. He may ride it in the house, in the yard, or where there is an *eruv*. It is advisable to remove the bell or horn or to make it unusable before the Sabbath. See Part III, note 108.

one will come to repair it. Hence one may not even produce a musical sound on any instrument or any sound on a musical instrument[17] or on a device designed for that purpose, such as a bell[18] or a knocker on a door.[19]

6.   The Rabbis have furthermore prohibited creating something new (מוֹלִיד) on the Sabbath, inasmuch as it resembles the performance of a *melachah*. Thus, one may not crush snow[20] or hail so that the water

---

17.   Use of a Tuning Fork by the Ḥazan   Opinions differ with regard to the use of a tuning fork by the *hazan* while leading the prayer service on *Shabbat*. Some authorities prohibit its use, as it entails producing a sound on a musical instrument. Others, however, condone its use by the *hazan,* noting that the tuning fork emits a fixed tone which is heard momentarily only by the *hazan,* who deems it essential in order to ascertain the proper pitch, so that he may perform the *mitzvah* of leading the congregation and inspiring the worshipers to devotion in prayer. For further discussion of the use of a tuning fork and a pitch pipe, see Part I, Chapter 6, note 7.

18.   Sounding a Bell or a Rattle for a Child   One should refrain from sounding a bell or a rattle for a child's amusement. However, it may be countenanced if it is done in order to keep the child from crying. One may dress a child with shoes or slippers that are fitted with bells which tinkle when they walk, as it gives the child pleasure and helps to know the child's whereabouts. See also Part III, paragraph 87 and notes.

19.   Sounding a Doorbell or a Knocker   In case of necessity, as when one cannot enter the house otherwise, it is permitted to ring a doorbell or sound a knocker that operates mechanically. If possible, he should sound the bell or knocker in a manner different from the usual, with his foot, his left hand or an elbow, and the like. The above also applies in the case of a door that has a bell attached to it, which is set to ringing when one enters. If it is urgently necessary, one may use the door to enter and leave the premises. For the laws pertaining to a bell that operates electrically, see Melachah 36, *Electrical Equipment and Appliances,* note 11.

20.   Melting Ice in a Glass of Water   It is not permitted to melt ice in an empty container in order to drink the water. However, one may put ice into a glass of water, wine or other liquid so that the ice will melt and cool the

will melt[21] and begin to flow, for in doing so one brings the water into existence on the Sabbath.[22] One is also not permitted to put any perfume on a garment, because it generates a fragrance (מוֹלִיד רֵיחָא) in the garment;[23] nor may one pour a perfume into water in order to impart an aroma to it, because it produces a fragrance in the water.[24]

---

drink. Some authorities even permit crushing the ice, since the water flowing from it mixes with the liquid immediately and is not discernible. In an automatic ice cube dispenser one should take care that the electrical circuit is not activated when removing the ice cubes. The mechanism should be deactivated before the Sabbath. See Melachah 5, note 11.

21. Spreading Rock Salt on Ice One may spread rock salt or sand on ice, where it is permissible to carry on the Sabbath, in order to prevent one from slipping on the ice. This should be done not in public view, and in a manner different from the usual, by pouring it from the bag or container and the like. If possible one should have it done by a non-Jew.

22. Making Ice Cubes and Refreezing Ice Cream Opinions differ regarding the permissibility of making ice cubes on the Sabbath by placing water in trays to be frozen in the freezer. Many authorities permit it in case of necessity. Ice cream that has begun to melt may be returned to the freezer to be frozen. One may put milk, cooked meat and the like into the freezer, and when needed they may be removed and thawed out. See Melachah 5, note 10; Part V, Chapter 3, note 9.

23. Use of Perfume, Air-freshener, and Insect Repellent One may apply perfume to one's hands, face and other parts of the body, but not to a handkerchief or an article of clothing. One may spray an air-freshener in order to clear a foul odor in a room. One may spray an insect repellent on one's person and in the air in order to repel, but not to kill, mosquitos and other insects.

24. Scenting Food and Drink While it is not permitted to scent water for washing or for its fragrance, one may add an aromatic essence or spice to food or liquid in order to improve its taste, or to make the food or drink more pleasant.

7. It is forbidden to prepare (הַכָנָה) on the Sabbath for a weekday.[25] Neither is it permitted to do so for *Yom Tov* or for the coming Sabbath. The prohibition applies to whatever a person does, of which he has no need for that Sabbath. Hence, it is not permitted to prepare food on the Sabbath for the express purpose of eating it after *Shabbat*. One may not fold garments[26] in their original folds[27] for use after the Sabbath; neither may one arrange the beds[28] for use after the

---

25.   Prohibition of הַכָנָה   The prohibition of preparing on the Sabbath for a weekday is not classified under this *melachah,* although in several instances of הַכָנָה, as in folding garments, making the beds, and washing the dishes on the Sabbath, the *Tiferet Yisrael,* and probably Rambam as well, take the prohibition to be that of forming or improving a utensil (תִּיקוּן מָנָא).

26.   Folding Garments on the Sabbath   Occasionally folding a garment in order to put it away in a drawer would not be prohibited, inasmuch as the prohibition originally applied to garments that had to be folded and pressed to retain their proper shape. Garments are presently folded usually because one is not concerned with retaining their shape, and folding them would in all likelihood not serve to do so in any event. However, one should not fold, sort and store garments that have accumulated after a wash, as this would be engaging in a weekday activity on the Sabbath. See also Part III, paragraph 91 and notes.

27.   Folding a Tallit on Shabbat   Authorities, such as *Magen Avraham* and *Mishnah B'rurah,* do not permit folding a *tallit* on *Shabbat* morning after prayer, except where it is customary to wear a *tallit* again during the *Minḥah* service. Others permit it if the *tallit* is not folded in its original folds. Some permit folding it in the same folds, especially if one wears that *tallit* only on *Shabbat*. The reason given for permitting it is that it is a טַלִית שֶׁל מִצְוָה, a *tallit* used in performance of a *mitzvah,* and the duty to beautify a *mitzvah* (הִידוּר מִצְוָה) requires that the *tallit* be kept in good condition and not subject to being torn and soiled when left unfolded every Sabbath. See also Part V, Chapter 12, note 26.

28.   Making the Beds on the Sabbath   It is permitted to make the beds, and change the sheets and pillow cases on Friday evening for use on the Sabbath, although it is best to arrange the beds before the Sabbath. It is also

Sabbath, nor wash dishes that are not needed again for use on the Sabbath.[29]

8. Whatever one does without deliberation, which does not require effort, may be done on the Sabbath even if it results in a benefit for the weekday, provided one does not specify that he is doing it in preparation for the weekday. Thus, if one brought a *tallit* to the synagogue on *Shabbat,* he may take it home after the prayer service, provided it is permissible to carry. It is permitted, likewise, to put leftover food back into the refrigerator. Upon leaving the house on *Shabbat* one may take along a sweater to wear in the evening, if there is an *eruv* and it is permitted to carry.

9. One is permitted to do something that is not forbidden and does not require excessive effort, which cannot be done after *Shabbat,* and failure to do it will result in a considerable loss. Thus, one may soak meat, if the third day after it was slaughtered is a Sabbath, and he failed to soak it before *Shabbat,* in order to prevent the meat from being prohibited to be cooked afterwards (see Melachah 28, note 2; Volume One, Part III, Chapter 7, paragraph 28 and notes). One is permitted to remove utensils that may be handled on the Sabbath to keep them from being stolen, and to take in clothing from the yard,

---

permitted to make the beds and straighten the covers on Sabbath morning in order to keep the house tidy in honor of *Shabbat.* See Part III, paragraph 93 and note.

29. Washing Dishes and Other Utensils It is permitted to wash the dishes and silverware on the Sabbath for use at the Sabbath meals until the third meal (*seudah shlishit*), and even later if they will be used afterwards as well. Glasses and other drinking utensils may be washed all day, because there is no fixed time for drinking and they are likely to be used at any time. If the dirty dishes are unsightly and will attract insects or cause a foul odor, they may be placed in water, or rinsed, and if necessary washed, even if they will not be used again on *Shabbat.* In any event, it is permitted to put the dishes into a dishwasher to be washed after the Sabbath. See Part V, Chapter 5, note 8.

provided it is permitted to carry, in order to keep it from getting wet in the rain, so that he can wear it after *Shabbat*.

10.   The prohibition of הֲכָנָה does not apply when one provides for the Sabbath and also for the following day without additional effort. Likewise, whatever it is permissible to do on the Sabbath, which does not require undue effort, may be done even if it is intended for after *Shabbat*.[30] Thus, one may go to the Sabbath limit (*tehum Shabbat*) and wait there until nightfall, so that he will be able to go beyond the limit immediately after *Shabbat* in order to engage in an activity that would also be permissible on the Sabbath, such as taking a stroll, retrieving a permitted article, caring for the needs of a bride and groom, and attending to the needs of a dead person in preparation for the funeral.

39. CARRYING

הוֹצָאָה

1.   The *Av Melachah* of Carrying[1] comprises the transfer of an object

---

30.   Study in Preparation for an Examination   One may study on the Sabbath in preparation for a *shiur* or an examination, since study is in itself a permissible and useful activity which satisfies a need on the Sabbath. See Part V, Chapter 5, note 21.

1.   Biblical Sources for the Prohibition of Carrying on the Sabbath   Carrying was one of the 39 *melachot* performed in connection with the Sanctuary. The Rabbis note that the term *melachah* is used with reference to it in the verse, "And Moses commanded, and they caused it to be proclaimed throughout the camp, saying: Let neither man nor woman make any more work (*melachah*) for the Sanctuary. So the people were restrained from bringing" (Exodus 36:6). This is presumed to have occurred on the Sabbath. The prohibition of carrying is indicated in the verse, "Let no man go out of his place on the seventh day" (Exodus 16:29). The Rabbis understand this to have been a directive to the people not to go out on the Sabbath with a vessel in hand in the expectation of gathering manna. The severity of the

from a private domain to a public domain, or vice versa; and moving an object a distance of four *amot* (4 cubits, approximately seven feet) in the public domain. Whether a domain is considered private or public in this regard is not a question of ownership, but is determined by certain physical features and halachic requirements.

2.   There are four kinds of domain with respect to carrying on the Sabbath*: a private domain (*reshut ha-yaḥid,* רְשׁוּת הַיָּחִיד), a public domain (*reshut ha-rabim,* רְשׁוּת הָרַבִּים), a semi-public domain (*karmelit,* כַּרְמְלִית), and a free place (*mekom petur,* מְקוֹם פָּטוּר).

3.   A private domain (רְשׁוּת הַיָּחִיד) is an enclosed area no less than four *tefaḥim* (four handbreadths, approximately fifteen inches) square, surrounded by a wall, a fence, or other partition no less than ten *tefaḥim* (ten handbreadths, approximately three feet) high. Thus, an apartment, a house, an enclosed garden or yard is a private domain, irrespective of whether it is under private or public ownership. In addition an object, whether movable or immovable, such as a box, a wagon, or a car, or a depression in the ground such as a pit or a ditch, or an elevation such as a mound of earth or of stones, no less than four *tefaḥim* square and ten *tefaḥim* high or deep, even when located in a public domain, is considered a private domain. The airspace above a private domain is, to an unlimited height, considered a private domain. It is permitted to carry and to move permissible objects to any distance within a private domain.

4.   A public domain (רְשׁוּת הָרַבִּים) is an area frequented by the public, such as a street, road or public square, that is unroofed and open at both ends, and whose width is not less than sixteen *amot* (sixteen

---

* For more particulars concerning the four domains and carrying on the Sabbath, see Part IV, Carrying on the Sabbath.

---

prohibition is underscored by the fact that the Sages voided two *mitzvot* of the Torah in order to avoid carrying on the Sabbath. The *shofar* is not blown on Rosh Hashanah, and the *lulav* is not taken on Sukkot, when the festivals occur on the Sabbath, lest one carry them in the public domain.

cubits, approximately twenty-eight feet). Any elevation or object in the public domain that is less than three *tefaḥim* (three handbreadths, approximately eleven inches) in height, or a depression in the public domain less than three *tefaḥim* deep, is considered to be part of the public domain. The airspace above the public domain to a height of ten *tefaḥim* is considered public domain.[2] It is a violation of a Biblical prohibition (*Av Melachah*) to carry from a private domain to a public domain, or from a public domain to a private domain, or to carry a distance of four *amot* (four cubits, approximately seven feet) in a public domain. A public area may be made to conform to the requirements of a private domain in order to permit carrying on the Sabbath by enclosing it with partitions (מְחִיצוֹת) or by constructing a צוּרַת הַפֶּתַח. For a discussion of the relevant conditions and regulations, see Part IV, Chapters 2, 3.

5.   A third type of domain designated by the Rabbis as a *karmelit* (כַּרְמְלִית), a semi-public domain, is an area which does not conform to the above specifications and is not frequented by the public. Among such areas are a side street less than sixteen *amot* wide, an alley-way closed off at one end, an open field, open country, seas and rivers. The airspace above a *karmelit* to a height of ten *tefaḥim* is subject to the rules of a *karmelit*. It is Rabbinically forbidden to carry from a private or public domain to a *karmelit,* or from a *karmelit* to a private or public domain, or a distance of four *amot* (four cubits, approximately seven feet) in a *karmelit.*

6.   A fourth type of domain, termed a *mekom petur* (מְקוֹם פְּטוּר), a free place, is an area in the public domain measuring less then four *tefaḥim* (four handbreadths, approximately fifteen inches) square

---

2.   Carrying Above a Public Domain   The airspace over a public domain is limited to a height of ten *tefaḥim*; above that is considered a *mekom petur.* One is therefore permitted to carry from one private domain to another over a plank or a walkway that is suspended over a public domain at least ten *tefaḥim* (ten handbreadths, approximately three feet) above ground.

that is enclosed by partitions three or more *tefaḥim* in height; and an elevation or an object in the public domain that is more than three *tefaḥim* (three handbreadths, approximately eleven inches) above ground, measuring less than four *tefaḥim* square; or a ditch in the public domain that is more than three *tefaḥim* deep, but less than four *tefaḥim* square. The above constitute a *mekom petur* only if situated in a public domain, but not in a *karmelit*. The airspace ten or more *tefaḥim* above a public domain or a *karmelit* is considered to be a *mekom petur*. There is no prohibition of carrying to or from a *mekom petur* and the other three domains, or within a *mekom petur*.

7. Where carrying on the Sabbath is forbidden, whether as a Biblical or as a Rabbinical prohibition, one may not move, throw, extend, transfer, or carry any object by any means, whether by hand, or on one's person,[3] such as over the arm or shoulder, or in the pockets of one's clothing.[4] Thus, it is forbidden to carry any food[5] or beverage,

---

3. Carrying Identification and Information in Case of Emergency One who has a medical condition requiring special treatment may go out with a bracelet around his wrist, or a tag on a chain around his neck and the like, bearing his blood type and instructions as to medication and medical treatment in case of an emergency. One may go out in time of war or emergency with an identity card or certificate, carried in a manner different from the usual, when going to perform a *mitzvah*. A soldier on combat duty or on a security mission may go out wearing a disc with identification and other vital information around his neck or wrist.

4. Carrying Money and Valuables Home When Sabbath Arrives If one is still on his way when the Sabbath has arrived and he has something of value or money in his pocket, in his hand, or on his person, and he cannot entrust it to a non-Jew, or leave it on the way lest it be lost, he should do as follows. If he has a companion with him they should take turns, each of them carrying it a distance of less than four *amot* and handing it to the other, until they approach the house. If he is alone, he should carry it in stages for a distance of less than four *amot* at a time, stopping each time and if possible depositing it on the ground. Upon reaching the house he (or his companion) should throw it into the house or the courtyard in a backhanded manner. If this

any article[6] of whatever size or weight, even a key, a handkerchief, a *tallit,* or a *Siddur,*[7] or any article of clothing. However, it is permitted to go outdoors while wearing an article[8] of clothing[9] or an orna-

---

procedure is not practicable one may proceed in the following manner. He should run home quickly without stopping, and upon arriving he should throw it into the house or courtyard in a backhanded manner. If one sets out on the Sabbath and finds that he is carrying something, he should drop the object. If it is of value and he cannot abandon it, he should proceed as above.

5.   Carrying Candy or Gum in the Mouth   One is not permitted to go out into the street on the Sabbath where there is no *eruv* with candy or chewing gum in the mouth.

6.   Carrying Medication in Case of Emergency   One who must carry with him medication to take in case of emergency, such as a cardiac patient who takes sublingual nitroglycerin tablets with the onset of chest pain, or a diabetic receiving insulin who takes sugar with the onset of hypoglycemic symptoms may, according to some authorities, carry several tablets or cubes of sugar, as required, on the Sabbath. They should be carried in a manner different from the usual, if, especially in the case of nitroglycerin tablets, it will not affect their stability and potency. This is permitted when going to the synagogue to pray or to learn Torah, or for the sake of a *mitzvah.* Some permit it, as well, when going out for a stroll, if one's condition of health requires it. If one must take the sugar or medication while on the way, he should if possible enter a private building or courtyard, and leave after having swallowed it.

7.   Having a Child Carry One's Siddur   It is forbidden to accustom a child to desecrate the Sabbath or a *Yom Tov.* Thus one may not give the child a key to carry on *Shabbat,* where there is no *eruv,* unless it is for a *mitzvah.* However, one may give the child a *Siddur* and a *Ḥumash* to carry to the synagogue for his own use. He may then share its use with the child. A young child who has not reached the age of instruction in the observance of *mitzvot* (less than 6–7 years of age) may be permitted to carry food and the like for his own use.

8.   Wearing a Necktie and Tie Clip Outdoors   It is permissible to wear an article of clothing and whatever is normally attached to the clothing or is

ment,[10] if it is worn in a normal manner. For a detailed discussion of the laws of carrying see Part IV, Chapters 2, 4.

8.   In the view of many authorities an area is not deemed a public domain unless it is frequented daily by six hundred thousand people. Accordingly, since our cities and streets do not, for the most part, meet this condition, as well as other pertinent halachic requirements, they do not constitute a public domain where carrying would be Biblically forbidden, but they are rather considered to be a *karmelit* where carrying is only Rabbinically prohibited. The Rabbis have, consequently, sanctioned the establishment of what is commonly known as an *eruv* in a designated community or in a city, thereby transforming it into a private domain where carrying is permissible.[11]

---

worn to service it. Thus, one is permitted to wear a necktie and a tie clip outdoors on the Sabbath.

9.   Going Out With a Label Sewn on a Garment   One may go out on the Sabbath wearing a garment with an identification label sewn inside the garment, such as a manufacturer's label, or a label indicating that the garment was tested for *sha'tnez.*

10.   Carrying a Purse or Handbag   While it is customary to go out wearing jewelry and ornaments, it is not permissible to carry any of these articles in the hand, even if that is the way in which they are normally used. A woman is, therefore, not permitted to carry a purse, handbag, or evening bag where there is no *eruv,* even if its use is only ornamental.

11.   Institution of the Eruv   The requirement that six hundred thousand people frequent the area if it is to be considered a public domain is predicated on the presumption that it must conform to the Israelite encampment in the wilderness in all respects. The number of adult, male Israelites of military age in the camp is set at this figure in the Torah. This requisite condition for a public domain has been generally accepted as the basis for establishing an *eruv* to permit carrying on the Sabbath. Rabbinic authorities have in the past been instrumental in instituting an *eruv* in many historic Jewish communities, and have advocated the establishment of an *eruv* wherever it is halachically feasible. Following historical precedent, the *eruv* has in recent

This is done by encompassing the entire area with a fence, or other partitions, either actual or nominal, including certain natural boundaries, such as a steep hill or a river embankment, in accordance with prescribed regulations.[12] Inasmuch as complex halachic rules are involved, the *eruv* should be instituted under the guidance and supervision of a Rabbinical authority. For further particulars, see Part IV, Chapter 1.

9. While carrying is permissible in a private domain, such as a house or an apartment, carrying and the transfer of an object between adjacent apartments or dwellings of two or more tenants or homeowners in the same building[13] or courtyard, and in the areas used by them in common, such as the hallway and the courtyard, is Rabbinically prohibited on the Sabbath as a precautionary measure

---

times become more prevalent in growing Jewish communities, as well as in some already established, in a concerted effort to provide greater convenience in engaging in personal and religious activities on the Sabbath, to prevent desecration of the Sabbath, and to preserve the vitality of Jewish communities. For further discussion of the *eruv* see Part IV, Chapter 1, end of paragraph 3 and notes; Part V, Chapter 10, paragraph 24 and notes.

12. Natural Boundaries Qualifying for the Eruv   A body of water such as a river or a lake qualifies as a מְחִיצָה, provided the height of the embankment at the shore line or the river bank is ten *tefaḥim* or more in an incline of less than four *amot*. A trench with the above dimensions qualifies as well. However, other factors, such as whether the place is the terminus of a bridge or of boats navigating the coast line, or if the water freezes over in winter, come under halachic consideration, and in some instances the place may require a צוּרַת הַפֶּתַח.

13. Bringing in Mail From the Mail Box   One may not bring in mail from the mail box that is situated outside the house, unless it is permissible to carry there. Neither may one bring the mail into his apartment from the mail box situated in the hallway, or in the entrance hall, in an apartment building that is occupied by several tenants, unless there is an *eruv ḥatzerot* on the premises and it is permissible to carry. See also Part V, Chapter 10, paragraph 5 and note.

to prevent carrying from a private to a public domain. This restriction, however, may be removed and carrying and the transfer of objects in these areas can be made permissible by establishing an *Eruv* of Courtyards, known as *Eruvei Ḥatzerot* (עֵירוּבֵי חֲצֵרוֹת). This is done by depositing a loaf of bread or a *matzah* in one of the dwellings, which is thus designated as the joint property of all the Jewish tenants or homeowners. If there are non-Jewish tenants or homeowners, it is necessary to obtain from them the right of way (שְׂכִירוּת רְשׁוּת) on the premises. By this means of *Eruvei Ḥatzerot* the individual families combine and share their rights of possession so that their separate dwellings are considered to be common property and accessible to all. The regulations regarding *Eruvei Ḥatzerot* are discussed in Part V, Chapter 10.

Part III

Select Sabbath Laws

"The principal *melachot* that are forbidden on the Sabbath are already known to most Jewish people. We will discuss here only such common activities that are not generally known."

SOME OF THE MELACHOT FORBIDDEN ON THE SABBATH

קְצָת מְלָאכוֹת הָאֲסוּרוֹת בְּשַׁבָּת

1. It is forbidden to use the light of an oil lamp for something that requires concentration. The Rabbis have prohibited this lest one forgets and tilts the lamp in order to bring the oil to the wick, thereby violating the prohibition of kindling a light.[1] However, two people may read by the light from one book about the same subject, because if one will want to tilt the lamp the other will remind him. It is now customary to permit the use of candles made of tallow or wax, as they adhere firmly to the wick. But one should take precautions not to knock off the ash from the top of the wick. According to Rambam this would be a violation of a Biblical prohibition. It is even forbidden to ask a non-Jew to remove the ash from the wick.

2. It is forbidden to open a door or a window opposite a candle that is burning nearby lest it be extinguished,[2] but it is permitted to close the door or the window. It is forbidden to open or close the door of an oven in which a fire is burning,[3] because one is thereby either kindling or extinguishing the fire.

---

1. Reading by the Light of an Electric Lamp One is permitted to read and study by the light of an electric lamp, inasmuch as the restrictive enactment of the Rabbis with regard to an oil lamp does not apply in the case of an electric lamp. Some authorities permit one to read by the light of an oil lamp as well if he puts up a sign or some other reminder that it is *Shabbat*. See Melachah 36, note 3.

2. Opening the Door Near a Burning Candle Where necessary one may open a door near a burning candle, provided he does so slowly so as not to cause a draft that might extinguish the flame. See Melachah 36, note 8.

3. Opening and Closing a Radiator Valve One may not open the valve on

239

3. It is forbidden to pour boiling hot soup on pieces of bread or *matzah*. One should first pour the soup into a plate, and when it has cooled somewhat, so that it is fit to be eaten, the bread or the *matzah* may be placed in it. But as long as the soup is boiling hot, even if it is in the plate, it is not permitted to put bread or *matzah* in it.[4] One should not put salt or spices into soup even if it is in the plate,[5] and certainly not if it is in the pot, as long as it is boiling hot, but he should wait until it cools somewhat so that it is fit to be eaten. Some are lenient with salt that was cooked while processed, [6] but it is more commendable to be strict even in this. One should not pour hot coffee or tea into a cup containing sugar, but he should first pour the coffee

---

a radiator which is heated by means of hot water that courses through the pipes, as he would be causing the boiler to operate and heat the water in the pipes and in the coils of the radiator. The same restriction applies if it is heated by steam. Opinions differ on closing the valve to shut off the steam. While some do not permit it, other authorities permit one to close the valve to keep the steam from coming into the radiator, if he cannot bear the heat in the room. See Melachah 11, note 5.

4. Putting Bread into Hot Soup One should wait before putting bread or *matzah* into the soup until it is no longer hot to the degree of *yad soledet bo*. The degree of *yad soledet bo* can be practically assumed when it is still so intensely hot that a person would normally refrain from drinking it. One can, if need be, use a spoon or a ladle to serve the hot soup, rather than pour it directly into the plate, so that the plate would then be considered a third vessel (*keli shlishi*), and thus not subject to the restriction. Pouring the soup first into a serving pot and then into the plate would serve the same purpose. See Melachah 11, note 12.

5. Putting Spices into Hot Soup Many authorities are of the opinion that it is permitted to put spices into a plate of hot soup that is a second vessel (*keli sheini*), even if it is *yad soledet bo*. See Melachah 11, note 10.

6. Dissolving Bouillon Cubes in Hot Water Bouillon cubes may be dissolved in a cup or plate of hot water (a *keli sheini*) to make soup on the Sabbath. Some require that the cubes be dissolved in a *keli shlishi*.

or tea into the cup and then put the sugar in it.[7] In case of necessity, one may be lenient regarding this.

4.   It is forbidden to place fruit or water on a heated stove because the water might boil and the fruit might bake. Even if one's intention is only to warm them, it is forbidden to put them where they could be cooked or baked. A *pashtida* containing fat should not be placed in front of a fire or on a stove where it could heat up, even if his intention is only to warm it. However, one may place the above where they cannot possibly heat up and cook, but will only warm up somewhat.[8] This may be done even if the fat in the *pashtida* is congealed or the water is frozen. But one is not permitted to put anything cold to be warmed in an oven where food is stored so as to keep it warm, even if it cannot heat up and cook while it is there.[9] If it is for a person who

---

7.   Using Instant Coffee and Tea   When using instant coffee or instant tea on the Sabbath one should follow the same procedure as with sugar, namely to pour the hot water into the cup first, and then put the coffee or tea in it. Tea essence, made with tea leaves and boiled water, should be prepared before the Sabbath. See Melachah 11, notes 13, 14.

8.   Warming a Pashtida Pie or a Piece of Meat   A *pashtida* is a pie consisting of a double layer of dough filled with pieces of meat and fat. The *pashtida,* as well as a piece of meat, may be warmed on the Sabbath even though the congealed fat will melt again, because the prohibition of cooking would in any event not apply, as in its present state it is still considered dry food which had previously been fully cooked. See Melachah 11, note 28.

9.   Warming Food on the Sabbath   It is permitted to put a dish of cold food near the fire to take the chill away and to warm it, provided it is put at a distance from the fire where it cannot heat up to the degree of *yad soledet bo* (113^0F/45^0C), even it it will stand there for a long time. One may not place it close enough to the fire so that it could reach the degree of *yad soledet bo,* even if he does not intend to heat it to such a degree, but only to keep it there for a brief period of time. However, if it is urgently necessary to warm the food, as for a child or for a sick person, it is permissible, provided the food was fully cooked and he is careful to remove it before it heats up to the

is somewhat ill one should consult a Rabbinical authority.[10] Some are accustomed to return food to the oven on the Sabbath as long as it is still warm, but not if the food has cooled off completely. One who is meticulously observant should be strict in all instances.

5.   It is forbidden to wrap hot food on the Sabbath to retain its heat, even with something that does not add to its heat. It is therefore not permitted to take a pot containing food that was cooked or heated in it and wrap it or cover it with pillows or blankets, and the like, in order to retain its heat.[11]

6.   Food which cannot be eaten at all without rinsing it may not be rinsed on the Sabbath even in cold water. However, salted fish (herring) may be soaked in cold water because it is also edible before soaking.

7.   If one did not put vinegar into the mustard or horseradish before the Sabbath he may not do so on the Sabbath, unless it is done in a manner that is different from the way it is usually done, that is, by first putting the vinegar into a bowl and then putting in the mustard

---

degree of *yad soledet bo*. See Melachah 11, paragraph 12–14 and relevant notes.

10.   Removing the Chill From Food or Drink   In case of need, as for one who is ill or cannot tolerate cold food or cold liquids, it is permitted to place it on the stove to remove the chill, provided he is careful to keep it there only for a brief period of time and to remove it before it heats up.

11.   Covering Hot Food to Preserve Its Heat   Placing food under a covering, or embedding it in a substance to retain its heat (*hatmanah*) is forbidden on the Sabbath. The prohibition applies to the vessel in which the food was cooked or heated (*keli r'ishon*), and as long as it has not cooled below the degree of *yad soledet bo*. If one transfers the food to another pot, even though the food is still too hot to touch, or even if the hot food is returned to the original pot, *hatmanah* is permitted in a substance that does not add heat. See Melachah 11, paragraph 15 and notes.

or the horseradish. One should not make it a thick mixture, but he should pour in a great amount of vinegar so that the mixture is thin. Nor should one mix it with a spoon and the like, but rather with his finger, or by shaking the bowl until it is mixed.

8.   If one finds fruit beneath a tree on the Sabbath he may not even handle it, for it may have fallen off that very day. The fruit of a non-Jew may likewise not be handled on the Sabbath if there is a doubt as to whether or not it was picked on that day.

9.   It is forbidden to remove honey that is still attached to the bee-hive. It is likewise forbidden to crush the honeycombs, even if they had been detached from the hive before the Sabbath. If the honeycombs were not crushed before the Sabbath, honey that flows from them on the Sabbath is forbidden. But honey that flows in the hive is permitted.[12]

10.   It is permitted to gather up fruit scattered about in one place in the house or in the yard. But if it is dispersed in several places it is not permitted to gather it into a basket, as it involves undue exertion, but it may be picked up individually and eaten.[13]

11.   It is permitted to remove peas and the like from their pods if the pods are still green and edible, because it is like separating food from food. However, if the pods are dry and no longer edible it is not permitted to remove the peas. One should, likewise, be careful not to

---

12.   Taking Honey From the Hive   Honey that flows in the hive is permitted if the honeycombs were crushed before the Sabbath, even if they remain in the hive, or if the honey had already been flowing in the hive from before the Sabbath. See Melachah 11, note 1.

13.   Gathering Up Fruit Scattered About the Floor   One may not gather the fruit scattered about the floor into a basket because it has the appearance of a weekday activity. Some permit picking the fruit up into one's lap or into a garment, and the like, even if he does not eat it.

remove nuts from their green shells, nor sesame seeds from their shells.[14]

12.   It is forbidden to squeeze fruit to extract its juice. It is therefore, forbidden to squeeze lemons into water to make lemonade.[15] Some even prohibit sucking the juice out of fruit with one's mouth. One should therefore be careful at least not to suck the juice out of grapes and discard the skins.[16] If one does not require its juice it is permitted. Hence, it is permissible to squeeze the water out of lettuce or cucumbers since it goes to waste.

13.   A woman should not squeeze milk from her breasts into a cup or into a vessel for her child to drink. But she may squeeze out some milk so that the baby will take hold of the breast and suckle. However, she is not allowed to sprinkle some of her milk as a remedy in a case where there is no danger or severe pain.[17]

---

14.   Removing Nuts and Seeds From Their Shells   It is permitted to break the hard shell and to peel off the thin covering of a nut immediately prior to eating it. Some permit removing sesame seeds from their shells as well, but only a few at a time and in a manner different from the usual.

15.   Putting Lemon into Tea and into Food   It is permitted to put a slice of lemon into a cup of tea. Some permit squeezing out a lemon onto sugar and then adding water to make a lemon-flavored drink, as well as squeezing out a lemon into cooked food or any other food to add to its taste. See Melachah 5, note 2.

16.   Sucking Juice From Grapes and Olives   One who follows the stringent opinion need only refrain from sucking grapes or olives without putting them into his mouth. But if he puts them inside his mouth he may suck out the juice and throw away the remainder, as this is considered a way of eating them.

17.   A Woman Expressing Milk to Relieve Pain   A woman is permitted to express some of the milk from her breasts in order to relieve her pain. This is allowed as it does not violate the prohibition of מְפָרֵק because the milk is not being used and is going to waste, and since the woman is in pain even the Rabbinical prohibition does not apply. See Melachah 5, note 5.

14.   It is permitted to put congealed fat on hot food even though it will melt. Snow or hail may not be crushed so that the water will flow from it, but one may put it into a cup of wine or water to cool it, and one need not be concerned since it melts of its own accord.[18] One should be careful in the winter not to wash his hands with water containing snow or hail, and if he does he should take care not to press the snow or hail between his hands so as not to crush it.[19] It is permitted to break the ice in order to obtain the water beneath it. If possible one should refrain from urinating in snow, as well as on mud or loose earth.

15.   It is permitted to sort out foodstuff (אוֹכֶל) from worthless matter (פְּסוֹלֶת), but not the worthless matter from the foodstuff. And even food may not be separated by means of a utensil, but only by hand,[20] and only what one needs to eat immediately.[21] When separating food that one needs for immediate consumption from the remainder, one

---

18.   Making Ice Cubes   In case of necessity, as for example to provide for cold drinks in hot weather, or to apply ice to reduce a swelling, one may make ice cubes on the Sabbath by freezing water in a freezer. See Melachah 38, note 22.

19.   Walking in Snow   One need have no concern about walking in snow on the Sabbath and trampling it underfoot, even if the snow melts, since he does not intend this. Moreover the Sages did not prohibit it, as it is not possible to avoid it.

20.   Using Cutlery to Separate Food   Food may not be sorted or separated by means of a utensil that is specifically designed for that purpose. However, utensils that are ordinarily used for cutting and eating food such as spoons, forks, and knives are considered as one's hand. See Melachah 7, note 8.

21.   Preparing Food for Immediate Consumption   Whatever food is required for the meal under preparation is considered to be for immediate consumption, provided the food is prepared reasonably close to the meal. This includes food that is to be eaten during the course of the meal, regardless of its duration. One may prepare the food for others as well. See Melachah 7, notes 6, 9.

must be careful to separate only what he wishes to eat now and not what he intends to set aside for later, because in this regard what he needs for immediate consumption is considered foodstuff, while what he intends to set aside for later is considered worthless matter. It is even forbidden to peel garlic or onions with the intention of putting them aside for later,[22] as it involves the prohibition of selecting (בּוֹרֵר).[23] It is permissible to peel only what needs to be eaten imme-

---

22. Shelling Nuts and Removing Pits and Peel From Fruit   One may not remove the shells from nuts and eggs or the pits from plums, peaches and the like, unless he intends to eat them immediately or at the meal. In the latter case one may crack open and remove the hard shell of a nut even with a nutcracker. Some prohibit peeling apples if one only intends to set them aside for later. Others, however, permit it since the peel is edible and is therefore considered food. See Melachah 5, paragraph 2; Melachah 7, note 2.

23. Removal of Waste Matter From Food   Opinions differ as to whether the prohibition of selecting (בּוֹרֵר) applies only before the meal or also during the meal, as in removing bones and other waste matter from food while eating. While some authorities do not permit it at any time, others permit it when done in the course of eating. Where possible, it is advisable to follow the stricter view. Thus, when eating meat and chicken one should remove the meat from the bones. In the case of small bones, as in fish, while it is preferable to remove them from the mouth while eating, it is permissible to remove the bones beforehand, where necessary, as for young children. To avoid the problem, some are accustomed to eat only *gefilte* fish on the Sabbath. As to fruit, such as watermelon which contains many seeds, some require removal of the seeds, if possible, by eating the fruit and spitting out the seeds. Others permit removal of the seeds by hand, preferably in a manner different from the usual, as with the handle of a spoon. One may peel fruits and vegetables such as apples, oranges, and onions, and remove the shell from eggs for immediate use because the removal of the waste matter from the food (פְּסוֹלֶת מִתּוֹךְ אוֹכֶל) in this case is the normal way of eating it (דֶּרֶךְ אֲכִילָה). It is, likewise, permissible to remove the inedible part of the food when required for immediate consumption, such as removing the soiled or rotten leaves from a head of lettuce, or the burnt portion of a piece of bread. See Melachah 7, notes 3, 4, 5, 12.

diately. The outer shell of the garlic which encloses all its parts should not be removed even for immediate consumption, as it entails the act of separation (מְפָרֵק), a subsidiary of the *melachah* of threshing (תּוֹלָדָה דְּדִישָׁה).

16.   The prohibition against selecting (בּוֹרֵר) applies also to non-edible items, such as utensils and the like, for whatever one wishes to use at the time is considered as foodstuff, and the rest is considered as waste matter.[24]

17.   One should not filter any liquid, as it involves many different laws.[25] However, it is permitted to drink through a cloth filter, for the prohibition against selecting is only applicable when the food or drink is prepared prior to eating or drinking, but in this case he only prevents the waste from going into his mouth. Nevertheless, some do not permit drinking water through a cloth filter because of the prohibition against laundering (כִּיבּוּס). In a pressing situation, as when one has no pure water to drink, one may be lenient.

18.   When pouring coffee that has coffee grounds as sediment at the bottom, and any other beverage that has lees or other waste matter as sediment at the bottom, one must be careful not to pour out all of the clear liquid, but to leave over some of it with the sediment. One may collect the cream from the top of milk that has curdled, but only what he needs for immediate consumption. Even then he should take care

---

24.   Selecting Utensils and Clothing for Immediate Use   One may select utensils and cutlery and arrange them in preparation for the meal. One may, likewise, select the clothing one is about to wear from a pile of clothing or from a closet full of clothing. In either case it does not matter if one has to first remove the utensils or the clothing that are on top of the ones he intends to use. See Melachah 7, notes 13, 14.

25.   Pouring Tea and Coffee Through a Strainer   It is permitted to pour tea or coffee from a coffee pot or teapot with a strainer on the spout, so as to keep the tea leaves and coffee grounds from falling into the cup, as one is only pouring out the liquid and not straining it. See Melachah 7, note 17.

not to take off all of the cream, but to leave some of it on top of the curdled milk remaining at the bottom.[26]

19.   If a fly or some other refuse fell into food or in a beverage, one should not remove only the fly or the refuse, but he should remove some of the food or liquid with it.

20.   If one needs to crush pepper or salt and the like for seasoning food he may pound it with the handle of a knife on the table, or in a similar way, but not with a pestle or in a mortar.

21.   It is forbidden to cut up onions and other vegetables unless it is done before a meal, and even then one should not cut them into very small pieces.[27]

22.   It is forbidden to salt any substance upon which the salt acts to soften it or to make it less pungent, as this is similar to tanning (מְעַבֵּד).[28] It is, therefore, forbidden to salt raw cucumbers, as well as

---

26.   Pouring a Beverage and Removing Cream From Curdled Milk   If one intends to drink the coffee or the beverage, or to eat the cream immediately, he may pour off all of it, since it is permitted to separate food from waste matter on the Sabbath if one does not do it with a special utensil, and if he intends to eat the food immediately. See Melachah 7, note 16.

27.   Cutting Up Vegetables   Some follow a lenient view and are accustomed to cut the vegetables such as onions and radishes into tiny pieces, with added salt and vinegar or oil. However, this should be done only before the meal. The vegetables should be cut up with a knife, and not with a special utensil designated for that purpose, such as a chopping knife. Some have the custom of including in the Sabbath day meal a dish of chopped eggs and onions with some oil added. Preparation of the dish on the Sabbath is sanctioned by authorities, some of whom even permit use of a chopping knife for chopping the eggs with the onions. See Melachah 9, note 2.

28.   Soaking and Salting Raw Meat   It is forbidden to salt raw meat on the Sabbath. It is also not permitted to soak unsalted meat on the Sabbath, even if it is the third day after the meat was slaughtered, and one wishes to prevent the meat from becoming prohibited to be cooked afterwards. (For the regulation regarding meat kept for three days without washing and soaking

radishes or onions, even what one needs for that meal. But he should dip each piece in salt and eat it. However eggs and meat that are cooked, and other foods that are not affected by the salt, but only receive a salty flavor, may be salted to be eaten soon at the next meal, but not to be set aside for another meal.[29]

23. One should not salt a large quantity of cooked beans or peas together, because the salting helps to soften them. This is forbidden even if he intends to eat them immediately.

24. Salads made of lettuce, cucumbers and onions, and the like, may be salted before the meal, because the oil or vinegar that is immediately added to it weakens the effect of the salt. But it is forbidden to salt the salad and let it stand for some time.

25. The prohibition against building (בּוֹנֶה) applies also to food, as for instance making cheese, or joining fruit together and arranging them to give them a better appearance. Therefore, when cutting up onions with eggs or with the milt of herring, one should take care not to smooth and shape them, but to leave them as they are.[30]

---

in the interim, see Volume One, Part III, page 247). One may not have a non-Jew soak the meat in these circumstances, as there is no great loss involved since the meat can still be eaten roasted. This rule applies to an individual at home. However, if the meat belongs to a butcher, who must sell it to customers, and is therefore faced with a considerable loss, he may have the meat soaked by a non-Jew. See Melachah 28, note 2.

29. Salting Cooked Eggs and Meat Salting cooked eggs and meat to be put aside for later use is prohibited because it resembles tanning and pickling. Some authorities take the prohibition to apply if it is done to prepare the eggs and meat for a later meal on the Sabbath. Others, however, take it to apply only if one intends to set it aside for after the Sabbath, and they permit salting meat and eggs for another meal on the Sabbath. One may be lenient in this matter, particularly in hot weather when the salting prevents the eggs and meat from becoming putrid and malodorous.

30. Preparing a Platter of Eggs and Onions It is permissible to smoothen a platter of onions and eggs or herring, as this cannot be considered under

26. When washing utensils with hot water, one should not pour the water over them, but rather into another vessel and then put the utensils in it.[31] He should not wash them with a cloth because of the prohibition against wringing the water out of it (סְחִיטָה). But he may wash them with a rag that is used especially for this purpose, and which he is not particular to wring out even on weekdays. One should not wash glassware with oats and the like.[32] Only utensils needed for the Sabbath may be washed on the Sabbath.[33]

---

the prohibition of building on the Sabbath. Unlike making cheese and pressing fruits, such as figs pressed into the form of a cake, where the *melachah* of Building is involved in forming a solid mass, the onions and eggs or herring only form a soft mixture. In preparing the platter it is permitted to use a scoop, but one should not form distinctive shapes or designs.

31. Washing and Drying Dishes Pouring hot water on soiled dishes and utensils might result in cooking the leftover food or grease adhering to them. In washing them one should not use a cloth or a sponge as it absorbs water and would result in squeezing out the water. One may use synthetic materials, such as pot scourers, rubber bladed scrapers, and rubber or plastic gloves, that are not absorbent. One may use liquid soap, but not bars of soap or scouring powder. One should dry them with a dish towel used for that purpose and take care not to use it to the point where it becomes saturated with water, as he might come to wring it out between one dish or utensil and another. See Melachah 11, note 15; Melachah 13, note 1; Melachah 30, note 1.

32. Polishing Glasses and Silverware Glassware and silverware may be washed clean and dried on the Sabbath. However, one may not polish them with dry or liquid polish or with a polishing cloth.

33. Washing Dishes and Utensils on the Sabbath One may wash dishes and utensils on the Sabbath as needed, and in preparation for the next meal, even if there are others available and even several dishes of the same kind although he needs only one or two. After the meal, dishes and utensils may be placed in the dishwasher to be washed after the Sabbath. They may also be placed in a pan of water to soak, even if they will not be used again on the Sabbath. Drinking utensils, such as glasses, cups, saucers, teaspoons, and

27. Whatever a Jew is forbidden to do on the Sabbath, he may not have done by a non-Jew. Nevertheless, in the winter when it is permissible to have a non-Jew light the fire in the stove in order to heat the house, it is customary to have the non-Jew put the pots with food that has cooled onto the stove before lighting the fire. Since the intention in lighting the fire is not to warm the food, but rather to heat the house, it is permitted, provided the dishes are placed on the stove before lighting it and not afterward. Obviously, if the intention in lighting the fire is not for the sake of heating the house, but rather for the sake of warming the food, it is forbidden. Some forbid it even if the intention is to heat the house. Although the custom is according to those who permit it, a pious, God-fearing person should follow the more stringent view and refrain from the practice when it is not necessary,[34] especially when it involves a stove that is regularly used for cooking, even when the fire is made on the Sabbath for the sake of heating the house, and the non-Jew places the dishes on the stove before lighting the fire.

28. One who spills liquid on the ground in soil where something will grow is in violation of the prohibition of sowing (זוֹרֵעַ), because the liquid may cause it to grow. Therefore, one should refrain from eating in the garden, as it is difficult to avoid spilling liquids on the ground. It may also not be permissible to carry in the garden.

---

other utensils which are constantly used between and after meals, may be washed the whole day, even after the last meal, unless it is evident that they will no longer be used that day. See Melachah 38, note 29. On the use of a dishwasher on the Sabbath, see Part II, Melachah 36, Electrical Equipment and Appliances, note 17.

34. Having a Non-Jew Warm Food When needed for the Sabbath meal and one has no other recourse, some authorities permit having a non-Jew place a pot of cooked food that has cooled, even one that contains a broth or soup, near a fire or on the *blech* in order to warm it. See Melachah 11, note 47.

29. A sponge may not be used for wiping unless it has a handle.[35]

30. It is forbidden to spit in a place where the spittle will be scattered by the wind.[36]

31. A maiden may not braid her hair on the Sabbath, and she may not undo her braids, but she is allowed to arrange her hair with her hands.[37] It is forbidden to comb one's hair with a comb made of coarse and rigid bristles, so that it is not possible to comb without plucking out hairs. But if the bristles are not stiff it is permitted to arrange one's hair with it, especially if it is set aside expressly to be used on the Sabbath for that purpose.[38]

---

35. Use of a Sponge or a Brush   A wet sponge which absorbs water should not be used for wiping a table or a plate when it will result in squeezing out the water. One may use a brush, whose bristles are synthetic and do not absorb water, to clean dishes or utensils such as baby bottles. See also note 31.

36. Spitting in the Street   This ruling in the *Kitzur Shulḥan Aruch* is generally disregarded as it is not considered valid under the *melachah* of זוֹרֶה (Winnowing) cited by Rama. According to one view, however, it may apply with regard to carrying in the public domain.

37. Braiding and Curling the Hair   Braiding one's hair is not permitted by men and women, young and old alike, because it resembles the *melachah* of Building (בּוֹנֶה). This is inferred from the verse, "And God built the rib which he had taken from the man" (Genesis 2:22), which the Sages expound as intimating that God braided Eve's hair and brought her to Adam. The inference is that making braids is akin to building. It is not considered weaving, because the hair is attached to the head and will also not remain permanently braided. If one braids strands of detached hair, or a wig, it involves the *melachah* of Weaving (אוֹרֵג). The *Mishnah B'rurah* notes that protesting the practice is not called for when the protest will not be heeded. One is not permitted to curl the hair with curlers. However, a woman may put hairpins, clips, or combs in her hair to hold it in place. See Melachah 34, paragraph 11, and notes.

38. Cutting, Combing and Brushing the Hair   It is forbidden to cut and

32.   If a garment has dirt on it one may wipe it off with a rag and the like, but he should not pour water on it as that would be like laundering it.[39] Therefore, if a child urinates on a garment it is forbidden to pour water on it. (But if he urinates on the ground, or on an article made of wood or leather, it is permitted to pour water on it.) When one washes his hands, and he wants to dry them with a cloth, it is desirable to rub his hands against each other thoroughly in order to remove the water, so that wiping the small amount of water remaining on his hands only soils the cloth and is not considered laundering. One need not be concerned with this when one uses a colored cloth (as it does not involve laundering).[40]

33.   A jar containing water or some other liquid may not be covered with a cloth that is not intended for this purpose, lest one come to

---

otherwise remove one's hair, whether on the head or any other part of the body, either with an instrument, a powder, or an ointment. Neither may one tear out one's hair, whether by hand, with one's teeth, or with an instrument. One may not comb one's hair or wig or brush it with a brush that is likely to pull out hairs. However, one may use a soft brush, which is not likely to pull out any hair, to arrange the hair to keep it from appearing disheveled. One is allowed to part the hair with his hands. It is permitted to scratch one's head or beard with one's fingernails.

39.   Removing a Stain and Cleaning a Garment   It is forbidden to clean or to remove a stain from a garment on the Sabbath with water or any cleaning fluid or cleaning agent, such as a spray or powder that removes a stain or dirt or absorbs oil and grease. Plastic or rubber pants and sheets, and socks or other clothing made only from synthetic material may be cleaned by soaking in water if needed for use on the Sabbath.

40.   Drying the Hands With a Towel   In the view of some authorities there is no difference between a white cloth or a colored cloth with regard to the question of laundering. In any event, the prevailing practice is to be lenient in the matter of drying the hands, since no laundering is involved, as the towel has no dirt on it, and it is actually soiled when the hands are wiped on it. However, if one's hands are dripping wet, he should not wipe them with a cloth that he would normally be particular to wring out. On use of a paper towel, see Melachah 13, note 2.

wring it out. However, it is permitted to cover it with a cloth that is meant for that purpose, since we need not be concerned that he will wring it out.

34.   If water spills on the table it is forbidden to wipe it with a cloth that one minds being wet, because when it soaks up a lot of water we are concerned that one might wring it out.[41] One should also not use a cloth to dry cups and other vessels that have a narrow opening, because the water will be squeezed out of the cloth while drying them.[42]

35.   If while one is walking it begins to rain on him and on his clothes, he may continue on his way home.[43] When he removes his clothing he may not spread them out to dry.[44] He may not spread

---

41.   Cleaning a Windowpane and Eyeglasses   It is permitted to wipe the mist from a window with one's hands or with a rag. One may clean eyeglasses by wetting the lenses and wiping them with a dry cloth.

42.   Drying Cups and Jars   If necessary, one may dry a cup or a jar, or other vessel that has a narrow opening, with a cloth that he does not mind if it gets wet and will not come to wring it out. He should, however, first pour out whatever water is in the vessel. See Melachah 13, note 1.

43.   Wearing Wet Garments   The Sages did not prohibit wearing wet clothing for fear that one may wring them out. In case of need, one may even put on garments while they are still wet and go about in them.

44.   Handling and Drying Wet Clothes   Clothes that are wet from the rain may be put away or hung in their usual place. Some authorities maintain that the prohibition of spreading out clothing because of *mar'it ha'ayin,* that people might suspect they were laundered, applies if the clothes are soaked, but not if they are only moderately wet. Others do not make this distinction. One should refrain from handling a garment if it is soaked, but it may be handled when it is only moderately wet. Rags that are constantly soaked in water may be handled, since one does not mind if they remain wet and will not wring them out. Clothes, such as a raincoat and other items made of synthetic material, may be hung up to dry, but not near a heater or radiator.

them out even if they are only moist from perspiration.[45] And it is surely forbidden to spread out one's wet clothes before a fire.[46] Even while wearing them one may not stand before a fire where it is very hot. It is also forbidden to shake out the water from a garment. A garment about which one is particular that it should not be wet may not even be handled after he takes it off, lest he wring it out.[47]

36.   If when walking one comes to a stream of water, he may skip or jump over it even if it is wide and requires exertion. It is preferable to skip over it rather than walk around it, because the latter would be more tiring as it would add to his walking distance. It is forbidden to pass through the water so that he will not come to wring the water out of his wet clothes. One may not walk on the Sabbath in a place where he can slip and fall into the water, lest his clothing get soaked and he will come to wring them out.

37.   One who goes to perform a *mitzvah,* such as to visit his father, or his Torah teacher, or one who is greater than he in wisdom, may pass through a river, provided he alters his usual manner, such as

---

45. Hanging Up Diapers to Dry   Baby diapers, if needed on the Sabbath, may be hung up to dry in the house or in the sun in the courtyard, as this is common practice and people will not think that they were laundered. See Melachah 13, note 6.

46. Spreading Wet Clothes Near a Fire   Spreading wet garments on a stove or near a fire is forbidden if they are put in a place where they would reach a temperature of *yad soledet bo,* where the hand recoils because of the heat. Otherwise it is allowed, provided one does not spread them out in the manner that he would spread out laundered garments to dry.

47. Shaking Water Out of a Garment   One may not shake the water out of a new garment about which he is concerned that the water may cause it to shrink. However, even with an old garment one should take care not to shake the water out too vigorously, lest it result in wringing the water out of the garment. A raincoat made of non-woven plastic material may be shaken out even vigorously.

keeping his hand beneath his cloak so that he will remember and not come to wring it out. One is forbidden to pass through the water while wearing sandals, because they cannot be securely tightened and tied, and we are afraid that they will fall off and he will come to carry them, but one may pass through while wearing shoes. And since he went for the sake of a *mitzvah* he may return the same way. But if he went to guard his produce, he may pass through the water on the way there (since protecting one's property is also somewhat of a *mitzvah*), but not on his return.

38. Mud on one's clothing may be scraped off with a fingernail or with a knife if the mud is wet, but if it is dry it is forbidden to scrape it off, as that would be similar to grinding (טוֹחֵן).

39. It is forbidden to shake off snow or dust from a black garment,[48] but it is permitted to remove feathers by hand, although some refrain from doing this as well.[49]

---

48. Shaking Out Snow and Dust From a Garment Shaking out and removing snow and dust from a garment is presumed to effect a recognizable improvement in its appearance. When the garment is relatively new and of a black or dark color, so that one is particular about its appearance before wearing it, removing the snow and dust is then considered like laundering it.

49. Removing Surface Dirt and Snow From a Garment Improving the appearance of a garment, even without water, by shaking out the dust, dirt or snow, comes under the prohibition of cleansing (מְלַבֵּן). However, one may remove snow that has not yet melted by shaking the garment lightly. A raincoat made of non-woven plastic, or similar non-absorbent material may even be shaken vigorously. Dust, lint, feathers, and dirt that is only on the surface and is not embedded in the garment or stuck to it, does not come under the restriction and may be removed by shaking the garment or by brushing it lightly with one's hands or with a dry cloth. If the dust is embedded in a garment it may be removed in the above manner if the garment is not new, or he is not particular as to its appearance. Opinions differ on the use of a clothes brush. Some permit it, provided it is one whose bristles will

40. Mud that is on one's foot or on one's shoes may be removed with something which may be handled on the Sabbath.[50] One may also wipe it off against a wooden beam, but not against a stone or a brick wall or on the ground. In an extreme circumstance, as when there is excrement on one's foot or on his shoes and there is nothing available which may be handled on the Sabbath, he may wipe it off against a wall, and if there is no wall he may wipe it off on the ground. If there is water available he may rinse the shoe with water if the shoe is made of leather (because in the case of leather the mere rinsing is not considered laundering, unless he rubs one side against the other in the manner of launderers). But one may not scrape mud or excrement from a leather shoe with a knife. One may not scrape the mud from his shoes on the iron bar in front of the house if the bar is sharp-edged, but if it is not sharp-edged it is permitted.

41. If one's hands become dirty with mud, he should not wipe them with a cloth which is used for wiping the hands (as he may then inadvertently wash out the cloth).[51]

---

not fall out. Others forbid the use of any kind of brush. In any case, it is advisable to keep one's Sabbath clothes clean, and to be careful in the synagogue and elsewhere to put one's hat and coat where they will not fall to the ground and become dirty and soiled. See Melachah 13, note 9.

50. Cleaning and Polishing Shoes One may remove dirt and dust from one's shoes by hand or with a cloth, or by rinsing them with water, but without rubbing or making them shine. It is forbidden to apply shoe polish or liquid polish, or to smear one's shoes with oil and the like. It is also not allowed to shine them with a brush or a cloth, even without polish. The cleaning of suede and cloth shoes is governed by the rules outlined above regarding the cleaning of clothing.

51. Wiping One's Hands With a Cloth or Paper Towel One should wipe his muddied hands on a cloth or towel which he does not mind being dirty. One may wipe one's hands with a paper towel or napkin which is disposed of after use, even though it is likely to tear while being used. One may use a cloth or paper napkin at the meal to wipe one's mouth and hands.

42.   It is forbidden to paint anything even with a dye that is not durable. A woman is therefore forbidden to paint her face.[52] If one's hands are stained from fruit which he ate, he should be careful not to touch his clothing because he will color them.[53] One should also not use a cloth to wipe blood from his nose or from a wound.[54]

43.   One should not put saffron into cooked food because it colors it.[55]

44.   It is forbidden to plait (alt. reading: to tear) or to twine even two threads or two detached hairs.

---

52.   Applying Cosmetics   Painting one's body on the Sabbath is a Rabbinic prohibition under the *melachah* of Dyeing (צוֹבֵעַ). It is therefore forbidden to color the face, eyes, or any part of the body. A woman may use face powder, even if it is colored, if it does not actually adhere to the skin. But she may not use a cream or powder mixed with cream. It is not permitted to use nail polish, even if it is colorless. See Melachah 15, note 5.

53.   Staining a Cloth or One's Clothing   If one's hands and face become soiled from eating food or fruit, he should if possible wash them before wiping with a cloth napkin or towel. While one should be careful not to touch his clothes if his hands are stained, he may be lenient if it is unavoidable, since the dyeing is not constructive, as it is done in a way that dirties the garment. See Melachah 15, note 6.

54.   Applying a Cloth to a Wound   In case of necessity it is permitted to apply a cloth to a bleeding wound. On bandaging a wound see Part II, Melachah 15, note 7, and Part V, Chapter 7, paragraphs 9,10 and notes.

55.   Adding Color to Food   The *halachah* as stated in the *Shulḥan Aruch* is that the prohibition against dyeing (צוֹבֵעַ) does not apply to coloring foods. The above ruling is based on the *Ḥayye Adam* who nevertheless advises one to be stringent. Prevailing practice, however, follows the lenient view. Coloring may be added to food for flavor, provided the coloring is itself edible, and one's intention is to eat the food that has been colored. It is preferable, if possible, to add the food to the coloring. One should, however, refrain from putting coloring into food merely to change its color. It is therefore not allowed to color water or brandy for the purpose of giving it an attractive appearance.

45.   When tying something with two threads or cords, or when winding a thread or cord around it and tying the two ends together like a belt, it is customary to make two knots, one over the other, because one knot will not hold. On the Sabbath it is forbidden to make a double knot, even if it is something that is usually untied on the same day.[56] One should be careful with the kerchief one wraps around the neck not to tie it with a double knot on the Sabbath.[57] Even if one puts it on *erev Shabbat,* he should not tie it with a double knot because it would be forbidden to untie it on the Sabbath. It is also forbidden to make even a single knot at one end of a thread or cord, or to take the two ends and to make one knot on both together, because in this case even one knot will hold fast. It is permitted to tie the two ends with one knot and a bow over it, if it is something that is customarily untied the same day, but if not it is forbidden, even if in this instance he intends to untie it the same day. It is permitted to make two or more bows one over the other, even if one intends it to remain that way for many days.

46.   It is forbidden to untie a knot which one is not permitted to make on the Sabbath. In a case of distress it is permitted to have a non-Jew undo the knot.

---

56.   Tying and Untying a Knot in Case of Need   In a case of pressing need, as for example in order to secure a dressing on a wound, one may tie a loose double knot if it will be untied within twenty-four hours. Where there is no other way of securing it, one may tie a firm double knot if it is intended to last less than seven days. In case of distress, one is likewise permitted to untie a double knot on the presumption that it was not intended to remain tied permanently, and the Rabbinical prohibition does not apply in such a circumstance. It is permitted to untie a double knot if it is loose. See Melachah 21, note 1.

57.   Tying a Necktie and Shoelaces   Shoelaces may be tied with a bow over a single knot, as they are customarily untied within twenty-four hours. One may, likewise, tie a necktie if it is untied the same day. A necktie can also be tied in such a way that it can be untied by pulling one end, or it can be tied before the Sabbath in a way that the loop can be enlarged or tightened so that it can be put on and removed at will. See Melachah 21, note 2.

47. It is customary with tailors that before sewing a garment properly they baste the pieces of cloth together with long stitches, and then they remove the basting threads. On the Sabbath it is forbidden to remove the basting threads.[58]

48. Some garments, such as trousers, shoes, or skirts are made so that a band or strap is inserted in them. If the garment is new it is forbidden to insert the band or the strap on the Sabbath because this is considered as forming or improving a utensil (תִּיקוּן מָנָא).[59] If the garment is old and the hole is not narrow, so that it can be inserted without difficulty, it is permitted. But if it requires effort it is forbidden.[60]

49. At times, when a seam comes apart and the parts of a garment separate, the thread is pulled and they join and come together. It is forbidden to do this on the Sabbath because of the prohibition of sewing (תּוֹפֵר).[61]

---

58. Articles of Clothing Packaged or Tied Together   Articles of clothing which are tied or secured together should be untied before the Sabbath. If one neglected to do so, one may part a new pair of socks and other new articles of clothing, which are tied or sewn together, by severing the connecting threads. If necessary, one may tear open sealed bags containing new clothes, taking care not to tear through any lettering or pictures. If stapled, one may remove the staples. See Melachah 38, note 2.

59. Inserting a Belt   A belt may be inserted, even in a new dress or a new pair of trousers, if it is one that is not left there permanently, but is constantly taken out and inserted again.

60. Inserting and Threading Shoelaces   A shoelace that has torn or has slipped out of the eyelets may be rethreaded if it can be done without undue difficulty. One may insert new shoelaces into shoes, irrespective of whether the shoes are old or new, provided it can be done without undue difficulty. Authorities who take a more stringent view require that this be done in a way that will ensure their subsequent removal by using laces of a different color, or by not threading them through all of the eyelets. See Melachah 21, note 2; Melachah 38, note 7.

61. Inserting and Removing Pins   It is permissible to use an ordinary pin

50.   If sheets of paper are by chance stuck together, as the pages of a book sometimes are stuck together by the ink used by the bookbinder to color the front edges of the book, or some of the pages are stuck together by wax, it is permissible to separate them.[62]

51.   A vessel whose opening is wrapped with a cloth and bound with a band may be torn open on the Sabbath,[63] as this spoils it,[64] and it is permissible when needed on the Sabbath.[65]

---

or a safety pin to fasten one's clothing or a baby's diaper, or to join parts of a torn garment, and the like, if it is not meant to be permanently secured. In the case of a safety pin, some are of the opinion that one should stick the pin through the cloth only once. One may, likewise, remove the pins from a new shirt or garment on the Sabbath.

62.   Separating Pages Stuck Together   It is forbidden to separate the pages of a book, if they were not cut to allow the book to be opened without tearing the pages apart, or if they are stuck together on some of the letters which would be defaced if the pages were separated. On opening a book with lettering on the edges of the pages, see Melachah 33, note 2.

63.   Tearing Off a Wrapper or a Seal   Utensils fastened by a cloth or cord may be undone, torn, or cut open because these bindings were not meant to remain tied, but were intended to be undone frequently. While the binding is damaged and spoiled, it is not considered complete demolition and is therefore not in violation of the prohibition of demolishing. A plastic or paper bag that is stapled may be opened by removing the staples. When needed for the Sabbath, one may tear off the wrapper or seal, whether of paper or other material, from a bottle, a jar, a box or other container, taking care not to tear through any lettering, pictures, or diagrams.

64.   Opening a Container   Inasmuch as the law pertaining to opening containers of food and beverages on the Sabbath is complex, and opinions vary on the matter, it is advisable to open all sealed boxes, cartons, cans, and other containers before the Sabbath. Some authorities do not permit opening containers on the Sabbath except in a case of pressing need. Others permit it if the container is made to be discarded when emptied of its contents, or it is torn or broken open in a way that renders it no longer usable as a container. Some authorities also permit opening one that remains usable as a container. Thus, it would be permissible to twist the cap off a bottle of

52.   It is forbidden to trap any living creature on the Sabbath.[66] It is even forbidden to catch a flea. But if it is on a person's body and stinging him, it is permitted to grab it and throw it away, because of the distress that it is causing him. However, it is forbidden to kill it, because it is forbidden to kill any living creature on the Sabbath.[67] Lice that are in clothing may not be killed, but should be taken and thrown away.

---

wine or soda, with the metal ring breaking off at the bottom, on the ground that this does not involve breaking, constructing or repairing a vessel, since the cap served as a vessel before the bottom ring was severed and continues to serve as such afterward. Where possible, the container should be opened in a manner different from the usual, or in a way that makes it no longer usable as a container. Thus a can of sardines or tuna should be opened only partially. A carton of milk or juice, which upon opening forms a spout, should preferably be torn or cut open. In any case, care should be taken not to cut or tear through any letters, pictures or designs on the container. See Melachah 24, note 5.

65.   Diapers With Self-sealing Tapes   Disposable diapers made with self-sealing tapes may be used on the Sabbath and removed after use even if it becomes necessary to tear the tapes to do so. The adhesive tapes should be opened and the plastic covering peeled off before the Sabbath. See Melachah 23, note 4.

66.   Trapping or Killing a Living Creature   It is forbidden to trap any animals, fish or other living creatures on the Sabbath. One may not trap mice and other rodents. However, one may kill any creature or animal, such as a mad dog or a poisonous snake, whose bite is fatal. Harmful creatures, whose bite is not fatal but can cause injury and distress, may be killed only if one is pursued or threatened by them. See Melachah 25, notes 6, 7.

67.   Ants and Other Insects   It is forbidden to kill ants and other insects by spraying them with an insecticide, or by washing them away in a manner that will kill them. Nor may one deliberately tread on ants and other harmless insects, even if he does so while in the course of walking. See Melachah 25, note 8.

53.   When one wishes to close a box or cover a vessel in which there are flies, he should first take care to chase them away, because if he does not do so they will be trapped there. Nevertheless, he does not have to examine and search the vessel to be sure there are no flies left. He only has to chase away those that he can see.[68]

54.   It is not permitted to draw blood, not even to suck blood from the gums.[69] It is likewise forbidden to put a plaster on a wound to draw out some of the blood and the pus. And it is certainly forbidden to squeeze blood or pus from the wound.[70]

55.   Hangnails, which are thin strips of skin hanging loose at the side or root of a fingernail, may not be severed, neither with an instrument, by hand, or with the teeth. A fingernail, the greater part of which is severed and is close to coming off and is causing pain, may be pulled off by hand, but not with an instrument.[71] If the greater

---

68.   Use of Insect Repellent   While it is forbidden to catch flies or insects on the Sabbath, it is permitted to spray an insect repellent in the air, when necessary to keep them away from a sick person or a baby, but not directly on the flies or the insects, provided there is a door or window open for them to fly out. One may apply a liquid insect repellent on one's hands or body, but not a cream or ointment. See Melachah 26, note 4.

69.   Using a Toothbrush or a Toothpick   As to brushing one's teeth on the Sabbath, while some permit the use of a toothbrush without toothpaste, it is the practice not to brush one's teeth even without toothpaste. One may use a toothpick to clean particles of food from one's teeth. See Melachah 30, note 6.

70.   Opening a Boil or Abscess   It is permitted to open a boil or an abscess, but without squeezing it, in order to let the pus out and relieve the pain, even if there is also an accumulation of blood. If possible, one should have this done by a non-Jew. On cleansing and treating a wound, see Part V, Chapter 7, paragraph 9 and note 12.

71.   Cutting or Tearing Off a Nail   It is forbidden to file, trim, cut, or tear

part of the fingernail is not severed, it is not permitted to pull it off even by hand.

56.   It is forbidden to pour any liquid into vinegar[72] in order to convert it into vinegar.[73]

57.   Meat that was left unsalted, which would be forbidden if not soaked before three days have elapsed, should be soaked by a non-Jew if the third day is a Sabbath, but not by a Jew.[74]

58.   It is not permitted to smear plaster, nor is it permitted to smear wax or tar. It is therefore forbidden to put wax or thick oil in a hole to seal it, or to stick it onto something as a mark. But it is permitted to smear food, such as butter on bread, and the like.

59.   It is forbidden to break or to cut anything that is not food.[75] But

---

off one's nails, neither with an instrument, by hand, or with the teeth. If the greater part of the nail is detached and is causing one pain, or he is afraid it will cause him pain, it is permitted to remove it by hand or with the teeth, but not with an instrument.

72.   Diluting Vinegar, Wine, or Whiskey   It is permitted to pour a liquid into vinegar on the Sabbath in order to dilute the strength of the vinegar. Similarly, one may dilute the strength of wine or whiskey by adding water.

73.   Pickling Cucumbers   Pickling is prohibited on the Sabbath. It is therefore not permitted to put raw cucumbers, and the like, into brine or vinegar to turn sour or to pickle.

74.   Meat Left Unsoaked for Three Days   Unsalted meat left unsoaked for three days after slaughter may not be cooked, but it can be roasted. If the meat belongs to a butcher who stands to suffer a loss in not being able to sell the meat to his customers it may be soaked by a non-Jew on the Sabbath. Some authorities permit a Jew to soak the meat if a non-Jew is not available. See Melachah 28, note 2.

75.   Cutting Food and Animal Fodder   Cutting (מְחַתֵּךְ), one of the principal *melachot* forbidden on the Sabbath, does not apply to foodstuff. Hence, one may break off a piece of straw to use as a toothpick, or crush a detached

if it is food, even if only for an animal, it is permitted.[76] It is therefore permissible to cut off a piece of straw to pick one's teeth with it. It is permitted to lop off pieces from detached fragrant twigs, and to rub them in order to smell them, even if they are as hard as wood. But it is not permitted to lop them off to pick one's teeth.

60. One may not make use of a tree, whether fresh and moist or dried up, even if he does not shake it (as the mere shaking of the tree would involve the prohibition of *muktzeh*). One may not climb up on it, or suspend oneself from it. It is forbidden to place any object on it, or to take it off, or to tie an animal to it, and the like. It is even forbidden to make use of the "sides" of the tree. Therefore, if there is a basket hanging from it, it is not permitted to take something out of the basket or to put something in it, because the basket is considered as the "side" of the tree. But if there is a peg stuck in the tree and the basket is hanging from it, it is permitted to take something from it, or to put something in it, because then the basket is only a "side of the side" of the tree. However, it is not permitted to remove the basket or to hang it there, because one is then making use of the peg, which is considered the "side" of the tree.[77]

---

twig or plant to enjoy its fragrance, so long as it qualifies as food or animal fodder. One may, likewise, break off a piece from a detached twig or plant or a cluster of grapes to give it to someone else to smell or to eat.

76. Cutting Food into Shapes and Designs While it is permissible to break or cut up food, one may not use an instrument designed to form food, such as melons and the like, into special shapes and decorative designs. See Melachah 34, note 3.

77. Prohibited Use of a Tree The prohibition against use of a tree on the Sabbath, while enacted to prevent one from climbing the tree and tearing off a leaf, a branch or some fruit, applies to all kinds of trees, even those without fruit or foliage. It includes, as well, the use of the "sides" of the tree (צְדָדִים), that is something attached to the tree. Thus, it is forbidden not only to climb a tree, but one may not climb a ladder that is leaning on a tree as well. One is not permitted to hang a jacket or some other object, such as a

61. Plants or flowers that are grown in a pot for their beauty or fragrance may not be plucked, just as it is forbidden to pluck something that grows on a tree.[78] One should not move the pot from the ground to put it in another place, because when it stands on the ground it receives nourishment from it, and when one removes it from there it is as though he were detaching it from the ground. And if the pot is standing in another place, it is forbidden to take it and put it on the ground, because it is as though he were planting it. One should be careful with regard to the above, whether the pot is of wood or of clay, and whether or not it has a hole on the bottom.

62. It is forbidden to write or to make a drawing, even with one's finger and water on the table, or on a misty or frosty windowpane, or

---

basket, on a tree or on a branch of the tree, or on a nail or peg protruding from it. Neither may he remove the object. It is permitted, however, to make indirect use of the "sides" of the tree (צְדֵי צְדָדִים), that is use of an object that is connected to something attached to the tree. Thus, one may put an article into a basket or into the pocket of a jacket that is hanging on a nail or on a peg protruding from the tree. One may not use a clothesline that is directly tied to a tree, unless it is on a pulley that is attached to the tree, and provided the tree will not move. It is permitted to use a swing or a hammock if it hangs from a rope or a chain attached to the tree, or if it is suspended from a pole that connects two trees. provided the tree does not move. However, some advise caution in this instance, because it might mistakenly be used under conditions that are not permissible. One may not retrieve a ball stuck in a tree, either by hand or with a stick, and surely not by climbing the tree or shaking it. See Melachah 3, note 5.

78. Handling and Smelling Flowers While it is permissible to smell flowers that are still attached to a tree or to the soil, some authorities advise that one refrain from doing so. Cut flowers in a vase may be handled and their fragrance savored. One should not put flowers into a vase of water on the Sabbath, even if they were cut and prepared before the Sabbath, as the water will cause the buds and flowers to open. One may not change the water in the vase or add to it. See Melachah 3, note 2; Part V, Chapter 3, note 17. On handling a flowerpot, see Melachah 2, note 1.

anything similar, even if the writing or drawing is not permanent.[79] It is also forbidden to make a mark as a sign on something with one's fingernail. If wax, or the like, is found to have dripped on a book, even if only on one letter, it may not be removed.

63.   Just as it is forbidden to write on the Sabbath, so is it forbidden to erase what has been written. It is, nevertheless, permitted to break and to eat cakes that have letters or designs on them.[80]

64.   Some authorities forbid opening or closing books that have lettering on the outer edges of the pages. Others permit it, and this is the prevailing practice. However, since some do not permit it, such inscriptions should not be placed on books.[81]

---

79. Writing That Is Not Durable   While it is a violation of the Biblical prohibition only if the writing will last, as with ink on parchment or on paper, one is nevertheless Rabbinically forbidden to write or to erase even where the writing is not durable. Hence, it is forbidden to write, or draw, or make markings in dust or in sand. It is, likewise, forbidden to cut letters or designs into the rind of a melon, or the peel of an orange or some other fruit. It is, however, permitted to outline the shape of letters with one's fingers on a dry board or in the air, as there is no visible sign of the writing. See Melachah 32, paragraph 1 and notes.

80. A Cake or Chocolate Bar Decorated With Letters or Designs   It is not permitted to form any lettering or designs when putting icing or whipped cream on a cake. One may squeeze the icing or the whipped cream out of a tube or container, but not with a tip made to form it into a special shape. Cakes decorated with letters and designs made of icing or other foodstuffs may be eaten on the Sabbath. The cake should be cut into portions before the Sabbath. If it is to be cut on the Sabbath, one should avoid cutting or breaking of the lettering or the designs. If the decorations are of honey or fruit juices, or of the same ingredients as the food itself such as lettering raised or impressed on a cake or chocolate bar, it may be cut or broken and eaten on the Sabbath. Cookies formed and baked in the shape of letters or figures of animals and other objects may, likewise, be broken and eaten. See Melachah 32, note 12; Melachah 33, paragraph 5 and notes.

81. Opening and Closing a Book With Letters Stamped on the Edges

65. It is permitted to say to one's fellow, "Fill up this vessel for me," even if the vessel is used specifically for measuring, and even if it belongs to the seller, so long as the buyer takes it home. It is surely permissible if the buyer brings his own vessel and says, "Fill up this vessel for me." However, it is forbidden to measure with a vessel that is used specifically for measuring which belongs to the seller, and to pour its contents into the buyer's vessel. One may say to one's fellow, "Give me fifty nuts," and the like, provided he does not mention a measure or an amount of money. Nor may one make a reckoning and say, "I already owe you for fifty nuts, give me another fifty and I will owe you for a hundred." And he should certainly not speak of buying and selling, even if he does not stipulate the price, and even if it is needed for the Sabbath.[82] It is forbidden to make a purchase on the Sabbath through a non-Jew,[83] even if one pays him for his services.

Accepted practice permits opening and closing a book with an inscription bearing letters and words stamped on its front edges. Inasmuch as a book is intended to be opened and closed, and the letters and words are only separated and combined temporarily, opening and closing the book on the Sabbath is not subject to the prohibition of erasing and writing. Nevertheless, if one has another copy of the book without such an inscription, it is preferable that he use that copy. See Melachah 33, note 2.

82. Buying and Selling on the Sabbath Buying and selling merchandise is forbidden on the Sabbath. Measuring, unless it is for the sake of a *mitzvah,* is likewise not permitted. However, one may ask for what he needs in the manner indicated, so long as he does not stipulate a price, or use the language of buying and selling. See Melachah 32, paragraphs 4–6 and notes.

83. Requesting a Non-Jew to Make a Purchase A Jew is forbidden to request a non-Jew to make a purchase for him on the Sabbath. However, he may ask him to buy it for himself, with the understanding that if he needs it he will buy it from him after the Sabbath. One may also give a non-Jew money before the Sabbath to buy some merchandise for him, promising to compensate him for his services. He should not, however, stipulate that he is to buy it on the Sabbath, and if the non-Jew then makes the purchase on the Sabbath, he will be doing it for his own benefit. If there is ample time for the

66. It is permitted to say to one's fellow, "Fill up this vessel for me," or "Give me up to this mark, and tomorrow we will measure it or weigh it."

67. Just as it is forbidden to build even a temporary structure on the Sabbath, so it is forbidden to add even a temporary addition to a permanent structure. An entrance which was not made to be used constantly[84] to go in and out, but only infrequently, and for which one made a door that does not swing on its hinges (a hinge in this instance being a wooden or iron bar that projects from the door and is inserted at the bottom into a hole in the threshold, and at the top into the lintel, so that the door will turn in both directions), but he tied it to the doorway and hung it there for closing the entrance, then if the door has a hinge, or even if it does not have a hinge now, but it once had a hinge that broke and its place is still evident, it is permitted to close the entrance with it on the Sabbath. Even if the door is made in such a way that when it is opened it drags on the ground, and when it is closed it is raised and placed on the threshold, it is still permitted. Since it is tied to the doorway and hangs there, and there is indication of a hinge, it is evident that it is a door made to be closed and opened, and it does not appear as though one were building. It is certainly permitted to use the door if it still has a hinge, provided one does not return the hinge to its place, as then it would be considered building.

68. If, however, there is no indication of a hinge it is forbidden to close the entrance with it on the Sabbath. For since it was made for the entrance only to be used infrequently, and it does not look like it was meant to be a door, closing it would appear as though he were

---

non-Jew to make the purchase before the Sabbath, compensation for his services is not a requirement, and the non-Jew can then make the purchase when he sees fit to do so. But in this instance, as well, he may not stipulate that he buy it on the Sabbath.

84. An Entrance In Constant Use   An entrance that is used at least once in less than thirty days is considered as one that is in constant use.

building. But if it is securely tied and hung in a way that it does not drag on the ground when it is opened, even if it is only a hairbreadth above the ground, it has the appearance of a door and it is permitted to close the entrance with it.

69.   If the door is not attached and suspended from the doorway at all but, upon opening it, it is removed entirely, it is forbidden to close up an entrance with it, when the entrance is not intended to be used constantly to go in and out. But if the entrance is made to be used constantly it is permitted to close the entrance with it, even if it has no indication of a hinge.

70.   A door that consists of a single plank may not be used to close an entrance that was not intended to be used constantly to go in and out, even if it has hinges but it does not swing on its hinges. For since the door consists of one plank, and it does not swing on its hinges, it appears as though one were building and closing up an opening. But one may be lenient and use the door to close an entrance that was made to be used constantly, provided there is a threshold, for then it is evident that it is an entrance.

71.   It is permitted to close up a window with a shutter or some other object that is used for that purpose, even if it is not attached to the window, provided it was already used once before the Sabbath for closing up the window, or one had it in mind before the Sabbath to use it for that purpose. But if it was never used to close up the window, and he did not have it in mind to use it for that purpose, it is forbidden to close up the window with it on the Sabbath, if it is something that would normally be left there for a long time. But if it is something that would usually be left there only for a short time, such as a garment and the like, it is permissible to use it to close up the window under all circumstances.[85]

---

85.   **Inserting a Bar in a Door or Window**   Adding to a structure is considered building, which is forbidden on the Sabbath. However, something that is erected temporarily and made to be removed that very day is not con-

72. It is forbidden to remove or to reset doors and windows on the Sabbath,[86] even when they hang on iron hinges and are easily removed and reset, because when one hangs them it is as though he were building, and when he removes them it is as though he were demolishing.

73. It is forbidden to sweep the house, even if the floor is made of stone or of boards. It may, however, be done by a non-Jew. But if it is done in an unusual manner, such as sweeping it with goose feathers and the like, it may even be done by a Jew.[87]

74. One should not rub spittle on the ground with his foot because he will level the ground, but he may step on it without rubbing it.

75. It is forbidden to relieve oneself in a plowed field on the Sabbath. (If the field belongs to someone else, it is forbidden to enter it even on weekdays, because he will tread on the furrows and spoil them.)

---

sidered building. Thus, one may insert a bar or a bolt in a window or in the door on Friday night and remove it on Sabbath morning, provided it is adapted for that purpose. For the laws of building and demolishing, see Melachah 34, and Melachah 35.

86. Removing Frozen Ice From a Door One may remove ice that has frozen over a door and sealed it shut on the Sabbath, even by using a spade or iron bar to dislodge the ice.

87. Sweeping and Cleaning the Floor Many authorities permit sweeping the house on the Sabbath when the flooring is of a hard, smooth surface, such as wood, cement or marble, or covered with linoleum or tiles as is customary, and when one uses a soft broom or a broom whose bristles will not break off. It is not permitted, however, to sweep a carpeted floor, neither with a brush nor with an ordinary carpet sweeper, even if it is not electrically operated. One may sweep the carpet and gather up crumbs with a soft broom that will not pull out any of the nap from the rug or carpet. It is not permitted to polish a floor of wood, tiles or linoleum with wax or floor polish. See Melachah 1, note 4; Melachah 34, paragraph 10.

76.   It is forbidden to construct a partition, however temporary, on the Sabbath and on *Yom Tov*, if it is to make something permissible. Hence, it is not permitted to make a partition by putting up a curtain, and the like, in front of the light of a candle so that one may have marital relations, or in front of holy books so that one may have marital relations, or to relieve himself, for since the partition renders these acts permissible, it creates a separate premise and it is as though he were making a tent. However, it is permissible to cover the holy books with two covers, one on top of the other, as this does not constitute a tent. If the curtain hanging in front of the bed was already spread out a handbreadth (*tefaḥ*) before the Sabbath, whether on the side or on top, it is permitted to spread it out fully on the Sabbath, because it is regarded as an addition to a temporary tent. However the part of the curtain that is always folded up at one end does not count toward the required handbreadth, since it is not intended to serve as a tent. It is likewise forbidden to open a folding partition, commonly known as a "Spanish wall," unless it was already slightly open from before the Sabbath. The fact that it stands folded, although the screen is wider than a handbreadth, does not qualify it. It is, however, permitted to make a temporary partition that is not intended to make something permissible, but serves only as a protection against the sun, or to keep the wind from extinguishing the candles and the like.[88]

77.   It is forbidden to make a tent, that is a roof that shelters, even when it is intended to shield one from the sun or the rain and the like, and it is only a temporary tent, if it is one handbreadth by a handbreadth and a handbreadth high. Hence it is forbidden to spread a sheet over the arched wooden frame of a baby's cradle on the Sab-

---

88.   A Partition Before a Candle or Holy Books   If the partition is made sufficiently high to completely block out the candle light or the holy books from view, it is permitted in time of need, as it is then regarded not as a partition but rather as a cover. In the case of holy books, they should be covered and then partitioned off, so that they are in effect doubly covered.

bath and on *Yom Tov,* unless it was already spread a handbreadth from before the Sabbath, so that it is regarded only as an addition to a provisional tent, which is permissible. If the staves are close together within three handbreadths of each other, they are considered as already forming a tent—for it is a ruling given to Moses on Mount Sinai (הֲלָכָה לְמשֶׁה מִסִּינַי) that where a space in a partition is less than three handbreadths it is considered as joined (לָבוּד), that is, as attached and closed—and it is therefore permitted to spread a sheet over them.[89]

78.   One is forbidden to remove the cover from a chest if it is not attached to it with hinges,[90] because he is thereby demolishing a tent. One is, likewise, forbidden to place the cover on the chest because he is thereby making a tent. When placing a board on a barrel to make a table, the barrel should be set down with the open end on the bottom, for if the board were placed on the open end he would be making a tent.

79.   It is permissible to close the opening at the side of a chimney,

---

89.   Spreading a Sheet Over a Baby's Crib   Spreading out a mat or a sheet to form a permanent tent is forbidden on the Sabbath, because making a tent is a sub-labor (*Toladah*) of the *melachah* of Building. The Rabbis prohibited making a temporary tent in order to prevent one from making a permanent tent. Hence, one is permitted to spread a sheet over a baby's crib on the Sabbath only when it conforms to the conditions indicated. Likewise, if one of the arched staves is a handbreadth wide, or there is a space less than three handbreadths in one place, it is permitted to spread a sheet over it, since a tent already exists.

90.   Opening an Awning and the Hood of a Baby Carriage   It is permitted to open and extend the hood of a baby carriage that serves to shield the child from the sun and rain, because it is fastened to the carriage and is made to open and close by turning on its hinges like a door. It is, likewise, permitted to open the awning over a window or a balcony, as it is attached with hinges and is made to fold out and roll up, especially if it is left open a handbreadth from before the Sabbath. See Melachah 34, note 6.

for it is merely adding to the partition. But if the opening is on the top one is forbidden to close it on the Sabbath and on *Yom Tov,* because he is making a tent. However, if there is an iron door that swings on hinges attached to it, it is permitted to close it, for since it is fastened there permanently it is similar to any door that swings on hinges.[91]

80.   A cloth that is spread over a cask should not be drawn over the entire opening if the cask is not completely full, and there is an empty space of a handbreadth between the liquid it contains and the cover, because of the prohibition of making a tent,[92] but one should leave part of the opening uncovered.

81.   Any partition or tent which it is forbidden to make may not be removed, because it is like demolishing a tent.

82.   One is forbidden to carry an umbrella made to shield one from the sun or the rain, because he is making a tent.[93]

83.   Utensils made up of parts inserted into one another, that have been taken apart, may be reassembled if the parts are normally held

---

91.   Closing the Opening of a Chimney   If there are glowing coals in the oven it is in any case forbidden to close the opening on top of the chimney, quite apart from the prohibition of making a tent, as he would then be causing the coals to be extinguished.

92.   Covering a Utensil   It is advisable to follow the stringent view of the *Shulḥan Aruch,* as stated above, not to cover a large water cask completely on the Sabbath if it is not entirely full. However, inasmuch as other authorities are of the opinion that the prohibition of making a tent does not apply to the covering of utensils, one should not protest against those who are accustomed to be lenient in this matter.

93.   Carrying an Umbrella   It is forbidden to open or close an umbrella on the Sabbath. It is likewise not permitted to carry an umbrella that was opened before the Sabbath, even where there is an *eruv* and it is ordinarily permissible to carry. See Melachah 34, note 7.

together loosely.[94] But if they are normally fastened tightly it is forbidden to reassemble them even loosely. If the parts are joined with screws they may not be reassembled even loosely if they have come apart, since they are normally fastened tightly.[95] However, the covers of utensils may be removed and reattached, since they are not made to remain attached but to be regularly opened and closed.[96]

84. A clothes press consisting of two boards, one on top of the other, between which the garments are pressed, if it belongs to an ordinary person may be opened to remove the garments needed for use on the Sabbath or *Yom Tov*. But one may not press any garment, as this would be using it for a weekday need. If the press is that of a presser or another craftsman it is forbidden to open it, for since it is tightly clamped, to open it would resemble the *melachah* of demolishing. Even if it was opened before the Sabbath it is not permitted to

---

94. Children Playing With Building Blocks It is permissible for young children to play with building or interconnecting blocks that are readily assembled into various forms and shapes, since they are made to be put together and taken apart, and are not intended to remain permanently attached. See Melachah 34, note 1.

95. Setting Up a Folding Bed, Crib, Chair, or Table A folding bed, such as a hi-riser, a couch, a wall bed, or a cot whose parts are attached to one frame, may be set up or opened up on the Sabbath and folded up again after use. One may set up a folding or portable crib, fasten the latches, and insert the bars to keep the sides steady, but he may not tighten or loosen any screws. A folding table may be set up, as well as lengthened by extending the side leaves and by inserting an additional board. A folding chair or a lawn chair may be set up, but the awning may not be attached to it to shield one from the sun. If the awning was already attached it may be opened and closed as needed.

96. Removing and Reattaching a Cover of a Utensil The covers of utensils may be removed and reattached, even if they are made to be screwed on, because the covers are not intended to remain attached to the vessels but only to be used constantly for opening and closing them.

remove the garments on the Sabbath or *Yom Tov,* lest one come to open it on the Sabbath or *Yom Tov.*[97]

85.   If one of the legs of a bench came off it is forbidden to replace it, and it is also forbidden to lean it against another bench, unless one already sat on it before the Sabbath while it was in this condition.[98] But it is permitted to rest a board on two stools or on two blocks of wood which have been prepared before the Sabbath for this purpose.

86.   A watch, even if it is still going, may not be wound on the Sabbath or on *Yom Tov* to keep it going. On the second day of *Yom Tov* one may be lenient and wind the watch if it is still going, but only when it is needed for that day. One may not wind it for the following day. For the sake of a sick person it is permitted under all circumstances, if a non-Jew is not readily available to do it.[99]

---

97.   Removing Garments From a Clothes Press   According to some authorities if the press was completely open from before the Sabbath it is permitted to remove one's clothing from it. The above stated rulings apply to a press used to press garments after they have been laundered, which operates mechanically and involves no other violations of the Sabbath.

98.   Using a Broken Bench   It is forbidden to use the leg as a support for the bench, or to rest the broken bench on another bench, for fear that one would come to reattach the leg and wedge it in tightly. Therefore, if the leg is broken or no longer available the prohibitions do not apply. Also, if there is a danger that the bench might fall and cause injury it is permitted to remove it or to rest it on another bench in order to sit on it.

99.   Winding a Watch   It is forbidden to start the movement of a watch that has stopped, neither by winding it nor by shaking it. Opinions differ on the permissibility of winding it while it is still going in order to keep it going for a longer period of time. All agree that for the sake of a sick person a Jew is permitted to wind the watch if it is still going, and to have it wound by a non-Jew even if it has stopped. Some authorities permit one to wind the watch when it is still going also for the sake of a *mitzvah* or for some other pressing need. It is permitted to wear a self-winding watch, so long as it is going. A digital watch powered by a battery may be worn on the Sabbath, provided one does not have to light up the numbers for them to be seen. One

87.   It is forbidden to make a musical sound on the Sabbath, either with an instrument[100] or with one's limbs (except the mouth). One should not snap his fingers or tap them on a board to make a sound, or make a rattling noise with nuts or with a rattle to keep a child from crying. Nor should one clap his hands or dance. It is, however, permissible to clap and dance in honor of the Torah. Neither are we to prevent one from doing this for a baby to keep it from crying, since some authorities permit it.[101]

88.   It is permissible to make a sound that is not musical. Therefore, one is permitted to knock on the door so that it will be opened, and the like. Some authorities maintain that it is nevertheless forbidden to make a sound with a specially designed instrument, such as knocking with a metal ring or a gong attached to the door.[102] Clocks that

---

may not adjust the time on this type of watch, or cause the numbers or letters to appear or disappear. See Melachah 38, paragraph 4 and notes. For the laws regarding going out into the street where there is no *eruv* wearing a wristwatch or a pocket-watch, see Part IV, Chapter 4, paragraph 2 and notes.

100.   Playing Music on the Sabbath   It is forbidden to play a record on a phonograph, even one that is operated manually. It is forbidden to set a phonograph or some other instrument or appliance, such as a radio, stereo, microphone, and television, on an automatic timer before the Sabbath to play on the Sabbath. See Melachah 36, Electrical Equipment and Appliances, notes 5, 10; Melachah 38, paragraph 5 and notes.

101.   Playing With Toys That Emit a Sound   A child should not play on the Sabbath with a bell, horn, whistle, record player, and the like, as well as with toys that emit a distinctive sound when wound up, or when handled, such as a toy telephone. Such toys should be put away before the Sabbath. Young children may be allowed to play with toys that only incidentally emit a sound when pulled or squeezed. It is permissible to give a baby a rattle to play with, and some authorities permit one to shake the rattle or sound a bell to quiet a crying baby. See Melachah 38, note 18.

102.   Using a Door Knocker   In the case of need, where one has no other recourse to enter the house, it is permissible to use the door knocker to sum-

are made to sound the hour by striking them or by pulling on a cord may not be operated on the Sabbath[103] or on *Yom Tov.*

89.   One who watches over fruit or grain to protect them from animals or birds should not clap his hands, or slap his thighs, or stamp his feet in order to chase them away, as he is accustomed to do on weekdays.

90.   One should not play[104] with nuts[105] and the like[106] on the

---

mon someone to open the door. See Melachah 38, note 19. For particulars regarding a doorbell that operates electrically, see Melachah 36, Electrical Equipment and Appliances, note 11.

103.   Resetting an Alarm Clock   If an alarm clock (non-electric) has been set before the Sabbath to ring at a designated hour for prayer or Torah study, one may shut off the alarm on Friday night so that it will not ring at that hour, and then open it so that it will ring at the designated hour on *Shabbat* morning. If necessary, one may reset the time for the alarm to ring, provided he does not cause it to ring immediately. Once the alarm rings at the designated time, it is permitted to shut it off. However, it is not permitted to set the alarm on the Sabbath. One may not shut off the alarm on a clock that operates on electricity. See Melachah 38, note 13.

104.   Attending a Sporting Event   One should not attend a sporting event, such as a game of football, soccer, hockey, or basketball, even when admission to the stadium is free, as such events are generally associated with desecration of the Sabbath and are not in keeping with the sanctity of the Sabbath.

105.   Playing Ball and Playing With Marbles   Playing with nuts or marbles on the ground is prohibited, for fear that one may level the earth to prepare a path for rolling them. The restriction applies outdoors even when the ground is paved, because one might conclude that if it is permissible on paved ground it is also permitted on unpaved ground. It is permissible to play with nuts or marbles on a table or mat, or on the floor in the house. Some also permit table tennis with a ping-pong ball. Playing ball is allowed in the house, or outside the house where there is an *eruv,* on a paved surface such as a cemented court, and the like. The above applies to young children,

ground, even if it is paved. Nevertheless, it is advisable not to protest against children[107] who do it, as they will surely not listen, and it is better that they transgress unwittingly rather than willfully.[108]

---

that is boys under thirteen and girls under twelve years of age. Older children and adults should refrain from such games on the Sabbath, but should rather devote their time to Torah study and activities in keeping with the holiness of the day. Even younger children should engage in some Torah study, and should be involved in other activities in the spirit of the Sabbath. See Melachah 1, note 5.

106. Playing Chess, Checkers and Other Games Games in which the score is kept and normally written down, and games that involve the use of play money, especially in the form of coins, should not be played on the Sabbath. Games like chess, checkers and dominoes are generally permitted on the Sabbath. The Rama specifically permits chess, provided it is for pleasure and not for gain. The *Magen Avraham* and *Mishnah B'rurah* note that it is the practice to have silver chess pieces especially designated for the Sabbath so that it would not resemble a weekday activity. However, other authorities cited do not permit these games on the Sabbath, including chess, and do not approve of them even on weekdays. It is generally agreed that it is more appropriate to devote one's time to Torah study and activities in keeping with the spirit of the Sabbath. See Melachah 32, note 26.

107. Building With Blocks and Assembling a Jigsaw Puzzle Children may play with building blocks, provided they are of the kind that are put together loosely and are made to be put together and taken apart. Games in which letters are put together to form a word, or parts of pictures are placed side by side to form a picture are permissible, provided they are not set and held together firmly in a frame or interlocked as in a jigsaw puzzle. See Melachah 32, note 26.

108. Riding a Tricycle, Running, Skipping Rope A young child may be allowed to ride a tricycle, a scooter, or a bicycle with training wheels in the house, or outside where there is an *eruv,* as it is apparent that it is a child's vehicle used for play. He should be cautioned not to repair it, and the bell or horn should be removed. Running, jumping, rope skipping, and the like are permissible games. See Melachah 38, note 16.

91. There are many particular laws regarding the folding of garments,[109] hence no garment[110] should be folded on the Sabbath.[111]

92. If a garment catches on fire it is permissible to pour a liquid on the part of the garment that is not burning, so that when the fire reaches the part that is wet it will be extinguished. But it is not permitted to pour water on the garment.[112]

---

109. Folding a Garment It is permissible to fold a garment on the Sabbath if the garment is folded in a manner different from the way it is usually folded, although it is preferable to be stringent in this as well. Hence, when folding articles, such as sheets, tablecloths, and the like, they should not be folded in their original creases. Articles in which there is no recognizable crease, such as rubber sheets, plastic tablecloths, and woolen garments, may be readily folded without regard to their creases. It is likewise permitted to fold articles of clothing, and the like, when one is not particular about the way in which they are folded, but only wishes to put them away properly and to keep the house tidy. The prohibition also does not apply to restoring a garment to its normal shape. Hence, one may restore the dents in a hat that has been crushed, and turn up a turned down trouser cuff, or adjust a shirt collar to its proper shape. See Melachah 38, note 26.

110. Inserting Shoe Trees In Shoes One may insert shoe trees into his shoes on the Sabbath, provided they are not intended to widen and reshape the shoe. Shoe trees may also be inserted into shoes that are wet from the rain in order to keep their shape.

111. Folding a Tallit Some authorities permit folding a *tallit* on the Sabbath, but advise that one should not fold it in its original folds. Some do not permit folding it at all, while others permit folding it in the usual manner, especially if it is a *tallit* that is regularly set aside for use on the Sabbath. For particulars, see Part II, Melachah 38, note 27; Part V, Chapter 12, note 26.

112. Saving an Article That Has Caught on Fire It is forbidden to extinguish a fire on the Sabbath, where there is no danger to life, merely to save an article such as a garment or a tablecloth that has caught on fire. It is permitted, however, to cause the fire to be extinguished by pouring a liquid and wetting down the area that is not burning. The restriction against pouring water is because of the prohibition of cleansing and laundering. Should

93. One should not make the bed on the Sabbath for use after the
Sabbath, even when there is enough time for one to sleep on it on the
Sabbath. Since it is not his intention to sleep on it until after *Shabbat,*
one is in fact preparing on the Sabbath for the weekday, which is
forbidden.[113]

---

there be a possible danger to life, one must of course act quickly and take
any measure to extinguish the fire. For a further discussion of the laws that
pertain in the case of a fire, see Part II, Melachah 37, note 7; Part IV,
Chapter 5.

113. Making the Beds One should arrange the beds with sheets, covers
and pillowcases before the Sabbath. If the beds were not prepared in
advance one may do so Friday evening as well. Inasmuch as it is now customary for the beds to be made daily by arranging the sheets, the pillows, and
the bedspreads in order to keep the house from appearing unsightly, and not
necessarily to prepare them for later use, it is permissible to do so in honor
of the Sabbath. Indeed, if the beds were left in disarray it would be dis-
respectful of the Sabbath. See Melachah 38, note 28.

Part IV

Carrying On The Sabbath

1. FOUR DOMAINS WITH REGARD TO THE SABBATH

אַרְבַּע רְשׁוּיוֹת לְשַׁבָּת

1. There are four kinds of domain with regard to carrying on the Sabbath: a private domain (*reshut ha-yaḥid,* רְשׁוּת הַיָחִיד), a public domain (*reshut ha-rabim,* רְשׁוּת הָרַבִּים), a semi-public domain (*karmelit,* כַּרְמְלִית), and a free place (*mekom petur,* מְקוֹם פְּטוּר). For a formulation of the *melachah* which prohibits carrying on the Sabbath, see Part II, Melachah 39.

2. A private domain (רְשׁוּת הַיָחִיד) is an area at least four *tefaḥim* (four handbreadths, approximately fifteen inches) by four *tefaḥim*— this being a sufficiently useful space—that is enclosed by partitions no less than ten *tefaḥim* (ten handbreadths, approximately three feet) high—even if the partitions are not whole; or the area is bounded by a trench ten *tefaḥim* deep and four *tefaḥim* wide. Similarly, an excavation such as a pit, or an elevation such as a mound of earth or stones,[1] or an object such as a box, or a vessel such as a barrel, that measures ten *tefaḥim* in depth or in height, and is four *tefaḥim* square, forms a separate premise and is considered to be private domain, even when it is situated in a public domain[2] or in a *karmelit.* The airspace above

---

1. Slope of the Pit or Mound The pit or excavation, and the mound or elevation, must reach a depth or a height of ten handbreadths within a slope of less than four cubits for it to be considered private domain. But if it is more than four cubits, with a more gradual incline affording greater accessibility to people, it is regarded as part of the public domain.

2. A Tower in a Public Domain A structure such as a tower and the like, which stands in the public domain upon one or more pillars or posts, and measures ten *tefaḥim* in height and four *tefaḥim* square is considered a private domain, although the space beneath it is public domain.

285

a private domain is, to an unlimited height, private domain. The tops of the partitions that enclose the area are also private domain. Any holes on the inner side of the walls or partitions are likewise considered private domain, even if they extend through to the outer side, inasmuch as they are of use from within the premises. Indeed, whatever is in a private domain, irrespective of its size or dimensions, is subordinate to it and is considered to be private domain.

3. A public domain (רְשׁוּת הָרַבִּים) is an area, such as a public square or a market place,[3] which measures sixteen *amot* (sixteen cubits, approximately twenty-eight feet) by sixteen *amot,* or an intercity highway that is sixteen *amot* wide—this being the width of the road in the camp of the Levites in the wilderness. Anything in the public domain that is less than three *tefaḥim* (three handbreadths, approximately eleven inches) in height from the ground, such as a mound of earth or stones, even thorns and dung which people avoid stepping on, is subordinate to the ground and considered public domain.[4] A ditch less than three *tefaḥim* deep that is in the public domain is considered to be a part of the public domain. A hole in the side of a wall facing the public domain that does not extend through the wall into the private domain, if situated less than three *tefaḥim* from the ground, is subordinate to the ground and considered public domain. If it is three *tefaḥim* or more from the ground it is judged in accordance with its measurements. If it measures four *tefaḥim* by four *tefaḥim* and is lower than ten *tefaḥim* from the ground it is considered a *karmelit.* If it is more than ten *tefaḥim* from the ground it is considered a private domain. If it does not measure four *tefaḥim* by four

---

3. A Public Square and Market Place To be considered a public domain the public square or market place should have no roof and no walls. If it has walls it should be open at both gates and its doors unlocked at night, so that it is accessible to the public at all times.

4. Airspace Above a Public Domain The airspace over a public domain to a height of ten handbreadths is considered to be public domain; above ten handbreadths it is regarded as a "free place" (מָקוֹם פָּטוּר).

tefaḥim it is considered a *mekom petur,* irrespective of whether it is more or less than ten *tefaḥim* from the ground. An alley leading into the public domain is at times regarded as public domain and at times as a *karmelit,* inasmuch as its status is subject to many particular laws. Some authorities are of the opinion that any place that does not have six hundred thousand people (שִׁשִּׁים רִבּוֹא) passing by daily,[5] equal to the number of Israelites encamped in the wilderness, is not considered to be a public domain, but is regarded as a *karmelit.* Hence, according to this view, there is presently no area that has the status of a public domain.[6] Every God-fearing person should adopt the stricter view for himself.[7]

---

5.   Six Hundred Thousand People in a Public Domain   It is uncertain whether the requisite condition of שִׁשִּׁים רִבּוֹא means that six hundred thousand people must actually pass through an area daily if it is to be regarded as a public domain. The *Shulḥan Aruch* so states it, but the *Mishnah B'rurah* points out that the previous authorities do not mention this fact. He therefore maintains that it suffices if there is that number of people present or residing in the area. See Melachah 39, note 11.

6.   A Primary Consideration in Establishing an Eruv   The presence of six hundred thousand people (שִׁשִּׁים רִבּוֹא) as a requirement for an area to be regarded as a public domain is not explicitly stated in the Talmud, and it is therefore the subject of controversy among halachic authorities. The question turns on whether the area must conform to the Israelite encampment in the wilderness in this respect. Rashi, Rosh, Semag, Semak and other authorities believe שִׁשִּׁים רִבּוֹא to be a requisite condition. Rambam, Ramban, Rashba and others, however, are of the opinion that if the place has the essential characteristics, namely, that it is a public square or a road that is unroofed, measuring sixteen cubits in width, and open at both ends, it is considered a public domain.

The view which deems שִׁשִּׁים רִבּוֹא a requisite condition is cited in the *Shulḥan Aruch* and has come to prevail. This is significant because it is a condition that is of primary consideration in the establishment of an *eruv* in cities and populous metropolitan areas of considerable size. If the area does not qualify as a רְשׁוּת הָרַבִּים it is regarded as a כַּרְמְלִית, and carrying on the Sabbath does not violate a Biblical prohibition, but is only Rabbinically prohibited. Hence, carrying can be made permissible by constructing a צוּרַת הַפֶּתַח and

4.   A *karmelit* (כַּרְמְלִית) is a semi-public domain[8] that does not serve
as a public thoroughfare, and is also not properly enclosed by partitions. Some examples of a *karmelit* are the following: an open field;
the sea; a river that is at least ten *tefahim* deep and four *tefahim* wide;[9]
an alley that has partitions on three sides; a portico at the entrance to
a shop (where the merchants sit) and a balcony (used as a stand for
traders' stalls) erected in front of columns in the public domain,
which measure four *tefahim* in width and from three to ten *tefahim* in
height; an area in the public domain that is four *tefahim* by four *tefahim* and enclosed by partitions that are less than ten *tefahim* high; a
mound in the public domain which measures four *tefahim* by four

---

encompassing the area with what is commonly known as an *Eruv,* consisting
of natural boundaries and wires or cables strung along a series of posts,
forming actual and nominal partitions, in accordance with halachic specifications. For further discussion of this subject, see Melachah 39, notes 11, 12;
Part V, Chapter 10, paragraph 24 and notes.

7.   Stringency in Personal Practice Regarding the Eruv   While there is due
regard for the prevailing view as stated above, and general acceptance of the
validity of the *eruv* which permits carrying on the Sabbath even in some
populous metropolitan areas, some authorities advise those who are more
stringent in religious observance to be stricter in their personal practice and
to refrain from carrying even where there is an *eruv*. However, they caution
against imposing such restriction on those who are inclined to be lenient
whether for reasons of convenience or necessity, as in the case of families
with young children who in the absence of an *eruv* would be confined to their
apartments and dwellings on the Sabbath.

8.   Airspace Above a Karmelit   A *karmelit* extends only to a height of ten
handbreadths. The airspace above that is regarded as a "free place" (מָקוֹם
פָּטוּר).

9.   A Stream Coursing Through a Public or Private Domain   A small
stream that is less than ten handbreadths deep or four handbreadths wide is
considered subsidiary to and part of the domain, whether public or private,
through which it runs.

tefaḥim and is from three to ten *tefaḥim* high;[10] and a pit in the public domain that is four *tefaḥim* by four *tefaḥim* and from three to ten *tefaḥim* deep. The above, and others of a similar nature,[11] cannot be classified as private domain since they do not have adequate partitions, nor as public domain since they do not serve as a public thoroughfare. Their designation is, therefore, that of a *karmelit*.

5.   A *mekom petur* (מָקוֹם פָּטוּר), a "free place," is an area in the public domain that is raised three *tefaḥim* or more above ground level and measures less than four *tefaḥim* by four *tefaḥim*;[12] or a ditch that is three *tefaḥim* or more deep and measures less than four *tefaḥim* by four *tefaḥim*; or a space measuring less than four *tefaḥim* by four *tefaḥim* that is enclosed by partitions three *tefaḥim* or more in height. In the above instances it is a *mekom petur* only if it is in a public domain. If it is in a *karmelit* it is regarded as a *karmelit*.

---

10.   An Article in the Public Domain   An article or utensil in the public domain that is less than ten handbreadths in height does not have the status of a *karmelit*, but is considered as part of the public domain. If it is attached to the ground it is considered a *karmelit*, provided it is four handbreadths square.

11.   An Enclosed Park   The status of a *karmelit* is also accorded an area, such as a park, which though enclosed by a wall, a fence, or other partition, is more than seventy cubits and four handbreadths square, and is not enclosed for dwelling purposes, nor does it serve as a courtyard of a dwelling. See Chapter 3.

12.   Measurements of a Mekom Petur   An area is considered a *mekom petur* so long as it measures less than four handbreadths in width regardless of its length, no matter how great.

2. THE PROHIBITION OF CARRYING

FROM ONE DOMAIN TO ANOTHER

אִסּוּר הַעֲבָרָה וְהוֹצָאָה מֵרְשׁוּת לִרְשׁוּת

1. In the public domain or in a *karmelit* it is forbidden to move, carry, throw, or hand over any object a distance of four *amot* (four cubits, approximately seven feet). It is also forbidden to move it in stages of less than four *amot* at a time.[1]

2. It is forbidden to carry, throw, or hand over any object from a private domain to a public domain or to a *karmelit*, and from a public domain or a *karmelit* to a private domain. It is also forbidden to carry from a public domain to a *karmelit*, or from a *karmelit* to a public domain. But it is permitted to carry from a *mekom petur* to a private or public domain or to a *karmelit*, and from the latter domains to a *mekom petur*,[2] provided the article is not moved four *amot* in the public domain or in the *karmelit*. As there are many particulars, in addition to those cited above, to be considered in determining what constitutes a public domain, a *karmelit*, or a private domain, it is advisable that, in a city that has no *eruv*, one who is not well versed in the Law should refrain from carrying anything on the

---

1. **Carrying Less Than Four Cubits**   In an emergency this restriction may be relaxed. Thus, if one finds himself on the road as the Sabbath is about to begin, and he has a purse of money with him, he may carry the purse in stages for short distances, each less than four cubits. For the procedure to follow in this situation, see Part II, Melachah 39, note 4. There is no restriction for moving an object once for a distance of less than four cubits.

2. **Carrying by Way of a Mekom Petur**   While it is permissible to carry to and from and within a *mekom petur*, it is not permitted for one who is standing in a private domain to remove, retrieve, throw or hand over an object into a public domain, or vice versa, by way of a *mekom petur*. Neither may one stand in a *mekom petur* and receive or take an object from a public domain and hand it over or deposit it in a private domain, or vice versa.

Sabbath from one place to another, unless it is in a place where he is certain that it is permissible to carry.

3.   Lifting an article from the place where it lies is called *akirah,* and putting it down is called *hanahah.* Although one is not liable according to Biblical law unless he does both the *akirah* and the *hanahah,* it is nonetheless Rabbinically prohibited to lift the article even without depositing it, or to set it down even without having lifted it. Therefore, a Jew is not permitted to hand an article to a non-Jew for him to carry it out from a private domain to a public domain or to a *karmelit* because the Jew is doing the *akirah.* The non-Jew must take the article himself. Likewise, when a non-Jew brings an article the Jew should not take it from his hand because he will then be doing the *hanahah.* The non-Jew must deposit the article himself. Hence, when an infant is to be carried[3] by a non-Jewess to the synagogue on the Sabbath to be circumcised,[4] the non-Jewess herself should lift the infant and carry him from the house, and upon reaching the courtyard of the synagogue she should put the infant down, and then a Jewess can take him.

4.   In the event that there is a breach in the partition of a courtyard, then if there remains a part of the partition on one side measuring four *tefahim* in width, and ten *tefahim* in height from the ground, or

---

3.   **Wheeling a Child in a Carriage or Walker**   It is not permitted to carry a child or to wheel him in a baby carriage or a walker where there is no *eruv.* It is, however, permitted to have a non-Jew carry the child or wheel him in his carriage or walker. One who does not carry even where there is an *eruv,* because of a self-imposed stringency, may carry a child or wheel him in his carriage or walker with its usual accessories, such as a blanket and the like, within the area of a properly instituted *eruv.*

4.   **Carrying an Infant to the Synagogue for Circumcision**   Some authorities do not permit having a non-Jew carry an infant to the synagogue to be circumcised on the Sabbath. The *Magen Avraham* and *Mishnah B'rurah* are of the opinion that, where there is no *eruv* and it is not permissible to carry, the circumcision should take place in the home.

there remains a part of the partition measuring one *tefah* in width and ten *tefahim* in height on each side, the partition need not be repaired, provided the breach is no wider than ten *amot*, because the breach is considered as an entrance. But if the breach is more than ten *amot*, or there does not remain a part of the partition on one side measuring four *tefahim*, or one *tefah* on each side,[5] and surely if the breach extends the full length so that there is no partition on one side of the courtyard, then even if the breach is only three *tefahim* it is forbidden to carry in the courtyard until the partition is repaired.[6] The best way to repair it is to do it in the form of a doorway (צוּרַת הַפֶּתַח). If there are two or more tenants or homeowners dwelling in the courtyard they also need to make *Eruvei Hatzerot,* as will be explained later (Part V, Chapter 10).

5.   The above-stated rule that if the breach is no wider than ten *amot* it is considered as an entrance and the partition need not be repaired applies if there is only one breach. But if there are two or more breaches, then what remains standing of the partition must be at least equal to what has been breached. But if what has been

---

5.   A Breach at a Corner of the Partition   A breach at one of the corners, where the partitions on two sides meet, is not considered as an entrance, even if the opening is less than ten cubits wide, and it needs to be repaired in the form of a doorway (צוּרַת הַפֶּתַח) to permit carrying in the courtyard.

6.   Repairing a Breached Partition   While it is permitted, according to Biblical law, to carry in an area that is enclosed by partitions on three sides, the Rabbis declared it prohibited until the fourth side is partitioned off as well, so that it should not have the appearance of a public domain. In the event of a breach that requires repair of the partition enclosing a courtyard, one can do so by replacing the partition on one side for a distance of at least four *tefahim,* or by putting up a board on each side of the breach. In the latter case, the board can be of any width even less than a *tefah,* since it is evident that it is put there to repair the breach and to render the area permissible for carrying. For the laws regarding repair of an *eruv* that becomes defective and inoperative on the Sabbath, and the procedure to be followed in the event it cannot be repaired, see Part V, Chapter 10, note 18.

breached is greater than what remains standing of the partition, then wherever the breach is more than three *tefaḥim* it must be repaired by closing the breach or by forming a doorway.

6. What forms a doorway (צוּרַת הַפֶּתַח)? One puts up posts no less than ten *tefaḥim* high at each end of the opening,[7] and places a stick or a cord on top, reaching from one post to the other.[8] The stick or the cord must be on top of the posts and not by their sides. If one drives nails into the top of the posts and ties a cord to them, reaching from one post to the other, it is also valid. Neither of the posts should be at a distance of three or more *tefaḥim* from the partition, or three or more *tefaḥim* removed from the ground. If it is not possible to form the doorway except by placing the posts three or more *tefaḥim* from the partition, one may be lenient with regard to this requirement.

7. The doorway of a courtyard or a house that opens onto the street, with the door opening inwards, and the doorposts, lintel and doorstep facing towards the street, is at times considered a private domain and at times a *karmelit*. Inasmuch as not everyone is well versed in the Law, the strictures of both a private domain and a *karmelit*, apply in this instance. Hence, one may not carry from the doorway into the street, which is either a public domain or a *kar-*

---

7. **Use of an Archway for a צוּרַת הַפֶּתַח**   An archway qualifies as a doorway, provided the side posts or side walls reach a height of ten *tefaḥim* before they begin to arch.

8. **Use of Wires and Telephone Cables for the Eruv**   While the partitions or the posts must be able to stand against an ordinary wind, the cord or wire strung on top of the posts to form a doorway may sway in the wind, although they must be firmly attached so that they are not torn or blown away. Some authorities, however, require the cord or wire to be tightly drawn so that it does not sag or sway in the wind. Telephone and electricity wires and cables strung on posts may, likewise, serve for a צוּרַת הַפֶּתַח, and thus be considered for the purpose of an *eruv,* if they conform to the halachic requirements.

melit, and from the street into the doorway, as it may have the status of a private domain. Nor may one carry from the house or the courtyard into the doorway, or from the doorway into the house or courtyard, as the doorway may have the status of a *karmelit.* Therefore, if the door is locked and it has to be unlocked, one should be careful to have the non-Jew put the key into the lock, and after unlocking it the non-Jew should remove the key before the Jew opens the door. For if the Jew should open the door while the key is in the lock, he will have brought the key from a *karmelit* into a private domain.[9]

8.   In many places there are houses where the roof extends beyond the wall of the house into the street, where it is supported by pillars. It is forbidden to carry from the house into the space beneath the projection, and from there into the house. It is also forbidden to carry anything a distance of four *amot* in the area itself, since it is considered as the street, in which case it may have the status of a public domain or a *karmelit.* Although that part of the roof rests on pillars, giving it the form of a doorway, which the law regards as a partition, it is not regarded here as a partition, as there are no partitions on either side. It is therefore necessary to put up a post on one side, adjacent to the wall of the house and opposite the pillar supporting the roof, and another post on the other side, thus forming a doorway on both sides. If there are several adjoining houses whose roofs project

---

9.   Opening the Door With a Key Attached to a Belt   One may open the door himself by using a key that serves as an integral part of a belt worn on the Sabbath. Where the keyhole penetrates into the house, which is usually the case, the key should be inserted while it is attached to the belt. If the door opens inward, one should remove the key from the lock and refasten the belt before opening the door and entering the house. If the doorway, consisting of the doorposts and lintel, covers an area that extends outward four *tefaḥim* or more from the door, one may not remove the key which he is wearing in order to insert it into the lock until he is standing in the doorway. After unlocking the door, he should remove the key from the lock and refasten it in the belt before opening the door into the house and entering the house.

in the same manner, it suffices to put up the posts at the end of the last house on either side of the row of houses. They must also make *Eruvei Ḥatzerot*.

9.   One may give food to a non-Jew in the courtyard or in the house, even though he knows that the non-Jew will carry it outside, so long as he does not place it directly in his hands, for he would then be doing the *akirah*.[10] This is permissible provided the non-Jew is allowed to eat it there if he should wish to do so. But if he is not allowed to eat it there, or if the food is in so great an amount that he could not eat it all there, or if he wants to give him some other article which it is evident that he will carry outside, it is not permitted, as it appears that he is giving it to him for the express purpose of carrying it outside.

10.   A woman may lead her child even in the public domain, provided she does not pull him along. The child should be led in such a manner that he will lift up one foot at a time, while the other foot is on the ground, so that he will always be supporting himself on one foot. But if she drags him along by both his feet it is as though she were carrying him, and this is forbidden even in a *karmelit*. Carrying a child, even if he is old enough to walk by himself, is forbidden on the Sabbath even in a *karmelit*.[11] The rule that "a living person car-

---

10.   Extending Food to a Non-Jew   According to some authorities, when one invites a non-Jew to partake of food on the Sabbath, it is permitted to give him the food in his hand, provided the non-Jew is standing with him in the house or courtyard and it is not for the express purpose of carrying it outside. All authorities permit it if the non-Jew takes the food from the Jew's hand in order to eat it on the premises.

11.   Carrying a Sick Child   A child who is able to walk by himself may be carried in a *karmelit* if he cries and wants to be carried, or he is otherwise distressed or in pain. If he is ill, any child even an infant may be carried in a *karmelit*. A sick child who knows how to walk by himself may be carried in a public domain to be taken to the doctor. If there is a possible danger to life it is, of course, permissible to carry any child under all circumstances. When

ries himself'' (הַחַי נוֹשֵׂא אֶת עַצְמוֹ) applies only insofar as it absolves one from a sin-offering. It is nonetheless a Rabbinical prohibition (שְׁבוּת), and in a *karmelit* it involves the transgression of two concurrent Rabbinical prohibitions (שְׁבוּת דִּשְׁבוּת). It is therefore advisable to caution the public who err in this matter.[12]

11.   It is forbidden to draw water from a stream or a canal that runs through a courtyard.[13]

---

it is permitted to carry a child, it is also permitted to take him in a crib or carriage with its usual accessories, such as a sheet and blanket. In the above instances, where it is permissible to carry the child, one should take care that he does not have an object in his hand or in his clothes. However, if the child is hurt or fearful, it is permitted for him to carry a doll or a toy and the like to calm his fears.

12.   Carrying a Child in the Street   It is permitted to help a child to walk, but it is not permitted on the Sabbath to carry a child in one's arms or on one's shoulders in the public domain or from a private domain to a public domain or *karmelit,* and vice versa. Those people who carry a small child in the street where there is no *eruv,* thinking that if the child is capable of walking by himself it is permissible, are in error and they transgress a Rabbinical prohibition. Nevertheless, the *Mishnah B'rurah* advises that one refrain from telling them that they are transgressing a Rabbinical prohibition, because they will surely not listen, and it is better that they should transgress in ignorance than that they should do so willfully. One who does not usually carry on the Sabbath where there is an *eruv,* because of a self-imposed restriction, may allow himself to carry a child or an infant in order to relieve the child and the mother from distress.

13.   Drawing Water From a Stream or a Reservoir in a Courtyard   A stream or water canal, measuring ten *tefahim* deep and four *tefahim* wide, that flows into and out of a courtyard is considered an independent domain, having the status of a *karmelit.* Hence, one is forbidden to draw water from it because he would be transferring the water from a *karmelit* to a private domain. The water can be made accessible by cutting it off from the flow of water outside the courtyard and rendering it a part of the private domain. This can be done, even if only nominally, by erecting partitions ten *tefahim*

12. While standing in one domain, whether it is private, public, or a *karmelit,* one may not pass water or spit into another domain.

13. It is permitted to pour out waste water in a courtyard which measures four *amot* square, even if it runs off into the public domain.[14]

3. ENCLOSURE OF AN AREA FOR DWELLING PURPOSES

הֶקֵּף מְחִיצוֹת לֹא מְהַנֵי אֶלָּא כְּשֶׁהוּקַף לְדִירָה

1. Enclosing an area with partitions in order to be permitted to carry is of no avail unless the enclosure is for dwelling purposes. What is considered an enclosure for dwelling purposes? If one built a house to dwell in, or if he opened up a doorway from his house and fenced the area around it with partitions, in the way one makes a

---

in height at the points of entry and exit. If the partition is placed above ground, one *tefaḥ* should be below the water line, and if submerged, one *tefaḥ* should be above the water. If the stream or water canal does not have the above dimensions, or if it does not run through the courtyard but flows into a pool and remains within the premises, it need not be partitioned off. It is considered a part of the courtyard and within the private domain, and one is permitted to draw water from it on the Sabbath.

14. Pouring Waste Water into the Courtyard While it is not permitted to pour from a private domain into a public domain or a *karmelit,* in this case it is permissible to pour the water into the courtyard because it is estimated that the amount of water that a person normally uses for his personal needs daily, when poured out as waste water, can be absorbed in the ground in an area four cubits square. Hence, one is not particular that it flow out into the street, because it will not soil the ground if it should remain on the premises. Therefore, even if it does flow off into the street, that was not his intention when he poured out the waste water, and on the Sabbath a forbidden act must be intentional for it to be considered a transgression. However, one should be careful to pour the waste water at a distance from the street, so that if it flows out it will not be a direct result of his pouring the water.

courtyard around the house, then no matter how large the enclosure it is in every respect a private domain. But if the enclosure is not for dwelling purposes, as in the case of vegetable gardens and orchards which are fenced in for the purpose of guarding their contents, it depends on the size of the area. If the area is of a size that requires no more than two *seahs* of seed to be sown there it is permitted to carry in it;[1] but if it is a larger area it is considered a *karmelit,* and it is not permitted to carry in it.

2.   An enclosure that is not for dwelling purposes but which is not larger than would require two *seahs* of seed and where carrying is permissible, if there is a courtyard adjacent to it, it is permitted to carry from the enclosure to the courtyard, and vice versa, utensils that are in either place during the Sabbath, because the enclosure and the courtyard are considered as one domain. However, it is not considered to be one domain with the house, so that utensils that are in the enclosure on the Sabbath may not be carried into the house, and utensils that are in the house may not be carried into the enclosure.

---

1.   Dimensions of an Area Enclosed for Dwelling An area, whatever its shape, of such size that it requires no more then two *seahs* of seed is the equivalent of the court of the Tabernacle, where it was permissible to carry, which measured one hundred cubits in length and fifty cubits in width (Exodus 27:18). Since one *seah* of seed is estimated to cover an area 50 cubits by 50 cubits, or 2500 square cubits, two *seahs* would cover an area 5000 square cubits. In a quadrangle it is taken to be an area approximately 70 cubits and four handbreadths by 70 cubits and four handbreadths. According to present measurements, which take the cubit to be of a greater length, it would be approximately 53 cubits by 53 cubits square, or 2809 square cubits. The area in question is variously estimated to be approximately 125–130 feet square. An area of greater size, even if enclosed by walls or partitions ten handbreadths high, which does not serve as a courtyard or garden adjacent to a dwelling is accorded the status of a *karmelit,* and the Rabbis prohibited carrying a distance more than four cubits therein as a precautionary measure; although according to Torah law an area of any size, no matter how large, enclosed by partitions ten handbreadths high, is considered a private domain.

3. An enclosure that was not made initially for dwelling purposes, that is, one first enclosed the area with partitions and then built a house, or he opened up a doorway from his house leading into it, can be converted into an enclosure for dwelling purposes by making a breach in the partitions more than ten *amot* wide (an opening of ten *amot* is considered a doorway, while a larger opening is a breach), thus invalidating the partitions. After that he should repair the breach, and it will be considered enclosed for dwelling purposes.[2]

4. If one planted trees is an enclosed courtyard comprising an area that would require more than two *seahs* of seed, even if he planted them over the greater part of the courtyard, it does not invalidate it as an enclosure for dwelling purposes, because people usually take shelter in the shade of trees. But if he planted vegetables over the greater part of the courtyard, even if not in one place but scattered throughout the courtyard, it invalidates it as an enclosure for dwelling purposes, and the entire courtyard is considered a vegetable garden. If one planted the vegetables in the lesser part of the courtyard, and the planted area would require less than two *seahs* of seed, it is subordinate to the courtyard, and the entire area is considered as a courtyard. However if the vegetables cover an area that would require more than two *seahs* of seed (in any one place), the sown area is considered a *karmelit,* and the rest of the courtyard is regarded as being completely breached to the prohibited area, and it is forbidden to carry a distance of four cubits in the entire courtyard.

5. A courtyard comprising an area that would require no more than two *seahs* of seed or less is subject to the following considerations in

---

2. Converting an Enclosure for Dwelling Purposes One need not take apart all of the partition to its full height to convert the enclosure for dwelling purposes. It is sufficient if he breaches a part of it, so that it is no longer ten handbreadths high. He can also breach the partition and repair it one cubit at a time. If there is a breach already in the partition, he can extend it somewhat beyond the ten cubits. One can also repair the breach by forming it into a doorway.

the event that one planted a part of it with vegetables. If the vegetables are planted over the greater part of the courtyard, while it is permissible to carry in the courtyard because it is of a size that does not require more than two *seahs* of seed, it is nevertheless not permitted to carry out into the courtyard utensils that are in the house on the Sabbath. One should therefore erect a partition in front of the vegetable garden so that he will be permitted to carry from the house into the courtyard.

4. LAWS OF CARRYING WITH REGARD TO

GARMENTS AND ORNAMENTS

דִּינֵי הוֹצָאָה דֶּרֶךְ מַלְבּוּשׁ וְתַכְשִׁיט

1. One may not go out in the public domain or in a *karmelit* with any article that is not a garment (מַלְבּוּשׁ) or an ornament (תַּכְשִׁיט).[1] It is forbidden for a man to go out with a needle or a pin stuck in his clothing.[2] A woman, however, may go out with a pin (but not with a

---

1. **Wearing a Garment or an Ornament**   The *melachah* of Carrying relates to any article that is halachically considered a burden (מַשָּׂא). It forbids removing an article from one domain to another, or carrying it a distance of four cubits in the public domain or in a *karmelit*. The prohibition, however, does not apply to a garment or an ornament. An article of clothing that serves to protect one's person or provide for his bodily needs, and is worn in the normal manner is considered a garment (*malbush,* מַלְבּוּשׁ). An article of a decorative nature, such as jewelry, or an article (other than clothing) that serves a bodily need, such as a cotton pad or a bandage on a wound, is regarded as an "ornament" (*tachshit,* תַּכְשִׁיט). One is permitted to go out in a *karmelit* or in the public domain wearing a garment or an ornament, provided it is worn in the usual manner, and it is not likely to fall off or to be removed and carried in hand.

2. **Wearing a Pin to Secure a Garment or a Yarmulke**   A safety pin that is used to fasten two parts of a garment, or a pin used to secure a *kipah,* or *yar-*

needle), if the pin is required for her apparel,[3] for example to fasten a shawl, since it is customary for women to fasten their garments with pins.[4]

2.   Our Rabbis, of blessed memory, have also forbidden going out on the Sabbath with ornaments that one might remove in order to show them to someone. Thus, some ornaments are forbidden to men, and some are forbidden to women. While it is now common practice to wear such ornaments, and reasons have been advanced by the authorities to permit it,[5] a God-fearing person should nevertheless be

---

mulke, may be worn outside, where there is no *eruv,* by a man as well. See also Part II, Melachah 23, note 5; Part III, note 61.

3.   Wearing Accessories on One's Person and Apparel   A woman may go out on the Sabbath with a comb, headband, hair pins, clips, and the like, to hold the hair in place, provided it is customarily worn in this manner, and she will not remove it, nor will it fall off. A belt that is tied or sewn to the garment may, likewise, be worn. A woman may wear gloves when they are customarily worn, as in cold weather.

4.   Wearing Cuff Links   Anything that is normally attached to a garment or an article of clothing, or is required or serviceable as an accessory to it, is considered subsidiary to the garment or article of clothing, regardless of its intrinsic value. Hence, one may go out on the Sabbath where there is no *eruv* while wearing cuff links to button the sleeves of his shirt, and a stud to fasten the shirt collar, as these are appropriate accessories especially for formal attire. If the cuff links and the stud are gold or silver, and the like, they may be considered to be ornamental.

5.   Wearing Ornaments on the Sabbath   The reasons given by authorities to justify the prevalent practice of wearing ornaments are: (1) since many authorities maintain that we do not have true public domains nowadays, there is no need for a precautionary decree to forbid wearing ornaments in a semi-public domain; (2) since women go out wearing ornaments nowadays even on weekdays, and not just on *Shabbat* as in former times, there is no longer any reason to fear that a woman might remove the ornament to show it to someone and carry it four cubits in the street.

more strict in his personal practice. A man should especially be careful not to go out with a ring on which there is no engraved seal.[6] Nor
should one carry a watch, even if it is attached to a gold chain and
worn about the neck as an ornament. A pocket watch is certainly not
permitted,[7] as it is considered a burden.[8]

---

6. Wearing Jewelry on the Sabbath   The Rabbis prohibited wearing an
ornament or jewelry that is likely to fall off and be carried in the hand, or
removed and shown to someone. It is, however, presently common practice
to wear jewelry, such as rings, bracelets, brooches, and necklaces, provided
they are securely fastened. It is customary to wear such articles of a decorative nature even when they are covered by one's clothing and are not visible.
Authorities are inclined to leniency because people nowadays are not in the
habit of removing jewelry in the street in order to show it to somebody. A
ring is generally deemed to be an appropriate ornament, and even men are
accustomed to wear rings that have no engraved seal. However, a man who
is meticulous in his religious observance will avoid going out wearing any
kind of a ring on the Sabbath.

7. Wearing a Watch on a Chain   One is not permitted to go out on the
Sabbath with a pocket watch on a chain, even if both the chain and the
watch are of gold. Even if attached to a gold chain worn about the neck as
an ornament it is prohibited, because the watch is essentially made, and
generally carried, for its utility as a timepiece, and only incidentally as an
ornament. Indeed, one is not likely to wear it or to carry it when it is not
working. Moreover, it is customary even for a man to take the watch in
hand to check the time and to show it while carrying it. Some permit a
woman to wear a watch attached to a gold chain around the neck, since in
her case it is generally worn as an ornament. Others do not permit it even if
both the watch and the chain are of gold.

8. Wearing a Wristwatch   Some authorities do not permit going out wearing a wristwatch where there is no *eruv,* even if the band or the watch is
made of gold or silver and ornamentally designed, as it is worn essentially
for its practical use. Others, however, are of the opinion that it is not forbidden to wear a gold wristwatch as it is considered an ornament. Some permit an ordinary wristwatch with an ordinary band as well. However, a *Ben
Torah* and one who is meticulous in observance of the Sabbath should

3. It is common practice to go out on the Sabbath wearing a silver key, although it is designed for practical use,[9] since it also serves as an ornament.[10] However, it is not permitted to go out wearing eyeglasses, even if they are framed in silver.[11]

4. A woman is not permitted to place a cloth on her kerchief,[12] nor

---

refrain from doing so. On wearing a self-winding wristwatch, see Melachah 38, note 12.

9. Wearing a Key as a Tie Clip or on a Belt One or more house keys made in the form of a tie clip or a brooch, pinned or clipped to the garment and regularly worn as an ornament, may be worn where there is no *eruv* on the Sabbath. A house key may also be worn if the key is attached to one's belt to serve as a clasp with which to buckle the belt.

10. Carrying an Ornament Although it is permissible to wear an ornament on the Sabbath, it is not permitted to carry it in hand. A woman may, therefore, not carry an evening bag, and the like, even if it is wholly ornamental. Nor may a man go out carrying a cane with a silver knob or some other ornamental decoration or insignia.

11. Wearing Eyeglasses and Contact Lenses The prohibition originally applied to spectacles that were worn clipped to the nose, or fastened to a ribbon or chain encircling the neck or attached to one's garment, because they were likely to fall off and to be carried. One may go out with eyeglasses that are firmly secured and normally worn to improve or correct vision. However, one may not go out with eyeglasses that are used only for reading, nor with sunglasses that are worn casually, unless they are intended to shade the eyes from the sun, as one is likely to remove them and carry them in the street. Eyeglasses that have bifocal lenses, and dark or tinted glasses that are worn to protect the eyes or for medical reasons are permissible. Contact lenses to which one has become accustomed are also permissible.

12. Wearing a Rain Bonnet One may go out with any article of clothing, even if it is intended to protect one's other garments, if it is worn in the usual manner. If the article of clothing is not worn in the usual manner, it is permitted to wear it to protect one's garments only if it also serves one's bodily needs. Hence, putting a cloth over a kerchief or hat to protect it from the

is a man permitted to place a cloth[13] on his hat,[14] to protect it from the rain, because it is not then worn in the manner of clothing. But if their intention is to prevent the rain from causing them distress it is permitted.

5.   A person who is lame,[15] and one who is recovering[16] from an

---

rain is not permissible. However, if the cloth also serves to protect the person from the rain it is permitted. A woman may therefore go out with a cloth, a scarf, or a plastic rain bonnet on her head or over her hat, if it also envelopes her head and face, thereby affording protection from the rain and the wind, provided it is tied securely and she will not take it off outside if it stops raining.

13.   Wearing a Plastic Cover Over a Hat   Authorities differ on wearing a plastic or nylon cover that is fitted over one's hat to protect it from rain or snow. Rabbi Moshe Feinstein ל״ז forbids it, since it does not provide the person himself with additional warmth or protection, unlike galoshes or rubbers worn over one's shoes which serve to keep out the dampness and add warmth. Other authorities permit it, provided it is not removed when the rain stops, because it is considered an article of clothing worn in the normal manner. Some who deem it permissible, however, refrain from public approval in deference to the authorities who forbid it, but nevertheless will not deter one who is inclined to be lenient.

14.   Wearing a Feather in the Hatband   While a man is permitted to go out with a feather or a similar accessory in his hatband, as it is considered decorative and of an ornamental nature, one is advised to refrain from it.

15.   Going Out With Dentures, Braces, Artificial Limbs   One may go out on the Sabbath wearing a prosthetic device, such as an artificial limb, and dentures. Dental plates and braces are likewise permissible if they must be worn constantly.

16.   Going Out With a Sling or Surgical Belt   One may go out with a sling to support a broken or aching arm. One may go out wearing a truss, a brace or a surgical belt, and the like. These are not regarded as a burden for those who require them, but as a *tachshit*.

illness,[17] or a very old person[18] who is unable to walk without a cane, is permitted to walk with a cane in hand. But if one is able to walk without a cane, and he does so at home, but uses a cane only when walking outdoors in order to steady himself, he is not permitted to walk with a cane on the Sabbath. A blind person who is able to walk without a cane may not walk with a cane in a city where there is no eruv.[19] One who has no need for a cane at all is not permitted to go out with a cane, even where there is an eruv, because it shows a disregard for the Sabbath.[20]

6. One who is bound in chains may go out with them on the Sabbath.

---

17. Going Out in a Wheelchair An invalid, who is confined to a wheelchair, may go out with it, and he may be wheeled in it on the Sabbath, where there is an eruv. Where there is no eruv, he may use it only for a mitzvah, such as to attend a prayer service in the synagogue, provided it is wheeled or he is helped to wheel it by a non-Jew.

18. Going Out With a Hearing Aid A hearing aid that is attached to one's eyeglasses may be worn outdoors. Where the receiver is pinned to the pocket, some permit wearing the hearing aid outdoors in case of necessity. A hearing aid which is placed behind the ear, and which operates automatically without batteries, may be worn on the Sabbath as one would on weekdays. See Part II, Melachah 36, Electrical Equipment and Appliances, note 23.

19. A Blind Person Carrying a Cane A blind person is permitted to carry a cane on the Sabbath, even where there is no eruv, when the lack of it would put him in danger of falling, or of injuring himself, or going off into the street in the midst of traffic.

20. Carrying a Cane Due to Infirmity or Danger of Falling One is permitted to carry a cane where there is an eruv, according to some authorities, if he has to walk on an icy sidewalk, or on a slippery road where he is in danger of falling. One who must walk with a cane at all times, due to illness or old age, may carry a cane on the Sabbath even where there is no eruv.

7. It is not permitted to go out with stilts, that is, tall wooden poles with footrests, that are used to walk through mud and water.[21]

8. One may go out with a medicated compress or plaster on a wound, for since it is for the purpose of healing it is considered a *tachshit*. (On treating a wound on the Sabbath, see Part V, Chapter 7.) The compress may be wrapped with an inexpensive or disposable bandage, which is then considered an accessory to the compress. One may not wrap it with an article of value such as a kerchief and the like, as that would neither be subordinate to the compress nor would it serve as a garment, and would then be regarded as a burden.[22]

9. One may go out with a wad of cotton placed in one's ear to absorb the fluid that excretes from the ear, provided it is firmly plugged into the ear so that it will not fall out.[23] One may, likewise, go out with a pad or straw in one's shoe, provided it is put there in such a manner that it cannot fall out.[24]

---

21. Walking With Snowshoes The reason for the prohibition against walking with stilts is that they are not worn in the manner of clothing (דֶּרֶךְ מַלְבּוּשׁ). It would seem then that the prohibition would not apply to the use of snowshoes in regions that are snowbound, and where it is not possible to walk outdoors without them. Inasmuch as the shoe with its wooden frame is firmly attached to the foot, and is designed to enable one to walk on snow, it may be regarded as part of one's normal footgear.

22. Going Out With a Dressing on a Wound Inasmuch as the dressing on the wound is used for its healing effect it serves a bodily need and is therefore considered to be a *tachshit*. One may go out with a bandage, irrespective of its value, if it covers the wound itself, and serves as a protection to keep the wound from being irritated. On carrying medication in case of emergency, see Melachah 39, note 6.

23. Going Out With Cotton in the Ear One may go out on the Sabbath with absorbent cotton in his ear if the ear is infected or it aches, if there is an excretion from the ear, or to protect it from the wind.

24. Going Out With Orthopedic Supports or Insoles One may go out on

10. A woman may not go out with a pad or a belt which she wears during her menstrual period, if it is intended only to keep her clothing from being soiled, unless it is fashioned as a garment.[25] However, if she wears it in order to avoid discomfort, so that the blood will not drip on her body and dry up causing her distress, she may go out with it.[26]

11. When walking in mud or in dirt one may lift his garments somewhat to keep them from becoming soiled,[27] but he may not lift them completely.[28]

---

the Sabbath wearing orthopedic supports inside one's shoes, as well as insoles for comfort, for a better fit, for warmth, or to absorb perspiration, provided they will not fall out.

25. Wearing a Sanitary Napkin or Tampon A woman may go out with a sanitary napkin or tampon if it is needed to prevent the menstrual flow from covering her body and causing her discomfort. A sanitary napkin with adhesive that sticks to the undergarment may be worn as protection against soiling one's body and clothing.

26. Going Out With a Catheter or a Colostomy Bag One who is incontinent, and is equipped with a catheter designed to control a urinal discharge that empties into a receptacle attached to it, is permitted to go about with both the catheter and the receptacle even where there is no *eruv*. (For the laws pertaining to performance of his religious duties, see Volume One, Chapter 4, notes 2, 3). Similarly, a patient with a colostomy or ileostomy bag attached may go out with it on the Sabbath. It is preferable in the above instances to empty the bag or receptacle before going outdoors.

27. Wearing a Garment in a Customary Manner A garment must be worn and should remain on one's body in a usual manner of dress. The garment may be lifted to keep it from being soiled, or if it hinders walking. It may be folded over one's shoulder, or draped around the neck, as with a scarf, if it is customarily worn in this manner.

28. Wearing a Coat Over the Shoulders One may wear a topcoat over one's shoulders, or a raincoat over an overcoat, without his arms in the sleeves, as in hot weather or if he finds it uncomfortable to put his arms into

12. One is permitted to go out on the Sabbath with two similar garments worn one over the other, although he does not need the second garment for himself, but is only taking it out for someone else's benefit or for some other reason, provided he is at times accustomed to wearing two such garments on weekdays as well,[29] since it is then worn in the manner of clothing.[30] But if it is not customary ever to wear two such garments it is forbidden to go out with them on the Sabbath because the second garment is considered as though it were a burden. The same rule applies to wearing two socks, and a large hat over a small hat or cap, and the like.[31]

13. Where it is customary to wear both an ordinary belt and a more attractive one over it, it is permissible to go out with two belts on the Sabbath, although at the time he needs only one belt and is taking out the second one for someone else's benefit. But if it is not customary to wear two belts it is forbidden, even though he wants to wear both for his own sake; since one belt suffices, the second one is considered as though it were a burden. In any case, it is permissible to go out with two belts if there is a garment separating them, as for instance when the belt underneath is on the trousers and the one above is on the cloak, for then he has the use and benefit of both.[32]

---

the sleeves, as it is customary to wear coats and capes in this manner, provided the coats are arranged securely.

29. Wearing a Plastic Raincoat One may wear a raincoat over an overcoat, and a thin, plastic raincoat or cape usually worn to protect one's clothing, as these can normally be worn in this manner.

30. Wearing Galoshes and Rubber Overshoes It is permitted to wear galoshes and rubbers over one's shoes, since they serve as added protection and warmth, and are considered articles of clothing that are normally worn in this manner.

31. Wearing Two Pairs of Socks or a Hat Over a Skull Cap It is permitted to wear two pairs of socks, or a hat over a skull cap, as on occasion they are normally worn in this manner during the week as well.

32. Going Out Wearing a Gartel One is permitted to go out with a *gartel*

14. It is customary to carry a handkerchief by tying it around one's trousers under the upper garment. One should take care not to tie two knots, one on top of the other. The pious are careful to remove the suspenders so that the handkerchief will be of use to support the trousers. Some are accustomed to wrap the handkerchief around the neck. This is not permitted unless he is not wearing another kerchief, and he is used to wearing one occasionally in cold weather. The handkerchief should be tied loosely in a permissible manner. It is forbidden merely to put the handkerchief around the neck with the ends hanging in front. It is likewise forbidden to go out with the handkerchief wrapped around the leg or the hand.[33]

15. Some authorities permit one to go out on the Sabbath wearing gloves, while others forbid it.[34] One may be more lenient in the case of a muff which is made to warm[35] both hands together.

(a special belt usually worn by *Hasidim* during prayer) over a jacket or a capote, even if he is already wearing a belt or suspenders on his trousers, inasmuch as there is a garment intervening. In the opinion of Rabbi M. Feinstein one is not permitted to wear a *gartel* over his shirt or trousers without a garment intervening when the trousers are already supported by a belt.

33. Carrying a Handkerchief It is not permissible to carry a handkerchief in the pocket or in one's hand, or tucked under a bracelet or a watchband. One may go out with it wrapped around the neck and tied loosely, for it then serves as a garment by keeping the neck warm and free of perspiration. Some permit wearing it around the neck together with a scarf. Some also permit binding it around a sock or a stocking in place of a garter. A handkerchief may be sewn into a pocket so that it becomes part of one's clothing. However, attaching it with a safety pin is not sufficient.

34. Wearing Gloves or a Muff Gloves are considered to be garments as they are generally worn to keep the hands warm, and it would therefore be permissible to wear them even where there is no *eruv*. Some authorities, however, forbid wearing them on the Sabbath because of the likelihood that one will forget them in the coat pockets or remove them in the street and carry them. While it is customary nowadays for people to be lenient and to wear gloves, one who is more meticulous in his religious observance is

16.   It is permissible to go out with a *tallit* that is properly equipped with *tzitzit* and worn in the normal manner of clothing. But if the *tallit* is folded and wrapped around one's neck, it is forbidden where it is not customary to wear it that way.[36]

17.   If a garment has two straps or bands with which it is tied, or if it has clasps with which it is fastened, and one of them is torn off, although the one remaining is of no value, nevertheless if he intends to repair it by replacing the one that is missing, the one remaining is not regarded as subordinate to the garment and consequently is considered a burden. One is therefore forbidden to go out wearing the garment on the Sabbath. But if he does not intend to repair it, then since the one remaining is of no value, it becomes subordinate to the

---

advised to follow the stricter view in his personal practice and to refrain from going out with gloves on. Women, however, may allow themselves greater leniency, especially in cold weather, as they are less likely to forget to put the gloves on, or to remove them in the street. A muff is deemed to be preferable, since even if one should for some reason remove his hand from it, he will still be wearing the muff on the other hand. However, some are of the opinion that the likelihood of carrying applies to the muff as well, perhaps more so because it can slip off easily from both hands. Attaching the gloves or the muff to the coat is suggested as a means of keeping one from inadvertently carrying them in the street.

35.   Wearing Earmuffs   It is permissible to wear earmuffs in cold and windy weather, as they are not likely to be removed outdoors.

36.   Wearing a Tallit to the Synagogue   One may bring a *tallit* to the synagogue on the Sabbath by wearing it, even beneath his coat. The *tallit* should be worn draped around and below the shoulders, although it may be partly lifted above the shoulders so that it does not hang down. The *tallit* should be properly equipped with *tzitzit* that comply with the halachic requirements. The same applies to a *tallit katan*. If the *tzitzit* are deficient the *tallit* may not be worn where there is no *eruv*. A *tallit* or *tallit katan* properly equipped with *tzitzit* may be worn outdoors at night as well as during the day. Some question the propriety of wearing a *tallit* exposed in the street among non-Jews, as it is exclusively worn for prayer.

garment and one is permitted to go out with the garment. However, if it is something of intrinsic value, such as a silk band or a silver clasp, even if he does not intend to repair it, it is not subordinate to the garment, and one is forbidden to go out with the garment.

18. A baldheaded person who wears a toupee or a wig of combed flax or carded wool (a peruke) made to look like hair on his head may go out with it in the public domain on the Sabbath,[37] as it is considered an ornament, provided it was prepared before the Sabbath.

19. One who wears an amulet should consult an authority as to whether or not he may go out with it on the Sabbath.[38]

5. CARRYING OUT BELONGINGS IN CASE OF FIRE

ON THE SABBATH

דִּין אִם נָפְלָה דְּלֵיקָה בְּשַׁבָּת

1. Should a fire, God forbid, break out on the Sabbath, our Rabbis, of blessed memory, were concerned that if the owner of the house and the members of his household would engage in saving their belongings, while in a state of alarm and confusion for fear of losing them in the fire, they might forget that it is *Shabbat* and they would endeavor to extinguish the fire. The Rabbis, therefore, prohibited carrying any of the belongings out of the house, including things that may be han-

---

37. **Wearing a Wig** A woman may go out on the Sabbath wearing a wig or *shaitel,* as well as the hemispherical, dome-like form underneath which is worn to hold it in place on the head.

38. **Wearing an Emblem or a Name Tag** One may go out on the Sabbath with a medal, an emblem, or some other token of distinction pinned to his garment, as these are ornamental in nature. However one may not go out with a name tag, or a tag identifying his position, and the like, which is not decorative or ornamental.

dled on the Sabbath, even to where it would be permissible to carry them out. One is permitted to carry out and salvage only the food and drink that would be required for the day, or that can be carried out at one time, and whatever utensils would be needed for the day. One may also ask others to do likewise.[1]

2.   The above items may be taken only to where it is permissible to carry them out on the Sabbath, but to a place where it is forbidden to carry it is not permitted to salvage anything. However, one is permitted to put on as many clothes as he can wear, and carry them out

---

1.   Salvaging One's Possessions From a Fire   There are two concerns involved in this situation. One concern is that the owner and the residents, in their confusion, may think that once they are permitted to save their material belongings, they are also permitted to desecrate the Sabbath for that purpose. The other concern is that if they are permitted to take things out into a courtyard where there are many dwellings, they may think that it is permissible to take them out into a public domain as well.

An earlier authority, cited by *Shulḥan Aruch* and *Ḥayye Adam,* maintains that one is permitted to save whatever may be handled on the Sabbath, if he can take them out to his own court or to his neighbor's house with whom he shares an *eruv.* Others, such as neighbors, who are not members of the family and are not likely to be as alarmed, may salvage whatever is possible, even money, and carry it to where it is permissible to take it out. *Ḥayye Adam* favors this lenient view because people today, when alarmed at the prospect of losing their material possessions in the fire and cannot find a permissible way, will resort to forbidden means of saving their belongings and desecrate the Sabbath.

Ḥayye Adam cites another more lenient view that the owner of the house and members of the family may save whatever they can, even money and other things that are *muktzeh,* because if they would not be permitted to do so they might in their panic come to extinguish the fire, even when there is no possible danger to life. Moreover, since according to many authorities there is no true public domain but only a *karmelit,* they are permitted to carry things out of the house, without regard to the prohibition of carrying in a *karmelit* or in a courtyard without an *Eruvei Ḥatzerot,* as these are not violations of Biblical prohibition.

even to a public domain. He may then take them off and return to the house and put on other clothes and bring them out, and keep doing it repeatedly. He may also call upon others to come and salvage the clothing, and they can do it in the same manner.

3. The residents of nearby houses which are not on fire, who fear that the fire will spread to them, are allowed to salvage everything and to take it to where it is permissible to carry it out, since they are not so alarmed.

4. Some authorities even permit one to save money and other valuables from a sudden great loss, such as a fire, a flood, or a robbery by putting some food on top and carrying them out together. (In any other case it is not permitted to handle a *muktzeh* article in this way.) Some are more lenient, and permit one to carry the money and valuables out by themselves, because in the case of a sudden great loss the prohibition of *muktzeh* is set aside,[2] provided one does not take them to where it is forbidden to carry them out.

5. All sacred books (*sifrei kodesh*), whether written or printed, should be saved from a fire, or a flood, or a similar loss. They may be brought into a courtyard or an alley, even if it does not have an *eruv* and where it would ordinarily be forbidden to carry them out, provided the courtyard or the alley is suitable for instituting *Eruvei Ḥatzerot* or *Shitufei Mevo'ot* (an *eruv* permitting the removal of objects on the Sabbath to and from the house and the courtyard or

---

2. Picking Up a Purse One Finds in the Street The *Shulḥan Aruch* forbids one who finds a purse in the public domain on the Sabbath to pick it up because it is *muktzeh*. In this instance it is not permitted on the grounds of monetary loss, since it did not yet come into his possession. However, some authorities are inclined to leniency, and permit one to pick up the purse or other article of value if he is afraid someone else may take it and he is unable to forgo the loss. Some advise that he move it with his foot for short distances of less than four *amot* until he gets it to a safe place.

the alley, respectively).³ It is permitted to ask a non-Jew to save them, even if he has to carry them into a public domain.⁴

6.   One may save the case in which the *sefer* is kept together with the *sefer*, and the container in which the *tefillin* are kept together with the *tefillin*.

7.   Rescuing a *Sefer Torah* takes precedence over the rescue of other *sefarim*.⁵

8.   When there is any question of a possible danger to life,⁶ one is

---

3.   Saving Sacred Books From a Fire   The sacred books that one must save from a fire include *Tanach* (Scriptures, i.e., Torah, Prophets, Writings), Talmud (Mishnah, Gemara), and all other Torah books and writings, even those that are written in a language other than Hebrew. They may even be carried into a courtyard or alley that does not have an *Eruvei Hatzerot*, provided it is adequately fenced.

4.   Calling a Non-Jew to Put Out a Fire   It is permissible to call a non-Jew to put out a fire that has broken out, even if only to save the *sefarim* and the *mezuzot* in the house.

5.   Precedence in Rescuing From a Fire   Rescuing books of the Written Torah (*Tanach*) takes precedence over the rescue of books and writings of the Oral Torah (Talmud etc.). Rescuing a dead body from a fire takes precedence over the rescue of sacred books. For the regulations regarding the removal of a dead body from a fire on the Sabbath, see Part V, Chapter 3, paragraph 16 and notes. The rescue of a living human being, of course, takes precedence over all, and must be done expeditiously, superseding all Sabbath restrictions and prohibitions.

6.   Extinguishing a Fire in Case of Danger   Permission, presently, to extinguish a fire anywhere is based on this ruling, since it is possible that someone may be in danger. *Mishnah B'rurah* states that it is a *mitzvah* to proclaim publicly that it is permissible to extinguish a fire when there is even a remote possibility of danger to life. It is permitted to sound the alarm and to phone the fire department. See Part II, Melachah 37, note 7.

permitted to extinguished the fire.[7] Therefore, in places where Jews live among non-Jews it is permitted to extinguish a fire, even if it is in the house of a non-Jew. In the above instances it is only permissible to extinguish the fire, but it is forbidden to desecrate the Sabbath in order to save one's possessions.[8]

If one transgressed and desecrated the Sabbath, he should consult a Rabbi who will advise him as to the proper procedure to follow in order to repent and atone for his transgression.[9]

---

7. Cutting the Power From a Live Electrical Wire   In the case of a live electrical wire that is exposed in the house, and it is not possible to vacate the house for the Sabbath to prevent possible contact with it, one is permitted to cut the power or to summon the electric company, because it presents a danger to life. The same applies if the electric wire falls in the yard or in the street and there is the danger that someone might come into contact with it and be electrocuted.

8. Causing a Fire to Be Extinguished Indirectly   It is permitted to cause a fire to be extinguished by indirect means, even where there is only a monetary loss involved. Thus, if a candle or a spark from a flame falls on the tablecloth, one is permitted to shake it off, although he may indirectly cause it to be extinguished. If it is feared that the tablecloth might catch on fire, he may take hold of the candle and remove it from the table.

9. Repentance for Desecration of the Sabbath   One who desecrated the Sabbath, either intentionally or unintentionally, and wishes to repent is instructed to fast from a minimum of three days, on Monday, Thursday, and the following Monday, to a maximum of forty days, which need not be consecutive. The duration of the fast depends on whether one transgressed a Biblical or a Rabbinical prohibition, the severity of the transgression, whether it was intentional or unintentional, and whether out of necessity or merely to gratify one's desires. He must also give charity in accordance with his means. One may, if need be, redeem the fast by giving charity. Atonement is not required for an act which, in a given situation, is permissible. Thus, if one turns on the light on the Sabbath for a woman in childbirth, he should not fast since the act is permissible and there is no need for repentance.

Part V

*Muktzeh and
Additional Sabbath Laws,
Concluding the Sabbath*

1. BATHING

דִּין רְחִיצָה

1. It is not permitted to wash one's whole body or even the greater part of the body in hot water, even if the water was heated before the Sabbath.[1] It is forbidden even if one does not wash his body all at once, but only a part of his body at a time. Neither is it permitted to enter a bathhouse for the express purpose of sweating. However, it is permitted to wash one's face, hands and feet with water that was heated before the Sabbath.

2. It is permitted to bathe, even immersing one's whole body, in water flowing hot naturally from its source in the ground, such as the hot springs of Tiberias, provided the water is still in the ground and the place is not covered over with a roof. However, if the water is in a vessel or the place is roofed it is forbidden. Some permit bathing there even if the place is roofed, so long as the water is in the ground.

---

1. Bathing on the Sabbath The prohibition of bathing or washing one's whole body, or most of it, with hot water on the Sabbath is a Rabbinical enactment (*gezerah*) to prevent one from transgressing and heating the water on the Sabbath. It applies to water that is of a temperature normally considered to be hot, but not to lukewarm water. One is permitted to wash his face, hands and feet, or any part of the body, but not the greater part of the body. Thus, one may soak his aching feet or take a sitz bath to relieve a hemorrhoid condition. In special circumstances, however, as when suffering from an ailment, one may even bathe to relieve his discomfort. A baby may be bathed on the Sabbath. A woman may perform *tevilah,* immersing herself in a *mikveh* at the appointed time following her menstrual period. The *mikveh* should preferably be lukewarm. In such instances the Rabbinical edict is not invoked, providing the water was heated before the Sabbath. See Melachah 11, note 9.

3. One is permitted to bathe his whole body in cold water,[2] but he must not afterwards stand before a hot oven to warm up, as that would be like washing himself with hot water. Even if one only washed his hands he should not warm them by an oven while they are still moist, as it would be like washing with water that was heated that day. He should first rub his hands together to remove most of the water, and then dry them well before warming them.

4. When bathing one should be careful not to squeeze the water from his hair.[3] He must also refrain from swimming, as it is forbidden to swim on the Sabbath and on a Festival.[4] It is likewise forbidden to float anything, such as a piece of wood, on the water. If one is bathing in a place where it is not permitted to carry, he must also be careful to shake the water from his body and his hair, and dry himself

---

2. Bathing and Showering in Hot Weather   It is customary not to bathe on the Sabbath even in cold water. Some permit showering or bathing in cold or lukewarm water to relieve one's discomfort, as in very hot weather. One should take care, however, not to squeeze the water from his hair.

3. Washing and Drying Oneself   One may wash oneself, including his beard and the hair on his head, provided he does not press the water out of his hair. One should not wash with a washcloth or a sponge, as the water is absorbed and then squeezed out, involving the prohibition of *seḥitah*. When drying oneself with a towel, one should take care not to press the water out of the towel. One may use a paper towel or a paper napkin to dry one's hands, even if it is likely to tear, as that is not his intention.

4. Swimming on the Sabbath   The prohibition of swimming or floating something on the water would not strictly apply in the case of a pool in a private courtyard or in the house, as the pool is considered like a vessel since the water is contained within its walls and cannot flow beyond its enclosure. However, because of the likely involvement of other violations of the Sabbath, bathing or swimming in a pool, with or without a bathing suit or in any body of water other than in a *mikveh* for the purpose of purity or sanctity, has been generally regarded as an activity prohibited on the Sabbath. See also Melachah 38, note 15.

well so that he will not carry the water from one domain to another.[5] Even while in the river itself one must be careful not to carry the water on his person a distance of four cubits, as the river is considered a *karmelit*. Since not everyone is sufficiently informed to be careful in these matters, the prevailing custom is not to bathe at all on the Sabbath even in cold water, unless it is for the sake of a *mitzvah*, as in the case of a woman following her menstrual period and a man after a nocturnal pollution.[6]

5.   One may stand on a riverbank and wash his hands in the river, as there is no prohibition in his lifting the water on his hands from the river to the riverbank, since the river and its bank are each considered a *karmelit*, and it is permissible to carry from one *karmelit* to another a distance less than four cubits. But one should take care to dry them well before walking a distance of four cubits.

6.   It is permitted to rub one's hands with a coarse bran even when they are wet, provided he does not pour the water on the bran itself. However, it is forbidden to rub one's hands with salt, and certainly not with soap, [7] because it melts.[8]

---

5.   **Walking in Rain and Snow**   One is permitted to walk in the street on the Sabbath while it is raining or snowing, even though the rainwater and the snow will accumulate on his person and on his clothing. Since it is not possible to avoid this, as it often rains suddenly while one is in the public domain, the Sages did not prohibit it.

6.   **Bathing in a Mikveh for Purification and Sanctification**   Some among the pious are accustomed as well to bathe in a *mikveh* for sanctification before prayer on Sabbath morning. In any case care should be taken that the water in the *mikveh* is only lukewarm when immersing oneself on the Sabbath, whether for sanctification, or for purification following the menstrual period and after a nocturnal emission.

7.   **Use of Soap Made of Animal Fat**   Some refrain from using soap made from non-kosher ingredients, such as animal fat. While commendable if other soap is obtainable, it is generally accepted practice to use soap for bathing and washing oneself, even if made from non-kosher ingredients.

8.   **Washing With Soap**   Authorities differ on the use of soap on the Sab-

7.   It is not permitted to bathe on the Sabbath in turbid waters
where it is not usual to bathe except for medical purposes. The prohibition applies when one remains in the water for a while and it is
evident that he is bathing for healing purposes. But it is permitted if
he does not remain in the water, as it is apparent that his intention is
merely to cool off. In waters such as the hot springs of Tiberias,
where it is not usual to bathe except for healing, it is forbidden to
bathe on the Sabbath for medical purposes, even if one does not
remain in the water for a while.[9]

2.   LAWS CONCERNING CATTLE, ANIMALS, AND FOWL

דְּבָרִים שֶׁצְּרִיכִין לִיזָּהֵר בִּבְהֵמוֹת, חַיּוֹת, וְעוֹפוֹת

1.   It is written, "Six days you shall do your work, but on the
seventh day you shall rest; that your ox and your ass may have
rest . . ." (Exodus 23:12). The Torah hereby admonishes us that cattle
belonging to an Israelite must also rest on the Sabbath. This refers
not only to cattle, but to all animals.[1] A Jew is thus duty-bound to
keep his animals from doing any work that is prohibited on the

---

bath. Sefardim follow a lenient view, while Ashkenazim have adopted a
strict view and forbid the use of soap unless it is necessary for hygienic
reasons, as a doctor who must wash his hands with soap in examining a
patient. Liquid soap prepared before the Sabbath is generally permitted,
although some advise refraining from using it as well. Salt water is likewise
permissible.

9.   Bathing for Reasons of Health   Bathing on the Sabbath for therapeutic
purposes is not permitted a healthy person who is only somewhat indisposed. One who is ill and must bathe for the treatment of a disease or for
safeguarding his health may do so.

1.   Resting One's Animals   The Biblical injunction that one's animal
should rest on the Sabbath applies to animals on land, to fowl, as well as to

Sabbath, not even by themselves or by a non-Jew working with them.[2] Prohibited activities include plowing, planting, harvesting, threshing, pulling a wagon, carrying a load out into the public domain, and the like. The Torah likewise forbids work done jointly by man and animal, such as leading or driving a beast of burden (מְחַמֵּר) by directing it with his voice, or by striking it with a whip, and the like.[3]

2. A Jew may, therefore, not permit his beast to carry a burden into the public domain, as it would be a violation of the Biblical precept, even if it goes out by itself. The prohibition applies to any kind of burden, even if it is on the beast as an ornament. However, if it is for the purpose of healing, such as a bandage on a wound, or for its normal protection, it is permitted,[4] because it is not considered a

---

species of creatures of the sea. One may not allow his animal to do any *melachah,* or place any burden on it, apart from bridle and reins or whatever is necessary for its protection. If the animal does a *melachah* for its own satisfaction, as in the course of feeding and the like, one is not obligated to prevent it.

2. An Animal Hired From a Non-Jew If one hired an animal from a non-Jew he must likewise keep it from doing work on the Sabbath. If he hired the non-Jew for delivery or transport and the like, neither specifying the animal, nor assuming responsibility for it or for feeding it, he is not dutybound to keep the animal at rest on the Sabbath. Similarly, if he hired an animal from a non-Jew, he may hire it out to another non-Jew to work it as he sees fit on the Sabbath.

3. Driving an Animal Carrying a Load The prohibition against leading or driving an animal (מְחַמֵּר) that is carrying a load on the Sabbath is derived from the verse, "You shall not do any manner of work, you . . . nor your cattle" (Exodus 20:10), which the Sages take to mean "you together with your cattle." Unlike the admonition that one's animal must rest on the Sabbath (שְׁבִיתַת בְּהֶמְתּוֹ), the prohibition of מְחַמֵּר applies to all animals, even those belonging to a non-Jew.

4. A Dog Wearing a Collar, Leash and Blanket A dog may go out on the

burden but rather as a garment for a human being. Hence, a horse may go out with a halter or a bridle, but not with both if one suffices. One may bind the halter loosely around the neck so that he can readily slip his hand between the rope and the neck to restrain the horse if it should try to break away. One is permitted to handle the halter and put it on, but he should not lean on the horse, as it is not permitted to support oneself on an animal on the Sabbath. A donkey may not go out with an iron bit, as that is an unnecessary safeguard for it. An ox and a cow, which ordinarily do not require that they be guarded, may not go out with a rope around the neck unless they are in the habit of running away.

3. Neither a horse nor any other animal may go out with a pack-saddle. A donkey may go out with a saddle-like cover that serves it as a garment to protect it from the cold, as it is its nature to suffer from the cold, provided it was tied on before the Sabbath. It may not go out with the cover if it is not tied on, as it may fall off and one will come to carry it. One cannot tie it on the Sabbath because he would have to come close to the animal and lean on it, which is not permitted. But if the donkey is in the courtyard one may put the saddle-like cover on it to protect it from the cold, provided it does not go out with it. One may not put a saddle-like cover on a horse unless it is to protect him from intense cold, or it is to keep the flies from tormenting him in the summer, in which case one should take care not to lean against the animal while covering him. One may not remove the covering from the horse or the donkey on the Sabbath if the animal does not suffer from it.

4. An animal may not go out wearing a bell even when it is plugged and makes no sound,[5] and even in a city that has an *eruv*. The animal

---

Sabbath wearing a collar and leash, as it is needed for safeguarding. A collar that protects the dog from ticks and fleas, or one that glows in the dark and protects it from being struck by a car on the road, would likewise be permitted. Similarly, it may wear a blanket to keep it warm.

5. A Bell on a Animal The reason for the prohibition is that it appears as

may wear the bell while it is in the courtyard, provided it is plugged and makes no sound.

5.   It is permitted to lead a horse by a rope attached to the bridle, provided one holds onto the end of the rope so that it does not hang out of his hand a handbreadth, and the length of rope between his hand and the animal does not reach down to within a handbreadth of the ground.[6] If the rope is too long he should wind it around the horse's neck. One may not lead two or more animals that are tied together by holding on to the halter of one and having the others follow. This may not be done even in a city where there is an *eruv,* as it appears as if he is taking them to market. He may, however, lead them individually in the manner indicated above.[7]

6.   Chickens may not go out with strings tied on to their feet for identification or to keep them from breaking utensils. One may, however, tie their feet together to prevent them from running away. One may, likewise, tie together two legs of a horse that is grazing in the field to keep it from running away. It is forbidden, however, to tie

---

if it is dressed up and is being taken to market to be sold. Some authorities infer from the reason given that animals, such as cats and fowl which are not taken to be sold in this manner, may go out with a muffled bell which produces no sound. Others, however, consider the bell a burden and do not permit it in any case.

6.   Leading an Animal by a Leash   In leading an animal by a leash the rope must be held in such a way that it is evident that he is using it to guard the animal and not just carrying it as a burden. If the rope hangs from his hand, or he allows it to trail close to the ground, it appears as if he is carrying it and not holding it to guard the animal. In walking a dog outside one should follow the same procedure, preferably using a short leash. However, some authorities do not permit leading an animal by a leash, even where there is an *eruv.*

7.   Walking With a Seeing-Eye Dog   A blind person may walk in the street with a Seeing-Eye dog on the Sabbath. If necessary he may enter the synagogue for prayer accompanied by his Seeing-Eye dog. See Volume One, Part I, Chapter 10, note 15.

the horse's foreleg to the hind leg, or to shackle a horse by bending one of its legs and tying it up so that it can walk only on three legs. This may not be done even on weekdays, as it is forbidden to cause suffering to an animal. See Volume One, Part IV, Chapter 9.

7.   One need not prevent his non-Jewish servant from riding an animal while taking it to water, since the prohibition of riding on the Sabbath is not because it is a burden on the animal, for a living being carries itself. Indeed, it is a Rabbinical prohibition[8] which does not apply to the animal but to the person, and only a Jew is forbidden to ride an animal on the Sabbath.[9] A non-Jew is not bound by the prohibition. He may even put a saddle or a blanket on the animal in order to ride it, as these are incidental to the rider, but he may not place anything else on the animal.

8.   It is permitted to tell a non-Jew to milk one's cows on the Sabbath, because the accumulated milk causes the animal pain, and one is duty-bound to prevent an animal from suffering.[10] However, the

---

8.   Riding an Animal on the Sabbath   Apart from the general admonition to keep one's animals at rest on the Sabbath, a Jew is forbidden by Rabbinical ordinance to ride an animal on the Sabbath lest he break off a branch to use as a whip to spur the animal on. Indeed, the Sages prohibited any utilization of an animal, such as sitting on it, and leaning or supporting oneself on it. The Rabbinical ordinance applies even when there is no reason to fear that one may break off a branch, because the Sages generally made no exceptions in their enactments. The prohibition, however, does not apply to a non-Jew. Moreover, any distress he may cause the animal in this instance is compensated by the fact that he is taking it to water.

9.   Riding in a Carriage Drawn by an Animal   A Jew is forbidden to ride in a carriage or wagon drawn by an animal on the Sabbath, even if it is driven by a non-Jew, because it is not permitted to make use of the animal, and for fear of breaking off a branch, as in the Rabbinical ordinance noted above. If the Jew drives the carriage himself, he also transgresses the Torah prohibition of מְחַמֵּר, namely, driving a loaded animal on the Sabbath.

10.   Milking to Relieve the Animal   If a non-Jew is not available, the Jew

milk may not be used or even handled that day, but the non-Jew can store it until after the Sabbath. It is also permitted to tell a non-Jew to feed the geese once during the day to prevent them from suffering.[11]

9.   It is forbidden to lend or hire out one's animal to a non-Jew, unless it is on condition that he returns it before the Sabbath. If he does not return it the Jew should renounce ownership of it before the Sabbath, even if only in private, so that he will be spared a transgression. However, he may not at the outset lend or hire it out with this intention in mind.[12]

10.   One is duty bound to feed one's animals. It is therefore permitted to place food before one's cattle, fowl and other animals on the Sabbath. However, one should not measure out the feed, but only estimate the amount needed. One may untie a bundle of fodder to give to his cattle, so long as it is not tied in a durable double knot. One may cut up hard gourds for his cattle, provided they were detached before the Sabbath, but if they are soft and can be eaten as they are, it is not permitted to cut them up.

---

may do the milking to relieve the animal from suffering. For the procedure to be followed in such a case, see Part II, Melachah 5, paragraph 4, and note 4.

11.   Feeding Geese   Since the geese are used to being stuffed and cannot feed themselves, it would be cruel not to feed them. If a non-Jew is not available a Jew, preferably a minor, may feed them.

12.   Hiring Out an Animal   The prohibition applies only to animals that are hired for labor, but not to animals that are not used for work. Some authorities permit hiring out an animal for a period of time inclusive of the Sabbath by declaring it ownerless property before three people, as then it will be widespread knowledge that he renounced ownership. The pious are advised to be more strict in this matter. In any case it should be done only if there is a pressing need, as when one has a field which he rents to a non-Jew under a profit sharing arrangement and he must provide him with oxen to plow the field.

11.   It is permitted to put out one's cattle to graze, as pulling up the grass from the ground is not considered labor for them, because they are content to do so in order to eat it. However, one may not set the cattle to eat grass that was cut from the ground by a non-Jew on the Sabbath, lest he come to handle the grass which is *muktzeh*.[13] If they have nothing else to eat it is permitted, for one may not cause the animals to suffer. Likewise, if the cattle have nothing to drink, he may tell a non-Jew to bring water from a well that is in a *karmelit*.

12.   One may not hang a pouch or another container of feed on the animal so that it can eat without bending its neck, as this is merely for its comfort and one is not permitted to exert himself unnecessarily on the Sabbath for an animal's pleasure. However, it is permitted for calves or foals whose necks are short causing them distress to eat from the ground. But they should be kept in the courtyard and are not to go out with it, as it is considered a burden for them.

13.   In feeding fowl one should not throw the grain on moist ground, as some of the grain may remain and afterwards begin to sprout.[14]

14.   When giving fodder to cattle one may not first put it in a sieve to sift it and clean out the chaff. But if he does not intend this, he may carry it in a sieve and put it in the feeding trough.

15.   When giving bran to cattle or fowl one may not add water to it. If he added water to it before the Sabbath he may not knead it on the Sabbath, but it is permitted to pour it from one vessel to another in order to mix it.

---

13.   Feeding Cattle Cut Grass   One may stand before the cattle so that they will of their own accord come to feed on the cut grass. In case of need one may tell a non-Jew, who cut the grass on the Sabbath, to feed it to the cattle.

14.   Putting Out Grain for Fowl   In a place where people walk about it is permitted because any of the grain that might remain on the ground will not sprout. In any case it is allowed to put out an amount of grain that will be eaten up in a day or two.

16.   One is permitted on the Sabbath to feed cattle, animals and fowl that are raised by him, as it is his duty to provide them with food.[15] But he is not permitted to trouble himself to feed those that are not raised by him and whom he is not obliged to feed.[16] Hence it is not permitted to feed roosting pigeons, since they can fly out and eat in the field. One may place food before his dog. Indeed it is a *mitzvah* to provide food for any dog, even if it has no owner, for the Holy One, blessed be He, has compassion on it on account of its meager supply of food, causing the food it eats to remain undigested in its stomach, thereby nourishing it for three days. Some are accustomed to put out wheat-grain for the birds on *Shabbat Shirah,* the Sabbath on which the Song at the Sea (Exodus 15:1–19) is read in the synagogue. However, it is not proper to do so, as one is not obliged to provide them with food.[17]

---

15.   Feeding Fish in an Aquarium   Fish should be fed by putting the food into the aquarium before the Sabbath. However, if necessary the fish may be fed on the Sabbath. If the tank contains grass weeds and the like one should not change the water or add water. It is permitted to have the water changed automatically. One should not move a fish bowl or aquarium on the Sabbath, nor should one remove the fish from the water.

16.   Feeding Animals   One may not feed animals for whom he is not obliged to provide sustenance, either because they can find food for themselves, such as birds, or because they are not to be kept around the house, such as pigs. However, it is permitted to feed animals whom one is duty bound to provide with food, such as geese, chickens, birds in the house, a dog and a cat kept in the house, even if the animals do not belong to him. One may also feed a stray dog as it requires special consideration. In feeding animals or birds one should be careful not to handle them because all living creatures, whether domestic or not, are *muktzeh* and may not be handled on the Sabbath.

17.   Feeding the Birds on Shabbat Shirah   Some authorities favor retaining the custom of putting out feed for the birds on *Shabbat Shirah,* or at least shaking off the crumbs from the tablecloth, where there is an *eruv* and it is permissible. They consider it a *mitzvah* to feed the birds, who are said to

17.   Animals, beasts and fowl that are not yet trained to return to their cages in the evening, or if they are trained but have rebelled and fled, may not be driven into the cage or into the house. Even if they are already in the house or in the cage one may not close the door or the gate thereby trapping them, as this would be a violation of the *melachah* of Trapping. If they are trained and domesticated, and are accustomed to return to their places in the evening, but they went out and one is concerned lest they be stolen, one is permitted to drive them into a safe place.[18] However, one may not take hold of them, as they are *muktzeh*.

18.   One may not deliver the young of an animal, or assist in the birth of an animal on the Sabbath.[19]

19.   One may smear oil on the fresh wound of an animal to relieve it of its pain, but not when the wound is already healing and it is only for its pleasure. If one's animal is in pain from overfeeding on vetch or other plants, he may make it run about in the courtyard until it becomes tired and is relieved. If the animal has an attack of congestion, that is, an excessive fullness of the blood vessels, it may be made to stand in water to be cooled. If it is critically ill and needs bleeding, it is permitted to tell a non-Jew to bleed it. Other remedies as well should be administered by a non-Jew.

---

have burst forth in song when the Israelites were saved from Pharaoh and the Egyptians. It is thus a reminder of the joyous song of deliverance sung by Moses and Israel upon crossing the sea.

18.   Domesticated Animals Cows and horses which are naturally tame and domesticated, even if newly acquired and not yet accustomed to return of their own accord, may be caught and enclosed in a restricted area, provided they have not rebelled and fled. A cat is not considered a fully domesticated animal, hence the prohibition against trapping applies to it as to animals or birds.

19.   Delivering an Animal It is permitted to have a non-Jew deliver the animal. If a non-Jew is not available, and while giving birth the animal or its young is in danger, it is permitted for the Jew to make the delivery on the Sabbath.

3.   LAWS OF MUKTZEH

דִּינֵי מוּקְצָה בְּשַׁבָּת

1.   In order to safeguard and preserve the Sabbath as a day of rest, the Sages enacted the *gezerah* of *muktzeh* (מוּקְצָה), prohibiting the moving and handling of certain objects on the Sabbath, other than those that are needed and permissible of use.[1] The following rules pertain to the various types of *muktzeh*.[2]

---

1.   Reasons for Muktzeh   Rambam sets forth the following reasons for the enactment of *muktzeh*. Inasmuch as people are confined to the house and are unoccupied on the Sabbath they would look for something to do in their free time. Were it not for this prohibition they would spend the day arranging and moving things about, or engaging in similar activities, and the Sabbath would come to be regarded as just another weekday, and it would cease to be a holy day of rest. Another reason is that, if one were permitted to handle a tool or an implement which is normally used in an activity that is forbidden on the Sabbath, he might inadvertently engage in the prohibited activity itself and thereby violate the actual *melachah*. Moreover, some people are not laborers, have no occupation, and are always at leisure. Were they permitted to go about doing things in their usual manner they would not be resting on the Sabbath in any meaningful way. Therefore, so as to make the Sabbath a day of rest equally for all, the Sages instituted the law of *muktzeh*. According to Rabad the Rabbinical enactment is intended to keep one from inadvertently carrying an object from the house into the public domain. By limiting the objects that may be handled only to such that are necessary and prepared for use on the Sabbath one will avoid a possible violation of the *melachah* of Carrying.

2.   Types of Muktzeh   The term *muktzeh* means set aside, or excluded and not counted on for use on the Sabbath. Various types of *muktzeh* are listed by halachic authorities, all essentially explications of the basic concept. The types herein enumerated are:

1.   Articles intentionally set aside (מוּקְצָה מְדַעַת).

2.   *Nolad* (נוֹלָד), literally, newly born, that is it has come into being on the Sabbath.

3.   Utensils designed for work prohibited on the Sabbath (כֵּלִים הַמְיוּחָדִים לִמְלָאכָה אֲסוּרָה בְּשַׁבָּת).

An object intentionally set aside (מוּקְצֶה מִדַּעַת). Food which one had set aside with the intention of not eating it, either because it is unfit and can be eaten only with great difficulty, or it is readily edible but had been set aside to be sold, even if it was placed in storage; and food that is fit to be eaten that day by dogs, even though it was not so intended before the Sabbath, such as cattle and fowl that died on the Sabbath, may be handled on the Sabbath.[3] Likewise permitted is an article that has changed from what it was the previous day but which is nevertheless fit for some use, such as a utensil that broke on the Sabbath but can still be used for a similar purpose as a receptacle for food or drink, and bones that were detached from the meat on the Sabbath and are fit to be fed to dogs. All of the above may be handled on the Sabbath, except for whatever one has deliberately set aside, such as figs and raisins that have been set out to dry, and are put out of mind because they are inedible during the drying process.

---

4. *Muktzeh* due to concern for monetary loss (מוּקְצֶה מֵחֲמַת חֶסְרוֹן כִּיס).

5. An object which is not considered a utensil (דָּבָר שֶׁאֵין עָלָיו שֵׁם כְּלִי כְּלָל); this is also referred to as inherently *muktzeh* (מוּקְצֶה מֵחֲמַת גּוּפוֹ).

6. *Basis* (בָּסִיס), something which serves as a base or support for a *muktzeh* object.

Additional types listed are:

1. *Muktzeh* because the object is repulsive (מוּקְצֶה מֵחֲמַת מִיאוּס).

2. *Muktzeh* due to a prohibition (מוּקְצֶה מֵחֲמַת אִיסוּר), that is, an object such as *hametz* on Passover, or a garment that contains *sha'tnez,* whose use involves violation of a prohibition.

3. *Muktzeh* due to *mitzvah* (מוּקְצֶה מֵחֲמַת מִצְוָה), that is, an object, such as a *lulav,* which is reserved for use in the performance of a *mitzvah.*

Specific rules vary as to whether *muktzeh* applies and to what extent on the Sabbath and on *Yom Tov.*

3. Edible Food and Usable Items Food that is edible, whether by humans or animals, is not *muktzeh*. Objects, even pieces of broken utensils, that are of some use are not *muktzeh*. However, food that is unfit for either human or animal consumption is *muktzeh*. Items, such as sticks and stones, unless designated for some use, and broken utensils that are of no use, are *muktzeh*. The above is the general rule; specific rulings may vary depending upon the circumstances and halachic considerations, as will be explained.

2. Food which in its present uncooked state is wholly unfit for human consumption, although it is fit food for cattle or dogs, but since it is intended to serve later as food for humans it is not now ready to be given to cattle and dogs, may not be handled on the Sabbath. Likewise forbidden are objects that are unfit for any use on the Sabbath, such as pieces of wood, bird feathers, cattle skins, wool, flax, living creatures, even those that are domesticated,[4] shells of nuts and egg shells,[5] hard bones that are not even fit for dogs, doors and windows that are forbidden to be hung up on the Sabbath, pieces of broken utensils that are not fit for any further use, and the like. All these may not be handled on the Sabbath.[6] It is permitted, however, to remove pieces of broken glass from where they may cause injury.[7]

---

4. Animals and Pets   All animals including pets are *muktzeh*. Hence it is not permitted to handle and fondle dogs, cats, and other animals on the Sabbath. It is, however, permitted to give them food, as indeed it is one's duty to feed his animals. One is permitted to feed one's birds and fish, although it is advisable to place a sufficient amount of food in the cage and aquarium before the Sabbath. Inasmuch as the birds and the fish are *muktzeh* one may not move the bird cage and aquarium or fish bowl. If the animal is in distress, or it is necessary to prevent its suffering, one may hold it by the neck and lead it. A blind person is permitted to use a Seeing Eye dog on the Sabbath. Inasmuch as it is designated for this purpose it is not *muktzeh* and may be handled as necessary. See also Part V, Chapter 2 and relevant notes.

5. Removing Shells, Pits and Peels   Fruit peels which are edible either by humans or animals are not *muktzeh*. Nut shells, egg shells, fruit pits, and the like, which are inedible are *muktzeh*. However, they may be removed from the table indirectly by shaking out the tablecloth, or by brushing them off the table with a napkin or a knife. If they are unsightly on the table one may pick them up if need be and remove them directly. It is advisable to remove the shells from nuts before the Sabbath. One may clear the table of *muktzeh* objects to make room for guests, even if there is a clean table available elsewhere.

6. Articles of Forbidden Usage   Articles which may not be used on the Sabbath are *muktzeh*. Hence, eye color, nailpolish, and cosmetics of a similar nature are *muktzeh*. Insecticides and poisons, such as are designed to

3.   Food which a Jew is forbidden to eat but from which he may derive benefit, and it is fit food to be given to a non-Jew to eat in its present state, such as cooked meat and like, may be handled on the Sabbath. But if it is not fit to be eaten by a non-Jew as is, such as raw meat (nor can it be considered for dogs since it is fit for human consumption), or if one cannot give it to a non-Jew because it does not belong to him, may not be handled on the Sabbath.

4.   *Nolad* (נוֹלָד), that is, something that has come into being on the Sabbath.[8] Examples of this type of *muktzeh* are ashes from a fire kindled by a non-Jew on the Sabbath, an egg laid on the Sabbath, and juice exuding from trees on the Sabbath. Even if it did not come into being on the Sabbath, but is the result of an activity which is forbidden on the Sabbath, such as fruit which fell from a tree or was plucked by a non-Jew on the Sabbath, or milk that was milked on

---

kill ants, roaches and rodents, are *muktzeh,* as they may not be used on the Sabbath. Insect repellents, such as sprays and salves, which are designed to repel flies and mosquitoes may be used on the Sabbath and are not *muktzeh.*

7.   Removing Hazardous Objects   The law of *muktzeh* allows for leniency in a hazardous situation. In this case the broken glass should be cleared away in an indirect manner, if possible, by pushing the pieces away with one's foot or by using a broom and dust pan, and not moved directly by hand. If that is not practical they may be picked up and removed. Similarly, if the gas on the stove should accidentally be extinguished one is permitted to turn the knob and shut off the flow of gas.

8.   Types of Nolad   There are two types of *nolad.* Absolute *nolad* (נוֹלָד גָמוּר) is something that actually came into existence that very day, such as the ones enumerated, which are *muktzeh* on the Sabbath and on *Yom Tov.* Ordinary *nolad* is something which existed before in some form but underwent a change, such as a utensil made by a non-Jew, which is *muktzeh* on Yom Tov but not on the Sabbath. Rain or snow that fell on the Sabbath is not considered *muktzeh* according to most authorities. While young children may play with the snow, however, older children and adults are not permitted. See Melachah 5, note 7.

the Sabbath, and the like[9] may likewise not be handled on the Sabbath.

5 *Utensils used primarily to do a melachah that is forbidden on the Sabbath*[10] (כֵּלִים שֶׁהֵם מְיוּחָדִים לַעֲשׂוֹת בָּהֶם מְלָאכָה הָאֲסוּרָה לַעֲשׂוֹת בְּשַׁבָּת). This type of *muktzeh* includes a mortar, a mill, a hammer, an axe, a broom, a *shofar,* a candlestick,[11] a sewing needle, whole candles whether of tallow or of wax, cotton wicks, a garment of wool and

---

9.   Making Ice Cubes   In the opinion of many authorities freezing water to make ice cubes and melting ice do not constitute *nolad,* and ice cubes, whether made before or on the Sabbath or *Yom Tov,* are not *muktzeh* and are permissible. Since some take a stricter view, one should not make ice cubes on the Sabbath or *Yom Tov* except in a case of necessity. An automatic ice cube dispenser, which involves activating an electrical circuit, should not be used unless the mechanism has been deactivated. It is not permitted to make ice cream on the Sabbath. See also Melachah 5, note 10; Melachah 38, notes 20, 22.

10.   Utensils of Prohibited Use   While other *muktzeh* articles may not be moved at all, a utensil of prohibited usage may be handled for some permissible secondary use, or for the place it occupies, but not to protect or preserve the utensil itself unless it involves a considerable loss. Utensils of this type include cooking and baking equipment, grinders, percolators, and the like. If the utensil contains some food it is subordinate to the food and is not *muktzeh.* Other such utensils are mechanical and gardening tools, electrical appliances, radios, calculators, tape recorders, flashlights, scissors, pens, pencils, staplers, glue, paints, paint brushes, and the like.

11.   Moving a Candlestick or Lamp   The candlestick herein referred to as a utensil of prohibited usage is one that is not now lit, nor was it lit at twilight (*bain ha-shemashot*) of that Sabbath. A candlestick, or a lamp which is presently lit, or it was lit during twilight, even if the light is no longer burning, is totally *muktzeh* and may not be moved at all, even לְצוֹרֶךְ גּוּפוֹ וּמְקוֹמוֹ. Since it was totally *muktzeh* with the onset of *Shabbat,* it remains totally *muktzeh* the entire Sabbath day. However, one may have a non-Jew move it. A candlestick or lamp that was never used for kindling a light is not yet considered a utensil of prohibited use and may be moved for any reason.

linen which may not be worn, because it is *sha'tnez,* and the like.[12] These articles and utensils[13] may be handled for permissible use (לְצוֹרֶךְ גּוּפוֹ).[14] Thus a hammer may be used to crack open nuts, an axe to cut

---

12. Moving an Electric Lamp, Clock, and Urn An electric lamp or flashlight that is lit may not be moved on the Sabbath. The table or stand which is a base to the lamp may also not be moved. If the light was on during twilight with the advent of *Shabbat* it may not be moved even after the light is turned off by a time-clock or by a non-Jew. If the light was off during twilight and it was turned on during the Sabbath and then turned off it may be moved, but only לְצוֹרֶךְ גּוּפוֹ וּמְקוֹמוֹ, as when its place is needed. An appliance, such as an electric clock, or an electric urn whose indicator light is on, may be moved for its permitted use or if its place is needed (לְצוֹרֶךְ גּוּפוֹ וּמְקוֹמוֹ).

13. Moving Electrical Appliances Electrical appliances, such as electric clocks and fans, are utensils of prohibited usage. While such an appliance is *muktzeh,* it may nevertheless be moved for its permitted use or for its place (לְצוֹרֶךְ גּוּפוֹ וּמְקוֹמוֹ). Thus, an electric clock plugged in before the Sabbath may be moved if necessary to see the time, or removed from a table if the place is needed, taking care not to unplug the cord. Similarly, one may move an electric fan to direct the breeze as desired, or remove it to clear its place on the table. A cold water vaporizer plugged in before the Sabbath may likewise be moved closer to the patient, or in a particular direction as needed. Water may be added to it through the sprout. It is not permitted to add water to a hot water vaporizer, as this involves the prohibition of cooking on the Sabbath. One is permitted to use an electric blanket that has been plugged into the outlet before *Shabbat,* and one is assured of its safety, provided the controls are set and taped or covered before the Sabbath. See Melachah 36, Electrical Equipment and Appliances, note 19.

14. Removing Articles From a Car An automobile which is primarily a utensil of prohibited usage also has a secondary use for storing objects. In case of urgent need one may remove permissible items left in the car or in the trunk, provided no light is activated as the door or trunk is opened. As a rule, however, one should avoid this practice. Moreover, it may be done, when necessary, only if the car is parked where it is permitted to carry, and in a private place where there is no fear of *mar'it 'ayin,* giving the appearance of driving the car on the Sabbath. The door or trunk may also be closed normally if an object of value is left in the car, otherwise it should be closed

food, and a needle to remove a splinter. They may also be moved if their place is needed (לְצוֹרֶךְ מְקוֹמוֹ), that is, if one needs to utilize the place on which the utensil is lying. As long as one was permitted to take hold of the utensil, or if he inadvertently took it in his hands, he may handle it further and put it wherever he wishes. However, if one does not need to move the utensil for some permissible use nor for the place it occupies, but only for its own sake so that it will not be stolen or damaged, it is forbidden to move it. It is not permitted to handle *tefillin* on the Sabbath. But if they are in an unseemly place, or where they might be soiled, it is permitted to move them and put them where they will be safe.[15]

6.   *Muktzeh due to concern for monetary loss* (מוּקְצֶה מֵחֲמַת חֶסְרוֹן כִּיס). Articles which a person intentionally withholds from use to keep them from being impaired may not be handled on the Sabbath. Included are utensils or instruments about which one is concerned lest they may be damaged or impaired through handling or excessive use, such as a workman's tools, a penknife, a knife used for slaughtering, the cutting instrument used for circumcision, writing paper, notes of indebtedness, accounts, letters held for safekeeping, precious utensils which one does not use, valuable articles which are not used and are kept in a special place, utensils that are kept in one's shop for sale, even such that are for culinary use, but one does not lend them

---

indirectly. The keys to the car door, the glove compartment and trunk are not *muktzeh.*

15.   Handling Tefillin, Mezuzah, Shofar, Lulav and a Tallit With Torn Tzitzit   Since *tefillin* are not worn on the Sabbath they may not be handled unless it is necessary to protect them from being damaged or stolen. They may be moved, as well, to allow removal of a *sefer* from a bookshelf, or one's *tallit* from a *tallit* bag, if one forgot to remove it before the Sabbath. The above also applies to a *shofar,* but not to a *lulav* which may not be handled at all. A *mezuzah* that falls to the ground may be picked up and put away lest it be defiled. It is likewise permitted to handle its container. A *tallit* whose *tzitzit* are torn or defective and has become *pasul* is not *muktzeh* and may be handled.

out, a purse used exclusively for keeping money, and the like. These are *muktzeh* due to concern for monetary loss, and may not be handled even for a permissible use or for use of the place it occupies.

7. *An object which is not considered a utensil* (דָּבָר שֶׁאֵין עָלָיו שֵׁם כְּלִי כְּלָל). Wood, stones, pieces of metal,[16] and the like, may not be handled, even for a permissible use or for use of the place they occupy, unless one designated them before the Sabbath for some permanent use.[17] Therefore, it is not permitted to take a chip of wood to pick one's teeth. Candles which are not whole are not considered utensils and may not be handled. A ladder is also not considered a utensil.

8. A utensil which has a permissible use,[18] or if it is used for a forbidden *melachah* as well as for a permissible use, such as a pot which is used for cooking and for storing food, may be handled on the Sab-

---

16. Money and Coins Used as an Ornament Money, whether in script or in coin, is *muktzeh*. Gold pieces and coins of silver or some other metal, if perforated and strung as a necklace or chain, or otherwise fashioned as an ornament, are not *muktzeh* and may be handled on the Sabbath.

17. Artificial and Live Flowers and Plants Artificial flowers and plants may be handled on the Sabbath, as they are ornamental objects in the home and are not *muktzeh*. Live, growing plants are *muktzeh* and may not be moved on the Sabbath or *Yom Tov*. A vase with flowers is not *muktzeh* and may be moved, but one may not place the flowers in the vase containing water. See Melachah 3, note 2.

18. Watches and Clocks Watches and alarm clocks which operate mechanically, and electronic watches which display the time without pressing a button, are not *muktzeh*, so long as they are operational and running. If the watch is primarily regarded as jewelry, as it is generally by women, and it is normally worn even when it is not running, it is not *muktzeh*. As to considerations other than *muktzeh*, such as winding the watch or wearing it in the street, these questions are discussed relative to the *melachot* involved. A clock that hangs on the wall or stands on the floor, such as a grandfather clock, is *muktzeh* and may not be moved unless its space is needed. See Part II, Melachah 38, notes 11–13; Part IV, Chapter 4, paragraph 2 and notes.

bath, even if only for its own sake to keep it from being stolen or broken. An unclean utensil may, likewise, be moved, as the prohibition of *muktzeh* because the object is repulsive does not apply on the Sabbath. The above utensils, however, should not be handled if there is no need to do so.[19] Holy books and food stuff may be handled, even if there is no need to handle them.[20]

---

19. Handling Toys, Games and Household Articles Articles and utensils of permitted usage, such as furniture, clothing and the like, may be moved and handled for any purpose. However, they should not be moved and handled needlessly. This restriction does not apply to holy books and food stuff, and in the view of some authorities to tableware, such as plates, cups, glasses, knives, spoons etc., as well.

Toys, games, balls, sporting goods and equipment, such as baseball bats, gloves, tennis rackets and the like, are not *muktzeh*. Their use, however, may be restricted or forbidden, as other prohibitions may be involved, such as writing, building, or carrying in a public domain. Toys which emit a sound, such as musical toys, whistles, toy phones, talking dolls and the like, are not *muktzeh* and may be moved, provided it can be done without causing the sound to be made. Such toys should not be given to children on the Sabbath, but if a child too young to be taught the Sabbath rules takes the toy, he may be allowed to play with it. Mechanical toys, while not *muktzeh,* are not to be wound up on the Sabbath. Games, such as checkers, chess, and other board games are not *muktzeh,* but those that involve keeping score are not to be used on the Sabbath. Children's tricycles are not *muktzeh* and may be used in the house or within an *eruv*. Two wheel bicycles should not be used even within an *eruv.*

Household items of permissible usage are not *muktzeh*. A broom, with nylon or synthetic bristles which do not break off, that is used indoors on floored surfaces, such as tile, wood and linoleum, is not *muktzeh*. Perfumes and deodorant and perfume sprays are not *muktzeh* and may be used on one's person, but may not be applied to one's clothing. Air freshener and room deodorizer sprays are not *muktzeh* and may be used on the Sabbath. Furniture may be moved unless it is a base or a stand for an object that is *muktzeh.*

20. Handling Books One may move and handle all books that one is permitted to read on the Sabbath.

9. Just as it is forbidden to move whatever is *muktzeh* or *nolad,* so is it forbidden to place a vessel underneath for the object to fall into it, for then the vessel may not be moved due to the *muktzeh* object in it, and he will have rendered the vessel unsuitable and useless, as though he had cemented it down.[21] However, it is permitted to turn over a basket for the young chicks to climb up into or down from the coop, for when they are not on the basket it would be permissible to move it. But if they were on it at twilight on the eve of the Sabbath, it is not permitted to move the basket all of the Sabbath day.[22]

10. One is permitted to move earth and sand that had been gathered in a heap in a corner of the yard or the house, for since it was heaped up it is considered prepared for use.[23] But if it is scattered about, it is subordinate to the ground and may not be handled. Similarly, if one cuts off a branch from a tree before the Sabbath to use it to chase away the flies[24] and the like, it is permitted to use it on the Sabbath, since he designated it for that purpose and made a utensil of it. But

---

21. Placing a Vessel Under a Lamp or Candle The Sages prohibited rendering a vessel unsuitable for its designated purpose and useless, because it is akin to demolishing it. Thus, one may not place a vessel under a lamp on the Sabbath to catch the dripping oil. He may, however, do so before the Sabbath. One is permitted to place a vessel under a burning candle, even on the Sabbath, if he fears that it may fall and start a fire.

22. Muktzeh With the Onset of Shabbat A general rule with regard to *muktzeh* is that an object which is *muktzeh* with the commencement of the Sabbath on Friday evening during twilight (בֵּין הַשְּׁמָשׁוֹת), that is, between sunset and nightfall, remains *muktzeh* for the rest of the Sabbath.

23. Covering Waste With Earth and Sand One may prepare a sack or heapful of earth or sand before the Sabbath to be used to cover excrement or refuse, provided he does not cause a pit to be formed as he removes some of the earth or the sand.

24. Using a Flyswatter It is permitted to use a flyswatter on the Sabbath to chase away flies, but one should take care not to kill them.

one may not remove a twig from the broom on the Sabbath, as it is *muktzeh* and may not be handled even if it was removed by a non-Jew.

11. Boards belonging to private individuals which are not intended for sale may be handled on the Sabbath. But if they belong to a craftsman they may not be handled, unless he had in mind before the Sabbath to make use of them on the Sabbath.

12. All *muktzeh* articles are only forbidden to be handled, but merely touching a *muktzeh* article without moving it is permitted.[25] Hence, it is permitted to touch a standing candelabrum even when the candles are burning. But it is forbidden to touch a hanging lamp, because by merely touching it one moves it. One may also remove an object that one is permitted to handle, even if it is resting on something that is *muktzeh*. It is also permitted to cover an article that is *muktzeh* with something that is not *muktzeh* to protect it from the rain, and the like.[26]

13. It is permissible to move an object that is *muktzeh* if it is done in an indirect manner.[27] Thus, if one left a *muktzeh* article on some uten-

---

25. **Touching a Muktzeh Object** While touching a *muktzeh* object without moving it is not forbidden, it is nevertheless customary to refrain from touching it altogether unless it is for the sake of retrieving a permitted article, and the like.

26. **Covering a Lamp** One may remove a permitted object even if it is resting on a *muktzeh* article that is suspended and will move as the object is removed, because the movement is considered to be indirect handling (טִלְטוּל מִן הַצַּד) for the sake of the permitted object, and moving a *muktzeh* article indirectly is permissible. By the same token, one may place a permitted object on a *muktzeh* article even if it will move. Hence, it is permitted to cover a lamp in order to darken the room, even if it is a hanging lamp that will move as it is covered.

27. **Moving a Muktzeh Object Indirectly** Moving a *muktzeh* article with an object such as a stick or a knife is considered by some authorities as in-

sil and forgot to remove it, or if it fell there on the Sabbath, and he needs the utensil or the place it occupies he may shake it off, or carry the utensil to another place and shake it off there. He may do the same if he forgot money in the pocket of his clothes and he needs that garment. But this may not be done if it is only for the sake of the *muktzeh* article.[28] However, if he intentionally placed the *muktzeh* article on the utensil before the Sabbath and purposely left it there, the utensil becomes a base for the *muktzeh* article and it is forbidden to move it.

14.   If one does not need the utensil which may be handled it is forbidden to move it if there is a *muktzeh* object on it. Therefore, one is not permitted to take a child in his arms, even in a private domain, if the child is holding in his hand a stone or some other object that is *muktzeh*. However, if the child yearns to be held and will be distressed and sicken if one does not pick him up, and one cannot make him drop the stone or the *muktzeh* object because he will scream and

---

direct handling, while others consider it an extension of the hand. Moving it with a part of one's body other than one's hands is considered indirect handling and is permitted. One may; therefore, sit or lie on a *muktzeh* object, even if it moves under him. One may kick it out of the way with his foot, or move it by blowing on it. Some authorities advise that the above indirect methods of handling a *muktzeh* object be resorted to only in case of necessity.

28. When a Muktzeh Object May Be Handled Directly   If one should forget and pick up a *muktzeh* object he need not drop it immediately, but he may carry it and put it down elsewhere, where it belongs or where it will be safe. A *muktzeh* object may, furthermore, be handled directly in the following instances: (a) Where it is necessary for the sake of human dignity, as in the removal of foul matter, or in the care of the deceased, (b) Where it involves a hazard to safety or health, (c) Where there is a monetary loss involved due to fire, looting, or when delayed on the road with one's valuables at the onset of *Shabbat,* (d) For the sake of a person who is ill. Even in these instances, when feasible, one should endeavor to move the objects in some other permissible way, either indirectly or through a non-Jew.

cry, one is permitted to take him in his arms in a private domain. But if the child is holding a coin it is forbidden even to hold his hand while he is walking by himself, even in a private domain and even if he longs for him, for fear that the coin may fall from the child's hand and, forgetting that it is the Sabbath, one will pick it up and actually handle a *muktzeh* object.[29] This is forbidden even if it is possible that the child may become unwell, as there is no danger to life if he does not hold him.

15.   It is forbidden to move the body of a dead person on the Sabbath.[30] But it is permitted to slip the pillow out from beneath him so as to prevent giving off a malodor, provided one does not move any of his limbs. If his mouth keeps opening one may bind the jaw in a way that will keep it from opening further, but not so that it will close what has already opened, for then he would be moving a limb.[31]

---

29.   Holding a Child Carrying a Coin   Some authorities maintain that one is only forbidden to carry a child who has a coin in his hand, but it is not forbidden to hold the child's hand while he is holding a coin.

30.   Moving a Dead Person   In the event of a death occurring on the Sabbath, only such minimal arrangements are made as are deemed necessary in respect of the deceased and in accord with the Sabbath laws. Funerals are not permitted on the Sabbath. The body of a deceased person is considered *muktzeh* and may not be moved. If it is necessary to move the body, as for example to keep it from decaying by moving it out of the sun, or to protect it from indignity or from fire, one may move the body in the manner further indicated. In this regard no distinction should be made between a pious and righteous person and a wicked person.

31.   Closing the Eyes and Straightening the Limbs of a Dead Person   The deceased must be treated with due respect. Thus, if the mouth is distending it is permitted to fasten the jaw to keep it from opening further. Some are accustomed to close the dead person's eyes and to straighten his limbs so that they would not become bent. While this custom has no basis in law, but is attributed to the Zohar, it is customary to be lenient with regard to this practice on the Sabbath.

16.   If a fire broke out and it is feared that the dead person will be
burned it is permitted to move the body by way of an object that may
be handled, that is, by placing some food on the body or by its side
and moving them together. If there is no food available a utensil or
an article of clothing that is permitted to be handled may be used. If
this too is not available it is permitted to move the body by itself. In
any event, the body is to be carried only to a place where it is permitted to carry. If it is to a place where it is not permitted to carry, it
should be done by a non-Jew.[32]

17.   Any foul object,[33] such as excrement, vomit or discharge of
humans or fowl that is in a house or in a courtyard where people
reside may be removed[34] and taken to the garbage pile. When a bed-
pan or urinal is removed to be emptied, so long as it is still in one's
hand he is permitted to return it, in keeping with the rule that while a
muktzeh object is in one's hand he may continue to handle it and put

---

32.   Carrying the Deceased Outside   In the view of some authorities, in
order to prevent dishonoring the dead in these circumstances, one is permitted to carry the body outside the permissible premises into a *karmelit*. A
non-Jew may carry it out into the public domain as well.

33.   Removing Diapers, Bedpans, Garbage Cans   Soiled diapers, urinals,
bedpans and the like, while *muktzeh* may be removed from one's living
quarters. Garbage cans, which may contain *muktzeh* items should not be
moved on the Sabbath or on *Yom Tov* if possible. However, if a foul odor
from the garbage causes discomfort they may be removed to a permissible
place.

34.   Removing Untidy, Dirty and Foul Objects   *Muktzeh* objects lying on
the table or scattered about the house which make one's living quarters
slovenly and unpleasant may be removed, preferably indirectly. If this is not
possible, one may remove them directly. Thus, one may remove bones,
shells, peels and other such objects that are on the table or on the floor, giving the house an untidy appearance. One may, likewise, remove dead bugs,
roaches, rodents etc., as well as live ones, provided he does so without trapping them.

it wherever he pleases. But after one has put it down, it is forbidden to handle it because it is extremely replusive and considered inherently *muktzeh,* and therefore dealt with more stringently than objects which are *muktzeh* because they are repulsive. However, if it is still needed, it is permitted to return it to its place in deference to human dignity. If one can add some water, so that it is moderately clean, he may return it under any circumstance.

18.   It is permitted on the Sabbath to place a vessel beneath dripping water, and when it is full it may be emptied and returned to its place, provided the water is fit for washing. But if the water is putrid it is not permitted to put the vessel there, as it is forbidden to make a receptacle for putrid matter on the Sabbath. However, if he did put it there, and it is in a place where it is repulsive to him, he may remove it.

4.   LAWS CONCERNING A BASE

FOR A FORBIDDEN ARTICLE

דִּין בָּסִיס לְדָבָר הָאָסוּר

1.   If on *erev Shabbat* one placed an article that is *muktzeh* on a utensil that belongs to him with the intention that it should remain there at the coming of the Sabbath, the utensil becomes a base (*basis*) for a forbidden article. Even if the *muktzeh* article is removed on the Sabbath, nevertheless since it lay there at twilight (בֵּין הַשְּׁמָשׁוֹת) and the utensil became a base for a forbidden article, it may not be handled afterward the entire Sabbath day, even if there is need for the utensil or for the place it occupies (לְצוֹרֶךְ גּוּפוֹ וּמְקוֹמוֹ).[1]

---

1.   Conditions Regarding a Base to a Muktzeh Article   The utensil becomes a base for a *muktzeh* article (בָּסִיס לַדָּבָר הָאָסוּר), with the same restrictions as to movement and handling applying to it as apply to the *muktzeh* article that is resting on it, under the following conditions: (1) The *muktzeh* article is on it

2. If, at the coming of the Sabbath, there was also a non-*muktzeh* article on the utensil, so that it thus became a base for both a forbidden article and for a permitted article, then if the permitted article is of greater value to him he may move the utensil, but if the forbidden article is of greater value to him he may not move it. Therefore, it is best to put the *hallot* on the table before twilight,[2] so that it will be permissible to move the tablecloth and the table on the Sabbath, since they will be a base for both the candles and the *hallot*.[3] If one did not do so, then the tablecloth and the table have become a base

---

during twilight (בֵּין הַשְּׁמָשׁוֹת) on *erev Shabbat*. (2) He had in mind that it remain there all of the Sabbath. This is the view of many authorities, which can be relied upon in case of necessity. (3) It was put there intentionally for the Sabbath, but not if one intended to remove it before the Sabbath and left it there inadvertently. (4) The *muktzeh* article is placed on one of his own utensils, but not on someone else's, unless it is with his permission. (5) The *muktzeh* article is deliberately put in place and not just by chance, or casually as one might pile objects one upon the other. While some authorities consider it a base regardless of how it is placed, the former view may be followed in case of necessity. (6) The *muktzeh* article is put on the utensil itself and not on something subordinate to it. (7) The *muktzeh* article is on the utensil by itself, and not if there is with it also a permissible article of greater value to him.

2. Placing the Ḥallot on the Table First Women are accustomed to place the *hallot* on the table before the Sabbath candles. While the order is not essential, so long as the *hallot* are on the table before twilight when the candles are kindled, the custom is commendable, as one will then be permitted to move the table even while the candles are still burning, since the table did not become a base for a forbidden article. In the view of many authorities the tablecloth may be moved in any case, as it is not considered a base for a *muktzeh* article, since the tablecloth serves the table and one's intention is that the candles rest on the table and not necessarily on the tablecloth.

3. A Costly Candlestick The *hallot* in this case are more important because they are needed for the Sabbath meal. This is so even if the candlestick is made of silver and more costly, because it is only a base for the burning flame of the candle which is the actual forbidden article.

for the *muktzeh* candles alone and may not be moved. However, in a case of necessity, as when a candle should fall on the table, it is permitted to shake it off the table. In this case one may rely on the opinion of those authorities who hold that the utensil becomes a base only if he intends that the *muktzeh* article remain there the entire Sabbath day,[4] and since it is customary to have the candlesticks removed in the morning by a non-Jew,[5] it is not considered a base for the *muktzeh* article.

3.   If there is money in a pocket that is sewn into one's garment, he may handle the garment, because only the pocket and not the entire garment is considered a base to a *muktzeh* article, and the pocket is subordinate to the garment.[6] However, one should not wear the garment even in the house, lest he goes out with it in the public domain.

---

4.   Removing a Muktzeh Object From a Sefer   One should not put an object that is *muktzeh* on a *sefer* before the Sabbath. Nevertheless, if he did so, he may tilt the *sefer* and remove the *muktzeh* object so that he can use the *sefer* for reading and study.

5.   Moving a Candlestick and Tray   Candles, even when unlit, are *muktzeh*. The candlestick on which the Sabbath candles are kindled becomes a base for a *muktzeh* object, and one may not move it after the candles have burned out. The device of placing a permitted object of value on the candlestick does not, in the opinion of many authorities, render it permissible to be moved, since it is essentially made to serve the candle and the flame, and it is therefore considered a base for a *muktzeh* object. It is, however, permitted to have a non-Jew remove the candlestick from the table. The tray upon which the candlestick rests is, likewise, considered a base for a *muktzeh* object, and one may not move it even if a non-Jew removed the candlestick. Placing a non-*muktzeh* object such as a *Kiddush* cup, a *siddur,* and the like on the tray is not, in the view of many authorities, deemed sufficient to permit the tray to be moved. Unlike the table which is made to hold many things, the tray is intended essentially as a base for the candlestick and the candles.

6.   Money in the Pocket of a Garment   Before handling the garment the money should in any case be removed, if possible by shaking it out of the pocket.

However, if there is money in the drawer of a table, it is not permitted to move the table, because the drawer is considered a vessel by itself[7] and is not subordinate to the table.[8]

4.   A utensil does not become a base for a forbidden article unless the *muktzeh* article was on it at twilight (בֵּין הַשְּׁמָשׁוֹת) *erev Shabbat.*[9] If

---

7.   Money in the Drawer of a Table or Desk   A drawer in a table, a dresser or desk is considered a vessel by itself only if it is removable. If it is not removable it is considered subordinate and the table may be moved. If the drawer contains, in addition to the money, other non-*muktzeh* items of greater value it is permitted to open and close the drawer as well. If the drawer containing the money, even if removable, is primarily intended as a receptacle for other articles that are permitted to be handled, such as silverware and the like, it is permitted to move the table even when the permitted articles are not in the drawer at the time. Likewise, if there is on the table a permitted article of greater value to him than the money in the drawer, and it was there at the onset of the Sabbath, it is permitted to move the table. The money in the drawer should be an appreciable amount if the drawer is to be considered a base for a *muktzeh* object. If it is only a few pennies, the drawer does not lose its individual status.

8.   A Purse Hanging on a Door   If a purse containing money is hanging on a doorknob or on the door itself, one may open and close the door on the Sabbath, as it has not become a base for the forbidden article because it is considered to be a part of the house.

9.   An Article That Is Muktzeh Bain Ha-Shemashot   An article which was *muktzeh bain ha-shemashot* (בֵּין הַשְּׁמָשׁוֹת) on Friday evening, that is at twilight between sundown (שְׁקִיעָה) and nightfall (צֵאת הַכּוֹכָבִים), remains *muktzeh* all of the Sabbath day. Opinions differ as to whether or not the object must be *muktzeh* during the entire *bain ha-shemashot* period. Rabbi M. Feinstein ז״ל is of the view that if it is *muktzeh* for any part of the *bain ha-shemashot* period it remains *muktzeh*. Accordingly, if a *muktzeh* article was on a vessel during *bain ha-shemashot* with the onset of the Sabbath, it becomes a base and remains *muktzeh* for the entire Sabbath, even if the *muktzeh* article is removed.

it was not there at twilight,[10] but was only put there afterwards, the utensil does not become a base and it is permitted to move it even when the *muktzeh* article is still lying on it. Hence it is permitted to tilt the table or shake the tablecloth to remove the bones and peels, so long as they have not become a base for the candles, as noted above.

5.   A utensil does not become a base for a forbidden article unless the *muktzeh* article was deliberately placed on it with the intention that it remain there during *bain ha-shemashot* on Friday evening. But if it was left there inadvertently because he forgot, or it fell there of itself, the utensil does not become a base.

6.   A utensil does not become a base for a forbidden article unless it belongs to him. But if he put a *muktzeh* article on someone else's utensil it does not become a base, because one cannot make someone else's utensil prohibited without his consent.[11]

---

10.   Status of Muktzeh After Kabbalat Shabbat Before Twilight   The principle of *muktzeh* applies in this instance only if the *muktzeh* article is on the vessel during twilight (בֵּין הַשְׁמָשׁוֹת). Hence if one made *Shabbat* early and the *muktzeh* article was only there before twilight, even though he was מְקַבֵּל שַׁבָּת and had concluded the *Maariv* prayer and recited *Kiddush,* but it was not there at twilight, it is not considered a base and may be moved.

11.   Making Someone Else's Vessel Muktzeh   One cannot make someone else's vessel a base for an article that is forbidden to be handled even if the *muktzeh* article also belongs to the other person. However, if it is done for the other person's benefit, and he would be pleased by it and would deem it to be in his interest, it does become a base. Thus, if one placed a vessel beneath his neighbor's candlestick so that if a candle should fall it would not start a fire, and the candle fell into the vessel before the Sabbath and remained there until nightfall, the vessel is considered a base for a forbidden article and may not be moved on the Sabbath.

5. WEEKDAY ACTIVITIES FORBIDDEN ON THE SABBATH

דִּין עֲשִׂיַּת חֲפָצָיו בְּלֹא מְלָאכָה

1. Certain activities are forbidden on the Sabbath although they neither resemble a *melachah* nor do they lead to doing a *melachah*.[1] Why, then, are they forbidden? Because it says, "If you turn away your foot because of the Sabbath, from attending to your affairs on My holy day . . . and shall honor it, not doing your wonted ways, nor pursuing your business, nor speaking thereof" (Isaiah 58:13). Our Rabbis, of blessed memory, have explained (Shabbat 113a) that "and shall honor it, not doing your wonted ways"[2] means that your

---

1. Activities of a Weekday Nature Some authorities consider all activities that are Rabbinically prohibited on the Sabbath as weekday activities (עוּבְדִין דְּחוֹל). Others, however, distinguish between Rabbinic prohibitions that relate to *melachot* which are termed שְׁבוּתִים, and other Rabbinic prohibitions that are intended to preserve the unique spiritual, festive and tranquil character of the Sabbath. It is in keeping with the latter objective that the Sages prohibited certain activities because they are of a weekday nature (עוּבְדִין דְּחוֹל) and as Rambam notes, if one would engage in such activities the Sabbath would appear in his eyes as an ordinary weekday.

2. Playing Ball and Other Games Authorities take a lenient view and permit playing with a ball on the Sabbath provided it is not in the street, or where the ball may fall out of bounds, where it is not permitted to carry. Certain sports, however, such as soccer, golf, and football, are in any case forbidden, for fear that one may dig up or level the ground. One may be lenient with children playing ball, as it is better that they transgress in ignorance rather than they should do so willfully. Ball games that are played on a board, a mat, or a table, such as table tennis, are permitted. Nevertheless, while some games as noted are not forbidden, it is improper to spend the Sabbath day engaged in sports, as this is not in the spirit of *Shabbat* as a day of rest and holiness. One should also not attend such games, even if only to view the sport. Games, such as dominoes and chess, preferably with a distinctive design for *Shabbat,* are permitted to be played by young boys and girls, although it is best that they occupy themselves with activities more in keeping with the spirit of *Shabbat*. See Melachah 1, note 5; Part III, notes 105, 106.

walking on the Sabbath shall not be like your walking on weekdays. Therefore, it is forbidden to run on the Sabbath.[3] But since it is written "your wonted ways," it implies that your ways are forbidden, but the ways of Heaven are permitted. Hence, for the sake of doing a *mitzvah* it is permitted to run, indeed it is a *mitzvah* to hasten to do it.[4]

2.   Our Rabbis, of blessed memory, have taken the words "nor pursuing your business" to mean that one's business may not be attended to on the Sabbath, even if it does not entail doing any forbidden labor (*melachah*).[5] Accordingly, one may not inspect his property to see what requires to be done the next day. It is also forbidden to walk about the city in search of a horse, a boat, or a wagon to hire after the Sabbath, if it is apparent that he is going for that purpose. However, one is permitted to watch over his property and belongings, or that of his neighbor.

3.   On the Sabbath one is forbidden to go to the end of the Sabbath limit (תְּחוּם שַׁבָּת), or even a lesser distance towards the *teḥum,* and wait there until nightfall in order to be able to set out on his journey from there sooner.[6] By starting out from there at the conclusion of the Sab-

---

3.   Jogging and Exercise   One is permitted to go walking, but not running or jogging. Youths who enjoy jumping and running may do so on the Sabbath, as this is their enjoyment. One is not permitted to do exercises on the Sabbath that involve physical exertion and are intended to work up a sweat and tire oneself. Some permit one to follow a daily routine of calisthenics intended to maintain physical fitness. One may do breathing exercises to correct an impairment. One may use a small, hand exerciser to strengthen the hand and the fingers.

4.   Running to the Synagogue and to Do a Mitzvah   It is a *mitzvah* to run to the synagogue to pray, or to the *Bet Hamidrash* to learn Torah, or to do a *mitzvah.* It is proper to hasten for the sake of the above even on the Sabbath.

5.   Moving Furniture, Checking Schedules   Activities of this nature would include moving furniture around the house, rearranging one's library, checking on train, bus or airline schedules, and the like.

6.   Going to the Station or Airport   One may not go to the bus or train sta-

bath[7] it is evident that he went there principally for that purpose. This is forbidden only if he goes and waits until nightfall in order to set out to do something which he cannot do on the Sabbath, such as to hire workers, or to pick fruit, or to bring back fruit which is *muktzeh,* as there is no way that it would be permissible to do these things on the Sabbath. However, one is permitted to go and wait at the *tehum* border until nightfall in order to bring in his cattle, for if there were houses on the way there within seventy cubits of each other it would be permitted even on the Sabbath. He is, likewise, permitted to go in order to bring fruit that was already plucked and is not *muktzeh,* as that would be permitted even on the Sabbath if the road were enclosed by partitions. One is also permitted to go to his orchard that is within the *tehum* in order to pick fruit at the close of the Sabbath, as it is not evident that he went there for that purpose,[8] because

---

tion, or to the airport on the Sabbath, and wait until nightfall in order to board a bus, train or airplane at the close of the Sabbath so as to embark on his journey sooner, unless it is an emergency, or it is necessary for the sake of performing a *mitzvah.*

7.   Carrying a Bus Pass for Use After Shabbat   One who sets out to walk a considerable distance on the Sabbath may not take along a bus ticket or a transit pass for return transportation after *Shabbat,* even where it is permissible to carry, because it is *muktzeh* and one would, moreover, be preparing on the Sabbath for the weekday.

8.   Loading a Washing Machine and a Dishwasher   Whether preparing on the Sabbath for a weekday activity is permitted depends on what is evident as to the purpose one has in mind. Thus, one may not put soiled clothes into a washing machine to prepare them for washing after the Sabbath. But if one is accustomed to store dirty clothes in the washing machine until they are washed it is permissible, provided there is no water in the machine. It is permitted to put dishes into the dishwasher, without meticulously sorting them in place, as it is customary to do so after a meal and to store them there until it is time to wash them, and it is not evident that his intention is to prepare them for a weekday activity. It is permitted to open the door of the dishwasher or washing machine, since it is for a permissible use. It is advisa-

people who would see him would say that he went for a walk, or to look for lost cattle, and once he was there he decided to remain until nightfall[9] in order to pick some of his fruit.

4.   The words "nor speaking thereof" are explained by the Rabbis to mean that your speech on the Sabbath should not be the same as on weekdays.[10] Hence, one may not say, "I will do this work tomorrow," or "I will buy this merchandise tomorrow." This is forbidden only if one speaks of doing what may not be done on the Sabbath under any circumstances. But if it can be done in some way, even though it is not feasible at the time, it is permitted. Therefore, one may say "I will go to that place tomorrow," provided he does not use an expression that implies that he will ride there in a carriage. Nor should he talk too much about it. It is likewise not permitted to engage excessively in idle conversation.[11] It is forbidden on the Sabbath to recount anything of a grievous nature. One is forbidden to

---

ble to take some precautionary measure so that one does not inadvertently start the machine in operation. One should check the nature of the operation of the newer models to determine whether it is permissible to open them on the Sabbath.

9.   Dressing Children in Pajamas Before the Sabbath Is Over   One may dress children in their pajamas before the Sabbath is over, even though they will not be going to bed until after nightfall. This is not considered preparing on the Sabbath for the weekday, as children are usually dressed for bed some time before bedtime for various reasons.

10.   Sabbath Greetings   When meeting or visiting a friend on the Sabbath one should not greet him in the same manner as he would on an ordinary weekday. He should rather greet him, whether in Hebrew or in another language, with a Sabbath greeting, such as *Shabbat Shalom* or *Guten Shabbos,* in fulfillment of the Biblical directive, "Remember the Sabbath day" (Exodus 20:8).

11.   Speaking in Hebrew on the Sabbath   It is deemed praiseworthy not only to refrain from idle talk on the Sabbath, but to speak only in the holy tongue, that is in Hebrew, in keeping with the holiness of the day.

make calculations verbally on the Sabbath, neither of future transactions, nor of past transactions that he still needs to know, as for
example, if he reckons how much he spent for the workers' wages on
a certain building and there are still wages due them, so that he needs
to know the full reckoning. But one is permitted to make calculations
for which he has no need, provided he does not do it excessively, as it
is forbidden to engage in too much idle talk on the Sabbath.

5. Since it says "nor pursuing your business," our Rabbis, of
blessed memory, have inferred that only personal business affairs are
forbidden,[12] but the affairs of Heaven are permitted.[13] Therefore it is
permitted to go to the *teḥum* border on the Sabbath and wait until
nightfall for the sake of performing a *mitzvah*.[14] One may also attend
to matters of communal concern on the Sabbath, such as going to
meet with a government official or the ruling council to speak on
behalf of the people, because the needs of the community are
regarded as heavenly affairs. One may talk with a teacher about
teaching his child, even to teach him a trade, as this is also considered
a *mitzvah,* because if he will not have a trade to support himself he
will turn to robbing people. However, it is forbidden to hire the
teacher on the Sabbath, because hiring is an actual violation of a

---

12. Pledging Money to the Synagogue or to Charity It is permitted to
pledge a sum of money as a donation to charity or to the synagogue on the
Sabbath. It is also permitted to record the pledge by placing a paper clip
next to the name of the donor.

13. Arranging a Betrothal and Providing for a Bride It is permitted to
arrange for a betrothal on the Sabbath. One may also go to the *teḥum*
border on the Sabbath and wait there until nightfall in order to attend to the
needs of a bride. These, too, are *mitzvot* that come under the category of
heavenly affairs.

14. Attending to the Dead One may go to the *teḥum* border on the Sabbath and wait there until nightfall in order to attend to the needs of a dead
person, such as to arrange for a coffin or shrouds, as this is a *mitzvah* which
comes under the category of heavenly affairs.

Rabbinical ordinance (שְׁבוּת) and is not permitted even for the sake of a *mitzvah*. Only what is forbidden because of the admonition "nor pursuing your business, nor speaking thereof" is permitted for the sake of a *mitzvah*.[15] It is also permitted to announce the loss of an article on the Sabbath, for returning a lost article is a *mitzvah*.

6.   Since it says "nor speaking thereof," our Rabbis, of blessed memory, have inferred that only speech is forbidden but thought is permitted. Hence, thinking about one's weekday affairs is permitted.[16] Nevertheless, it is a *mitzvah* not to think about them at all because of *Oneg Shabbat,* for the enjoyment of the Sabbath, and one should consider it as though all of his work is done. This is the explanation of the Biblical verse, "Six days shall you labor and do all your work" (Exodus 20:9). But it is not possible for a person to complete all his work in six days. Therefore, this means that every Sabbath one should view all his work as though it were accomplished, there being no greater joy than this (*Mechilta,* ibid.). One should particularly refrain from thinking about something that will trouble him or cause him anxiety.[17]

---

15.   Buying a House From a Non-Jew in Israel   It is permitted to buy a house from a non-Jew in the Land of Israel on the Sabbath. While one may not violate Sabbath laws by writing or making any actual payment, he can arrange for the purchase and provide assurance of payment. The non-Jew may sign the deed of sale and register it in the courts. The Rabbis permitted this because of the *mitzvah* of Jewish settlement in *Eretz Yisrael.*

16.   Reading or Listening to Business Reports   Permission to think about one's weekday affairs refers to thoughts that normally come to one's mind, since it is not expected that one should be able to banish such thoughts altogether. It is, however, not permitted to deliberately set one's thoughts on weekday business affairs by reading the business section in the newspaper, or by listening to the business and stock market report on the radio.

17.   Visiting a Sick Person or a Mourner   One is permitted to visit the sick and to visit the house of a mourner on the Sabbath, although this may cause him pain and anxiety. Since it is a *mitzvah* to visit and comfort the sick (בִּיקוּר

7.   One is permitted to say to a worker, "Do you think that you will be able to meet me tonight?", even though he will understand from the question that he needs him that evening in order to hire him for work, because only an explicit statement is forbidden. But he should not say to him, "Be ready to meet me tonight," for this is as though he were telling him explicitly that he wants to hire him.

8.   If one hires a worker as a watchman, he may not take any wages specifically for the Sabbath alone. However, if he is hired by the week or by the month he may take wages for the entire period including the Sabbath.[18]

9.   It is not permitted to give someone a gift, unless it is something that is needed for the Sabbath.[19] It is also forbidden to give someone

---

חוֹלִים) and to bring consolation to those in mourning (נִיחוּם אֲבֵלִים), it is permitted. But one should not do so only for convenience, failing to take time during the week and deliberately postponing the visit for the Sabbath.

18.   Hiring a Ḥazan for Shabbat and Yom Tov   While some do not countenance hiring a *ḥazan* specifically to conduct the services on a Sabbath or on a *Yom Tov,* the prevailing *minhag* is to permit it because it is for the sake of a *mitzvah.* The same applies to hiring someone to blow the *shofar* on *Rosh Hashanah.* It is preferable that the *ḥazan* be hired by the month or by the year, and that his contract include some additional duty besides leading the services on *Shabbat* and *Yom Tov.*

19.   Presenting a Gift to a Bar Mitzvah   In presenting a gift to someone the object leaves the possession of the giver and enters the possession of the recipient. Since it resembles buying and selling it is forbidden on the Sabbath, unless it is needed for use on the Sabbath. This is also the reason for not giving something as a pledge. If a gift is presented to someone on the Sabbath, as is customary to a *Bar Mitzvah,* or a bridegroom, when he delivers a Torah discourse, he should have in mind not to acquire possession until after the Sabbath, or someone should take possession of it for him before the Sabbath. When giving a gift to a *Bar Mitzvah* in the synagogue, as is the custom in some synagogues, care should be taken also that he does not take it with him after the services where it is not permitted to carry.

an article as security, unless it is for the sake of a *mitzvah,* or it is needed for the Sabbath. When giving it one should not say "Here is the pledge," but he should just give it to him.

10.   It is forbidden to read secular documents, such as due bills, accounts, and personal letters. Even to peruse them without reading them aloud is not permitted. Although one is only thinking about them it is still forbidden, because thinking is permitted only when it is not apparent that one is thinking about weekday affairs, but in this case it is obvious that he is thinking about weekday affairs that are forbidden on the Sabbath, and this comes under the prohibition against "pursuing your business" on the Sabbath. But one who receives a letter and does not know its contents is permitted to read it, because it may contain something of a personal nature which is important to him. However, he should not read it aloud. If he knows that the letter is only about business matters, he may not even read it, and it is also forbidden to handle it because it is *muktzeh.*[20]

11.   One may not read secular literature,[21] such as books about

---

20.   Personal and Business Letters   Personal letters are forbidden because they may be confused with secular documents. A letter dealing with business matters is *muktzeh* only if he intends to retain it for safekeeping, as is common among merchants who file business letters. A business letter may not be read even if written in Hebrew, but a personal letter in Hebrew may be read. It is customary not to accept a letter from the mailman directly when it is delivered on the Sabbath, but to instruct him to put it on a table or on the floor. One should not tell a non-Jew directly to open the letter, but rather indirectly by saying, for example, "I cannot read it as long as it is not opened," thus intimating that he wants him to open it.

21.   Reading Secular and Scientific Literature   While some authorities forbid it, others permit reading and studying proper secular literature, and scientific books and journals on chemistry, biology, physics, astronomy, medicine and the like. A God-fearing person should be stringent and refrain from reading such books and secular literature of a similar nature, and devote himself to studying Torah and reading Torah literature on *Shabbat.* However, if necessary, as in the case of a student who must prepare for

wars, historical accounts of the kings of the gentile nations, and proverbs and fables of a secular nature, even if they are written in Hebrew. Erotic literature is surely forbidden to be read even on weekdays because of the admonition against "the company of scoffers" (Psalms 1:1). In the case of erotic literature there is an additional prohibition in that he incites evil desires (*yaitzer ha-ra*). However, it is permitted to read history books from which one can derive moral lessons and the fear of God, such as the book of Josephus, even if they are written in a language other than Hebrew.[22] Nevertheless, it is improper to read too much of this literature as well. One should rather devote himself on *Shabbat* and *Yom Tov* to the study of Torah.[23]

12. It is not permitted on the Sabbath to take the measure of anything that needs to be measured,[24] unless it is for the sake of a *mitzvah*.[25]

---

examinations in these subjects, one may rely on the authorities who permit reading secular and scientific literature on the Sabbath.

22. Reading Newspapers and Hebrew Writings Rama permits reading secular writings of this nature if written in Hebrew. *Mishnah B'rurah* explains that it is because the language itself is holy, and one may learn Hebrew and words of Torah. Other authorities, however, do not permit it. With regard to reading a newspaper, while some forbid it as well, others permit it, especially if written in Hebrew, as it is deemed necessary to keep abreast of current events. However, one should not read business newspapers or newsletters, as well as the business and stock market sections in regular newspapers.

23. Torah Study on Shabbat One who is busy all week in business, in his profession, or at work and he does not have the time or the opportunity to learn Torah should be especially assiduous in devoting himself to Torah study on *Shabbat*. Even scholars, who are engaged in Torah study all week long, should not neglect their Torah study on the Sabbath.

24. Filling a Measuring Vessel With Food Where the measurement is not of the nature of a business transaction and it does not have the appearance

13.   Where one may otherwise suffer a loss, it is permitted to discuss one's needs, whether with a Jew or with a non-Jew.

6.   WORK ON THE SABBATH BY A NON-JEW

מְלָאכָה עַל יְדֵי אֵינוֹ יְהוּדִי

1.   Whatever a Jew is forbidden to do on the Sabbath he is not permitted to tell a non-Jew to do for him, because instructing a non-Jew to do a *melachah* (אֲמִירָה לְנָכְרִי) is a *shevut* (שְׁבוּת), that is, a violation of a Rabbinical ordinance.[1] One may not even hint to him to do it. Nor

---

of a weekday activity, it is permitted. Thus, one may request that a vessel ordinarily used for certain measurements be filled with food or other products. One may also ask for a quantity of eggs or other products, provided he does not stipulate a price.

25.   Measuring for a Mitzvah   Measurements that pertain to a *mitzvah* which are permitted on the Sabbath include measuring a *mikveh* to determine whether it contains the required forty *seah* of water, and measuring a mixture of food to ascertain if it contains a sufficient quantity to neutralize the forbidden ingredient in the mixture in order to render it permissible. Taking one's temperature with a thermometer is also considered to be for the sake of a *mitzvah* and is permitted on the Sabbath.

1.   Instructing a Non-Jew to Do a Melachah   Rambam states that the reason a Jew is forbidden to instruct a non-Jew to do a *melachah,* even though the non-Jew is not commanded to observe the Sabbath, is in order that he should not take the Sabbath lightly and come to do the *melachah* himself. It is Rabbinically prohibited when it involves a *melachah* that the Jew is forbidden to do, either because of a Biblical prohibition, (מְלָאכָה דְּאוֹרַיְיתָא) or because of a Rabbinical prohibition (שְׁבוּת דְּרַבָּנָן). Thus, one is not permitted to tell a non-Jew to buy or sell something for him on the Sabbath, to hire workers for him, or to perform any labor that is forbidden on the Sabbath. The prohibition applies in situations where the *melachah* is done for the sake of the Jew, or it is done with something that belongs to him, even if it is not for his sake. However, one may instruct a non-Jew to do what is forbidden only by custom or as a restrictive measure (חוּמְרָא בְּעָלְמָא).

may one tell him before the Sabbath that he should do it on the Sabbath.[2] It is also not permitted to tell a non-Jew on the Sabbath to do the work after the Sabbath. The latter is prohibited not because it is a *shevut,* since the work is to be done when it is permissible, but rather because of the admonition "nor pursuing your business." Hence, if it is for the sake of a *mitzvah* it is permitted.

2.   Even if the non-Jew comes of his own accord to do some work for the Jew on the Sabbath he is required to prevent him from doing it.

3.   If one is faced with a possible loss, for example if something needs to be repaired in an emergency, such as a barrel of wine that has sprung a leak, he may summon a non-Jew, even if it involves an actual *melachah,*[3] but he should not directly request him to repair it.

---

2.   Contracting for Work by a Non-Jew   If the Jew does not instruct the non-Jew to do the work on the Sabbath, but he does so of his own accord, it is permitted. A Jew may, therefore, contract with a non-Jew before the Sabbath to clean his clothing, to repair his shoes, to repair his automobile, or to do other work. The non-Jew can then proceed to do the work on his own time, even on the Sabbath, provided he does it in his shop or garage so that it is not apparent that he is doing the work for the Jew. However, this does not include work in the field or on a building, where other restrictions apply. See Part I, chapter 3, for a full discussion of this subject.

3.   When It Is Permissible to Tell a Non-Jew to Do a Melachah   It is permitted to tell a non-Jew to do a *melachah* on the Sabbath in the following circumstances:

1. In the case of an illness. Thus, for example, one may request a non-Jew to extract a tooth that gives one severe pain, to cook food for a child who cannot eat uncooked food, or to light the furnace in severely cold weather, because everyone is subject to becoming ill when exposed to the cold.

2. For the sake of settling *Eretz Yisrael* it is permitted to buy a house from a non-Jew, assuring him of due compensation for it but without making payment, and having him sign the deed and record it in the courts.

3. In a situation where one is extremely distraught, for example if

He can say, "Whoever prevents this loss will not go unrewarded." However, this should not be done unless it involves a considerable loss.

4. One may tell a non-Jew to do something that does not constitute an actual *melachah*, but is only Rabbinically prohibited as a *shevut*,[4] if it needs to be done for the sake of a *mitzvah* or for one who is slight-

---

someone is on his way home *erev Shabbat* and it is getting dark, he may give his wallet to a non-Jew to carry it for him.

4. To protect Torah scrolls and other holy books from desecration or from fire. Thus it is permitted to request a non-Jew to put out the candles in the synagogue or in the home because of the possible danger of a fire.

5. To prevent the suffering of an animal. Hence one may instruct a non-Jew to milk his cows. The milk, however, may not be used that day.

6. At twilight, even if one has already ushered in the Sabbath, he may request a non-Jew to light a *Yahrzeit* candle, or lights for the Sabbath meal, to repair the *eruv*, or to do other work necessary for a *mitzvah*, or to prevent a loss.

7. Where the *melachah* is not intended, although it is inevitable. Thus it is permitted to tell a non-Jew to remove a pot from the fire, even though some coals will thereby be extinguished and others rekindled.

8. Where one stands to suffer a considerable loss. Thus if one's merchandise is being ruined by rain, or if a barrel of wine has broken and the wine is leaking out, and the like, one may summon a non-Jew and indirectly indicate that he needs him to prevent the loss.

9. For the sake of a *mitzvah* when urgently necessary. Thus it is customary to request a non-Jew to kindle the lights in the home for the Sabbath meal, for the *seudah* at a wedding or a circumcision, or for prayer in the synagogue.

4. Permissibility of a Shevut De-Shevut Instructing a non-Jew to do work on the Sabbath is Rabbinically prohibited as a *shevut*. If the activity itself is only Rabbinically prohibited on the Sabbath, it constitutes a *shevut de-shevut*, that is, an act involving two separate Rabbinical prohibitions that would be permissible if the Rabbis had not enacted any one of the two prohibitions. In such a case it is permitted under certain conditions, as indicated.

ly ill. Accordingly, it is customary to send a non-Jew for a beverage or whatever else is needed for the Sabbath, even where there is no *eruv*. This should not be permitted except in a case of necessity when one does not have anything to drink, but if it is merely for one's pleasure it should not be allowed. One is not permitted, however, to tell a non-Jew to bring something[5] from outside the Sabbath limit (*tehum*), and if he did so whatever he brought is forbidden on the Sabbath. Some authorities maintain that where a loss is involved, it is permitted to instruct a non-Jew to do what is necessary to prevent the loss, for example to remove merchandise that is being damaged by rain. This opinion may be relied upon in a case involving a great loss.[6]

5.   In cold weather it is permitted to instruct a non-Jew to light the furnace[7] because everyone has the status of a sick person with regard to suffering from the cold.[8] But if it is not urgent it should not be

---

5.   Home Delivery of a Newspaper on Shabbat   When subscribing for home delivery of a daily newspaper, some authorities advise that one arrange not to have the paper delivered on the Sabbath.

6.   Instructing a Non-Jew in a Case of Extreme Need   One may be lenient as well in requesting the aid of a non-Jew in a case of extreme need, even where no great loss is involved. Any judgment as to need or loss is to be made on an individual basis, with due consideration to the circumstances.

7.   Repair of Furnace and Delivery of Oil on the Sabbath   If one's furnace breaks down, or it runs out of oil on the Sabbath, it is permitted to request a non-Jew to summon the gas or oil company to repair the furnace and to deliver the oil. This is permissible because of the danger of illness due to the cold, especially if there are children or old and sickly people in the house.

8.   Having a Non-Jew Turn the Air Conditioner On or Off   It is permitted to instruct a non-Jew to turn the air conditioner off on the Sabbath if there is a change in the weather and it is making the house intensely cold. This may be done in the synagogue as well. It is similarly permitted to instruct a non-Jew to turn on a fan or an air conditioner on the Sabbath to cool the room in hot weather, as people are just as likely to suffer from the heat as from the cold, particularly older people who are more prone to heatstroke in very hot weather.

done.[9] It is forbidden to have a non-Jew light the furnace on Sabbath afternoon so that it will be warm at night.

6.   It is forbidden to send a non-Jew outside the Sabbath limit (*teḥum*) to summon the relatives[10] of the deceased, or to summon someone to deliver the eulogy at the funeral.

7.   If non-Jews bring a Jew grain in repayment of their debts, the Jew may give them the key to his granary and allow them to measure and count the grain and leave it there, because the non-Jew does the work for himself, since the grain does not belong to the Jew until after it has been measured out. The Jew may stand there and watch that he does not cheat him, provided he does not discuss the transaction with him. But if they bring the Jew grain that belongs to him, he may not instruct them to unload it from the wagons and put it in his granary. Even if the non-Jews want to unload it of their own accord, he must prevent them from doing so.

8.   A non-Jew may make cheese on the Sabbath from milk that belongs to him, while the Jew watches the milking and the cheese making so that it will be permissible to Jews[11] and he will be able to

---

9.   Instructing a Non-Jew to Make the Furnace   Instructing a non-Jew to make the furnace on the Sabbath depends on the degree of cold and the discomfort of the people in the house at the time. It is surely permissible if the house is cold, and when there are children or old people in the home, as they are more likely to suffer from the cold. It is best to contract with the non-Jew to make the furnace and to service it on the Sabbath throughout the winter, so that it will not be necessary to instruct him to do so on the Sabbath.

10.   Summoning Relatives of One Who Is Critically Ill   If one who is critically ill requests that his relatives be summoned, it is permitted to send a non-Jew beyond the *teḥum* on the Sabbath, and even to hire him if need be, so that the sick person should have peace of mind.

11.   Cheese Produced by Non-Jews   Cheese made by non-Jews is not permitted unless the process was under Jewish supervision. Indeed, some authorities prohibit it even when under supervision. However, current prac-

buy it after the Sabbath. It is permitted, even though his intention is to make the cheese in order to sell it to the Jew, because the cheese still belongs to the non-Jew who is producing it for his own benefit. Moreover, the Jew may even tell him on the Sabbath to do it, because one may say to a non-Jew "Do your work," even if the Jew derives benefit from it.

9.   If a non-Jew bought merchandise from a Jew and he comes to collect it on the Sabbath, he should be kept from taking it, if possible, in order not to accustom the non-Jew to doing this, as people will suspect the Jew of selling it to him on the Sabbath.

10.   If one has *Yahrzeit* on the Sabbath, and he forgot to light the *Yahrzeit* candle, he may tell a non-Jew to light it Friday evening at twilight (*bain ha-shemashot*), but not on the Sabbath.

11.   One may invite a non-Jew to his home to have a meal with him on the Sabbath. Although he may not do so on *Yom Tov,* lest he cook extra food on his account, we need have no such concern on the Sabbath. It is even permitted to serve him alone, although he is not obliged to feed him and it would seem that he is troubling himself needlessly on the Sabbath.[12] Since we are duty-bound to provide for

---

tice follows the lenient view in permitting the use of such cheese, provided the ingredients are kosher. For a further discussion of the question of milk and cheese produced by non-Jews, see *The Concise Code of Jewish Law,* Volume One, pp. 271, 272.

12.   Providing Food for a Non-Jew   Although one must not exert himself needlessly on the Sabbath, one may provide food for a non-Jew, because he has a moral responsibility of being charitable towards a non-Jew as towards a Jew. Jewish law requires that poor Gentiles be provided for and receive maintenance like poor Jews. Hence, one may invite a non-Jew, whether he is a poor person, or a distinguished guest, to partake of his Sabbath meal. This is not the case on *Yom Tov,* when it is only permitted to cook what is necessary, and it is feared that he may come to cook additional food for the sake of the non-Jew whom he has invited to be his guest. However, if the

non-Jews as for Jews, because the ways of the Torah are ways of peace, it is considered as an obligation to feed him (*Kitzur Shulḥan Aruch* 87:19).

7. LAWS ON TREATMENT OF A MINOR AILMENT
AND ONE WHOSE ILLNESS IS NOT CRITICAL

דִּין מִי שֶׁיֵּשׁ לוֹ מֵיחוּשׁ בְּעָלְמָא וְחוֹלֶה שֶׁאֵין בּוֹ סַכָּנָה

The Halachah with regard to medication and medical treatment on the Sabbath (as will be further detailed) distinguishes among the following: (1) One who is indisposed and feels discomfort (מֵיחוּשׁ בְּעָלְמָא), and one who suffers from a minor ailment (חוֹלִי קְצָת). (2) One who is ill, but whose illness is not critical (חוֹלֶה שֶׁאֵין בּוֹ סַכָּנָה). (3) One who is critically ill (חוֹלֶה שֶׁיֵּשׁ בּוֹ סַכָּנָה).

1.   One who feels discomfort,[1] but is able to go about as a healthy

---

non-Jew comes to his home uninvited, he may have him share the meal and the food that was prepared for his household.

1.   Measuring Temperature and Blood Pressure   It is permitted to take the temperature with a mercurial thermometer on the Sabbath in order to ascertain if one has a fever. A woman who is required to take her temperature daily in order to determine the time of ovulation may do so on the Sabbath. It is permitted to readjust the level of mercury for immediate use or for further use on the Sabbath, but not to prepare it for use after the Sabbath. One may dip the thermometer in oil, or in a salve such as Vaseline. One may clean it with alcohol and then dry it with cotton, but he should not dip the cotton in alcohol and wipe it off. Some permit the use of a thermometer which registers the temperature on tape when placed on the skin by a change of color or by illuminating figures or numbers imprinted on the tape. It is advisable not to use one where the tape is blank and the figures become visible only when the temperature is taken. One may take other measurements such as pulse rate and blood pressure to determine a patient's medical con-

person, is not permitted any medical treatment[2] on the Sabbath,[3] even if it does not involve a *melachah*. Nor may one rub himself with oil, or have it done by someone else, even by a non-Jew.

2.   One may eat any food and drink any beverage that is normally consumed by people in good health, even if it is apparent that it is intended as a remedy.[4] Whatever is not considered a food or beverage

---

dition. The results may be recorded with clips attached to prepared charts, or written down by a non-Jew.

2.   Medication to Relieve a Slight Ailment   The Sages prohibited medication on the Sabbath for a localized minor ailment, or for slight aches and pains, even if it involves no forbidden labor, or the medicine was prepared before the Sabbath. For were medical treatment permitted in such a case, it would be mistakenly assumed that it is permissible to compound medicines on the Sabbath, which would entail a violation of the *melachot* of Grinding and Smoothening. However treatment which does not involve medication, such as applying pressure to prevent swelling, or heat where indicated, is permitted to relieve discomfort. The Rabbinical prohibition (*gezerah*) applies to one who only experiences discomfort due to a mild, localized pain or a slight ailment; it does not apply to one who is confined to bed or whose whole body is affected by the illness or by severe pain. It definitely does not apply to one who is critically ill, in which case one is duty-bound to administer medical treatment, even if it involves doing a *melachah* on the Sabbath.

3.   Medicine Prescribed to Be Taken Daily   Medicine that is prescribed to be taken daily for a period of time in order to achieve the desired therapeutic effect may be taken on the Sabbath, if its omission would result in illness or would delay or jeopardize one's recovery. A woman who is daily taking fertility pills, or oral contraceptive pills with medical and halachic sanction, is permitted to take them on the Sabbath. In general, one need not take a strict view regarding the use of medicines on the Sabbath, especially since people no longer prepare their own medicines, and most people are not even capable of doing so.

4.   Taking Vitamins, Sedatives and Aspirin   One is permitted to take vitamin pills on the Sabbath to supplement one's diet, as it is usual for normally healthy people to take vitamins to preserve their health and vigor and to

by healthy people is not permitted to be eaten or drunk as a cure.[5] One is permitted to drink a sweet syrup and to swallow a raw egg to make his voice more pleasant, as it is not medicinal since his throat is not sore.

3.   One who has a mild toothache and is not in great pain should not take some vinegar or liquor in his mouth for relief and then spit it out, but he should swallow it, or dip a piece of bread in it and eat it in the usual manner. Likewise, one who has a slightly sore throat should not just gargle with some liquor to relieve the soreness, but he should swallow it.[6]

4.   Where massaging with oil is done only for medical treatment, it is not permitted for one who has some pain in his loins or scabs on

---

prevent illness. Sedatives or tranquilizers taken to calm the nerves and relieve tension are likewise permitted on the Sabbath, because tension and lack of sleep can cause considerable pain or adversely affect one's whole body and prevent one from enjoyment of the Sabbath. Opinions differ on the permissibility of taking aspirin for a mild ache or pain. One who has a severe headache may take aspirin or other medication.

5.   Medication for Mild Aches or for Prevention   A normally healthy person with mild aches or pains, such as a stomachache and heartburn, may not take any medication on the Sabbath. But he may drink soda with lemon, or some other beverage, to obtain relief from these ailments, as such drinks are drunk for pleasure as well. But if the pain is severe and the ailment affects his whole body, it is permitted to take medicine to alleviate it. One is permitted to suck a candy even if it is to keep from coughing, but not medicated cough drops, unless he has a severe cough or cold, in which case he is considered ill. One is permitted to inhale menthol to relieve congestion and stuffiness in the nose. One may also take medicine that is intended as a preventive measure. Thus, one suffering from hemorrhoids may take a laxative.

6.   Rinsing With a Mouthwash   One may rinse his mouth with a mouthwash on the Sabbath, as it is not for a medicinal purpose but for clean breath. If the mouthwash has to be mixed with water, it should be prepared before the Sabbath.

his head to rub oil on the affected area on the Sabbath, as it is apparent that he is doing it for a medicinal purpose.[7]

5. One who has a stomachache may apply a vessel from which the hot water has been emptied, even though it still retains the heat. He may also heat a cloth and put it on his stomach.[8]

6. One who injures his hand or his foot[9] may apply wine to stop the bleeding, but not vinegar because it is strong and serves a medicinal purpose. If his skin is delicate he may not use wine either because it is like vinegar. If the blow was on the back of his hand or foot, or the injury was caused by a metallic object one may apply any remedy, as it is considered a serious wound. See Chapter 8, paragraph 5.

7. One who feels a slight discomfort in his eyes may not apply any-

---

7. Applying Baby Oil, Vaseline and Other Ointments   One may not apply Vaseline, moisturizers, hand creams, and the like on the hands or other parts of the body. However, it is permitted if necessary to apply oil or some other liquid lotion, but not Chapstick and the like, to dry, cracked lips or hands if the condition causes some pain. Vaseline or another ointment may be applied by a nursing woman to her nipples if they are sore, or on a baby to relieve or prevent diaper rash. This should be done without rubbing or smearing it on. The Vaseline or ointment can be applied to a gauze before the Sabbath and then placed on the affected part on the Sabbath. Baby oil may be applied, but not with cotton or a cloth. Baby powder may likewise be used.

8. Applying a Hot Water Bag   It is permitted to apply a hot water bag to the ear and to other parts of the body as well in order to obtain relief from pain. Applying heat to the stomach to relieve a stomachache at any time should be only upon the advice of a physician. When it is medically indicated one may apply a hot water bottle or a hot water bag on the Sabbath in the usual manner. It is, likewise, permitted to soak one's feet in warm water to obtain relief from pain.

9. Applying an Ice Bag   It is permitted to apply an ice bag to relieve a swelling caused by a blow or a fall, or to lower a high temperature.

thing for healing purposes, unless it is something intended merely to enable him to open his eyes.[10]

8.   One who suffers pain from overeating[11] may induce vomiting manually by thrusting the finger down the throat.

9.   One should not place a bandage with ointment or any medicated dressing on a superficial wound for the purpose of healing.[12] But one

---

10.   Cleaning the Eyes and Treating an Infection   It is permitted to wash out the secretion from one's eyes with a swab of cotton and warm water. A mild eye infection or inflammation may be treated with eye drops and ointment. In the case of disease of the eye, or severe pain or a serious infection it is permitted to administer treatment, even if it involves violation of the Sabbath. See Chapter 8, paragraph 7.

11.   Relief of Constipation and Diarrhea   It is permitted to relieve abdominal pain or illness due to constipation, preferably by taking an oral cathartic medication, and if necessary by means of a rectal suppository or an enema. Medicine for the relief of diarrhea may be taken by one who is ill, and for a severe case of diarrhea even by a healthy person. The practice of bulimia, that is, induced vomiting in order to sustain an abnormal and constant craving for food, is generally not permitted even on weekdays. In case of extreme need on the Sabbath it may be done manually.

12.   Cleansing and Treating a Wound   One may cleanse a wound on the Sabbath by first applying water or an antiseptic such as hydrogen peroxide, and then wiping it dry. One should not apply absorbent cotton that had been soaked with water or with the antiseptic. Since Iodine causes considerable staining, one should rather use Tincture of Iodides, which is colorless and does not stain. One may bandage a wound to keep it from becoming infected. It is permitted to apply ointment to a wound by pressing it out of the tube or dabbing it on, without rubbing or smearing it on, and then covering it with a cloth or bandage. It is advisable to prepare bandages of various types and sizes before the Sabbath. A medicated bandage may be applied to a wound if it was prepared before the Sabbath. The bandage should not be secured with a double knot, but with a single knot or bow, or with a clip or safety-pin. It may be removed on the Sabbath for adjustment. One may apply a bandage with adhesive tape, such as a Band-Aid, prepared

may cover the wound with a bandage to keep it clean and to protect it from irritation. If the dressing was on from before, one may cleanse the wound on the Sabbath by lifting the bandage partly at one end and then at the other without removing the bandage altogether. It is not permitted to instruct a non-Jew to prepare a bandage with ointment on the Sabbath, unless it is a severe wound that has affected his whole body.

10. It is not permitted to place a cloth on a wound that is bleeding slightly, because the blood will color it. One should first wash away the blood with water or wine and then cover the wound with a bandage. If this does not stop the bleeding, he should apply medication and bandages as necessary,[13] if possible by a non-Jew. It is forbidden to press a wound in order to extract the blood.

11. Piercing an abscess that is already draining in order to enlarge the opening of the wound is a violation of the Sabbath, as this is a medical procedure. But if one pierces it only to drain the pus which is causing him pain, and he does not mind if it closes up again, it is permitted. He should pierce it with a needle and the like, but not with his fingernails, because he is likely to tear the skin and tissue surrounding it. If possible the piercing should be done by a non-Jew, as he may intend to have the wound remain open for the pus to continue to drain.

12. One who has a hole in the arm called an *aptura* (a fontanel), that is, a membrane-covered opening in the bone or between the bones, and the hole became somewhat blocked, he may not insert pulse

---

for use before the Sabbath. One may not remove the adhesive from the skin if it will pull out the hair, unless it is essential to do so. It may be removed by moistening it with water or a prepared solvent. See Melachah 30, note 2.

13. Stopping Severe Bleeding One may use styptic powder on a wound to stop the bleeding. If the bleeding is severe, as in the case of arterial bleeding which is life-threatening, one should do whatever is necessary to stem the flow of blood.

inside the hole to open it, because he intends that it remain open. But it is permitted to cover it with a bandage that was prepared before the Sabbath in order to protect it. However, if the bandage is made to draw out pus or blood it is forbidden, because in this case the pus and blood are in the flesh and by extracting them he makes a wound, unlike an abscess where the pus and blood are localized and no wound is made when it is pierced. One is also not permitted to wipe it, if in doing so he will cause the blood or pus to come out.

13.   A sore that has healed may be covered with a bandage that was prepared before the Sabbath, as it is only for the purpose of protecting it.[14] It is permitted to remove a scab from a sore.

14.   One may remove a splinter with a needle, but he should take care not to cause bleeding, as he would be making a wound.

15.   If one is confined to bed due to illness,[15] although it is not life-threatening (חוֹלֶה שֶׁאֵין בּוֹ סַכָּנָה),[16] or if one suffers from an ailment

---

14.   Changing a Bandage   It is permitted to change the bandage on a wound to keep it from putrefying or if it is causing pain. The wound may be wiped and cleansed if one can avoid extracting blood, or if only the blood that was already collected there is drawn out. See note 12 above for further details on bandaging a wound.

15.   Ringing a Bell to Summon Help   A sick person who is confined to bed, even if he is not critically ill, may summon help by ringing an ordinary bell on the Sabbath. One who is in the hospital and must summon a nurse may ring an electric bell, provided it does not put on a light. In an emergency, and when he must use the toilet facilities, he may ring the bell, if possible in an indirect manner, even if it will result in putting on a light. One who is dangerously ill may ring a bell to summon help under all circumstances.

16.   One Whose Illness Is Not Critical   One who experiences severe pain, such as migraine or a severe headache, and a feeling of weakness and fatigue throughout his body, is considered to be ill, although not critically (חוֹלֶה שֶׁאֵין בּוֹ סַכָּנָה), and is permitted medication and medical treatment as indicated. It

which has affected his whole body,[17] so that he is considered as though he were bedridden, although he is able to walk about, one may instruct a non-Jew to administer medical treatment and to cook for him on the Sabbath. He is allowed to eat food that was cooked by a non-Jew, since he is permitted to have a non-Jew cook for him on the Sabbath. He is permitted to take medicines and to have medical treatment administered to him, either by himself or by others,[18]

---

is, likewise permitted to one who is subject to serious illness unless he receives treatment, as in the case of one who suffers from asthma, diabetes, rheumatic fever, and heart disease. One who is running a fever, above his normal temperature, is, likewise, considered to be non-critically ill (חוֹלֶה שֶׁאֵין בּוֹ סַכָּנָה). However, one who has an abnormally high fever, or who has fever accompanied by chills, or one whose fever, even if moderate, is not due to a cold or a sore throat and the like, but may be caused by an internal condition, is considered to be critically ill (חוֹלֶה שֶׁיֵּשׁ בּוֹ סַכָּנָה). In general, especially with children, where there is fever one should practice caution, unless it is manifestly clear that it presents no danger. For one who is seriously ill, whose condition is possibly life-threatening, every Jew is duty-bound to do whatever is necessary, even if it involves desecration of the Sabbath.

17. Medical Treatment for a Child   A child up to the age of nine or ten, or older, depending upon his physical condition and stage of development, is considered to be of a weak nature and in need of special care. It is therefore permitted to do whatever is necessary for him, just as for one who is considered a non-critically ill person (חוֹלֶה שֶׁאֵין בּוֹ סַכָּנָה). He may be given medicines and medical treatment as indicated. If the child feels ill and has a fever, even if moderate, he is considered to be critically ill (חוֹלֶה שֶׁיֵּשׁ בּוֹ סַכָּנָה), and the Sabbath is to be desecrated, when necessary, to provide food and medical treatment (see Chapter 9 note 11).

18. Use of a Vaporizer   When it is necessary to use a vaporizer on the Sabbath, as for a child who has difficulty breathing, if it is a cold water vaporizer one may add water as needed on the Sabbath. If it operates automatically one should take care that the water is not depleted, causing it to shut off and to begin operating when the water is added. If it is a hot water vaporizer one may not add water because of the prohibition of cooking, but he may instruct a non-Jew to do it. If the patient's condition is serious and a

provided it does not involve the transgression of a *melachah*, even if it is only Rabbinically prohibited. Whatever involves a Rabbinical prohibition may be done by a non-Jew. If a non-Jew is not available, and it only involves the transgression of a Rabbinical prohibition, it may be done by a Jew in a manner different from the way it is usually done.

16.   Where vaccination of children as required by health regulations is scheduled for the Sabbath, one should have vaccination of his child postponed until after the Sabbath. If this is not possible, and it must be done on the Sabbath,[19] one should not hold the child for the vaccination, but he should be held by a non-Jew.

---

non-Jew is not available, one may add boiled water to the vaporizer. It should be done in a manner different from the usual, as with the left hand. The water should be boiled before the Sabbath and kept on the fire to be added as needed. The vaporizer should be started before the Sabbath, or activated by means of a timer that is set before the Sabbath. If these preparations were not made before the Sabbath, and the patient is critically ill, one may activate the vaporizer on the Sabbath and add water as necessary.

19. Vaccination and Injections   It is permitted to administer a vaccination on the Sabbath when medically prescribed, as for smallpox, if it cannot be postponed. One is, likewise, permitted to give subcutaneous and intramuscular injections to a non-critically ill patient, or to one who must receive the injection daily, as in the case of a diabetic who requires daily injections of insulin. The area may be cleansed and disinfected with iodine, or by pouring some alcohol and wiping it dry with a wad of cotton. The needle may be similarly sterilized. The wrapper may be removed from the syringe, if possible without tearing the print. It is best to prepare the cotton, needle and syringe before the Sabbath. It is also permitted to attach the needle to the syringe as it is disposable and is subsequently discarded. One is not permitted to give an intravenous injection to a patient who is not seriously ill, but he may give it to a critically ill patient, if it is necessary to administer it on the Sabbath.

8. LAWS CONCERNING ONE WHO IS CRITICALLY ILL

AND ONE FORCED TO TRANSGRESS

דִּין חוֹלֶה שֶׁיֵּשׁ בּוֹ סַכָּנָה וְדִין אָנוּס לַעֲבֵירָה

1. The Sabbath laws, like all of the other laws of the Torah, are superseded when a human life is in danger.[1] It is, therefore, a *mitzvah* to desecrate the Sabbath[2] for one who is critically ill,[3] even for a day-

---

1. Desecrating the Sabbath to Save a Life   One must do everything possible, even if it involves desecration of the Sabbath, to save a life. Thus, if a person, whether child or adult, is critically ill, or in danger of drowning at sea or in a flood, or has fallen into a pit, or is buried by debris, or is trapped in a fire, or is pursued by a deadly snake, or by a wild animal, or by someone threatening to kill him, all efforts must be extended to save him. In these and in similar situations, one should act quickly and resolutely, without waiting to ascertain whether it is permissible to desecrate the Sabbath. Likewise, when attacked on the Sabbath, one is duty-bound to take up arms and defend oneself and others against those who threaten one's life. Suspension of the Sabbath laws when human life is in danger is inferred from the Biblical verse, "Wherefore the children of Israel shall keep the Sabbath, to observe the Sabbath throughout their generations for a perpetual covenant" (Exodus 31:16). The Rabbis state, "Desecrate one Sabbath on his account, so that he may keep many Sabbaths" (*Yoma* 85b).

2. Desecrating the Sabbath for One Who Is Dangerously Ill   All measures called for under the circumstances are to be taken promptly on the Sabbath for one who is dangerously ill, just as one would do on an ordinary weekday. This includes administering first aid, phoning for an ambulance, transporting the patient to a hospital, phoning for a doctor, driving to summon the doctor and to bring necessary medicines, giving injections, and administering prescribed treatment. Those who are on emergency call, such as volunteers for *Hatzolah,* may carry beepers which alert them to an emergency and enable them to respond without delay. For a more detailed study on the resolution of problems of a medical nature, and medical practice relating to the patient and the physician, consult the sources listed in the bibliography.

old infant.[4] If the sick person does not wish to have the Sabbath desecrated for his sake, he should be compelled to submit, for it is a grave
sin for one to be a pious fool who refuses medical attention because
of some prohibition. Of such a one it is said, "And surely your blood
of your lives will I require" (Genesis 9:5).[5]

Indeed, one who is quick in desecrating the Sabbath for the sake
of one who is dangerously ill[6] is praiseworthy. Even if a non-Jew is
present it should be done by a Jew.[7] Whoever desecrates the Sabbath

---

3. When an Illness May Be Critical A mild illness is considered non-
critical so long as there are no unusual circumstances. However, in the case
of one who is in delicate health and in a physically weakened condition, or in
the case of an infant and a frail child, an illness or a fever that is not usually
deemed serious may be critical for them. One should therefore be alert to the
potentially serious consequences of an illness and act accordingly. A person
is considered critically ill if there is a possible danger to his life, or if his condition may become graver and his life threatened if he is not attended to .

4. Saving the Life of a Fetus One is duty-bound to desecrate the Sabbath,
if need be, in order to save the life of a newborn infant. Desecration of the
Sabbath is called for, as well, to save the life of a fetus, even if it is less than
forty days since its inception, when there is a possible danger to the fetus,
although the mother is not in any danger.

5. A Patient Who Refuses Medical Treatment on the Sabbath The Rabbis
understand the verse to be a prohibition of suicide. One who is critically ill
and refuses medical treatment and help because it involves a desecration of
the Sabbath should be persuaded, and if need be compelled, to allow it.
Excessive piety in such a case is misguided, and contrary to Jewish law.

6. One Suffering From Mental Illness Jewish law considers a patient who
is afflicted with a mental illness to be in as serious a condition as one
stricken by a physical ailment. Hence, it is permitted to violate the Sabbath
for one suffering from severe mental illness, when it presents a danger to the
patient or to others, in order to provide him with necessary medical and
psychiatric care.

7. Violation of the Sabbath by a Jew in an Emergency The Rama states
that it is customary to have a non-Jew do whatever would be in desecration

for a person who is dangerously ill, even if it subsequently proves to have been unnecessary, has earned his reward. For example, if the doctor ordered a dried fig's bulk of food for the patient, and nine other people went and each one plucked a dried fig and brought it for him, they have all earned a goodly reward from the Lord, blessed be His Name, even if the patient had already recovered from the first. This applies whenever it is a matter of saving a life. Even when it is doubtful whether or not his life is in danger, it is a *mitzvah* to desecrate the Sabbath and to do whatever is necessary for him,[8] including

---

of the Sabbath, provided he will do it conscientiously and without delay. The Taz, however, maintains that in an emergency, when there is a possible danger to life, the Jew should do it himself even though he will desecrate the Sabbath. In his opinion reluctance on the part of the Jew to desecrate the Sabbath, and requiring that it be done by a non-Jew, may lead people to believe that even when a non-Jew is not present it is forbidden for a Jew to desecrate the Sabbath, and one must wait for the non-Jew thereby endangering a life. The Taz notes that in such a situation the Sages require that it should be done by a Jew, preferably the most distinguished of those present. In practice, whatever is not urgent and does not have to be done immediately, such as lighting the fire in the furnace to heat the house, if there is a non-Jew present it should be done by him.

8. Attending to One Who Is Critically Ill It is permissible to provide all necessary medical care and to attend to the needs of a critically ill person on the Sabbath, so that his physical and mental condition is not aggravated. Thus, one is even permitted to make the fire in the furnace, if a non-Jew is not readily available, in order to have heat in the house, because the cold could seriously affect him in his weakened condition. Other activities of a non-emergency nature that are required for his care, such as boiling water for medical or hygienic purposes, putting on a light in order to attend to the patient or for his comfort, extinguishing the light to allow him to sleep or to rest, and the like, may be performed by a Jew if a non-Jew is not readily available. However, only the essential activity is permitted. Thus, if it is necessary to turn on a light it may not be extinguished afterwards unless it is necessary to do so to allow him to sleep and rest. If possible his needs should be attended to in a manner that avoids desecration of the Sabbath or lessens its violation. Hence, one may not put on a light if the patient can be moved

the violation of Biblical prohibitions,[9] as there is nothing that supersedes the saving of a human life. For the Torah was given to live by it, as it is said, "You shall therefore keep My statutes and My ordinances, which if a man do them, he shall live by them" (Leviticus 18:5). The Sages expound on this, saying "He shall live by them, and not die on account of them" (*Yoma* 85b). However, the above does not apply to the three cardinal prohibitions of idolatry, illicit sexual intercourse involving adultery and incest, and murder, for which one is duty-bound to give up his life rather than violate them (*Sanhedrin* 74a).[10]

2. If there is no accredited physician present,[11] and someone

---

to a lighted room, or a light can be brought into his room. Nor may a light be extinguished if it can be screened or removed. As far as possible such activities should be kept at a minimum and the patient's needs should be anticipated and prepared for before the Sabbath.

9. Driving a Critically Ill Person to the Hospital In an emergency one is permitted to drive a patient to a doctor or to the hospital, but he may not drive home afterwards, as the permission to violate the Sabbath applies only to the time that there is a possible danger to life. In such a circumstance, it is best where possible to summon a taxi or a car driven by a non-Jew, so as to avoid unnecessary desecration of the Sabbath, provided it does not cause an undue delay. One is permitted to accompany the patient to ease his anxiety and to see that he receives proper treatment. An ambulance or a medical emergency vehicle driven by a Jew may return to its station on the Sabbath, as it is likely that it will be needed again in an emergency. In the event that one has to drive the patient to the hospital in his car, he should try to minimize violations of the Sabbath, provided it does not cause undue delay and endanger the patient. See also Chapter 9, note 3.

10. Three Cardinal Principles of Faith and Morality Inasmuch as these constitute cardinal principles of faith and morality in Judaism, one is called upon, under certain prescribed conditions and circumstances, to forfeit his life rather than violate them, in sanctification of the Name of God.

11. Volunteers Responding to an Emergency Volunteers who respond to

declares that in his estimation the sick person is critically ill, he is to be believed and the Sabbath is violated for the sake of the patient. Even if he does not declare it for certain, but only that it appears to him that his condition is critical, the Sabbath is violated, because the law requires leniency even when the matter is in doubt and there is only a possible danger to human life. If the doctors disagree in diagnosing his condition, and one doctor says that he is dangerously ill and requires a certain remedy and the other says that he does not need it, or if the patient says that he does not need it, we must listen to the doctor who believes that he is critically ill and requires the remedy. If the sick person says that he is critically ill and requires a certain remedy and the doctor says that he does not need it, we must pay heed to the sick person. However if the doctor says that the remedy or the treatment will be harmful to him, we must listen to the doctor.

3. If an accredited physician,[12] whether Jew or non-Jew, or someone who has competence in the matter, declares that while the sick person is not in immediate danger, if he will not receive a certain treatment[13] his condition may become critical and his life en-

---

an emergency, such as those in *Hatzolah,* are permitted to carry a beeper on the Sabbath so that they can be summoned at all times. When responding to an emergency the volunteer may travel by car, carry oxygen and other equipment, and do whatever is necessary in ministering to the patient. He is also permitted to return by car afterward, as he may be summoned for another emergency. If he can get a non-Jew to drive the car he should do so, provided there is no delay whatsoever in getting to the patient.

12. Summoning a Particular Doctor   One is permitted to call a family doctor on the Sabbath, or a particular physician requested by the patient who is critically ill or by his family, even if there is a competent, accredited physician readily available to attend to him. The physician summoned is, likewise, permitted to respond and attend to the patient (see also Chapter 9, note 2) even if other physicians are available and he will have to desecrate the Sabbath.

13. Surgery and Other Medical Procedures on the Sabbath   The Sabbath

dangered, even if the patient says that he does not require it, we must heed the advice of the physician and administer the treatment, no matter that it involves a violation of the Sabbath.[14] If the physician says that if the treatment is not administered he will surely die, and if

---

may be violated for medically prescribed procedures, such as surgery, X-rays, electrocardiogram, blood transfusion, injections, and the like, which the doctor declares must be done that very day. Elective surgery, however, should not be scheduled for the Sabbath, if the doctor's schedule permits it and its postponement will not endanger the patient. Similarly, radiation treatments, or intravenous injections, and the like, should not be scheduled for the Sabbath, providing the delay will not adversely affect his condition. Surgery of a non-emergency nature should, if possible, be performed early in the week, so as to avoid violations of the Sabbath in the post-operative procedures that are required in the days immediately following the operation. However if this might lead to further delay and complications, the operation may even be scheduled for Thursday or Friday. One who has undergone surgery is considered to be critically ill following the operation, and the Sabbath is violated on his account.

14. A Doctor Attending to Patients on the Sabbath   The medical profession devoted to healing the sick and preserving human life has been highly regarded in Jewish law and tradition. Indeed, the Sages of the Talmud and later Torah authorities throughout the generations possessed medical knowledge, and considered the study and practice of medicine a *mitzvah* and an exemplary way of helping one's fellowman and serving God.

In the course of his medical practice the Jewish physician is permitted to attend to his patients when necessary, and to respond to medical emergencies on the Sabbath, according to the guidelines set forth in Halachah. Nevertheless, the Jewish physician should endeavor to observe the Sabbath in the normal, traditional manner. As a rule he should not schedule office hours or appointments, but arrange to be free of duty on the Sabbath. Where he must be in attendance in the hospital, or he is summoned to a patient in case of an emergency, he is obliged to treat the critically ill patient even if it involves violating the Sabbath. For a detailed guide to the law as it pertains to travel to and from the patient or the hospital, the procedures to be followed by the doctor in the course of treatment and in the hospital, and his medical practice in general, so as to avoid or minimize desecration of the Sabbath, consult the relevant sources listed in the bibliography.

he receives it there is a chance that he might live,[15] the Sabbath should be violated for his sake as well.

4.   The Sabbath is violated for any internal injury resulting from a wound or abscess, and the like,[16] that is from the lips inward, including the teeth. In such a case it is not required to assess the illness as critical, so that even if there is no one present who is competent to offer a medical opinion and the sick person does not say anything, one should do for him everything that would normally be done on weekdays. However, if the nature of the illness is known, and one can see from his condition that treatment for the illness can be deferred, and there is no need to violate the Sabbath, it should not be violated. Ordinary aches and pains are not considered as injuries. If one has a severe toothache, and he suffers from it to such an extent that his whole body is ill because of it, he is permitted to instruct a non-Jew to extract the tooth.[17]

---

15.   When Recovery Is in Doubt or the Illness Is Terminal   Desecration of the Sabbath for one whose life is possibly in danger is mandated even if it is doubtful the treatment will be effective and the patient will survive, or when it is certain that his illness is terminal and his condition hopeless. It must be done if only to keep him alive for the moment, and even if it is doubtful his life will be prolonged at all. In the final analysis, the decision of life and death is in the hands of God.

16.   Treating Infections, Internal Disease and Injury   Any internal disease, or an infection of any member or part of the body that poses the danger of spreading throughout the body is considered to be life-threatening, and one may violate the Sabbath to treat the infection or the disease. Where there is a possibility of internal injury, as in the case of an automobile accident, it is permitted to provide treatment and to conduct diagnostic investigations as necessary.

17.   Treating a Severe Toothache and Extracting a Tooth   One who has a severe toothache may apply medication on the Sabbath. If there is severe pain in the tooth or swelling of the gums which is not relieved with medication, or if there is a possible infection or dental abscess, and immediate extraction of the tooth is medically indicated, it may be done by a Jew if a

5. The Sabbath is violated for a wound on the back of the hand[18] or on the front of the foot,[19] for a wound caused by a metal object, for an ulcer at the opening of the rectum,[20] for one who swallowed a leech, for one bitten by a mad dog, or by a reptile even if it is doubtful whether it is deadly or not. The Sabbath is also violated for one who has a very high fever, but not for an ordinary fever.[21] In the latter case he should be attended by a non-Jew.

---

non-Jewish dentist is not available, inasmuch as the teeth are considered to be organs of an internal nature.

18. A Condition Considered Life-Threatening by the Sages The Sages considered a blow on the back (dorsal) surface of the hand or on the upper (dorsum) side of the foot to be like an internal wound, usually resulting in swelling and possibly affecting the arteries and blood vessels in the area. For these injuries and other conditions which the Sages of the Talmud considered life-threatening the Sabbath is violated, regardless of medical opinion on the matter.

19. Resetting a Dislocated Limb It is permitted on the Sabbath to treat a fracture and to reset a dislocated limb, such as an arm or a leg, whether it is broken or not. This may be done for an adult, and certainly for children, when there is severe pain and if left unattended can result in a weakening of the limb. When a limb is endangered it is considered to be life-threatening and the Sabbath is desecrated to save it.

20. Treating Hemorrhoids One who suffers from hemorrhoids may use suppositories on the Sabbath, and bathe the area in warm water provided it was prepared in a permissible manner. He is permitted to take laxatives and the like to facilitate and ease the discharge, since one may take medicine on the Sabbath as a preventive measure. In the case of severe pain, medical treatment may be administered as necessary.

21. Violating the Sabbath for a Fever An abnormally high fever, a fever accompanied by chills, a typhus fever, or a fever attributable to a diseased lung or other organ, are considered life-threatening. However one may not violate the Sabbath for a fever that is simply due to a cold and it is manifestly not critical. In the case of a child the Sabbath is violated for any temperature above the normal.

6. One who suffers an attack of congestion may have blood-letting done immediately. If blood was let and he is overcome with a chill, one may make a fire to warm him even on the summer solstice (*teku-fat Tamuz*).

7. The Sabbath is violated for one who feels pain in his eyes, or who has pus in an eye, or if there is a discharge or bleeding from the eye, or if the eye is otherwise in danger.[22]

8. If one who is dangerously ill requires meat, and only forbidden meat is available, it is permitted to slaughter on the Sabbath for his sake in order to provide him with kosher meat. He should not be fed the non-kosher meat,[23] because when he realizes that he ate forbidden meat he may be sickened by it. But where there is no such concern, as in the case of a child or one who is mentally deranged, he should be fed the forbidden meat rather than slaughter on the Sabbath on his account.

9. When food is cooked by a Jew on the Sabbath for a patient who is dangerously ill,[24] it may not be eaten by a healthy person. Immediately after the Sabbath even a healthy person may eat it.

---

22. Treating an Eye Infection One who has a mild eye infection is considered to be non-critically ill, and may have eye drops or other medication administered. If the infection is serious and there is indication of disease of the eye, as manifested by severe pain or inflammation, or any of the symptoms enumerated above, one is considered to be critically ill. The Sabbath is violated in such instances, and wherever there is a danger of a possible loss of an eye or of blindness.

23. Non-Kosher Meat for One Who Is Critically Ill If a dangerously ill person requires the meat immediately, he should be given the available non-kosher meat without delay. But if the need is not immediate, one should prepare kosher meat for the patient if it is absolutely necessary that he eat the meat.

24. Cooking for One Who Is Critically Ill While it is permissible to boil water and cook food when it is necessary for one who is dangerously ill, one should as far as possible minimize the violation of the Sabbath. Thus, one

10.   If someone is being forced to transgress, one may not desecrate the Sabbath to save him even from a serious transgression.[25] However, if a Jew, whether he is an adult or a child, is being forced to convert from the Jewish faith and to abandon the community of Israel, everyone is duty-bound to exert all his efforts to save him, even if it requires desecrating the Sabbath in the violation of Biblical prohibitions, just as one is duty-bound to desecrate the Sabbath for a dangerously ill person. For it is written, "Wherefore the children of Israel shall keep the Sabbath" (Exodus 31:16); the Torah tells us, "Desecrate one Sabbath on his account so that he may keep many Sabbaths" (*Yoma* 85b). One is duty-bound to desecrate the Sabbath and do whatever he can to save one from apostasy, even if it is doubtful that his efforts will avail, just as one must desecrate the Sabbath even in a case of doubtful danger to human life. However, for one who willfully wishes to convert and forsake the Jewish faith it is not permitted to desecrate the Sabbath when it involves violating a Biblical prohibition. Since he does it willfully we do not say to a person, "Sin so that your fellow may benefit." Nevertheless, when it only involves violation of a Rabbinical prohibition, such as going beyond the Sabbath limit (*teḥum*), riding on a horse or in a wagon, or handling money, and the like, some permit violating the Sabbath in order to save him.

---

should have a non-Jew do the cooking, if there is no delay that might endanger the patient. If it becomes necessary for a Jew to do the cooking, he should cook only the required amount. While cooking he may adjust the flame, but not extinguish it afterwards. Food cooked on the Sabbath for a critically ill patient may not be eaten on the Sabbath even by another patient who is not critically ill. Utensils used for cooking on the Sabbath are permissible for further use and do not need to be *kashered*.

25.   Desecrating the Sabbath To Save One From Transgression   One is not called upon to transgress and desecrate the Sabbath in order to keep another from transgressing. However, if he is being compelled to transgress one of the three cardinal prohibitions, namely, idolatry, illicit sexual intercourse involving adultery or incest, and murder, for which he is likely to give his life to avoid transgressing them, there is reason to violate the Sabbath for his sake.

9. LAWS CONCERNING A WOMAN IN CHILDBIRTH

דִּינֵי יוֹלֶדֶת

1. As soon as a woman begins to experience signs of labor,[1] even if she is not certain of it, a doctor or a midwife should be summoned immediately,[2] even from a place many miles distant.[3]

2. A woman in childbirth is considered as one who is dangerously ill and the Sabbath is desecrated on her account for whatever she needs. However, if possible, this should be done in an indirect or

---

1. Preparing for Possible Delivery of the Baby on Shabbat If a woman is in the ninth month of pregnancy consideration should be given to the possibility of her giving birth on the Sabbath. Preparations should be made before *Shabbat* for whatever would be needed, such as putting on lights, assembling necessities for delivery of the baby, or arranging for transportation to the hospital, so that there will be a minimal desecration of the Sabbath in the event that she goes into labor. She need not, however, trouble herself to stay near the hospital so as not to have to travel on the Sabbath.

2. Summoning a Woman's Own Obstetrician It is permitted to summon a woman's own obstetrician, or the doctor of her preference, to attend to her on the Sabbath and to deliver the baby, even though it involves violating the Sabbath and there is another doctor readily available. The Halachah requires that everything be done for the sake of a woman who is in labor to ease her anxiety. See also Chapter 8, note 12.

3. Transporting a Woman in Labor to the Hospital At the first signs of labor one should phone for a cab or car service, or for an ambulance, or drive the woman to the hospital, as in the case of a person who is critically ill. See Chapter 8, note 9. If possible, and there is no undue delay, it is preferable that one call a cab or car service, rather than drive on the Sabbath. She may be driven to her designated hospital, or to the hospital of her choice, where her physician will attend to the delivery, although there is another hospital nearby or at a closer distance. The woman may be accompanied by her husband, or by someone else, in order to comfort her, and she may take along whatever she will need on the Sabbath.

unusual manner, or by a non-Jew.[4] A woman is considered to be in childbirth when she is in labor, or there is a flow of blood, or she is unable to walk by herself.[5] A woman who has a miscarriage forty days or more after her ritual immersion (*tevilah*) is likewise governed by the laws that apply to a woman in childbirth.[6]

3.   During the first three days following childbirth the Sabbath is violated for her sake, even if the woman who gave birth says that she does not require it. Thereafter, until after the seventh day, if she says that she requires it the Sabbath is violated for her sake, and if she says that she does not require it the Sabbath is not violated, provided she does not suffer any other illness except for the usual pains that follow childbirth. The above are calendar days reckoned from the day of birth and not from hour to hour in a twenty-four hour cycle.[7]

---

4.   Keeping Violations of the Sabbath at a Minimum   Since childbirth is a normal, natural process it is deemed advisable to keep violations of the Sabbath at a minimum, but only if it does not result in delay or in not properly attending to the woman's needs.

5.   A Woman in a Condition of Childbirth   A condition of childbirth would likewise be indicated by rupture of the membranes. These signs of actual labor, however, are required only for activities that are not immediately necessary. But calling a doctor or an ambulance, taking the woman to the hospital, and doing whatever else is immediately necessary, should be attended to directly and promptly as soon as she begins to feel what appear to be labor pains, even if she is not sure of it.

6.   Violating the Sabbath to Prevent a Miscarriage   The Sabbath is violated to prevent a miscarriage in order to save the fetus, even when there is no danger to the mother. This is permitted even in the case of a doubtful danger to the fetus, and even before the forty days from the time of conception. See Chapter 8, note 4.

7.   Reckoning the Period of Confinement   Many halachic authorities require the days to be reckoned in a twenty-four hour cycle. The first three days would thus constitute a period of seventy-two hours from the time of birth. During this period of confinement the Sabbath is violated on the

Thus, if she gave birth on Wednesday towards evening, the following Sabbath is already after the three days. And if she gave birth on Saturday towards evening, the following Sabbath is already after the seven days. However, if the woman is in frail health and there is a slight possibility of danger the days may be reckoned in a twenty-four hour cycle from the actual time of birth.

4. After the seventh day the Sabbath is not violated for her sake, even if she says that she requires it. From then until thirty days following childbirth she is considered as a non-critically ill patient and all her needs are attended to by a non-Jew.[8] However, if it is necessary to heat the house, this may be done by a Jew even during the summer solstice, if a non-Jew is not readily available, because a woman is considered in danger from the cold for thirty days following childbirth.

5. An infant born on the Sabbath[9] is bathed, his umbilical cord cut,

---

advice of a doctor or someone else competent in the matter even if the woman does not consider it necessary. Even after the first three days, if there are complications and it is deemed necessary, or if the woman says that she requires it even if the physician does not consider it necessary, the Sabbath is violated for her sake. However, as at the time of childbirth, this should be done, if possible, in an indirect or unusual manner or by a non-Jew. The above rules apply both in the case of a normal delivery, or a stillbirth, as well as a miscarriage.

8. Attending to a Woman's Needs Thirty Days Following Childbirth From the seventh day until after thirty days following childbirth, provided there are no complications in her medical condition, the law applies to her as to those who are non-critically ill. Activities that are only Rabbinically prohibited may be performed by a Jew for her sake. All manner of work may be done by a non-Jew.

9. Violating the Sabbath for an Infant Born Prematurely The Sabbath is violated for the sake of a newborn infant, even if it is only to sustain its life momentarily. Indeed, advances in neonatal medicine have greatly increased

his limbs straightened out, and everything that is required[10] is done for him.[11]

10. THE ERUV OF COURTYARDS
דִּינֵי עֵרוּבֵי חֲצֵרוֹת

1. Two or more Jews who reside in one courtyard, each in his own dwelling, are forbidden to carry on the Sabbath from the dwellings to the courtyard,[1] and from the courtyard to the dwellings. They are likewise forbidden to carry from one dwelling to another even if it is not through the courtyard, as for instance through a door or window

---

the prospects of survival for infants born prematurely or with serious ailments and deformities.

10. Nursing the Baby A woman nursing her baby on the Sabbath should nurse him at the breast. She should not express the milk into a vessel unless it is in exceptional circumstances, as when the baby is incapable of sucking at the mother's breast or is in the hospital and needs to be nourished with his mother's own milk fresh daily. Likewise, if she suffers pain from excess milk she may express the milk on the Sabbath, by means of a suction pump if necessary. In the latter case it should be done in a manner that renders the milk unfit for consumption and is discarded. See Part II, Melachah 5, note 5.

11. Attending to an Infant and Young Child An infant, as well as a young child, has the status of one who is ill but not critically so (חוֹלֶה שֶׁאֵין בּוֹ סַכָּנָה) with respect to the Sabbath laws (see Chapter 7, note 17). In the view of some authorities he is to be considered in possible danger as regards food and nourishment. In order to avoid unnecessary desecration of the Sabbath, however, whatever food and drink is required should be cooked and prepared before the Sabbath and properly stored and refrigerated. On the procedure for warming food and drink on the Sabbath so that the child may receive his nourishment as usual, see Melachah 11, notes 11, 21, 26.

1. Carrying Within the Courtyard Articles that are kept within the courtyard on the Sabbath may be moved about within the courtyard, even without an *Eruv Hatzerot,* provided it is otherwise permissible to carry there.

between the dwellings. In order to avoid transgression the tenants are obliged to establish *Eruvei Ḥatzerot,* (עֵירוּבֵי חֲצֵרוֹת),[2] an *eruv* of courtyards, in the manner outlined below, which will allow them to carry in these circumstances.

2. The tenants of two adjoining courtyards with a doorway between them may establish a separate *eruv* for each courtyard, permitting them to carry in their respective courtyards. They are, however, then forbidden to carry from one courtyard to the other vessels that are in the house on the Sabbath. All of the tenants in both courtyards can, if they wish, establish one *eruv,* permitting them to carry from one courtyard to the other, even vessels that are in the house on the Sabbath. They may also establish one *eruv* jointly even if there is only a window between the courtyards, provided it measures no less than four handbreadths in width and four handbreadths in height, and it is within ten handbreadths of the ground, and it has no grate. But if the window is of lesser dimensions they cannot make an *eruv* jointly. If there is a window between two of the dwellings, even if it is higher than ten handbreadths, the tenants may make an *eruv* jointly (because a house is as though it were filled to the ceiling, and the window is regarded as being within ten handbreadths of the ground).

3. If there are two courtyards, one within the other, and the residents of the inner courtyard have no exit to the street except by way

---

2. The Reason for an Eruv Ḥatzerot Where two or more Jews or Jewish families reside in adjoining houses or apartments which open onto a common courtyard, or in separate apartments in the same building which open onto a shared hallway, carrying while not a Biblical violation is nevertheless forbidden because of the similarity to private and public domains. If carrying were permitted it might lead one to think that it is permissible in the latter instance as well. The *Eruv Ḥatzerot* serves to join the residents in the building or courtyard so that they are considered as one family and their premises as common to all, thereby enabling them to carry on the Sabbath between the dwellings, and into or from as well as in the hallway or courtyard.

of the outer courtyard through a doorway that provides passage between them, the tenants of both courtyards can, if they wish, establish one *eruv* jointly. If they did not make an *eruv* jointly, and the tenants of the inner courtyard alone made an *eruv*, the latter are permitted to carry in their courtyard, while the tenants of the outer courtyard are forbidden to carry in theirs. If the tenants of the inner courtyard did not make an *eruv*, and the tenants of the outer courtyard alone made an *eruv*, the *eruv* does not avail them, for inasmuch as the residents of the inner courtyard have the right of passage through the outer courtyard they impose the prohibition of carrying on them as well. This is the case only if the tenants of the inner courtyard did not make an *eruv*, for since they restrict one another in their own place they impose the same restriction in the other place as well. But if the tenants of the inner courtyard also made an *eruv*, permitting them to carry in their own courtyard, they do not restrict the residents of the outer courtyard from carrying. If there is only one Jewish tenant residing in the inner courtyard, and he is therefore not restricted from carrying in his own place, he likewise does not restrict the tenants in the outer courtyard from carrying. But if there are two tenants residing in the inner courtyard and they did not make an *eruv*, then even if there is only one tenant residing in the outer courtyard they restrict him from carrying, for since they restrict one another in their own place, they impose the same restriction on the one tenant in his place as well.

4.   A building that has apartments on an upper floor, and a balcony from which the tenants descend by means of a stairway into a courtyard and proceed from the courtyard to the street, is likewise governed by the law as it applies to two courtyards, one within the other, with the balcony considered as the inner courtyard.[3]

------

3.   A Balcony With an Exit to a Courtyard   The balcony with an exit to a courtyard must be at least ten handbreadths above the courtyard for it to be considered as a separate inner court, otherwise it would be considered as part of the lower courtyard.

5. Two tenants who reside in separate apartments in a building with a common hallway providing entrance to each of the apartments are forbidden to carry from the apartment into the hallway until they establish an *eruv*. Likewise, if one apartment is divided into two rooms which serve as separate dwellings for two tenants, even if the inner room has no exit other than a doorway opening into the outer room from which one exits into the courtyard, the tenants are forbidden to carry from one room to the other until they establish an *eruv*. If the two apartments or dwellings belong to one person and he rents them out, but he retains an interest in them, i.e., the right of storage, the tenants do not restrict him since they are considered his guests. Both the owner and the tenants are permitted to carry from their dwellings into the courtyard, even if they did not make an *Eruv Hatzerot*.[4] (See *Shulhan Aruch* 370, *Hayye Adam* 73:3, 4).

6. How is the *Eruv Hatzerot* established? On *erev Shabbat* one of the tenants in the courtyard takes a whole loaf of his bread and assigns a share therein to all of the residents in the courtyard, by handing it to another and saying the following to him in a language that he understands: "Take this loaf and acquire a share in it on behalf of all the Jews residing in this courtyard (or in these courtyards)." The latter then takes the loaf and raises it a handbreadth. Thereupon the one making the *eruv* takes it from him and recites the blessing, בָּרוּךְ אַתָּה ה', אֱ-לֹהֵינוּ מֶלֶךְ הָעוֹלָם אֲשֶׁר קִדְּשָׁנוּ בְּמִצְוֹתָיו וְצִוָּנוּ עַל מִצְוַת עֵירוּב. "Blessed are You,

---

4. Apartments Where the Owner Reserves the Right of Storage If the owner of several apartments or rooms reserved the right of storage, even if only in a designated place in the dwelling, it is considered as though they are residing together, even if the rental is for more than thirty days. They are permitted to carry without an *Eruv Hatzerot,* provided he has actually stored in the dwelling an article that cannot be moved on the Sabbath because it is very heavy, or it is *muktzeh* and may not be moved even for the space it occupies. According to some authorities if whatever is stored, such as a stove or refrigerator, is rented to the tenant, who has use of it under the terms of the rental, the owner is not considered as retaining an interest (*tefisat yad*) in the dwelling.

Lord our God, King of the Universe, who has sanctified us with His commandments and commanded us concerning the precept of *eruv*." He then continues and says the following: בַּהֲדֵין עֵירוּבָא יְהֵא שָׁרֵא לָנָא לְאַפּוּקֵי וּלְעַיּוּלֵי מִן הַבָּתִּים לֶחָצֵר וּמִן הֶחָצֵר לַבָּתִּים וּמִבַּיִת לְבַיִת לָנָא וּלְכָל יִשְׂרָאֵל הַדָּרִים בַּבָּתִּים שֶׁבְּחָצֵר הַזֶּה. "By virtue of this *eruv* be it permitted unto us to take out and to carry in from the houses into the courtyard, and from the courtyard into the houses, and from one house into another, for us and for all the Jews who reside in this courtyard." Since all of the residents have acquired a share in this loaf of bread, and with the onset of the Sabbath it is in the home of the one who made the *eruv,* it is considered as though they all reside in his house. They are, therefore, permitted to carry from the houses into the courtyard and from the courtyard into the houses, as well as throughout the courtyard.

7.   Assignment on behalf of the residents must be made through another person. Therefore one should not assign it through his own son or daughter who are minors, even if they are not dependent upon him for their support, because their hands are as his own. However, he can assign it through another minor (for in matters of a Rabbinical nature a minor can acquire rights for another person). If possible, one should not assign it through his own wife whom he supports, nor through his adult son or daughter if they are dependent upon him for their support, since some authorities are of the opinion that their hands are also as his own. Nevertheless, if there is no one else, he can make the assignment through them. If the son is married, even if he is dependent upon his father for support, all agree that he can assign it through him.

8.   What should be the size of the loaf of bread to be used for the *eruv*? If there are eighteen tenants or less, it should be of a quantity equal to a dried fig (about one-third of an egg) for each tenant, excepting the one who makes the *eruv* and keeps it in his house, because he does not need to place any bread as a token of residence since he lives there. If there are more than eighteen tenants, even if there are a thousand, it is sufficient if the *eruv* is enough for two meals, that is of a quantity equal to eighteen dried figs, which is the

equivalent of six eggs. Some maintain that it is the equivalent of eight eggs (in which case a dried fig would be about one-third and one-ninth of an egg).

9.   One should not mind if the bread with which he made the *eruv* is eaten by a neighbor, for if he does the *eruv* is not valid. Therefore, one should take care not to make the *eruv* with food that he has prepared for the Sabbath.

10.   The *eruv* must be put in a place where it is accessible at twilight on Sabbath eve to everyone of the tenants for whom it is intended. Hence, if there is a deceased person, God forbid, in the place where the eruv was deposited, or in the courtyard, and one of the tenants is a *kohen* who would be unable to come there at twilight on Sabbath eve, the *eruv* is not valid.

11.   The *eruv* should be established every *erev Shabbat* and eaten on the Sabbath, as it only needs to be available at the onset of the Sabbath.[5] However, if one is afraid that he may sometimes forget, he can make the *eruv* with one loaf of bread for all Sabbaths until Passover.[6]

---

5.   An Eruv Ḥatzerot That Is Consumed   As long as the *Eruv Ḥatzerot* was available with the onset of *Shabbat* it continues to serve the purpose for that Sabbath, even though it is subsequently eaten or completely destroyed. However, in such a case another *eruv* must be established for the following Sabbath.

6.   Establishing an Eruv Ḥatzerot for the Year   The custom, as recorded by the Rama, is to make an *Eruv Ḥatzerot* before Pesach for the entire year, using a *matzah* which can be kept over Passover and will last for a long period of time. The *eruv* is then valid for all, even those who will take up residence at a later date. Later authorities, however, maintain that it is best to make the *eruv* every *erev Shabbat,* for fear that if kept for a long time it will spoil or become wormy. In this case, when the *eruv* is for that Sabbath, it may be eaten Friday evening after dark, although it is customary to eat it at the Sabbath day meal.

In such a case, he should say the following after reciting the blessing:
בַּהֲדֵין עֵירוּבָא יְהֵא שָׁרֵא לָנָא לְאַפּוֹקֵי וּלְעַיּוּלֵי מִן הַבָּתִּים לֶחָצֵר וּמִן הֶחָצֵר לַבָּתִּים וּמִבַּיִת
לְבַיִת בְּשַׁבָּת הַבָּאָה וּבְכָל הַשַּׁבָּתוֹת שֶׁעַד הַפֶּסַח הַבָּא עָלֵינוּ לְטוֹבָה לָנָא וּלְכָל יִשְׂרָאֵל הַדָּרִים
בַּבָּתִּים שֶׁבֶּחָצֵר הַזֶּה. "By virtue of this *eruv* be it permitted unto us to take
out and to carry in from the houses into the courtyard, and from the
courtyard into the houses, and from one house into another, on this
coming Sabbath and on every Sabbath until Passover, may it come to
us for good, for us and for all the Jews who reside in this courtyard."
The loaf of bread should be thin and well baked, so that it will not
spoil. For the Sabbath during Passover the *eruv* should be made with
matzah that is kosher for *Pesach*.

12. An *Eruv Ḥatzerot* should not be made on *Yom Tov*. If *Yom Tov*
occurs on a Friday the *eruv* should be made *erev Yom Tov*.[7]

13. When one eats in one place and sleeps in another, the place
where he eats is considered his residence with regard to the *eruv*.[8] It is

---

7. Making an Eruv Ḥatzerot Conditionally on Yom Tov If one forgot to
make an *Eruv Ḥatzerot* before a *Yom Tov* which occurs on Thursday and
Friday, he can make the *eruv* conditionally on *Yom Tov,* without reciting the
blessing, in the following manner. On the first day of the Festival he should
say, "If today is an ordinary weekday, then let this be the *eruv* for the coming Sabbath. But if today is a holy day, then let my words be void." And on
the second day of the Festival, using the same loaf of bread, he should say,
"If today is holy, then I have already made the *eruv* yesterday. And if today
is an ordinary weekday, then let this be the *eruv* for the coming Sabbath."
This procedure can be followed in the diaspora where a Festival, because of
doubt, is observed for two days, but not on *Rosh Hashanah* when the two
days are regarded as one prolonged day.

8. One Who Resides Alone But Eats in the Home of His Parents One who
has his meals in the home of his parents and sleeps in his own apartment or
elsewhere, does not restrict others from carrying, neither where his parents
reside, as he is included in the *eruv* with his parents, nor where he sleeps,
since that is not considered his residence in this regard.

there, and not where he sleeps, that he restricts others from carrying, if he eats of his own in his private quarters.[9]

14.   If one is a temporary resident in a courtyard, and in the opinion of some authorities even if he occupies an apartment for himself, he does not restrict the other tenants from carrying, so long as he is a resident for thirty days or less. In such a case, all of the tenants may carry, both from his apartment and from the tenants' dwellings, and even if there are many temporary residents and only one tenant, provided the latter is a permanent tenant, even if he is a non-Jew, since the temporary residents are subordinate to him. But if they are all temporary residents, and each one eats in his own apartment, they restrict one another from carrying. If one of them is a non-Jew they must rent his premises, as will be explained later. Some authorities maintain that there is no difference between a temporary resident and a tenant, but whoever has his meals in separate quarters has the status of a tenant. It is advisable to follow the stricter opinion at the outset, and they should make an *eruv* without reciting the blessing. However, if they failed to do so, they may rely on the more lenient opinion.

15.   If a Jew and a non-Jew reside in one courtyard, the latter does not restrict the Jew, and he is permitted to carry from the house into the courtyard and from the courtyard into the house.[10] Even if there

---

9.   Guests in a Hotel   Guests in a hotel, and residents in a similar establishment, such as a dormitory, a camp or a kibbutz, who have their meals together, are not required to make an *Eruv Ḥatzerot,* even though they have separate sleeping quarters.

10.   A Jew Residing in a Building or Courtyard With Non-Jews   An *Eruv Ḥatzerot* is not required when only one Jewish family resides in a building or courtyard with non-Jews, since *Eruvei Ḥatzerot* was enacted for ordinary situations when Jews reside together as neighbors. However, once an *eruv* is required, the Jews are restricted from carrying on the Sabbath by a non-Jew residing there unless they rent his premises from him, providing them the right of access and with his right of way in the building or courtyard.

are two or more Jews residing there, but in a manner in which no *eruv* is required (as indicated above in paragraph 13), they are not restricted by the non-Jew as well. However, if there are two or more Jews residing there who are required to make an *eruv*, they are restricted by the non-Jew residing there, and they cannot make an *eruv* unless they rent the premises from him. If there are two or more non-Jewish tenants residing there, it is necessary to rent from each of them.

16. Even if the non-Jew resides in another courtyard but he has no exit to the street except by way of the courtyard where the Jews reside, or if he lives on an upper floor and the stairway leads into the courtyard he also restricts them.

17. If the courtyard is owned by a Jew and he rented or lent a dwelling to a non-Jew, the latter does not restrict the Jewish tenants because the owner did not rent or lend the dwelling to him so that he would restrict the Jewish tenants,[11] even if the owner himself does not reside in the courtyard.

18. How does one rent from a non-Jew? The Jew says to him, "Rent me your premises for this sum of money." He need not specify that it is in order to make it permissible to carry. But if he says, "Give me permission," even if he specifies that it is in order that he may carry in the courtyard, it is invalid.

19. The premises may be rented even from the non-Jew's wife or from his servant.[12]

---

11. **A Jew Who Rents to a Non-Jew** In the view of some authorities, a non-Jew who rents the dwelling from the Jewish owner does not restrict the other Jewish tenants provided the owner retains the right to have the non-Jewish tenant vacate the premises whenever he decides to exercise that right.

12. **Rental of a Non-Jew's Premises** The rental of the non-Jew's premises, by which the Jew obtains the rights in his premises and in the courtyard, can be made by one of the Jewish tenants on behalf of all. One can rent from a member of his household, from the landlord, from his agent, or from the superintendent of the building. The rental is valid even if contracted for

20.   If one rented the premises for an indefinite period of time, the rental is in effect so long as the non-Jew did not retract it and continues to live there. But if the non-Jew moved out and another moved in, it is necessary to rent anew from the second tenant. However, if he rented for a specified period of time, and in the interim the non-Jew rented his dwelling to another non-Jew, the original rental is sufficient. But if, in the interim, the non-Jew died or sold the dwelling to another, one must rent again from the heir or from the new owner. If he rented from the non-Jew's servant for an indefinite period of time, the rental is valid only so long as the servant remains there. But if he rented for a specified period of time, then even if the servant is no longer there the rental is valid for the time specified.

21.   Whenever the rental is terminated and it is necessary to rent again, one must make a new *Eruv Ḥatzerot,* as the *eruv* has also terminated and is not automatically renewed.

22.   If it is not possible to rent the non-Jew's premises, one of the Jewish tenants should request that he allow him to store something in a designated place in his premises. He should then deposit the article there, and thereby he acquires the rights to his premises. Even if he removed the article before the Sabbath, it is nevertheless considered as though he has a share in the dwelling, since he had the right to keep the article there on the Sabbath as well. The Jew can then rent the premises to all the tenants in the courtyard.[13]

---

a minimal amount, even less than a *perutah,* for food or anything else, inasmuch as it is but a token given as a gift to permit carrying in the courtyard. A verbal agreement suffices, there being no need for a written agreement. The rental ordinarily precedes establishment of the *Eruv Ḥatzerot,* although the *eruv* is valid even if it was made before the rental, since with the onset of the Sabbath, when the *eruv* takes effect, the rental will already have been arranged.

13.   A Non-Jew Who Allows Use of the Premises   If the non-Jew does not mind when the Jewish tenants use the premises or the courtyard for activi-

23. A Jew who is an apostate or one who desecrates the Sabbath in public (according to some authorities, even if he only transgresses a Rabbinical prohibition) is considered as a non-Jew in this regard, and it is necessary to rent his premises.[14]

24. In many communities all of the alleys and streets are enclosed with *Eruvim*[15] (by means of a nominal doorway (צוּרַת הַפֶּתַח) and the like),[16] and the premises are rented from the non-Jews residing there,

---

ties which he is not obliged to permit according to the terms of his lease, it is considered as though they had requested and were granted a place to store an article on his premises and thereby acquired the rights to his premises.

14. Renting the Premises From One Who Desecrates the Sabbath In the view of many authorities one is considered as a non-Jew with regard to the requirement to rent his premises only if he deliberately and habitually desecrates the Sabbath publicly, that is in the presence of ten Jews, or he knows that his conduct will become public knowledge.

15. Jewish Communities Advised to Institute an Eruv The Rabbis have exhorted Jewish communities to institute *Eruvim* by means of the proper partitions, installations and arrangements required by Jewish law in order to enable the Jewish residents to carry on the Sabbath, thereby preventing their inadvertent violation of the Sabbath, and enhancing their comfort and enjoyment of the Sabbath. The responsibility for instituting an *Eruv* rests upon the Rabbi of the community. See Part II, Melachah 39, note 11, Part IV, Chapter 1, notes 5, 7.

16. An Eruv in a Large City Whether or not an *Eruv* can be instituted on the basis of a צוּרַת פֶּתַח to permit carrying in a large city is a matter of controversy. The question involves the halachic determination of a public domain, more precisely whether it must be frequented by six hundred thousand people or more daily for it to be considered a public domain. While *Eruvim* have been instituted in a number of large cities in conformance with the lenient view, some authorities advise that one adopt a more stringent view in his personal conduct. They nevertheless caution against imposing one's will on others who wish to follow the more lenient practice. See the previous note for additional references.

in order to be able to carry throughout the city on the Sabbath. All of the arrangements should be made by a Rabbi who is expert in this matter. In these communities it is customary to store the *Eruv Hatzerot* in the synagogue (because the *eruv* is in the nature of a partnership and it need not be kept necessarily in a dwelling).[17]

25.   In communities where there are no *Eruvim* in the city, and an *Eruv Hatzerot* is established for the residents of a courtyard, even if the synagogue is located in that courtyard, the *eruv* may not be stored in the synagogue, but it should be kept in a dwelling.

26.   If the *Eruv* of a city becomes defective on the Sabbath and is rendered inoperative, it is still permissible to carry during the entire Sabbath in the courtyards that have proper enclosures which have not been breached, including those with several dwellings in them. Even if the *Eruv Hatzerot* is in a place that is now separated from the properly enclosed courtyard, it is nevertheless permitted to carry there, because in such a case the rule is that once it is permitted on that Sabbath it remains permitted the entire Sabbath. However, since there is the likelihood that many people will carry even in places where it is presently forbidden, because they have become accustomed to carrying when it was permissible it is permitted to have a non-Jew repair the *Eruv*. If the cord or wire forming the nominal doorway (צוּרַת הַפֶּתַח) was torn, it is preferable that the non-Jew repair it, if possible, by tying the ends together by means of a bow or a bow over a single knot.[18]

---

17.   Establishing an Eruv Ḥatzerot for the Community   Where the *Eruv Hatzerot* is established for the entire community the procedure is as follows: A representative of the Jewish community makes the necessary rental arrangement with the proper official in the city government. Having effected the rental in this manner, there is no further need to rent from individual tenants, whether they be non-Jews or Jews who are not observant of the Sabbath. The *Eruv Hatzerot* is then made on behalf of all of the Jewish residents, generally *erev Pesach,* with *matzot* which are placed in the synagogue and stored there for the year.

27. If a *Yom Tov* occurs on *erev Shabbat* and the *Eruv* becomes defective on *Yom Tov,* then although the *Eruv* serves also on *Yom Tov* to permit one to carry articles that are not needed, we do not rule that since it was permitted on *Yom Tov* it continues to be permitted on the Sabbath, because *Yom Tov* and *Shabbat* constitute two distinct sanctities.

11. THE ERUV OF BOUNDARIES

דִּין עֵרוּבֵי תְּחוּמִין

1. On the Sabbath or on *Yom Tov* it is forbidden to go beyond the Sabbath limit or boundary, the *tehum Shabbat*[1] (תְּחוּם שַׁבָּת), that is,

---

18. Repairing an Eruv on the Sabbath   While it is preferable that the repair be made in the manner suggested, it is nevertheless permitted to tell a non-Jew to repair the *Eruv,* even if it entails work that is Biblically forbidden on the Sabbath, since a *mitzvah* affecting the public is involved, namely to keep people from transgressing the prohibition of carrying on the Sabbath. If a non-Jew is not available, the *Eruv* may be repaired by a Jew, if he does it in a permissible way, that is by tying the ends in a bow or in a bow over a single knot, as indicated above. If the *Eruv* becomes defective and inoperative on the Sabbath and cannot be repaired it is best not to announce publicly that it is forbidden to carry, but rather to inform the pious who are certain to heed the warning.

1. The Sabbath Boundary   The Torah states, "Abide ye every man in his place, let no man go out of his place on the seventh day " (Exodus 16:29). The verse is understood to refer to the camp of the Israelites in the desert. Some halachic authorities, such as Rambam and Rif, maintain that it constitutes a Biblical prohibition of walking from one's Sabbath abode more than twelve *mil* (approximately 8.7 miles), which was the measure of the camp of the Israelites. The Sabbath boundary (*tehum Shabbat*) prescribed by the Rabbis would thus be a further restriction of the Sabbath limit to two thousand cubits (approximately three quarters of a mile). Others, however, are of the opinion that there is no Biblical prohibition, and they view the verse

more than a distance of two thousand cubits (about three quarters of a mile)[2] from the place where one has made his abode for the Sabbath or the Festival. A man's place is minimally considered to be the space of four cubits (about seven feet) that he occupies. Hence, if one is in an open field at twilight (בֵּין הַשְּׁמָשׁוֹת) *erev Shabbat* the Sabbath limit is measured from his place, that is, beyond the space of four cubits that is his place. If he is in a house or in a building in an open field, the Sabbath limit is measured from the outer wall and beyond. But if he is in the city, the entire city is considered his abode. In addition, the outskirts of the city, comprising an area of seventy and two-thirds cubits (about 133 feet), are also considered a part of the city, even if there are no buildings there. It is from the outer perimeter of this area, which is known as the city enclosure (קַרְפִּיף הָעִיר), that one begins to measure the Sabbath limit.

2. If it is a walled city, no matter how large, one may walk the entire length of the city and its outskirts, and from there until the Sabbath boundary. Similarly, in an unwalled city, if the buildings are close to each other, that is, there is not more than seventy and two thirds cubits between one building and the next, they are considerd to be joined and a part of the city,[3] even if it should take several days to walk the distance. It is from the last building that one then measures the outskirts or enclosure of the city and the Sabbath limit.

---

only as a Scriptural text offering support (*asmachta*) for the Rabbinical enactment of *teḥum Shabbat*.

2. Determining the Sabbath Limit If one is not certain of the Sabbath limit, he can walk a distance of two thousand paces, taking moderate steps, as each step of moderate length of a person of medium height measures approximately one cubit.

3. An Extension Formed by Uninhabited Buildings The buildings need not be inhabited, so long as they are minimally fit for habitation. A space of at least four square cubits enclosed by three partitions, even without a roof, or by two partitions with a roof above, is a building that is considered an extension of the city.

3.   An enclosure is added only to a city,[4] but not to a solitary building. In the latter case the Sabbath limit is measured from the outer wall of the building.

4.   If two cities are near each other, an enclosure is added to each. Therefore, if the distance between the two cities is not greater than the two enclosures, they are considered as one city.

5.   As there are instances allowing for leniency in measuring to determine the Sabbath limit, it should be done by one who is proficient in the law.

6.   One who needs to go farther than the Sabbath limit on a Sabbath or on a *Yom Tov* is required to establish an *Eruv Teḥumin* (עֵירוּבֵי תְּחוּמִין), an *eruv* of boundaries, before the Sabbath or the Festival within the Sabbath limits of the city, where he would be allowed to walk on the Sabbath. The place where he deposits the *eruv* is then considered his abode, and he thereby acquires the right to walk from that place a distance of two thousand cubits in any direction.[5] It is understood that what he gains on the side where he established the *eruv,* he loses on the other side. Thus, for example, if he established the *eruv* at the end of two thousand cubits on the eastern side he cannot walk any distance on the western side, because he is already distant from his dwelling the full length of the Sabbath limit.

7.   How is the *Eruv Teḥumin* established?[6] The principal means of

---

4.   Minimal Habitation of a City   A place consisting of at least three courtyards, with two permanent dwellings each, is considered a city in this regard, and the area normally allotted as a city enclosure is to be added to the Sabbath limit.

5.   Going Beyond the Teḥum in an Emergency   In case of an emergency it is permissible to go beyond the Sabbath boundary, regardless of the distance even where there is no *Erev Teḥumin*. This and all restrictive laws of the Sabbath are set aside when there is a possible danger to human life.

6.   Establishing an Eruv Teḥumin   One can establish an *Eruv Teḥumin* by

establishing an *Eruv Teḥumin* is by means of one's own presence, that is, by going to the Sabbath limit *erev Shabbat* and remaining there through the period of בֵּין הַשְּׁמָשׁוֹת until nightfall and the advent of the Sabbath. If one does not wish to trouble himself, or he cannot remain there until nightfall, the *eruv* may be established in the following manner. One takes bread sufficient for two meals[7] or a relish, such as onions or radishes and the like, sufficient to be eaten with bread for two meals (apart from salt and water which cannot be considered as part of the *eruv*). He then brings it to the place where the *eruv* is to be deposited and recites the blessing, בָּרוּךְ אַתָּה ה' אֱ-לֹהֵינוּ מֶלֶךְ הָעוֹלָם אֲשֶׁר קִדְּשָׁנוּ בְּמִצְוֹתָיו וְצִוָּנוּ עַל מִצְוַת עֵירוּב. "Blessed are You, Lord our God, King of the Universe, who has sanctified us with His commandments, and commanded us concerning the precept of *eruv*." Following the blessing he says, בְּזֶה הָעֵירוּב יְהֵא מוּתָּר לִי לֵילֵךְ מִמָּקוֹם זֶה אַלְפַּיִם אַמָּה לְכָל רוּחַ. "By virtue of this *eruv* be it permitted unto me to walk from this place two thousand cubits in any direction." He may then return to his home. One *eruv* suffices for many Sabbaths, provided he deposits it in a safe place where it will not be lost and it will not spoil.[8]

---

going to the Sabbath boundary *erev Shabbat* and remaining there until nightfall, thereby signifying that the place is his abode for the Sabbath, and then he may return home for the night. This is the procedure primarily intended in the enactment of *Eruv Teḥumin*. However, as an accommodation to relieve one of the obligation to go *erev Shabbat* and remain at the Sabbath boundary until nightfall, it was permitted to establish the *eruv* at one's convenience by depositing the food. Moreover, he can have someone else bring the food and deposit it for him, but he cannot delegate another person to go to the Sabbath boundary and remain there until nightfall on his behalf.

7. Amount of Food Required for the Eruv The quantity of bread sufficient for two meals for the average person is estimated to be the equivalent of six eggs by some authorities, and eight eggs by others. At the outset one should follow the stricter opinion.

8. Discovering That the Eruv Is Missing The *eruv* has to be in place and in edible condition *erev Shabbat* at twilight (בֵּין הַשְּׁמָשׁוֹת). If one comes there on the Sabbath and does not find the *eruv*, after having properly deposited it

8. One may delegate another Jew to deposit the *eruv* for him, in which case the one delegated recites the blessing and then says the following: בָּזֶה הָעֵירוּב יְהֵא מוּתָּר (לִפְלוֹנִי) לֵילֵךְ מִמָּקוֹם זֶה אַלְפַּיִם אַמָּה לְכָל רוּחַ. "By virtue of this *eruv* be it permitted unto (name) to walk from this place two thousand cubits in any direction." The person delegated must be an adult of sound mind, and not a minor. Even if the one delegated does not return and report that he deposited the *eruv,* one can rely on him to have done so, because the presumption is that one who is appointed to a task fulfills his mission.

9. One can make an *Eruv Teḥumin* for several people, provided there is the required amount of food for each one. Assignment on their behalf must be made through another person, as is the case with an *Eruv Ḥatzerot.* The *eruv* cannot be made for someone unless it is with his consent. The one who is appointed to deposit the *eruv* for the others should say, בָּזֶה הָעֵירוּב יְהֵא מוּתָּר (לִפְלוֹנִי וְלִפְלוֹנִי) וכו' "By virtue of this *eruv* be it permitted unto (names of the persons)" etc. If he is making the *eruv* for himself as well, he should say, בָּזֶה הָעֵירוּב יְהֵא מוּתָּר לִי (וְלִפְלוֹנִי וְלִפְלוֹנִי) וכו' "By virtue of this *eruv* be it permitted unto me and (names of the persons)" etc.

10. The *eruv* must be deposited where it is accessible and could be eaten *erev Shabbat* at twilight without violating a Biblical prohibition. Therefore, if he placed it in a pit and covered it with earth the *eruv* is not valid. But if he covered it with a stone the *eruv* is valid. If he placed it on a tree that is hard and firm the *eruv* is valid, but if he placed it on a tree or a stalk that is soft and tender the *eruv* is not valid.

11. If one deposited the *eruv* within a city, the entire city is deemed to be the place of the *eruv,* and it is considered as though he were residing in that city. He can then walk the entire city no matter how

---

there, he may still walk the additional distance of two thousand cubits on that Sabbath. If the *eruv* was intended for several Sabbaths, it should be checked periodically to see that it is not lost or spoiled.

large it is, and also outside the city the full distance of its enclosure and the Sabbath limit.

12.   If there is within the Sabbath limit a city that is surrounded by a wall or it has an *Eruv,* it is not included in the measurement and it counts for no more than four cubits, provided the *tehum Shabbat* extends beyond the city. Thus, for example, if the distance from the *Eruv Tehumin* to the city is five hundred cubits, and the length of the city is one thousand cubits, the city is reckoned as no more than four cubits, and he has an additional one thousand four hundred and ninety-six cubits beyond the city to the Sabbath boundary. In this regard there is no difference between one side of the *eruv* and the other. But if the Sabbath limit (*tehum Shabbat*) ends at some point in the city, he is forbidden to walk any farther because in this instance the city is not reckoned as four cubits.[9]

13.   Similarly, if one deposited the *eruv* close to two thousand cubits outside the city and he returns to the city, and the two thousand cubits from the place of the *eruv* end somewhere at the beginning of the city at a distance from his house, he is forbidden even to return to his house. (This is the opinion of most authorities, and it is the prevailing view).[10]

14.   An *Eruv Tehumin* should be established only for the purpose of

---

9.   When the Tehum Terminates in the City   The Rama cites a lenient view even in this instance where the *tehum Shabbat* terminates within the city. If he stays there for the night he is permitted to walk throughout the city, but not beyond it. See the following note.

10.   Returning Home Friday Night   In the more lenient opinion (see the previous note) cited by Rama, one who deposited the *eruv* close to two thousand cubits outside the city, but spends Friday night at home in the city, may return to his house and walk the entire length of the city as well, irrespective of the distance from the *eruv,* since that is his place of lodging for the night. He may not, however, go outside the city other than in the direction of the *eruv.*

performing a *mitzvah*,[11] as for instance to pray with a *minyan,* to greet one's Torah teacher or a friend who has returned from a journey, to participate in a *seudat mitzvah,*[12] to attend to matters of public concern, or if one returns from a journey and wishes to go home, and the like.

15.   An *Eruv Tehumin* may not be established on a Sabbath or on a *Yom Tov.* Therefore, if a *Yom Tov* occurs on the eve of the Sabbath (*erev Shabbat*), and one wishes to go beyond the Sabbath limit on the Sabbath, he must establish the *eruv* before *Yom Tov.* Likewise if a *Yom Tov* occurs on the day following the Sabbath, and he wishes to go beyond the limit on *Yom Tov,* he must establish the *eruv* before the Sabbath.

16.   One's utensils, livestock, and other possessions are as his own person with regard to the restrictions of the Sabbath limit. Hence it is forbidden for anyone to take them wherever the owner is restricted from going. However, if he loaned them or hired them out to another person, or he placed them in someone's care, they are considered as the one in whose charge they are. Even if the latter is a non-Jew the livestock and the utensils acquire their resting place for the Sabbath

---

11.   An Eruv Tehumin Made for Attending to Private Matters   In the view of some authorities the restriction of an *Eruv Tehumin* only for the purpose of a *mitzvah* applies when one symbolically acquires his abode at the *tehum* by depositing bread and food. But if he personally goes and remains there until nightfall, it is permissible even for the purpose of attending to private matters. In case of need, one may follow this view. In any event, if one already established the *eruv* and made it his place of abode, whether by his presence or by depositing food, it is valid even if it is for the purpose of attending to one's private affairs.

12.   An Eruv Tehumin to Attend a Brit or a Wedding Feast, or to Visit a Mourner   One may make an *Eruv Tehumin* in order to go to the house of a mourner, to a *Brit Milah,* or to a festive meal on the occasion of a wedding or an engagement, provided it will be conducted in accord with Jewish law and in a traditional manner.

with him. Moreover, even articles that belong to a non-Jew acquire their resting place for the Sabbath wherever they are *erev Shabbat* at twilight.

17.   If a non-Jew brought fruit on the Sabbath about which one need not be concerned that it was picked that day, or anything else about which he need not be concerned that it involved a *melachah* that day, only that it was brought from outside the Sabbath limit, then if he brought it for himself or for another non-Jew, a Jew is allowed to use it immediately, and even to eat it. However, it may not be carried more then four cubits unless it was brought into the house. If it was brought into a city that has an *Eruv,* one may carry it throughout the city, because wherever it is permissible to carry is considered as within the four cubits. But if the non-Jew brought it for a Jew, it is forbidden to him and to his family until after nightfall for the period of time that it takes to bring it on the Sabbath. Nevertheless, he is allowed to carry it within the space of four cubits or in a place where it is permissible to carry.[13] When it is a matter of doubt as to whether it was brought from outside the *teḥum* it is also forbidden, unless it can more readily be assumed that it was not brought from outside the Sabbath limit.

18.   It is an established rule that there are no Sabbath limits (*teḥumin*) above ten handbreadths from the ground. Therefore, if one boarded a vessel *erev Shabbat* before the onset of the Sabbath and the vessel sailed away, even if on a long voyage, if it reached port on the Sabbath he is permitted upon disembarking to walk a distance of two thousand cubits in any direction, as it is presumed that during the voyage the vessel was always more than ten handbreadths above the

---

13.   Fruit Brought From Outside the Sabbath Limit   One is permitted to handle and carry fruit that was brought to him by a non-Jew on the Sabbath from outside the Sabbath limit, as it is not considered to be *muktzeh* since it was not picked on the Sabbath. Moreover, although he and his family and his guests are not allowed to eat it, the prohibition is not extended to others, and another Jew may eat it.

ground, and he did not acquire a resting place for the Sabbath until
he reached land. However, if on the Sabbath he left the vessel and
then returned to it, he has acquired a resting place on land while he
was there on the Sabbath. If the vessel then sailed beyond the Sabbath limit he is subject to the restriction imposed on one who goes
beyond the *tehum,* and he has only the space of four cubits when he
reaches port on the Sabbath.[14] Likewise, if on the Sabbath the vessel
was in any one place less than ten handbreadths from the ground, he
has acquired his resting place there. If there is a doubt whether the
vessel was in such a place, we take a lenient view.[15]

---

14.   When a Boat Goes Beyond the Tehum   One who leaves the boat and
returns on the Sabbath, and it then sails beyond the *tehum,* may not disembark when it reaches port on the Sabbath. He must remain on board, and
the entire vessel is then considerd as the four cubits' space allowed him. In
case of emergency or in circumstances beyond his control, he may disembark. See Part I, Chapter 4 and relevant notes for travel on the Sabbath by
boat and other means of transportation.

15.   The Sabbath Limit and Travel by Boat   There is no Biblical restriction
of a Sabbath limit in travel on water because it is not comparable to the
Israelite encampment and travel in the wilderness. Hence the law is lenient
as regards travel on water. Moreover, it is unlikely that a boat would at any
time be less than ten handbreadths above the ground, as the size of vessels
today and the deep waters they require to keep afloat preclude such a possibility. For a full discussion of travel by boat on the Sabbath, see Part I,
Chapter 4, and notes.

12. THE EVENING (MAARIV) PRAYER AND HAVDALAH

דִּינֵי תְּפִלַּת עַרְבִית וְדִינֵי הַבְדָּלָה

1. It is customary to delay reciting the Evening (*Maariv*) Prayer at the close of the Sabbath,[1] and to prolong intoning וְהוּא רַחוּם and בָּרְכוּ, in order to add from the weekday to the holiness of *Shabbat*.[2] In the fourth benediction of the evening *Shemoneh Esreh* the prayer אַתָּה חוֹנַנְתָּנוּ is included.[3] If one forgot to say it, but remembered before

---

1. When the Sabbath Ends The Sabbath ends when three small stars are visible close together in the heavens. In accordance with the view held by Rabbeinu Tam, the *Shulḥan Aruch* reckons this to be seventy-two minutes after sunset. While advising general acceptance of this ruling of the *Shulḥan Aruch,* some authorities maintain that observable data in the United States would indicate a more minimal time limit to the conclusion of the Sabbath, which may be followed when necessary. According to Rabbi M. Feinstein ז״ל in New York the Sabbath comes to a close approximately fifty minutes after sunset. Similarly, Rabbi Y. E. Henkin ז״ל estimates it at about one hour after sunset in the summer, and about three quarters of an hour after sunset in winter. It is accepted practice to delay the *Maariv* Prayer beyond the prescribed time at the conclusion of the Sabbath in order to add part of the weekday to the holiness of the Sabbath. See also Part I, Chapter 5, notes 2, 3.

2. Chanting Psalms Before Maariv The *hazzan* would in times past prolong the chanting of וְהוּא רַחוּם and בָּרְכוּ, thus further delaying the evening service. It is customary also to chant Psalm 144 (לְדָוִד, בָּרוּךְ ה׳ צוּרִי) and Psalm 67 (אֱ־לֹהִים יְחָנֵּנוּ) before *Maariv,* thereby further delaying the service and keeping people from engaging in idle talk as well during that time. It is, moreover, a most fitting and beautiful way of accompanying the Sabbath, which is called the Sabbath Queen and Bride, as she departs, taking leave of her with song and praise. In many congregations these psalms are sung to a traditional, liturgical melody.

3. Saying a Havdalah Prayer One is required initially to say a *Havdalah* prayer, marking the end of the Sabbath, both in the *Shemoneh Esreh* (אַתָּה חוֹנַנְתָּנוּ) and over a cup of wine (הַמַּבְדִּיל). One may not perform any prohibited

pronouncing the Divine Name at the end of the benediction, he should say it then and continue with וְחָנֵּנוּ to the conclusion of the benediction. But if one did not become aware of the omission until after he had already pronounced the Divine Name, he should conclude the benediction with חוֹנֵן הַדָּעַת, and he does not repeat the *Shemoneh Esreh,* because he will afterwards recite *Havdalah* over a cup of wine. However, he must then take care not to do any labor (*melachah*) and not to partake of any food or drink before reciting *Havdalah* over a cup of wine. But if he did work or partook of some food or drink he must repeat the *Shemoneh Esreh* and include the prayer אַתָּה חוֹנַנְתָּנוּ. The rules differ as well in the case of one who does not have a cup of wine for *Havdalah* and forgot to say אַתָּה חוֹנַנְתָּנוּ.[4]

2. After *Shemoneh Esreh*[5] the half-*Kaddish* is recited. This is followed by וִיהִי נֹעַם (Psalm 90:17, Psalm 91), which is said because it is a psalm of blessing wherewith Moses blessed the People of Israel when

---

activity (*melachah*) before reciting the *Havdalah* prayer, or at least saying בָּרוּךְ הַמַּבְדִּיל בֵּין קוֹדֶשׁ לְחוֹל "Blessed is He who has made a distinction between the holy and the profane," without pronouncing the Divine Name and His kingship in the form of a blessing.

4. When One Neglects to Say אַתָּה חוֹנַנְתָּנוּ If one neglected to say אַתָּה חוֹנַנְתָּנוּ in the *Shemoneh Esreh* it suffices that he will say the *Havdalah* prayer later over a cup of wine. However, if he has no wine or beverage over which to recite *Havdalah,* and he does not expect to have any even on the next day, he must repeat the *Shemoneh Esreh* and include אַתָּה חוֹנַנְתָּנוּ. In this particular case if he remembered before concluding the benediction of שׁוֹמֵעַ תְּפִלָּה, he should say אַתָּה חוֹנַנְתָּנוּ there. Likewise, if he reminded himself before concluding the *Shemoneh Esreh,* he should return to the benediciton of אַתָּה חוֹנֵן.

5. Making Up an Omission of the Maariv Prayer If one neglected to recite the *Maariv* prayer, he can make up the omission by saying *Shemoneh Esreh* twice the following morning without אַתָּה חוֹנַנְתָּנוּ, provided he made *Havdalah* over a cup of wine at the close of the Sabbath. But if he did not make *Havdalah,* he must say אַתָּה חוֹנַנְתָּנוּ as he recites the *Shemoneh Esreh* the second time (which is in compensation for the *Amidah* he omitted the night before). Following that, he must also make *Havdalah* over a cup of wine.

they completed the work of the Tabernacle. It should be said while standing. It is customary to repeat the last verse, אֹרֶךְ יָמִים etc. Afterward וְאַתָּה קָדוֹשׁ and the order of *Kedushah* related to וִיהִי נֹעַם are said, because through the work of the Tabernacle the *Shechinah* (Divine Presence) dwelt among the People of Israel, as it says, "You are the Holy One, enthroned upon the praises of Israel" (Psalm 22:4). If there is a Festival during the following week, even if it occurs on Friday (*erev Shabbat*), וִיהִי נֹעַם and וְאַתָּה קָדוֹשׁ are omitted.[6] For inasmuch as וִיהִי נֹעַם contains the petition, "You establish the work of our hands," there must be six days in which work can be done. Since וִיהִי נֹעַם is not said, וְאַתָּה קָדוֹשׁ is also omitted, because they go together. After וִיהִי נֹעַם and וְאַתָּה קָדוֹשׁ the complete *Kaddish* is recited, followed by וְיִתֵּן לְךָ. The reason for thus prolonging the Evening service at the close of the Sabbath is so that Israel will delay concluding the *Kedushah* in the order of prayer (in וְאַתָּה קָדוֹשׁ), and thereby extend the holiness of the Sabbath, in order to delay the return of the wicked to *Gehinnom,* which is delayed until the last assembly in Israel has concluded the recitation of *Kedushah.*[7]

3.   Just as it is commanded to sanctify the Sabbath over a cup of wine upon its arrival, so is it commanded to sanctify it over a cup of wine upon its departure by reciting *Havdalah.* Blessings are also said over spices (בְּשָׂמִים) and the light of a candle.[8] Women are also obli-

---

6.   Omission Of וִיהִי נֹעַם Before a Festival   The omission of וִיהִי נֹעַם and וְאַתָּה קָדוֹשׁ when a Festival occurs during the following week applies only to an actual *Yom Tov,* but not to the festival of *Purim.*

7.   Prolonging the Maariv Service   The wicked who are given rest on *Shabbat* are summoned at the close of the Sabbath by the angel appointed as overseer of the souls, who calls out "Return to *Gehinnom,* for the Israelites have completed the recitation of *Kedushah.*" The prayer וִיהִי נֹעַם and the verses of sanctification in the order of *Kedushah* (וְאַתָּה קָדוֹשׁ) are therefore intoned slowly and melodiously, thereby delaying the return of the souls to *Gehinnom.*

8.   Reciting Havdalah Without a Light   If one has no light, he may recite

gated to observe the *mitzvah* of *Havdalah*.[9] They should therefore listen attentively to the blessings of the *Havdalah*.[10] Where wine is not available, *Havdalah* can be recited over beer or mead, or some other commonly accepted beverage (חֲמַר מְדִינָה),[11] except water.[12]

Havdalah over the wine and say the blessing בּוֹרֵא מְאוֹרֵי הָאֵשׁ later when he comes upon a light. However, this is only on the night following *Shabbat* (מוֹצָאֵי שַׁבָּת), for the blessing is in commemoration of the creation of light by Adam on the night after *Shabbat*.

9. A Woman's Obligation for Havdalah   Some authorities maintain that women are obligated to observe the *mitzvah* of *Havdalah,* since it is included in the command to remember the Sabbath day which is obligatory upon men and women alike, as is the case with all the laws relating to the Sabbath. Others, however, are of the opinion that women are not obligated because *Havdalah* is made after *Shabbat* and does not come under the above principle. Hence it comes under the rule that women are exempt from *mitzvot* that are performed at a set time. They maintain, therefore, that women should not make *Havdalah* themselves, but they should listen to it as it is being said by one who is obligated. The prevailing ruling and practice is that a woman should listen to *Havdalah* made by a male, but if need be she may recite *Havdalah* for herself. However, a man cannot fulfill his obligation by listening to *Havdalah* when recited by a woman.

10.   Listening to Havdalah on the Telephone   Listening to *Havdalah* over the telephone is problematic, since one does not hear the natural, human voice when it is transmitted over the telephone. Some authorities are of the view that one's obligation is not fulfilled, and one should not respond with Amen to the blessings. In case of emergency, however, as when a woman is ill and in the hospital where *Havdalah* cannot be made for her, it is the opinion of Rabbi M. Feinstein ז״ל that she should listen to *Havdalah* over the telephone and answer Amen on hearing the blessings.

11.   Reciting Havdalah Over Coffee, Tea, Milk or Soda   In the view of many authorities, one who has no wine, or cannot drink wine, may make *Havdalah* over grape juice, over coffee with or without milk, over sweetened tea, or any beverage except water. Some include milk. Rabbi M. Feinstein does not permit the use of soda, because one generally drinks soda in place of water to quench one's thirst or to cool off, unlike other beverages which

4. As soon as it is twilight (בֵּין הַשְּׁמָשׁוֹת) it is forbidden to eat, or to drink anything except water, before reciting *Havdalah*. However, if one prolongs the third meal (*seudah shlishit*), even into the night, it is permitted, since he began his meal while it was still day when it was permissible. One is also permitted to drink from the cup of wine over which Grace is said because that is also part of the meal, provided he is accustomed to say Grace over a cup of wine. But one who occasionally says Grace without a cup of wine, relying upon the authorities who are of the opinion that Grace need not be said over a cup of wine, is not permitted in this instance to drink the wine of the cup of Grace before *Havdalah*.[13]

5. No work should be done before *Havdalah*.[14] Women who need to

---

one drinks for sociability and are considered חֲמַר מְדִינָה. Rabbi Obadiah Yosef maintains that only intoxicating beverages, such as wine, or beer, are considered to be חֲמַר מְדִינָה and acceptable for *Havdalah*. When acceptable beverages are unavailable, one should listen to *Havdalah* in the synagogue or from someone else, or rely on the *Havdalah* prayer said in the *Shemoneh Esreh*.

12. Havdalah Is Not Recited Over Water or Bread Water is not acceptable for *Havdalah* because it is not considered חֲמַר מְדִינָה. *Havdalah* cannot be recited over bread. In this regard *Kiddush* which is recited over the *hallot* is different, because it is said where one partakes of the meal, and bread is therefore related to the *Kiddush*.

13. Drinking the Wine After Sheva Berachot at the Seudah Shlishit If the *seudah shlishit*, celebrated in honor of a bride and groom during the week following the wedding, is prolonged into the night, one is permitted to drink the wine from the cup of Grace over which the seven benedictions (*sheva berachot*) have been recited, even if one is not accustomed to say Grace over a cup of wine.

14. Doing Work Before Havdalah One is forbidden to do any *melachah*, whether it is labor that is Biblically or Rabbinically prohibited, before *Havdalah*, even after nightfall. For, since he has not made *Havdalah* he is, to a degree, still subject to the sanctity of the Sabbath. However, if he said the

put on the lights before *Havdalah*[15] should first say בָּרוּךְ הַמַּבְדִּיל בֵּין קוֹדֶשׁ לְחוֹל, בֵּין אוֹר לְחוֹשֶׁךְ, בֵּין יִשְׂרָאֵל לָעַמִּים, בֵּין יוֹם הַשְּׁבִיעִי לְשֵׁשֶׁת יְמֵי הַמַּעֲשֶׂה, בָּרוּךְ הַמַּבְדִּיל בֵּין קוֹדֶשׁ לְחוֹל "Blessed is He who has made a distinction between the holy and the profane, between light and darkness, between Israel and the nations, between the seventh day and the six days of work, blessed is He who has made a distinction between the holy and the profane." If a Festival occurs on the following day, the blessing should be concluded with הַמַּבְדִּיל בֵּין קוֹדֶשׁ לְקוֹדֶשׁ, "who has made a distinction between the holy and the holy" (that is, between the holiness of the Sabbath and the holiness of the Festival).

6.   One who delays reciting the *Maariv* prayer on the conclusion of the Sabbath, or he prolongs his meal into the night, is permitted to tell even a fellow Jew who has already prayed and said the *Havdalah* prayer (אַתָּה חוֹנַנְתָּנוּ) in the *Shemoneh Esreh* to do work for him.[16] He may benefit from the work, and eat from food that he has prepared, even though he will subsequently still make mention of the Sabbath in the Grace.

Havdalah prayer (אַתָּה חוֹנַנְתָּנוּ) in the *Shemoneh Esreh* it is permitted, even if he did not yet make *Havdalah* over a cup of wine. If he must do a *melachah* after nightfall before reciting the *Havdalah* prayer in the *Shemoneh Esreh*, he should first say בָּרוּךְ הַמַּבְדִּיל בֵּין קוֹדֶשׁ לְחוֹל, "Blessed is He who has made a distinction between the holy and the profane," thereby signifying the departure of the Sabbath.

15.   Women's Custom to Refrain From Work Motza'ai Shabbat   Women generally refrain from work until the conclusion of the *Maariv* service in the synagogue. Some women have adopted the custom of refraining from work all night following the Sabbath. It is proper for everyone not to engage in regular work, other than what is necessary for the preparation of food, until after the *Melaveh Malkah seudah*.

16.   Concluding the Sabbath Individually   An individual is not bound by the majority of the community with regard to concluding the Sabbath. Even if the majority has not done so, he may recite the *Maariv* Prayer, make *Havdalah*, and do work if need be when the Sabbath has come to a close.

7. The cup for *Havdalah* should be filled to the brim, so that some of the wine will overflow as a token of blessing. One should hold the cup in his right hand and the spices in the left hand until after he has said the blessing בּוֹרֵא פְּרִי הַגֶּפֶן. Then he should take the cup in his left hand and the spices in his right hand and say the blessing בּוֹרֵא מִינֵי בְשָׂמִים, following which he says the blessing בּוֹרֵא מְאוֹרֵי הָאֵשׁ over the light of the candle.[17] Afterward he should again take the cup in his right hand and say the blessing הַמַּבְדִּיל. On concluding he should sit down and drink the entire cup, but leave some wine in the cup to be poured out and used to extinguish the *Havdalah* candle, and to dab one's eyes as a token of love for the *mitzvah*.[18] It is the custom that women do not drink the wine from the *Havdalah*.[19]

---

17.   Blessing Over Spices and Light Recited on Motza'ai Shabbat   One who does not have wine over which to make *Havdalah* on the night following the conclusion of the Sabbath (*motza'ai Shabbat*) must nevertheless say the blessings over the spices and the light. The spices are meant to be a consolation for the aching soul as the Sabbath leaves us, and are intended to revive us on the departure of the additional soul (נְשָׁמָה יְתֵירָה) that a Jew possesses on *Shabbat*. The light is for the fire that was first produced by Adam after the Sabbath. Since both blessings thus relate to *motza'ai Shabbat,* they are therefore said only at that time.

18.   Procedure Followed When Reciting Havdalah   *Havdalah* is recited by Ashkenazim while standing, and by Sefardim while seated. As the *Havdalah* is said, all should gaze at the cup of wine and the *Havdalah* candle, so as not to divert their attention. The one who made *Havdalah* should drink all of the wine, so as to be able to say the blessing עַל הַגֶּפֶן afterward. For were he to drink only the minimum requirement of a mouthful, his obligation to say the concluding blessing would be in doubt. Those present should listen attentively, so as to fulfill their obligation for *Havdalah,* and refrain from conversing until he drinks the wine and the *Havdalah* is concluded. The candle is then extinguished in the wine that has been poured onto the plate to show that it was kindled only for the *mitzvah* of *Havdalah*.

19.   Why Women Do Not Drink the Havdalah Wine   A woman does not drink the wine of *Havdalah* unless she is obliged to make *Havdalah* herself. A

8. One should, if possible, mix into the spices some of the musk plant, as all are agreed that over it the blessing בּוֹרֵא מִינֵי בְשָׂמִים is said.[20] One should also take some of the myrtle (הֲדַס) used on *Sukkot,* since a *mitzvah* was once performed with it (as one of the four species) it is fitting that another *mitzvah* should be observed with it.

9. As to the *Havdalah* candle, it is preferable to perform the *mitzvah* with a wax candle of several strands twined together to form a torch. If such a candle is not available,[21] the blessing can be said over two candles held close together so that the flames merge to form a torch. After saying the blessing בּוֹרֵא מְאוֹרֵי הָאֵשׁ it is customary to look at the

---

reason given for the custom that women do not ordinarily drink the wine of *Havdalah* relates to the Biblical account concerning the Tree of Knowledge, which the Rabbis say was a grape vine. Eve crushed the grapes and gave Adam to drink. Since wine was the cause of her sin and her separation from Adam, women do not drink the wine of *Havdalah*.

20. The Blessing בּוֹרֵא מִינֵי בְשָׂמִים in Havdalah Is Said Over All Spices   The reason for the spices during *Havdalah,* as noted above (note 17), is to refresh one's spirit which is distressed because of the departure of the Sabbath. While a separate blessing is usually said over each species, depending upon whether the fragrance comes from a tree or a plant, or it comes from grass or herbs etc. (see Volume One, Part II, Chapter 18), in this instance the blessing בּוֹרֵא מִינֵי בְשָׂמִים is said uniformly regardless of the spices used. This is so that people who are not well versed in the individual blessings should not err, and this blessing fulfills one's obligation for all species. It is nevertheless best to use the kind of spices, such as cloves, whose blessing is generally taken to be בּוֹרֵא מִינֵי בְשָׂמִים.

21. Reciting Havdalah Over Electric Lights   If candles are not available for *Havdalah* it is permissible, according to many authorities, to say the blessing over an electric light, preferably one designated for this purpose aside from those used to light the house. The bulb should be clear and not frosted or colored, and the flame should be visible. The blessing is not said over a fluorescent light or a flashlight. Some authorities, however, are of the opinion that the blessing should not be said over an electric light bulb, as the glass intervenes and covers the light.

fingernails and the palm of one's right hand. One should fold the four fingers onto the thumb, bending them into the palm of the hand, and look at his fingernails and palm at the same time, and then stretch out the fingers and look at the fingernails from the back of the fingers.[22]

10. One who is blind does not say the blessing over the *Havdalah* candle,[23] and one who is unable to smell does not say the blessing over the spices.

11. If, after saying the blessing over the wine, and while holding the spices in his hand, one intended to say the blessing over the spices but erred and instead said the blessing בּוֹרֵא מְאוֹרֵי הָאֵשׁ, then if he immediately corrected himself and said בּוֹרֵא מִינֵי בְשָׂמִים, it is considered a valid blessing over the spices, and he should proceed to say the blessing over the light. But if he actually intended the blessing to be over the light, it is considered a valid blessing over the light and he should then say the blessing over the spices.

12. It is a *mitzvah* to kindle many lights on the night after *Shabbat* (מוֹצָאֵי שַׁבָּת), and to chant the traditional hymns[24] to escort the Sab-

---

22. Looking at One's Palm and Fingernails By looking at one's palm and fingernails one benefits from the light as he distinguishes between light and darkness. The fingernails are also a sign of blessing, inasmuch as they are constantly undergoing a process of growth and renewal.

23. A Blind Person Reciting Havdalah While a blind person does not say the blessing over the light, he does recite the other blessings and prayers of *Havdalah*.

24. Traditional Hymns Sung After Havdalah *Havdalah* is intoned in a traditional melody. Among the hymns sung after *Havdalah* are הַמַּבְדִּיל בֵּין קֹדֶשׁ לְחוֹל, and אָמַר ה' לְיַעֲקֹב. The best known of the hymns, אֵלִיָּהוּ הַנָּבִיא, proclaims the coming of Elijah the Prophet and the Messiah. A moving prayer in Yiddish, traditionally chanted by pious Jewish women in a haunting melody, begins "Gott fun Avraham, Yitzchok un Yakov, der lieber Shabbos koidesh geht avek . . ." "God of Abraham, Isaac and Jacob. The beloved holy Sabbath with honor[25] upon its departure,[26] even as a king is escorted as he departs from the city. Elijah the Prophet is to be remembered, and prayers offered that he may come and herald the Redemption. For tradition has it that Elijah will not come on the eve of the Sabbath in order not to stop Israel from preparing for the Sabbath. And on the Sabbath we do not pray for his coming, as we are in doubt whether the Sabbath limits apply above ten handbreadths, and he would not be able to come on the Sabbath. Therefore, when the Sabbath is over and he can come, we pray for him to come and bring us the good tidings. It is also stated in the Midrash that every *motza'ai Shabbat* Elijah enters *Gan Eden* where he seats himself beneath the Tree of Life and records the merits of the People of Israel who observe the Sabbath. We, therefore, remember him at this time with gratitude.

13.   One should, if he can, take leave of the Sabbath with a *seudat Melaveh Malkah* (סְעוּדַת מְלַוֶה מַלְכָּה)[27] at a well set table with bread and a hot dish in honor of the departure of the Sabbath. One who is unable to eat bread should at least eat some pastry or fruit.

---

bath is departing. May the new week come to us for health, for life and for good fortune. May it bring us sustenance, good tidings, deliverance and consolation. Amen."

25.   Wearing One's Sabbath Clothes on Motza'ai Shabbat   One should not remove his Sabbath clothes until after *Havdalah*. Some are accustomed to wear one's Sabbath clothes on *motza'ai Shabbat* until after the *Melaveh Malkah seudah*.

26.   Folding the Tallit After Shabbat   A custom, attributed to Maharil and followed by many, is to fold the *tallit* upon conclusion of the Sabbath, so as to occupy oneself with a *mitzvah* at the beginning of the new week. See Part II, Melachah 38, note 27 on folding a *tallit* on the Sabbath.

27.   The Melaveh Malkah Seudah   The festive meal on *motza'ai Shabbat* known as *seudat Melaveh Malkah* (lit. escorting the Sabbath Queen), is traditional, though not obligatory as are the three meals on Shabbat. It is preferably held early in the evening, and no later than midnight, so that it is close to the departure of the Sabbath.

14.   One who has already made *Havdalah* may recite *Havdalah* again for the sake of his children who have reached the age of religious training, and all the more so for an adult, so that they may thereby fulfill their obligation. Whoever makes *Havdalah* for others should smell the spices after saying the blessing בּוֹרֵא מִינֵי בְשָׂמִים, so that his blessing over the spices which are intended for his benefit will not be in vain. One who has already made *Havdalah* should not recite *Havdalah* again for the sake of women exclusively, because some authorities are of the opinion that women are exempt from *Havdalah*.[28]

15.   If one forgot, or was prevented, or willfully neglected to make *Havdalah* on the conclusion of the Sabbath (מוֹצָאֵי שַׁבָּת), he can recite it until the end of the third day (Tuesday).[29] However, he should not then say the blessing over the spices or over the light. He should only say the blessing בּוֹרֵא פְּרִי הַגֶּפֶן and the blessing הַמַּבְדִּיל. After the third day one cannot recite *Havdalah*. The reason for this is that the first three days of the week are called days that follow the Sabbath and are thus considered as *motza'ai Shabbat*, while the last three days of the week are called days preceding the coming Sabbath and therefore have no relation to the previous Sabbath.

---

28.   Reciting Havdalah for a Woman   Some authorities are of the view that one who has already made *Havdalah,* or heard it said in the synagogue, may not recite it again for the sake of a woman unless there are adult males or children present, and if not she should make *Havdalah* herself. Others, however, maintain that he may recite it again for a woman exclusively. In view of the differing opinions, it is advisable that one have in mind not to fulfill his obligation with the *Havdalah* recited in the synagogue, so that he may make *Havdalah* at home. On a woman's obligation for *Havdalah*, see note 9.

29.   One Who Does Not Recite Havdalah on Motza'ai Shabbat   While one who fails to make *Havdalah* on *motza'ai Shabbat* can do so until the end of the third day, that is until sunset on Tuesday, he should nevertheless endeavor to make *Havdalah* on the first day after the Sabbath, or as soon as possible. Indeed, when it becomes possible for him to make *Havdalah*, he is not permitted to eat before *Havdalah*.

Sources and References
Codes and Responsa
Glossary
Index of Subjects
Index of Passages Cited
Topical List of Halachic Annotations

SOURCES AND REFERENCES

The sources that appear in the headings relate to the text in each chapter. The individually numbered notes correspond to the halachic annotations in the chapter. The sources cited in the notes for reference may reflect varying halachic opinions, and one is advised to consult them for further study.

Part I
Welcoming the Sabbath, Prayers and Reading of the Torah on the Sabbath
1. The Holiness of the Sabbath
גודל קדושת שבת
קצור שלחן ערוך סימן עב, חיי אדם הלכות שבת כלל א

1. ירושלמי ברכות פ״א ה״ח, נדרים פ״ג הי״ד; חולין ה, א, הוריות ח, א; ספרי במדבר טו, כב; רמב״ם הל׳ שבת פ״ל, הט״ו, ועי׳ מגיד משנה שם שמחלל שבת הוי מומר לכל התורה לפי שהשבת מורה על החידוש, וכופר בחידוש כופר בכל התורה כולה, ולפיכך צריך אדם לקבוע בנפשו אמונת החידוש ולשמור השבת שהוא אות נאמן עליו, ועי׳ ש״ע או״ח סי׳ שפה ס״ג.

2. עי׳ שמ״ב מ״ת סי׳ ע״ב סק״ז דדינו כעכו״ם לחומרא ולא לקולא, ש״ע אבן העזר סי׳ מ״ד ס״ט. עי׳ רמב״ם הל׳ אישות פ״ד הט״ו; עי׳ רמב״ם הל׳ שבת פ״א ה״א שהעושה מלאכה ברצונו בזדון חייב כרת ואם היו שם עדים והתראה חייב סקילה.

3. ש״ע או״ח סי׳ שפה ס״ג, משנה ברורה ובאור הלכה שם, דמחלל שבת כשעושה זה בפריקת עול; ועי׳ קונטרס אחרון לשמ״ב סי׳ עב ס״ק ח ע״פ ש״ע או״ח סי׳ שפ״ה ס״א, ט״ז ומגן אברהם שם דמי שנתגדל ונתחנך עפ״י דרכי אבותיו הוי כתינוק שנשבה בין העכו״ם. ועי׳ יורה דעה סי׳ ב ס״ה, באר היטב ס״י סק״ט, וש״ך ס״ק יז אם צריך שיחלל כמה פעמים או אפילו רק פעם אחת בפרהסיא; ועי׳ מג״א סי׳ שפה ס״ק ב ומ״ב שם ס״ק ד, ומסגרת השלחן סי׳ עב ס״ק א, וסי׳ צד ס״ק יא דוקא כשרגילו בעון זה. ועי׳ יו״ד סי׳ ב ס״ה באר היטב שם ופתחי תשובה ס״ק ח אם מקרי מומר לחלל שבת אם עובר על איסור דרבנן, ועי׳ פרי מגדים בשפתי דעת שם ס״ק יז שהוא דוקא בדאוריתא; ועי׳ שו״ת שרידי אש ח״ב סי׳ קנו.

4. עי׳ לחם הפנים על קצש״ע סי׳ עב ס״ב; משנה ברורה סי׳ שפה ס״ק ה, ו; עי׳ שמ״ב מ״ת סי׳ עב ס״ק ח; שו״ת מלמד להועיל או״ח סי׳ כט.

5. דהכי מוכח בגמרא ופוסקים גבי והא אסתר פרהסיא הוה, עי׳ סנהדרין עד, ב; יורה דעה סי׳ קנז ס״א, ש״ך שם ס״ק ד; עי׳ פרי מגדים יו״ד שם סי׳ ב שפתי דעת ס״ק יז שפירסום הוי עשרה מישראל או שידע שיתפרסם.

6. ירושלמי עבודה זרה פ״א ה״א ותוס׳ שם מא, א ד״ה ככדור; ספר הכוזרי מאת ר׳ יהודה הלוי, מאמר שני, כ; ספר היומם מאת הרב יחיאל מיכל טיקוצינסקי, ירושלים תש״ג; מאמר „שבת בראשית ושבת סיני״ מאת הרב מנחם מ. כשר, תלפיות שנת תש״ד חוב׳ ב כרך א, ושנת תש״ה חוב׳ ג-ד; מאמר „לבעיית קביעת קו התאריך״ מאת הרב מ.מ. כשר, נועם כרך

421

יא, תשכ"ח; מאמר „ע"ד קו התאריך הישראלי" מאת הרב י.מ. טיקוצ'ינסקי, תלפיות שנת
תש"ה חוב' ג-ד; מאמר „הלכה ומדע בקביעת קו התאריך" מאת דר. אברהם י. ברוור,
הדרום תשרי תשכ"ט; ספר חזון איש, אורח חיים, הל' שבת סי' סד, קונטרס שמונה עשרה
שעות; מאמר „שבת היא לה'", ומאמר „על שבת בראשית ושבת סיני" מאת הרב יוסף
אליהו הענקין, פירושי לב איברא עמ' 51-60; פסקי עזיאל בשאלות הזמן סי' כא; שו"ת
באר משה ח"ז ק"ע סי' צד, קטו; שמ"ב מ"ת סי' עב ס"ק א; עי' שו"ת הר צבי או"ח ח"ב
סי' קלח.

2. Preparing For the Sabbath

דיני הכנת שבת

קצור שלחן ערוך סימן עב, חיי אדם הלכות שבת כלל א

1. משנה ברורה סי' רנ ס"ק א ובאור הלכה שם ד"ה ישכים בבוקר.

2. משנה ברורה סי' רנ ס"ק ד.

3. ויקרא כד, ח; תוספות חיים על חיי אדם כלל א, ס"ק ט; ש"ע או"ח סי' רמב, מ"ב ובה"ל
שם, ועי' מחצית השקל שם ס"ק ד, וקדשו"ע סי' עב ס"ו, כי אדם הראשון נברא בע"ש
וחטא עי' חוה בע"ש לכן התיקון ג"כ ראוי בע"ש.

4. ח"א הל' שבת כלל א ס"ד, מ"ב סי' רמב ס"ק ו, סי' רעד סק"ד.

5. שבת פ"ב, מ"ו ועי' רע"ב שם, ש"ע או"ח סי' רמב, מג"א ס"ק ד; יו"ד סי' שכח ס"ג, ט"ז
ס"ק ב, ועי' בית הלל שם ע"ד המנהג שאף היולדות אופין חלות וחושבין זאת למצוה רבה
ליטול חלה בע"ש.

6. ש"ע או"ח סי' רנז ס"ח רמ"א שם; עי' מ"ב ס"ק מט ותורת שבת עמ' לד מ"ש מספר
המאור לרבנו זרחיה הלוי, ועי' מ"ב ס"ק מח דמי שמזיק לו החמין מותר לאכול צונן.

7. ח"א כלל א ס"ה, ותוס' חיים שם ס"ק י, מג"א סי' רמב ס"ק א, ומ"ב שם ס"ק ב; ועי' מטה
משה ח"ד סי' תד טעם אכילת דגים; ועי' ט"י יו"ד סי' ריח ס"ק ד בשם ת"ה בענין תקנת
הקהל שלא למכור בשר ביוקר מהערכ.

8. ש"ע או"ח סי' רסב ס"א משנה ברורה ס"ק ד; ועי' באר היטב ס"ק ג שמביא מנהג רש"ל
שהיה לו שתי מפות על השלחן, ועוד טעם למנהג זה.

9. קצשו"ע סי' עב ס"ג; ש"ע או"ח סי' רמב משנה ברורה ס"ק ז; שמות טז, יד, רש"י שם.

10. מג"א סי' רנו ומחצית השקל שם, מ"ב שם ס"ק א וסי' רנא ס"ק א, בה"ל ד"ה העושה
מלאכה, שעה"צ ס"ק ד. ועי' בערוך השלחן סי' רנא ס"ד שיש ללמד זכות על הבעלי
מלאכות שאין מבטלין מלאכתן עד קרוב לשקיעה, אולי זה מדוחק הפרנסה, וגם שסומכים
על הנשים שהן מכינות הכל לצורך שבת.

11. משנה ברורה סי' רמט ס"ק יז.

12. מג"א סי' רמט ס"ק ד, מ"ב ס"ק י ובאור הלכה ד"ה מפני כבוד השבת.

13. משנה ברורה סי' רמט ס"ק ט.

14. ח"א כלל א ס"ח, מ"ב סי' רמט ס"ק יב, ועי' ש"ע הרב שם ס"ח שלדעתו אם הפדיון בע"ש
שלא בזמנו לא יעשה סעודה.

15. משנה ברורה סי' רפה ס"ק ב, ח, ט, יד; שו"ת יחוה דעת ח"ב סי' לז ספר לוית חן סי' כא;
ועי' שו"ת בית יעקב סי' קלז, ושו"ת הרדב"ז ח"ג סי' תקכט.

16. מג"א או"ח סי' רפה ס"ק א בשם האר"י ז"ל, וש"ע הרב שם ס"ג; עי' מ"ב שם ס"ק ב, וערוך השלחן שם ס"ה; ועי' שו"ת יחוה דעת ח"ב סי' לז; שו"ת ציץ אליעזר חט"ו סי' ז אות ד.

17. מסגרת השלחן סי' עב ס"ק ז; ש"ע הרב או"ח סי' רפה ס"י; מגן אברהם סי' רפה ס"ק יב.

18. משנה ברורה סי' רפה ס"ק ה, ו; עי' שו"ת תשובות והנהגות סי' רסא מ"ש בשם הגר"א בחובת שנים מקרא ואחד תרגום שהזהיר תלמידיו לא לקרא בלי להבין אלא ללמוד ולהבין דוקא, ולכן הסכים הגר"מ שטרנבוך לבעל תשובה שאינו מבין תרגום לקרא שנים מקרא ויקרא תרגום אנגלי מת"ח ויר"ש.

19. עי' פרי חדש או"ח סי' תיז שנוהגין להתענות כל ערב ראש חודש ומהר"ם קורדוויירו ז"ל היה קורא אותו יום כיפור קטן לפי שבו מתכפרין עוונות של כל החודש וכדאמרינן במוסף זמן כפרה לכל תולדותם; קצש"ע סי' צז ס"א ועי' משנה ברורה סי' רנ ס"ק ג שיהרהר בתשובה ע"ש כי שבת מקרי כלה מלכתא וכאלו מקבל פני המלך ואין נאה לקבלו כשהוא מכוסה בחלאת העוונות.

20. משנה ברורה סי' רסב ס"ק ה, עי' באר היטב שם ס"ק ד שמהרי"ל היה לו טלית מיוחד לשבת; ועי' שערי תשובה שם ס"ק ג.

21. ש"ע או"ח סי' רסב ס"ב, משנה ברורה ס"ק ה, ס"ג; סי' שא סט"ז רמ"א שם; שו"ת יחוה דעת ח"ה סי' כג; שו"ת ציץ אליעזר חי"ד סי' לד אות ב, ש"ע הרב סי' רסב ס"ג.

22. ש"ע או"ח סי' רנט ס"ז, ומ"ב שם.

23. ש"ע או"ח סי' רנג ס"א ומ"ב שם; מצודת דוד סי' עב קצור כללי בשול, הטמנה, שהיה, וחזרה; יסודי ישרון, מערכת ערב שבת עמ' 57, מסגרת השלחן סי' עב חלק ב ס"א-ו.

24. ש"ע או"ח סי' רנז ס"א, ג, ח ומ"ב שם; חיי אדם כלל ב ס"ה, כלל כ סכ"ב; מצודת דוד סי' עב קצור כללי בשול, הטמנה, שהיה, וחזרה.

25. ש"ע או"ח סי' רס ס"ב, מ"ב ס"ק יג; ש"ע יורה דעה סי' שכג; ש"ע הרב או"ח סי' רס ס"ה, מסגרת השלחן סי' עב ס"ק יג.

26. עי' גיטין ו, ב כל המטיל אימה יתירה בתוך ביתו סוף הוא בא לידי חילול שבת. ועי' ספר תפארת השבת עמ' יח שבזוהר ובמקובלים הזהירו שלא יהיה מחלוקת בשבת וסמכו על הפסוק לא תבערו אש בכל מושבותיכם ביום השבת, וצריך להראות חיבה יתירה ואהבה עם אשתו בע"ש.

3. Contracting Before the Sabbath For Work By a Non-Jew

לתת קודם שבת מלאכה לאינו יהודי

קצור שלחן ערוך סימן עג, חיי אדם הלכות שבת כלל ג

1. רמב"ם הל' שבת פ"ו ה"א; ספר מקור חיים ח"ג פ' קה.

2. ש"ע או"ח סי' רסא ס"א, משנה ברורה ס"ק יג; שו"ת אגרות משה או"ח ח"ד סי' עד ערך בישול אות מ.

3. ש"ע או"ח סי' רנב ס"ב ומגן אברהם שם ס"ק ו; חיי אדם כלל ג ס"ג; ש"ע הרב או"ח סי' רמד ס"א וסי' רנב ס"ד; קה"ש כלל יג סכ"ז.

4. ש"ע או"ח סי' רמז ס"ד, סי' רנב ס"ב משנה ברורה ס"ק יד, כא; חיי אדם הל' שבת כלל ג ס"ג, תוס' חיים שם ס"ק ב; מסגרת השלחן סי' עג ס"ק א.

5. ש"ע או"ח סי' רמז ס"א; חיי אדם כלל ג סי"א. שו"ת אגרות משה ח"ג סי' מו; יסודי ישרון הוצ' תשל"ט מערכת ערב שבת עמ' 44 וח"ג דף סב; שמ"ב מ"ת סי' עג ס"ק ה, מקור חיים ח"ג פ' קה ס"ט;

6. חיי אדם הל' שבת כלל ג ס"ד.

7. שו"ת יחוה דעת ח"ג סי' יז, ע"י שם שדעתו להתיר במקום צורך אפילו אם יצטרך הגוי לעבוד גם בשבת להשלמת התיקונים, אלא שפוסקים אשכנזים מחמירים בזה.

8. ש"ע או"ח סי' רמד ס"א, ומגן אברהם שם ס"ק ח; ועי' שמ"ב מ"ת סי' עג סק"ו שמביא בשם שו"ת חתם סופר או"ח סי' נט ושו"ת נודע ביהודה או"ח סי' יב שאף אם מנהג העיר בקבלנות דליכא חשש מראית העין, לא רצו להתיר בשבת; ועי' משנה ברורה סי' רמד ס"ק ז. ובשו"ת מהרש"ם ח"ב סי' קכג דן במי שמתחברנס מבניני בתים והבניה בקבלנות עם אומן אינו יהודי ולא נודע כלל אם המקום שייך לישראל, שיש צדדים להיתר דליכא בבנינים כאלו משום מראית העין.

9. שו"ת חתם סופר או"ח סי' ס; עי' תוס' חיים על חיי אדם כלל ג ס"ק ד.

10. ש"ע או"ח סי' רמה ס"א ומ"ב שם; עי' יסודי ישרון (הוצ' תשל"ט) מערכת קבלנות ואריסות עמ' 96, ועי' שמ"ב מ"ת סי' עג ס"ק ט בנדון מי שיש לו מניות (שערס) בעסק יחד עם נכרים שעוסקים בו בשבת.

11. ש"ע או"ח סי' רמד ס"ג, וסי' שכה סי"ד ומשנה ברורה שם; חיי אדם כלל ג ס"ז ותוספות חיים שם, ועי' בשמ"ב סי' עג ס"ק ו, ובשו"ת אגרות משה ח"ג סי' לה.

12. ש"ע או"ח סי' רמג ס"א וס"ב, ומשנה ברורה סק"ח.

13. משנה ברורה סי' רעו ס"ק יא; שש"כ מ"ת פ"ל סכ"ז; שו"ת באר משה ח"ז ק"ע סי' ל, לא.

14. ש"ע או"ח סי' שז סכ"א ומשנה ברורה ס"ק עג; מגן אברהם סי' רעו ס"ק ד; משנה ברורה סי' רמד ס"ק ל, חיי אדם כלל סד ס"ב ותוס' חיים ס"ב; מסגרת השלחן סי' עג ס"ק ח.

15. ש"ע או"ח סי' רנב ס"ד רמ"א שם.

16. ש"ע או"ח סי' רנב ס"ד, מ"ב שם ס"ק לא, לג.

17. שמ"ב מ"ת סי' עג ס"ק יז, יח וסי' צ ס"ק ז, וקונטרס אחרון שם.

4. Travel By Boat On the Sabbath

דין המפליג בספינה

קצור שלחן ערוך סימן עד, חיי אדם הלכות שבת כלל ד

1. ש"ע או"ח סי' רמח ס"ב וס"ד ורמ"א שם, ומשנה ברורה בהקדמה וס"ק א; ועי' משנה ברורה ס"ק ד מ"ש בשם הגר"א ע"י מג"א שם ס"ק יט; חיי אדם כלל ד ס"א.

2. טוש"ע או"ח סי' רמח ס"ד, סי' רמ"ב ס"א, ב"ח ומגן אברהם שם ס"ק א, באר היטב ומ"ב שם ס"ק א, ג; חיי אדם כלל א ס"ז ותוס' חיים שם ס"ק יד; מקור חיים פ' קעא ס"ט; עשה לך רב ח"א סי' לד.

3. ש"ע או"ח סי' רמח ס"א, ס"ג וס"ד ומ"ב ס"ק כב, וסי' שד, ש"ע הרב או"ח סי' רמח ס"ט; חיי אדם כלל ד ס"ג; מקור חיים ח"ג פ' קעא.

4. ש"ע או"ח סי' רמח ס"ב, ט"ז ומגן אברהם שם.

5. ש״ע או״ח סי׳ רמח ס״ג, מגן אברהם ומחצית השקל ומשנה ברורה שם, וסי׳ תד ס״א ומ״ב שם ס״ק י; חיי אדם כלל ד ס״ג; ש״ע הרב סי׳ רמח ס״ט.

6. ש״ע או״ח סי׳ שה סי״ח רמ״א שם, תפארת ישראל, כללכת שבת דיני מלאכת שבת אות ט; באור הלכה סי׳ תד ד״ה ואין בכל אחד; מצודת דוד על קצש״ע סי׳ עד ס״ד; תוס׳ חיים על ח״א כלל עו ס״ק יז; שו״ת חתם סופר ח״ו סי׳ צז; שו״ת מלמד להועיל או״ח סי׳ מא; שו״ת ציץ אליעזר ח״א סי׳ כא, חי״ד סי׳ קו; שו״ת מנחת יצחק ח״ב סי׳ קן; שו״ת אגרות משה יו״ד ח״א סי׳ מד, או״ח ח״ג סי׳ צר; שמ״ב מ״ת סי׳ עד ס״ק א, ג, ד; יסודי ישרון ח״ה עמ׳ קלז; מקור חיים פ׳ קעא ס״ח, פ׳ קעד סט״ו, טז; ועיין תלפיות שנת תרצד, נח. אולם עי׳ פסקי עזיאל סי׳ יג שמצדד להתיר נסיעה בקרונות קיטוריות או חשמליות בשבת בתנאי שהיא קבועה בתוך העיר, ושמתנהגות ע״י לא יהודים ועיקר נסיעתן בשביל לא יהודים, ושלא יצטרכו לשלם דמי כרטיס נסיעה, והיא לשם מצוה אבל לא לשם טיול ולא לשם צורך מסחרי.

7. ש״ע או״ח סי׳ רמח ס״ד, מגן אברהם ס״ק טו, משנה ברורה ס״ק כח; כתובות קיא, א; רמב״ם הל׳ מלכים פ״ה הי״א.

8. כללכת שבת, דיני מלאכת שבת אות ט; שמ״ד מ״ת סי׳ עד ס״ק ד; עי׳ שו״ת אגרות משה או״ח ח״א סי׳ צב, ושו״ת ציץ אליעזר ח״ה סי׳ ז בדבר נסיעה בשבת בספינה שמנהיגיה ומלחיה ישראלים.

5. Lighting the Sabbath Candles

דין הדלקת הנרות

קצור שלחן ערוך סימן עה, חיי אדם הלכות שבת כלל ה

1. שבת כה, ב רש״י ותוס׳ שם; רמב״ם הל׳ שבת פ״ה הי״א, פ״ל ה״ה.

2. חיי אדם כלל ה ס״א; ש״ע או״ח סי׳ רסא ס״ב וסי׳ רסג רמ״א שם, מ״ב סי׳ רסא ס״ק כ—כג; מסגרת השלחן סי׳ עה ח״א; שו״ת אגרות משה או״ח ח״א סי׳ צו, ח״ד סי׳ סב; שו״ת באר משה ח״ב סי׳ טו.

3. פסחים צד,א, תוס׳ ד״ה רבי יהודה אומר; ש״ע או״ח סי׳ רסא ס״א, ב, משנה ברורה ס״ק כ, כג, באור הלכה ד״ה מתחלת השקיעה, ד״ה שהוא, וד״ה קודם הלילה, שער הציון שם ס״ק כא. ועי׳ שערי תשובה או״ח סי׳ שד״מ ס״ק א בדין מקומות שהיום מתארך חודש וב׳ חדשים ויש גם ששה חדשים.

4. ש״ע או״ח סי׳ רסא ס״ד, וסי׳ רס״ג ס״י, יא; מ״ב סי׳ רסא ס״ק לא, עי״ש כשמקבל שבת בעוד יום אסור מדרבנן בכל מלאכה, עי׳ מ״ב סי׳ רנט ס״ק כו; עי׳ שו״ת אגרות משה או״ח ח״א סי׳ צו.

5. חיי אדם כלל ה ס״א; ש״ע או״ח סי׳ רסא ס״ב ומ״ב ס״ק כה, וסי׳ רסג ס״ד ובה״ל ד״ה קודם הלילה; ש״ע הרב סי׳ רסא ס״ה וסי׳ רסג ס״ו; עי׳ שו״ת באר משה ח״ב סי׳ טו, יט שתדליק כע״ה דקות לפני צה״כ ובתקופת תמוז בערך קה דקות קודם צה״כ; ועי׳ שו״ת אגרות משה ח״ג סי׳ לח שהאשה לא נמשכת אחר הבעל כשמקבל עליו שבת מבעוד יום, אולם אף שלא נאסרת במלאכת עצמה מן הראוי להחמיר במלאכה לצורך הבעל.

6. ש״ע או״ח סי׳ רסג סי״ב, מ״ב ס״ק נא, מגן אברהם ס״ק כד; חיי אדם כלל ה ס״ה; עי׳
שו״ת באר משה ח״ב סי׳ טז, יז, שו״ת אגרות משה או״ח ח״ג סי׳ לח.

7. ש״ע או״ח סי׳ רסג סי״א, ש״ע הרב שם ס״א וקונטרס אחרון ס״ק א, משנה ברורה שם ס״ק
ו, תוספות חיים על חיי אדם כלל ה ס״ק כא בשם השל״ה, שמ״ב מ״ת סי׳ עה ס״ק יג, יסודי
ישרון הל׳ שבת מערכת נר שבת עמ׳ 117, וח״ג עמ׳ קלה.

8. קצור שלחן ערוך סי׳ עה ס״ב, סדור אוצר התפלות, הנהגת ערב שבת, תפלה לאחר הדלקת
הנרות.

9. שו״ת מלמד להועיל או״ח סי׳ מז׳ ומצודת דוד סי׳ עה בשם שו״ת בית יצחק ח״א סי׳ קכ
אות ה וח״ב סי׳ לא אות ח; שו״ת יחוה דעת ח״ה סי׳ כד; שו״ת ציץ אליעזר ח״א סי׳ כ
פי״א, יסודי ישרון הל׳ שבת (תשל״ט) מערכת נר שבת עמ׳ 130, שמ״ב מ״ת סי׳ ע״ה ס״ק
ז; שו״ת באר משה ח״ו ק״ע סי׳ נח וח״ז ק״ע סי׳ ו; עדות לישראל עמ׳ 122.

10. שו״ת ציץ אליעזר חי״ג סי׳ כד; שו״ת יחוה דעת ח״ב סי׳ לא, שלא לברך שהחיינו, עי׳
שמ״ב סי׳ עה ס״ק ח מ״ש היעב״ץ בסידורו שתברך.

11. עי׳ שו״ת תשובות והנהגות סי׳ ער שמצא הנוסח ״להדליק נר של שבת קודש״ בסידור
הגרש״ז. אולם לא מצאתי נוסח זה בש״ע הרב (עי״ש סי׳ רסג ס״ח) אלא הנוסח המקובל
״להדליק נר של שבת״ המובא בש״ע או״ח סי׳ רסג ס״ה.

12. שו״ת יביע אומר ח״ב או״ח סי׳ טז, ח״ו או״ח סי׳ מח אות יא; ספר לוית חן סי׳ ה.

13. מסגרת השלחן סי׳ עה ס״ק ד.

14. תוספות חיים כלל ה ס״ק יח; מסגרת השלחן סי׳ עה ס״ק ו; ועי׳ מגן אברהם סי׳ רסג ס״ק
כ; באור הלכה סי׳ רסג ס״ה ד״ה אחר ההדלקה.

15. רמב״ם הל׳ שבת פ״ה ה״ג, משנה שבת פ״ב מ״ו, שבת נה, ב; רש״י שבת לב, א בשם
בראשית רבה (סוף פרק יז); טור או״ח סי׳ רסג; חיי אדם כלל ה ס״ט; קצש״ע סי׳ עה ס״ה.

16. ערוך השלחן סי׳ רסג ס״ז; שו״ת יחוה דעת ח״ב סי׳ לב.

17. באר היטב סי׳ רסג ס״ק ג בשם כנה״ג; עי׳ ערוך השלחן סי׳ רסג ס״ז; ועי׳ שו״ת ציץ
אליעזר חט״ו סי׳ לב אות ז. עי׳ שש״כ מ״ח פל״ו סט״ז.

18. ש״ע או״ח סי׳ רסג ס״י; יסודי ישרון מערכת נר שבת עמ׳ 118; שו״ת אגרות משה או״ח
סי׳ צו, ואין לאסור נסיעה אחר הדלקת הנרות משום מראית עין, שידוע לכל שהאנשים
עדיין מותרים במלאכה.

19. משננה ברורה סי׳ רסג ס״ק מה, מו, מח; עי׳ שו״ת תשובות והנהגות סי׳ ערב שמעדיפים
להדליק נרות שבת מן הצד, שבזמנינו עיקרם לכבוד שבת ובצד ניכר שכן הוא, ועל השלחן
לפעמים נכנסים לשאלות של כבוי ומוקצה.

20. שו״ת באר משה ח״ו סי׳ סד.

21. משנה ברורה סי׳ רסה ס״ק טז, יח.

22. שו״ת אגרות משה או״ח ח״ג סי׳ נא, ח״ד סי׳ עג.

23. יסודי ישרון (תשל״ט) מערכת נר שבת עמ׳ 119.

6. Prayers On the Sabbath and Festivals

דיני התפלות בשבת וביום טוב

קצור שלחן ערוך סימן עו, חיי אדם הלכות תפלה כלל כז, כח, לד

1. ש"ע או"ח סי' רלג ס"א מ"ב ס"ק ד ושעה"צ ס"ק י; סי' רסג ס"ד מ"ב ס"ק יט; מ"ב סי' רסז ס"ק ד, מ"ב סי' תמג ס"ק ח; מ"ב סי' נח ס"ק ד; קצש"ע סי' סט ס"ב; ועי' פסחים צד, ב שמהלך אדם בינוני ביום הוא עשר פרסאות דהוי ארבעים מיל.

2. ש"ע או"ח סי' רסו ס"ב, מגן אברהם ס"ק א ומ"ב ס"ק ו; חיי אדם כלל לד ס"ח והל' שבת כלל ו ס"א ותוס' חיים ס"ק א, ומסגרת השלחן סי' עו ס"ק א.

3. ש"ע או"ח סי' רסג סט"ו, טז, משנה ברורה ס"ק ס, סב; שו"ת ציץ אליעזר חי"ג סי' מב; שו"ת יחוה דעת ח"ו סי' יח; ספר לוית חן סי' ז.

4. עי' מגן אברהם סי' רסח ס"ק א ומ"ב שם ס"ק א, ולא נזכר שם „שבתות קדשך"; ועי' ב"י סי' רצב ד"ה סדר. בסידורי התימנים וברמב"ם איתא בכל התפלות „שבתות קדשך וינוחו בם", עי' סדור אוצר התפלות תפלת מנחה לשבת, עיין תפלה שם שהיה ראוי לומר „וינוחו בהן",ובהג"ה שם שבנוסח אשכנז אחזו בהנוסח „בם" בתפלת מנחה ע"פ קבלה ושבקו הנוסח „שבתות" והרי זה תרתי דסתרי, עי' ערוך השלחן או"ח סי' רסח ס"ק יד, שו"ת יחוה דעת ח"ה סי' ל ובס' מקור חיים פ' קיג ס"ק יח, והעמק שאלה להנצי"ב, שאילתות פ' יתרו סי' נד אות א, הטעם לשינויים בה, בו ובם.

5. טור וש"ע או"ח סי' רסח ס"ז, ט"ז ומגן אברהם שם; ש"ע שם סי"ב; מ"ב שם ס"ק יט, ובאור הלכה שם ד"ה ומעומד; ומ"ב בסי' רעא ס"ק מה; שו"ת ציץ אליעזר חי"ד סי' כד, וכשהאריך בתפלת הלחש אולי צריך להשתדל לומר ויכלו יחד עם הקהל.

6. ברכות לד, א; ש"ע או"ח סי' קיג ס"א, סי' רפא ס"א; עי' שו"ת ציץ אליעזר ח"ז סי' כג שיסודו של מנהג זה בתורת הנסתר של האר"י ז"ל שכותב שדברכת מעין שבע דינה כחזרת העמידה של הש"ץ.

7. ש"ע או"ח סי' שלח ס"א, משנה ברורה ס"ק ד, סי' שלט ס"ג רמ"א שם; עי' ערוך השלחן סי' שלח ס"ח; ספר מלמד להועיל או"ח סי' סג; שו"ת נהרי אפרסמון סי' ג; שו"ת צפנת פענח סי' נ.

8. משנה ברורה סי' רסח ס"ק כב.

9. משנה ברורה סי' רסח ש"ק כ, וסי' תפז ס"ק ט.

10. ט"ז או"ח סי' רסח ס"ק ח, ומגן אברהם שם ס"ק יד, משנה ברורה שם ס"ק כד וכה; חיי אדם כלל לד סי"ו; ש"ע הרב שם סט"ו; מקור חיים פ' קיג סכ"ג, ועי' שו"ת ציץ אליעזר ח"ז סי' כג מנהג ירושלים דהש"ץ אומר ברכת מעין שבע במקום שמתפללין תפלת ערבית אפילו אין שם ספר תורה.

11. ש"ע או"ח סי' רסט ס"א, מגן אברהם ס"ק ג ומ"ב ס"ק ה; שו"ת הרשב"א סי' לז וסי' שכג; שו"ת שרידי אש ח"ב סי' ב סי' קנז; שו"ת ציץ אליעזר חי"ד סי' כז; שו"ת יחוה דעת ח"ב סי' לד; שו"ת תשובות והנהגות סי' רנה.

12. ש"ע או"ח סי' רעג ס"ד, משנה ברורה ס"ק טז, שעה"צ ס"ק יז, ובה"ל ד"ה והוא, ומ"ב סי' רסט ס"ק ד.

13. ש"ע או"ח סי' עב, מ"ב וש"ע הרב שם; חיי אדם כלל לד סי"ב ותוס' חיים שם; מקור חיים

פ' קיב סי"א; ועי' שו"ת ציץ אליעזר חי"ג סי' נ מה שמביא מחדושי חתם סופר על התורה על טעמי המנהגים באמירת במה מדליקין, וטעם השל"ה ז"ל כדי לישב הנשמה יתירה בלימוד משנה (כי משנה אותיות נשמה) שמדבר מעניני נר, כדכתיב נר ה' נשמת אדם.

14. ש"ע או"ח סי' לא משנה ברורה שם.

15. ספר מהרי"ל הל' שבת; ש"ע או"ח סי' ח ס"א–ד, מגן אברהם ומשנה ברורה שם, סי' יז ס"ג, באר היטב ס"ק ד ומ"ב ס"ק י, שו"ת יחוה דעת ח"ה סי' א שו"ת באר משה ח"ג סי' ח.

16. טור וש"ע או"ח סי' רפא סי"א, רמ"א ומ"ב שם, ש"ע הרב שם; קצש"ע סי' עו ס"י; ועי' ברכות כו, ב, מגילה כג, א, רש"י שם ד"ה ובשבת ממהרין לבא.

17. ש"ע או"ח סי' קכד ס"ד, רמ"א שם ומ"ב שם ס"ק יז כ ועי' מגן אברהם שם ס"ק ח שמביא דעה שאם הלומדים מכוונים בסוף הברכה לענות אמן אין למחות בידם אבל מסוף דבריו משמע שדעתו להחמיר. עי' שו"ת יחוה דעת ח"ה סי' יא ושו"ת אגרות משה או"ח ח"ד סי' יט.

18. שו"ת ציץ אליעזר חי"ג סי' לח.

19. רמב"ם הל' תפלה פי"ב ה"כ; שו"ת ציץ אליעזר חי"ג סי' לח.

20. שעמ"ב מהד"ת סי' עו ס"ק ט בשם שו"ת מהר"ם שיק או"ח סי' קכ; ועי' ברכות כח, ב ורש"י שם מעשה דרב אויא כמקור למנהג הדרשה קודם מוסף.

21. ש"ע או"ח סי' רפח ס"א משנה ברורה ס"ק א, ב, ואם טעים קודם תפלת מוסף מותר להתאחר יותר משש שעות.

22. ש"ע או"ח סי' רפו ס"ד ומ"ב ס"ק יג, ש"ע הרב שם ס"ב וס"ה, ועי' סי' קח ס"ו ומגן אברהם ס"ק ט; חיי אדם כלל כז ס"ח.

23. עי' בסדור אוצר התפלות פירוש ענף יוסף על קדושה דמוסף לשבת שמביא דין זה בשם כתבי האר"י ז"ל והגר"א; עי' ש"ע או"ח סי' סא ס"ט ומשנה ברורה ס"י יא, כב שאסור לומר שמע ב' פעמים משום דנראה כאלו מקבל עליו שתי רשויות ח"ו.

24. שו"ת אגרות משה או"ח ח"ב סי' כב; עי' תשובה מאת הגרי"ד סולואייטשיק בחוברת אגודת החזנים ע"י ישיבה אוניברסיטה, חשון תשכ"ו, התשובה נכתבה ט"ז אלול תשכ"ג וז"ל, "אני מקפיד מאד שש"ץ לא יאמר דברי תפלה פעמים, אמנם כל זה שייך רק לחזרת הש"ץ ולברכות שמע או הלל או לפסוקי כה"ק אע"פ שאין אמירתם חובה, בפיוטים ובשאר דברי ריצוי שאינם מהווים גופה של תפלה או ק"ש ואינם מצטטים פסוקי מקרא אין לחוש," עי' שו"ת יביע אומר ח"ו או"ח סי' ז.

25. טור או"ח סי' רצב, ב"י וב"ח שם, באר היטב ומ"ב שם; מטה משה ח"ד סי' תפה, וי"א דאומרים צדקתך צדקתך להצדיק הדין על הרשעים שחוזרים לגיהנם במוצאי שבת.

26. משנה ברורה סי' רצב ס"ק ז; מטה משה ח"ד סי' תפה.

27. מגן אברהם או"ח סי' תכב ס"ק ב;מ"ב סי' קיז ס"ק יח; ש"ע הרב סי' רסח ס"ח; חיי אדם כלל כד סט"ו; קצש"ע סי' יט ס"ו.

28. משנה ברורה סי' תפז ס"א באור הלכה שם; חיי אדם כלל כח ס"י; מסגרת השלחן סי' עו ס"ק ד.

7. Kiddush and the Sabbath Meals

דיני הקידוש והסעודות בלילה וביום

קצור שלחן ערוך סימן עז, חיי אדם הלכות שבת כלל ו,ז.

1. עי' ספר מטעמים אות שבת סי' צג טעם שמברכים הבנים וסי' צד טעם המנהג לומר גוט
   שבת כשבא לביתו; ומובא מכתבי האר"י ז"ל שיש לומר שבת שלום ומבורך; וזכרני שכן
   היה נוהג אמו"ר ז"ל לומר שבת שלום ומבורך בניגון ובנעימות ג' פעמים קודם שלום
   עליכם. עי' באור הלכה סי' רעא ס"ב ד"ה דאיתקש מ"ש מחדושי רע"א דאולי יוצא המ"ע
   באמירת שבתא טבא בלבד, ולפלא דהרי הרמב"ם כתב דבעינן זכירת שבת וקידוש; עי' סדור
   אוצר התפלות פי' עיון תפלה שהמנהג לומר שלום עליכם נוסד על מאמר חז"ל שבת קיט, ב,
   וטעם שאומרים אשת חיל ע"פ כתובות סב, ב; ועי' תוס' חיים על ח"א כלל סא ס"ק א
   שהיוצא מביהכ"נ לא יאחר וישיח שיחת חולין ומעניני משא ומתן.

2. ש"ע או"ח סי' רעא ס"ח, מ"ב ס"ק מ.

3. שו"ת ציץ אליעזר חי"ד סי' כה; עי' ספר מנחת שלמה סי' ג שאין לקבוע מנהג זה בקביעות
   אלא באופן עראי בשעת הדחק. ולדעתו עדיף טפי שיכוין לקבל שבת, ואפי"ה יוכל לנסוע
   חזרה לביתו לפני כניסת השבת ע"י נהג נכרי, ולצורך גדול גם ברכב ישראל בלי תשלום.

4. מגן אברהם סי' רסז ס"ק א, מ"ב ס"ק ה; חיי אדם כלל ו ס"ב.

5. ש"ע או"ח סי' רעא ס"ד, מ"ב ס"ק יא; ש"ע הרב שם ס"ט; מסגרת השלחן סי' עז ס"ק א;
   מגן אברהם סי' רסט ס"ק א ומ"ב ס"ק א.

6. תוס' חיים על חיי אדם כלל ו, ס"ק ב.

7. משנה ברורה סי' ערב ס"ק טו, טז, כב; שו"ת באר משה ח"ו סי' נג.

8. ש"ע או"ח סי' תפג ס"א, מ"ב ס"ק ג, ובסי' רעא ס"ק מא, וסי' ערב ס"ק כח; מסגרת
   השלחן סי' עז ס"ק ג; חיי אדם כלל ו ס"ק ו וס"ו; ותוס' חיים שם.

9. ש"ע או"ח סי' רעא ס"י, ורמ"א שם, מ"ב שם ס"ק מה, מו; חיי אדם כלל ו ס"י; ש"ע הרב
   סי' רסח סי"ב וסי' רעא סי"ט; שו"ת חתם סופר או"ח סי' י; שו"ת ציץ אליעזר חט"ו סי'
   טז; מקור חיים פ' קיד ס"ז; ועי' סדור אוצר התפלות שהארי ז"ל היה עומד בכל הקידושין
   בשבת וביו"ט ואח"כ יושב וטועם מן הכוס של קידוש. ואמו"ר ז"ל היה עומד בקידוש בליל
   שבת והיה יושב בקידוש ביום ש"ק וכך אני נוהג, ועי' טעם נכון למנהג זה בשו"ת תשובות
   והנהגות סי' רנד.

10. ש"ע או"ח סי' רעא ס"ב, מ"ב ס"ק ג, ד.

11. ש"ע או"ח סי' ריג ס"ג, וסי' רעג ס"ד ומ"ב שם; שו"ת ציץ אליעזר חי"ב סי' כד.

12. קצש"ע סי' ו ס"ט; עי' ש"ע או"ח סי' קכד ס"ה וס"ו, משנה ברורה ומגן אברהם ודגול
    מרבבה שם; סי' ריג ס"ג מ"ב ס"ק יז, סי' רטו ס"ב ומ"ב ס"ק ח.

13. קצש"ע סי' קלה ס"ו; ש"ע או"ח סי' תרמג ס"א וס"ב ושערי תשובה שם; ועי' סי' תפח
    ס"א, באר היטב ס"ק ג, ומ"ב ס"ק ח, וסי' רעא סט"ז.

14. טור או"ח סי' ערב וב"י שם; שו"ת יחוה דעת ח"ב סי' לה.

15. רמב"ם הל' שבת פכ"ט ה"ז; משנה ברורה סי' רעא ס"ק מ"ב ס"ק מב; שו"ת אגרות משה
    או"ח ח"ג סי' לט; שו"ת ציץ אליעזר חי"ב סי' כג; שמ"ב מ"ת קונטרס אחרון סי' עז ס"ז.

‫16. ש״ע או״ח סי׳ רעא סי״ג סי׳ רעג ס״ד, וסי׳ קפב ס״ג ומשנה ברורה ס״ק יז; עי׳ סי׳ קע‬
‫סט״ז ומשנה ברורה ס״ק לז, סי׳ רעא סי״ז משנה ברורה ס״ק פג; וש״ע הרב סי׳ קץ ס״ה‬
‫שהכוס פגום לאחר ששתה ממנו המברך, אולם עי׳ שעה״צ סי׳ רעא ס״ק פט שאם שותין‬
‫כולם מכוס של ברכה אע״ג דהוא שותה מתחלה מקרי מכוס שאינו פגום; עי׳ ספר עדות‬
‫לישראל מדור ההלכה עמ׳ 160.‬

‫17. ש״ע או״ח סי׳ ערב ס״ט ומגן אברהם ס״ק ט, ש״ע הרב שם סכ״ה; חיי אדם כלל ו סט״ו.‬

‫18. משנה ברורה סי׳ קעד ס״ק ח.‬

‫19. ש״ע או״ח סי׳ רעא ורמ״א שם, מגן אברהם ומ״ב שם; חיי אדם כלל ו סי״ב.‬

‫20. ש״ע או״ח סי׳ רפט ס״א, מ״ב ס״ק ב, ג.‬

‫21. ש״ע או״ח סי׳ רפט ס״א, משנה ברורה שם ובאור הלכה שם ד״ה חובת קידוש; עי׳ מג״א‬
‫רסט ס״ק א, וסי׳ פט באר היטב ס״ק יב ומשנה ברורה ס״ק כג; שו״ת אגרות משה או״ח‬
‫ח״ב סי׳ כו, כח, וח״ד סי׳ קא אות א; קצש״ע סי׳ ח ס״ד; ועי׳ שו״ת תשובות והנהגות סי׳‬
‫רסג דאם אוכל מעט מזונות לבד בחולה להשקיט לבבו אין צורך לקדש לפני התפלה.‬

‫22. ש״ע או״ח סי׳ רפט ס״ב; סי׳ ערב סי״ט מ״ב ס״ק כט, ל, ועי׳ מ״ב שם שביין שרוף יזהר‬
‫ליקח כוס מחזיק רביעית וישתה מלא לוגמיו שהוא רוב רביעית, ובשעת הדחק שתיית כל‬
‫המסובין מצטרפין למלא לוגמיו, ועי׳ שו״ת באר משה ח״ו סי׳ נד; שמ״ב מ״ת סי׳ עז ס״ק‬
‫יב; עי׳ ט״ז או״ח סי׳ רי ס״ק א ובאר היטב ס״ק ב. עי׳ שו״ת מהרש״ם ח״א סי׳ קעה‬
‫שיכול לקדש על יי״ש בכוס קטן כדרך שתייתו.‬

‫23. חיי אדם כלל נה ס״ו קצש״ע סי׳ קעד ס״ק יא, וסי׳ רח ס״ק כד;‬
‫שו״ת יחוה דעת ח״ה סי׳ כ, ועי׳ תוס׳ חיים על ח״א שם ס״ק ט שאין להרבות בברכות ולכן‬
‫יכוין בשעת קידוש לפטור גם המשקין.‬

‫24. שו״ת ציץ אליעזר חי״א סי׳ כו.‬

‫25. ש״ע או״ח סי׳ רעג ס״ה, מ״ב ס״ק כה, ושערי תשובה ס״ק ב.‬

‫26. ש״ע או״ח סי׳ רפו ס״ג, משנה ברורה ס״ק ט; משנה ברורה סי׳ תרלט ס״ק יג, וסי׳ קסח‬
‫ס״ק כד.‬

‫27. שבת קיז, ב; חיי אדם כלל ז ס״א; משנה ברורה סי׳ רצא ס״ק א.‬

‫28. ש״ע או״ח סי׳ רצא רמ״א שם ומשנה ברורה ס״ק ה.‬

‫29. קצש״ע סי׳ מ ס״ה; ערוך השלחן סי׳ רעד ס״ד, ומ״ב שם ס״ק ב; שו״ת תשובות והנהגות‬
‫סי׳ רנח.‬

‫30. ש״ע או״ח סי׳ קפח ס״ה, וקצש״ע סי׳ מד סי״ב, יג; ועי׳ חיי אדם כלל מז סי״ח ומ״ב שם‬
‫ס״ק כג שצריך לחזור רק אם כבר התחיל ברכה רביעית ולא מקרי התחלה עד שאמר הא–ל,‬
‫אבל אם אמר רק בא״י אמ״ה יסיים אשר נתן שבתות למנוחה וכו׳ ואח״כ אומר ברכת הטוב‬
‫והמטיב.‬

‫31. ש״ע או״ח סי׳ רצא ס״א וס״ה, מ״ב שם ס״ק ג. עי׳ ס״ה שם דאפילו בפירות יכול לקיים‬
‫סעודה שלישית ולא נזכר דוקא מבושלים.‬

‫32. ש״ע או״ח סי׳ רצא ס״ב ועי׳ מ״ב שם ס״ק ז וס״ק יא.‬

‫33. שו״ת ציץ אליעזר חי״א סי׳ כד, כה, וחי״ב סי׳ כה, כו; עי׳ ש״ע או״ח סי׳ קסח ס״ג.‬

‫34. שבת קיז, ב; משנה ברורה סי׳ רעד ס״ק א; ש״ע הרב שם ס״ב; מסגרת השלחן סי׳ עז ס״ק‬
‫יז; שמ״ב מ״ת סי׳ עז ס״ק יח, כב.‬

35. ש״ע או״ח סי׳ קסז ס״א, מ״ב ס״ק י, וסי׳ רעד ס״ק ב, ה; קצש״ע סי׳ מא ס״ג וסי׳ עז סי״ז.

36. שו״ת ציץ אליעזר חי״ד סי׳ מ; שו״ת מנחת יצחק ח״ט סי׳ מב.

37. ש״ע או״ח סי׳ רפה ס״ד, מ״ב שם ס״ק ט ושער הציון שם אות יד.

38. ש״ע או״ח סי׳ רפח ס״א, מ״ב ס״ק ב; ש״ע הרב שם ס״א; מסגרת השלחן סי׳ עז ס״ק כ.

39. ש״ע או״ח סי׳ רפז ס״א, מ״ב ס״ק א.

40. שבת יב, א, ש״ע או״ח סי׳ רפז ס״א, וסי׳ רפח ס״י, מגן אברהם שם ס״ק יד, ומ״ב שם ס״ק כח.

41. מגן אברהם סי׳ רטו ס״ק ו, ש״ע או״ח סי׳ רצ ס״א, מחצית השקל שם, ומ״ב שם ס״ק ב.

42. מגילה יב, ב „שישראל אוכלין ושותין [ביום השביעי], מתחילין בדברי תורה ובדברי תשבחות". רמב״ם הל׳ שבת פ״ל ה״ז; מקור חיים פ׳ קיז ס״י; עי׳ ספר הזהר פ׳ עקב (דף רבע ע״ב) וז״ל למהוי על פתורא מלי דאוריתא . . . וצריכין לאתערא לאתערא שירה וחדוה לפתורא לגבה; עי׳ ספר חסידים סי׳ תט וז״ל בשבת . . . יש לרנן שבחו של מקום שני מזמור שיר ליום השבת טוב להודות לה׳ ולזמר לשמך עליון; עי׳ ספר המטעמים אות שבת סי׳ צז, צח בשם יעב״ץ שמזמרין זמירות בסעודת שבת ומקיים בזה זה השלחן אשר לפני ה׳; ועי׳ שו״ת שרידי אש ח״ב סי׳ יד שהתירו גדולי אשכנז לאנשים ונשים לשיר זמירות ביחד.

43. טור וש״ע או״ח סי׳ רצ ס״ב, בית יוסף, מגן אברהם, ומשנה ברורה שם.

8. Reading the Torah On the Sabbath and Festivals

הלכות קריאת ספר תורה בשבת ויום טוב וחיובם

קצור שלחן ערוך סימן כג, עח, חיי אדם הלכות קריאת התורה כלל לא.

1. ש״ע או״ח סי׳ קמט מג״א ס״ק ג; קצש״ע סי׳ כג ס״א; שו״ת ציץ אליעזר חי״ב סי׳ מ.

2. שו״ת שרידי אש ח״ב או״ח סי׳ י׳ וסי׳ קנו; שו״ת אגרות משה או״ח ח״ב נ, וח״ג יב; שו״ת דבר יהושע ח״ב או״ח יט.

3. ש״ע או״ח סי׳ רפב ס״א, מגן אברהם ס״ק א, ובאר היטב ס״ק ג, ומ״ב ס״ק ד, ה.

4. משנה ברורה סי׳ קלה ס״ק לה.

5. יומא פ״ו מ״ב, סוטה לח, ב, קדושין עא, א; עי׳ רמב״ם מורה נבוכים ח״א פרק סא, סב; ספר הכוזרי, מאמר שני ס״ב, ומאמר רביעי ס״א.

6. שו״ת ציץ אליעזר חי״ג סי׳ לו; ועי׳ ש״ע או״ח סי׳ רפח. ס״י ומ״ב ס״ק כח דכשעושין מי שברך לחולה שאין בו סכנה אומר שבת היא מלזעוק ורפואה קרובה לבוא.

7. ש״ע או״ח סי׳ רפב ס״ו, משנה ברורה ס״ק לג.

8. משנה ברורה סי׳ קמג ס״ק כג; חיי אדם הלכות כלל לא, סל״ג; מסגרת השלחן סי׳ עח ס״ק ג.

9. עי׳ מגן אברהם סוף סי׳ רפב, ובאור הלכה סי׳ קלו ד״ה בשבת שחתן ביום חופתו דהיינו בחול הוא קודם לכל החיובים, ואלמן אף שאין מזמרין אותו יש לקרותו קודם לאחרים אם אינם חיובים.

10. שו״ת שרידי אש ח״ב או״ח ה; שו״ת אגרות משה ח״ד סי׳ סה, ועי׳ שם סוף סי׳ כג.

11. ביאור הלכה או״ח סי׳ קלו ד״ה בשבת.

.12 עי' באר היטב או"ח סי' רפב ס"ק יג שכתב בשם ספר הכוונות דהעולה ששי הוא המעולה שבקרואים ולפי הקבלה הוא בבחינת יסוד בספירות; ול"נ דאולי הוא מטעם ששלשה קוראים העשרת הדברות בפ' יתרו ופרשת שמע בפ' ואתחנן, שהם יסודי התורה והאמונה, ולכן מכבדין לאדם חשוב. עי' ברכות נה, א דמי שנותנין לו ספר תורה לקרות ואינו קורא הוי מג' דברים שמקצרים ימיו ושנותיו של אדם.

.13 ביאור הלכה ש"א או"ח סי' קלו ד"ה בשבת.

.14 ש"ע או"ח סי' קלט רמ"א שם; עי' שמ"ב סי' כג ס"ק ח; יסודי ישרון ח"ב מערכת קריאת התורה סי' ה; ועי' נועם ספר ח שער הלכה עמ' רפו; שו"ת חתם סופר אה"ע סי' עא; שו"ת מנחת יצחק ח"א קלו וח"ב קטו.

.15 ש"ע או"ח סי' קלט ס"ד, מ"ב ס"ק יז ובה"ל ד"ה ורואה; מצודת דוד על קצש"ע סי' כג.

.16 ש"ע או"ח סי' קמב ס"א; שו"ת ציץ אליעזר חי"ב סי' מ.

.17 ש"ע או"ח סי' רפב מגן אברהם ס"ק ו, משנה ברורה ס"ק יב יג', ועי' שעה"צ ס"ק טז ודרישה ופרישה שם ס"ק ה; ולע"ד משמע דבעת הצורך כשקורין קטן למפטיר לאחר שבעה קרואים וכשגמרו קריאת הפרשה יכול הוא לחזור ולקרא מה שקרא השביעי כרגיל. עי' שו"ת יחוה דעת ח"ד סי' כג וח"ה סי' כה; וספר לוית חן סי' יט.

.18 שו"ע או"ח סי' קמו ס"ד, ט"ז ס"ק א, מג"א ס"ק ו, מ"ב ס"ק יח, יט; עשה לך רב ח"א סי' לח, קצש"ע סי' כג ס"ו.

.19 ש"ע או"ח סי' קמב ס"א, משנה ברורה ובאור הלכה שם; עי' שו"ת באר משה ח"א סי' ד.

.20 שו"ת באר משה ח"ז ק"ו סי' קי, קיט; עי' ספר מנחת שלמה סי' ט שהשומע קול שופר או מקרא מגילה ע"י רם-קול או מיקרופון לא יצא, ואין להשתמש בביהכ"נ במכשירים כאלה לצרכי תפלה, שאינו שומע רק קול תנודות מכניות של הממברנה, אולם עי' מ"ש בהערה ד שם בשם החזו"א שיתכן דכיון שהקול הנשמע נוצר ע"י המדבר והקול נשמע מיד כדרך המדברים אין זה כ"כ פשוט שלא יצא כלל ידי חובתו.

.21 ש"ע או"ח סי' קלה ס"ב רמ"א שם, ומ"ב ס"ק ה ושער הציון ס"ק ה; שו"ת ציץ אליעזר חי"ג סי' כז.

.22 מגן אברהם סי' קמג ס"ק ב, ג, משנה ברורה שם ס"ק ט, י; עי' שו"ת אגרות משה או"ח ח"ג סי' יט.

9. Reading the Maftir and Haftarah

דיני מפטיר

קצור שלחן ערוך סימן עט, שלחן ערוך אורח חיים הלכות שבת סימן רפד

.1 ש"ע או"ח סי' רפב ס"ד, וסי' רצב מגן אברהם ס"ק ב ומ"ב ס"ק ד; קצש"ע סי' כג סכ"ו.

.2 שמ"ב מ"ת סי' עט ס"ק ב; עי' לוח מנהגי ביהכ"נ עפ"י פסקי הגרי"א הנקין ז"ל.

.3 שו"ת מנחת יצחק ח"ט סי' כב; עי' ש"ע או"ח סי' רפד ס"ד מ"ב ס"ק ז, ח.

.4 מגן אברהם ריש סי' רפד; ש"ע הרב שם ס"ד, ומ"ב שם ס"ק יא.

.5 שו"ת חתם סופר חלק או"ח סי' סח.

.6 ש"ע או"ח סי' רפב ס"ד משנה ברורה ס"ק כג, כד, ובאור הלכה שם; עי' קצש"ע סי' קמ ס"ג.

7. שו״ת אגרות משה או״ח ח״א סי׳ קב; שו״ת ציץ אליעזר ח״ו סי׳ לו.

8. משנה ברורה סי׳ קמג ס״ק כג, כט; עי׳ מגן אברהם שם ס״ק ד.

Part II
Principal Classes Of Labor (Melachot) Forbidden On the Sabbath
ל״ט מלאכות האסורות בשבת

Introduction
The Nature of Melachah

כללת שבת, כללי ל״ט מלאכות; חיי אדם, הלכות שבת כלל ט; רמב״ם, הלכות שבת
פרק א, ב, ח, י, כא, כג, כד; שלחן ערוך הלכות שבת סימן שז, שכא, שלא

1. אע״פ דכתיב „אל יצא״ דרשו כמו כן דכתיב „אל יוציא״ והכי משמע שאל יצא בשבת עם
כליו ללקוט את המן, עי׳ עירובין יז, ב, רש״י ותוס׳ שם; ועי׳ שבת צו, ב דילפינן איסור
הוצאה בשבת מ„ויצו משה ויעבירו קול במחנה" (שמות לו, ו), ומלבד הטעם דתוס׳ שם
לשתי הדרשות לאיסור הוצאה, עי׳ תורה תמימה שם דילפינן גם מפסוק דכתיב במלאכת
המשכן משום דהיסוד אבות מלאכות בשבת ילפינן ממלאכות שהיו במשכן.

2. שבת עד, ב שבק תנא דידן בישול סממנין... סידורא דפת נקט, אבל עי׳ רש״י שם ודף עג,
א ד״ה האופה דלא שייך אפיית פת במלאכת המשכן, עי׳ אגלי טל בהקדמה דהוי מחלוקת
רש״י ורבנו חננאל שלפי ר״ח ילפינן ל״ט מלאכות לא רק מבנין המשכן אלא גם ממנחת
התמיד והחביתין.

3. שבת פ״ז מ״ב, שם עג, ב, ורש״י שם; רמב״ם הל׳ שבת פ״ז ה״א; ספר מצות גדול, מצות
לא תעשה סה; חיי אדם הל׳ שבת כלל ט, י, יא.

4. שבת עד, ב; רמב״ם הל׳ שבת פ״ט ה״א וז״ל „אחד האופה את הפת, או המבשל את המאכל
או את הסממנין או המחמם את המים, הכל ענין אחד"; ועי׳ מ״ש לעיל שלפי רש״י שם
ובדף עג, א לא שייך אפיה במלאכת המשכן כלל.

5. עי׳ שבת עה, ב, היינו מולח והיינו מעבד, אפיק חד מינייהו ועייל שירטוט; רמב״ם הל׳ שבת
פ״ז ה״א, פי״א ה״א, יז; חיי אדם כלל לב, לג ס״ב, לד, לה ס״א; כלכלת שבת, כללי ל״ט
מלאכות סי׳ ד, כח, כט.

6. עי׳ רמב״ם הל׳ שבת פ״א ה״א, ופ״ז ה״ז שהעושה אב מלאכה או תולדה במזיד חייב כרת,
ואם היו שם עדים והתראה נסקל, ואם עשה בשוגג חייב קרבן חטאת קבועה, עי׳ חיי אדם
כלל ט סי״ב דמחלל שבת בשוגג אפילו באיסור דרבנן יתענה ויתן צדקה.

7. עי׳ ביצה יג, ב; סנהדרין סב, ב; כריתות יט, ב.

8. שבת קכ, ב; ש״ע או״ח סי׳ שלד סכ״ב ובאור הלכה ד״ה שודאי וד״ה דגרם, רמ״א שם
סכ״ו, ומ״ב ס״ק עג, עד, ספר הלכות שבת ח״א פ״ג עמ׳ לט.

9. רמב"ם הל' שבת פ"א הט"ו טז; חיי אדם הל' שבת כלל ט ס"ט; כללת שבת סי' ב, א.

10. עי' שבת יב, א, כט, ב; לא, ב; עג, ב מחלוקת ר' יהודה ור' שמעון; והרמב"ם בהל' שבת פ"א ה"א פוסק כר' יהודה דחייב, ורוב ראשונים פוסקים כר' שמעון דפטור אבל אסור מדרבנן, עי' ש"ע או"ח סי' רעח ומשנה ברורה ס"ק ג; כללת שבת, כללי ל"ט מלאכות סי' ב, ב.

11. שבת צד, ב; קג, א; כללת שבת סי' ב, ג; חיי אדם ט, ב; ש"ע או"ח סי' שמ ס"א משנה ברורה ס"ק ב; מגן אברהם סי' שלו ס"ק יא.

12. רמב"ם הל' שבת פ"א ה"ה; ש"ע או"ח סי' שלו ס"ג; חיי אדם הל' שבת כלל ט ס"ד; כללת שבת סי' ב, ד.

13. שבת עה, א; רמב"ם הל' שבת פ"א ה"ו, ש"ע או"ח סי' שלו ס"ג, ועי' שם סי' שכ סי"ח, משנה ברורה ס"ק נג, דרק לענין שבת דבעינן שיהא מלאכת מחשבת ליכא חיובא בפסיק רישא דלא ניחא ליה, אבל לענין שארי איסורי תורה אסור, ואיסורו מן התורה עי' בה"ל שם ד"ה דלא , ועי' מגן אברהם שם סי' שכ ס"ק כ; חיי אדם הל' שבת כלל ט ס"ו; כללת שבת סי' ב, ד, ולענין פסיק רישא באיסור דרבנן עי' ש"ע או"ח סי' שיד ס"א וסי' שטז ס"ג, רמ"א ומשנה ברורה שם, ומשמע דבחד איסור דרבנן אסור ובתרי דרבנן מותר.

14. שבת קה, ב; רמב"ם הל' שבת פ"א הי"ז, יח; ערוך השלחן סי' רמב סכ"ג וסל"ז; כללת שבת סי' ב, ה.

15. רמב"ם הל' שבת פ"ט הי"ג, דכל שאין מלאכתו מתקיימת בשבת פטור, עי' פ"י ה"א, פי"א הט"ו; ש"ע או"ח סי' שיז ס"א, כללת שבת סי' ב, ו; שעה"צ סי' שג ס"ק סח; ועי' כללת שבת מלאכת בונה שדוקא לזמן מרובה דהיינו לח' או ט' ימים.

16. מקור חיים פ' קעד ס"ב.

17. משנה ברורה סי' שיח ס"ק ה; חיי אדם כלל ט סי"א.

18. עי' רמב"ם הל' שבת פכ"א ה"א; רמב"ן ויקרא כג, כד; ערוך השלחן סי' רמג ס"ג וסי' שח ס"ד; ועי' רא"ש שבת פ"ב דף כד, א; בית יוסף או"ח הל' פסח סי' תסב; ועי' מגיד משנה הל' חמץ ומצה פ"ה ה"כ דאין לנו לגזור גזירות מדעתנו אחר דורות הגאונים; ועי' שו"ת יחוה דעת ח"ה סי' כח.

19. רמב"ם הל' שבת פ"א ה"ג, חיי אדם הל' שבת כלל ט ס"י, וסי"ב, תוס' חיים שם ס"ק יד.

20. רמב"ם הל' שבת פכ"ב ה"כ; ש"ע או"ח סי' שא סמ"ה ומ"ב ס"ק קסה; שו"ת באר משה ח"א סוף סי' לב; שו"ת אגרות משה או"ח ח"א סי' צו.

Melachah 1. Plowing

חרישה

כללת שבת, החורש; חיי אדם כלל י

1. מקור חיים פ' קמב ס"ד; ששכ"ז מ"ח פכ"ח סמ"ב וס"ק צט; ספר הל' שבת ח"ב, פ"ד עמ' מג; שער המזרח סי' פ ס"ק נה; שמ"ב מ"ת סי' פ ס"ק ק.

2. ש"ע או"ח סי' שלז ס"א, מגן אברהם ס"ק א, משנה ברורה ס"ק ג; כללת שבת, החורש.

3. רמב"ם הל' שבת פ"ח ה"א, פ"י הי"ב; משנה ברורה פתיחה לסי' שלו, עי"ש ס"ב רמ"א ומשנה ברורה שם ובסי' שיב ס"ק כד; ועי' כללת שבת, מלאכת החורש ומלאכת הבונה.

4. ש"ע או"ח סי' שלז ס"א, ב, ג, משנה ברורה שם, כלכלת שבת, החורש; שו"ת באר משה
ח"א סי' לב; מקור חיים פ' קמב ס"ה, ו; שש"כ מ"ח פכ"ג ס"ג ד.

5. ש"ע או"ח שח סמ"ה רמ"א שם, ומשנה ברורה שם ס"ק קנח, ואין למחות בנשים
וקטנים דמוטב שיהיו שוגגין ואל יהיו מזידין; ועי' סי' שלח ס"ה ומשנה ברורה שם ס"ק כ;
ועי' ערוך השלחן סי' שח ס"ע; כלכלת שבת, החורש; מקור חיים פ' קמב ס"ז; שש"כ מ"ח
פ' טז ס"ה; ועי' פסקי הל' שבת ח"א תשובות הגר"מ שטערן שאלה יב, שנוטה לאסור
משחקי כדור בשבת ויום טוב.

Melachah 2. Sowing

זריעה

כלכלת שבת, הזורע; חיי אדם כלל יא

1. רמב"ם הל' שבת פ"ח ה"ד; ש"ע או"ח סי' שלו ס"א, משנה ברורה ס"ק מג, מד ושער
הציון ס"ק לז, ובאור הלכה ד"ה אפילו; חיי אדם כלל יא ס"ד די"א דכל כלי חרס או כלי עץ
דינו כנקוב וא"כ צריך להחמיר בכולן; כלכלת שבת, הזורע.

2. שו"ת באר משה ח"ז קע סי' עא; עי' ש"ע או"ח סי' רנב ס"ה ומ"ב ס"ק לה דמותר לפתוח
מים לגינה בע"ש והם נמשכים והולכים בכל השבת, ועי' שש"כ מ"ח פכ"ו ס"א שמתיר
לפתוח ממטרות השקאה מבעוד יום כדי להשקות את השדה או את הגינה, עי' שו"ת ציץ
אליעזר ח"ד סי' לא, ח"ה סי' ו אות ג; יסודי ישרון ח"ג עמ' שלח; מנוחה נכונה פ"ג עמ'
לג. בכל זאת בנדון דידן לא יעשה כן בחצרו שלפני ביתו בפני בני אדם ההולכים שם.

3. מקור חיים פ' קמב ס"ו; ערוך השלחן סי' שלו ס"ל.

4. ש"ע או"ח סי' שלו סי"א משנה ברורה שם ס"ק נד ושעה"צ שם ס"ק מח; ועי' חיי אדם
כלל יא ס"ג שדעתו לאסור להעמידים בשבת במים לכתחלה אם לא עמדו מאתמול, ועי' תוס'
חיים שם ס"ק ה; ערוך השלחן סי' שלו ס"ל; כלכלת שבת, הזורע; שש"כ מ"ח פכ"ו סכ"ה,
שו"ת יחוה דעת ח"ב סי' נג; ועי' סי' הלכות שבת ח"ב פ"ה ס"ק סד ס"ק צו מ"ש בשם
הגר"מ פיינשטיין ז"ל דמותר לטלטל אגרטל בשבת.

5. ש"ע או"ח סי' שכא סי"א, ומשנה ברורה סי' שלו ס"ק נא; חיי אדם כלל יא ס"ב ותוס'
חיים שם ס"ק ג; כלכלת שבת, הזורע.

6. ש"ע או"ח סי' שלו ס"ג, משנה ברורה שם, עי"ש שמותר להשתין שם שמי רגלים שורפים
את הזרעים ומונעים מלהצמיח; חיי אדם כלל יא ס"א ותוס' חיים שם; כלכלת שבת, הזורע.

Melachah 3. Reaping

קצירה

כלכלת שבת, הקוצר; חיי אדם כלל יב

1. רמב"ם הל' שבת פ"ח ה"ג, לחם משנה שם; כלכלת שבת, הקוצר; משנה ברורה סי' שה ס"ק
סא.

2. ש"ע או"ח סי' שלו ס"י, משנה ברורה ס"ק מח; חיי אדם כלל יב ס"ח; מקור חיים פ' קמד
ס"ו; שש"כ מ"ח פ"כו סכ"ב; שו"ת הגר"מ שטערן אות לה בפסקי הל' שבת ח"ג.

3. שמות כג, יב, רש"י ומכילתא שם; שבת קכב, א ותוס' ד"ה מעמיד; רמב"ם הל' שבת פכ"א
הל"ו; ש"ע או"ח סי' שכד סי"ג ומשנה ברורה ס"ק לג.

4. ש"ע או"ח סי' שלו ס"ג, משנה ברורה ס"ק כד; כלכלת שבת, הקוצר; חיי אדם כלל יב ס"ו;
ספר זכרו תורת משה סי' טז ס"ג, קהלת יום טוב שם ס"ק יא.

5. ש"ע או"ח סי' שכב ס"ג ומשנה ברורה שם; חיי אדם כלל יב ס"ז; כלכלת שבת, הקוצר.

6. ש"ע או"ח סי' שלו ס"א, יג ומ"ב שם; כלכלת שבת, הקוצר; ערוך השלחן סי' שלו סי"ח.

7. ביצה לו, ב; ירושלמי ביצה פ"ה ה"ב; רמב"ם הל' שבת פכ"א ה"ט; ש"ע או"ח סי' שה
סי"ח, ומשנה ברורה שם ושעה"צ שם ס"ק נב; חיי אדם כלל יב ס"ט; כלכלת שבת הקוצר;
ועי' בתקון דוד ושאול על קיצור הלכות שבת כלל ג, סט"ו ס"ק טו מה שמביא בשם החתם
סופר להשוות טעם הירושלמי שאסרו רכיבה ע"ג בהמה משום שביתת בהמתו וטעם הבבלי
שאסור שמא יחתוך זמורה.

Melachah 4. Binding Sheaves

עימור

כלכלת שבת, המעמר; חיי אדם כלל יג

1. ערוך השלחן סי' שם ס"ג; משנה ברורה סי' שם ס"ק לז, לח; חיי אדם כלל יג ס"א.

2. ספר הלכות שבת ח"ב פ"ז עמ' 83 ס"ק כא בשם הגר"מ פיינשטיין, דאסור אף שלא במקום
גידולו משום דהוי כמתקן.

Melachah 5. Threshing

דישה

כלכלת שבת, הדש; חיי אדם כלל יד; שלחן ערוך, הלכות שבת סימן שכ

1. ש"ע או"ח סי' שכא סי"ג, ומשנה ברורה שם.

2. ש"ע או"ח סי' שכ משנה ברורה ס"ק כב; כלכלת שבת, הדש; זכרו תורת משה סי' יח ס"ג,
קהלת יום טוב שם ס"ק ו; שו"ת באר משה ח"ו סי' קט.

3. ש"ע או"ח סי' שכ ס"ז, משנה ברורה ס"ק כד, כה; חיי אדם כלל יד ס"ה, ו; כלכלת שבת,
הדש.

4. ש"ע או"ח סי' שה ס"כ, מגן אברהם ס"ק יג, משנה ברורה ס"ק עג; ערוך השלחן שם ס"כ;
חיי אדם כלל יד ס"ח ותוס' חיים שם ס"ק ג; כלכלת שבת, הדש; שש"כ מ"ח פכ"ז
סמ"ו–מח; שו"ת ציץ אליעזר ח"ב ס"י ג; שו"ת שרידי אש ח"ב סי' כד; ועי' תורת השבת
פ"ז, ה באם אין גוי ואין לו מכונה חשמלית דיש מתירין בהפסד מרובה לחלוב ע"י שימת
צבע או אורז לתוכו בכדי להפכו ממשקה לאוכל וצ"ע.

5. ש"ע או"ח סי' שכח סל"ד, לה, וסי' של ס"ח ומשנה ברורה שם ס"ק לב; חיי אדם כלל יד
ס"ט; כלכלת שבת, הדש; זכרו תורת משה סי' יח ס"ד קהלת יום טוב ס"ק י; שו"ת ציץ

אליעזר ח"ח סי' טו פי"ב; שש"כ מ"ח פל"ו ס"כ, כא עי' תשובת הגר"מ שטערן בחוב' עם התורה י"ד עמ' נא ועי' ס' הלכות שבת ח"ב פ"ח עמ' קיד ס"ק רעד דבמשאבה חשמלית אם היא מחוברת לשעון שבת אפשר דיש להקל במקום צער בפרט היכא דא"א בע"א.

6. רמב"ם הל' שבת פ"ח ה"י, פ"ט הי"א, פכ"ב הט"ו; ערוך השלחן סי' שכ סכ"ז, כח; משנה ברורה שם ס"ק נה, ובאור הלכה שם סי"ח ד"ה יש מי שמתיר; ועי' כללכת שבת, הדש, הסוחט משקין מבגד והוא צריך למשקין היוצאין הוי תולדת דש, ואם בלוע מים או משקין המלבנין חייב משום מלבן, ולרמב"ם ולרמב"ן בין סוחט משקין או מים מבגד אינו רק תולדת מלבן, דאין דישה רק כשהדבר שסוחטין ממנו הוא גדולי קרקע.

7. שש"כ מ"ח פט"ז סמ"ד; מנוחה נכונה ג, ה; ספר קיצור הלכות שבת כלל ה סי"ג שו"ת הגר"מ שטערן, שאלה ו בפסקי הלכות שבת ח"ב; ועי' מ"ב סי' שלח ס"ק ל דאין על מטר שיורד בשבת שם מוקצה או נולד.

8. ש"ע או"ח סי' שכ סי"א משנה ברורה ס"ק לז.

9. חיי אדם כלל יד סי"א; ערוך השלחן או"ח סי' שכ סכ"ד.

10. ספר הלכות שבת ח"ב פ"ח עמ' 118, 120 וס"ק שלג בשם הגר"מ פיינשטיין ז"ל; שו"ת באר משה ח"ב סי' כה, כו; שו"ת יחוה דעת ח"א סי' ל; שש"כ מ"ח פ"י ס"ד; שו"ת ציץ אליעזר ח"ו סי' לד, ח"ח סי' יב.

11. משנה ברורה סי' שכ ס"ק לב; שש"כ מ"ח פ"י ס"א; שו"ת ציץ אליעזר ח"ו סי' לד ס"ק לט, וחי"ד סי' מט; שו"ת באר משה ח"ב סי' כה, כו.

Melachah 6. Winnowing

זריה

כללכת שבת, הזורה; חיי אדם כלל טו

1. שבת עג, ב ורש"י שם, שבת עה, ב רש"י שם ד"ה הרי; רבינו חננאל שבת עד, א; ערוך השלחן או"ח סי' שיט ס"ב; מקור חיים ח"ג פ' קמז; קיצור הל' שבת כלל ו תד"ו ס"ק א; ספר הלכות שבת ח"ג פ"ט עמ' 123, 122.

Melachah 7. Selecting

ברירה

כללכת שבת, הבורר; חיי אדם כלל טז; שלחן ערוך, הלכות שבת סימן שיט

1. משנה ברורה, הקדמה לסי' שיט.

2. משנה ברורה סי' שיט ס"ק כד; שו"ת אגרות משה ח"ד סי' עד ערך בורר אות ח, יג; תשובת הגר"מ פיינשטיין בהל' שבת ח"ב שאלה ח; שש"כ מ"ח פ"ג סל"א, לד, לח; עי' שו"ת באר משה ח"ו סי' מז, דמותר בדרך אכילה.

3. באור הלכה סי' שיט ס"ד ד"ה מתוך אוכל; שש"כ מ"ח פ"ג סי"א–טו; שו"ת אגרות משה או"ח ח"ד סי' עד ערך בורר אות ז; מקור חיים פ' קמז סי"ט; שו"ת באר משה ח"ו סי' סט.

4. משנה ברורה סי' שכא ס"ק פד ושעה"צ ס"ק צט; שו"ת אגרות משה או"ח ח"ד סי' עד ערך

בורר אות ז; תשובת הגר"מ פיינשטיין בהל' שבת ח"ב שאלה ז; שש"כ מ"ח פ"ג סט"ז, יז, לג; מקור חיים פ' קמז סכ"ב, כג.

5. ט"ז או"ח סי' תקו ס"ק ג וסי' שיט ס"ק יג, ומשנה ברורה שם ס"ק סא; חיי אדם כלל טז סי"ב ותוס' חיים שם ס"ק ח, י; זכרו תורת משה סי' כ ס"ו וקהלת יום טוב שם ס"ק יט; ש"ע הרב סי' שיט סכ"ד; שש"כ מ"ח פ"ג סי"ח, לו.

6. משנה ברורה סי' שיט ס"ק ד, ה, ו.

7. מגן אברהם או"ח סי' שכא ס"ב ס"ק טו, ובאר היטב שם בשם ר"ן, ובאור הלכה סי' שיט ס"א ד"ה כדי לאכול לאלתר בשם פמ"ג; תוס' חיים על חיי אדם כלל יז ס"ק ג.

8. שו"ת אגרות משה או"ח ח"א סי' קכד; שו"ת מנחת יצחק ח"א סי' עו; שש"כ מ"ח פ"ג סמ"ה.

9. ש"ע או"ח סי' שיט ס"א, משנה ברורה ס"ק י, וסי' שכא ס"ק מה; תשובות הגר"מ פיינשטיין ז"ל בהל' שבת ח"ב שאלה יג; ועי' מגן אברהם סי' שכא ס"ב ס"ק טו לגבי טוחן וה"ה לגבי בורר דבעינן סמוך לסעודה ממש, ויש לעשות רק אחרי יציאת בית הכנסת.

10. חיי אדם כלל טז ס"ה, תוס' חיים שם ס"ק ה בשם הפמ"ג; משנה ברורה סי' שיט ס"ג ס"ק טו.

11. משנה ברורה סי' שיט ס"ק טו, ובאור הלכה ד"ה לאכול מיד.

12. ש"ע או"ח סי' שיט ס"א, באור הלכה שם ד"ה מן העלין, ובס"ד שם ד"ה מתוך אוכל; ספר הל' שבת ח"א פ"י ס"ק מג בשם הגר"מ פיינשטיין ז"ל; שו"ת באר משה ח"ו סי' סט.

13. ערוך השלחן או"ח סי' שיט ס"ח, ט, ועי' בט"ז שם ס"ק יב; שש"כ מ"ח פ"ג סע"ח; מקור חיים פ' קמז סל"ז; ועי' בשו"ת יביע אומר ח"ה סי' לא.

14. משנה ברורה סי' שיט ס"ג ס"ק טו, באור הלכה ד"ה לאכול מיד; ערוך השלחן שם ס"ח, ט, תשובת הגר"מ פיינשטיין בספר הל' שבת ח"ב שאלה יב.

15. שו"ת באר משה ח"ו סי' סח; תשובת הגר"מ פיינשטיין ז"ל בספר הל' שבת ח"ב שאלה יב; שש"כ מ"ח פ"ג סס"ט.

16. ש"ע או"ח סי' שיט סי"ד; ערוך השלחן שם סל"ה; חיי אדם כלל טז ס"ט; זכרו תורת משה סי' כ ס"ג; מקור חיים פ' קמז ס"ל.

17. ש"ע או"ח סי' שיט סי"ד; שו"ת ציץ אליעזר חי"ד סי' מו; שו"ת יחוה דעת ח"ב סי' נא; מקור חיים פ' קמז ס"ל; שש"כ מ"ח פ"ג סנ"ז.

18. חיי אדם כלל טז ס"י; כללת שבת, הבורר; משנה ברורה סי' שיט ס"ק נה, סב, ושעה"צ ס"ק נט.

19. ש"ע או"ח סי' שיט ס"ח משנה ברורה ס"ק כט; שו"ת אגרות משה או"ח ח"א סי' קכה; קה"ש כלל ז תד"ו ס"ק ט; ועי' מקור חיים פ' קמז סכ"ח, מ"ש דהכל שוטפים פירות וירקות בתוך כלי מים או בברז, והנה להם לישראל.

20. ש"ע או"ח סי' שכא שיט רמ"ח שם, ומשנה ברורה ס"ק פד ושעה"צ ס"ק צז, מגן אברהם שם ס"ק ל; ועי' מקור חיים פ' קמז בהקדמה לסכ"ו מ"ש בשם שדי חמד, כללים מערכת ב, כלל לב, שמתיר לקלוף תפוחים בשבת אפילו להניח דהרי הוא כחותך מגוף התפוח ואין זה דומה לקילוף שומים ובצלים; ועי' תשובת הגר"מ פיינשטיין בהל' שבת ח"ב תשובה ח שנוטה לאסור כהמגן אברהם; עי' שש"כ מ"ח פ"ג ס"ל, לא.

Melachah 8. Sifting

הרקדה

כלכלת שבת, המרקד; חיי אדם כלל יח

1. ש"ע או"ח סי' שיט ס"י, משנה ברורה ס"ק לד; מקור חיים פ' קמז ס"ל; ושש"כ מ"ח פ"ג סנ"ו בשם החזון איש ועי' שם ס"ק קסג מ"ש מכף החיים דבירושלים עיה"ק היו נוהגים לסנן המים משום ספק תולעים.

2. ש"ע או"ח סי' שיט סט"ז, משנה ברורה ס"ק ס, ושער הציון ס"ק נב.

3. שבת קלט, ב, ש"ע או"ח סי' שיט ס"י, יא, משנה ברורה ס"ק לד, לה, מ, ערוך השלחן שם סכ"ט; כלכלת שבת, המרקד; תשובת הגר"מ פיינשטיין בספר הלכות שבת ח"ב, אות ד; ועי' שש"כ מ"ח פ"ג סנ"ג שאוסר לסנן מיצי פירות.

4. משנה ברורה סי' שיט ס"ק מח; הלכות שבת ח"ג פי"א עמ' 195 ותשובת הגר"מ פיינשטיין שם אות א; ועי' שש"כ מ"ח פ"ג סנ"ג שאוסר סינון הרוטב מירקות מבושלים, אבל מותר לסחוט ביד את הירקות מן המים המיותרים.

5. הל' שבת ח"ב תשובת הגר"מ פיינשטיין שם אות ה; שש"כ מ"ח פי"ב סט"ז.

Melachah 9. Grinding

טחינה

כלכלת שבת, הטוחן; חיי אדם כלל יז; שלחן ערוך, הלכות שבת סימן שכא

1. ש"ע או"ח סי' שכא ס"ז ומשנה ברורה ס"ק כה; חיי אדם כלל יז ס"א.

2. ש"ע או"ח סי' שכא סי"ב, מגן אברהם ס"ק טו, ש"ע הרב ס"י, משנה ברורה ס"ק מב, מד, מה, ובאור הלכה ד"ה מידי; שו"ת אגרות משה או"ח ח"ד סי' עד ערך טוחן אות א; חיי אדם כלל יז ס"ב; ערוך השלחן סי' שכא סט"ט; תשובות הגר"מ פיינשטיין ז"ל בס' הל' שבת ח"ד תשובה א; ועי' קיצור הל' שבת כלל ט תד"ו ס"ק ב דעת המתירין לחתוך בצלים עם ביצים ושומן דאין בזה איסור משום לישה.

3. כלכלת שבת, הטוחן; מקור חיים פ' קמח ס"ט; שו"ת אגרות משה או"ח ח"ד סי' עד ערך טוחן אות ב; תשובות הגר"מ פיינשטיין ז"ל בס' הל' שבת ח"ד תשובה ב; שו"ת יחוה דעת ח"ה סי' כז; שש"כ מ"ח פ"ו ס"י.

4. ש"ע או"ח סי' שכא סי"ב, משנה ברורה ס"ק מ, באור הלכה שם ד"ה לפרר לחם.

5. ש"ע או"ח סי' שכא ס"ט משנה ברורה ס"ק לא, לב, תשובות הגר"מ פיינשטיין ז"ל בס' הל' שבת ח"ד תשובה ד; שש"כ מ"ח פ"ו סי"א, יד.

6. ש"ע או"ח סי' שב ס"ז, משנה ברורה ס"ק לו; כלכלת שבת, הטוחן; מקור חיים פ' קמח ס"י.

7. ש"ע או"ח סי' שכח ס"א ומשנה ברורה שם; חיי אדם כלל סט ס"ה.

8. רמב"ם הל' שבת פכ"א הי"ח, יט, לה, לו; ש"ע סי' שכא וסי"ב, משנה ברורה ס"ק לג, מד, וסי' שכד ס"ד-י"א, משנה ברורה שם ושעה"צ שם ס"ק יד.

9. רמב"ם הל' שבת פכ"א הל"ה; כלכלת שבת, הטוחן; ש"ע או"ח סי' שכד ס"י-יג ומשנה ברורה שם.

Melachah 10. Kneading

לישה

כלכלת שבת, הלש; חיי אדם כלל יט; שלחן ערוך, הלכות שבת סימן שכא

1. משנה ברורה סי׳ שכא ס״ק סח; שש״כ מ״ח פ״ח ס״ד.

2. רמב״ם הל׳ שבת פ״ח סט״ז, משנה ברורה סי׳ שכא ס״ק נ, סי׳ שכד ס״ק ס״ג ומשנה ברורה שם, ובאור הלכה שם ד״ה אין גובלין.

3. ש״ע או״ח סי׳ שח סל״ח משנה ברורה ס״ק קמג, קמד, סי׳ שכא משנה ברורה ס״ק נ; שש״כ מ״ח פט״ז ס״ד; שו״ת הגר״מ שטערן בס׳ פסקי הל׳ שבת ח״ב אות ו; מקור חיים פ׳ קמט ס״ח; שו״ת באר משה ח״ו סי׳ לא, לד.

4. שו״ת ציץ אליעזר חט״ו סי׳ כה ואין בו משום איסור בונה ולא משום איסור לישה; שו״ת הגר״מ שטערן בפסקי הל׳ שבת ח״ג אות מד דאינו מתכוין והוי כלאחר יד והאבק הוא מעט מזעיר ולא שייך ביה לישה; אולם עי׳ שש״כ מ״ח פי״ד סל״ה שאוסר באבק משום לישה.

5. ש״ע או״ח סי׳ שכא סי״ב והוא משום מלאכת טוחן, עי׳ משנה ברורה ס״ק מה, באור הלכה שם ד״ה המחתך; שו״ת ציץ אליעזר חי״א סי׳ לו; שש״כ מ״ח פ״ח סכ״ג; שו״ת באר משה ח״ו סי׳ מג, מד; עי׳ ס׳ הל׳ שבת פי״ג עמ׳ 237, ופסקי הל׳ שבת ח״א פ״א סי״ג, יד; קיצור הל׳ שבת כלל ט תד״ו סק״ב.

6. שש״כ מ״ח פ״ח סי״ח, כד; ספר הל׳ שבת ח״ד פי״ג עמ׳ 223, ותשובות הגר״מ פיינשטיין שם אות ו.

7. שו״ת אגרות משה או״ח ח״ד סי׳ עד ערך לש אות ג, יב; שו״ת באר משה ח״א סי׳ לה; עי׳ שו״ת באר משה ח״ו סי׳ מה, ושש״כ מ״ח פ״ח סכ״ה שאוסרים באבק פודינג אפילו בבלילה רכה; ועי׳ כלכלת שבת מלאכת האופה שמתיר לטרוף ביצה ללבן הקפה; עי׳ שו״ת ציץ אליעזר חי״ב סי׳ לב.

Melachah 11. Baking and Cooking

אפיה ובישול

כלכלת שבת, האופה, כללי הטמנה ובשולי שבת; חיי אדם כלל ב, כ; שלחן ערוך,
הלכות שבת סימן רנג, רנד, רנז, שיח

1. עי׳ כשרות ושבת במטבח המודרני ח״א פ״ז דיון על שימוש במיתקנים לאחזקת חום באמצעות קיטור.

2. שו״ת אגרות משה או״ח ח״ג סי׳ נב.

3. שבת כ, א רש״י שם, עי׳ שבת מ, ב שיעור יס״ב כל שכריסו של תינוק נכוית; רמב״ם הל׳ שבת פ״ט ה״ה; ש״ע או״ח סי׳ רנד ס״ב, ה, סי׳ שיח ס״ד, יד, משנה ברורה סי׳ רנג סל״ז לח; מצודת דוד על קצש״ע סוף סי׳ עב; שש״כ מ״ח פ״א ס״א; מקור חיים פ׳ קנ ס״א; שמ״ב מ״ת סי׳ פ ס״ק ז, קונטרס אחרון שם; הל׳ שבת דיני אופה ס״ק כ, צט, ותשובות הגר״מ פיינשטיין שם אות טז; ועי׳ שו״ת אגרות משה או״ח ח״ד סי׳ עד ערך בישול אות ג, דבשעור ק״ס מעלות יש לחוש ליד סולדת בו ובמדת ק״ס הוא ודאי יס״ב אף לקולא; עי׳ שו״ת מהרש״ם ח״א סי׳ קצז; שו״ת יביע אומר ח״ג או״ח סי׳ כד; ספר לוית חן סי׳ מח.

4. ש"ע או"ח סי' שיח סי"ב ומשנה ברורה שם; שו"ת אגרות משה יו"ד ח"ב סי' לג; ספר עדות לישראל עמ' קכב; שו"ת באר משה ח"ז ק"ע סי' קה; שש"כ מ"ח פ"א סל"ט; קיצור הל' שבת כלל יא סמ"ד מה ותד"ו ס"ק מב, מג; שו"ת מנחת יצחק ח"ג סי' קלז; שמ"ב מ"ת סי' עב ס"ק מג; שו"ת מלמד להועיל או"ח סי' מד; ועי' ספר דברי דוד סי' פז מאת הרב דוד קראנגלאס שמצדד להקל פתיחת הברז של המים החמים בשבת מכמה טעמים; ועי' ספר משנה הלכות ח"ז סי' נד שכותב שאין לסמוך על פלפולו להתיר. עי' חימום מים בשבת מאת הרב לוי יצחק הלפרין ח"ג וח"ד דיון הלכתי על חימום מים בבוילער ופתרונות טכניים.

5. ספר עדות לישראל עמ' קכב; שו"ת באר משה ח"ו ק"ע סי' מ, מא, ח"ז סי' כ; קה"ש פי"א סמ"ז ותד"ו שם.

6. רמב"ם הל' שבת פכ"ב ה"י; ש"ע או"ח סי' שכא ס"ג ומשנה ברורה שם; מגן אברהם שם ס"ק כד; כלכלת שבת, מלאכת האופה.

7. ש"ע או"ח סי' שיח ס"ג משנה ברורה ס"ק כא; תוס' חיים על חיי אדם כלל כ ס"ק ג; שש"כ מ"ח פ"א סמ"ה והערה קכז; שו"ת אגרות משה ח"ג סי' נב.

8. שש"כ מ"ח פ"א סמ"ה, ועי' מקור חיים פ' קנ סט"ז שמתיר להשתמש במים שהוחמו בדוד שמש אף שנכנסים מים קרים, שאין דין בישול בחמה דומה לאש; ועי' שו"ת יביע אומר ח"ד סי' לד; שו"ת ציץ אליעזר ח"ז סי' יט.

9. ש"ע או"ח סי' שכו סי"א, ס"ט, סי' שלט ס"ב, משנה ברורה סי' שכו ס"ק ה, ז, כא, כד, כה, באור הלכה שם ס"ח ד"ה אדם מותר, מג"א שם ס"ק ח; ערוך השלחן שם ס"ג וס"י; ש"ע הרב שם ס"ו; שו"ת אגרות משה ח"ג סי' פז; מקור חיים פ' קנ ס"ל; שו"ת באר משה ח"ו סי' עג.

10. ש"ע או"ח סי' שיח ס"ד, מג"א ס"ק לא, משנה ברורה ס"ק עא; חיי אדם כלל כ ס"ד.

11. משנה ברורה סי' רנח ס"ק ב; ש"ע או"ח סי' שיח סי"ג, משנה ברורה ס"ק פו, פז ובאור הלכה ד"ה אבל; מקור חיים פ' קנ סכ"ה; שש"כ מ"ח פ"א ס"נ; הל' שבת ח"ד דיני אופה ס"ק שעד בשם הגר"מ פיינשטיין ז"ל; ועי' שמ"ב מהד"ת סי' עב ס"ק מה מ"ש בשם החזון איש דאין נתינה במים חמים בכלל הטמנה ומותר.

12. ש"ע או"ח סי' שיח ס"ה, משנה ברורה ס"ק מה.

13. שש"כ מ"ח פ"א סמ"ט, סנ"ו; שו"ת באר משה ח"ב סי' כא; עי' שו"ת אגרות משה או"ח ח"ד סי' עד ערך בישול אות טז שכותב שהוא מחמיר על עצמו בקפה נמס ליתן בכלי שלישי, אבל לדינא אין להחמיר. עי' שו"ת תשובות והנהגות סי' ריט שיש לשפוך המים חמין לכלי שלישי; ועי' שו"ת מנחת יצחק ח"ט סי' כז, ועי' שו"ת יחוה דעת ח"ב סי' מד שדעתו להתיר לערות אפילו מכלי ראשון מכיון שהקפה נתבשל לפני כן; ועי' קיצור הל' שבת כלל יא סל"ו ול"ז ותד"ו שם ס"ק לד, לה.

14. משנה ברורה סי' שיח ס"ק לט ושעה"צ ס"ק סד, סה, ואין לחוש לצביעה דאין צביעה באוכלין, ואם התמצית תה חמה, טוב יותר שיערה המים לתוכה לצאת דעת החוששים לצביעה, עי' שש"כ מ"ח פ"א סמ"ו, מז, נג, נה; שו"ת יביע אומר ח"ב סי' כא וספר לוית חן סי' מו; הל' שבת ח"ד דיני אופה עמ' 294; מקור חיים פ' קנ סי"ז.

15. ש"ע או"ח סי' שכג ס"ו, ומשנה ברורה ס"ק כט, מג"א ס"ק ט ובסי' רנג ס"ק מא; חיי אדם כלל כ ס"י"ט; שש"כ מ"ח פ"א סמ"א.

16. מגן אברהם סי' שיח ס"ק לא, משנה ברורה ס"ק כג, לה; שו"ת אגרות משה או"ח ח"ד סי' עד ערך בישול אות יח; שו"ת ציץ אליעזר חי"ד סי' לב; שו"ת מלמד להועיל או"ח סי' נט;

ששכ"ך מ"ח פ"א סנ"א ג-נו, אולם עי' כללת שבת, כללי הטמנה ובישולי שבת אות א, שאוסר ליתן חלב צונן לתוך כלי שני ביס"ב.

17. חיי אדם כלל כ, סכ"א, משנה ברורה סי' שכא ס"ק סח.

18. חיי אדם כלל כ ס"ו; משנה ברורה סי' שיח ס"ק לו; ששכ"ך מ"ח פ"א סנ"ז.

19. משנה ברורה סי' שיח ס"ק מז; ערוך השלחן שם ס"ק כח; שו"ת חתם סופר יו"ד סי' צה; פתחי תשובה יו"ד סי' צד ס"ז; הל' שבת ח"ד פי"ד ס"ק צא, ועי' תשובות הגר"מ פיינשטיין שם אות כו שכותב שלא נראה כלל לומר דאיכא דברים שמתבשלים בכלי שלישי.

20. מגן אברהם סי' שיח ס"ק לא, משנה ברורה ס"ק סה; שו"ת אגרות משה או"ח ח"ד סי' עד ערך בישול אות ה; תשובות הגר"מ פיינשטיין בהל' שבת ח"ד אות יח; ששכ"ך מ"ח פ"א סנ"ח.

21. עי' טור או"ח סי' רנג בית יוסף שם ד"ה ומ"ש רבינו כל זמן, דמיירי בתבשיל שרובו רוטב; ש"ע או"ח סי' שיח סט"ו, משנה ברורה שם ס"ק צט, ש"ע הרב שם ס"ק, ששכ"ך מ"ח פ"א ס"ז, ח, ט, הל' שבת ח"ד דיני אופה עמ' 261, 312. ועי' תשובות הגר"מ פיינשטיין שם אות כו דאין זה ברור אם בענין רובו רוטב, ולכן ראוי להחמיר, ובשעת הדחק גדול יש להתיר. עי' ספר לוית חן שהעלה להתיר להניח תבשיל לח שנתבשל כל צרכו מע"ש כגון מרק, חלב, ודייסא של תינוק והוא צונן, כנגד האש על גבי המיחם או פלטה חשמלית אפילו במקום שהיס"ב כדי להפשירו בלבד ומיד אחר שיפשור יסירנו משם.

22. ש"ע או"ח סי' שיח ס"ח משנה ברורה שם ס"ק קיז, שעה"צ שם ס"ק קלו, מגן אברהם שם ס"ק מב; כללת שבת, האופה; תשובות הגר"מ פיינשטיין בס' הל' שבת ח"ד אות כא.

23. מקור חיים פ' קן סכ"ו; ששכ"ך מ"ח פ"א סס"א; הל' שבת ח"ד דיני אופה עמ' 265.

24. משנה ברורה סי' שיח ס"ק מה; עי' משנה ברורה ס"ק פז דאם משהה הכף בתוך הקדירה עד שמעלה רתיחה מקרי כלי ראשון, אבל עי' ששכ"ך מ"ח פ"א סנ"ט ס"ק קפ מ"ש בשם החזון איש דיש להבדיל בין קדירה שע"ג האש דאז אמרינן דדין כף ככלי ראשון, לקדירה שהעבירה מע"ג האש דאין דין על מה שבכף אלא דין כלי שני.

25. עי' שו"ת אגרות משה ח"ד סי' ס; שו"ת ציץ אליעזר ח"ב סי' ו, ז; ח"ג סי' יח; חי"ב סי' לא; יסודי ישרון ח"ג מערכת ע"ש עמ' מב; שמ"ב מהד"ת סי' עב ס"ק מב; שו"ת מלמד להועיל אה"ז סי' נח; עדות לישראל אות כ עמ' 122 ח"ל להעריך מע"ש מורה שעות... שיבעיר תנור העלעקטרי לחמם התבשיל שעומד בו מע"ש מותר אבל לבשל עי"ז תבשיל מחדש נראה דאסור, עי' ששכ"ך מ"ח פ"א סכ"ו, פל"א ס"ח; שו"ת באר משה ח"ז ק"ע סי' ה; פסקי עזיאל בשאלות הזמן סי' יז.

26. ש"ע או"ח סי' שיח ס"ד ה, ח, טו, משנה ברורה ס"ק לג, צב, צד, שעה"צ ס"ק מו; שו"ת אגרות משה או"ח ח"א סי' צד שמותר בדבר יבש ובלח למקום שלא אפשר לבא לידי יס"ב, או"ח ח"ד סי' עד ערך בישול אות לב; ועי' שו"ת באר משה ח"ז ק"ע סי' ד דעתו לאסור בפלטה חשמלית דהמאכל מתחמם יותר מיס"ב; ועי' ששכ"ך מ"ח פ"א ס"י, כה; אולם עי' שו"ת יחוה דעת ח"ב סי' מה שמתיר לחמם תבשיל צונן, שנתבשל כל צרכו בע"ש והיה מונח במקרר, על פלטה חשמלית אפילו חום שהיס"ב, ובלבד שרוב התבשיל יבש אף שיש בו קצת רוטב.

27. ש"ע או"ח סי' שיח ס"ח, משנה ברורה ס"ק ס; ששכ"ך מ"ח פ"א סל"ו.

28. משנה ברורה סי' שיח ס"ק קה.

29. ש"ע או"ח סי' רנג ס"א רמ"א שם ומשנה ברורה ס"ק כח, וש"ע הרב שם ס"ז; שו"ת

אגרות משה או"ח ח"א סי' צג; ועי' הל' שבת ח"ד דיני אופה ס"ק תרצט שכן דעת הגרי"א
הענקין ז"ל; ועי' תשובות הגר"מ פיינשטיין ז"ל שם אות לב; עי' כשרות ושבת במטבח
המודרני עמ' קפא.

30. ש"ע או"ח סי' רנג ס"ג מג"א שם ס"ק לא, משנה ברורה ס"ק פא, קג, שעה"צ ס"ק עה;
שו"ת אגרות משה או"ח ח"א סי' צג, וח"ד סי' עד ערך בישול אות כט, הל' שבת ח"ד
תשובות הגר"מ פיינשטיין שם אות לד; שו"ת יביע אומר ח"ו או"ח סי' לב; שו"ת ציץ
אליעזר ח"ח סי' כו; ששכ"ח מ"ח פ"א סכ"ד, כה; שו"ת באר משה ח"ו ק"ע סי' ב, ח"ז ק"ע
סי' ג, ד, שמ"ב מ"ת סי' ע"ב ס"ק מא; מקור חיים פ' קנ סכ"ח; כשרות ושבת במטבח
המודרני עמ' קפא.

31. רמב"ם הל' שבת פ"ג ה"י; ש"ע או"ח סי' רנג רמ"א שם, מגן אברהם ס"ק כג, ומשנה
ברורה ס"ק סב; שו"ת אגרות משה או"ח ח"ד סי' עד ערך בישול אות יב; שו"ת באר משה
ח"ו ק"ע סי' יב; שו"ת ציץ אליעזר חי"ב סי' צא.

32. חיי אדם כלל כ ס"ק.

33. שבת כ, א, כד, שיצלו מבעוד יום כמאכל בן דרוסאי, ועי' רש"י שם שהוא שליש בישולו;
ועי' טור או"ח סי' רנג וב"י שם; ובש"ע או"ח סי' רנד ס"ב פסק כרמב"ם שהוא חצי
בישולו, ועי' מג"א שם ס"ק ח דאע"ג דביו"ד סי' קיג ס"ח פסק כרש"י פסק הכא לחומרא
משום חומרא דשבת; ועי' ש"ע הרב סי' רנג סי"ג דבדיעבד יש להתיר התבשיל אם נתבשל
שליש בישולו מבעוד יום; ועי' משנה ברורה סי' רנג ס"ק לח; ששכ"ח מ"ח פ"א סס"ג.

34. ש"ע או"ח סי' רנז ס"א רמ"א שם, ומשנה ברורה ס"ק מח, מט.

35. כלכלת שבת כללי הטמנה ובישולי שבת אות ה, ש"ע או"ח סי' רנג ס"ב, ס"ד, מגן אברהם
ס"ק לב, משנה ברורה ס"ק נה, וסי' שיח ס"ד משנה ברורה ס"ק כד; תשובת הגר"מ
פיינשטיין ז"ל בס' הל' שבת ח"ד אות כד; תשובות הגר"מ שטערן בפסקי הל' שבת ח"ג
אות ג.

36. שו"ת אגרות משה או"ח ח"ד סי' עד ערך בישול אות כא, כב, כג; תשובות הגר"מ
פיינשטיין ז"ל בהל' שבת ח"ד אות כט; שו"ת ציץ אליעזר ח"ב סי' יח; שו"ת באר משה
ח"ז ק"ע סי' מא, קד; ששכ"ח מ"ח פ"א ס"מ.

37. ש"ע או"ח סי' רנג ס"ד מגן אברהם ס"ק לב; שו"ת אגרות משה או"ח ח"ד סי' עד ערך
בישול אות יג, תשובות הגר"מ פיינשטיין ז"ל בהל' שבת ח"ד אות כד; עי' שו"ת יחוה דעת
ח"ד סי' כב; ששכ"ח מ"ח פ"א סט"ז.

38. שבת לו, ב, רש"י ד"ה לא מחזירין תוס' ד"ה ובית הלל; ר"ן שם ד"ה איבעיא להו; עי' ש"ע
או"ח סי' רנג ס"ב; סי' שיח ס"ד; עי' כשרות ושבת במטבח המודרני ח"א פ"ה.

39. ש"ע או"ח סי' רנג ס"ב רמ"א שם, משנה ברורה ס"ק כג, סז, סח, עו; ערוך השלחן שם
סל"ג; ש"ע הרב שם סכ"א.

40. ש"ע או"ח סי' שיח סטו ומ"ב ס"ק צט; סי' רנג ס"ב משנה ברורה ס"ק נו, סה, שעה"צ ס"ק
נ, ובאור הלכה שם ד"ה ודעתו; כלכלת שבת, כללי הטמנה ובישולי שבת ב, עי' שו"ת אגרות
משה או"ח ח"ב סי' סט; ששכ"ח מ"ח פ"א ס"ד וס"ק סו; מקור חיים פ' קנ ס"ח, עי' כשרות
ושבת במטבח המודרני ח"א פ"ו דיון על העברת תבשילים מסירי בישול גדולים לכלים
קטנים שנתונים ע"ג מיתקנים מחזיקי חום חשמליים, בכדי למנוע קלקול מאכלי שבת ביחוד
במלונות ומוסדות, והצעות לפתרון הבעיה ההלכתית לגבי חשש איסור חזרה בנדון זה.

41. ש"ע או"ח סי' רנג ס"ב משנה ברורה ס"ק נז, נח, צב; חיי אדם כלל כ סי"ד; ועי' הל' שבת

ח"ד דיני אופה ס"ק תתקסג שמביא דעתו של הגר"א קטלר זצ"ל להתיר חזרה בתנורים
שלנו בתנאי חזרה, אבל דעת הגר"מ פיינשטיין זצ"ל לאסור, אלא שאם שם בתוך התנור
בלעך מד' דפנות כקופסא כמו שעושים בפסח מותר להחזיר, עי"ש תשובות הגרמ"פ אות
כו, כז, לב, לג; ועי' ששה"כ מ"ח פ"א סי"ז סכ"ט; קיצור הל' שבת כלל יא ס"ח תד"ו שם
ס"ק ח; ועי' ש"ע הרב סי' רנג סכ"א שדעתו לאסור חזרה לתוך התנור או לתוך הכירה אף
אם אין יד סולדת בו. עי' או"ח סי' רנג ס"ה מגן אברהם ס"ק לו ומשנה ברורה שם, ובה"ל
שם ד"ה להחם שמצדד להקל בדבר יבש שנתבשל כל צרכו ליתנו תוך התנור ע"י אינו יהודי
לצורך שבת ואין לו עצה אחרת, ועי' שערי תשובה סי' שיח סט"ו ס"ק ו; עי' כשרות ושבת
במטבח המודרני ח"ז שמצדד להחמיר שלא לפתוח את דלת התנור הפועל על בסיס
טרמוסטטי ושלא להכניס מאכלים קרים בתוכו בשעה שאין גוף החימום דלוק, אכן בשעה
שגוף החימום דלוק יש להקל בשינוי באופן מיקרי בלבד לצורך עונג שבת, עי"ש הצעות
טכניות לפתרון הבעיה, אולם עי' שו"ת אגרות משה או"ח ח"ד סי' עד ערך בישול אות כח
שהתיר לפתוח התנור כשאינו פועל משום שאינו פסיק רישא ואינו מתכוין.

42. ש"ע או"ח סי' רנז ס"ח, שעה"צ שם ס"ק מג, משנה ברורה סי' רנג ס"ק יח; תשובות
הגר"מ פיינשטיין ז"ל בהל' שבת ח"ד אות לג.

43. ש"ע או"ח סי' רנז ס"ב וס"ד, משנה ברורה שם ס"ק יד; שו"ת אגרות משה או"ח סי'
צה.

44. ש"ע או"ח סי' רנז ס"ה, משנה ברורה ס"ק כט; שו"ת מלמד להועיל או"ח סי' מה; שו"ת
אגרות משה או"ח ח"א סי' צה; שמ"ב סי' פ ס"ק יג וק"א שם; שו"ת ציץ אליעזר חי"א סי'
כט; שו"ת יביע אומר ח"א סי' יב; ששה"כ מ"ח פ"א ס"ע; מצודת דוד על קצש"ע סי' עב;
עי' קיצור הל' שבת כלל יא סכ"ו תד"ו ס"ק כד שיש לערותו מקודם לכלי שני ומשם
לטרמוס.

45. הל' שבת ח"ד פי"ד עמ' 399 והערות שם.

46. ש"ע או"ח סי' שיח ס"א, ב משנה ברורה ס"ק ד, יא.

47. עי' ש"ע או"ח סי' רנג ס"ה רמ"א שם ומשנה ברורה ס"ק צט, ק, בה"ל שם ד"ה להחם;
ערוך השלחן שם סל"ז; סי' רעו ס"ה משנה ברורה ס"ק מ; מגן אברהם סי' שי"ח סט"ו ס"ק
מב; שערי תשובה ס"ק ו; שו"ת אגרות משה או"ח ח"א סי' צד; ששה"כ מ"ח פ"א סי' צד,
פל"א ס"ח; הל' שבת ח"ד פי"ד עמ' 319, 368, 369.

Melachah 12. Shearing

גזיזה

כלכלת שבת, הגוזז; חיי אדם כלל כא

1. זכרו תורת משה סי' כה וקהלת יום טוב שם ס"ק א; עי' ששה"כ מ"ח פ"ג ס"ל.

2. ש"ע או"ח סי' שמ ס"א, משנה ברורה ס"ק א, ב; קיצור הל' שבת כלל יב, ס"ד וס"ה;
ששה"כ מ"ח סמ"א.

3. רמב"ם הל' שבת פ"ט ה"ט; חיי אדם כלל כא ס"ד; כלכלת שבת, הגוזז; קצש"ע סי' פ
סנ"ה; ששה"כ מ"ח פי"ד סנ"ד.

4. קיצור הל' שבת יב ס"י; ששה"כ מ"ח פי"ד סמ"ו.

5. ש"ע או"ח סי' שג סכ"ו, כז, משנה ברורה ס"ק פה-פח; שו"ת אגרות משה או"ח ח"ב סי'
עח; כללת שבת, הגוזז; שש"כ מ"ח פי"ד סמ"ד.

Melachah 13. Cleaning

ליבון

כללת שבת, המלבן; חיי אדם כלל כב; שלחן ערוך, הלכות שבת סימן שב

1. משנה ברורה סי' שב ס"ק נט; תוס' חיים על ח"א כלל כ ס"ק טז; יסודי ישרון מערכת הל'
שבת (תשל"ט) עמ' 367.

2. שו"ת אגרות משה ח"ב סי' ע.

3. מגן אברהם סי' שב ס"ק כז, ומשנה ברורה שם ס"ק ס, וסי' שכ ס"ק נה; שש"כ מ"ח פי"ב
סל"ז-מא; מקור חיים פ' קנב ס"ו.

4. שו"ת באר משה ח"א סי' מג אות ז; שש"כ מ"ח פי"ב סט"ו.

5. ש"ע או"ח סי' שב ס"י, עי' משנה ברורה ס"ק לט, ומגן אברהם שם ס"ק כא; כללת שבת,
המלבן.

6. חיי אדם כלל כב ס"ז; כללת שבת, המלבן; משנה ברורה סי' שא ס"ק קסד, ובאור הלכה
סי' שב ס"י ד"ה דלא אמרינן, ועי' סי' שכח רמ"א שם דצרכי קטן כחולה שאין בו
סכנה דמי, ולכן יש להתיר איסור דרבנן בשבילו ובלבד שיזהר שלא יסחוט. ועי' שו"ת באר
משה ח"א סי' לב אות יד, ח"ו סי' פ, ח"ז ק"ע סי' סא; שו"ת יחוה דעת ח"ג סי' יח;
ושש"כ מ"ח פט"ו סכ"ב שמותר ליתן בגדים המלוכלכים במכונת כביסה כשרגיל בכך ואין
לאסור לא משום הכנה ולא משום עובדא דחול.

7. ש"ע או"ח סי' שא סמ"ה-מז ומשנה ברורה ס"ק קע; חיי אדם כלל כב ס"ו; כללת שבת,
המלבן.

8. משנה ברורה סי' שכו ס"ק כה, שש"כ מ"ח פי"ד ס"כ.

9. ש"ע או"ח סי' שב ס"א, מג"א ס"ק ג, מ"ב ס"ק ו, באור הלכה שם ד"ה ועיין, סי' שב ס"ט,
סי' שלו ס"ב; חיי אדם כלל כב, ס"ט; כללת שבת, המלבן; שש"כ מ"ח פט"ו סכ"ה, כו. עי'
שו"ת יביע אומר ח"ד סי' לו.

10. ש"ע או"ח סי' שלו ס"ב רמ"א ובאור הלכה ד"ה שלא, וסי' שב ס"א רמ"א ובאור הלכה
ד"ה ועיין; שו"ת באר משה ח"א סי' לב; שו"ת מנחת יצחק ח"ה סי' לט אות א; שש"כ
מ"ח פכ"ג ס"ד; קה"ש כלל יב סי"ג ותד"ו ס"ק יג וכלל יג סי"ט.

11. ש"ע או"ח סי' שב ס"ו, ח, ט, ומשנה ברורה ס"ק לז; חיי אדם כלל כב סי"א; כללת
שבת, המלבן; שש"כ מ"ח פט"ו סל"ח-מ.

Melachah 14. Combing Raw Materials

ניפוץ

כללת שבת, המנפץ; חיי אדם כלל כג

Melachah 15. Dyeing

צביעה

כללת שבת, הצובע; חיי אדם כלל כד

1. רמב״ם הל׳ שבת פ״ט הי״ג; חיי אדם הל׳ שבת כלל כד ס״א ותוס׳ חיים שם ס״ק ב; משנה ברורה סי׳ שכ ס״ק נט; ועי׳ שבת צד, א, וצה, ב כוחלת משום צובעת, וחכמים אוסרים משום שבות כיון שצבע הכחל אינו מתקיים; ועי׳ שער הציון בסי׳ שג ס״ק סח דמספקא ליה אם בעינן שיהיה מתקיים תמיד או שדי אם מתקיים על יום השבת לחוד.

2. שו״ת יחוה דעת ח״ב סי׳ מז; שו״ת באר משה ח״ו סי׳ מו; עי׳ שו״ת אגרות משה או״ח ח״ג סי׳ מה דאין בזה איסור משום צובע או מתקן מנא.

3. שו״ת ציץ אליעזר חי״ד סי׳ מז דאין לחוש לצביעה ולא למוליד ריחא דאין צביעה באוכלין ומשקין ואין כוונתו לצביעה רק לניקוי, וגם למעשה הוא מושך המים שכבר נצבעים במיכל, ורק בגרמתו נכנסים מים חדשים אל המיכל שנצבעים לאח״כ ע״י החומר המונח שם, ואין מכוין לעצם הריח כי אם שריח זה יעביר הריח הרע, עי׳ שו״ת באר משה ח״ח סי׳ כב וסי׳ כה שטוב להחמיר אלא שמתיר אם מצטמצם מריח רע בבית.

4. ש״ע או״ח סי׳ שכ סי״ט, ס״כ, משנה ברורה ס״ק נו; חיי אדם הל׳ שבת כלל כד ס״ה ותוס׳ חיים ס״ק ו.

5. ש״ע או״ח סי׳ שג סכ״ה מ״ב ס״ק עט ושעה״צ ס״ק סח; חיי אדם הל׳ שבת כלל כד ס״ב; רמב״ם הל׳ שבת פ״ט הי״ג פכ״ב הכ״ג, ועי׳ רמב״ם פכ״ג הי״ב שאסור לכחול מפני שהוא ככותב, ועי׳ רש״י שבת צד, ב, שמפרש שמוליך המכחול סביב העין כאדם המוליך קולמוס סביב האות, וצ״ע שהגירסא במסקנת הגמרא שבת צה, א היא „כוחלת משום צובעת״. אבל עי׳ בעין משפט נר מצוה שם שאפשר שהגירסא הנכונה היא „כוחלת משום כותב״, ועי׳ רמב״ם הוצ׳ מוסד הרב קוק עם פירוש לעם שם הערה עא שכך היא הגירסא בכ״י מינכן, עי׳ ערוך השלחן או״ח סי׳ שג ס״ל של״ד כך היתה גירסת הרמב״ם בגמרא, וכן הגירסא בערוך. עי׳ שו״ת אגרות משה או״ח ח״א סי׳ קיד; שו״ת יחוה דעת ח״ד סי׳ כח; ובשו״ת יביע אומר או״ח ח״ו סי׳ לז מתיר לנשים לתת אבקת פודרה צבעונית על פניהם בשבת כיון שאינו דבר המתקיים ואין צביעה בעור אדם ובזה לא גזרו חכמים; ועי׳ שש״כ מ״ח פי״ד סנ״ז, נח, נט דנכון שלא לתת פודרת איפור על הפנים, ועי׳ שו״ת באר משה ח״ח סי׳ כה באחד שבתו צובעת פניה ואת השפתחים ואביה בקשה שלא לעשות כן בשבת, דאם יודע בבירור שלא יועיל מוטב שתהי׳ שוגגת, ועי׳ מגן אברהם סי׳ שג ס״ק יט שצביעת אשה אינו אלא איסור דרבנן.

6. ש״ע או״ח סי׳ שכ ס״כ משנה ברורה ס״ק נט, ועי׳ באר היטב שם ס״ק כב ש מ״ש בשם אליה רבה; זכרו תורת משה סי׳ כח וקהלת יו״ט שם ס״ק ג; שש״כ מ״ח פי״ד סי״ט.

7. ש״ע או״ח סי׳ שכח סמ״ח, מחצית השקל ס״ק נד, משנה ברורה ס״ק קמו; חיי אדם הל׳ שבת כלל כד ס״ו; שש״כ מ״ח פל״ה סי״ח; מקור חיים פ׳ קעג סנ״ה.

Melachah 16. Spinning

טוייה

כלכלת שבת, הטווה; חיי אדם כלל כה

1. רמב״ם הל׳ שבת פ״ט ה״ז; משנה ברורה סי׳ שמ ס״ק ה, שעה״צ ס״ק יב.

Melachah 17. Stretching the Threads

הנסכת המסכת

כלכלת שבת, המסיך; חיי אדם כלל כה

Melachah 18. Making Meshes

עשיית הנירין

כלכלת שבת, העושה שתי בתי נירין; חיי אדם כלל כה

Melachah 19. Weaving

אריגה

כלכלת שבת, האורג; חיי אדם כלל כה

1. ש״ע או״ח סי׳ שג סכ״ו, מג״א ס״ק כ, משנה ברורה ס״ק פב, וסוף סי׳ שדם אות ו; חיי אדם כלל כה ס״ו, וכלל מד ס״י; כלכלת שבת, האורג.

Melachah 20. Separating the Threads

בציעה

כלכלת שבת, הפוצע שני חוטין; חיי אדם כלל כה

1. מנוחה נכונה פ״ג ס״כ; שש״כ פי״ד סכ״ט, פל״ה סי״ט.

Melachah 21. Tying a Knot

קשירה

כלכלת שבת, הקושר והמתיר; חיי אדם כלל כו, כז, שלחן ערוך, הלכות שבת סימן שיז

1. שבת קיא, ב, רש״י שם; רמב״ם הל׳ שבת פ״י ה״א; ש״ע או״ח סי׳ שיז ס״א, משנה ברורה שם בהקדמה ובס״ק ו; חיי אדם כלל כו, כז ס״א וס״ב ותוס׳ חיים שם ס״ק א; כלכלת שבת, המתיר; שש״כ מ״ח פט״ו סנ״ב.

2. ש״ע או״ח סי׳ שיז ס״ב וס״ה, מגן אברהם ס״ק ז, יא, טו, ומשנה ברורה ס״ק ז, טז, יח, כט, ש״ע שם ס״א; שש״כ מ״ח פט״ו, ס״ס, ועי׳ שם שאוסר בשרוך חדש אא״כ בשעת הדחק

ושעתיד להוציאו, אבל עי' שו"ת הגר"מ שטערן בפסקי הל' שבת ח"ב שאלה לג שמתיר
להכניס שרוך חדש בנעל ואפילו בנעל חדש, אם יכולים להכניסו בנקל, ואין בזה איסור
משום מתקן מנא בנעלים שלנו דלא דמי למנעלים שלהם שהיו עשוים פרקים והיו
מתחברים ע"י הרצועה.

3. שש"כ מ"ח פט"ו. סנ"ח; שו"ת הגר"מ שטערן בפסקי הל' שבת ח"ג שאלה נז.

Melachah 22. Untying a Knot

התרה

כלכלת שבת, המתיר; חיי אדם כלל כו, כז

1. כלכלת שבת, המתיר; חיי אדם כלל כו, כז ס"ב; מג"א סי' שיז ס"ק יא.

2. חיי אדם כלל כו, כז ס"ה; כלכלת שבת, המתיר; משנה ברורה סי' שיז ס"ק ז; שש"כ מ"ח
פט"ו סי"ד, טו.

Melachah 23. Sewing

תפירה

כלכלת שבת, התופר; חיי אדם כלל כח

1. ש"ע או"ח סי' שמ ס"ו, משנה ברורה ס"ק כז, שעה"צ ס"ק ס, דאסור מדרבנן אפילו בלא
קשר; שש"כ מ"ח פט"ו סס"ז.

2. שבת קיא, ב; ש"ע או"ח סי' שמ ס"ז משנה ברורה ס"ק כט; חיי אדם כלל כח ס"ב, כלכלת
שבת, התופר; שו"ת אג"מ או"ח ח"ב סי' פד.

3. חיי אדם כלל כח ס"ה; תורת השבת פ"ז סי' כג ס"ב; שש"כ מ"ח פכ"ח, ס"ה.

4. שו"ת באר משה ח"ו סי' יד, טו; שש"כ מ"ח פט"ו ספ"א.

5. משנה ברורה סי' שמ ס"ק כז; תוס' חיים על חיי אדם כלל כח ס"ק ג; מקור חיים פ' קנז
ס"ד; שו"ת אגרות משה או"ח ח"ב סי' פד; ועי' שו"ת באר משה ח"ב סי' כט שלא לתוחבו
יותר משתי תכיפות אף שמעיקר הדין מותר שאין זה דומה לתפירה, ועי' תשובתו בפסקי
הל' שבת ח"ב שאלה ב.

6. שש"כ מ"ח פט"ו סע"ד.

Melachah 24. Tearing

קריעה

כלכלת שבת, הקורע; חיי אדם כלל כט

1. רמב"ם הל' שבת פכ"ב הכ"ד; חיי אדם הל' שבת כלל כט ס"ג, משנה ברורה סי' שמ ס"ק
מה.

2. שש"כ מ"ח פ"ט ס"ט והערה לד, פכ"ח ס"ה והערה יז, דבחיבור הסיכות הוה ע"מ לתקן,

אבל בהסרתן קיל טפי מכיון שאינן תפורות ואינן של קיימא, שהשקית והמעטפה עומדת להפתח.

3. כלכלת שבת, המחתך; משנה ברורה סי' שמ ס"ק מא; וע" מקור חיים פ' קנז ס"י ופ' קסד ס"ב דאיסורו משום קורע כשקורע סתם, וכשקורע במקום המנוקב שהוא חיתוך לפי מדה איסורו משום מחתך, ובתורת השבת פ"ח סי' כד ס"ד מביא בשם הרה"ר לישראל רב"צ עוזיאל ז"ל להתיר בניר המנוקב אם שכח ולא הכינו מע"ש משום דנקביו מעידים עליו שעומדים להפרד זמ"ז; וע" שמ"ב מ"ת סי' פח ס"ק כב וקונטרס אחרון שם; וע" שו"ת ציץ אליעזר חי"א סי' ל שיעשה ע"י שינוי; ושש"כ מ"ח פ"ט סכ"ה.

4. מג"א סי' שז ס"ק כ, משנה ברורה שם ס"ק נו, ושעה"צ ס"ק סז, וע" שערי תשובה שם ס"ק ה דלצורך גדול מתיר אפילו ע"י ישראל, ובסי' שם מ"ב ס"ק מא ובאור הלכה ד"ה הניר דלצורך גדול יש להקל ע"י נכרי; שמ"ב מ"ת סי' פ סס"ק מו.

5. חיי אדם כלל כט ס"ד, כלכלת שבת, מלאכת התופר והקורע; מג"א סי' שיד ס"ק יד; ערוך השלחן שם ס"ח; שו"ת באר משה ח"ו סי' פט, וסי' צא; מ"ח פ"ט; שו"ת הגר"מ שטערן שליט"א בפסקי הל' שבת ח"א אות ג, ה; שש"כ מ"ח פ"ט, וע" שו"ת אגרות משה ח"א סי' קכב שדעתו להחמיר בקופסאות ובפחים שרגילים להשתמש בהם אחרי פתיחתם והוצאת תוכנם אם לא לצורך גדול, וע" שם סי' צג, ובח"ד סי' עח שנוטה לאסור למעשה; וע" שש"כ מ"ח פ"ט סי"ז שמביא דעת הגרש"ז אויערבך שליט"א לאסור להסיר את מכסה הפח מבקבוק אשר עם פתיחתו נעשה ראוי לתשמיש כפקק; וע" שו"ת ציץ אליעזר ח"ו סי' לה, חי"ד סי' מה; ושו"ת יחוה דעת ח"ב סי' מב שדעתם להתיר משום שכבר נקרא עליו שם כלי לפני הידוקו בצואר הבקבוק; וע" ספר משנה הלכות ח"ז סי' מז שנוטה להתיר.

6. מג"א סי' שם ס"ק יח ומשנה ברורה שם ס"ק מה; חיי אדם כלל כט ס"ב; כלכלת שבת, התופר.

Melachah 25. Trapping

צידה

כלכלת שבת, הצד; חיי אדם כלל ל; שלחן ערוך, הלכות שבת סי' שטז

1. רמב"ם הל' שבת פ"י הכ"ד ומגיד משנה שם; משנה ברורה סי' שטז ס"ק כה.

2. רמב"ם הל' שבת פ"ג ה"ב; ש"ע או"ח סי' רנב ס"א, משנה ברורה ס"ק ז, ובסי' שטז ס"ק יח.

3. חיי אדם כלל ל ס"ט, כלל לא ס"ב; כלכלת שבת, הצד; משנה ברורה סי' שטז ס"ק ד, יג, לג; ש"ע או"ח סי' שכה ס"ה, ו, ואם האינו יהודי צד דגים בשבת בשביל ישראל אסורים לישראל בו ביום וצריך להמתין לערב בכדי שיעשו.

4. חיי אדם כלל ל ס"ד; משנה ברורה סי' שטז ס"ק נז; קצש"ע סי' פז סכ"א.

5. ש"ע או"ח סי' שטז ס"ב, מגן אברהם שם ס"ק ה, באר היטב ס"ק ג; משנה ברורה ס"ק יא; חיי אדם כלל ל ס"ה, ותוס' חיים שם ס"ק ה.

6. ש"ע או"ח סי' רנב ס"א, סי' ש"ח סל"ד ומשנה ברורה שם ס"ק קל, סי' שטז ס"ד מגן אברהם שם ס"ק ט, ומשנה ברורה שם ס"ק יח, שש"כ מ"ח פכ"ז סמ"ב, פכ"ה ס"ו, ז.

7. ש"ע או"ח סי' שטז ס"י משנה ברורה ס"ק מד, מה.

8. ש"ע או"ח סי' שטז ס"ט, ס"י, משנה ברורה ס"ק כז, לו, לז, מב, מו, כלכלת שבת, הצד;
ששכ"ג מ"ח פכ"ה ס"א–ג.

Melachah 26. Slaughtering

שחיטה

כלכלת שבת, השוחט; חיי אדם כלל לא

1. רמב"ם הל' שבת פכ"ה ה"ח; ש"ע או"ח סי' שח סי"א ובה"ל שם ד"ה הקרץ; מג"א סי'
שכח ס"ק לב ומ"ב ס"ק פח; ששכ"ג מ"ח פל"ה סי"ז.

2. ש"ע או"ח סי' שכח ס"ג, מג"א ס"ק ג, מ"ב ס"ק י-יב ובסי' שטז ס"ק ל, ועי' בה"ל סי'
שכח סי"ג ד"ה ומצטער, ש"ע הרב שם ס"ג; ששכ"ג מ"ח פל"ח ס"ז ופל"ח ס"ה; ועי' מקור
חיים פ' קעג סי"ג, ושו"ת ציץ אליעזר ח"ח סי' טו פ"י שאם יקבע רופא שמטעם סכנה יש
הכרח מיידי בעקירת השן מותר גם ע"י ישראל.

3. ש"ע או"ח סי' שכח ס"ח מ"ב ס"ק ל; ששכ"ג מ"ח פ"מ סכ"ה, כז.

4. ש"ע או"ח סי' שטז ס"ט, מג"א סק"ט, משנה ברורה ס"ק יח, מח; ששכ"ג מ"ח פכ"ה ס"ד,
ה; קיצור הל' שבת תד"ו ס"ק ה; מנוחה נכונה פ"ג סכ"ו ע"פ פסקי חזון איש; שו"ת באר
משה ח"ב סי' כג.

5. מקור חיים פ' קסא ס"ח; ששכ"ג מ"ח פכ"ה ס"ו.

6. מקור חיים פ' קסא ס"ו דהוה פסיק רישיה.

Melachah 27. Skinning

הפשטה

כלכלת שבת, המפשיט; חיי אדם כלל לב, לג

1. שבת עט, ב, תוס' שם ד"ה קלף; רמב"ם הל' תפילין פ"א ה"ר–ח; משנה ברורה סי' שכו ס"ק
טז.

Melachah 28. Tanning

עיבוד העור

כלכלת שבת, המולח והמעבד; חיי אדם כלל לב, לג

1. משנה ברורה סי' שכא ס"ק כא.

2. חיי אדם הל' שבת כלל לב, לג ס"י; כלכלת שבת, המולח; משנה ברורה סי' שכא ס"ק כא.

Melachah 29. Marking

שרטוט

כלכלת שבת, המשרטט; חיי אדם כלל לד, לה

1. משנה ברורה סי' רעד ס"ק ה; שש"כ מ"ח פי"א סט"ו.

2. ש"ע או"ח סי' שמ ס"ה ומשנה ברורה שם; חיי אדם כלל לז ס"ג; ש"ע הרב סי' שם ס"ז.
   עי' מקור חיים פ' קסה ס"ב שמתיר לרשום בצפורן על הספר לסימן שאין זה דבר המתקיים.

3. קיצור הל' שבת כלל ל תד"ו ס"ק ג; מנוחה נכונה פ"ג סי' ל.

Melachah 30. Scraping and Smoothening

מחיקת העור

כלכלת שבת, הממחק; חיי אדם כלל לד, לה.

1. ש"ע או"ח סי' שכג ס"ט משנה ברורה ס"ק לח, לט; שש"כ מ"ח פי"ב סי"ד; שו"ת הגר"מ
   שטערן אות יב בפסקי הל' שבת ח"ג.

2. כלכלת שבת, הממחק; שש"כ מ"ח פל"ג סי"ד, פל"ה ס"ח; שו"ת באר משה ח"א סי' לו
   אות ד, ח"ב ל, ח"ד סי' צב אות ז; שו"ת הגר"מ שטערן שליט"א אות מ בפה"ש ח"ג.

3. שו"ע או"ח סי' שכו ס"א, משנה ברורה סי' שג ס"ק פא, סי' שכח ס"ק ע; שו"ת באר משה
   ח"א סי' יט; שו"ת אגרות משה או"ח ח"א סי' קיד; שו"ת הגר"מ שטערן שליט"א אות מא
   בפה"ש ח"ג, שש"כ מ"ח פי"ד סמ"ח; קיצור הל' שבת כלל כט ס"ד.

4. ש"ע או"ח סי' קכח קכה משנה ברורה ס"ק כג, וסי' תקיא תקיא ס"ד ברמ"א שם; שו"ת באר משה
   ח"ב סי' כג; שו"ת הגר"מ שטערן בפה"ש ח"ג סי' לט; שש"כ מ"ח פי"ד סל"ב, נא, עי"ש
   הערה צב, דבגוף האדם לא שייך בו משום מוליד ריח, אולם בש"ע הרב סי' תקיא ס"ז וכף
   החיים ס"ק מד מחמירים.

5. ש"ע או"ח סי' שכו ס"י משנה ברורה ס"ק ל; שש"כ מ"ח פי"ד סט"ז; מקור חיים פ' קסג
   ס"ד; ועי' שו"ת אגרות משה או"ח ח"א סי' קיג שראוי להחמיר אפילו בסבון נזיל.

6. עי' שו"ת ציץ אליעזר ח"ז סי' ל דעתו לאסור במשחת שיניים; עי' מקור חיים פ' קסא
   סי"ב; שש"כ מ"ח פי"ד סל"ד; שו"ת יביע אומר ח"ד סי' כז-ל; ועי' שו"ת שרידי אש ח"ב
   סי' כח; שו"ת אגרות משה או"ח ח"א סי' קיב שמתיר בלי משחה ומבלי ללחלח המברשת
   במים.

7. ש"ע או"ח סי' שב ס"ו-ט, משנה ברורה ס"ק כו, ובה"ל שם ד"ה או על מנעליו, משנה
   ברורה סי' שכו ס"ק טז ושעה"צ שם ס"ק יז; ערוך השלחן סי' שכו ס"ד; חיי אדם כלל לה,
   לו ס"ג; כלכלת שבת, הממחק; קצש"ע סי' פ ס"מ; שמ"ב סי' פ ס"ק יט; שש"כ מ"ח פט"ו
   סל"ז-מ, ובעכו"ם אסור למוצאי שבת שיעשה בכדי שיעשה ככל מלאכה שעשה העכו"ם לצורך
   ישראל.

8. ש"ע או"ח סי' שיד ס"א, משנה ברורה סי' שכא ס"ק נ; שש"כ מ"ח פט"ז סי"ג; מקור חיים
   פ' קסג ס"ה.

Melachah 31. Cutting

חיתוך העור

כלכלת שבת, המחתך; חיי אדם כלל לו

1. ש"ע או"ח סי' שמ סי"ג, משנה ברורה ס"ק מא; שו"ת ציץ אליעזר חי"א סי' ל; שש"כ מ"ח פ"ט סכ"ה, פי"ד סכ"א, פכ"ג סט"ז.

2. חיי אדם כלל לו ס"ג; משנה ברורה סי' שכב ס"ק יב, יח; שש"כ מ"ח פי"א סי"ב, סט"ו.

Melachah 32. Writing

כתיבה

כלכלת שבת, הכותב; חיי אדם כלל לז; שלחן ערוך, הלכות שבת סימן שו, שז

1. משנה, שבת פי"א מ"א, רש"י, ר"ן ורע"ב שם, ופי"ב מ"ה; רמב"ם הל' שבת פי"ג הי"ג, ופי"א הט"ו, ועי' מגיד משנה שם; ושער הציון שו"ע או"ח סי' שג סכ"ו ס"ק סח.

2. רמב"ם הל' שבת פי"א הי"ד, משנה ברורה סי' שמ ס"ק כד.

3. שמ"ב מ"ת סי' פ ס"ק נח; קיצור הל' שבת כלל תד"ו ס"ק ט, כ; ועי' מג"א סי' שמ ס"ק י.

4. שמ"ב מ"ת סי' פ ס"ק נז.

5. שש"כ מ"ח פט"ז סכ"ו, שמ"ב מ"ת סי' פ ס"ק נד בשם הגר"י שטייף ז"ל.

6. שש"כ מ"ח פט"ז סכ"ה.

7. שו"ת אגרות משה או"ח ח"ד סי' מ אות י.

8. שמ"ב מ"ת סי' פ ס"ק נה.

9. קיצור הל' שבת כלל לב ס"ק תד"ו שם; שו"ת באר משה ח"ז ק"ע קין; עי' שו"ת מנחת יצחק ח"ב סי' לח; ועי' יסודי ישרון ח"ה עמ' מה, קכ; ושו"ת יחוה דעת ח"ב סי' נז.

10. שש"כ מ"ח פט"ז סכ"ב.

11. חיי אדם כלל לז ס"ה; משנה ברורה סי' שו ס"ק מז.

12. שש"כ מ"ח פי"א סי"ד, פט"ז סכ"ז; שו"ת הגר"מ שטערן בפה"ש ח"ג שאלה א, ב; שו"ת באר משה ח"ו סי' מג.

13. שו"ת ציץ אליעזר חי"ג סי' מד; שמ"ב מ"ת סי' פ ס"ק סב; תשובות הגר"מ שטערן בפה"ש ח"ג שאלה נד.

14. חיי אדם כלל לז ס"ו; שש"כ מ"ח פט"ז סכ"ג, וסכ"ד; שו"ת באר משה ח"ו סי' כו, עב; שו"ת הגר"מ שטערן בפסקי הל' שבת ח"א שאלה כא, ח"ב שאלה ו, וח"ג שאלה עט; מקור חיים פ' קסה ס"ב; ועי' שו"ת אגרות משה או"ח ח"א סי' קלה.

15. שו"ת אגרות משה או"ח ח"א סי' קלה.

16. משנה ברורה סי' שכב ס"ק יח.

17. שו"ת חתם סופר, חושן משפט סי' קצה, ע"פ הרמב"ן ויקרא כג, כד, והמכילתא שמות יב, יז.

18. בבא קמא פ, ב, גיטין ח, ב, "ואע"ג דאמירה לעכו"ם שבות, משום ישוב ארץ ישראל לא גזרו רבנן", ועי' רש"י בגיטין שם ד"ה משום ישוב א"י, "לגרש עכו"ם ולישב ישראל בה".

עי' ש"ע או"ח סי' שו סי"א ומשנה ברורה שם, ועי' מג"א ס"ק יט, מ"ש בשם הריב"ש
והרא"ש דכשקנה מע"ש אז מותר לומר לעכו"ם לכתוב בשבת.

19. ש"ע או"ח סי' שו ס"ד, ס"ה, ומשנה ברורה שם, ועי' מג"א סי' תקפה ס"ק יב; מקור חיים
פ' קסה סכ"ד, כה; עי' שו"ת ציץ אליעזר ח"ז סי' כח, שלפי הרבה מגדולי הפוסקים מותר
גמור הוא השכירה לדבר מצוה ולצורך שבת ובפרט כשהוא לשם תפילה לזכות את הרבים.

20. משנה שבת פכ"ג מ"א; רמב"ם הל' שבת פכ"ג הל' יב; ש"ע או"ח סי' שז סי"א, משנה
ברורה ס"ק מב, מג.

21. ש"ע או"ח סי' שז סי"א, מג"א סי' שו ס"ק טז, וסי' שכה ס"ק ח, כלכלת שבת, המוחק.

22. שמ"ב מ"ת סי' פ ס"ק נג.

23. חיי אדם כלל ג סי"א, שו"ת אגרות משה או"ח ח"ג סי' מו; שמ"ב מ"ת סי' עג ס"ק ה;
ששכ"ז מ"ח פל"א ס"כ; קצוה"ש כלל לב תד"ו ס"ק יט.

24. משנה ברורה סי' שו ס"ק לג; קה"ש כלל לב, ס"ק לח; ועי' מקור חיים ח"ג פ' קסה סכ"ו;
וששכ"ז מ"ח פכ"ד סכ"ט; שו"ת שרידי אש ח"ב סי' כו; שו"ת יחוה דעת ח"ג סי' כא, וטוב
שיקנה לו את המתנה ע"י אחר מבעוד יום.

25. ש"ע או"ח סי' רמ"א שלט ס"ד ומשנה ברורה שם, והוא שלא קיים פו"ר, וכבר הכינו צרכי
סעודה ויש הפסד רב, וגם ביוש לחתן וכלה, ובאין כל התנאים הנזכרים אין להתיר, ובבין
השמשות אין להחמיר בדיעבד, ועי' חיי אדם כלל לח סי' שרמ"א התיר בתשובה והוא
בעצמו סידר הקדושין מפני שגדול כבוד הבריות.

26. חיי אדם כלל לח ס"ק יא; ש"ע או"ח סי' שלח ס"ה מגן אברהם ס"ק ח ומשנה ברורה ס"ק
כא ועי"ש דנוהגין לעשות השח"מט מכסף שיהיו מיוחדין לשבת; שו"ת באר משה ח"ב סי'
כז, ח"ו סי' עב, וסי' ק; שו"ת הגר"מ שטערן בפסקי הל' שבת ח"א סי' כא, וח"ג סי' עט;
ששכ"ז מ"ח פט"ז סי' כ"ג, ל"א לב, לד; עי' שו"ת אגרות משה או"ח ח"א סי' קלה; שו"ת
מנחת יצחק ח"ג סי' לג.

27. שבת קנ, א; רמב"ם הל' שבת פכ"ג סי"ח; ש"ע או"ח סי' שו ס"ו ומשנה ברורה שם.

Melachah 33. Erasing

מחיקה

כלכלת שבת, המוחק; חיי אדם כלל לח

1. ש"ע הרב סי' שמ ס"ד; שמ"ב מ"ת סי' פ ס"ק סב, שו"ת אגרות משה ח"ד סי' מ אות כב.

2. שו"ת הרמ"א סי' קיט; חיי אדם כלל לח ס"ה, כלכלת שבת, המוחק; מג"א סי' שמ ס"ק ו,
ש"ע הרב שם ס"ד, משנה ברורה שם ס"ק יז ושעה"צ שם; שו"ת ציץ אליעזר חי"ג סי' מד.

3. ששכ"ז מ"ח פי"א ס"ז, ועי"ש פ"ט הערה מח מ"ש בענין לחתוך בין האותיות, דאולי אין
לאסור בכזה וצ"ע; ועי' מקור חיים פ' קסה ס"ו שיכול לחתוך בין תיבה לתיבה אבל לא בין
האותיות שבתיבה; ועי' שערי תשובה סי' שמ ס"ג ס"ק א בשם דגול מרבבה שכתב היתר
גמור בעיקר הדין, והמחמיר לא יחמיר לאחרים.

4. משנה ברורה סי' שמ ס"ק טו, יז, ושעה"צ ס"ק כב, ויזהר שלא לשבור בידו רק בפיו דרך
אכילה; שו"ת באר משה ח"ו סי' צב; שו"ת ציץ אליעזר חי"א סי' כ; ששכ"ז מ"ח פי"א
ס"ח.

Melachah 34. Building

בנייה

כללכת שבת, הבונה; חיי אדם כלל לט-מב; שלחן ערוך, הלכות שבת סימן שיג-שטו

1. שו״ת ציץ אליעזר חי״ג סי׳ ל; שו״ת יחווה דעת ח״ב סי׳ נה; שש״כ מ״ח פט״ז סי״ח; שו״ת הגר״מ שטערן אות ד בפה״ש ח״ב; מקור חיים פ׳ קנח סי״ג.

2. ש״ע או״ח סי׳ שז סי״ז; שש״כ מ״ח פט״ז סמ״ה; שו״ת הגר״מ שטערן אות לז בפסקי הל׳ שבת ח״ג; מקור חיים פ׳ קנח סי״ב.

3. חיי אדם כלל לט ס״א; כללכת שבת מלאכת הבונה; קצשו״ע סי׳ פ סכ״ה; שש״כ מ״ח פי״א סי״א, יב.

4. ש״ע או״ח סי׳ שטו ס״ה, משנה ברורה ס״ק כג, כז; כללכת שבת, הבונה; שש״כ מ״ח פכ״ד סכ״ג.

5. שש״כ מ״ח פכ״ד סכ״ג; קה״ש כלל לד ס״ק יח, כ; שו״ת הגר״מ שטערן בפה״ש ח״ג סי׳ כ-כב.

6. שש״כ מ״ח פכ״ד סי״ג עפ״י החזון איש; שו״ת באר משה ח״ו סי׳ צז; עי׳ שו״ת אגרות משה או״ח ח״ד סי׳ קה אות ג שיש להחמיר שיהיה פרוס לרוחב טפח מבעוד יום; עי׳ משנה ברורה סי׳ שטו סי״א.

7. כללכת שבת, הבונה; שו״ת נודע ביהודה מהדורא תנינא סי׳ ל; חיי אדם כלל מב ס״ל; שערי תשובה סי׳ שא ס״ק ה; באור הלכה סי׳ שטו ס״ח ד״ה טפח, שש״כ מ״ח פכ״ד סט״ו; שו״ת יחוה דעת ח״ב סי׳ מג; ספר מנוחה נכונה פ״ג סי׳ לד; שו״ת באר משה ח״ו סי׳ קח; מקור חיים פ׳ קנח סכ״ח; ועי׳ שו״ת חתם סופר או״ח סי׳ עב.

8. ש״ע או״ח סי׳ שח סמ״ה, רמ״א שם ומ״ב שם ס״ק קנד; שש״כ מ״ח פט״ז ס״ו; ועי׳ שו״ת באר משה ח״ב סי׳ כז.

9. שש״כ מ״ח פי״ד סמ״ד, נב, נג, פי״ח ס״ח; קה״ש כלל לד סנ״ג.

10. מגן אברהם סי׳ שג ס״ק כג; שו״ת באר משה ח״א סי׳ לד, ח״ד סי׳ כו; עי׳ שש״כ מ״ח פי״ד סמ״ח, נ, נא שמתיר להתיז מי בושם על השערות, אבל לא על פאה נכרית דאית ביה משום מוליד ריח.

11. שבת צד, ב ותוס׳ שם ד״ה וכי דרך, צה, א; רמב״ם הל׳ שבת פכ״ב הל׳ כו; טוש״ע או״ח סי׳ שג סכ״ו; משנה ברורה שם ס״ק פב, ועי׳ בית יוסף שם ד״ה וכי ומ״ש שמביא בשם הכל בו דמוטב שיהיו שוגגות שא״א למנען שלא יתגנו על בעליהן, אולם עי׳ דרכי משה שם דנשי דידן נזהרין.

Melachah 35. Demolishing

סתירה

כללכת שבת, הסותר; חיי אדם כלל מג, מד; שלחן ערוך, הלכות שבת סימן שיד

1. מגן אברהם סי׳ שיד ס״ק יא; חיי אדם הל׳ שבת כלל מג ס״א ותוספות חיים שם ס״ק א, כללכת שבת, הסותר; משנה ברורה סי׳ שיד, ס״ק לז, וסי׳ שכח ס״ק לח, ועי׳ בשערי תשובה

סי' שיד ס"ז, ובמקום מצוה כגון שנאבד המפתח של ארון הקודש יש מתירין להביא עכו"ם
לשבור המנעול כיון דמקלקל הוא ושבות דשבות במקום מצוה לא גזרו רבנן.

2. שש"כ מ"ח פכ"ד ס"י וס"ג; ש"ע או"ח סי' תרכו ס"ג רמ"א שם; ומשנה ברורה סי' תרמ
   ס"ק כה.

3. משנה ברורה סי' שיד ס"ק יז, שש"כ מ"ח פ"ט ס"כ; עי' כללת שבת, הסותר.

4. מקור חיים פ' קנה סט"ו; שו"ת אגרות משה ח"א סי' צג, קכב, ח"ד סי' עח; שו"ת באר
   משה ח"ו סי' פט, צא; שש"כ מ"ח פ"ט.

Melachah 36. Kindling a Fire

הבערה

כללת שבת, המבעיר; חיי אדם כלל מה, מו

1. שש"כ מ"ח פי"ג ס"א; יסודי ישרון ח"ה עמ' קכד.

2. שו"ת יחוה דעת ח"ב סי' מו; שו"ת ציץ אליעזר ח"ז סי' י; שו"ת באר משה ח"ו ק"ע סי'
   לז; יסודי ישרון ח"ה (תשכ"ו) עמ' קכט, דניצוצות אלה אינם ראוים להבעיר, ועי' שש"כ
   מ"ח פט"ו סע"ב, ופכ"ב הערה קם דמוליד שאינו מתכוין ואין בו ממשות מותר.

3. חיי אדם כלל מה-מו סי"ד ותוס' חיי שם; לחם הפנים על קצש"ע סי' פ ס"ק ט; משנה
   ברורה סי' ערה ס"ק ד ובה"ל ד"ה לאור הנר; שו"ת יחוה דעת ח"ג סי' כ; שו"ת יביע אומר
   ח"א סי' טז; שו"ת באר משה ח"ו ק"ע סי' כא וח"ז ק"ע סי' מ; שש"כ מ"ח פי"ג סל"ב;
   יסודי ישרון מערכת הל' שבת תשל"ט עמ' 278.

4. שו"ת באר משה ח"א סי' מג אות ח.

5. ש"ע או"ח סי' רעו ס"ה משנה ברורה שם; שש"כ מ"ח פכ"ג סכ"ד.

6. שמ"ב מ"ח פ"ח סי' פ ס"ק ג; שו"ת מנחת יצחק ח"ג סי' כד; שש"כ מ"ח פכ"ג ס"כ כא, ועי"ש
   שאין להנמיך בשבת את פעולת החימום באמצעות הטרמוסטאט אלא דוקא בזמן שפעולת
   החימום מופסקת, ועי' הערה סח שם דלית ביה משום מוקצה.

7. חיי אדם כלל מה, מו סי"ג; עי' שו"ת באר משה ח"ז ק"ע סי' קו, שש"כ מ"ח פ"א סכ"ט,
   ויסודי ישרון ח"ה עמ' קכ"א; אבל עי' שו"ת אגרות
   משה או"ח ח"ד סי' עד ערך בישול אות כח, ותשובות הגר"מ פיינשטיין זצ"ל בספר הלכות
   שבת ח"ד שאלה לג שאין לאסור לפתוח דלת התנור כשהאש נסגר דאין בזה פסיק רישא
   והוא דבר שאין מתכוין, ועי' שו"ת מנחת יצחק ח"ג סי' כד.

8. ש"ע או"ח סי' רעז ס"ב, משנה ברורה שם; כללת שבת המבעיר; חיי אדם כלל מה-מו
   סי"ב; יסודי ישרון ח"ה (תשכ"ו) עמ' קס.

9. שו"ת מלמד להועיל או"ח סי' מט; שו"ת ציץ אליעזר ח"א סי' כ, ח"ג סי' יז; שו"ת באר
   משה ח"ו ק"ע סי' כב, כג, וח"ז ק"ע סי' כד; מקור חיים ח"ג פ' קס"ו ס"א; שו"ת מנחת
   יצחק ח"ג סי' לח; יסודי ישרון ח"ה (תשכ"ו) עמ' קמג; קה"ש כלל לו ס"ק א; ויש חוששין
   גם לאיסור משום עובדא דחול; חזון אי"ש או"ח הל' שבת סי' נ ס"ק ט, הלופי מכתבים
   בין החזון אי"ש והג"ר שלמה זלמן אויערבאך בספר מנחת שלמה סי' יא; ועי' החשמל
   בהלכה ח"ב פ"ב, ה, ח, ואנציקלופדיה תלמודית כרך יח ערך חשמל.

10. עי' שו"ת אגרות משה או"ח ח"ד סי' ס שאסור להעמיד שעון שבת בע"ש שיעשה מלאכה בשבת מטעם זילותא דשבת, אבל אין לאסור לכבות ולהדליק נרות חשמל דכבר נהגו להקל. ועי' שם ס"מ אות ב'; ועי' שו"ת באר משה ח"ז ק"ע סי' עא וששכ"ז מ"ח פי"ג סכ"ג שמתירין, ועי' ש"ע או"ח סי' רסה ס"ד ברמ"א ובאור הלכה ד"ה גרם כיבוי, ובנוגע לשנות את הזמנים בשעון כדי לאחר את שעת ההדלקה או את שעת הכיבוי עי' שו"ת באר משה ח"ו ק"ע סי' לו, לט וח"ז ק"ע סי' עג דעתו לאסור, וששכ"ז מ"ח פי"ג סכ"ה והערה צא שם, ופכ"ג סכ"ד, ושו"ת יביע אומר ח"ג או"ח סי' יז, יח דעתם להתיר.

Electrical Equipment and Appliances

1. שו"ת אגרות משה או"ח ח"ד סי' ס וסי' צא אות ה; שו"ת באר משה ח"ז ק"ע סי' עא; שו"ת ציץ אליעזר ח"א סי' כ פ"ח, פ"ט ח"ג סי' יז; שמ"ב מהד"ת סי' עה ס"ק יא; יסודי ישרון ח"ג עמ' מ; שו"ת באר משה ח"ז ק"ע סי' לח, לט; ח"ז ק"ע סי' כח, לה, מז, עא; שו"ת מנחת יצחק ח"א סי' נח; ששכ"ז מ"ח פי"ג ס"ל, ספר מנחת שלמה סי' יב, יג; ועי' מקור חיים פ' קסו ס"ג שמתיר להזיז מחוגי השעון כדי שיכבה בשעה מאוחרת יותר, וגם להקדים כיבויו בשעה מוקדמת יותר לחולה שמצטער ואינו יכול לישון, ומתיר להזיז מחוגי השעון כדי שידליק בשעה יותר מאוחרת, וגם שידליק בשעה יותר מוקדמת לצורך מצוה.

2. עי' שו"ת ציץ אליעזר ח"ח סי' י"ב וחי"ב סי' צב, וששכ"ז מ"ח פ"ח פ"ט ס"ט וסי"ב, וספר מנחת שלמה סי' י, דעת הגרא"י וולדינברג והגרש"ז אויערבאך שלדינא מותר לפתוח את המקרר בכל עת; ועי' ספר עדות לישראל עמ' 122, 151, ושו"ת אגרות משה ח"א סי' קכח וח"ב סי' סח, ושו"ת באר משה ח"ו ק"ע סי' ד, ז, ט, דעת הגרי"א העניקן ז"ל והגר"מ פיינשטיין ז"ל ויב"ל הגר"מ שטערן שליט"א שיש לפותחו בזמן שהוא פועל, ולפי הגרמ"פ שם ופסקי החזו"א במנוחה נכונה פ"ג מלאכת הבערה, ושו"ת מנחת יצחק ח"ב סי' טז יש לחברו לשעון אוטומטי אשר יפסיק את זרם החשמל לפרקי זמן קבועים, ועי' שו"ת יביע אומר ח"א סי' כא; מקור חיים אורח ח"ג פ' קסו ס"ח; יסודי ישרון מערכת הל' שבת (תשל"ט) עמ' 279; שמ"ב מ"ח סי' פ ס"ק ב, ג ובק"א שם; שו"ת תשובות והנהגות סי' רכ; וששכ"ז פ"י סי"ד.

3. ששכ"ז מ"ח פי"ג סל"ה.

4. שו"ת באר משה ח"ז ק"ע סי' יט, עא, סג; יסודי ישרון ח"ה (תשכ"ו) עמ' קלח; ששכ"ז מ"ח פי"ג סל"ד, פכ"ג סכ"א, פ"ל סי"א, פל"ו ס"ט; עי' שו"ת אגרות משה או"ח ח"ג סי' מד; שו"ת מנחת יצחק ח"ג סי' כג, כד.

5. ערוך השלחן או"ח סי' שלח ס"ה; עדות לישראל עמ' 122; שו"ת אגרות משה או"ח ח"ד סי' פד; שו"ת ציץ אליעזר ח"ג סי' טז פי"ב, ח"ז סי' כא, וחי"ג סי' נד; שו"ת יביע אומר ח"א סי' כ, וח"ו או"ח סי' לד; שו"ת באר משה ח"ז סי' קכא ובק"ע סי' יג; מנוחה נכונה פ"ג, לו ע"פ פסקי חזון אי"ש; יסודי ישרון ח"ג עמ' נ, נה; שו"ת מנחת יצחק ח"א סי' קז; פסקי עזיאל סי' ח; ספר מנחת שלמה סי' ט; עשה לך רב ח"א סי' לה.

6. שו"ת באר משה ח"ז ק"ע סי' כא.

7. ספר עדות לישראל עמ' 122; שו"ת ציץ אליעזר ח"א סי' כ פ"י; שו"ת יביע אומר ח"א סי' כ; פסקי עזיאל סי' ו, ז; שו"ת באר משה ח"ו ק"ע סי' מז; יסודי ישרון ח"ה (תשכ"ו) עמ'

קלב; שש״כ מ״ח פל״ב ס״מ-מג, פל״ו ס״ח, פ״מ סע״ב, פמ״א ס״א וסכ״ה, ועי׳ שם פי״ג
סל״ז שאם שכח להפסיק את חיבורו של הטלפון מבעוד יום, שמתיר להפסיק את החיבור
ע״י הוצאת התקע מן השקע בשעה שאין הפעמון פועל, לצורך חולה שהצלצול יפריע לו.
עי׳ שמ״ב סי׳ פ ס״ק פב; מצודת דוד על קצש״ע סי׳ פ ס״ק פח.

8. שו״ת באר משה ח״ז ק״ע סי׳ כה, כו, עי״ש שלדעתו מוטב להשכיר שרות לקבל את
הקריאה ולהשיב לקורא.

9. שו״ת אגרות משה או״ח ח״ג סי׳ נה וח״ד סי׳ פד; שו״ת יביע אומר ח״א סי׳ יט; שו״ת
מנחת יצחק ח״א סי׳ לז וח״ג סי׳ לח; ספר מנחת שלמה סי׳ ט; שו״ת באר משה ח״ו ק״ע
סי׳ טז; קה״ש לו, כו; ספר עדות לישראל עמ׳ 122; יסודי ישרון ח״ה (תשכ״ו) עמ׳ קמח;
ועי׳ שו״ת תשובות והנהגות סי׳ רטז שאוסר ברמקול אפילו בלתי חשמלי דאוושא מילתא
ויש כאן משום זילותא דשבת, עי׳ שו״ת אגרות משה יו״ד ח״ב סי׳ ד, ה, בדין חזן המתפלל
ברמקול בשבת, אם הוא ראוי להיות שוחט.

10. שו״ת באר משה ח״ז ק״ע סי׳ מב, קיז; שו״ת יחוה דעת ח״ב סי׳ נז; יסודי ישרון ח״ה עמ׳
מה, קכ; עדות לישראל עמ׳ 122; שש״כ מ״ח פל״א סכ״ה.

11. שו״ת באר משה ח״ז ק״ע סי׳ קיג; יסודי ישרון ח״ה עמ׳ קלד.

12. שו״ת באר משה ח״ז ק״ע סי׳ כח; שש״כ מ״ח פכ״ג סנ״ג; שו״ת מלמד להועיל ח״א או״ח
סי׳ נ; מקור חיים פ׳ קסו ס״ו; שמ״ב מ״ח סי׳ פ ס״ק ב. ועי׳ יסודי ישרון ח״ה (תשכ״ו) עמ׳
קל דלהוכנס לבית סתם היכא דלא יודעין אם הדלת נפתחת ע״י חשמל אין לאסור משום ספק
פסיק רישא, ועי׳ מ״ש בשם שו״ת מלמד להועיל ח״א אה״ע סי׳ קב דמלאכת מחשבת אסרה
תורה ואם המלאכה אינה ברורה במחשבתו אז מותר באינו מתכוין.

13. שו״ת באר משה ח״ז ק״ע סי׳ לא, וח״ז ק״ע סי׳ כב.

14. ספר עדות לישראל עמ׳ 121; פסקי עזיאל סי׳ טז; שש״כ מ״ח פכ״ג סמ״ט, נא, נב, ופ״ל
סנ״ד; שמ״ב סי׳ עד ס״ק ה; יסודי ישרון ח״ה עמ׳ קלה; שו״ת באר משה ח״ז ק״ע סי׳ קז.

15. שש״כ מ״ח פכ״ג סנ״ב.

16. שו״ת באר משה ח״ו ק״ע סי׳ יח; שו״ת תשובות והנהגות סי׳ רל.

17. שש״כ מ״ח פי״ב סל״ה; שו״ת באר משה ח״ג סי׳ מח, ח״ו ק״ע סי׳ פא; ח״ז ק״ע סי׳ סא;
כשרות ושבת במטבח המודרני, כשרות ח״ב; שמ״ב בק״א סי׳ צ ס״ג.

18. שו״ת אגרות משה או״ח ח״ג סי׳ נ; שו״ת באר משה ח״ו ק״ע סי׳ עא; שש״כ מ״ח פל״ח
ס״ז.

19. שו״ת אגרות משה ח״ג או״ח סי׳ נ; שו״ת יחוה דעת ח״ב סי׳ מט וח״ה סי׳ כח; שו״ת באר
משה ח״ו ק״ע סי׳ כ; קה״ש לו, תד״ו כו.

20. שו״ת ציץ אליעזר ח״ט סי׳ כא; שו״ת באר משה ח״ו סי׳ לב, ק״ע סי׳ יד; מקור חיים ח״ג
פ׳ קסו ס״י; יסודי ישרון ח״ה עמ׳ קכז.

21. עי׳ החשמל בהלכה ח״ב פרק מ מ״ש בשם שו״ת זכרון יעקב ע״ד מנעול דלת המחובר לחוט
אלקטרו-מגנט הנפתח ע״י לחיצה בכפתור, שדן בהולדת ניצוצות בפסיק רישיה ואינו מתכוין
וגם לא ניחא ליה, ודעתו להתיר במקום צורך, אבל לע״ד בהופעת מכשירים חדשים מסוג זה
יש לדון גם עם בעיות חמורות ואיסורים הנוגעים לחילול שבת ממש.

22. שו״ת ציץ אליעזר חי״ד סי׳ לח, שו״ת באר משה ח״ו ק״ע סי׳ עג, וח״ז ק״ע סי׳ סו; שו״ת
יחוה דעת ח״ב סי׳ מט; שש״כ מ״ח פכ״ח סכ״ד.

23. שו"ת אגרות משה או"ח ח"ד סי' פה; שו"ת באר משה ח"ו ק"ע סי' יד וח"ז ק"ע סי' י;
ספר עדות לישראל עמ' 122; שו"ת ציץ אליעזר ח"ו סי' ו; יסודי ישרון ח"ה (תשכ"ו) עמ'
קלט; שמ"ב סי' פ ס"ק פא; מקור חיים פ' קסו ס"ט; שו"ת מנחת יצחק ח"א סי' לז, ח"ב
סי' יח, קיב וח"ג סי' מא; עי' שש"כ מ"ח פל"ד סכ"ח, וספר מנחת שלמה סי' ט הערה ג.

Melachah 37. Extinguishing a Fire

כיבוי

כלכלת שבת, המכבה; חיי אדם כלל מה, מו

1. רמב"ם הל' שבת פ"ה הי"ז; ש"ע או"ח סי' רעז ס"א ומגן אברהם שם ס"ק ב; משנה ברורה
שם; כלכלת שבת, המבעיר; חיי אדם כלל מה, מו סי"א; יסודי ישרון ח"ה עמ' קס.
2. שו"ת אגרות משה ח"ד סי' עד ערך בישול אות לט; שש"כ מ"ח פ"א סכ"ח.
3. משנה שבת ב, ה, ופירוש המשניות להרמב"ם שם; רמב"ם הל' שבת פ"ב ה"ב; ש"ע או"ח
סי' רעח ס"א, משנה ברורה שם.
4. שש"כ מ"ח פי"ג סכ"ח; שו"ת תשובות והנהגות סי' רכא; וע"י שו"ת מנחת יצחק ח"א סי'
נח וח"ב סי' קי, יסודי ישרון ח"ה עמ' קסה; שו"ת ציץ אליעזר ח"א סי' כ פ"ט, ח"ה סי' ח,
ח"ו סי' ה אות ג, וקה"ש לז, יא שאין להתיר, מטעם מוקצה.
5. שש"כ פי"ג הכ"ו; מקור חיים פ' קסו ס"ה בשם הגרא"ה קוק והגרא"פ פרנק שהתירו, אף
שיש אוסרים מטעם מוקצה.
6. עי' המקורות המובאים ביסודי ישרון ח"ה עמ' קמג, קנט; שו"ת ציץ אליעזר ח"ג סי' יז,
ובספר החשמל בהלכה ח"ב פ"ה; ספר מנחת שלמה סי' יב.
7. ש"ע או"ח סי' שלד סכ"ו רמ"א ומשנה ברורה שם; בית יוסף שם סוף סי' שלד; ערוך
השלחן שם ס"ט וסמ"ג, מד; כלכלת שבת, המכבה; מקור חיים פ' קסו; מנוחה נכונה ג, לו
ע"פ פסקי חזון איש; יסודי ישרון ח"ה עמ' קסז; שו"ת ציץ אליעזר ח"ז סי' כ.
8. ש"ע או"ח סי' שלד ס"ב, וע"י קצש"ע סי' פה ס"ד דבהפסד גדול פתאומי נדחה איסור
מוקצה, ובלבד שלא יוציא למקום שאסורין להוציא; וע"י שמ"ב מ"ח שם.
9. ש"ע או"ח סי' רס"ה ס"ד, משנה ברורה שם.

Melachah 38. Striking the Final Hammer Blow

מכה בפטיש

כלכלת שבת, המכה בפטיש; חיי אדם כלל מד

1. שו"ת באר משה ח"ב סי' כ, ח"ו סי' כג; תשובות הגר"מ שטערן בפה"ש ח"א שאלה יג
וח"ב שאלה ה; עי' יסודי ישרון מערכת הל' שבת עמ' 403, ושש"כ מ"ח פט"ז ס"ח.
2. ש"ע או"ח סי' שיז רמ"א שם ומשנה ברורה ס"ק כה; שש"כ מ"ח פט"ז סס"ג; תשובות
הגר"מ שטערן בפה"ש ח"ג שאלה נב; ואין לעשות כן בפני עם הארץ שלא יבוא להקל
באיסורים אלה בכלל.
3. שש"כ מ"ח פט"ז סס"ד; שו"ת באר משה ח"א סי' כב.

4. שש"כ מ"ח פט"ז סי"ד וע"י הערה לט מ"ש בשם הגרש"ז אויערבך שליט"א שאין זה שייך לכינון שעון, אבל ע"י ספר טלטולי שבת הל' מוקצה עמ' 28 הערה 36 מ"ש בשם הגר"מ פיינשטיין ז"ל דעריכת צעצועים כאלה דומה לכינון שעון ומ"מ אינם מוקצה דעומדים ומיוחדים לילדים.

5. שו"ת באר משה ח"א סי' כט, ח"ג סי' ע; שו"ת אגרות משה או"ח ח"ד סי' מ אות ט; עי' ש"ע או"ח סי' שלו ס"ט, משנה ברורה ובאור הלכה שם, שש"כ מ"ח פ"ט ס"י, יא; שו"ת מנחת יצחק ח"ה סי' עה, שמ"ב מ"ת סי' פ ס"ק סט; וע"י מקור חיים פ' קנט ס"ה מ"ש בשם שו"ת יביע אומר ח"ה סי' לג שיש להתיר לשפוך מים רותחים בכיור שנסתם כדי לפתחו, שהשומן המצטבר והוא הסותם כבר מבושל ואין בישול אחר בישול.

6. תוס' חיים על ח"א כלל מד ס"ק ד; קה"י כלל לד סמ"ב; שש"כ מ"ח פט"ו סע"ז; פה"ש ח"ב פ"ו סכ"א בשם הגר"מ שטערן שליט"א.

7. שו"ת הגר"מ שטערן שליט"א בפה"ש ח"ב סי' לג; עי' שש"כ מ"ח פט"ו ס"ס; כללת שבת, המכה בפטיש.

8. משנה ברורה סי' שיז ס"ק טז דלא מבטל ליה התם ולא הוי מתקן מנא.

9. ש"ע או"ח סי' שכג ס"ז רמ"א ומשנה ברורה שם; חיים אדם כלל סי"ז; כללת שבת, המכה בפטיש.

10. ש"ע או"ח סי' רסא משנה ברורה ס"ק ד; כללת שבת, המכה בפטיש; חיי אדם כלל מד סכ"ב; וע"י יסודי ישרון מה"ש עמ' 85 מה שמביא מהמקורות שבארץ ישראל עוד נוהגים לומר בע"ש „עשרתם, הפרשתם חלה", הואיל ואין תקנה בא"י להפריש אח"כ כמו בחו"ל.

11. חיי אדם כלל מד סי"ט, תוס' חיים שם ס"ק ט; משנה ברורה סי' שלח ס"ק טו ושעה"צ שם ס"ק יז; כללת שבת, המכה בפטיש; שו"ת יביע אומר ח"א או"ח סי' לה; שו"ת יחוה דעת ח"ב סי' מח; עי' מקור חיים פ' קנט ס"י, יא; שש"כ מ"ח פכ"ח סי"ט, כ, כג.

12. שו"ת יביע אומר ח"ו או"ח סי' לה; שו"ת ציץ אליעזר ח"ז סי' כ; שו"ת באר משה ח"ז ק"ע סי' ט; שש"כ מ"ח פכ"ח סי"ט; יסודי ישרון תשל"ט עמ' 334; שו"ת יחוה דעת ח"ב סי' מה שאלה ד, וע"י שם סי' כט שמתיר לשאת שעון יד אלקטרוני המופעל ע"י מצבר כל שאינו לוחץ על הכפתור אלא הוא הולך מעצמו.

13. ש"ע או"ח סי' רנג ס"ה רמ"א שם; תוס' חיים על ח"א כלל מד ס"ק ט; מקור חיים פ' קנט סי"ב; שש"כ מ"ח פכ"ח סכ"ט; שו"ת ציץ אליעזר ח"ח סי' יג; שו"ת הגר"מ שטערן בפה"ש ח"ג אות מח; שו"ת באר משה ח"ז ק"ע סי' לו, מג, עי"ש שעפ"י עיקר ההלכה שרי לצו"ג להוציא ולהכניס את המעצר קודם הזמן כדי שיצלצל או שלא יתחיל לצלצל, אלא שטוב להחמיר ולהיות נזהר בעניני חשמל בשבת.

14. ביצה לו, ב, גזרה שמא יתקן כלי שיר; ש"ע או"ח סי' שלט ס"ג, עי' רמ"א שם דאין אנו בקיאין בעשיית כלי שיר וליכא למגזר ונהגו להקל; משנה ברורה שם ושעה"צ ס"ק ז; ערוך השלחן שם ס"ט; כללת שבת מלאכת מכה בפטיש; חיי אדם כלל מד סי"ט; עי' יסודי ישרון, תשל"ט, עמ' 321 מ"ש בשם שו"ת מנחת אלעזר ח"א סי' כט כט שחסידים ואנשי מעשה נהגו שמרקדין ומספקין בשמחות ורננות בשבת ויו"ט; וע"י שו"ת יחוה דעת ח"ב סי' נח שהספרדים ועדות המזרח קבלו עליהם הוראת הש"ע לאסור טיפוח וריקוד אף בזה"ז; אולם עי' עשה לך רב ח"ב סי' ל שאין למחות בבני הישיבה בין שהם אשכנזים בין שהם ספרדים הרוקדים בשבת לכבוד התורה, ומצטט מ"ש ר' יהודה הלוי בכוזרי מאמר שני ס"נ

וז"ל ואין כניעתך בימי התענית יותר קרובה אל האלקים משמחתך בימי השבתות והמועדים
כשתהיה שמחתך בכוונה ולב שלם . . . ואם תעבור בך השמחה אל הנגון והריקוד היא עבודה
ודבקות בענין האלקי.

15. אף שלדינא אין אסור לשחות בבריכה שבחצר כשיש לה כותלים גבוהים מכל צד ואין המים
יוצאין ונמשכין בחצר, מכ"ז כתבו הפוסקים דנהגו שלא לרחוץ כלל בנהר או במקוה דמצוי
לבא לידי סחיטת שער, ועוד כמה טעמים. עי' רמב"ם הל' שבת פכ"ג ה"ה; ש"ע או"ח סי'
שלט ס"ב משנה ברורה ובאור הלכה שם, ומשנה ברורה סי' שכו סכ"א; חיי אדם כלל מד
ס"כ ותוס' חיים שם ס"ק יב; כללת שבת, מכה בפטיש; שש"כ מ"ח פי"ד סי"ב, ופט"ז
סל"ח; קצה"ש כלל לח סי' לג; מקור חיים פ' קנט סט"ו. תורת השבת פ"ז סי' כו; עי' שו"ת
באר משה ח"ג סי' נו. וכבר נהגו להתיר טבילה במקוה לנשים בזמנן ולאנשים לטבילת קרי.
עי' משנה ברורה סי' שכו ס"ק כד, וביה"ל ד"ה אדם; שש"כ מ"ח פי"ד הערה ד.

16. שו"ת הגר"מ שטערן בפה"מ ח"ב סי' ג; מקור חיים פ' קנט סט"ו, יז; מנוחה נכונה פ"ג סי'
לח; שש"כ מ"ח פט"ז סי"ז, ועי' יסודי ישרון מה"ש עמ' 385 שמביא עוד טעמים לאיסור
רכיבה באופניים בשבת מלבד שמא יתקן, והוא גזירה שמא יצא חוץ לתחום ומשום עובדין
דחול. עי' שו"ת ציץ אליעזר ח"א סי' כא אות כז, וח"ז סי' ל.

17. עי' משנה ברורה סי' שלח ס"ק ד שדעתו לאסור דכלי שיר הוא, ושמ"ב סי' פ ס"ק עט) וכן
בשש"כ מ"ח פכ"ח סל"ד; ועי' ערוך השלחן שם ס"ח, ושו"ת מלמד להועיל או"ח סי' סג
שיש ללמד זכות על החזנים וכן נהגו בקהלות שהיו מלפנים ולא מיחו, ועכ"פ יוכיחו לחזן
שלא יכוון למצוא חן בעיני השומעים אלא לכבד את ה' מהונו ומגרונו. ובשם שו"ת נהרי
אפרסמון מביאים עוד טעמים להתיר דאין אנו בקיאין בעשיית כלי שיר, ובפרט שהדבר
ברבים ואין כאן חשש שמא יתקן. עי' יסודי ישרון מה"ש עמ' 318, מקור חיים פ' קנט
סי"ג.

18. חיי אדם כלל מד סי"ט; שו"ת הגר"מ שטערן בפה"ש ח"ב שאלה מו; שו"ת באר משה ח"ו
סי' פו.

19. ש"ע או"ח סי' שלח ס"א משנה ברורה שם וביה"ל ד"ה הואיל; ערוך השלחן שם ס"ב;
כללת שבת, מכה בפטיש, תוס' חיים על חיי אדם כלל מד ס"ק יא; שש"כ מ"ח פכ"ג
סמ"ה; יסודי ישרון מה"ש עמ' 318.

20. ש"ע או"ח סי' שכ ס"ט, משנה ברורה ס"ק לד, לה; שש"כ מ"ח פ"י סי"ב.

21. ש"ע או"ח סי' שכ סי"ד משנה ברורה ס"ק מא; שו"ת באר משה ח"א סי' כח; שש"כ מ"ח
פכ"ה הערה מט; יסודי ישרון (תשל"ט) עמ' 366.

22. שו"ת ציץ אליעזר ח"ו סי' לד, חי"ב סי' לד; שו"ת באר משה ח"ו סי' יא, ע"ה, וח"ז
ק"ע סי' לד; שש"כ מ"ח פי"ז סי"ד, ה, ז; שמ"ב סי' פ ס"ק יח; עי' ספר הל' שבת ח"א-ג
עמ' 120 מלאכת דש הערה שלג מ"ש מפי הגרמ"פ ז"ל שיש להתיר במקום צורך כגון
לצורך אורחים; ועי' יסודי ישרון (תשל"ט) עמ' 284; וקצה"ש כלל לח סנ"ג ס"ק נא.

23. שו"ת יביע אומר ח"ו או"ח סי' לו; שמ"ב מ"ת סי' פו ס"ק ו וק"א שם; שש"כ מ"ח פי"ד
סל"ב; שו"ת באר משה ח"ב סי' כג; ספר משנה הלכות חי"ב סי' מו.

24. ש"ע או"ח סי' תקיא ס"ד; שערי תשובה שם ס"ק ז; ערוך השלחן שם סי"ב; ועי' משנה
ברורה סי' קכח ס"ק כג; שו"ת יביע אומר ח"ו או"ח סי' לו; שש"כ מ"ח פי"א סל"ט.

25. כללת שבת, מלאכת המכה בפטיש; ועי' חיי אדם כלל מד סכ"א, כד; עי' שבת קיח, א
רש"י שם ד"ה שוב; רמב"ם הל' שבת פכ"ב הכ"ב, פכ"ג ה"ז, וז"ל הרמב"ם "ואסור להדיח

קערות . . . מפני שהוא כמתקן", והראב"ד חולק עליו וכותב שאינו אסור אלא מפני שהוא
טורח לחול, ועי' מגיד משנה שם שאף הרמב"ם סבור כך שתקון זה אינו אסור אלא מפני
שהוא לצורך חול. ועי' שש"כ מ"ח פכ"ח ביאור דיני הכנה.

26. שבת קיג, א ורש"י שם, טוש"ע או"ח סי' שב וב"י שם ד"ה מקפלין בשם הכלבו, דקיפול
דידן לא דמי לקיפול שלהם. ועי' יסודי ישרון מה"ש עמ' 343 שמביא דברי הכלבו בשם
הארחות חיים בדיני שבת סי' שצא; מקור חיים פ' קנט סט"ז.

27. שבת קיג, א תוס' שם ד"ה מקפלין; ש"ע או"ח סי' שב ס"ג, מגן אברהם ס"ק ו ומשנה
ברורה ס"ק יב, יג, יח; חיי אדם כלל מד סכ"ד ותוס' חיים שם ס"ק יח; שו"ת יחוה דעת
ח"ב סי' מ; שו"ת ציץ אליעזר חי"ד סי' לד; ועי' מקור חיים פ' קנט ס"כ שמנהג קהלות
הספרדים לקפל הטלית כסדר קיפולו הראשון; ערוך השלחן סי' שב סי"ב.

28. רמב"ם הל' שבת פכ"ג ה"ז, מגן אברהם סי' שב ס"ק ז, ערוך השלחן שם סי"ג, משנה
ברורה שם ס"ק יט, כלכלת שבת המכה בפטיש; שו"ת ציץ אליעזר חי"ב סי' לו; ועי' קה"ש
כלל לח ס"ק יד ויסודי ישרון מה"ש עמ' 343 מ"ש בשם בדי השלחן שבימי התלמוד לא היו
המצעות על המטה כל היום לכן הוה הכנה משבת לחול, משא"כ בזמננו שהכרים והכסתות
על המטה כל היום ופשיטא שמותר לסדרם יפה ולפרוש מכסה עליהם לכבוד השבת. עי'
שש"כ מ"ח פכ"ח סע"ח.

29. שבת קיח, א; ש"ע או"ח סי' שכג ס"ו, מג"א ומ"ב שם, כלכלת שבת המכה בפטיש; חיי
אדם כלל מד סכ"א, מקור חיים ח"ג פ' קנט ס"כ, יסודי ישרון מה"ש עמ' 341. שו"ת ציץ
אליעזר חי"ד סי' לז אות א; שו"ת אגרות משה ח"ד סי' עד ערך רחיצה אות ד; שו"ת באר
משה ח"ג סי' מח; שו"ת הגר"מ שטערן בפה"ש ח"ג סי' יב; שש"כ מ"ח פי"ב ס"ב, ג.

30. שש"כ מ"ח פכ"ח ספ"ד והערה קסט, רד, ומסתפק אם מותר להכין גם בלימודי חול במי
שאין כונתו בשביל לדעת, אלא רק כדי להצליח בבחינה שתיערך ביום חול.

Melachah 39. Carrying

הוצאה

כללת שבת, המוציא מרשות לרשות; פתיחה למסכת שבת; חיי אדם כלל מז-נב;
שלחן ערוך, הלכות שבת סימן שמה, שמו

1. שבת צו, ב, עי' תוס' שם ד"ה ממאי; ירושלמי שבת פ"א ה"א; פירוש רע"ב שבת פ"א
מ"א; רמב"ם הל' שבת פי"ב ה"ח; משנה ברורה הקדמה לסי' שמה; ראש השנה כט, ב;
סוכה מב, ב; ועי' מגילה ד, ב; וש"ע או"ח סי' תרפח ס"ו.

2. ש"ע או"ח סי' שמה סי"ב, משנה ברורה ס"ק מד, שעה"צ ס"ק מח; תורת השבת פי"ד סי'
לט ס"ו.

3. שמ"ב מ"ת סי' פד ס"ק יט; שש"כ מ"ח פי"ח סכ"ב, פ"מ ס"ז.

4. ש"ע או"ח סי' רסו סי"א, יב משנה ברורה שם, וס"ז משנה ברורה ס"ק כב; חיי אדם כלל
נד ס"א, ב; שש"כ מ"ח פי"ח סנ"ב; מקור חיים פ' קסט סי"ג; יסודי ישרון ח"ה עמ' ריב,
שו"ת באר משה ח"ו סי' קג.

5. שבת קב, א; שש"כ מ"ח פי"ח ס"ב; שו"ת באר משה ח"א סי' מ.

6. שש"כ מ"ח פל"ב סנ"ד, פ"מ ס"ז; ספר משנה הלכות ח"ז סי' נו; שו"ת הגר"מ שטערן,

שאלה כח בפה"ש ח"ג; כל בו על אבלות ח"ב עמ' 21; אולם עי' שו"ת ציץ אליעזר חי"ג
סי' לד שדעתו להחמיר.

7. ש"ע או"ח סי' שמג משנה ברורה ס"ק ו, באור הלכה שם ד"ה מד"ס וכן; שו"ת באר משה
ח"ו סי' יח; שש"כ מ"ח פי"ח סנד; עי' מ"ש הבאר היטב סי' שמו ס"ק ה בשם הט"ז
והמרדכי שמותר להביא המפתח של בית הכנסת ע"י תינוק, דאין לנו רשות הרבים אלא
כרמלית שהוא מדרבנן, עי' שו"ת חתם סופר ח"ו סי' יג שדעתו להתיר במקום מצוה, והוא
להביא המפתח לבית הכנסת וגם הקטן בעצמו נכנס להתפלל שם. ולענין גיל קטן שהגיע
לחינוך עי' משנה ברורה ס"ק ו עא ס"ק ו. ועי' יסודי ישרון ח"ה עמ' ריג מ"ש בשם שו"ת ארץ
צבי סי' ע"ה ע"ה שמלמד זכות על מנהגם של ישראל שנותנין לקטן להוציא ספר או שאר חפצי
מצוה במקום שאין לו עירוב, דקטן שאין לו כוונה דינו כדבר שאינו מתכוון, ועי"ש עמ' ריז.

8. שש"כ מ"ח פי"ח סכ"ט והערה קכו שם; עי' שו"ת אגרות משה או"ח ח"ג סי' מו דהעניבה
אינה בגד אלא תכשיט.

9. ש"ע או"ח סי' שא סכ"ג רמא שם; שש"כ מ"ח פי"ח סמ"ד; שו"ת הגר"מ שטערן, שאלה
כה בפה"ש ח"ג, ולדעתו הוא בתנאי שהפתק בפנים הבגד או במקום שאינו נראה בחוץ;
שו"ת מנחת יצחק ח"ג סי' לו, שמ"ב מהד"ת סי' פד ס"ק יח.

10. ש"ע או"ח סי' שא ס"ז ובאור הלכה ד"ה כל; ערוך השלחן שם סנ"א; שש"כ מ"ח פי"ח
סכ"ג.

11. רש"י עירובין ו, א ד"ה ר"ה, ותוס' שם ד"ה כיצד, רש"י שם ו, ב ד"ה ירושלים, נט, א ד"ה
עיר של יחיד; ש"ע או"ח סי' שג סי"ח, סי' שמה ס"ז; מגן אברהם שם ס"ק ז, ט"ז ס"ק ו;
רמ"א סי' שמו ס"ג; משנה ברורה סי' שמה ס"ק יז ובה"ל שם ד"ה שאין ששים רבוא,
ומשנה ברורה סי' שסד ס"ק ח ועי' שש"כ מ"ח פי"ז הערה יח, כא, ויסודי ישרון ח"ה עמ'
קפט שלדעת החזון איש אין לנו רשות הרבים גמורה מדאורייתא בזמן הזה. עי' חיי אדם
כלל מט סי"ג, תוס' חיים כלל עא ס"ק א; קצש"ע סי' פא ס"ג וסי' צד סכ"ד; ועי' מ"ש
החתם סופר או"ח סי' צט שהשכל הפשוט גוזר שראוי' ומחוייב לתקן החצרים והמבואות
בעירוב המתיר טלטול כדי שלא יכשלו רוב המון עם בהוצאה מרשות לרשות ביום שבת
קודש; עי' עדות לישראל עמ' 151; עי' שו"ת אגרות משה או"ח ח"א סי' קלח-קמ, או"ח
ח"ד סי' פו עמ"ש עמ"ש ע"ד העירוב בקיו גארדענס הילס שרואה בזה תועלת גדולה והצלה
ממכשול בשוגג ובמזיד, וסי' פז-פט ע"ד העירוב בפלעטבוש ובמאנהאטען שדעתו להחמיר
באלו המקומות. עי' הפרדס (תשל"ט) חוב' ה-ו. עי' ערוך השלחן סי' שמה סט"ז-כב, כו;
ש"ע הרב שם סי"א; יסודי ישרון ח"ה עמ' קפח, רמז, רפו; תורת השבת עמ' סז; ועי' שו"ת
ציץ אליעזר חי"ד סי' צ מ"ש בשם הג' אבני נזר ז"ל או"ח סי' רסו דהמונע מלהעמיד
עירובין הוא מחטיא את הרבים ועתיד ליתן את הדין, ועי' קונטרס אום אני חומה (תמוז
תשמ"א) מאת הרב מנשה קליין בענין תיקון עירובין בעיירות, וספר משנה הלכות ח"ז סי'
ס-סב.

12. ש"ע או"ח סי' שסג סכ"ט, מגן אברהם ס"ק ל, משנה ברורה ס"ק קיח, קכא ושעה"צ ס"ק
צג, צה; ש"ע או"ח סי' שמה סי"א, סי"ד, משנה ברורה ס"ק מא; עי"ש דעת אחרונים
דבמקום הגשר, ובמקום שהספינות עוברות שם לנמל, וכשהמים נקרשין בימות הגשמים
בטלה המחיצה וצריך לעשות צורת הפתח; עי' חיי אדם כלל מז, עא סט"ו.

13. שש"כ מ"ח פי"ז סי"א, פל"א סכ"א; שו"ת הגר"מ שטערן בפה"ש ח"ג שאלה כו; עי'
משנה ברורה סי' שז ס"ק נו.

Part III
Select Sabbath Laws
Some of the Melachot Forbidden on the Sabbath
קצת ממלאכות האסורות בשבת
קצור שלחן ערוך סימן פ

1. שו"ת יחוה דעת ח"ג סי' כ; שמ"ב מ"ת סי' פ ס"ק א בשם שו"ת לבושי מרדכי ח"ב סי' נב, דאין בחשמל חשש לשמא יטה לצורך הבערה, ואין לנו לגזור מעצמינו גזירה שמא יכבה.
2. משנה ברורה סי' רעז ס"ק ג.
3. ספר עדות לישראל, מדור ההלכה ס"כ עמ' 122; שמ"ב מ"ת סי' פ ס"ק ד; קיצור הל' שבת, כלל יא סמ"ז.
4. משנה ברורה סי' שיח ס"ק מה; שמ"ב מ"ת סי' פ ס"ק ז; ששכ"ך פ"א סנ"ט.
5. ש"ע או"ח סי' שיח ס"ט, משנה ברורה ס"ק סה; שמ"ב מ"ת סי' פ ס"ק ח; ששכ"ך פ"א סנ"ה.
6. שמ"ב מ"ת סי' פ ס"ק י דכבר נתבשל החומר בבית החרושת, ועי' ש"ע או"ח סי' שיח מגן אברהם ס"ק לא ומשנה ברורה ס"ק עא; ששכ"ך פ"א סמ"ט, נה; ועי' פה"ש ח"ג פ"א סל"ב מ"ש מפי הגר"מ שטערן דבעינן לערבו עם מים חמים שבכלי שלישי.
7. שמ"ב מ"ת סי' פ ס"ק ט; ששכ"ך מ"ח פ"א סמ"ט, נה, נו, פ"ח סכ"ד.
8. ש"ע או"ח סי' שיח סט"ו, טז ומשנה ברורה ס"ק צג, ק, קה.
9. ש"ע או"ח סי' שיח סי"ד, טו, משנה ברורה שם ובאור הלכה ד"ה להפיג צינתן, סי' שכח סי"ז רמ"א שם; ששכ"ך מ"ח פ"א סי"ג.
10. ש"ע או"ח סי' שיח סט"ז, משנה ברורה ס"ק קז; חיי אדם כלל כ סי"ג; שמ"ב מ"ת סי' פ ס"ק יב בשם צמח צדק סי' לז.
11. ש"ע או"ח סי' רנג ס"ב, וסי' רנז ס"ה, ומשנה ברורה שם ס"ק כח, ל.
12. ש"ע או"ח סי' שכא סי"ג, משנה ברורה ס"ק מט, ובאור הלכה שם ד"ה שנתרסקו.
13. משנה ברורה סי' שלה ס"ק יז, באור הלכה שם ד"ה אחד הנה.
14. משנה ברורה סי' שיט ס"ק כא, כד; ששכ"ך פ"ג סל"ח.
15. ש"ע או"ח סי' שכ ס"ק ד, ס"ו, ס"ז, משנה ברורה ס"ק יז, כב; שמ"ב מ"ת סי' ח בשם חזון איש.
16. משנה ברורה סי' שכ ס"ק יב; ששכ"ך מ"ח פ"ח ס"י.
17. ש"ע או"ח סי' של ס"ח, משנה ברורה ס"ק לב; ש"ע הרב שם ס"ט.
18. ששכ"ך מ"ח פ"י ס"ד; שמ"ב מ"ת סי' פ ס"ק ח, שו"ת באר משה ח"ב סי' כה; ספר הלכות שבת ח"ב, מלאכת דש עמ' 120 ס"ק שלג בשם הגר"מ פיינשטיין ז"ל.
19. ש"ע או"ח סי' שכ סי"ג, משנה ברורה ס"ק לט.
20. שער המזרח סי' פ ס"ק יט; ששכ"ך מ"ח פ"ג סמ"ה.
21. ש"ע או"ח סי' שיט ס"א, משנה ברורה ס"ק ד, ו.
22. משנה ברורה סי' שיט ס"ק כד, שכא ס"ק פד, מגן אברהם שם ס"ק ל, ושער הציון שם ס"ק צז; חיי אדם כלל יד ס"א; ספר הלכות שבת ח"ב פ"ח עמ' 94, ובתשובת הגר"מ פיינשטיין שם הל' בורר בשבת אות ח.
23. ש"ע או"ח סי' שיט ס"ד באור הלכה שם ד"ה הבורר, וד"ה מתוך אוכל, באור הלכה סי'

שיט ס"א ד"ה מן העלין, וסי' שכא סי"ט ד"ה לקלוף, ספר הלכות שבת ח"ג פ"י, ותשובות
הגר"מ פיינשטיין שם הל' בורר בשבת אות ז, ח; כף החיים סי' שיט אות מז.

24. משנה ברורה סי' שיט ס"ק טו; שו"ת יביע אומר ח"ה סי' לא.

25. ש"ע או"ח סי' שיט סי"ד; שו"ת יחוה דעת ח"ב סי' נא.

26. משנה ברורה סי' שיט ס"ק נה, ש"ע הרב שם סי"ח.

27. ש"ע או"ח סי' שכא סי"ב, משנה ברורה ס"ק מד, מה, ערוך השלחן שם ס"ט; שמ"ב מ"ת
סי' פ ס"ק כג בשם האלף לך שלמה סי' קלט דמנהג ישראל תורה היא.

28. משנה ברורה סי' שכא ס"ק כא, ועי' מ"ש בשם א"ר ותשובת נודע ביהודה דאם אי אפשר
ע"י אינו יהודי מותר גם ישראל להדיח הבשר, אך אם מונח בכלי טוב שירחוץ ידיו עליו עד
שיהיה הבשר שרוי במים.

29. ש"ע או"ח סי' שכא ס"י, משנה ברורה ס"ק כא.

30. שו"ת באר משה ח"ו סי' מג, עי' מ"ש בשם המנ"ח דלא דמי דבילה לגבינה שנעשה לגוף
אחד, ולכן בודאי מסתבר להקל בבצלים עם ביצים וחלב דג מלוח, ולא כבקצש"ע שאוסר
להשוותן וליפותן משום איסור בונה, ועי"ש סי' מד שמותר לערב ביצים עם בצלים ושמן
ואין לחוש משום לישה משום דלא נעשה גוש אחד, וכן נוהגים ומנהג ישראל תורה.

31. ש"ע או"ח סי' שב סי"ב, משנה ברורה ס"ק נח, נט, וסי' שכ סי"ז, משנה ברורה ס"ק מה;
ששכ"כ מ"ח פי"ב סי"ג, יד; יסודי ישרון תשלט עמ' 367.

32. מגן אברהם סי' שכג ס"ק טו, משנה ברורה ס"ק לח; מסגרת השלחן סי' פ ס"ק נט; ששכ"כ
מהד"ב פי"ב סכ"ד.

33. ש"ע או"ח סי' שכג ס"ו, משנה ברורה ס"ק כו, כז, כח; ששכ"כ פ"ט מ"ח פי"ב ס"א; שו"ת
באר משה ח"ו ק"ו סי' פא, וסי' פב; ח"ז ק"ו סי' סא.

34. באור הלכה סי' רנג ס"ה ד"ה להחם הקדרה.

35. ש"ע או"ח סי' שכ סי"ז, משנה ברורה ס"ק מו, מז; ששכ"כ מ"ח פי"ב סי' יא, טו, פי"ד
סי"ג.

36. ש"ע או"ח סי' שיט סי"ז, משנה ברורה ס"ק סז דאין מי שחושש לזה, ועי' באור הלכה שם
ד"ה מפזר די"ל דהוא כמעביר ארבע אמות בר"ה ע"י הרוח.

37. ש"ע או"ח סי' שג סכ"ו, משנה ברורה ס"ק פב, ושער הציון שם ס"ק סח; מסגרת השלחן
סי' פ ס"ק סג; ששכ"כ מ"ח פי"ד סמ"ז, נג.

38. ש"ע או"ח סי' שמ ס"א, משנה ברורה ס"ק א, וסי' שג סכ"ז, משנה ברורה ס"ק פו, פז, פח;
ששכ"כ פי"ג סכ"ה, כו, ל; ובמ"ח פי"ד סמ"א-מט.

39. ש"ע או"ח סי' שב ס"ט, ש"ע הרב שם ס"כ; ששכ"כ פי"ד סט"ז, ובמ"ח פט"ז ס"ה, ו, כד.

40. ש"ע או"ח סי' שב ס"י רמ"א שם, משנה ברורה ס"ק נא, ש"ע הרב שם ס"ק כא; מסגרת
השלחן סי' פ ס"ק סח, סט.

41. שמ"ב מ"ת סי' פ ס"ק לה ע"פ מג"א סי' שב ס"ק כז, עי' משנה ברורה שם ס"ק ס; ששכ"כ
מ"ח פט"ו סל"א.

42. באור הלכה סי' שב סי"ב ד"ה משום; שמ"ב מ"ת סי' פ ס"ק לה.

43. ש"ע או"ח סי' שא סמ"ה, משנה ברורה ס"ק קסב.

44. ש"ע או"ח סי' שא סמ"ה, מו, משנה ברורה ס"ק קסג, קעא, קעב; ששכ"כ מ"ח פט"ו סי"א,
לה.

45. משנה ברורה סי' שא ס"ק קסד.

46. ש"ע או"ח סי' שא סמ"ו, משנה ברורה ס"ק קע; מסגרת השלחן סי' פ ס"ק עז.

47. ש"ע או"ח סי' שב ס"א, משנה ברורה ס"ק ד, שש"כ מ"ח פט"ו סל"ד.

48. ש"ע או"ח סי' שב ס"א, משנה ברורה ס"ק א, ב.

49. ש"ע או"ח סי' שב ס"א, משנה ברורה ס"ק ה, ו, וסי' שלז ס"ב משנה ברורה שם ס"ק יג, ובאור הלכה סי' שב ס"א ד"ה מן הטל, וד"ה ועי' לקמן, ושער הציון שם ס"ק ט; מסגרת השלחן סי' פ ס"ק פ; שש"כ מ"ח פט"ו סכ"ה, ל. ובנוגע לניקוי בגדים במברשת בשבת, עי' שו"ת יביע אומר ח"ד סי' ל שמתיר להשתמש במברשת בגדים, ועי' בתפארת ישראל, כללת שבת, המלבן, שנהגו לאסור אפילו ע"י מברשת העשויה משערות מדהו"ל עובדין דחול ומחזי כמתקן מנא.

50. ש"ע או"ח סי' שב ס"ט, משנה ברורה ס"ק מא, באור הלכה שם ד"ה זה על זה, משנה ברורה סי' שכז ס"ק יב, טז; כללת שבת, ממחק, דצחצוח נעליים במשחה אפילו ע"י עכו"ם אסור, ועי' ערוך השלחן סי' שכז ס"ד; זכרא תורת משה כלל לט סי' ב; שש"כ מ"ח פט"ו סל"ח.

51. משנה ברורה סי' שב ס"ק נז; שש"כ פי"ג סי"ד, יט.

52. רמב"ם הל' שבת פ"ט הי"ג, ש"ע או"ח סי' שג סכ"ה, משנה ברורה ס"ק עט, מג"א סי' שכ ס"ק כה; שו"ת אגרות משה או"ח ח"א סי' קיד; שו"ת יחוה דעת ח"ד סי' כח; שש"כ מ"ח פי"ד סנ"ז-נט.

53. משנה ברורה סי' שכ ס"ק נז, נט; שש"כ מ"ח פי"ד סי"ט.

54. חיי אדם הל' שבת כלל כד ס"ו; משנה ברורה סי' שכח ס"ק קמו.

55. ש"ע או"ח סי' שכ סי"ט, מגן אברהם שם ס"ק כה, ומשנה ברורה ס"ק נו; חיי אדם הל' שבת כלל כד ס"ה; ועי' שער הציון סי' שיח ס"ק סה; שער המזרח סי' פ ס"ק מג בשם בן איש חי.

56. ש"ע או"ח סי' שיז רמ"א שם, משנה ברורה ס"ק ו, יב, ועי' מ"ש בס"ק ז דכל קשר שמותר להתירו, אם אינו יכול להתירו מותר לנתקו אם הוא לצורך; עי' מסגרת השלחן סי' פ ס"ק פג, פו, פז; שער המזרח סי' פ ס"ק מד בשם כף החיים; שש"כ מ"ח פט"ו ס"נ.

57. שש"כ מ"ח פט"ו סנ"ח.

58. שש"כ מ"ח פ"ט ס"ט, פט"ו סס"ג, פ.

59. משנה ברורה סי' שיז ס"ק טז; שש"כ מ"ח פט"ו סס"ב.

60. שו"ת הגר"מ שטערן בפה"ש ח"ב שאלה לג; שש"כ מ"ח פט"ו ס"ס.

61. שערי תשובה סי' שמ ס"ק ג; שו"ת אגרות משה או"ח ח"ד סי' פד; שו"ת ציץ אליעזר חי"ג סי' מג; שו"ת מנחת יצחק ח"ב סי' יט; שמ"ב מ"ח סי' פ ס"ק מו בשם כף החיים; שש"כ מ"ח פט"ו סס"ד, ע; שו"ת באר משה ח"א סי' כב, ח"ב סי' כט.

62. משנה ברורה סי' שמ ס"ק מה.

63. ש"ע או"ח סי' שיד ס"ו, ס"ז, משנה ברורה ס"ק כה, ל, לא, וסי' שיז רמא שם, שש"כ מ"ח פ"ט ס"ק.

64. ערוך השלחן סי' שיד ס"ח; שו"ת אגרות משה או"ח ח"א סי' קכב, ח"ד סי' עח, שו"ת ציץ אליעזר חי"ד סי' מה, שו"ת יחוה דעת ח"ב סי' מב; שש"כ מ"ח פט"ו ס"ג, ד, ט, שמ"ב מ"ח סי' פ ס"ק מו; עי' ספר משנה הלכות ח"ז סי' מז.

65. שמ"ב מ"ח סי' פ ס"ק מה בקונטרס אחרון שם; שו"ת הגר"מ שטערן בפה"ש ח"ב, שאלה א; שש"כ, מ"ח פט"ו ספ"א.

66. ש"ע או"ח סי' שטז ס"ג, י, מגן אברהם ס"ק ב, משנה ברורה ס"ק מו; ש"ע הרב שם ס"ו.

67. ש"ע או"ח סי' שטז ס"ט, משנה ברורה ס"ק מב, מח; שש"כ מ"ח פי"ד ס"כ.

68. ש"ע או"ח סי' שטז ס"ג; עי' שו"ת יביע אומר ח"ג סי' כ, שש"כ מ"ח פי"ד סל"א, פכ"ה ס"ה, שו"ת באר משה ח"ב סי' כג.

69. שו"ת אגרות משה או"ח ח"א סי' קיב; שו"ת מנחת יצחק ח"ג סי' מח; שש"כ מ"ח פי"ד סל"ד; שמ"ב מ"ת סי' פ ס"ק מח ובקונטרס אחרון שם.

70. ש"ע או"ח סי' שכח סכ"ח, משנה ברורה ס"ק פח, פט.

71. ש"ע או"ח סי' שמ, ס"א, משנה ברורה ס"ק א; שש"כ מ"ח פי"ד סנ"ד.

72. משנה ברורה סי' שכא ס"ק טו; שמ"ב מ"ת סי' פ ס"ק מט.

73. ש"ע או"ח סי' שכא ס"ג, משנה ברורה ס"ק טו.

74. ש"ע יו"ד סי' סט סי"ב, יג, משנה ברורה סי' שכא ס"ק כא; ובשו"ת נודע ביהודה מהדורא תנינא סי' כז כתב דאם אי אפשר ע"י אינו יהודי מותר גם ע"י ישראל, וטוב שירחוץ ידיו עליו עד שיהיה שרוי הבשר במים.

75. ש"ע סי' שכב ס"ד, ה, משנה ברורה ס"ק יח; שער המזרח סי' פ ס"ק נב בשם כף החיים.

76. שש"כ מ"ח פי"א סי"ב; עי' משנה ברורה סי' תקו ס"ק יז.

77. ש"ע או"ח סי' שלו ס"א, י"ג ומשנה ברורה שם, ושערי תשובה שם ס"ק א; שש"כ מ"ח פט"ו ס"כ, פט"ז ס"ז; שו"ת הגר"מ שטערן שאלה ו אות ג בפסקי הל' שבת ח"ב.

78. ש"ע סי' שלו ס"י, יא, משנה ברורה ס"ק מח, נד, שש"כ מ"ח פכ"ו סכ"ב, כה, כו, שמ"ב מ"ת סי' פ ס"ק נב.

79. ש"ע סי' שמ ס"ד, משנה ברורה ס"ק כ, כב, שש"כ מ"ח פט"ז סכ"ז.

80. ש"ע או"ח סי' שמ ס"ג, משנה ברורה ס"ק טו, טז, יז, ועי' שער הציון שם ס"ק כב דמקילין מטעם עונג שבת; שמ"ב מ"ת סי' פ ס"ק ס; שש"כ מ"ח פי"א סי"ז; תשובות הגר"מ שטערן בפה"ש ח"ג אות א, ב.

81. חיי אדם כלל לח ס"ה; משנה ברורה סי' שמ ס"ק יז; ש"ע הרב שם ס"ד; שו"ת ציץ אליעזר חי"ג סי' מד.

82. ש"ע סי' שו ס"ז, סי' שכג ס"א, ד, משנה ברורה ס"ק א.

83. ש"ע סי' שז ס"ג, ד, משנה ברורה ס"ק יד, טו, ובאור הלכה שם, ועי' באור הלכה בס"ג ד"ה אסור, שמביא דעת הפרמ"ג שמסתפק לאסור אפילו כשאין נותן לו מעות, כיון דאומר לו שיקנה בשבילו, עי' שש"כ מ"ח פל"א סט"ז.

84. באור הלכה סי' שיג ס"ג, ד"ה שאין נכנסים.

85. ש"ע סי' שיג ס"א מ"ב ס"ק ו; שמ"ב מ"ת סי' פ ס"ק סה ובקונטרס אחרון שם בשם שו"ת חתם סופר או"ח סי' עב; וש"ע הרב סי' שיג סכ"א וסי' שיד סי"ט.

86. שמ"ב מ"ת סי' פ ס"ק סו בשם שו"ת מהרש"ם.

87. ש"ע סי' שלז ס"ב, באור הלכה שם ד"ה ויש מחמירין; שו"ת מנחת יצחק ח"ג סי' נ ס"ק ה, וח"ה סי' לט (א); שו"ת באר משה ח"א סי' לב; שש"כ מ"ח פכ"ג ס"א-ד.

88. ש"ע סי' שטו ס"א, משנה ברורה ס"ק י.

89. ש"ע או"ח סי' שטו ס"א וס"ב משנה ברורה ס"ק א, יג.

90. שמ"ב מ"ת סי' פ ס"ק עג בשם חזון איש; שש"כ מ"ח פכ"ד סי"ג, טו.

91. משנה ברורה סי' שטו ס"ק כב; מצודת דוד סי' פ סע"ט.

92. ש"ע סי' שטו ס"ג, משנה ברורה ס"ק מט; ש"ע הרב סי' שטו ס"כ.

93. כללכת שבת, הבונה; באור הלכה סי' שטו ס"ח ד"ה טפח; שו"ת יחוה דעת ח"ב סי' מג;
שמ"ב מ"ת סי' פ ס"ק עה; ושו"ת נודע ביהודה מהדורא תנינא סי' ל דאסור לפותחה בשבת
מה"ת ואם העמידה מע"ש ראוי לאסור מפני מראית העין; וע"י שו"ת חתם סופר או"ח סי'
לב שחולק דאין זה אלא בנין לשעה, אלא ששומר נפשו ירחק ממנו, אבל מותר לפותחה ע"י
גוי; וע"י שש"כ מ"ח פכ"ד סט"ו בשמשית גינה שתקועה בקרקע מבעוד יום שמותר
לפותחה ולקפלה.

94. שו"ת יחוה דעת ח"ב סי' נה, שש"כ מ"ח פט"ז סי"ח; שו"ת הגר"מ שטערן בפה"ש ח"ב
שאלה ד.

95. כללכת שבת, הבונה; ש"ע סי' שיג ס"ו, סי' שטו ס"ה ומשנה ברורה שם ובאור הלכה שם
ד"ה לכתחלה; שש"כ מ"ח פכ"ד סט"ו, כג, שו"ת הגר"מ שטערן בפסקי הל' שבת ח"ג
שאלה כ, כא.

96. משנה ברורה סי' שיג ס"ק מה.

97. ש"ע סי' שב ס"ד, משנה ברורה ס"ק כא.

98. ש"ע סי' ש"ח סט"ז, משנה ברורה ס"ק סט, באור הלכה שם ד"ה דאסור לטלטלה.

99. ש"ע או"ח סי' שלח ס"ג שערי תשובה ס"ק ב, משנה ברורה ס"ק טו; כללכת שבת, המכה
בפטיש; תוס' חיים על ח"א כלל מד ס"ק ט; עי' שו"ת באר משה ח"ו ק"ע סי' עג, ושו"ת
הגר"מ שטערן בפה"ש ח"ג שאלה עז; שמ"ב מ"ת סי' פ ס"ק עז; שו"ת יביע אומר ח"ו סי'
לה; שו"ת ציץ אליעזר ח"ט סי' כ; שש"כ מ"ח פכ"ח סי"ט, כ, כג, כח.

100. שמ"ב סי' פ ס"ק עח; עי' ערוך השלחן סי' שלח ס"ה דאסור להעמיד כלי שיר מע"ש
דשמא יתקן כלי שיר, ולהעמידו בשבת אסור משום מתקן מנא.

101. שש"כ מ"ח ס"ב וס"ג, וע"י שם הערה יא; שו"ת באר משה ח"ו סי' כח; שו"ת הגר"מ
שטערן בפסקי הל' שבת ח"ב שאלה מו, מז, דיש להקל לנענע צעצועים המשמיעים קול
בשביל תינוק שלא יבכה מפני עונג שבת וצערא דינוקא, וע"י שם פ"ד סכ"ד, כה.

102. ש"ע סי' שלח ס"א באור הלכה ד"ה הואיל; כללכת שבת, מלאכת מכה בפטיש; שמ"ב
מ"ת סי' פ ס"ק פג.

103. שש"כ מ"ח פכ"ח סכ"ט; שו"ת הגר"מ שטערן בפה"ש ח"ג שאלה מח; שמ"ב מ"ת סי' פ
ס"ק פד.

104. באור הלכה סי' שא ס"ב ד"ה כל דבר; שש"כ מ"ח פט"ז, ס"ט.

105. ש"ע סי' שח סמ"ה משנה ברורה ס"ק קנח, סי' שלח ס"ה משנה ברורה ס"ק כ, כא; ערוך
השלחן סי' שלח ס"ע; שש"כ מ"ח פט"ז ס"א, ו; שו"ת באר משה ח"ב סי' כז.

106. ש"ע או"ח סי' שלח ס"ה, רמ"א שם, מגן אברהם ס"ק ח, ומשנה ברורה ס"ק כא; חיי אדם
כלל לח סי"א; שש"כ מ"ח פט"ז סל"ד; שו"ת באר משה ח"ב סי' כז; שו"ת הגר"מ
שטערן בפה"ש ח"א שאלה יד; שו"ת מנחת יצחק ח"ג סי' לג.

107. עי' שו"ת אגרות משה או"ח ח"א סי' קלה; שש"כ מ"ח פט"ז, סכ"ג; שו"ת הגר"מ שטערן
בפה"ש ח"ב שאלה ד.

108. ש"ע סי' שא ס"ב; שש"כ מ"ח פט"ז סי"ז לט; שו"ת באר משה ח"ו סי' טז, יז; שו"ת
הגר"מ שטערן בפה"ש ח"ב שאלה ג.

109. ש"ע סי' שב ס"ג משנה ברורה ס"ק יח, יט, ערוך השלחן שם סי"א, שש"כ מ"ח פט"ו
סמ"ו, מז.

110. שש"כ מ"ח פט"ו סמ"ח; שו"ת הגר"מ שטערן בפה"ש ח"ג שאלה נא.

111. ש"ע סי' שב ס"ג משנה ברורה ס"ק יג, יח; ערוך השלחן שם סי"ב; שש"כ מ"ח פט"ו סמ"ה; שו"ת יחוה דעת ח"ב סי' מ, ודעת כמה פוסקים שכ"ש שמותר בטלית המיוחד לשבת שהקיפול הוא הידור מצוה ולצורך שבת אחרת.

112. ש"ע סי' שב ס"ט, משנה ברורה ס"ק לט, מח, ובאור הלכה שם ד"ה שיש, סי' שכט ס"א, סי' שלד סכ"ד, כו, משנה ברורה נח, נט, ס, עג.

113. משנה ברורה סי' שב ס"ק יט, עי' פסקי הל' שבת ח"ג פ"ב סכ"ד, הערה לח מ"ש בשם קצות השולחן.

Part IV
Carrying on the Sabbath
1. Four Domains With Regard to the Sabbath

ארבע רשויות לשבת

קצור שלחן ערוך סימן פא; חיי אדם כלל מז, מט, נ;
תפארת ישראל, פתיחה למסכת שבת

1. תפארת ישראל, פתיחה למס' שבת; חיי אדם כלל מז ס"ד.

2. חיי אדם כלל מט סי"ב; משנה ברורה סי' שמה ס"ק מד.

3. ש"ע או"ח סי' שמה ס"ז; חיי אדם כלל מט ס"א.

4. רמב"ם הל' שבת פי"ד ה"ג; ש"ע או"ח סי' שמה סי"ב ועי' משנה ברורה שם ס"ק מד ושעה"צ ס"ק מח; חיי אדם כלל מט סי"ב.

5. ש"ע או"ח סי' שג סי"ח, וסי' שמה ס"ז משנה ברורה שם ס"ק כד ושעה"צ ס"ק כה; עי' רש"י עירובין ו, א ד"ה ר"ה, ו, ב ד"ה ירושלים, נט, א ד"ה העיר של יחיד, תוס' עירובין ו, א ד"ה כיצד; רע"ב שבת פי"א מ"א.

6. תפארת ישראל, פתיחה למס' שבת; ש"ע או"ח סי' שמה ס"ז, משנה ברורה ס"ק כג, באור הלכה שם ד"ה וי"א שכל וד"ה שאין ששים רבוא; ערוך השלחן שם סט"ז-כ; עי' משנה הלכות ח"ז סי' ס-סב, יסודי ישרון ח"ה עמ' קפט, קצ, ושש"כ פי"ז ס"ג והערה יח, כא, דעת החזון איש באו"ח סי' קז דבזמן הזה כמעט אין לנו רשות הרבים דאורייתא.

7. חיי אדם כלל מט סי"ג; עי' ט"ז סי' שמה ס"ק ו שהמחמיר יחמיר לעצמו ואין בידו למחות למה שנוהגין עכשיו כאותן הרבים שמקילין; ועי' מ"ש במשנה ברורה סי' שסד ס"ק ח, אף דאין למחות לאחרים הנוהגין להקל ע"י צורת הפתח שכן נהגו מעולם ע"פ דעת הפוסקים המקילין בזה מ"מ כל בעל נפש יחמיר לעצמו שלא לטלטל ע"י צורת הפתח לבד.

8. שבת ז, א; רמב"ם הל' שבת פי"ד ה"ה; ש"ע או"ח סי' שמה סי"ח.

9. תפארת ישראל, פתיחה למס' שבת; מגן אברהם סי' שמה ס"ק יא; ש"ע או"ח סי' שנו ס"א, באר היטב ס"ק א, משנה ברורה ס"ק ג, ושעה"צ ס"ק ג.

10. מגן אברהם סי' שמה ס"ק ד; משנה ברורה שם ס"ק טז ושעה"צ שם ס"ק טו, יז.

11. שבת ז, א; ש"ע או"ח סי' שמו ס"ג, משנה ברורה ס"ק טז, יז; קצש"ע סי' פג ס"א, ב; תפארת ישראל למס' שבת.

12. מגן אברהם סי' שמה סי"ק טו, משנה ברורה שם ס"ק פא; תפארת ישראל, פתיחה
   למס' שבת; תוס' חיים על חיי אדם כלל נ ס"ק א.

2. The Prohibition of Carrying From One Domain to Another

איסור העברה והוצאה מרשות לרשות
קצור שלחן ערוך סימן פב, חיי אדם כלל מח, נב

1. ש"ע או"ח סי' רסו ס"ז, עי' משנה ברורה ס"ק יז, יח דזה אינו מועיל אלא לענין טלטול
   בר"ה או בכרמלית אבל לא בהוצאה מרשות לרשות, עי"ש איך לטלטלו ומה לעשות כשהוא
   בא סמוך לביתו, עי' חיי אדם כלל נד; ש"ע או"ח סי' שמט ס"ט מ"ב ס"ק טז.
2. ש"ע או"ח סי' שמו ס"א ומשנה ברורה שם.
3. משנה ברורה סי' שח ס"ק קנד; שו"ת ציץ אליעזר חי"ג סי' לב; יסודי ישרון ח"ה עמ' רכו.
4. מגן אברהם סי' שלא ס"ק ה, משנה ברורה שם ס"ק כ, ערוך השלחן שם ס"ו. עי' ש"ו הרב
   שם ס"ח דיש מתירין משום ברב עם הדרת מלך ויש לנהוג כן במקומות שנוהגים להביא
   התינוק לבהכ"נ ע"י שאחד נותנו לחבירו וחבירו לחבירו בפחות מד"א, ושיוציאוהו מרה"י
   ע"י נכרי ויכניסוהו ע"י נכרי, ועי' ט"ז סי' שמט ס"ק א.
5. ש"ע או"ח סי' שסא, משנה ברורה שם.
6. ש"ע או"ח סי' שסג ס"א, ב ומשנה ברורה שם; חיי אדם כלל עא ס"א-ג.
7. ש"ע או"ח סי' שסב ס"ב, ועי' סי"א שם וחיי אדם כלל מח ס"ו, שאפילו אם אין קנה
   העליון נוגע בקנים שלמטה כשר דאמרינן גוד אסיק, ובלבד שיהיו הקנים שלמטה מכוונים
   ממש נגד הקנה שלמעלה, ועי' תוס' חיים שם ס"ק ח דאם יש ביניהם ה' או ו' אמות לא יפה
   עושים.
8. ש"ע או"ח סי' שסב ס"א משנה ברורה ס"ק סו ושעה"צ ס"ק נו; תוס' חיים על חיי אדם
   כלל מח ס"ק יא; יסודי ישרון ח"ה עמ' רפג; מקור חיים פ' קסז ס"ט.
9. ש"ע או"ח סי' שמה ס"ד, סי' שמו ס"ג ט"ז שם ס"ק ו, משנה ברורה ס"ק כח; ש"ע הרב
   שם סי"א; שש"כ מ"ח פי"ח סמ"ט.
10. ש"ע או"ח סי' שכה ס"א משנה ברורה ס"ק ג.
11. שו"ת אגרות משה או"ח ח"ד סי' צא אות א; יסודי ישרון ח"ה עמ' רכו; מקור חיים פ' קסט
   סי"ב; שש"כ מ"ח פי"ח סנ"א והערה ריא.
12. משנה ברורה סי' שח ס"ק קנד; שו"ת ציץ אליעזר חי"ג סי' לב.
13. ש"ע או"ח סי' שנו ס"א, משנה ברורה וביה"ל שם; חיי אדם כלל נג סט"ז.
14. ש"ע או"ח סי' שנז ס"א משנה ברורה שם; מסגרת השלחן סי' פב ס"ק ו.

3. Enclosure of an Area for Dwelling Purposes

היקף מחיצות לא מהני אלא כשהוקף לדירה
קצור שלחן ערוך סימן פג, חיי אדם כלל נא

1. ש"ע או"ח סי' שנח ס"א, משנה ברורה שם; חיי אדם כלל נא ס"א ותוס' חיים שם ס"א א;

תורת השבת עמ' סט; קצש"ע סי' פג ס"ב, וכנראה טעות סופר שם בחשבון האמות
המרובעות.

2. ש"ע או"ח סי' שנח ס"ב משנה ברורה שם.

4. Laws of Carrying With Regard to Garments and Ornaments

דיני הוצאה דרך מלבוש ותכשיט
קצור שלחן ערוך סימן פד, חיי אדם כלל נו

1. ש"ע או"ח סי' שא ס"ז, באור הלכה שם ד"ה כל, וסי' כב, נא, משנה ברורה ס"ק נא; חיי
אדם כלל נו ס"א; שש"כ מ"ח פי"ח ס"ג, יב.

2. שש"כ מ"ח פי"ח סכ"ט, ועי' ביה"ל סי' שא ס"ה ד"ה ובשאינה נקובה.

3. ש"ע או"ח סי' שג ס"ט, מגן אברהם ס"ק ח, ומשנה ברורה ס"ק כג; שש"כ מ"ח פי"ד
סמ"ז, פי"ח ס"ז; שו"ת באר משה ח"א סי' כז; שו"ת אגרות משה יו"ד ח"א סוף סי' מח,
ח"ו סי' עז, פא.

4. ש"ע או"ח סי' שא סכ"ג, משנה ברורה ס"ק פא, פב; שו"ת אגרות משה או"ח ח"א סי' קז;
שש"כ מ"ח פי"ח סכ"ט; קצה"ש כלל לט תד"ו ס"ק י, כא.

5. ש"ע או"ח סי' שג סי"ח, משנה ברורה ס"ק סב; ערוך השלחן שם סכ"ב.

6. ש"ע או"ח סי' שג סי"ח, ביה"ל ד"ה כי בזה, משנה ברורה ס"ק טז, סה; ערוך השלחן סכ"ב;
משנה ברורה סי' שא ס"ק לח ושעה"צ ס"ק לג; חיי אדם כלל נו ס"א; שש"כ מ"ח פי"ח
סי"ב, סכ"ד; מקור חיים פ' קסט ס"ב; שמ"ב מ"ת סי' פד ס"ב בק"א שם; שו"ת אגרות
משה או"ח ח"א סי' קיא.

7. ש"ע או"ח סי' ש"א סי"א, משנה ברורה ס"ק מה וביה"ל שם ד"ה בזה; ערוך השלחן שם
סעי' סב; חיי אדם סי' נו ס"ב; זכרו תורת משה סי' מה סכ"א וקהלת יום טוב שם ס"ק לו;
לחם הפנים על קצש"ע סי' פד ס"ב; שש"כ מ"ח פי"ח סעי' כו, כז; שמ"ב סי' פד ס"ק ג
וקונטרס אחרון שם.

8. שו"ת אגרות משה או"ח ח"א סי' קיא; שו"ת יחוה דעת ח"ג סי' כג; מקור חיים פ' קסט
ס"ד; שש"כ מ"ח פי"ח סכ"ז; עי' מנוחה נכונה עמ' סח דמוטב שלא לשאתו אם לא לצורך
גדול; ושו"ת ציץ אליעזר חי"א סי' כח שדעתו לאסור וכן בשו"ת מנחת יצחק ח"א סי' סז.
ועי' שמ"ב סי' פד ס"ק ג מ"ש בשם המג"א סי' שא ס"ק טו דבעניין תכשיט תלוי הדבר לפי
המקום והזמן.

9. ש"ע סי' שא סי"א, משנה ברורה סי' מב, מה; שש"כ מ"ח פי"ח סמ"ח; פסקי הל' שבת
ח"א פ"ג ס"א, ושו"ת הגאב"ד דעברעצין שם ח"ג תשובה ל.

10. ש"ע או"ח סי' שא ס"ז ובה"ל שם ד"ה כל היוצא; שש"כ מ"ח פי"ח סכ"ג.

11. מצודת דוד על קצש"ע סי' פד ס"ג; תוס' חיים על חיי אדם כלל נו ס"ק ה; שש"כ מ"ח
פי"ח סט"ז, יז, יח; מקור חיים ח"ג פ' קסט ס"ה; מנוחה נכונה עמ' סח; שמ"ב מ"ת סי' פד
ס"ק ד; ספר משנה הלכות ח"ז סי' נז.

12. ש"ע או"ח סי' שא סי"ד, משנה ברורה ס"ק נג, נד, ושעה"צ ס"ק נז, מגן אברהם שם ס"ק
כג; שש"כ מ"ח פי"ח ס"י; ועי' שו"ת מנחת יצחק ח"ג סי' כו אות ח.

13. שו"ת אגרות משה או"ח ח"א סי' קח-קי ושו"ת תשובות ומנהגות סי' רמב דעתם לאסור;

ועי' שו"ת באר משה ח"א סי' ל דעתו להתיר אבל לא בפומבי, וכן מביא דעת הג' ר' משה
צבי ארי' ביק שם בח"ב סי' לא, אלא שאינם מוחים במי שמקיל בדבר; ובשש"כ מ"ח פי"ח
ס"י מביא דעת הגרש"ז אויערבך להקל במקומות שאין מקפידין להסיר הציפוי בשעה
שהגשם פסק דבטיל לגבי הכובע וחשיב דרך מלבוש, וכן שו"ת ציץ אליעזר ח"י סי' כג,
ומקור חיים פ' קסט ס"ג להתיר; ועי' חיי אדם כלל נו ס"ד ומ"ב סי' שא ס"ק נה, שו"ת
מנחת יצחק ח"ג סי' כו אות ח; שמ"ב מ"ת סי' פד ס"ק ה; שו"ת יביע אומר ח"ה או"ח סי'
כג, כד.

14. שש"כ מ"ח פי"ח סכ"ה; שו"ת באר משה ח"ג סי' סט.

15. עי' ש"ע או"ח סי' שא סט"ו סי' שג סי"ב; שש"כ מ"ח פי"ח סט"ו, פל"ד סכ"ט; שו"ת
הגר"מ שטערן שאלה מג, בפסקי הל' שבת ח"ג.

16. ש"ע או"ח סי' שא סנ"א, משנה ברורה ס"ק קפ; שש"כ מ"ח פי"ח ס"כ; שו"ת באר משה
ח"א סי' יז אות ה, וסי' יח.

17. שערי תשובה סי' שא ס"ק ג; שו"ת נודע ביהודה מהדו"ק סי' יא ומהדו"ת סי' כח; ערוך
השלחן או"ח סי' תקכב ס"ב; שמ"ב סי' פ ס"ק ע וסי' פד ס"ה בק"א שם; שש"כ מ"ח
פל"ד סכ"ז; עי' שו"ת מנחת יצחק ח"ב סי' קיד; ועי' ספר לב אברהם פכ"ג ס"ב שכן הורה
לו הגר"ע יוסף והגרש"ז אויערבך.

18. עי' שו"ת ציץ אליעזר ח"ו סי' ו; שש"כ מ"ח פל"ד סכ"ח; שו"ת באר משה ח"ו בקונטרס
עלעקטריק סי' יד; שמ"ב מהדו"ק סי' פ ס"ק לט אות ה; יסודני ישרון ח"ה עמ' רכז; קצה"ש
כלל לט תד"ו ס"ק יא; מקור חיים פ' קסט ס"ו; ספר עדות לישראל עמ' קכב; עי' שו"ת
אגרות משה או"ח ח"ד סי' פה שיש חשש פקוח נפש כשירצה לילך החוצה שלא ישמע
נסיעת המכוניות; ועי' מקור חיים פ' קסו ס"ט; שו"ת תשובות והנהגות סי' רמד.

19. שש"כ מ"ח פי"ח סי"ג הערה סב.

20. ש"ע או"ח סי' שא סי"ז, רמ"א שם, ט"ז ס"ק יב, באר היטב ס"ק יז, משנה ברורה ס"ק סד,
סה; שו"ת נודע ביהודה מהדו"ת סי' כח; תוס' חיים על ח"א כלל נו ס"ק יג; שש"כ מ"ח
פי"ח סי"ב.

21. עי' משנה ברורה סי' שא ס"ק ע הטעם מפני שאין זה דרך מלבוש, וכן ברמב"ם הל' שבת
פי"ט הט"ו. ועי' במשנה שבת ו, ח, "אנקטמין טהורין ואין יוצאין בהן" ופיה"מ לרמב"ם,
"אנקטמים כמו מנעל מעץ", אלא שמבואר שם הטעם שאין מקבלין טומאת מדרס, "שלא
תקבל ההליכה בהם", ובנעלי שלג כאלה כן מקבלים ההליכה בהם ורגילים להשתמש בהם
בימי החורף במקומות האסורים בשלג, כנ"ל.

22. ש"ע או"ח סי' שא סכ"ב, משנה ברורה ס"ק עז, קח.

23. שו"ת ציץ אליעזר חי"ג סי' מט; שש"כ מ"ח פי"ח ס"כ; שו"ת הגר"מ שטערן, שאלה כט,
בפסקי הל' שבת ח"ג.

24. ש"ע או"ח סי' שג סט"ו, משנה ברורה ס"ק מב; שש"כ מ"ח פי"ח סכ"א.

25. ש"ע או"ח סי' שא שג סי"ג, סי' שג סט"ו ומשנה ברורה ס"ק מה; שו"ת באר משה ח"א סי' טז,
וח"ב סי' סו; שש"כ מ"ח פי"ח ס"כ.

26. שו"ת ציץ אליעזר חי"ד סי' נח; עי' ש"ע הרב סי' שא ס"י, וערוך השלחן סי' שא סס"ה;
ועי' ספר לב אברהם פ"י ספ"ב מ"ש בשם הגרא"י וולדינברג שמותר משום שהוא מונע
מכאב וצער וגם מזיהום בשלפוחית השתן שהוא יותר חשוב מצער הגוף.

27. ש"ע או"ח סי' שא ס"ל, לא, לד, ומשנה ברורה ובאור הלכה שם.

28. שו"ע או"ח סי' שא סל"א, משנה ברורה ס"ק קי"ח; שו"ת ציץ אליעזר חי"ג סי' לג; עי' ששכ"ז מ"ח פי"ח ס"ד, ושו"ת באר משה ח"ג סי' סג, דמותר אלא שבר"ה גמורה נכון להחמיר דיש לחשוש שמא יפול.

29. שו"ע או"ח סי' שא סי"ד; ששכ"ז פי"ח ס"י והערה מו.

30. שו"ת אגרות משה או"ח ח"א סי' קח; ששכ"ז מ"ח פי"ח ס"י; שמ"ב מ"ח סי' פד ס"ק ה; ועי' ש"ע או"ח סי' שא סל"ו.

31. שו"ע או"ח סי' שא סל"ו, משנה ברורה ס"ק קלו, קלז.

32. שו"ע או"ח סי' שא סל"ו מחבר ורמ"א שם, משנה ברורה ס"ק קלד; חיי אדם כלל נו סי"א; שו"ת אגרות משה ח"ב סי' עו וח"ד סי' קא אות ה; ששכ"ז מ"ח פי"ח ס"ה; יסדי ישרון ח"ה עמ' רמו; ועי' פה"ש ח"א פ"ג סי' לג שמביא בשם הגר"מ שטערן שאוסר אם לא שלובש הגרטל כל השבת ולא רק בעת התפלה; עי' שו"ת באר משה ח"ג סי' סד.

33. שו"ע או"ח סי' שא סכ"ג, ט"ז ס"ק יד, ובאר היטב ס"ק כא, משנה ברורה ס"ק קלג; ערוך השלחן סמ"ח; חיי אדם כלל נו סי"א וע"י תוס' חיים שם ס"ק יז דבמקום שרגילים גם בחול לכורכה מסביב לצואר והקצוות תלויים מותר אף בשבת. עי' שו"ת ציץ אליעזר חי"ג סמ"ט; שמ"ב מ"ת סי' פד ס"ק יא-יג; ועי' ששכ"ז מ"ח פי"ח סמ"ז שאם אי אפשר לו באחד האופנים הנ"ל והוא זקוק למטפחת מאד, כגון שהוא מצונן ויש משום כבוד הבריות התירו איסור דרבנן ויכול לכורכה מסביב לידו או להכניסה בתוך מגבעתו, אלא שיש להיזהר בזה שרבים נכשלים בו, ועי"ש סכ"ה מ"ש במטפחת הנתונה בכיס לקישוט.

34. שו"ע או"ח סי' שא סל"ז, משנה ברורה ס"ק קלט, קמא; ששכ"ז מ"ח פי"ח ס"ד; מנחה נכונה פ"ג סי' לט; שו"ת באר משה ח"ו סי' פא; ועי' פה"ש ח"ג סי' סו מ"ש בשם הגר"מ שטערן דאם הכפפות מחוברין לבגד ע"י מהדקים ולא ע"י תפירה אסור לצאת לר"ה כשהן תלויין אלא שצריך להכניס ידיו לתוכן.

35. ששכ"ז מ"ח פי"ח ס"ד; שמ"ב מ"ת סי' פד ס"ק יד; עי' קצה"ש כלל לט תד"ו ס"ק יח שמפקפק בדבר.

36. שו"ע או"ח סי' יג ס"ב וס"ג, ומשנה ברורה ס"ק ד; סי' שא סכ"ט, ל, לח, ומשנה ברורה ס"ק קיא-קיג, קמג; ששכ"ז מ"ח פי"ח ס"ו וסל"ח; עי' ערוך השלחן סי' שא ס"ק ח שמותר לצאת בטלית גדול בליל יום כיפור לבד דאז לובשין אותה בלילה, אולם בסי' יג ס"ב כותב שמותר לצאת לר"ה בשבת בין בטלית קטן בין בטלית גדול ואפילו בלילה שאינו זמן ציצית שהרי הם נוי הבגד. ועי' קצש"ע סי' קלא סט"ו שלא ילך ברחוב לבוש בקיטעל שהוא בגד מיוחד לתפלה. ונ"ל שמטעם זה יש למנוע גם לצאת ברחוב לבוש בטלית וכ"ש בין נכרים.

37. שו"ע או"ח סי' שג סי"ד, משנה ברורה ס"ק לו ושעה"צ ס"ק לב; ערוך השלחן שם סי"ז; ששכ"ז מ"ח פי"ח ס"ז; שו"ת הגר"מ שטערן בפה"ש ח"ב שאלה כט.

38. שו"ע או"ח סי' שא סכ"ג רמ"א שם, ומשנה ברורה ס"ק פג; משנה ברורה סי' שא ס"ק מה; ש"ע הרב סי' שא ס"ב; ששכ"ז מ"ח פי"ח סכ"ה. עי' שמ"ב מ"ת סי' פד ס"ק יט שמסתפק במי שנושא מזוזה על צוארו אם מותר לצאת בשבת, דבקמיע שאינו מומחה אסור לצאת לרה"ר ואף לכרמלית, עי' ש"ע או"ח סי' שא סכ"ה וסי' שח סל"ג ומשנה ברורה שם, ובתוס' יו"ט כלים פי"ז מט"ז כתוב שהיו אנשים בזמן המשנה נושאים מזוזה עמם וחשבו זה למצוה ולשמירה. ונ"ל שמי שנושא מזוזה לשם זיהוי כיהודי, כאלה שנושאים מגן דוד על צוארם, הרי היא כתכשיט.

5. Carrying Belongings Out of a House In Case of Fire on the Sabbath

דין אם נפלה דליקה בשבת

קצור שלחן ערוך סימן פה, חיי אדם כלל מה, מו

1. טוש"ע סי' שלד סי"א בשם שם יש אומרים; חיי אדם כלל מה, מו ס"ג-ז שדעתו להקל לפי ספר התרומה שלחצר שלו ולבית חביריו שעירב עמו יכול להוציא כל מה שירצה, ועי' משנה ברורה סי' שלד ס"ק א, ד; לחם הפנים על קצש"ע סי' פה ס"ק א. ותי' חיי אדם שם ס"ח מ"ש בשם או"ה והמרדכי; עי' שמ"ב סי' פה ס"ק א; שש"כ מ"ח פמ"א ס"ה, ו.

2. ש"ע או"ח סי' רסו סי"ג משנה ברורה ס"ק לח ובאור הלכה ד"ה מצא ארנקי ד"ה פן יקדמנו אחר; חיי אדם כלל נד ס"י; שש"כ מ"ח פכ"ב סל"ד. עי' שמ"ב מהד"ת סי' פה ס"ק ב בשם נשמת אדם שסמך עצמו על הרמב"ם הל' שבת פי"כ ה"ז. לפי הרמב"ם אם יכול להחשיך עליה יחשיך ואם לאו מוליכה פחות פחות מארבע אמות. והקשו עליו מפרשי הרמב"ם שהרי בגמרא שבת קנג, א מבואר שדוקא כיסו אבל מציאה לא, ותי' מגיד משנה ומגדל עוז שם מה שהשיב הרמב"ם בתשובה לחכמי לוניל.

3. ש"ע או"ח סי' שלד סי"ב יז, משנה ברורה ס"ק ל, לא, מח; שש"כ מ"ח פמ"א סי"ג.

4. ש"ע או"ח סי' שלד סכ"ו משנה ברורה שם, עי' מגן אברהם שם ס"ק ל, באר היטב ס"ק כב; ש"ע הרב שם סכ"ה; מסגרת השלחן סי' פה ס"ק ב שמותר לומר לנכרי לכבות משום כתבי הקודש, והמזוזות שקבועים בכל חדר, ותי' מג"א שם ס"ק כג דשבות דאמירה לעכו"ם שרי מפני בזיון כתבי הקודש; עי' חיי אדם כלל מה, מו ס"ט; עי' שש"כ מ"ח פ"ל סי"ב, פמ"א סט"ו.

5. משנה ברורה סי' שלד ס"ק ל, סח.

6. ש"ע או"ח סי' שכט ס"א, סי' שלד סכ"ו רמ"א שם, משנה ברורה שם ס"ק עג, עד; שש"כ מ"ח פמ"א ס"א.

7. שש"כ מ"ח פמ"א סכ"א, כב.

8. ש"ע סי' רעז ס"ג משנה ברורה ס"ק יג, יד, סי' שלד סכ"ב; שמ"ב מהד"ת סי' פה ס"ק ג; שש"כ מ"ח פמ"א סי"ז, יח.

9. ש"ע או"ח סי' שלד סכ"ו רמ"א ומשנה ברורה שם.

Part V
Muktzeh and Additional Sabbath Laws, Concluding the Sabbath
1. Bathing

דין רחיצה

קצור שלחן ערוך סימן פו, חיי אדם כלל ע

1. ש"ע או"ח סי' שכו ס"א רמ"א ומ"ב שם ס"ק א, ז, יז, כד, לו, ובאור הלכה שם ד"ה במים שהוחמו מע"ש; ש"ע הרב שם ס"א; ערוך השלחן שם ס"ג; מסגרת השלחן סי' פו ס"ק ב;

שו"ת נודע ביהודה מהדו"ת או"ח סי' כד; ששכ"ד פי"ג ס"א ס"ק א, ב; ועי' מ"ב סי' שכח ס"ק קלו.

2. שו"ת אגרות משה או"ח ח"ד סי' עד ערך רחיצה אות א, ג, וסי' עה אות א; שו"ת נודע ביהודה מ"ת או"ח סי' כד; שערי תשובה סי' שכו ס"ק א, מ"ב שם ס"ק כד, ובאור הלכה שם ד"ה במים שהוחמו; שמ"ב מ"ת סי' פו ס"ק ב; ששכ"כ מ"ת פי"ד ס"א, יד.

3. ש"ע או"ח סי' שכו מ"ב שם ס"ק כה; שו"ת אגרות משה או"ח ח"א סי' קלג; שמ"ב מ"ת סי' פו ס"ק ד; ששכ"כ מ"ח פי"ד ס"כ, כא.

4. ש"ע או"ח סי' שלט ס"ב, ו, מ"ב ס"ק לד, ובאור הלכה ד"ה ואם יש לה שפה, מ"ב סי' שכו ס"ק כא; חיי אדם כלל מד ס"כ, תוס' חיים שם ס"ק יב; ערוך השלחן סי' שכו ס"ט וסי"י; ועי' ספר הלכות שבת ח"ד עמ' 393; שער המזרח סי' פו ס"ק ד בשם כף החיים; ספר מנוחה נכונה פ"ג סי"ג עפ"י פסקי חזו"א; וששכ"כ פ' יג ס"י; מקור חיים פ' קנ סל"א; ששכ"ח פי"ד סי"ב, פט"ז סל"ח.

5. ש"ע או"ח סי' שכו ס"ז, טז ס"ק ב, ומשנה ברורה ס"ק כג.

6. שו"ת אגרות משה או"ח ח"ג סי' פז; ועי' מגן אברהם סי' שכו ס"ק ח ומ"ב שם ס"ק ז, כד ובאור הלכה שם ד"ה האדם מותר; חיי אדם כלל ע ס"א; חכמת אדם כלל קכב ס"כ; ועי' שו"ת נודע ביהודה מ"ת או"ח סי' כד.

7. באור הלכה סי' שכו ס"י ד"ה בשאר חלב, עי"ש מ"ש בשם ביאור הגר"א דאסור בבורית שנעשה מחלב מטעם דסיכה כשתיה, מיהו מנהג העולם להתיר אלא שנכון לחוש לדעת המחמירין אם מצוי להשיג בורית שלא מחלב.

8. ש"ע או"ח סי' שכ ס"י וסי' שכו ס"י ומ"ב שם ואיסורו משום נולד, עי"ש בשם תפארת ישראל בדבורית שלנו שהיא רכה אסור משום ממחק ומנהג כל ישראל להחמיר. עי' סי' שכו ס"י במגן אברהם ובאר היטב שם בשם ש"ג ותשובת גנת ורדים דיש מתירין ואין למחות ביד העושים כן. ועי' בערוך השלחן סי' שכו ס"א שמתיר בבורית שניתך מע"ש, ועי' מ"ב סי' שכו ס"ק לח שמותר ליטול ידיו במי מלח. עי' שו"ת אגרות משה או"ח ח"א סי' קיג; שו"ת יחוה דעת ח"ב סי' נ; ששכ"כ מ"ח פי"ד סט"ז.

9. תוס' חיים על ח"א כלל ע ס"ק ה; קצשו"ע סי' פו ס"ז, לחם הפנים שם.

2. Laws Concerning Cattle, Animals and Fowl

דברים שצריכין ליזהר בבהמות, חיות, ועופות
קצור שלחן ערוך סימן פז, חיי אדם כלל נז-נט

1. ש"ע או"ח סי' שה ס"א, משנה ברורה ס"ק א וסי' רמו ס"ג באור הלכה שם ד"ה שביתת בהמה; מכילתא, שמות כג, יב; ועי' רש"י שם, ותוס' שבת קכב, א, ד"ה מעמיד אדם בהמתו.

2. מגן אברהם סי' רמו ס"ג ס"ק ח וסי' רסו ס"א ס"ק א; כלכלת שבת, ערך דיני שביתת בהמה ומחמר ס"ה.

3. חיי אדם כלל נח ס"א; כלכלת שבת שם ס"ב.

4. ש"ע או"ח סי' שה ס"א, ה, ז ומ"ב שם.

5. שבת נד, ב, רש"י שם, משנה ברורה סי' שה ס"ק מב, מג.

6. שבת נד, א, ב, רש"י שם, ש"ע או"ח סי' שה סט"ז; שמ"ב מ"ת, קונטרס אחרון סי' פז
   ס"א; ששכ"ג מ"ח פכ"ז ס"כ; עי' שו"ת באר משה ח"ו סי' צה ובפה"ש ח"א שאללה ט.

7. שו"ת אגרות משה או"ח ח"א סי' מה; ששכ"ג מ"ח פי"ח הערה כב.

8. ביצה לו, ב; ש"ע או"ח סי' שה סי"ח, משנה ברורה ס"ק סא; חיי אדם הל' שבת כלל נז ס"י
   וסט"ז.

9. ש"ע או"ח סי' שה סי"ח ומ"ב ס"ק סו, ועי' שער הציון שם ס"ק נח דאם הבהמה שלו עובר
   גם על שביתת בהמה.

10. עי' שמ"ב מ"ת סי' פז ס"ק ה; מקור חיים סי' פ' קמו ס"ט-יד; ששכ"ג מ"ח פכ"ז סמו-נג.

11. ש"ע או"ח סי' שה ס"כ, מגן אברהם שם ס"ק יב; חיי אדם כלל נט סי"ב; משנה ברורה סי'
    שה ס"ק עא.

12. ש"ע או"ח סי' רמו ס"ג, באור הלכה שם ד"ה בהמתו לא"י, משנה ברורה שם ס"ק יד, לב
    ומגן אברהם שם ס"ק ט בשם הב"ח; חיי אדם כלל נז, סי"ד; תפארת ישראל, כלכלת שבת,
    ערך שביתת בהמה ס"ו.

13. ש"ע סי' שכד סי"ג; חיי אדם כלל נט, ס"ח, כלל סב, ס"ח; משנה ברורה סי' שכה ס"ק סד,
    ושער הציון שם.

14. ש"ע או"ח סי' שלו ס"ד.

15. חיי אדם הל' שבת כלל לא ס"ב; שו"ת באר משה ח"ב סי' כח, וח"ח סי' סט אות ד; מקור
    חיים פ' קעב סמ"ד; אולם עי' ששכ"ג מ"ח פכ"ז הערה צו דעת המתירים לטלטל דגים במים
    בתוך הזכוכית המיוחדים לנוי.

16. ש"ע או"ח סי' שכד סי"א ומ"ב שם; חיי אדם כלל נט ס"ז; ערוך השלחן סי' שכד ס"ב,
    וס"ג; ש"ע או"ח סי' שח סל"ט, ומ"ב סי' שכד ס"ק כח; ששכ"ג מ"ח פכ"ז סכ"א, כג.

17. עי' מגן אברהם סי' שכד ס"ג ומ"ב ס"ק לא דאינו נכון לתת חטים לפני העופות בשבת
    שירה; אולם עי' ערוך השלחן סי' שכד ס"ג דעתו להתיר דמנהג ישראל תורה; עי' תוס' חיים
    על ח"א כלל נט ס"ק ג; שמ"ב מ"ת סי' פז ס"ק ח; שו"ת ציץ אליעזר חי"ד סי' כח; ששכ"ג
    מ"ת פכ"ז סכ"א.

18. ש"ע או"ח סי' שטז סי"ב, מ"ב שם ס"ק נט, סא.

19. באור הלכה סי' שלב ס"א ד"ה אין מילדין; מנוחה נכונה פ"ד עמ' עה עפ"י פסקי החזון
    איש.

3. Laws of Muktzeh

דיני מוקצה בשבת

קצור שלחן ערוך סימן פח, חיי אדם כלל סה, סו, כלכלת שבת, כללי מוקצה

1. רמב"ם הל' שבת פכ"ד הי"ב, יג, השגת הראב"ד שם.

2. חיי אדם כלל סה, כלכלת שבת, ערך כללי מוקצה, משנה ברורה, הקדמה לסי' שח.

3. ש"ע או"ח סי' שח ס"ו, כ, כא, כב, כו, כט; חיי אדם כלל סה ס"ג; ספר טלטולי שבת פ"ד,
   פ"ה.

4. ספר טלטולי שבת, הל' מוקצה פ"ז; שו"ת באר משה ח"ב סי' כח; שו"ת אגרות משה או"ח
   ח"ד סוף סי' טז. ששכ"ג מ"ח פכ"ז סכ"ה הערה פה, ופי"ח הערה סב.

5. ש"ע או"ח סי' שח סכ"ז, וס"ל, ט"ז ומשנה ברורה שם; חיי אדם כלל טז ס"ד ותוס' חיים שם ס"ק ד; שו"ת באר משה ח"א סי' כא.

6. ספר טלטולי שבת, הלכות מוקצה פ"ה עמ' 110, 109.

7. ש"ע או"ח סי' שח ס"ו, מ"ב ס"ק ל; ספר טלטולי שבת, הל' מוקצה פ"ד עמ' 87; שמ"ב מ"ח סי' פח ס"ק ד.

8. ש"ע או"ח סי' שלח ס"ח משנה ברורה ס"ק ל; חיי אדם כלל ס"ה ס"ג, כלכלת שבת, ערך כללי מוקצה ס"ו; ספר טלטולי שבת, הל' מוקצה פי"ב, יג; שו"ת באר משה ח"א סי' כ, ח"ו סי' ל; ששכ"ח מ"ח פט"ז סמ"ד.

9. ש"ע או"ח סי' שיח סט"ו ומ"ב שם, שו"ת ציץ אליעזר ח"א סי' לד וח"ח סי' יב, ששכ"ח מ"ח פ"י ס"ז; מקור חיים ח"ג י' קעב סכ"א וכב, ספר טלטולי שבת, הל' מוקצה פי"ב עמ' 165, עשיית גלידה אסורה משום שמוליד ועושה בריאה חדשה.

10. ש"ע או"ח סי' שח, ס"ג ומשנה ברורה שם; ספר טלטולי שבת, הל' מוקצה פ"ב.

11. ש"ע או"ח סי' רעט ס"א, ב, ד, ומ"ב שם, ובאור הלכה ס"א ד"ה נר; ובס"ג משמע דאין לטלטל נר ע"י שנותנים עליו לחם מבעוד יום, ועי' שו"ת ציץ אליעזר חי"ב סי' ל שבא לישב המנהג להסיר הטס והמנורות לאחר שיכבו בשעת הצורך בליל שבת או ביומו ע"י שישימו על הטס מע"ש לחם או סידור וכדומה כדי שהטס יהא בסיס להיתר ולאיסור, ועי' מגן אברהם שם ס"ק ה ומחצית השקל הטעם שפוסק הש"ע שאין לסמוך על היתר זה.

12. ספר טלטולי שבת, הל' מוקצה פי"ז עמ' 213; תשובות הגר"מ פיינשטיין שם אות יא; שמ"ב מ"ח סי' פח, ס"ה בקונטרס אחרון שם; ועי' שו"ת אגרות משה או"ח ח"ד סי' צא אות ה; שו"ת מנחת יצחק ח"ג סי' מג; שו"ת ציץ אליעזר ח"ו סי' ו אות ד; שו"ת באר משה ח"ו ק"ע סי' כו; ששכ"ח מ"ח פכ"ח סכ"ד.

13. ספר טלטולי שבת, הל' מוקצה פ"ב עמ' 52, 60, 62, תשובות הגר"מ פיינשטיין שם אות ח, ותשובות הגרש"ז אויערבך שם אות ד; שו"ת אגרות משה או"ח ח"ג סי' מט, נ, וח"ה סי' ג; שו"ת יחוה דעת ח"ה סי' כח.

14. ששכ"ח מ"ח פ"כ ס"ע; ספר טלטולי שבת, הל' מוקצה פ"ב עמ' 50, תשובות הגר"מ פיינשטיין שם אות ז, ותשובות הגרש"ז אויערבך שם אות ג; שו"ת באר משה ח"א סוף סי' כו.

15. ש"ע או"ח סי' שח, ס"ד משנה ברורה שם, ועי' סי' לא, משנה ברורה ובאור הלכה שם; חיי אדם כלל סו, ס"ב, ולולב אסור לטלטלו אפילו לצורך גופו ומקומו דאין עליו שם כלי כלל; ספר טלטולי שבת, הל' מוקצה פ"ב עמ' 55, פ"ה עמ' 158; ששכ"ח מ"ח פ"כ ס"ד והערה לג; שו"ת הגר"מ שטערן בפה"ש ח"ג שאלה לב; שו"ת באר משה ח"ח סי' עב, עג; ספר משנה הלכות ח"ז סי' ד.

16. ש"ע או"ח סי' שא סל"ב מ"ב ס"ק ס"ד קכא, ומגן אברהם ס"ק מה, וסי' שג סכ"ב ומ"ב שם; כלכלת שבת, ערך כללי מוקצה ס"ב.

17. ש"ע או"ח סי' שח, ס"כ ומ"ב שם, וסי' תצד, ס"ג ומ"ב שם ס"ק ט, ששכ"ח מ"ח פכ"ו סכ"ה, כו; ספר הלכות שבת עמ' 61, 64; ספר טלטולי שבת, הל' מוקצה פ"א עמ' 31, ופ"ד עמ' 86.

18. ש"ע או"ח סי' שח סנ"א משנה ברורה ס"ק קסח; ספר טלטולי שבת, הל' מוקצה פ"א עמ' 21-19.

19. ש"ע או"ח סי' שח ס"ד, באר היטב ומשנה ברורה שם; ערוך השלחן או"ח סי' שח, ס"י, יא; ספר טלטולי שבת, הל' מוקצה פ"א; שו"ת באר משה ח"ו סי' כד, כה.

20. משנה ברורה סי' שח ס"ק כב.

21. ש"ע או"ח סי' רסה, ס"ג, משנה ברורה שם; קצש"ע סי' עה סי"א.

22. ש"ע או"ח סי' שי ס"ז.

23. ש"ע או"ח סי' שח סל"ח משנה ברורה שם.

24. ש"ע או"ח סי' שח, סכ"ג, משנה ברורה ס"ק צט.

25. שער המזרח על קצש"ע סי' פח סי"ב בשם כף החיים.

26. ש"ע או"ח סי' שח, ס"ג, משנה ברורה ס"ק יט, ש"ע הרב שם סי"ד; שמ"ב מ"ת סי' פח, סי"ב בקונטרס אחרון שם.

27. ש"ע או"ח סי' שח, ס"ג, מג, וסי' שיא ס"ח ומ"ב שם; חיי אדם כלל סז, סי"ד; מסגרת השלחן סי' פח ס"ק כו, כז; ש"ע הרב או"ח סי' שח, סי"ד, טו, כ; ועי' ט"ז סי' שח ס"ק יח שמתיר ע"י סכין, ועי' באר היטב שם ס"ק לד שהט"ז חזר בו בסי' שיא ס"ק ב; ועי' ספר טלטולי שבת הל' מוקצה פי"ט ותשובות הגר"מ פיינשטיין שם אות לב.

28. כללכת שבת ערך כללי מוקצה ס"ג וס"ז; ספר טלטולי שבת, הל' מוקצה פכ"א.

29. ש"ע או"ח סי' טש ס"א, משנה ברורה שם ובאור הלכה שם ד"ה וי"א.

30. ש"ע או"ח סי' שי"א ס"א, ב, ד, סי' תקכו ס"ג; ועי' גשר החיים פ"ג סי' ב אות ג שמותר להוריד המת על הארץ ע"י דבר המותר ולהפשיט בגדיו, ובמקום שא"א מטלטלין אותו בלאו הכי דכבוד הבריות דוחה איסור טלטול בשבת; שו"ת ציץ אליעזר חי"א סי' לה.

31. חיי אדם כלל סז סי"ח, משנה ברורה סי' שיא ס"ק כב, עי"ש איך ליישר האברים בשבת במקום שנוהגין להקל.

32. ש"ע או"ח סי' שיא ס"א, וס"ב, ט"ז שם ס"ק א, משנה ברורה שם ס"ק יב, ובאור הלכה שם ד"ה וכל זה; ש"ע הרב שם ס"א, ב.

33. ש"ע או"ח סי' שח סל"ד, לה; ספר טלטולי שבת, הל' מוקצה פ"ו עמ' 114, 113.

34. ש"ע או"ח סי' שח, ט"ז שם ס"ק יח, ומשנה ברורה שם ס"ק קטו, ספר טלטולי שבת, הל' מוקצה פכ"א עמ' 268, 264.

4. Laws Concerning a Base for a Forbidden Article

דין בסיס לדבר האסור

קצור שלחן ערוך סימן פט, חיי אדם כלל סז, כלכלת שבת, כללי מוקצה

1. חיי אדם כלל סז ס"א.

2. חיי אדם כלל סז ס"ד, תוס' חיים שם ס"ק ד, משנה ברורה סי' רעו ס"ק יח; ש"ע הרב או"ח סי' שט ס"ט; מסגרת השלחן סי' פט ס"ק ג; תוס' חיים על ח"א כלל סז ס"ק ב.

3. חיי אדם כלל סז ס"ד, תוס' חיים שם ס"ק ג.

4. שו"ת אגרות משה או"ח ח"ד סי' עב.

5. חיי אדם כלל סז ס"ה, תוס' חיים שם ס"ק ב; ש"ע או"ח סי' רעט ס"ג, משנה ברורה שם ס"ק י ספר טלטולי שבת, הל' מוקצה תשובות הגר"מ פיינשטיין שם אות ל; ועי' תשובות

הגרש"ז אויערבך שם אות טו שמתיר לטלטל הטס לאחר שנכבו הנרות אם מונח עליו דבר
חשוב כגון כוס של כסף וכדומה, ועי' בפמ"ג א"א סוף סי' רעט. ועי' שו"ת ציץ אליעזר
חי"ב סי' ל דעת המתירין שם.

6. מגן אברהם סי' שי ס"ז, ומשנה ברורה שם ס"ק כט.

7. חיי אדם כלל סז ס"י וסי"א, משנה ברורה סי' שי ס"ק לא.

8. משנה ברורה סי' רעז ס"ק ז, וש"ע הרב שם ס"ג.

9. ש"ע או"ח סי' שי ס"ג; ספר טלטולי שבת, הל' מוקצה פ"כ עמ' 238; תשובות הגר"מ
פיינשטיין שם אות לג.

10. ספר טלטולי שבת הל' מוקצה פ"כ עמ' 238; פרי מגדים א"א סוף סי' רעט.

11. ש"ע או"ח סי' טש ס"ד, מגן אברהם ס"ק ח, ומשנה ברורה ס"ק כז.

5. Weekday Activities Forbidden on the Sabbath

דין עשיית חפציו בלא מלאכה

קצור שלחן ערוך סימן צ, חיי אדם כלל ס, סא

1. כללכת שבת סי' א; ר"ן שבת ג, ב ד"ה אמר רב ביבי; רמב"ם הל' שבת פכ"ד הי"ב.

2. ש"ע או"ח סי' שח סמ"ה, משנה ברורה ס"ק קנח, סי' שלח ס"ה, משנה ברורה ס"ק כ, ועי'
סי' שא ס"ב באור הלכה שם ד"ה כל; ששכ"כ פט"ז ס"ו, לד; תורת השבת פי"ח ס"ו; מנוחה
נכונה פ"ד עמ' עד; שו"ת מנחת יצחק ח"ג סי' לג; ועי' שו"ת באר משה ח"ב סי' כז שאוסר
משחק טניס השולחן מטעם השמעת קול ועובדא דחול.

3. ש"ע או"ח סי' שא ס"ב, מגן אברהם ומשנה ברורה שם, סי' שכח סמ"ב ומשנה ברורה שם;
שו"ת ציץ אליעזר ח"ו סי' ד, וחי"ב סי' מה; מקור חיים ח"ג פ' קעג סמ"ג.

4. ש"ע או"ח סי' שא ס"א; קצש"ע סי' יב סי"א.

5. מנוחה נכונה פ"ד עמ' עב, עד, סידור ספרים אסור גם מטעם בורר.

6. מנוחה נכונה פ"ד עמ' עג.

7. שו"ת ציץ אליעזר חי"ד סי' לז אות ב; עי' ששכ"כ מ"ח פ"כ ס"כ.

8. ש"ע או"ח סי' שז ס"ט, מגן אברהם ומ"ב שם; שמ"ב מ"ת סי' צ ס"ג קונטרס אחרון שם;
ששכ"כ מ"ח פט"ו סכ"ב, ופ"כ סע"ז; שו"ת באר משה ח"א סי' לב אות יד.

9. שו"ת אגרות משה ח"ד סי' קה אות ג.

10. משנה ברורה סי' שז ס"ק ה בשם השל"ה; תוס' חיים על חיי אדם כלל סא ס"ק ז.

11. משנה ברורה סי' שז ס"ק ה; תוס' חיים על חיי אדם כלל סא ס"ק ג בשם זוה"ק פ' מקץ.

12. ש"ע או"ח סי' שו ס"ו, משנה ברורה סי' שכג ס"ק כ.

13. משנה שבת פכ"ג מ"ד; ש"ע או"ח סי' שו וס"ו, הגירסא שם ולשדך התינוק, ועי' משנה
ברורה שם ס"ק כט שצ"ל ולשדך התינוקת כדאיתא בכתובות ה, א, וכן במה ידידות בזמירות
ליל שבת כתוב ולשדך הבנות, אכן בשבת קנ, א הגירסא משדכין על התינוקות ליארס בשבת,
ומפירוש המשניות להרמב"ם ממסכת שבת פכ"ג משמע דמיירי בבנים ובנות וז"ל מלבד אם
הוא דבר מצוה ויהיה דבור חפצי שמים כגון שידבר בו אדם בשדוכי הנערים והנערות.

14. משנה שבת פכ"ג מ"ד, ש"ע או"ח סי' שו ס"ג.

15. ש"ע או"ח סי' שו סי"א, ומשנה ברורה שם.

16. שערי תשובה סי' שו ס"ק ג בשם שאלת יעב"ץ סי' קסב; עי' שמ"ב מ"ת סי' צ ס"ק ו ומ"ש בשם המאירי שבת קיג טעם ההיתר בהרהור משום דלא נתנה תורה למלאכי השרת.

17. שבת יב, א; רמב"ם הל' שבת פכ"ד ה"ה; ש"ע או"ח סי' רפז ס"א ועי' שערי תשובה שם ס"ק א דמי שהוא מיצר על יסורי החולה אין לו לילך בשבת לבקר דלעונג ניתן ולא לצער; עי' חיי אדם כלל סא ס"א ותוס' חיים שם ס"ק ד; שו"ת ציץ אליעזר חי"ג סי' לו, וספר רמת רחל סי' יד.

18. ש"ע או"ח סי' שו ס"ה, ומשנה ברורה שם; ש"ע הרב סי' שו סי"א, שער המזרח סי' צ ס"ק ה בשם כף החיים; עי' שו"ת יביע אומר ח"ה סי' כה; שו"ת ציץ אליעזר ח"ז סי' כח.

19. משנה ברורה סי' שו ס"ק לג; שמ"ב מ"ת סי' צ ס"ק ח; פסקי הלכות שבת ח"ג פ"י הל' מח בשם הגר"מ שטערן שליט"א.

20. משנה ברורה סי' שז ס"ק נב, נה, נו, סג; חיי אדם כלל סא ס"ח, ותוס' חיים שם ס"ק ט.

21. ש"ע או"ח סי' שז סט"ז, יז ומשנה ברורה ס"ק סה, וסי' שח ס"נ ומשנה ברורה ס"ק קסד עי"ש שמותר להביט באצטרולוב (משקפת) בשבת וכן לטלטלה ולכוון אותה; שש"כ מ"ח פט"ז סמ"ה; ספר טלטולי שבת הל' מוקצה עמ' 140; עשה לך רב ח"א סי' לו.

22. ש"ע או"ח סי' שז סט"ז רמ"א שם, ומשנה ברורה ס"ק סג; כללת שבת מלאכת המוחק; מנוחה נכונה פ"ד ס"ד קי"ז; שמ"ב מ"ת סי' צ ס"ק י; תוס' חיים על ח"א כלל סא ס"ק ג.

23. ש"ע או"ח סי' רצ ס"ב וב"י סי' רפח בשם ירושלמי; משנה ברורה סי' שז ס"ק ד.

24. ש"ע או"ח סי' שכג ס"א-ד, ומשנה ברורה שם; ועי' ש"ע הרב סי' שו סי"ט.

25. ש"ע או"ח סי' שו ס"ז, משנה ברורה ס"ק לה; שמ"ב מ"ת סי' צ בקונטרס אחרון שם.

6. Work on the Sabbath By a Non-Jew

מלאכה על ידי אינו יהודי

קצור שלחן ערוך סימן צ, חיי אדם כלל סב, כללת שבת, אמירה לעכו"ם

1. ש"ע או"ח סי' שז ס"ג וס"ג ומשנה ברורה ס"ק ח; כללת שבת דיני אמירה לעכו"ם; עי' טעם איסור אמירה לעכו"ם ברמב"ן שבת פ"ו ה"א, וטעם אחר ברש"י עבודה זרה טו, א, דאף שבני נח לא נצטוו על השבת "אסור לישראל לומר לעכו"ם עשה לי כך משום ממצוא חפצך ודבר דבר (ישעיה נח, יג) דבור אסור".

2. ש"ע או"ח סי' רמה ס"א, ס"ה, סי' רנב ס"ב; רמב"ם הל' שבת פ"ו הי"ב-יד; מקור חיים פ' קה ס"א-ו.

3. תפארת ישראל, כללת שבת, דיני אמירה לעובד כוכבים.

4. חיי אדם כלל סב ס"ו; כללת שבת דיני אמירה לעכו"ם.

5. תשובות הגר"מ שטערן בפה"ש ח"ב שאלה לט; עי' שו"ת תשובות והנהגות סי' רעט דנראה שאסור להניח גוי להביא לו בשבת שמוציא מרשות לרשות בשבילו, וגם זהו מקח הנעשה בשבת שישראל זוכה ונתחייב בדמים בשבת.

6. ש"ע הרב או"ח סי' שז סי"ב; מסגרת השלחן על קצש"ע סי' צ ס"ק טז; תוס' חיים על ח"א כלל סב ס"ק יא; ועי' מגן אברהם סי' רסא ס"ק ו מ"ש בשם רש"ל דאין חילוק בין צורך גדול להפסד מרובה; שמ"ב מ"ת סי' צ ס"ק יב בקונטרס אחרון שם; עי' משנה ברורה סי' שז ס"ק כד.

7. שו"ת באר משה ח"ז ק"ע סי' ל, לא.

8. שו"ת אגרות משה או"ח ח"ג סי' מב; שמ"ב מ"ת סי' צ ס"ק כ.

9. חיי אדם כלל ס"ב ס"י; ש"ע או"ח סי' רעו ס"ה משנה ברורה שם.

10. ש"ע או"ח סי' שו ס"ט, משנה ברורה ס"ק מא; קצש"ע סי' קצג ס"ח.

11. ש"ע יו"ד סי' קטו ס"ב ש"ך וט"ז שם ופתחי תשובה ס"ק ו; ועי' קצש"ע כאן סי' צ סכ"א שכותב שכיון שהחלב והגבינות עדיין של הנכרי מותר, ובסי' לח סי"ד כותב שאם הגבינות בשעת עשייתן של עכו"ם אסורות וצ"ע.

12. ש"ע או"ח סי' שכה ס"א וסי' תקי"ב ס"א ומשנה ברורה שם; קצש"ע סי' פז סי"ט, סי' פב ס"ט, וסי' צח סל"ו; שבת יט, א, ותוס' שם ד"ה נותנין; גיטין סא, א; רמב"ם הל' עכו"ם פ"י ה"ה.

7. Laws on Treatment of a Minor Ailment and One Whose Illness Is Not Critical.

דין מי שיש לו מיחוש בעלמא וחולה שאין בו סכנה
קצור שלחן ערוך סימן צא, חיי אדם כלל סט

1. ש"ע או"ח סי' שו ס"י ומשנה ברורה ס"ק לו; שו"ת אגרות משה או"ח ח"א סי' קכח; שו"ת ציץ אליעזר ח"ג סי' י, חי"א סי' לח, חי"ב סי' מד, חי"ד סי' ל, לא; שו"ת מנחת יצחק ח"ג סי' קמב; שו"ת יחוה דעת ח"ד סי' כט; ששכ"ח מ"ח פ"מ ס"ב; שו"ת באר משה ח"ב סי' כב, וח"ו סי' נו ועי' ח"ו ק"ע סי' עז שיותר טוב למדוד החום ע"י מד-חום.

2. רמב"ם הל' שבת פכ"א ה"ך; ש"ע או"ח סי' שכח ס"א, ב, יז; חיי אדם כלל סט ס"א, ה; קצש"ע סי' צא, מצודת דוד שם.

3. שו"ת ציץ אליעזר חי"א סי' לז וחי"ב סי' מה; ששכ"ח מ"ח פל"ד סי"ז-יט; שו"ת באר משה ח"א סי' לג, וח"ו סי' לט; עי' שו"ת אגרות משה או"ח ח"ג סי' נג שמתיר רק במצטער טובא או שלא יוכל להתרפא ויחלה; עי' שמ"ב מ"ת סי' צא ס"ק ב וק"א שם מ"ש בשו"ת רדב"ז ח"ג סי' אלף ס"ה בשם גדולי הראשונים דהך איסורא משום שחיקת סממנין היא גזירה דרבנן בעלמא וקולא טפי אפילו מאמירה לעכו"ם בשבות דרבנן, ועי' באור הלכה סי' שכח סל"ז ד"ה וכן שמרמז לדברי הרדב"ז, ועי' שו"ת ציץ אליעזר חי"ד סי' נ וח"י סי' טו פט"ו. עי' רמ"א סי' שלט ס"ג מ"ש בשם י"א בנוגע לגזירה דשמא יתקן כלי שיר, דבזמן הזה ליכא למגזר דאין אנו בקיאין בעשיית כלי שיר, ומלתא דלא שכיח הוא, ולכן נהגו להקל.

4. מקור חיים ח"ג פ' קעג סמ"ז; שו"ת אגרות משה או"ח ח"ג סי' נד; שו"ת ציץ אליעזר חי"ד סי' נ; שו"ת באר משה ח"א סי' לג, ח"ו סי' לט, עי' ח"ב סי' לב שהרה"ג ר' יונתן שטייף ז"ל התיר אספירין בשבת; שמ"ב מ"ת סי' צא ס"ק ג, ובק"א שם ועל סט"ז.

5. ש"ע או"ח סי' שכח סל"ז; מקור חיים ח"ג פ' קעג סמ"ה, מח; שו"ת באר משה ח"א סי' לג אות ה, יב; שו"ת ציץ אליעזר חי"א סי' לז.

6. ש"ע או"ח סי' שכח סל"ז; שמ"ב מ"ת סי' צא ס"ק ד; שו"ת באר משה ח"א סי' לד אות ז.

7. שו"ת באר משה ח"א סי' לו אות ד, ח"ב סי' ל; ששכ"ח מ"ח פי"ד סכ"ח, ל, ופל"ז ס"ו.

8. שבת מ, ב, רש"י ותוס' שם; ש"ע או"ח סי' שכו ס"ו ומ"ב ס"ק יט; קצש"ע סי' לג סי"ב;

שו"ת באר משה ח"א סי' לג אות טו; שש"כ מ"ח פל"ג סט"ו; שו"ת ציץ אליעזר ח"ח סי' טו פט"ו.

9. שו"ת באר משה ח"א סי' לג אות יז, יח.

10. ש"ע או"ח סי' שכח ס"ט; שש"כ מ"ח פל"ד ס"ח; שו"ת ציץ אליעזר ח"ח סי' טו פ"י, ח"ט סי' יז פ"ב אות יט, חי"ג סי' פג.

11. ש"ע או"ח סי' שכח סמ"ט ומשנה ברורה שם; חיי אדם כלל סט סכ"ב; שו"ת ציץ אליעזר ח"ח סי' טו פט"ו; שש"כ מ"ח פל"ג סי"ב; מקור חיים ח"ג פ' קעג סמ"ה; שו"ת באר משה ח"א סי' לג אות טו; שמ"ב מ"ת סי' צא ס"ק ו, ע"ש בשם הגהות מהרש"ם שעשיית חוקן במים לבד בלי תרופות מותרת במקום צער, ועי' שו"ת ציץ אליעזר ח"ח סי' טו פט"ו אות יא שבמקום כאב בבטן מותרת בכל גוונא.

12. ש"ע או"ח סי' שכח, סכ"ה, משנה ברורה ס"ק פב, שש"כ מ"ח סי' לה ס"ב, ח, כ, כז, שו"ת ציץ אליעזר ח"ז סי' ל, ח"ח סי' טו פ' יד, חי"ב סי' מא; ספר לב אברהם פ"י ס"ע, עא; שו"ת באר משה סי' לו אות א, ח"ו סי' לח; מקור חיים ח"ג פ' קעג ס"ס.

13. משנה ברורה סי' שכח ס"ק קמו; שו"ת ציץ אליעזר ח"ח סי' טו פי"ד אות טו; לב אברהם פ"י סס"ב.

14. משנה ברורה סי' שכח ס"ק צ, ושער הציון שם ס"ק סז, סח.

15. שש"כ מ"ח פ"מ סי"ט.

16. ש"ע או"ח סי' שכח ס"ב, ז, יז, ומשנה ברורה שם; שו"ת אגרות משה או"ח ח"א סי' קכ"ט; שו"ת ציץ אליעזר ח"ח סי' טו, פט"ו; שש"כ מ"ח פל"ג ס"א; שו"ת באר משה ח"ו סי' נז.

17. ש"ע או"ח סי' רעו ס"א רמ"א שם, וסי' שכח סי"ז רמ"א שם, שו"ת אגרות משה או"ח ח"א סי' קכ"ט; שו"ת ציץ אליעזר ח"ח סי' טו פ"י; שש"כ מ"ח פל"ז.

18. שש"כ מ"ח פל"ז סט"ו; עי' שו"ת באר משה ח"ו סי' נא, נב ובפה"ש ח"ב שאלה י, יא; ועי' הל' שבת ח"ב דיני זורה ס"ד ס"ק סד בשם הגר"מ פיינשטיין ז"ל; עי' החשמל בהלכה ח"ב פל"א.

19. שו"ת ציץ אליעזר ח"ח סי' טו פי"ד אות ח, ט, יב, ופט"ו; ח"ט סי' יז פ"ב אות כ, סי' טו פ"ח אות ב, פי"ד אות כב, וסי' כח אות י, חי"ג סי' מה, מו; שו"ת יחוה דעת ח"ב סי' נו; מקור חיים פ' קעג סל"ט; שש"כ מ"ח פל"ב סנ"ז, נח, ופל"ג ס"ז, כא; יסודי ישרון מערכת הל' שבת עמ' 292; שמ"ב מ"ת סי' צא ס"ק יא וק"א שם.

8. Laws Concerning One Who Is Critically Ill and One Forced To Transgress

דין חולה שיש בו סכנה ודין אנוס לעבירה
קצור שלחן ערוך סימן צב, חיי אדם כלל סח

1. רמב"ם הל' שבת פ"ב ה"א, טז, יז, יח, כג, כד; ש"ע או"ח סי' שכח ס"ב, יג, סי' שכט ס"א, ג, ו, ח.

2. רמב"ם הל' שבת פ"ב ה"א, ב; ש"ע או"ח סי' שכח ס"ב; מקור חיים פ' קעג ס"ב; שש"כ פי"ט ס"ד, ובמ"ח פל"ב; ועי' שו"ת אגרות משה או"ח ח"ד סי' פא שמתיר יציאה בשבת

במכשיר קשר (ביפער) הנצרך להצלת נפשות; וע" שו"ת ציץ אליעזר ח"ח וח"ט קונטרס בדיני רפואה בשבת.

3. ש"ע או"ח סי' שכח משנה ברורה ס"ק יז; ששש"כ מ"ח פל"ב ס"ח; מקור חיים ח"ג פ' קעג סל"ב.

4. שו"ת ציץ אליעזר חי"א סי' מג; ששש"כ מ"ח פל"ב ס"ג הערה יג; עי' יומא פ"ח ברא"ש סי' יג בשם הרמב"ן וקרבן נתנאל שם ס"ק י; טור או"ח סי' תריג וב"י שם, ש"ע או"ח סי' ס"ז, באור הלכה שם ד"ה או ספק.

5. בבא קמא צא, ב, משנה ברורה סי' שכח ס"ק ו בשם הרדב"ז.

6. שו"ת ציץ אליעזר ח"ד סי' יג ס"ג, סי' יז אות ג, ח"ח סי' טו פ"י, יב, סי' טז פי"ב ס"ה; חי"ג סי' לה; לדעתו של הגרא"י, וולדינברג שליט"א חולה במחלת הנפילה מוגדר כחולה שיש בו סכנה.

7. ש"ע או"ח סי' שכח רמ"א שם וט"ז ס"ק ה, ומשנה ברורה ס"ק לז; עי' יומא פד, ב, ורמב"ם הל' שבת פ"ב ה"ג; ששש"כ מ"ח פל"ח ס"א, ב.

8. רמב"ם הל' שבת פ"ב ה"א, ב; ש"ע או"ח סי' רעח ס"א, משנה ברורה ס"ק ב; סי' שכח ס"ד ומ"ב ס"ק יד, סב ובסי' של ס"ק כא; מגן אברהם סי' שכח ס"ק ד; חיי אדם כלל סח ס"ט; שו"ת יחוה דעת ח"ד סי' ל; מקור חיים פ' קעג סכ"א, כד, כו; ששש"כ פי"ט ס"ה, ו, ובמ"ח פל"ב סי"ח, כז-כט, לד, נב, סג, סד, ע, פא, פג.

9. מקור חיים ח"ג פ' קעג סכ"ה; שו"ת ציץ אליעזר ח"ח סי' טו פ"ז אות יב; ששש"כ (תשכ"ה) פי"ט סי"ג, כג, כז, כט, במ"ח פל"ב; וע" שמ"ב מ"ת סי' צב ס"ק ז ובקונטרס אחרון שם מ"ש בדבר היתר ליסע למקום החולה המסוכן לזרז להרופאים ולפקח על החולה ולשמשו.

10. רמב"ם הל' יסודי התורה פ"ה ה"ב; ש"ע יו"ד סי' קנז ס"א; חיי אדם הל' ברכות כלל כא סי"ג.

11. שו"ת אגרות משה או"ח ח"ד סי' פ, פא.

12. שו"ת ציץ אליעזר חי"ג סי' נה, נו, והוא שלא מכל אדם זוכה להתרפאות; וע" ששש"כ מ"ח פל"ב סמ"ו ופ"מ ס"ט שמותר לרופא להיענות לצלצול הטלפון כל שקיים חשש שחולה שיש בו סכנה מתקשר אתו, ושיעשה זאת בשינוי. וע" שו"ת באר משה ח"ו ק"ע סי' נג.

13. ששש"כ פי"ט ס"ז, ח, יד, טו, יט, ובמ"ח פל"ב ס"ג, נז, ופ"מ סל"א, לב, לח; שו"ת ציץ אליעזר חי"ב סי' מג; מקור חיים פ' קעג ס"ו; שו"ת באר משה ח"ז ק"ע סי' נ.

14. ש"ע יורה דעה סי' שלו ס"א; רמב"ם פיה"מ נדרים פ"ד; שו"ת ציץ אליעזר ח"ה, ספר רמת רחל סי' כא, עי"ש דמלבד הלימוד מורפא ירפא (שמות כא, יט) שנתנה רשות לרופא לרפא נלמד עוד מקרא דואהבת לרעך כמוך (ויקרא יט, יח) חיוב לרפות; שו"ת אגרות משה או"ח ח"א סי' קלא וח"ד סי' עט; שו"ת ציץ אליעזר ח"ח סי' טו, חי"א סי' יז, חי"ב סי' לט, מ, ובדין חילול שבת בשביל חולה נכרי עי' ש"ע או"ח סי' של ס"ב ומשנה ברורה ס"ק ח; ששש"כ מ"ח פ"מ סי"ד; שו"ת ציץ אליעזר ח"ח סי' טו פ"י, ובמקורות שם.

15. ש"ע או"ח סי' שכט ס"ד, ובאור הלכה שם ד"ה אלא לפי שעה, דהתורה חסה על חיי שעה וע" מ"ש בשם המאירי, עי' משנה ברורה סי' שכח ס"ק לז; עי' שו"ת ציץ אליעזר חי"ס סי' טו פ"ג; ששש"כ מ"ח פל"ב ס"ב.

16. שו"ת ציץ אליעזר ח"ח סי' טו פ"י, פי"ד אות לא; מקור חיים פ' קעג ס"ל; ששש"כ מ"ח פל"ב סי"א; שו"ת באר משה ח"ז ק"ע סי' נ.

17. חיי אדם כלל סט סי"א; שו"ת ציץ אליעזר ח"ח סי' טו פ"י; מקור חיים פ' קעג ס"ז.

18. שבת קט א, משנה ברורה סי׳ שכח ס״ק ח; מקור חיים פ׳ קעג ס״י; עי׳ שו״ת ציץ אליעזר
ח״ח סי׳ טו פ״י, דכשחז״ל קבעו שישנו בדבר משום סכנה אין בידי חות דעת הרופאים
לשנות הדינים האמורים בזה בהחלטיות, ולכן לו גם אם יש רק ספק בדבר הרי ספק נפשות
להקל, וכל מה שקבעו חז״ל בזה הוא ע״פ סוד ה׳ ליראיו ואת אשר ראו בחכמתם הקדושה
ברוח אלקים אשר עליהם.

19. ש״ע או״ח סי׳ שכח סמ״ז, משנה ברורה ס״ק קמה; וערוך השלחן שם סל״ט וס״מ; שו״ת
ציץ אליעזר ח״ח סי׳ טו פ״י, חי״ד סי׳ נא, פט; ששכ״כ מ״ח פל״ג סי״ז.

20. ש״ע או״ח סי׳ שכו ס״א; שו״ת ציץ אליעזר ח״א סי׳ לג אות יג, ח״ח סי׳ טו פ״י, חי״א סי׳
לז, חי״ב סי׳ מד; מקור חיים פ׳ קעג סי״ד.

21. ש״ע או״ח סי׳ שכח ס״ז, משנה ברורה ס״ק יט, כ; שו״ת ציץ אליעזר ח״ח סי׳ טו פ״י;
ששכ״כ מ״ח פל״ב סי״א; שו״ת אגרות משה או״ח ח״א סי׳ קכט; שו״ת באר משה ח״ו סי׳
נז.

22. ש״ע או״ח סי׳ שכח ס״ט, משנה ברורה ס״ק כב, כג; ששכ״כ פ״כ ס״א ס״ק ו, פכ״א ס״ו
ובמ״ח פל״ד ס״ח; שו״ת ציץ אליעזר ח״ח סי׳ טו פ״י, חי״ד סי׳ פט.

23. ש״ע או״ח סי׳ שכח סי״ד, באר היטב ומשנה ברורה שם; חיי אדם כלל סח ס״י, ועי״ש
מחלוקת הפוסקים אם שבת הותרה או דחויה אצל פקוח נפש, וגם טעם הר״ן דבאכילת נבלה
וטרפה עובר על כל כזית וכזית; ועי׳ תוס׳ חיים שם שצריך לברך על השחיטה, אבל אסור
ליקח שכר על שחיטה זו; ועי׳ שמ״ב מ״ת סי׳ צב ס״ק יב וקונטרס אחרון שם דיש גם
למלוח הבשר; עי׳ שו״ת מהרש״ח ח״ז סי׳ נא.

24. חיי אדם כלל סח סי״א, משנה ברורה סי׳ שכח סל״ט, מד; ששכ״כ פי״ט סכ״ד, כה, כו וס״ק
קיז שם, כז, ובמ״ח פל״ב סע״ב-עד.

25. משנה ברורה סי׳ שכח ס״ק לא; ועי׳ משנה ברורה סי׳ שו ס״ק נח דמ״ש הרמ״א בסי׳ שכח
ס״י שאין מחללין עליו השבת כדי להצילו מעבירה גדולה מיירי שרוצים לאנסו שיעבור
העבירה רק פעם אחת, משא״כ כאן שרוצים להוציאו מכלל ישראל ושיחלל שבת לעולם.

9. Laws Concerning a Woman in Childbirth

דיני יולדת

קצור שלחן ערוך סימן צג, חיי אדם כלל סח

1. ש״ע או״ח סי׳ של ס״א מגן אברהם ומשנה ברורה שם, תוס׳ חיים כלל ס״ח ס״ק יז; ששכ״כ
מ״ח פל״ו ס״א, ז.

2. שו״ת ציץ אליעזר חי״ג סי׳ נה; עי׳ רמב״ם הל׳ שבת פ״ב הי״א; ש״ע או״ח סי׳ ס״א.

3. שו״ת אגרות משה או״ח ח״א סי׳ קלב; ששכ״כ מ״ח פל״ו ס״ח, יא, ופ״מ ס״ע; עי׳ שו״ת
באר משה ח״ו ק״ע סי׳ נא.

4. משנה ברורה סי׳ של ס״ק ה.

5. משנה ברורה סי׳ של ס״ק ט; ששכ״כ פכ״ג ס״ו, ובמ״ח פל״ו ס״ט.

6. שו״ת ציץ אליעזר חי״א סי׳ מג, ששכ״כ (תשכ״ה) פי״ט ס״ט והערה נח שם; ובמ״ח פל״ב
הערה יג, פל״ו ס״ב.

7. משנה ברורה סי׳ של ס״ק י-יד; ששכ״כ פכ״ג ס״ב, ובמ״ח פל״ו סי״ג, יד, טו.

8. .משנה ברורה סי' שכח ס"ק נז, וסי' של ס"ק טו, ושער הציון שם ס"ק יג.

9. .שש"כ פכ"ג ס"ו, ובמ"ח פל"ו סי"ו סעיף כד; עי' שמ"ב מ"ת סי' צג ס"ק ג.

10. ש"ע או"ח סי' שכח סל"ד, לה, וסי' של ס"ח ומשנה ברורה שם; שו"ת ציץ אליעזר ח"ח סי'
   טו סי"ב; שש"כ פכ"ג סי"ג-טו, ובמ"ח פל"ו ס"כ, כא.

11. ש"ע או"ח סי' רעו ס"א רמ"א שם, וסי' שכח סי"ז רמ"א שם; מקור חיים פ' קעג סע"ג
   בשם החזון איש; שש"כ מ"ח פל"ז ס"א, ב.

10. The Eruv of Courtyards

דיני עירובי חצרות
קצור שלחן ערוך סימן צד, חיי אדם כלל עב-עה

1. .משנה ברורה סי' שעב ס"ק ג.

2. עירובין כא, ב; רמב"ם הל' עירובין פ"א ה"א-ד; ש"ע או"ח סי' שסו ס"א, ומשנה ברורה
   שם; חיי אדם כלל עב ס"א; תפארת ישראל פתיחה לעירובין.

3. .משנה ברורה סי' שעה ס"ק א.

4. ש"ע או"ח סי' שע ס"ב, משנה ברורה שם, חיי אדם כלל עג ס"ג, ד; שו"ת אגרות משה
   או"ח ח"א סי' קמא; אולם עי' שו"ת מנחת יצחק ח"ד סי' נה מ"ש בשם תשו' מהרש"ם
   ח"ה סי' לד, דכלי הבית המושכרין להשוכר לא נקרא תפיסת יד לבעה"ב. וכן בשו"ת באר
   משה ח"ח סי' יב אות יא בשם מהרש"ם.

5. .משנה ברורה סי' שסח ס"ק א, וט"ז שם ס"ק א.

6. ש"ע או"ח סי' שסו ס"ט ומשנה ברורה ס"ק נב, נג; סי' שסח ס"ה רמ"א שם ומ"ב ס"ק כא,
   וסי' שצד ס"ב רמ"א שם ומ"ב ס"ק ד.

7. ש"ע או"ח סי' שצג ס"א, ומשנה ברורה שם.

8. ש"ע או"ח סי' שע ס"ד ומ"ב ס"ק מג, ועי' בה"ל שם ד"ה וישן מ"ש בשם הפמ"ג
   דתלמידים שאוכלים בבית בעלי בית ולנים בבית רבם דאזלינן בתר לינה דניחא להו טפי.

9. ש"ע או"ח סי' שע ס"ד וס"ד ומשנה ברורה שם; מקור חיים פ' קסח ס"ז; שש"כ פכ"ז
   הערה לד, ובמ"ח פי"ז הערה פו.

10. עירובין סא, ב, משנה וגמרא שם; ש"ע או"ח סי' שפב ס"א, משנה ברורה שם, דחכמים גזרו
   דליאסר עליו כדי שלא ידור עם העכו"ם וילמוד ממעשיו, ולא גזרו אלא בדבר דשכיח דהיינו
   במקום שדרים כמה ישראלים, ועי' תפארת ישראל, פתיחה לעירובין.

11. משנה ברורה סי' שפב ס"ק ז בשם הגר"א, ובשער הציון שם ס"ק ו, ועי' באור הלכה סי'
   שפד ס"א ד"ה אינו אוסר.

12. ש"ע או"ח סי' שפב ס"ד, ה, ט, משנה ברורה שם, ושער הציון שם ס"ק לא, ובאור הלכה
   ריש סי' שפב ד"ה צריך שישכירו; ועי' תשובת הגר"מ קליין בקובץ שערי הלכות תשרי ה'
   תש"ל חוב' ד דיכול לקנות רשות מבעל הבית הנקרא לענדלארד או מן שכירו הנקרא סופער
   ולכתחילה יותר טוב לשכור מבעה"ב.

13. שמ"ב מ"ת סי' צד ס"ק טו בשם חזון איש, ועי' שם ס"ק י בשם מהרש"ם דבשעת הדחק יש
   לצרף דברי המקילים.

14. ש"ע או"ח סי' שפה ס"ג מגן אברהם ומשנה ברורה ובאור הלכה שם; חיי אדם כלל עה
סכ"ו; מסגרת השלחן סי' צד ס"ק יא; ועי' בש"ע הרב סי' צב ס"ג מ"ש בשם תוס' עירובין
סט, א ד"ה הוציא, שאינו נקרא מומר לחלל שבתות בפרהסיא אלא כשרגיל בכך ואינו נזהר
כלל; ועי' ש"ך יו"ד סי' ב ס"ה ס"ק יז, דנעשה מומר אפילו חילל שבת פעם אחת בפרהסיא,
ואפשר דלענין עירוב מקילין כהפוסקים דבחד זימנא לא מקרי מומר; עי' מחצית השקל סי'
שפה ס"ק ב.

15. עי' שו"ת חתם סופר או"ח סי' צט וז"ל „השכל הפשוט גוזר שראוי ומחוייב לתקן החצרים
והמבואות בעירוב המתיר טלטול". ועי' שמ"ב מ"ת סי' צד ס"ק יז מ"ש עוד מתשובת
הרא"ש כלל כא סי' ח ושו"ת תשב"ץ ח"ב סי' לח.

16. ש"ע או"ח סי' שמה ס"ז וסי' שסד ס"ב משנה ברורה ובאור הלכה שם, ועי' מגן אברהם סי'
שמה ס"ק ז שדעת רוב הפוסקים להקל וכ"פ בש"ע סי' שג סי"ח דהשתא לית לן רה"ר גמור
וכל רה"ר שלנו כרמלית.

17. ש"ע או"ח סי' שסו ס"ג רמ"א שם; חיי אדם כלל עב ס"א; מקור חיים פ' קסח ס"ז; שמ"ב
מ"ת סי' צד ס"ק יט.

18. משנה ברורה סי' רעו ס"ק כה; קצש"ע סי' פ סמ"ה; מחצית השקל סוס"י שסה; שמ"ב מ"ת
סי' צד ס"ק כג; שש"כ מ"ח פ"ל סכ"ב ופי"ז סכ"ה שלא להכריז ברבים דמוטב שיהיו
שוגגים.

11. The Eruv of Boundaries

דין עירובי תחומין

קצור שלחן ערוך סימן צה, חיי אדם כלל עו-עח

1. רמב"ם הל' שבת פכ"ז ה"א; חיי אדם כלל עו ס"א ותוס' חיים שם; משנה ברורה סי' שצז
ס"ק א.

2. חיי אדם כלל עו ס"א; משנה ברורה סי' שצז ס"ק ה, ובאור הלכה שם.

3. חיי אדם כלל עו ס"ב; משנה ברורה סי' שצח ס"ק יט.

4. ש"ע או"ח סי' שצח ס"י, ומשנה ברורה ס"ק לח.

5. ש"ע או"ח סי' תטו ס"א, משנה ברורה ס"ק ו; מנוחה נכונה פ"ח עמ' צב.

6. ש"ע או"ח סי' תט ס"ז, משנה ברורה ובאור הלכה שם.

7. ש"ע או"ח סי' שסח ס"ג וסי' תט ס"ז, ומשנה ברורה שם.

8. ש"ע או"ח סי' תט ס"ו, משנה ברורה סי' תטז ס"ק ט; מסגרת השלחן סי' צה ס"ק ג.

9. ש"ע או"ח סי' תח ס"א רמ"א ומ"ב שם.

10. רמ"א סי' תח ס"א, משנה ברורה ס"ק יא, יב; מסגרת השלחן סי' צה ח"א ס"י.

11. ש"ע או"ח סי' תטו ס"א ומשנה ברורה שם.

12. ש"ע או"ח סי' תטו ס"א, משנה ברורה ס"ק ב, ד, ה, ועי' מ"ש רמ"א שם שהרוצה לילך
לטייל ביו"ט או שבת בפרדס שיש בו שמחה בזה מקרי דבר מצוה.

13. ש"ע או"ח סי' שכה ס"ח, משנה ברורה ס"ק לו, וסי' תקטו ה"ד משנה ברורה ס"ק מז, מח.

14. ש"ע או"ח סי' תד ס"א, רמ"א שם, ומשנה ברורה ס"ק י; ועי' מ"ב ס"ק טו דאם מחמת

אונס נכנס בתוך עיר מוקפת מחיצות נחשב לו כל העיר כד"א; חיי אדם כלל עו סל"ג;
מנוחה נכונה פ"ח עמ' צב.

15. ש"ע או"ח סי' תד ס"א, משנה ברורה ס"ק ז, ח; ועי' שמ"ב סי' צה ס"ק ז, דכמו דאין
תחומין למעלה מעשרה טפחים כך אין תחומין למטה מעשרה מתחת לארץ.

12. The Evening (Maariv) Prayer and Havdalah

דיני תפלת ערבית ודיני הבדלה
קצור שלחן ערוך סימן צו, חיי אדם כלל ח

1. ש"ע או"ח סי' רסא ס"ב משנה ברורה שם ובה"ל ד"ה שהוא, וסי' רצג ס"ב ומ"ב שם;
שו"ת אגרות משה או"ח ח"ד סי' סב; ספר עדות לישראל מדור ההלכה עמ' 150; שמ"ב
מ"ת סי' צו ס"ק א.

2. משנה ברורה סי' רצג ס"ק א; עי' ערוך השלחן סי' רצז ס"ב על מנהג החזנים לומר והוא
רחום וברכו באריכות ובנעימות כדי להוסיף מחול על הקודש.

3. ש"ע או"ח סי' רצד ס"א ומ"ב ס"ק ג, וסי' רצט ס"י ומ"ב ס"ק לד.

4. ש"ע או"ח סי' רצד ס"ב, מ"ב ס"ק ו.

5. משנה ברורה סי' רצד ס"ק ב; קצש"ע סי' כא ס"ו.

6. משנה ברורה סי' רצה ס"ק ג.

7. טור וש"ע או"ח סי' רצה ס"א, ומ"ב ס"ק ב.

8. ש"ע או"ח סי' רצח ס"א מ"ב ס"ק א, ב, וסי' רצט ס"ו.

9. ש"ע או"ח סי' רצו ס"ח מ"ב שם, מגן אברהם שם ס"ק יא; חיי אדם כלל ח סי"ב ותוס'
חיים שם ס"ק יא; עי' שו"ת יביע אומר ח"ד סי' כד.

10. שו"ת באר משה ח"ג סי' קסו, וח"ז ק"ע סי' קי, קיט; ספר מנחת שלמה סי' ט, שאין לענות
אמן על ברכה ששומע ע"י טלפון הואיל ושומע את הברכה רק ממברנה ולא מפי אדם, ועי'
מ"ש בשם בעל החזו"א שלדעתו אין זה כ"כ פשוט, ויתכן דכיון שהקול הנשמע נוצר ע"י
המדבר וגם הקול נשמע מיד כדרך המדברים אפשר דגם זה חשיב כשומע ממש מפי המדבר,
ועי' שו"ת אגרות משה או"ח ח"ב סי' קח וח"ד סי' צא אות ד שגם לדידיה מספקא טובא
ואפשר שנחשב כקולו ממש, וכן צריך לענות אמן על ברכה ששומעין ע"י טלפון ומייקרופון
מספק, אך כיון שלא ברור להיתר יש למחות מלהשתמש במכשירים אלו.

11. ערוך השלחן סי' ערב סי"ד, וסי' רצו ס"ב; שו"ת ציץ אליעזר ח"ח סי' טז, יח, וחי"ד סי'
מב; שו"ת באר משה ח"ו סי' נג; שו"ת אגרות משה או"ח ח"ב סי' עה; שו"ת יביע אומר
ח"ג סי' יט; שו"ת יחוה דעת ח"ב סי' לח; ועי' מ"ב סי' ערב ס"ק כה וסי' רצו ס"ק ט
שלדעתו אין חלב בכלל חמר מדינה, ושאין כדי להבדיל על יי"ש וכשאין לו משקה אחר
יכול להבדיל עליו, ואך שיזהר לשתות כמלא לוגמיו שהוא רוב רביעית.

12. ש"ע או"ח סי' רצו ס"ב, מ"ב ס"ק ז וס"ק י.

13. תוספות חיים על חיי אדם כלל ח ס"ק יד.

14. ש"ע או"ח סי' רצט ס"י, מגן אברהם ומ"ב שם; מסגרת השלחן סי' צו ס"ק ה.

15. מגן אברהם סי' רצט ס"ק טו בשם אבודרהם; מ"ב סי' ש ס"ק ב, שערי תשובה שם ס"ק א.

16. משנה ברורה סי' רסג ס"ק סז בשם הפמ"ג.

17. ש"ע או"ח סי' רחץ ס"א רמ"א שם; חיי אדם כלל ח סכ"ב; ש"ע הרב סי' רצז ס"א ורחץ
ס"ג; עי' אוצר התפלות עמ' תלו פי' ענף יוסף ועיון תפלה שם; ועי' שבלי הלקט סי' קל,
ומ"ב סי' רצז ס"ק ב, ושו"ת שרידי אש ח"ב סי' כג טעם שמברכים על בשמים במו"ש.

18. ש"ע או"ח סי' רצו ס"א וס"ו, מ"ב שם.

19. משנה ברורה סי' רצו ס"ק לה, עי' מגן אברהם סי' רצו ס"ק ד ואוצר שלם למנהגי ישראל
עמ' 265 טעם השל"ה שגרמה חוה להיות נבדל מאדם ע"י היין מצד נדותה, שבא לאשה דם
נדות סוד הזוהמה שהטיל הנחש בחוה, ועי' שו"ת ציץ אליעזר חי"ד סי' מג מ"ש מס' רוח
חיים שלכן אין הנשים טועמות יין של הבדלה וגם אינן מבדילות. ועי' ספר טעמי המנהגים
ומקורי הדינים ח"א, עניני שבת אות תיז, עוד טעם שחוה כבתה נרו של עולם.

20. משנה ברורה סי' רצו ס"ק א, ב.

21. עי' ש"ע או"ח סי' רחץ סט"ו ומ"ב שם, עי' דעת המתירים בשו"ת ציץ אליעזר ח"א סי' כ
פי"ג, וחי"ד סי' לח, עי"ש מ"ש בשם ספר נחלת שמעון סי' טו שהג"ר חיים סאלאוויציק
בירך על החשמל, ועי"ש חט"ו סי' ג אות ה שהג"ר חיים עוזר היה מבדיל לפעמים על
חשמל כדי להראות שהבערתו היא אש מדאוריתא. ועי' שו"ת באר משה ח"ו ק"ע סא
דבאין לו נר יש להתיר, עי"ש סי' סב אות כא, סג אות כב ובק"ע סי' סו, וח"ז ק"ע סי' ו,
וכן בס' עדות לישראל עמ' 122, ובשמ"ב מ"ת סי' צו ס"ק ו. ועי' שו"ת יחוה דעת ח"ב סי'
לט, ושו"ת יביע אומר ח"א סי' יז, יח דלא מברכין על החשמל, עי' ספר יסודי ישרון ח"ה
עמ' תצד.

22. טור או"ח סי' רחץ ב"י וב"ח שם, מ"ב שם ס"ק ט, עי' שבלי הלקט השלם סי' קל.

23. ש"ע או"ח סי' רצח סי"ג, מ"ב ס"ק לד.

24. ספר מהרי"ל, הל' שבת; או"ח סי' ש ב"י וט"ז שם בשם שבלי הלקט; סדר תפלות כל השנה
ע"י הרב יוסף צבי הערץ, רב הכולל דבריטאניא עמ' 749.

25. חיי אדם כלל ח סל"ה ותוס' חיים שם ס"ק כז בשם האר"י ז"ל.

26. מגן אברהם או"ח סי' ש; עי' ספר מהרי"ל הל' שבת שמהר"י שבת סגל היה לו טלית מיוחד
לשבת והיה כופלו בכל מוצאי שבת כי אמר יש להתעסק במצוה בהתחלת ימי החול; ועי'
תוס' חיים על ח"א כלל ח ס"ק כו שהמנהג הוא תיכף אחר הבדלה.

27. משנה ברורה או"ח סי' ש ס"ק ב; עי' חיי אדם כלל ח סל"ו ותוס' חיים ס"ק כז; ספר יסודי
ישרון ח"ה עמ' תצח; עי' ספר טעמי המנהגים מאת אי"ש שו"ב, חלק עניני שבת סי' תכה
טעם שאומרים במו"ש דא היא סעודתא דדוד מלכא ע"פ מ"ש (שבת ל, א) שאמר הקב"ה
לדוד שימות בשבת ע"כ כשעברה השבת ולא מת היה דוד שמח עם כל ב"ב ועשה סעודה
גדולה בכל מו"ש.

28. משנה ברורה סי' רצו ס"ק לו.

29. משנה ברורה סי' רצט ס"ק טז, ושער הציון שם ס"ק כח, וכן מוכח מלשון הרמב"ם הל'
שבת פכ"ט ה"ד.

הערה מאת הגאון הרב אהרן הלוי סולוביציק שליט״א

בענין מלאכה דאורייתא משום סכנת אבר גרידא

אני רוצה להעיר הערה קטנה בקשר עם מלאכה דאורייתא משום סכנת אבר גרידא בלי
סכנת נפשות, דהמחבר בשולחן ערוך אורח חיים סימן שכח פסק דדוחה רק מלאכת שבות ולא
מלאכה דאורייתא, ופסק המחבר מבוסס על שיטת הרמב״ן, הרא״ש והר״ן דרק בסכנת עורון
מחללין במלאכה דאורייתא משום דשורייתא דעינא בליבא תלי, ורוב הפוסקים האחרונים פסקו
כוותיה — שזה אינו דבר פשוט כלל. ישנם כמה ראשונים דסוברים דכל סכנת אבר נחשב לפקוח
נפש ממש ודוחה כל התורה כולה.

המרדכי בפרק יז ממסכת שבת מזכיר מחלוקת בין ר״י בר שלמה ורבינו תם בענין זה, דר״י
בר שלמה סובר כמו הרמב״ן, הרא״ש והר״ן דרק סכנת עורון דוחה מלאכה דאורייתא אבל לא
שאר סכנת אבר, ורבינו תם אומר „שכל חסרון גוף וחסרון אבר ועובר" נחשב לפקוח נפש
ומחללין במלאכה דאורייתא, ועיין בתוספות סוכה דף כו ד״ה ואפילו חש בעיניו דכתב „דסכנת
אבר כסכנת נפשות אפילו לחלל עליו את השבת". ועיין בהרב המאירי בע״ז דף כ״ח דסכנת אבר
נחשב לפקוח נפש ודוחה כל התורה כולה. ועיין בש״ך ביורה דעה סימן קנז סעיף ג שכתב וז״ל
„ואם יש סכנת אבר צ״ע אי דמי לממון או לנפש, עיין בריב״ש סימן שכו ובאו״ח סימן שכח
סעיף יז ונראה לקולא". ועיין בב״י סימן תריח בהלכות יום הכפורים שמביא בשם רבינו ירוחם
שאם ישנה מחלוקת הפוסקים אם איזה דבר נחשב לסכנת נפשות או לא ורוב פוסקים סבירי להו
דאינו נחשב לפקוח נפש דאז אין אנו סומכין על רוב פוסקים משום דספק נפשות להקל ואין
הולכין בפקוח נפש אחר הרוב.

לכך לפי דעתי יכולים להקל בסכנת אבר גרידא ולחלל שבת במלאכה דאורייתא. ועיין
בתשובות שרידי אש שפסק ג״כ דמחללין מלאכה דאורייתא במקום סכנת אבר גרידא וסמכין
על שיטת הש״ך ביו״ד סימן קנז נגד שיטת המחבר באו״ח סימן שכח, ועיין בפרי מגדים או״ח
סימן שכח שכתב שהש״ך בי״ד סימן קנז מכון לאיסור של לאו גרידא שסכנת אבר דוחה לאו
גרידא שאין בו כרת, אבל סכנת אבר אינה דוחה מלאכה דאורייתא בשבת שיש בה כרת, כמו
שפוסק המחבר באו״ח סימן שכח, ברם דברי הפרי מגדים הם מוזרים וקשים עד מאד. הפשט
הפשוט בש״ך הוא שהש״ך חולק על המחבר והוא פוסק כמו ר״ת ותוספות בסוכה דף כו (את
דברי הרב המאירי בע״ז הש״ך בודאי שלא ראה).

ויש מעשה רב בענין דומה. לפני מאה שנה מרן הגר״ח ז״ל פסק שמחללין את השבת
במלאכה דאורייתא בשביל חיי שעה של ולד בן ח אפילו בן ח ודאי שלא בהתאם לפסק המחבר
באו״ח סימן של סעיף ז דאין מחללין את השבת בשביל בן ח ואפילו בשביל ספק סן ח. עיין במגן
אברהם שם שכתב שם שפסק המחבר שאין מחללין את השבת בשביל בן ח תלוי בשני הלשונות
ברמב״ן ביומא אם מחללין את השבת בשביל סכנת ולד לחודיה אפילו לחודיה דליכא למיחש
לדידה דשיטת בעל ההלכות דמשום סכנת ולד לחודיה מחללין, והשיטה של לשון שני ברמב״ן

היא דלא מחללין בשביל וולד לחודיה, והמחבר פוסק כמו לשון השני ברמב"ן, לכך פסק הגר"ח ז"ל דצריכין אנו לחלל את השבת בשביל בן ח אפילו בשביל חיי שעה של בן ח.

ועיין בחזון איש על אורח חיים שפסק גם כן דהיום מחללין את השבת בשביל בן ח משום שנשתנה הטבע, ברם הגר"ח ז"ל פסק לפני מאה שנה קודם שנשתנה הטבע דמחללין את השבת על בן ח משום דבמקום פקוח נפש אנו מחויבים לסמוך על מיעוט פוסקים לקולא, וכמו שכתב הב"י באו"ח סימן תריח בשם רבינו ירוחם.

CODES, RESPONSA, AND OTHER WORKS

The following is a list of the sources cited and the codes and responsa consulted in the preparation of this volume, in addition to the standard Biblical, Talmudic, and Rabbinic sources.

ספרי הלכה

משנה תורה, הוא היד החזקה, לרבנו משה בן מיימון (רמב"ם), עם
השגות הראב"ד לרבנו אברהם ב"ר דוד, ופירושי וחידושי
אור שמח מה"ר מאיר שמחה הכהן
הגהות מיימוניות מה"ר מאיר הכהן
כסף משנה מה"ר יוסף קארו
לחם משנה מה"ר אברהם די בוטן
מגדל עוז מה"ר שם טוב ב"ר אברהם
מגיד משנה מה"ר דון וידל די טולושא
משנה למלך מה"ר יהודה רוזאניס

טור אורח חיים (או"ח) מה"ר יעקב ב"ר אשר, עם פירושי
בית חדש מה"ר יואל ב"ר שמואל סירקיש
בית יוסף מה"ר יוסף קארו
בית ישראל, הנקרא בשם דרישה ופרישה, מה"ר יושע פאלק הכהן
דרכי משה מה"ר משה איסרלש

שלחן ערוך (ש"ע) לרבנו יוסף קארו, ומפה פרושה עליו מה"ר משה איסרליש (רמ"א)
ונושאי כליהם:
באר היטב מה"ר יהודה אשכנזי
דגול מרבבה מה"ר יחזקאל הלוי לאנדא
טורי זהב (ט"ז) מה"ר דוד ב"ר שמואל הלוי
מגן אברהם (מג"א) מה"ר אברהם אבלי סג"ל גומבינר
מחצית השקל מה"ר שמואל הלוי מקעלין

491

פרי חדש מה"ר חזקיה די סילוא

פרי מגדים מה"ר יוסף תאומים

פתחי תשובה מה"ר אברהם צבי הירש אייזענשטאט

שערי תשובה מה"ר חיים מרדכי מרגליות

שפתי כהן (ש"ך) מה"ר שבתי ב"ר מאיר הכהן

קצור שלחן ערוך (קצש"ע) מה"ר שלמה גאנצפריד, ופירושי
מסגרת השלחן, ולחם הפנים, מה"ר חיים ישעיה הכהן
מצודת דוד מה"ר דוד פעלדמאן

חיי אדם מה"ר אברהם דאנציג, ופירוש תוספות חיים (תוס' חיים על ח"א) מה"ר משולם
פינקלשטיין

תפארת ישראל, פתיחה ראשונה הנקרא בשם קופת הרוכלים, וכולל כללת שבת על כללי
ל"ט מלאכות, מה"ר ישראל ליפשיץ

משנה ברורה, עם באור הלכה (בה"ל), ושער הציון (שעה"צ), מה"ר ישראל מאיר הכהן

זכרו תורת משה מה"ר אברהם דאנציג, עם פירוש קהלת יום טוב מה"ר יום טוב נעטיל
בראנשפיגעל

ספר חזון איש, אורח חיים, קונטרס שמונה עשרה שעות מה"ר אברהם ישעיהו קארעליץ

ספר החינוך, מחברו מבית לוי ברצלוני

חכמת אדם מה"ר אברהם דאנציג

יסודי ישרון מה"ר גדליה פעלדער

לוית חן על הלכות שבת מה"ר עובדיה יוסף

ספר מהרי"ל מה"ר יעקב ב"ר משה הלוי

מטה משה מה"ר משה מפרעמסלא

מנוחה נכונה מה"ר חיים ביברפלד, עם פסקי חזון איש, וקונטרס הערות מה"ר שריה
דבליצקי

מנחת שלמה מה"ר שלמה זלמן אויערבאך

מקור חיים, חלק שלישי, מה"ר חיים דוד הלוי

עדות לישראל מה"ר יוסף אליהו העננקין

ערוך השלחן מה"ר יחיאל מיכל הלוי עפשטיין

פירושי לב איברא מה"ר יוסף אליהו העננקין

פסקי הלכות שבת מה"ר אפרים אליעזר פאדאווער

קצור הלכות שבת (קה"ש), עם תקון דוד ושאול (תד"ו) מה"ר ש"ב שיעו"ר

קצור שלחן ערוך עם לקט בני איש מה"ר אליקים שלנגר

קצור שלחָן ערוך עם שער המזרח מה"ר יצחק בר־דע

שבלי הלקט לרבנו צדקיה ב"ר אברהם הרופא

שלחן ערוך הרב מה"ר שניאור זלמן מליאדי

שמירת שבת כהלכתה (שש"כ), שנת תשכ"ה, ומהדורה חדשה (מ"ח), מה"ר יהושע ישעיה נויבירט

שערים מצויינים בהלכה (שמ"ב), שנת תש"ט, ומהדורה תליתאה (מ"ת) עם קונטרס אחרון (ק"א), מה"ר שלמה זלמן ברוין

תורת השבת מה"ר ברוך ישר

שאלות ותשובות (שו"ת)

אגרות משה (אג"מ) מה"ר משה פיינשטיין

באר משה, עם קונטרס עלעקטעריק (ק"ע), מה"ר משה שטערן

דבר יהושע מה"ר יהושע מנחם מענדל אהרנברג

העמק שאלה על ספר שאילתות דרב אחאי גאון מה"ר נפתלי צבי יהודה ברלין

הרדב"ז מה"ר דוד אבן זמרא

חתם סופר מה"ר משה סופר

יביע אומר מה"ר עובדיה יוסף

יחוה דעת מה"ר עובדיה יוסף

מהרש"ם מה"ר שלום מרדכי הכהן

מלמד להועיל מה"ר דוד צבי האפפמאנן

מנחת יצחק מה"ר יצחק יעקב וייס

משנה הלכות, מדור התשובות, מה"ר מנשה הקטן קליין

נהרי אפרסמון מה"ר יעקב טעננענבום

נודע ביהודה מה"ר יחזקאל סג"ל לנדא

עשה לך רב מה"ר חיים דוד הלוי

פסקי עזיאל בשאלות הזמן מה"ר בן ציון מאיר חי עזיאל

ציץ אליעזר, עם קונטרס בדיני רפואה בשבת, מה"ר אליעזר יהודה וולדינברג

צפנת פענח מה"ר יוסף ראזין

רשב"א מה"ר שלמה בן אדרת

שרידי אש מה"ר יחיאל יעקב וויינברג

תשובות והנהגות מה"ר משה שטרנבוך

ספרים שונים ולועזים

אום אני חומה, משנה הלכות בהלכות עירובין, מה"ר מנשה הקטן קליין

אוצר שלם למנהגי ישראל מה"ר אברהם אליעזר הירשאוויץ

אנציקלופדיה תלמודית, כרך שמונה עשר, נספח לערך חשמל

הדרום, קובץ תורני, בעריכת הרב חיים דוב שעוועל

ספר הזהר מהתנא רבי שמעון בן יוחאי

ספר חסידים לרבנו יהודה החסיד

החשמל בהלכה מה"ר אליהו וייספיש

ספר הכוזרי מה"ר יהודה הלוי

ספר הלכות שבת מה"ר שמעון איידער

ספר טלטולי שבת, הלכות מוקצה מה"ר ישראל פנחס באדנער

טעמי המנהגים מה"ר אי"ש שו"ב

יסודות הלכות שבת מה"ר משה חיים שלנגר

כשרות ושבת במטבח המודרני מה"ר לוי יצחק היילפרין

לב אברהם מה"ר אברהם-סופר אברהם

מורה נבוכים לרבנו משה בן מיימון (רמב"ם)

מטעמים החדש מה"ר יצחק ליפיעץ

נועם, שנתון לבירור בעיות בהלכה

סדור אוצר התפלות עם פירושי עיון תפלה מה"ר אריה ליב גורדון, ועץ יוסף וענף יוסף מה"ר חנוך זונדל בה"ר יוסף

עקדת יצחק מה"ר יצחק בן עראמה

הלכות ערובין מה"ר אלימלך לנגה

פירוש בעל הטורים על התורה לרבנו יעקב בן אשר

פירושי התורה לרבנו משה בן נחמן (רמב"ן)

תלפיות, רבעון לעניני הלכה, אגדה ומוסר היהדות בעריכת הרב שמואל ק. מירסקי

ספר רמת רחל מה"ר אליעזר יהודה ולדינברג

ספר תפארת השבת מה"ר דוד יהושע רוזנוואלד

Code of Jewish Law by Rabbi Solomon Ganzfried (קצור שלחן ערוך), trans. by
Rabbi Hyman E. Goldin

Guide of the Perplexed of Maimonides (מורה נבוכים), trans. by Dr. M.
Friedlander

Halacha, Medical Science and Technology, by Rabbi Faitel Levin

Halakha and Medicine: A Physician's Hospital Manual, Hilchot Shabbat, by Dr. Binyomin Sokol

Halachos of Muktza (ספר טלטולי שבת, הלכות מוקצה), by Rabbi Yisroel Pinchos Bodner

Halachos of Shabbos (ספר הלכות שבת), by Rabbi Shimon D. Eider

Horeb by Rabbi Samson Raphael Hirsch, trans. by Dayan Dr. I. Grunfeld

Jewish Medical Law by Dr. Avraham Steinberg, trans. by Dr. David Simons

Journal of Jewish Music and Liturgy, ed. Macy Nulman

Kuzari by Rabbi Yehuda Halevi, trans. by Dr. Hartwig Hirschfeld

Laws and Customs of Israel (דת ודין), by Rabbi Gerald Friedlander

The Laws of Shabbos: A Digest, by Rabbis Aron and Avrohom Pessin

Medical Halachah for Everyone (לב אברהם), by Dr. Abraham S. Abraham

Mishnah Berurah, Hebrew-English Edition, Volume III, ed. by Rabbis Aharon Feldman and Ariel Orenstein

The Sabbath, by Dayan Dr. I. Grunfeld

Shabbat and the Modern Kitchen, by Rabbi L.I. Halpern, trans, by Rabbi Dovid Oratz

Shemirath Shabbath, Volume I, by Rabbi Yehoshua Y. Neuwirth, trans. by W. Grangewood

GLOSSARY

AGGADAH, lit., tale, lesson; portions of Rabbinic literature which comprise homiletic expositions of the Bible, maxims, folk-lore, legends, historical data, anecdotes, and similar material, as distinguished from Halachah.

AHARON, one called last to the reading of the Torah.

AKIRAH, lifting an object from the place where it lies, with relation to the laws of carrying on the Sabbath.

ALIYAH, pl. ALIYOT, lit., ascent; the honor of being called up to the reading of the Torah.

AMAH, pl. AMOT, cubit; a unit of length based on the length of the forearm, from the elbow to the tip of the middle finger, estimated to measure 22.7 inches according to the *Hazon Ish,* and 18.9 inches according to Rabbi Avraham Hayyim Na'eh.

AMEN, traditional response to a blessing, expressing solemn confirmation.

AMIDAH, lit., standing; prayers recited three times daily while standing, comprising nineteen benedictions on weekdays, and seven on *Shabbat* and Festivals; also called *Shemoneh Esreh.*

AMUD, lectern at the front of the synagogue from which the one who leads the service recites the prayers.

ASHKENAZI, pl. ASHKENAZIM, lit., German; a Central or East European Jew and one who follows their customs, religious ritual, and liturgical tradition, as distinguished from Sefardi.

ASMACHTA, a Scriptural text interpreted and used as a nominal support for a Rabbinical enactment.

AV MELACHAH, pl. AVOT MELACHOT, one of the thirty-nine principal categories of labor forbidden on the Sabbath.

BAIN HASHEMASHOT, twilight; the period between sunset and the appearance of the stars, when it is doubtful whether it is day or night.

BAR MITZVAH, lit., one who must observe the Law; a boy who is thirteen years of age or older, and performs religious duties as an adult; also a common reference to the occasion when a boy who has reached his religious majority is called to the Torah.

BET HAMIDRASH, house of Torah study.

BIMAH, raised platform from which the Torah is read at a prayer service.

BIRKAT HAMAZON, blessing of Grace recited after a meal.

BLECH, metal sheet covering the fire on the stove, required on the Sabbath.

BRIT, BRIT MILAH, the covenant or rite of circumcision.

CHULENT, a dish of hot food, consisting usually of meat, beans and potatoes, kept on the fire overnight to be eaten at the Sabbath day meal.

CUBIT, see *Amah*.

DAYAN, judge (Rabbinical).

ERETZ YISRAEL, Land of Israel, the Holy Land.

EREV SHABBAT, eve of the Sabbath; the day (Friday) or the period immediately preceding the Sabbath.

ERUSIN, betrothal.

ERUV, pl. ERUVIN, lit., mixture, combination; a Rabbinically sanctioned device or provision by which community, continuity of space, or continuity of time is established, whereby carrying and certain other activities ordinarily forbiddehn on the Sabbath or *Yom Tov* become permissible; see also *Eruv Ḥatzerot, Eruv Teḥumin.*

ERUV ḤATZEROT, an *eruv* which permits carrying on the Sabbath into and between courtyards and adjacent dwellings; also the food deposited in one of the dwellings on behalf of all the residents, rendering their premises common to all and enabling them to carry on the Sabbath.

ERUV TEḤUMIN, an *eruv* which permits walking beyond the *teḥum,* or Sabbath boundary; the food deposited on the eve of the Sabbath a distance of two thousand cubits from the city limit in order to allow walking beyond it a similar distance.

ETROG, citrus; one of the four species of plants used in observance of the Festival of Sukkot.

GABAI, a functionary in the synagogue who usually distributes the *aliyot* and other honors during the service.

GAN EDEN, Garden of Eden, a heavenly Paradise, where the righteous receive their eternal reward.

GARTEL, belt usually worn by *Ḥasidim* during prayer.

GEFILTE FISH, Yiddish, lit., filled fish; a dish of stewed or baked fish, stuffed with bread crumbs and seasoning, usually eaten on the Sabbath.

GEHINNOM, Hell, where the wicked souls suffer punishment after death.

GELILAH, tying the Torah scroll, an honor bestowed at the prayer service following the reading of the Torah.

GEZERAH, a Rabbinical enactment or prohibition issued as a guard or preventive measure.

GUT SHABBOS, Yiddish, lit., a good Sabbath, a customary greeting on the Sabbath.

HAFTARAH, the section from the Prophets read at the prayer service after the reading of the Torah portion on Sabbaths, Festivals and Holy Days.

HAGBAH, raising of the open Torah scroll, an honor bestowed at the prayer service following the reading of the Torah.

HAGOMEL, blessing recited on recovery from a serious illness, on returning from a perilous journey, on being saved from danger, and on release from prison.

HALACHAH, Jewish Law; the final decision of the Rabbis.

ḤALITZAH, the ceremony (see Deuteronomy 25:9) instituted in place of levirate marriage.

ḤALLAH, pl. ḤALLOT, loaf of bread, usually the Sabbath bread; also a portion of dough, originally designated as the priest's portion (see Numbers 15:21), separated from the dough to be burned.

ḤANAḤAH, setting an object down, with relation to the law of carrying on the Sabbath.

ḤANUKAH, Festival of Dedication, observed for eight days, beginning on the 25th of *Kislev,* by the kindling of lights in commemoration of the rededication of the Temple by the Maccabees.

ḤAROSET, a condiment made of nuts, fruit, and spices mixed with wine, used to sweeten the bitter herbs at the *Seder* on Passover night.

ḤASID, pl. ḤASIDIM, member of a religious group or community which follows the practices and beliefs of *Ḥasidism.*

ḤATAN, bridegroom.

ḤATAN TORAH, one who is honored by being called to the reading of the concluding section of the Torah on *Simḥat Torah.*

ḤATMANAH, covering a dish or a pot of food with a substance in order to retain the heat or to add to it.

HATZOLAH, lit., rescue; an organization of volunteers who respond to calls for help in medical emergencies.

HAVDALAH, lit., separation; the blessing recited and the ceremony performed to mark the conclusion of the Sabbath or holy day.

ḤAZAN, pl. ḤAZANIM, cantor; one who leads the congregation in prayer, also referred to as *Sh'liaḥ tzibur*.

ḤILLUL HASHEM, desecration of the Divine Name.

ḤOL HAMOED, Intermediate Days of a Festival.

ḤUMASH, pl. ḤUMASHIM, the Torah; the first five books of the Bible (Pentateuch).

KABBALAT SHABBAT, acceptance of the sanctity of the Sabbath; the prayer service on Sabbath eve which signifies the acceptance of the Sabbath.

KADDISH, prayer recited at various times during the service by the *ḥazan* and by the mourners.

KARAITE, a follower of the doctrine of Karaism, which based its tenets solely on Scripture, and rejected the Talmud and Rabbinical authority.

KARMELIT, an area which is neither a private nor a public domain, and which is subject to special laws with regard to carrying on the Sabbath.

KASHER, lit., to make fit; a cleansing process rendering utensils fit for use by restoring them to their original kosher state.

KEDUSHAH, lit., holiness; the third benediction of the *Amidah*; a prayer proclaiming the holiness of God recited during the repetition of the *Amidah* and at various other times during the prayers.

KELI RISHON, lit., the first vessel; a vessel that is on the fire, and after it is removed from the fire, when it retains heat capable of cooking.

KELI SHEINI, lit., the second vessel; a vessel that is not on the fire, into which food has been transferred from a first vessel.

KELI SHLISHI, lit., the third vessel; a vessel that is not on the fire, into which food has been transferred from a second vessel.

KEZAYIT, a measure the size of an olive's bulk.

KIDDUSH, blessing recited, usually over wine, in sanctification of the Sabbath or holy day at its arrival and during the day.

KILAYIM, diverse kinds (1) of seeds or plants for sowing, (2) of animals for propagation, (3) of material containing wool and linen for wearing.

KISHKE, Yiddish, a casing stuffed with flour, fats and spices and cooked.

KOHEN, a Jew of priestly descent, of the family of Aaron.

KOSHER, lit., fit; permissible according to Jewish law.

KUGEL, a pudding usually made from potatoes or noodles.

LEḤEM MISHNEH, two *ḥallot* over which the blessing is recited at the Sabbath meals in remembrance of the double portion of manna that the people of Israel gathered every *erev Shabbat* for the Sabbath (Exodus 16:22).

LEVI, LEVITE, a Jew descended from the tribe of Levi, but not of the family of Aaron.

LUBAVITCH, a *Ḥasidic* movement espousing the teachings of the *Ḥabad* school of *Ḥasidic* thought, as propounded by Rabbi Shneor Zalman of Liady.

MAARIV, the Evening Prayer.

MAFTIR, one called to the concluding reading of the Torah at the morning prayer service on the Sabbath and *Yom Tov,* followed by a reading of a section of the Prophets (*Haftarah*).

MAR'IT HA'AYIN, the appearance of wrongdoing; an act which may arouse suspicion that one thereby committed a transgression.

MEḤABER, lit., author; author of the *Shulḥan Aruch.*

MEKOM PETUR, a free place; one of the four domains, with regard to the laws of carrying on the Sabbath.

MELACHAH, pl. MELACHOT, work, labor; an activity forbidden on the Sabbath by Torah law, classed as a primary activity (*Av Melachah*) or a derivative, subsidiary activity (*Toladah*).

MELAVEH MALKAH, lit., escorting the Queen; the meal on the night after *Shabbat.*

MENORAH, candelabrum.

METURGEMAN, translator of the Torah reading into Aramaic at the services in former times.

MIDRASH, the homiletical commentary on the Scriptures.

MIKVEH, lit., a gathering [of water], a ritual bath.

MIL, a distance of two thousand cubits; a measure of the time it takes to walk the distance of a *mil.*

MINHAG, custom.

MINḤAH, the Afternoon Prayer.

MINḤAH GEDOLAH, the greater period for *Minḥah*; the early afternoon period, beginning at six and a half seasonal hours of the day until *Minḥah Ketanah.*

MINḤAH KETANAH, the shorter period for *Minḥah*; the late afternoon period, beginning at nine and a half seasonal hours of the day until nightfall.

MINYAN, ten adult males, the minimum number required for public worship.

MISHKAN, the Tabernacle (see Exodus 25:8,9).

MISHNAH, collection of the Oral Law and statements of the *Tanaim,* edited by Rabbi Yehudah Hanasi.

MITZVAH, pl. MITZVOT, commandment of the Torah; a religious, meritorious, or charitable deed.

MOHEL, one who performs the circumcision.

MOTZA'AI SHABBAT, the night after *Shabbat.*

MUKTZEH, lit., set aside; forbidden for use or handling on the Sabbath, and on a Festival or holy day.

MUSAF, Additional Prayer, recited on the Sabbath, Festivals and holy days.

NIDAH, a woman in the period of menstruation.

NISAN, first month in the Jewish calendar.

NOLAD, something that has come into being on the Sabbath; the prohibition against creating something new.

NUSAH, the liturgical tradition.

ONEG SHABBAT, delighting in the Sabbath.

PAROCHET, curtain overhanging the Ark in the synagogue.

PARSHAH, section of the Torah.

PARSHAT HAHODESH, the section of the Torah, dealing with the designation of the month of *Nisan* as the first of the months of the year (Exodus 12:2–20), read before the month of *Nisan.*

PARSHAT HASHAVUA, the portion of the Torah for the week.

PARSHAT PARAH, the section of the Torah, dealing with the precept of the *parah adumah* (the ritual of the red heifer (Numbers 19:1–22), read on the Sabbath before *Shabbat Parshat Hahodesh.*

PARSHAT SHEKALIM, the section of the Torah, dealing with the offering of half a *shekel* (Exodus 30:11–16), read on the Sabbath before the month of *Adar* that precedes the month of *Nisan.*

PARSHAT ZACHOR, the section of the Torah, invoking a remembrance of the iniquity of Amalek (Deuteronomy 25:17–19), read on the Sabbath before *Purim.*

PASHTIDA, meat pie.

PASUL, defective, unfit, disqualified.

PELAG HA-MINḤAH, lit., half of the short period for *Minḥah*; the period beginning at ten and three quarters seasonal hours in the day until nightfall.

PERUTAH, small copper coin; smallest coin of the currency.

PESAḤ, Passover, the festival commemorating the deliverance of the people of Israel from Egyptian bondage.

PIDYON HABEN, redemption of the first born son.

PIYUT, pl. PIYUTIM, liturgical poem.

RESHUT HA-RABIM, public domain.

RESHUT HA-YAḤID, private domain.

REVIIT, lit., a quarter (of a *log*), a measure equal to the quantity of liquid displaced by one and a half medium sized eggs, variously estimated at 5.3 ounces according to the *Ḥazon Ish,* and 3.0 ounces according to Rabbi Avraham Ḥayyim Na'eh.

RISHON, pl. RISHONIM, early halachic authority in the period from the *Gaonim* until the appearance of the *Shulḥan Aruch* in the sixteenth century.

ROSH HASHANAH, New Year, observed on the first two days of the month of *Tishri.*

ROSH ḤODESH, first day of the month.

SAGES, the Rabbis of the Talmud.

SANDAK, one who holds the infant for the circumcision; one who carries the infant to the circumcision.

SCHACH, roof covering of the *Sukkah.*

SEAH, a measure of volume for dry objects and for liquids.

SEASONAL HOURS, SHA'OT ZEMANIOT, hours calculated by dividing by twelve the length of the day, which varies with the season of the year. According to the *Shulḥan Aruch* the duration of the day is from dawn until nightfall, and according to the Gaon of Vilna from sunrise to sunset.

SEDER, lit., order; the ritual and recitations from the *Haggadah* on the first night [in the Diaspora on the first two nights] of Passover.

SEFARDI, pl. SEFARDIM, Spaniard; a Jew of Spanish origin, or from one of the Mediterranean countries, and one who follows their ritual, customs, religious practice, and liturgical tradition, as distinguished from *Ashkenazi.*

SEFER, pl. SEFARIM, book, usually referring to a Jewish book of a religious nature.

SEFER TORAH, pl. SIFREI TORAH, Scroll of the Torah.

SEḤITAH, pressing, wringing; an act forbidden on the Sabbath, classified as a subsidiary of the *melachah* of Threshing or of Cleaning.

SEUDAH, meal.

SEUDAH SHELISHIT, third Sabbath meal.

SEUDAT MITZVAH, a meal in connection with certain religious observances.

SHABBAT, Sabbath.

SHABBAT ḤAZON, the Sabbath preceding the Fast of the Ninth of *Av* which marks the anniversary of the Fall of Jerusalem, when the *Haftarah* reading is the opening chapter of Isaiah, which begins with the words, *Ḥazon Yeshayahu,* "the vision of Isaiah."

SHABBAT SHALOM, lit., a peaceful Sabbath; a Hebrew greeting extended on the Sabbath.

SHABBAT SHEKALIM, the Sabbath when the Torah reading is *Parshat Shekalim.*

SHABBAT SHUVAH, the Sabbath after Rosh Hashanah during the Ten Days of Repentance, when the *Haftarah* reading is from the concluding chapter of the prophecy of Hosea, beginning with the words *Shuvah Yisrael,* "Return O Israel."

SHAḤARIT, the Morning Prayer.

SHAITEL, wig.

SHALOSH SEUDOT, the three Sabbath meals; also used to refer to the third Sabbath meal.

SHAʻOT ZEMANIOT, see Seasonal Hours.

SHAʻTNEZ, a garment containing wool and linen, prohibited by Torah law (Deuteronomy 22:11).

SHAVUOT, Festival of Weeks, which commemorates the Revelation of the Torah on Mount Sinai.

SHECHINAH, Divine Presence.

SHEHIYAH, keeping food over the fire on the stove from before the Sabbath for use on the Sabbath.

SHEKEL, pl. SHEKALIM, coin or weight.

SHEM HAMEFORASH, the Divine Name, consisting of four letters, the Tetragrammaton.

SHEMA, the confession of Jewish faith recited twice daily, comprising three sections of the Torah (Deuteronomy 6:4–9, 11:13–21, Numbers 15:37–41).

SHEMONEH ESREH, Eighteen Benedictions (presently nineteen) recited at weekday morning prayers; the standard benedictions recited at every prayer service; see *Amidah.*

SHEVA BERACHOT, Seven Blessings, recited at the marriage ceremony and in the Grace after meals during the seven feast days following the wedding.

SHEVUT, something forbidden on the Sabbath because of an enactment of the Sages.

SHIR HASHIRIM, Song of Songs.

SHI'UR, a lesson or lecture on a subject of Torah study.

SIDDUR, pl. SIDDURIM, Prayer Book, usually for weekday and Sabbath prayers.

SIDRAH, pl. SIDROT, Torah portion read at the Sabbath service.

SIFREI KODESH, holy books.

SIMHAT TORAH, Festival of the Rejoicing of the Torah.

SUKKAH, pl. SUKKOT, the temporary booth erected in observance of the Festival of Sukkot.

SUKKOT, the Festival of Tabernacles, beginning on the fifteenth of the month of *Tishri.*

TA'AMIM, accents that indicate the cantillation of the Torah and *Haftarah.*

TAHANUN, prayers of supplication recited on weekdays following the morning and afternoon *Amidah.*

TALLIT, a four-cornered garment with fringes (*tzitzit*) worn by men during prayers.

TALLIT KATAN, a small four-cornered garment with fringes (*tzitzit*) worn by males.

TALMUD, a compilation of the discussion of the Sages on the Mishnah; usually a reference to the complete tractate consisting of the Mishnah, and the discussions on the Mishnah also known as *Gemara.*

TARGUM, Aramaic translation of the Torah.

TEFAH, pl. TEFAHIM, handbreadth, variously estimated as measuring 3.8 inches according to the *Hazon Ish,* and 3.2 inches according to Rabbi Avraham Hayyim Na'eh. There are six *tefahim* in an *amah.*

TEFILLAH, pl. TEFILLOT, prayer.

TEFILLIN, phylacteries, small leather cases containing parchment scrolls inscribed with certain passages from the Torah, traditionally worn on the arm and forehead during the weekday morning prayers.

TEHUM, the Sabbath boundary, which is two thousand cubits from the city limits, beyond which one may not walk on the Sabbath. This can be extended for another two thousand cubits by means of an *Eruv Tehumin.*

TEHUM SHABBAT, the Sabbath boundary; see *Tehum.*

TENA'IM, engagement agreement.

TEVILAH, immersion in a ritual bath (*mikveh*).

TISHRI, the seventh month of the Jewish calendar.

TOLADAH, pl. TOLADOT, an act classified as a derivative of, and subsidiary to, a primary category of labor (*Av Melachah*), and hence forbidden on the Sabbath.

TORAH, the first five books of Scriptures (Pentateuch); the whole body of Jewish law and religious literature.

TWILIGHT, see *Bain Hashemashot.*

TZE'ENAH URE'ENAH, a popular commentary on the Torah in Yiddish, based on Midrash, Talmud and other traditional sources.

TZITZIT, fringes or tassels, which must be tied to a four-cornered garment one wears, that serve as a reminder of the commandments; also refers to the garment bearing these fringes.

YAD SOLEDET BO, lit., the hand recoils on touching it; the temperature at which the hand is spontaneously withdrawn when touching the object, and at which temperature it retains sufficient heat to be capable of cooking.

YAHRZEIT, anniversary of the day of death.

YIDDISH, the language spoken by Jews chiefly of East European origin.

YOM TOV, a Festival; one of the major Festivals of the Jewish calendar when work is forbidden by Jewish law.

ZEMIROT, hymns sung at the Sabbath meal.

INDEX OF SUBJECTS

176, 259; bow, 176, 259; shoelaces, 176, 259; necktie, 176, 259; kerchief, 259; dressing on wound, 259

Typewriting, 192

Tzurat hapetaḥ, forming a nominal doorway, 287, 293, 397; in an archway, 293; use of wires, cables, 293

Ulcer, 381

Umbrella, opening, 202, 274; carrying, 203, 274

Untying, lasting knot, 176; bow, 177; food, food container, 177; container of beverage, medicine, 177

Urn, electric, use of, 160; moving, 336

Utensil, use of for eating, 136; for selecting, 138, 245; perforated, 141; washing, drying, 167, 228, 250; scouring, 188; polishing, 188; washing with liquid soap, 188; selecting for meal, 247; untying, 261; reassembling parts, 274; removing and reattaching cover, 275

Valuables, carrying home in emergency, 232, 290; saving, 311

Vaporizer, moving a cold water, 336; adding water to cold water, 336, 372; to hot water, 336, 372; use of, 372

Vase, see Flowers

Vegetables, washing, soaking, 125, 139; detaching from ground, 126; removing outer layer, 130; squeezing water out of, 131, 244; peeling, 139; 246; mashing cooked, 142; preparing salad of, 144; salting, 186, 187, 248, 249; cutting up, 248

Vessel, see also Utensil, covering on fire, 155; warming food on top of, 158; transferring between, 161; covering, 163; making, 200; assembling parts, 200; breaking open, 206; immersing in mikveh, 223

Video recorder, operating, 213

Vinegar, putting into horseradish, 242; pouring liquid into, 264

Vitamin, taking, 366

Wages, for work on Shabbat, 356; for services of ḥazan, 356; for blowing shofar, 356

Wall, making hole in, 200; plastering, 201; driving nail into, 201; hanging tapestry, 203; removing plank from, 205

Washing, with hot water, 150; with soap, 189, 321; body, 319; 320; face, hands, feet, 319; bathing, showering in hot weather, 320;

washing, drying, 320; hands in river, 321

Washing machine, storing soiled diapers, clothing, 168, 351; opening door of, 352

Watch, battery operated, 217, 276; digital, 217, 276; winding, 223, 276; setting time, 223, 276; self-winding wristwatch, 223, 276; going out wearing, 302; handling, 338

Water, preparing hot for Shabbat, 37, 160; drawing hot from faucet, 148; pouring hot on solid food, 149; from solar heater, 150; pouring hot onto instant coffee or tea, 152, 241; placing on heated stove, 241; passing through a stream, 255; coloring, 258; pouring out in courtyard, 297; placing vessel beneath dripping, 345

Wax, playing with, 145; heating, 149

Weaving, 173

Wedding, see Marriage

Weekday activity, 350ff.; nature of prohibition, 350; attending to business, 351f.

Whiskey, for Kiddush, 80; diluting with water, 264

Wig, combing, brushing, 166, 253; braiding, 174, 252; going out wearing, 311

Window, resetting, 200f., 271; locking with bolt, 201, 270; opening near fireplace, 208; wiping mist, 254; closing shutter, 270; opening awning, 273

Wine, handled by one who desecrates Sabbath, 22; filtering, 140; opening capped bottle, 180; corked bottle, 206; diluting, 263

Winnowing, 133

Woman, immersing in mikveh, 151, 224, 319; expressing milk from breast, 131, 244, 387; applying cosmetics, 258; coloring face, eyes etc. 258; using face powder, 258; nail polish, 258; going out with rain bonnet, 303; with sanitary napkin, 307; taking temperature to determine ovulation, 365; applying ointment, 368; in childbirth, 384; ff.; nursing baby, 387

Work, see Melachah

Work by a non-Jew, see also Non-Jew, 38ff., 359ff.; nature of prohibition, 38, 251, 359; reason for prohibition, 38, 359; contracting before Shabbat for, 38ff., 360; on building, in field, 40f., 360; repair in Jew's home, 42f.; cooking, baking, 164; buying, selling for Jew, 268 359; hiring workers for Jew, 359; cleaning clothes, 360; repairing shoes, 360; automobile repairs, 360; circumstances when Jew may request, 360;

Index of Passages Cited

The index is to quotations from the works cited.

119:48	83	118a	29
119:142	69	118b	16,17
134:2	83	Yoma	

Proverbs

		85b	374,377,383
3:9	12		
6:23	52	Betzah	

Nehemiah

		15b	29
9:13–14	21	Ketubot	
10:32	194	110b	17
13:17	194		

Mishnah

Mechilta

Shabbat

Exodus

		31:13	7
VII,2	108	31:14	11
XII,1	191		

Tamid

Pesikta

		Perek 23	6
VII,4	15		

Jerusalem Talmud

Midrash

Nedarim

Bereshit Rabbah

		11:3	17
III,14	21	11:9	7

Babylonian Talmud

Devarim Rabbah

Shabbat

		3:1	13
3a	113	Tanḥuma	
10b	18		
23b	52	Parshat Re'eh	12
49b	108		
73b	108	Zohar	
75a	114		
113a	33,350	Parshat Yitro	13

TOPICAL LIST OF HALACHIC ANNOTATIONS

The number preceding each annotation coincides with the number of the annotation in the chapter and in the section on Sources and References.

II. Principal Classes of Labor Forbidden on the Sabbath